Praise for *The Wobbling Pivot*

"Pamela Crossley, a leading historian of the Q⋯⋯⋯⋯⋯⋯ ⋯ely novel and stylish way of telling the story of C⋯⋯⋯⋯⋯⋯ ⋯he strikes a good balance between offering up b⋯⋯⋯⋯⋯⋯ ⋯them with revealing details, and she excels at limni⋯⋯⋯⋯⋯ ⋯ons between collective actions and state responses to unrest two centuries ago and patterns of protest and repression in the current era of Internet petitions and text message mobilization. The result is truly impressive, a high-level work of synthesis that is informed by deep knowledge of the past yet speaks with immediacy to the concerns of the present."

Jeffrey N. Wasserstrom,
University of California-Irvine,
author of China in the 21st Century:
What Everyone Needs to Know

"Pamela Crossley's book gives readers a new and original perspective on modern Chinese history by moving its focus away from the politics of the centre to give us a greater understanding of how China's regions and minorities have shaped this multi-voiced society in its transition from empire to nation-state."

Rana Mitter,
University of Oxford

"Original, conceptually bold, and unusually engaging. Crossley offers her readers a broader and deeper meditation on the shape and significance of China's historical trajectory, one that may indeed make Chinese history more meaningful in the context of teaching undergraduates."

Bryna Goodman,
University of Oregon

"*The Wobbling Pivot* is refreshingly ambitious in its interpretation of the whole scope of Chinese history since 1800. Its analysis of the often disastrous extremes of state authoritarianism and local implosion is told with a telling eye for detail that will grip general readers and specialists alike."

Frank Dikotter,
School of Oriental and African Studies,
University of London,
and the University of Hong Kong

For my teachers

Lillian M. Li

and

Jonathan D. Spence

THE WOBBLING PIVOT

CHINA
SINCE 1800

An Interpretive History

PAMELA
KYLE CROSSLEY

⟨W⟩WILEY-BLACKWELL

A John Wiley & Sons, Ltd., Publication

This edition first published 2010
© 2010 Pamela Kyle Crossley

Blackwell Publishing was acquired by John Wiley & Sons in February 2007. Blackwell's publishing program has been merged with Wiley's global Scientific, Technical, and Medical business to form Wiley-Blackwell.

Registered Office
John Wiley & Sons Ltd, The Atrium, Southern Gate, Chichester, West Sussex, PO19 8SQ, United Kingdom

Editorial Offices
350 Main Street, Malden, MA 02148-5020, USA
9600 Garsington Road, Oxford, OX4 2DQ, UK
The Atrium, Southern Gate, Chichester, West Sussex, PO19 8SQ, UK

For details of our global editorial offices, for customer services, and for information about how to apply for permission to reuse the copyright material in this book please see our website at www.wiley.com/wiley-blackwell.

The right of Pamela Kyle Crossley to be identified as the author of this work has been asserted in accordance with the UK Copyright, Designs and Patents Act 1988.

Wiley also publishes its books in a variety of electronic formats. Some content that appears in print may not be available in electronic books.

Designations used by companies to distinguish their products are often claimed as trademarks. All brand names and product names used in this book are trade names, service marks, trademarks or registered trademarks of their respective owners. The publisher is not associated with any product or vendor mentioned in this book. This publication is designed to provide accurate and authoritative information in regard to the subject matter covered. It is sold on the understanding that the publisher is not engaged in rendering professional services. If professional advice or other expert assistance is required, the services of a competent professional should be sought.

Library of Congress Cataloging-in-Publication Data

Crossley, Pamela Kyle.
  The wobbling pivot, China since 1800 : an interpretive history / Pamela Kyle Crossley.
    p. cm.
  Includes bibliographical references.
  ISBN 978-1-4051-6079-7 (hardcover : alk. paper) – ISBN 978-1-4051-6080-3 (pbk. : alk. paper) 1. China–History–19th century. 2. China–History–20th century. 3. China–History–2002–4. Central-local government relations–China–History. I. Title.
  DS755.C76 2010
  951–dc22
                                                        2009041257
A catalogue record for this book is available from the British Library.

Set in 10/12.5pt Galliard by SPi Publisher Services, Pondicherry, India

1 2010

Contents

List of Illustrations   vii
List of Maps   viii
Foreword and Acknowledgments   ix
Prelude   xi
Timeline   xv

 1   The Wobbling Pivot   1

 2   Sources of Order Under the Qing Empire   21

 3   Sources of Disorder Under the Qing Empire   44

 4   *Essay: Strategic Borders*   66

 5   Qing and the World   70

 6   *Essay: Rebel Heroines*   98

 7   Visionaries   100

 8   *Essay: Hunan Takes the Lead*   126

 9   *Essay: Water*   129

10   Beiyang Ascendancy   133

11   Cultural Revolution   155

12   *Essay: Manchus as Minorities*   177

13   War   180

14   The Ubiquitous Center   207

15   *Essay: Minerals*   240

Contents

16 *Essay: Health Risks*   243

17 Gravity   246

Bibliography   274
Index   295

List of Illustrations

1	Wu Bingjian	74
2	Grant and Li	124
3	Kang Youwei and family	145
4	Sun Yatsen	162
5	May Fourth demonstrators	170
6	Zhang Xueliang, Soong May-ling, Chiang Kaishek and Yan Xishan	197
7	The Gorbachevs and Deng Xiaping	264
8	Panorama of Tiananmen	266

The publishers gratefully acknowledge permission from the sources listed below to reproduce the illustrations:

1 courtesy of the Peabody Essex Museum. 2, 4 and 6 © Bettmann/CORBIS. 3 from *K'ang Yu Wei: A Biography and a Symposium* (1967) by Lo Jung-Pang. 5 © Tophams/ Press Association Images. 7 and 8 © Peter Turnley/CORBIS.

List of Maps

1	The Qing Empire to *c.* 1860	23
2	Qianlong and Jiaqing era rebellions	52
3	Changing strategic borders	67
4	Qing territorial losses	84
5	Qing rebellions and rebel kingdoms, 1821–78	106
6	China's waterways	130
7	The changing Yellow River	131
8	Republican China, *c.* 1930	156
9	Modern cultural variation	178
10	Communist spaces, 1928–49	189
11	Japanese incursions, 1932–43	193
12	The People's Republic of China	208
13	Known mineral deposits	241
14	Income disparities by province	268

Foreword
and Acknowledgments

THIS BOOK HAS put the pieces of Chinese history since roughly 1800 into a shape that makes sense to me. Nevertheless, I have attempted at every step to supply the reader sufficient pieces that he or she may rearrange them if the need to create a more sensible shape is felt. In scope and in content, this book can do no more than complement the dozen or so excellent books on modern China already in circulation. For a wealth of colorful detail or lengthy biographical digression, superb alternatives may be found. For incisive analysis and theoretical sophistication, there are also a handful of monographs that do what this book will not do. But for a narrative of scope and color sufficient to engage the reader of any level of knowledge about China, combined with a thematic orientation that I hope will interest specialists in the field, this book may, at present, stand alone.

This book has been strongly influenced by very recent scholarship in Chinese, most of which has not been cited in the book because of our assumption that the overwhelming majority of readers would be best served by being directed to works in English. Fortunately, all but the most current Chinese scholarship is reflected in the most recent works by historians and others writing in English. For that reason, I have attempted to include the most recent studies on the relevant subjects. Otherwise, I have included works chosen for their enduring impact, unique coverage, past points of view of which we should be reminded or best synthesis of complex subjects. Very many superb works have not been included, either because of my length considerations for the manuscript or because they are specialized to the degree that professionals will necessarily know them already and general readers will be unlikely to have a direct need of them. I regret that the printed medium imposes this rigidity upon us.

Some proper names and terms in the book have retained familiar forms, in contradiction of the rules of contemporary *pinyin* transliteration and of logic (for example, making English plurals of Chinese words or using mistaken English transmogrifications that have subsequently taken on a life of their own). These include but are not limited to: Canton (Guangzhou, not Guangdong), Howqua, Yangtze, Taipings, Yung Wing, Panthays, Boxers, KMT, Chiang Kaishek, Soong May-ling, Peking University, Jimmy Yen, Hu Shih, and so on. In addition, foreign treaties and events related to foreign relations retain whatever English name they assumed at the time: Treaty of Nanking, Convention of Peking, Tientsin Massacre, Rape of Nanking, Shanghai Communiqué, and so on.

It is impossible to name all the people who have influenced the generalities and particulars of this narrative. They are teachers, friends, colleagues, students, visiting research scholars, editors and the superb manuscript reviewers recruited by Wiley-Blackwell. I must thank Jon Taylor and Patrick Francis for early research assistance, Christopher Wheeler and Tessa Harvey for having encouraged the project and Tom Bates for seeing it through production. Naturally, I claim all errors of fact and ask the reader to delay judgment on errors of interpretation.

Pamela Crossley
Norwich, Vermont

Prelude

THE WORK OF classical Chinese philosophy, the *Zhongyong* – frequently cited in English as *The Doctrine of the Mean* – is a long meditation on the constancy of true virtue in times of change and temptation. In the interpretations of Chinese philosophers, the key to constancy was the ability of the man of perfect morality to allow unconsidered sincerity to guide his every action. Early political commentators in China considered *The Mean* as the ability of the sovereign to keep the state and the society balanced through all manner of turmoil, through the power of his virtue. In 1947, Ezra Pound first published his translation of the classic as "The Unwobbling Pivot." The title captures a persisting historical impression of an impartial and omnipresent state, oriented toward the unchanging fixtures of the material and the metaphysical world – the Pole Star, the *dao*, the ideal of benevolent government. What is striking to the historian is not any peculiarity of Pound's famous translation, but the precise contrast between the persisting ideal of unwobbling virtue in the person of the political leader and the reality of wobbling policy on the part of the state.

Inconstancy, flexibility, and a measure of cynicism have historically been the ingredients of government survival in China. In response to imbalances in the relationship between the state and the community, Chinese governance has swung between strategic and ideological imperatives for centralization at one extreme, and economic and social imperatives for decentralization at the other. Inside these cycles has been another set of epicycles, between initiative and power concentration at the center, and initiative and relative independence in the localities. All countries have periods of relative tranquility and of unrest. What is striking about the Chinese case is the constitutional opposition of perpetual resistance – peaceful or violent – between the localities and the center, a single process producing both stability and instability. Modern states in China, like their counterparts everywhere else, have several times in the past hundred years attempted to dismantle the complex self-sufficiency of the localities. Yet contemporary China finds itself again dependent upon a compact that strongly resembles the traditional one – in quality if not yet in magnitude – between center and locality, between state and society. In the historical pattern, it has been impossible to change Chinese government substantially from the center; instead, rebel kingdoms and regional insurgencies have tested their growth against the restraining power of the center, and sometimes won. How well such an ecology of power can support the needs of a modern state, or even a superpower, is a question raised with increasing urgency by observers within and without China. It is the ability to allow the pivot to wobble but not fall that has been the political art of the state in China for the last four hundred years and probably more, with a single dramatic exception in the later twentieth century.

Before about 1500 imperial government around the world was premised on a surface tension between coherent, resilient, complex local organization and a central authority of limited but precise reach. The key to stability lay partly in the ratios of size and wealth between the center and the locality. Hypertrophy at the local level could generate rebel states or policy imbalances that would allow concentrations of wealth, influence and military power in certain regions, fracturing the integrity of the realm. All this was true in China as well, and the Song empire may in some ways have represented a practical optimum in the ratios between center and locality, at least between 1000 and 1200. The Song economy was marked by agricultural productivity, burgeoning trade, and the ability to sustain a military force that not only fought two northern empires to a standstill, but remained the last Eurasian empire to resist the Mongols before the Song collapse in 1279. During the Mongol period, cultural and political China was reunited for the first time in three centuries, and the borders governed from China expanded to a size that approximates the size of the People's Republic of China. But the Mongol approach to government was to keep the center small – very small, in comparison to the Song – and to distribute peacekeeping and judicial functions to the provinces, particularly to aristocrats and professional bureaucrats tied to the capital in various ways.

The basic ratios of government size and income of the Ming and Qing periods approximated the scale of Yuan government much more than that of Song. Reliance upon the ability of the locality to feed itself, protect itself, and resolve its own internal conflicts was fundamental to government practice. In the early fourteenth century the Ming Yongle emperor experimented with massive court projects (including the Zheng He voyages and the building the Forbidden City in Beijing), but these were exceptions to the basic pattern of the era. The thinness of the government layer in the Ming period and vitality of both rural and urban organizations left the imperial order suspended in a delicate balance that could be easily disturbed. Unlike the Song, the Ming government was not good at transferring rapidly increasing local wealth to itself and its organs of adjudication, control, and defense. The Ming dynastic order collapsed not due to invasion by an overwhelming foreign force, but as a result of the explosion of organized regional opposition and even more organized nascent imperial orders at the borders. In the middle seventeenth century, the Qing conquest empire undertook to govern China on largely the Ming pattern, but diminished the depth of government even more by stretching a government apparatus the size and cost of the Ming over a territory that grew to be nearly twice as big, and within a century and a half became twice as populous.

The Qing balance between center and periphery was even more delicate than the Ming, partly by design: The Qing found that a light and highly delegated political apparatus suited the exigencies of the conquests that continued in south China, Yunnan, Mongolia, Turkestan and Tibet. Stability was the zone of balance between the threat of government terror, at one end, and the threat of popular violence at the other. It was a mechanism governed by popular tolerance, despite the claims of imperial omnipotence. From the Han period on, imperial edicts and imperially-approved social philosophy – usually called "Confucian" in English-language scholarship – had manufactured the image of a unified government apparatus under the guidance of morally-cultivated rulers and officials. Yet even in those days the Han government was flexed not only by popular resistance but by organized protests among its officials and scholars waiting to become officials. Many historians in the twentieth century have dismantled the illusion of government from the center legitimated by fulfillment of an ideal of "benevolent government," seeing in it a refusal to acknowledge local autonomy and the state's persisting need to negotiate with it. The history itself suggests something more: That the dependence of the small state on the huge society had the elements of a constitution, observed in not only policy but in legislation and ideology. It generated instability through state terror and frequently insuperable local disorder, but also stability through locally-shaped economic and trade patterns and a state economy that, for long periods of time, rested relatively comfortably on the shoulders of farmers and tradesmen.

When the outward conquest was completed in the eighteenth century the process of inward conquest continued, with some parts of the empire enduring sporadic revolts or secessionist movements and the occasional rise of rebel kingdoms. These episodes of local hypertrophy were generally met not by intensified centralization or thickening of the government on the ground, but by further delegation of power to perceived agents of order in the localities. The pattern resembled some earlier dynamics in Chinese history (particularly the Tang), in medieval Europe, and, in many ways, in the Russian and Ottoman empires of the eighteenth century. It was a strong contrast to other empires, such as France and England, which were increasing the size and wealth of government in rough parallel to the growing wealth of the society as a whole. As a trend it was a contrast to the life of the Qing court and the style of central Qing rule, which in its cultural and structural aspects showed a strong kinship with nearly all other early modern Eurasian rulerships. These elements of Qing emperorship aside, the scale and the grasp of Qing government over its territories was on a divergent trajectory from many other early modern empires.

In the ensuing two centuries, the space and the regional economic and environmental diversity that the sequential governments in China have attempted to control remained about the same as the under-governed mid-Qing. The precarious balance between center and locality was fatally disrupted by a confluence of many disparate factors in the nineteenth and twentieth centuries. Economic and cultural influences spread with a speed and volume not possible in earlier centuries. International currency became a set of standardized materials and practices, challenging the techniques used locally by old governments to adjust trade and taxation. Imperialism resulted in the further restriction of income for the state and a swelling of the wealth of merchant communities at Canton and Shanghai, beyond the ability of any government to restrain. Opium became the basis of a potent and coherent network of trade and management that battled the organizational strategies of all governments globally. Such influences affected many other societies, though the Qing may have been particularly ill-prepared to mitigate them. They faced peculiar obstructions, including Japan – a neighbor that adjusted quickly and aggressively to global changes, and at every point from the later nineteenth century to 1945 fused its industrialization, wealth accumulation and military aggrandizement to the inability of a government in China to re-center itself and gain traction. When the Qing empire died of the effects of dismemberment from within and without, virtually no fiscal or political space that could support a new government could be found. Attempts to reunite the country by military exertion never penetrated beyond an alliance of intact regional autonomies. For more than three decades China and its bordering regions suffered from absence of normative government or protection from brutal foreign invasion. In 1949 one military displaced another, but under the leadership of a generation intent upon establishing a government of sufficient size and depth to reverse the effects of decades of local hypertrophy. The project for large government mutated, for various reasons, into a project for totalizing the relationship between the individual and the state. The result was the novelty of a hypertrophied center, resembling nothing that had happened previously in Chinese history. The reversal failed spectacularly, at immense cost to individuals and to eastern Eurasia generally. The nature of the failure, as well as its magnitude, illuminates the history of stable and productive interdependency of state and locality in China, and clarifies the dynamics of the aftermath of the failed experiment. Though the Chinese political systems have not conformed to a European understanding of representative government, they have been based on principles of popular tolerance. The present government may be swinging back toward the center of the arc, for much the same reasons that earlier orders based in China did so.

Further reading

Ezra Pound saw the secret of the classic as the message that "absolute sincerity under heaven can effect any change." Mathews's definition of the title's meaning is "without inclination to either side and admitting no change." Pound's quotation on *The Unwobbling Pivot* is from *Confucius,* p. 95. The characterization of Pound's title "The Unwobbling Pivot" is from Wendy Stollard Flory's "Confucius against Confusion: Ezra Pound and the Catholic Chaplain at Pisa," p. 155. Pound's translation and commentaries have been revisited in the recent study by Feng Lan, *Ezra Pound and Confucianism* (2005); see especially pp. 42–4 where Feng speculates on the technical reasons for Pound omitting the last seven chapters of the *Zhongyong.* The title "The Wobbling Pivot" has been used once before, in 1972, by J. Z. Smith in an article on the illusion of chaos in some systems of religious thought – a parallel to the discussion here of apparent chaos in Chinese society and politics.

For an introduction to the theoretical issues of overall wobbling of the modern state in China, see Chen and Benton, *Moral Economy and the Chinese Revolution* (1986); Shue, *The Reach of the State* (1988); Kuhn, *Origins of the Modern Chinese State* (2002); and Thornton, *Disciplining the State* (2007).

Timeline

1796–1820	**Jiaqing reign period**	**1875–1908**	**Guangxu reign period**
1796–1804	White Lotus Rebellion	1882	Chinese legally excluded from residing in the USA
1813	Eight Trigrams Rebellion	1885	Qing naval defeat by France, establishment of Indochina colony
1821–50	**Daoguang reign period**		
1824–6	Grand Canal Crisis		
1839–42	Opium War ending in Treaty of Nanking, Britain receives Hongkong	1895	Treaty of Shimonoseki, Japan receives Taiwan
		1898	Hundred Days Reforms suppressed
1850–64	Taiping rebellion	1900–1	Boxers at Beijing
1853–64	**Taiping Heavenly Kingdom, capital at Nanjing**	1905	Sun Yatsen founds League of Alliances at Tokyo
1851–61	**Xianfeng reign period**	1908	Deaths of the Guangxu emperor and Xiaoqin
1855–72	**Muslim revolt in Yunnan, Panthay sultanate at Dali**	**1909–12**	**Xuantong reign period**
1856–8	Arrow War, Second Opium War	**1911**	**Nationalist uprising at Wuhan, provisional republican government**
1860	Allied sack of Beijing, Peking Conventions, Allies join war against Taipings	**1912**	**Qing emperor abdicates to republican rule**
1862–74	**Tongzhi reign period**		
1867–77	**Yakub Beg in control of Kashgar**	**1913–16**	**Yuan Shikai in power**
1868	Burlingame Treaty with USA	1913	Assassination of Song Jiaoren
1870	Tientsin Massacre		

1913–25	**Sun Yatsen in south China, where Nationalist Party rules**	1950–3	Korean War
1915	Twenty-One Demands	1949–54	Common Program, provisional constitution
1918	Treaties of Versailles and Paris	1954	First PRC constitution
1919–25	May Fourth Movement	1955	Bandung conference; USA–ROC mutual defense treaty
1921	Chinese Communist Party founded	1956	Hundred Flowers campaign
1925	Death of Sun Yatsen; May Thirtieth Incident	1957	Anti-rightist movement
1926–8	Northern Expedition	1958	Great Leap Forward initiated, rural collectivization achieved
1927	**Peng Pai's soviet at Nanchang**		
1927	White Terror	1959–60	Famine
1928–38	**Chiang Kaishek in control from Nanjing**	1959	Military occupation of Tibet
1931	Japanese forces seize Shenyang (Mukden)	1959	Lushan Plenum
1931–4	**Chinese Soviet Republic, based on soviets of southern China**	1960	Sino-Soviet split
		1960	Liu Shaoqi becomes Chairman of the PRC
1932–4	**Manchukuo Republic**	1962	Border conflict with India
1932	Japanese invade Shanghai		
1934–45	**Empire of Manchukuo**	1963–6	Socialist Education Movement
1934–6	Long March	1964	PRC successfully tests nuclear weapon
1935	Zunyi conferences		
1936	Chiang forced to Xi'an, agrees to second united front	1966–9	Cultural Revolution, first phase
1937	Japanese invade Beijing and Nanjing	1969–73	Cultural Revolution, second phase, return of Deng Xiaoping
1937–47	**Yan'an base area center of Mao's operations**	1969	Border clashes with USSR
1945	Japanese surrender, World War II ended	1971	PRC seated at the UN; death of Lin Biao
1946–9	Civil war between nationalists and communists	1972	Nixon and Kissinger in China;
1947–9	Nationalist transfers to Taiwan	1973	10th Party Congress
		1973–6	Cultural Revolution, last phase
1947	Local resistance in Taiwan against Nationalist arrival	1975	Death of Chiang Kaishek
1949	**Chiang arrives in Taiwan, declares continuity of Republic of China**	1976	Deaths of Zhou, first Tian'anmen incident; deaths of Zhu De and Mao; Tangshan earthquake; arrest of Jiang Qing and her collaborators
1949	**People's Republic of China declared**	1978–80	Democracy Wall

1979 Normalization of relations with the USA, PRC war with Vietnam; USA-Taiwan Relations Act

1980 Special economic zones introduced

1982 New constitution allows some privatization of land use and income

1984 Britain agrees to return Hongkong

1987 Martial law lifted in Taiwan by ROC

1989 Tian'anmen movement and suppression

1992 Deng Xiaoping retires from government power

1996 USA accuses China of expropriating weapons technology

1997 Death of Deng Xiaoping; Hongkong becomes part of PRC

1999 USA bombs Chinese embassy in Belgrade

2000 Removals from planned Three Gorges Dam reservoir space begin

2001 Air incident with USA above Hainan island; PRC joins WTO

2003 First PRC manned space mission

2005 Anti-secession law, evidently aimed at Taiwan

2006 Three Gorges Dam completed

2008 Tibetan unrest; Sichuan earthquake; Summer Olympics held in Beijing;

2009 Charter 08 activists arrested; Xinjiang unrest

1

The Wobbling Pivot

IT IS UNUSUAL for the contents of a semi-confidential email to become universally known on the Internet. But in March of 2009, after the nomination of Charles W. Freeman Jr. as chair of the American government's National Intelligence Council, his email to the ChinaSec listserv group of May 26, 2006 drew attention for this comment about the Tiananmen incidents of 1989: "I find the dominant view in China about this very plausible, i.e. that the truly unforgivable mistake of the Chinese authorities was the failure to intervene on a timely basis to nip the demonstrations in the bud, rather than – as would have been both wise and efficacious – to intervene with force when all other measures had failed to restore domestic tranquility to Beijing and other major urban centers in China. In this optic, the Politburo's response to the mob scene at 'Tian'anmen' stands as a monument to overly cautious behavior on the part of the leadership, not as an example of rash action."

Freeman's suggestion that the contrast is to tactics, and not to politics, leaves the comment dangling above the ground, out of contact with historical patterns of China's recent centuries. The hearts of China's political capitals have been occupied by state opponents and dissidents repeatedly over the centuries. State reaction is rarely swift, though it is often bloody. These events are products of a structural relationship between government and society that was strongly in evidence from at least 1644 to 1958, and since 1976 has been reestablishing itself to a modest degree. It is a system with a peculiar way of producing social and economic order, but one that in very extreme circumstances is vulnerable to catastrophic breakdown. Considered outside its historical context, it sometimes leads observers too quickly to words like "instability," "disorder," "chaos."

When I was following the thread that now runs through this book, my mind kept returning to scenes from contemporary China. I was in China for the first time in 1977. On an otherwise quiet afternoon in Luoyang, where the streets did not look particularly crowded, a loud discussion broke out between two men over a bicycle (in those days, bicycles were all *Flying Pigeon*, identical to any but the eye of love). A small knot of people quickly wound itself around the disputatious men, listening carefully, advising moderation and not, coincidentally, preventing the bicycle from going anywhere. The knot grew to a crowd large enough to block the narrow street.

A few men at the front of the throng had joined in the conversation, questioning the men in turn, and repeatedly advising calm and honesty. After some minutes the inevitable representative of local public security arrived. She was a small woman, not plump but solidly built, with the regulation even hair length and middle part, and a bright red arm band proclaiming her official status. The crowd shifted only enough to allow her to make her way to the front, a few people darting glances of blame at the bicycle men for having brought the authorities onto the scene. The public security woman asked a few questions of the men and appeared, for a moment, to be attempting to break up the congregation and send the men on their way. But she was a late arrival on the scene. The two men who had begun negotiations between the adversaries continued in their role, with polite acknowledgment of the official's presence. Occasionally Public Security would inject her questions or views, but at roughly the same rate and pitch as others at the center of the circle. After ten minutes, the contenders nodded agreement to each other, one moved off with the bicycle, and the crowd, including the woman distinguished by her bold red armband, moved on to their business.

I had the strong feeling that I had seen something that was not the least unusual. Everybody took the dispute, the resolution and the public participation in stride. The crowd was not merely bystanders, camp followers or observers for sport. The quickness with which they organized themselves for conflict containment and resolution, the precision with which certain individuals assumed and fulfilled their roles, suggested to me something basic about the social methods of the Luoyang inhabitants who had entered the street expecting to do their shopping or their chores, but instead became embroiled in the forensics, the philosophy and the administration of a dispute between two men over a bicycle. I did not know at the time, but am convinced now, that in 1977 such a social phenomenon in Luoyang evinced ancient practices that a decade before had been under extreme assault, and wounded seriously though not fatally.

Another side of this phenomenon seems to be evident in two anecdotes recently related by the journalist Tim Johnson in 2008. In the first, Johnson discovers that it is impossible to get taxi drivers in Changchun to actually use the meters and issue receipts from them. Since the law requires that the meters be used and the receipts issued, Johnson approached a "security guard" (the contemporary equivalent of the security maiden I spoke of in Luoyang in 1977) to complain. The guard merely shrugged. Johnson commented, "At first, I found this a little irksome. But on reflection, I sort of admired the taxi drivers. The local authorities apparently had imposed an impractical limit on fares, and the cabbies rebelled in the only way they could. The security guard understood and sympathized." In a second vignette, Johnson ends up on a bus after the flight he expected to take was cancelled. The airline had chartered the bus at no expense to the passengers, and had obviously provided the driver with sufficient cash to take the high-speed, well-maintained toll roads to the destination. The driver, however, took a meandering, pothole-riddled route, keeping the toll fees for himself. Passengers repeatedly pointed out to him the highway ramps he was passing, but otherwise took no issue or action. Johnson experienced some outrage at this, too, but then reconsidered after taking a comparative view: "It was a minor inconvenience. I thought back to times in South America, where bus drivers would be in cahoots with armed bandits, pulling buses over at remote spots where everyone would be robbed."

In Johnson's view, the passivity of the Chinese passengers was related to his philosophy of what is worth getting outraged about. But I see it in the same theme of social compact I witnessed in Luoyang. In the case of the Changchun taxi drivers, local officials and local riders permit the flaunting of law – and legally stipulated fares – in exchange for having reasonably numerous and reasonably efficient taxis accessible. There is also the assumption that taxis are not ridden in by the majority of people, but are usually hired by businessmen and foreigners who can arrange to be compensated for their inflated fares by filling in the blank receipts with the sum of their choosing. Losses will be passed on to a rich (possibly foreign) corporation. In the case of the bus driver, the riders could take the view that it was really the airline and not themselves that was being dunned to pay a little extra to a hard-working bus driver. If there was injustice, it was hard to define and seconded to a faceless, absent entity. Of course, being captives on the bus in question was not a trivial matter. Though it was not part of the scenes above in Luoyang or in Changchun, in Chinese history there is plenty of evidence of the complex role of coercion and terror in the workings of these social compacts.

Because of the uncertain balance between local and central power, coercion can go either way. There is nothing new about well-connected individuals using their status as leverage against local law enforcement, and in China there continue to be vivid examples of it. Cases of élites flaunting their privileges can be woven into an emerging popular discourse of heroic resistance to authority. In April of 2008, CCP party cadre Zhang Longping, aged 30, attached to the Hubei Automotive Institute, was out driving with some friends. Her car became involved in a minor collision with a police cruiser, which happened to be driven by the commander of the local constabulary. Both drivers jumped from their cars and began to shout. The police commander struck Zhang, and threw the keys to her car into a ditch. Zhang's friends spilled from her car and surrounded or disabled the police car so that it could not leave the scene. Zhang opened her cell phone and summoned twelve men to come help. When they arrived, they beat the police commander to death. Though Zhang was immediately arrested, she argued that the police commander had been drunk, and that his own behavior had precipitated his death.

In the days after her arrest, Zhang was publicly lauded by her friends and colleagues, who described her as sweet-natured, generous and loyal. Since the Hubei Automotive Institute has the status of a university, she was described in newspaper accounts as the "Female University Cadre Who is Charged with Beating a Policeman to Death." Photographs of her smiling with an earlier certificate for meritorious service became ubiquitous. In a way, she won her case: In a country where smugglers and con men are routinely sentenced to death (and it is frequently carried out), Zhang Longping was sentenced to ten years in prison for manslaughter and being a public menace. She became an Internet celebrity, inciting online shouting matches in which a considerable number of supporters lauded her as a valiant defender of people's rights. However meritorious Zhang may have been, her university and political connections gave her resources to call upon when in trouble, and may even have given her the sense of entitlement necessary to get into a slap-down with a police commander. Her ability to call upon twelve stalwarts who arrived to beat the officer to death is also intriguing. Zhang Longping, it would seem, is among the privileged in China, who have a community and a social compact (in addition to the tailored economic and political spaces they are known to inhabit) all their own.

News from China, much of it resembling news actually reported in China, suggests that the local initiative once essential to administrative cohesion under the empires continues to express itself, and is possibly increasing after the economic and political reforms of the late twentieth century. If individuals and crowds of individuals in China are slow to react to what may appear to be trivial violations of standards by private individuals, they are quick to respond to severe injustices at the hands of authority figures. A very typical case occurred in March of 2008, in Taishan, Guangdong, when a policeman stopped a moped rider for an equipment citation. The rider jumped into the river to escape impending arrest, but then thought better of his act and asked to come ashore. The policeman refused to allow him onto land, and also prevented bystanders from aiding the fugitive. In sight of a gathering crowd, the rider drowned in the river. Immediately, the onlookers set upon the officer. When police reinforcements in full riot gear arrived, they were stoned by the gathering, which now numbered somewhere between 8,000 and 10,000 people. One policeman, out of about a thousand present, was killed, though the policeman upon whom the crowd had originally set survived.

In the instance of the drowned moped rider, the policeman was judged in violation of the custom of tolerance and humane consideration. He pushed the rules regarding traffic misdemeanors to the point of causing a man's death, and at the same time demonstrated the arrogance of official conduct which most arouses the outrage of the Chinese public. Depending on circumstances, he could have got off with a scolding and mild rough-up from the crowd, or he might have been beaten to death with the consent of the majority. As it happened, the local authorities decided to fight to defend him, escalating the mêlée to the point where at least one (policeman) was killed and dozens were injured. The city came under the equivalent of martial law, and photographs document that the crowd for days ignored orders to disperse. We may surmise that traffic cops in Taishan are now hesitant to pester drivers over petty infractions.

Such incidents of public outrage at official presumption are microcosms of the upheavals that have shaken many rural communities, mostly in southern China, in the past decade as a result of public fury at official corruption. Dazhou, Sichuan, has for years been showing the stress of popular anger against its mining industries, prostitution rings, drug problems and a poorly managed outbreak of avian flu. County police were summoned on December 30, 2006, to the bar of a hotel known for its connections both to officials and to organized crime. They found the body of a 16-year-old waitress slumped over in a booth. Hotel employees told them that earlier in the evening they had seen three men known to be mine managers and cronies of the hotel owner indicate that they wished the young waitress to keep them company. The girl and the men left together, and the girl returned on her own some hours later; and still later, bar employees found her dead. The police promised a thorough investigation. Hotel employees, a few of whom had seen the body, spread reports that it showed signs of beating, forced injections of drugs and repeated brutal rape. By the middle of January, 2007, the police had made no arrests and had taken no statements. The family of the dead waitress and a few hundred other people gathered in front of the hotel where she had died, loudly demanding that the investigation progress. The Dazhou party secretary quickly made public statements to assuage the community, promising a speedy and impartial resolution, while the hotel offered the family money – reports ranged from 500,000 to 800,000 RMB (approximately US $90,000 to $140,000) – to not insist upon further inquiry. The family rejected the offers in favor of investigation and indictment. Days later a crowd burst into the hotel and set it afire. The riot eventually swelled to 10,000 participants, against which the Dazhou county security department deployed 5,000 armed police. By the end of the month police claimed the waitress had died of acute pancreatitis, but they arrested the hotel bartender for raping her after she returned from her tryst with the three mine managers. A policeman was demoted for having tampered with evidence. And a 24-year-old Dazhou mall worker had been sentenced to prison for spreading Internet reports about the alleged murder.

Environmental deterioration in rural China sparks public demonstrations and occasionally riots with increasing frequency. Weng'an, Guizhou, has been unsettled for years by anger over unsafe mines and polluted water. In June of 2008 the body of a 15-year-old girl was recovered from a river in Weng'an. Two sons of local officials and an additional friend were taken into custody, but soon released, and the police announced that the girl's death was due to suicide. Rumors and suspicion spread through the community quickly, claiming that the official's sons had raped and murdered the girl at the instigation of the jealous daughter of another official. The girl's parents stood vigil by the body to prevent the police from hastily cremating it. The girl's uncle, a well-known school teacher, went to the police station to ask for news of the investigation. He died there, apparently as a result of beating by police officers. News of the second death spread, and within a few days 30,000 people had surrounded the station. The building was torched and police cars were overturned. The county government sent in 2,000 police in riot gear; the people engaged in hand-to-hand combat with them. National and international reports eventually put the toll at 150 injuries (100 of them police), a gutted police station, and 20 charred police cars. Authorities restored order and the girl's funeral was held, but locals still made bold to adorn her coffin with a placard protesting that "killing people is not a crime." As the authorities announced that they would reopen an investigation into both the deaths and the riots, residents told journalists that riot leaders and peaceful protesters alike were being beaten and killed by local mobsters, either at the order of or with the permission of the police.

Incidents of popular unrest in China today, many linked to land rights, pollution, unsafe working conditions and the endless demands of local officials for bribes and sexual privileges, are too numerous to narrate or even quantify with precision. The most widely noted incidents involve heavy-handed local police responses that serve to escalate the conflicts, rather than resolving them, because the public finds organizational resources to continue resistance. Among the most famous was the incident at Dongzhou, Guangdong, in December of 2005, when farmers who felt themselves cheated in a land seizure by a state utility held a public demonstration. Police opened fire, killing at least five people at the scene. The incident drew attention when the police commander was denounced by officials and disciplined for using unnecessary violence. But many localities in Guangdong remain afflicted with frequent protests and outbreaks of violence. In nearly all cases, the government is quick to respond with statements intended to appease the public, and in a small number of incidents it actually goes the whole way with the convictions of low-level officials. The counter-productivity of strong police response has not changed the government strategy very much. An editorial in the official government Xinhua news service a year after the

Dongzhou incident proclaimed, "The huge number and broad scope of mass incidents has become the most outstanding problem that seriously impacts social stability ... We should stick to the principle of deploying police, using weapons and resorting to forceful measures prudently."

Despite Xinhua's urging that local authorities respond with a clenched fist, there is strong evidence that local officials and police commanders vary their responses, depending on circumstances. In Hunan province in September of 2008, officials and entrepreneurs cooperated in a plan to run a private, unregulated stock market in order to raise capital for local industries. Sellers of the shares promised quick profits, reported somewhere between 70 and 135 percent or more, to local investors – many of whom were underemployed and retired, attracted by the promise of rapid returns in an environment where interest rates were lower than inflation and few opportunities to exploit savings existed. According to reports from the press and from local Internet-based informants, between 2004 and 2006 the scheme raised over a billion dollars (in USD equivalence) for about fifty companies from about 150,000 local investors. But in June of 2008 the local officials lost their nerve when higher government levels began to learn of the scheme. The result was quick withdrawals by the well-informed, crashing the stocks and wreaking economic devastation on the local small investors. By the end of August it was clear that the losing investors had no hope of compensation, and tens of thousands of people took to the streets, demanding the arrest and prosecution of the entrepreneurs behind the disaster. Approximately 5,000 People's Liberation Army soldiers based in Hunan were sent to the scene. Injuries were minimal and only a small number of rioters were arrested. Instead the executives of Fuda Property Development Company were taken into custody by provincial authorities. In a similar incident in Gaodong, Sichuan, residents had lived for decades with the daily explosions from a network of manganese mines (their home county produces 20 percent of the world's mangenese). The blasts had deafened residents and undermined the foundations of their homes. In early 2008 they invited a county official to listen to their complaints, and were rewarded with the usual government bromides about tempering the drive for economic development with compassionate concern for the people's well-being. They took to the streets a few months later when their water supplies were poisoned, their crops ruined and rising incidences of cancer were starting panics. They surrounded and petitioned the company headquarters and officers. The provincial government took an unorthodox but not rare approach in this case, standing on the sidelines like a mildly interested observer, doing nothing as the locals pressured the company into paying token compensation for its assault on the local quality of life.

This is not to suggest that intermittent periods of government timidity in the face of public unrest correlate to the demonstrated boldness of individuals or groups in challenging the government. In all periods, public questioning or denunciation of the government in China is an act of serious courage, and may even be suicidal. This underscores the significance of the relative frequency with which individual Chinese proclaim their opposition to or skepticism of the government, or groups demonstrate on behalf of an individual or a cause. Overall it appears that people who take on the government without benefit of a resilient organizational connection fare worse, by far. In contrast to the cell-phone wielding/university student/party cadre/fashion plate Zhang Longping who was given ten years for having her friends beat a police commander to death, the Beijingers protesting destruction of their homes during the development frenzy that preceded the Olympics in 2008 were helpless. An estimated total of 1.25 million Beijing tenants from various neighborhoods were evicted on command; if they resisted, they were evicted by force. All were promised full compensation; very few received it. Riots were ruthlessly suppressed, lawsuits connected to tenants' rights were delayed or diverted, and petitions requesting the right to demonstrate during the Olympics against the removals were denied. Against the residents was arrayed the strongest axis of state capitalism in China: the party itself, almost wholly composed of investors in state-protected industries as well as privately-managed corporations that operate under CCP partnership. And arrayed behind them was the cohort of connected, predatory venture capitalists who intended to raze the neighborhoods not only for Olympic architecture but for "culture streets," dubious historical restorations designed to rake in dollars from credulous tourists. The residents themselves had been deprived of their only real resource – the organizational infrastructure of their neighborhoods, some of which had been inhabited by their ancestors for generations. Nevertheless, in a situation in which the state had optimal leverage and the society had none, protests continued. Thousands were fined and jailed. Most famous among them, perhaps, were Wu Dianyuan, 77, and Wang Xiuying, 79, who were convicted by the police, not the courts, of disturbing public order. The women, both of whom walked with canes, were sentenced to a year of "re-education through labor," though the police suggested they might waive the imprisonment if the convicts would go home and be quiet. Instead, Wang and Wu decried both the original injustice and the new injustices of their prison sentences, after which they were carted off to jail. During their imprisonment photographs of the two women sweltering in the mud-walled cell they shared were distributed across the Internet. Other Beijing residents whose petitions for redress had been denied continued to voice complaints to international reporters and to Chinese Internet writers.

More disturbing to state security planners are real or prospective combinations of traditional rages against government misbehavior with explosive tensions in the border and minority areas. Many of the most colorfully reported incidents of public disturbance are in Tibet, where riots provoked by local perceptions of government misconduct – or economic predation encouraged by government policies – have occurred off and on for decades. More relevant to this discussion might be the incidents of March 2008. Newspaper accounts and vivid television footage showed Tibetans attacking Han Chinese in Lhasa. The victims were not government officers but civilians, particularly shopkeepers. As the riots grew and police moved in to restore order, just under 1,400 shops were reported destroyed, along with 120 houses and over 80 cars and trucks. Though Lhasa is not one of the bigger cities in the PRC, casualties were very high for an incident of this sort. The official figures, which were probably lower than the actual numbers, listed 22 deaths (including at least one police officer) and over 600 injuries, of which at least 200 were suffered by the police. The statistics do not appear to include monks and nuns known to have been summarily executed, a normal feature of government crackdowns in Tibet. Trials that were concluded in November of 2008 sentenced another 55 Tibetans to prison terms for their roles in inciting, participating in or abetting the violence. Undoubtedly, there are aspects of civil conflicts in Tibet that are different from the civil conflicts in other parts of China. But the basic structure, in the case of March 2008, is similar. Because of government policies encouraging Han Chinese to migrate to Tibet from overpopulated and economically constrained parts of China, the Han merchants who operate in Tibet under the protection of the state are regarded as agents of the state – enriching themselves, as officials often do in other parts of China, with the leverage gained through family or, in this case, racial connections, at the expense of the local population. The implied compact of adjusting ambitions in order to preserve a basic comity was perceived to be broken, and as happens in other parts of the PRC when the compact is broken, the locals took matters into their own hands with violence.

The scale and the shape of public disorders in Tibet are being increasingly paralleled in Xinjiang province. In August of 2008 two police officers were killed and two others critically injured in what seemed a bizarre incident outside Kashgar, Xinjiang province. All involved in the incident, both attackers and attacked, were Uighurs (or Türki, as they call themselves). Witnesses claimed that a police troop of eight or ten soldiers, accompanied by the village mayor, were walking in a cornfield when they were attacked by six or seven individuals, wielding knives. Over 500 Han Chinese soldiers were brought in, ostensibly to apprehend the suspected attackers. Local Muslim men and women were closely questioned, but the suspects in the attack could not all be identified, and none could be located. Only weeks before, three Uighur policeman had been knifed to death in another Xinjiang village; a Uighur woman was a suspect, but had also not been apprehended, despite the posting of a 50,000 *yuan* (roughly US $8000) reward. And there were more incidents during the same month, involving both stabbings and bombings of police stations and police patrols. Though the state language describing such incidents in Xinjiang frequently mentions the word "Muslim," and often but not always suggests that there is a special issue in these conflicts (implying disrepute of and likelihood of terrorist connections among Xinjiang Muslims), the above incident has a shape that is similar to incidents that occur with great frequency in more central parts of China: The police were attacked by one or more local residents, and the locals supported the attackers (and perhaps the attack itself), in this case by shielding them from apprehension.

These incidents are symptomatic of tensions in Xinjiang. For decades government policy has encouraged migration to the region by Han Chinese from various parts of China, leaving the original Uighur inhabitants as half the provincial population and a mere 30 percent of the population in the provincial capital, Ürümqi. The government has exploited global apprehension of Muslim radicalism to pursue regulations limiting the public expression of Muslim identity. Recent policies have banned the use of Uighur as a school language, insisting that all education except for "foreign language study" (Uighur) be in Chinese. The city of Kashgar, central to the history of Uighur Muslim cultural history, has been subjected to the peculiarly brutal PRC practices of "restoration," already visited upon Beijing, Xi'an, and other historic treasure spots within China; in the case of Kashgar, the destruction was swift and carried out with virtually no acknowledgment of the protests and the anguish of the local population. In July of 2009, an open conflict of unprecedented proportions exploded in Ürümqi, resulting in at least 200 deaths, and thousands of injuries. The precipitating event was the beating to death of two Uighur factory workers sojourning in Guangdong province, and the apparent indifference of the Guangdong authorities to it. When crowds in Ürümqi protested the deaths and the lack of government action, riots involving thousands broke out. Subsequent investigation revealed that police forces had retreated or stood paralyzed in the face of the overwhelming numbers of protesters. The next day, Chinese media reported that Han Chinese were targeted by the rioters, and that more than 150 had been killed in one night. After the riots had been quelled by paramilitary police, Han Chinese in the city began to organize themselves to take revenge on the Uighurs. Disorders broke out in other Xinjiang cities, including Kashgar, and crowds of Uighurs continued for weeks to gather to demonstrate in front of the foreign media. The government massively augmented the troops on the scene, but promised to swiftly investigate the deaths in Guangdong and punish the killers. There are many indications, however, that the government response in border areas is leaning much more toward violent repression and much less toward civil concession. As in Tibet, the government seems to have responded to the magnitude of the challenge instead of its underlying character, while outbreaks of disorder in China's interior continue to be responded to with both repression and concession. In Tibet and Xinjiang the government may choose to use an inflexible approach as a possible backdoor solution to its "minority" problems. History suggests this would be a colossal mistake.

The broader historical energies behind public protests in China as well as minority areas are underscored by the fact that, in the aftermath of former Taiwan president Chen Shui-bien's independence-oriented government, the nationalist government of Ma Ying-jeou is having difficulty restraining crowds who gather to shower indignation upon visiting PRC officials. *Newsweek*'s online columnist Jonathan Adams described two incidents in the fall of 2008 that illustrate the point. In October, a PRC trade official touring southern Taiwan was surrounded by a crowd, "including, pathetically, an elderly woman who banged on the official's car with her crutch." In early November, PRC negotiator Chen Yunlin was unable to leave his hotel in Taipei for eight hours because it had been surrounded by a mob that scolded the PRC journalists trying to cover the event, and clashed with police who tried to disperse them. The willingness of the Taiwan public to take to the streets to demonstrate against China, or against corruption, or against the increasing authoritarianism of the Ma government is regarded in some quarters as destabilizing, in others as democratizing. Adams thought it was evidence of the fact that in Taiwan, unlike China, there are civil liberties. "For his part, Chen Yunlin was reportedly livid that Taiwanese police couldn't simply clear the hotel area of protesters – a simple enough task in the mainland, but not in freewheeling, democratic Taiwan, where there's such a thing as civil liberties."

There are civil liberties in Taiwan (where martial law was lifted in 1987 and where genuine democracy has evolved since) but there is another way of looking at these incidents. Clearing protesters from a site is not, in fact, a simple task in the PRC. This was demonstrated, not least of all, in 1999, when crowds in Beijing besieged both the Japanese embassy (in April) and the American embassy (in May). The Japanese embassy was subjected to relatively peaceful demonstrations by tens of thousands of Chinese as part of a series of public disorders (including assaults on Japanese in Beijing) relating to a controversies over new textbooks published in Japan that obscured Japanese atrocities committed in China in the 1930s and 1940s. In May, tens of thousands of demonstrators surrounded the US embassy in Beijing after American planes bombed the Chinese embassy in Belgrade, killing three staff outright and sending twenty to hospital. The USA apologized for using what it said was a faulty map of Belgrade, but otherwise made no public concessions. The crowd threw rocks, burning bottles and other debris at the embassy, destroying its windows and blockading its residents for days. International press compared the rampages of the spring to events 99 years before, when the Boxers had assaulted the foreign embassies, killing diplomats when possible and trapping foreign families in the walled embassy compounds. The American ambassador, James Sasser, survived the 1999 attacks unhurt like the rest of his staff (but soon returned to the USA and broke his arm after tripping on a cat his daughter had brought from China). In an interview with *The New York Times*, Sasser indicated that despite the mysterious ineffectiveness of the Beijing police in quelling the anti-American uprising, he had the strong impression that the PRC government, from the foreign ministry to then-president Jiang Zemin, had been helpless to avoid the prolonged assault on the embassy.

The above anecdotes are selected from hundreds of large incidents happening in recent years, and tens of thousands of smaller ones. In every province of China, workers and farmers are reported to resist or even drive off police teams sent to break up their demonstrations against the wholesale destruction of neighborhoods by developers, or for better wages, the protection of land rights, better housing standards and lower rents. Increasingly, environmental deterioration that ruins water supplies or threatens the health of children is the irritant behind public demonstrations. Even administrative issues can be subject to negotiation by mobilization, as when thousands protested a decision to diminish the status of Daye, Hubei, from a city to a district (and then protested again after police used dogs to break up the crowd) in August of 2005, or taxi drivers rioting from Guangdong to Qinghai to protest the failure to enforce regulations against unlicensed cabs. The Chinese government acknowledges these incidents are on the rise. Premier Wen Jiabao's deputy for financial and economic affairs, Chen Xiwen, made extensive comment on the matter in July of 2005, suggesting that rural incidents were a healthy sign that farmers were improving in democratic awareness without presenting a serious threat to the state. He told *South China Morning Post*, "There are at least 3 million villages [in which live about 800 million farming families] across the country and you can imagine how many problems crop up each day. If there are 30,000 villages having problems, that accounts for only 1 per cent of the total." Nevertheless almost as Chen spoke, Wen Jiabao's government made a public proposal to eliminate all taxes on the farming population by 2008, a program which has been largely realized. Though Chen Xiwen made no reference to it, the history of China is replete with popular action, both rural and urban, intended to limit the power of local officials or correct perceived injustices. It may or may not be "democratic." But it is certainly not novel, nor fundamentally related to claimed attempts by the contemporary government to introduce democratic education or reforms.

Collective expressions of discontent are not limited to the landless, homeless or laborers, agricultural or urban. Police themselves are not always unquestioning enforcers of the government will. Sometimes, as in Hunan province in December 2008, the police are doing the striking, the seizing of their own buildings, blocking a public intersection and clashing with paramilitary forces sent to quell them. The Hunan dispute was occasioned by what the police officers regarded as low wages (a type of incident with very strong resonance of events from Qing history, when the hereditary military forces, the Eight Banners, developed a rich history of riots protesting unpaid wages). Teachers and bureaucrats are also known to engage in work actions and public demonstrations if wages, benefits or working conditions are not satisfactory and attempts to lodge complaints are ignored. The explosion in condominium-style housing has produced a large class of homeowners, most of whom are sensitive to government and private land grabs that will displace them or diminish the value of their properties. Peaceful protest by these groups is increasing. In February of 2008 homeowners in Shanghai conducted a traffic-blocking "stroll" to protest a planned new maglev line which they feared would degrade the quality and safety of their neighborhood. Demonstrations of this sort are becoming more frequent. The educated middle class of China knows that the current laws permit applications for public protest – though in practice an application to protest during a sensitive time (for instance, before the Olympics) can in itself lead to arrest and imprisonment.

In the twenty-first century, professionals are clearly attempting to normalize the idea of petitioning as an implied protest against government repression of political activists, environmentalists, and leaders for minority rights. Petitioning is protected under traditional values, since all the empires and the Republican government have acknowledged the right of both common people and literati élites to petition for mercy or the righting of injustices; indeed, in imperial times petition and the appeal of legal convictions were essential tools for the central state to gain some ability to observe the conduct of its distant, local officials. Petitioning crossed cultural (but not class) divides when the dissident novelist Wang Lixiong (husband of a Tibetan blogger) led a widespread petitioning campaign for the release of Ilham Tohti, a Uighur economist arrested in the aftermath of the Xinjiang disorders of 2009. The government has every reason to expect that petitioning by professionals, bolstered as it now is by the international press, will become a more frequent feature of the public reaction to policies affecting speech, the environment, labor and cultural minorities.

In the most notorious incidence of a private citizen convicted for enraged violence against the police, journalists, lawyers, professors and other urban élites – though not members of the state–capitalist coalition – became visible as a layer of resistance against state authority. In 2007 Yang Jia was roughed up by police in Shanxi province who stopped him for questioning at a train station. Later Yang transferred to Shanghai, where he was unemployed, and was arrested by police because he was riding an unlicensed bicycle (which he had rented). He later attempted to file a lawsuit against the arresting officers, claiming that while in police custody he had been tortured and humiliated. The authorities, however, produced an audio tape of the arrest in which Yang could be heard becoming argumentative with the police as soon as they had stopped him. Yang's claim was rejected by the court. Just a month before the Olympics was held in Beijing in August of 2008, he went on a rampage inside the same Shanghai police station. He stabbed five officers to death and wounded four more, one of whom died of his wounds the next day. Yang told arresting officers that he was acting out of revenge, and that "I'd rather break the law than live with injustice my whole life." Yang was immediately sentenced to death by the local court, and he appealed the case to the municipal court, where angry crowds gathered demanding his exoneration. But the court confirmed the sentence in late October, and the appeal then went to the Supreme Court (*zuigao renmin fayuan*).

Newspaper editors, as well as the Shanghai public, were outraged at Yang's conviction. A man in nearby Suzhou claimed on the Internet that Yang's rage was due to the fact that beatings by the police had left him impotent; the blogger was arrested and interrogated by his own local police. Editors of the *Southern Weekly* newspaper, *Southern Weekend*, *Pearl River Evening News* and *Beijing News* came to Yang's defense. They pointed out that his lawyer at his trial was also the lawyer charged with handling legal affairs for the Shanghai police. They warned that executing Yang would lead to huge public disorders in the city. Lawyers in Beijing offered to represent Yang, but the Shanghai courts refused. As local leaders, journalists and lawyers continued to comment on the case and to petition the court for clemency, the government made more arrests, blocked more people's access to the Internet, and disappeared at least two legal advocates who were arrested for misdemeanors after publicly questioning the propriety of Yang's trials. This created a second and third round of public claims of power abuse and corruption.

By the time Yang's death sentence was upheld by the Supreme Court on November 3, 2008 he had become an icon – in the streets, in the press, and especially on the Internet – of the traditional Chinese ideal of steadfast if hopeless resistance by the helpless against the corrupt and capricious state. His personal flaws, which were not denied, were regarded as the products of social deformation, and his summary death sentence was seen as an act of inhumanity. National and international calls for commutation of the death sentence were accompanied by admonitions to the government that the case now involved so many detentions and disappearances that merely executing Yang could not make the problem go away. The case, if tried in some other countries, would likely be regarded as a case of an insane rampage against rational authority. But in the hands of journalists, lawyers and academic commentators in China it became a dramatization of the interplay of police thuggery, merciless government short-sightedness and malignant social imbalances. Courtrooms in which Yang's appeals were heard were packed with crowds of Shanghai-based supporters, and the artist Ai Weiwei led a petitioning campaign for the reduction of Yang's sentence. Lawyers and academics argued, before and after resolution of the case, that the refusal of the state to show any compassion for the fact that Yang had been literally driven mad when he was abused by corrupt and self-indulgent local police meant that the present government was not even graced by the compassion of the imperial governments, which had traditionally pardoned or softened punishments for the insane. The Yang Jia case came to be regarded as, and perhaps will continue to remain, the single most complex, and single most simple, test of the legitimacy of the PRC legal system. After Yang's execution on November 26, 2008, an Internet campaign to lionize him continued, warning that "millions and millions of Yang Jia's will follow him."

The mechanism for public trials of breakers of the peace is evolving, if somewhat erratically, in such a way as to allow a pause for public observation, comment and perhaps even intervention. In this enlarging interval between arrest and punishment, scholars, lawyers and journalists become involved in many cases. If the government response is crude enough, more arrests and trials result from the comments or claimed actions of the interveners, widening the pool of government violations and public mistrust. There are indications that the leaders of the CCP are undecided about the safest path. The rate of imposition of death sentences and actual executions is decreasing. Despite the risks, a few dozen lawyers in China continue to be full-time advocates for individual rights. They succeeded in having Deng Yujiao, a young waitress who stabbed to death a party official who was demanding sex from her, acquitted on the same grounds (mental distress or instability) that they had argued should have been applied in the Yang Jia case. Not long after Deng's acquittal in 2009, the government also announced that it would reduce the rate of execution to "a very small number" (Amnesty International had confirmed a minimum of 470 executions in China, but assumed the figure was far below the actual total; just enough is known of the total of annual executions in China to know that it kills far more convicts and prisoners per year than any other country, with Iran being a probable second). In cases such as tainted milk, poisoned groundwater or local corruption where the government would be inclined to find and punish scapegoats anyway, lawyers have been able to insert themselves and suggest that litigation might be a normal route of redress. They continue to work on behalf of dissidents whom the government has no apparent intention of treating with leniency, and in their persistence the lawyers hope to impress upon the Chinese public the idea that law has an innate validity, and that legal processes may, by their own power, lead to justice. The fight is a long and uncertain one, but the fact that the government has not silenced the lawyers – despite the fact that each year some of their number disappear into the state prisons – is testimony to their progress.

Between about 1998 and 2004, the government appeared to relax its censorship policies with the newspapers, regarding newspapers as commercial enterprises that would best thrive with minimal regulation. *Beijing News* (*BN*) was such a commercially-oriented outlet. It was founded in 2003 as a cooperative enterprise by two large and profitable newspapers, *Guangming Daily* (*Guangming ribao*) and *Southern Daily*. The editors of *Beijing News* were determined to print what the public wants to read, and what the Chinese public often wants to read is criticism of the government. *BN*'s frequent reports and editorials on official corruption were greeted as a breath of fresh air by the international press, and the paper's profits soared. It soon had smaller emulators, all challenging – if only implicitly – the voice of the party organ, *People's Daily*, and the official news service, Xinhua. It appears that in June of 2005 the *BN* went beyond the invisible limit of government forbearance. Residents of Dingzhou, Hebei province, had set out to protest and then to actually prevent the construction of new power plant. They threw up a small tent city for themselves at the construction site. Frustrated local officials, eager to get the facility operating, enlisted hundreds of local thugs to smash both the tents and the protesters; they killed six people outright and sent dozens to the hospital. Local knowledge of the event ignited public protests and property destruction spread. Plenty of journalists were on the scene, but only the *Beijing News* correspondent reported the role of government goons in the debacle. In December, after months of discussing whether and how *BN* should be punished, state officials demanded the resignation of its editor. If the intention was to remind the journalists at *BN* that, like all journalists in China, they publish and work only with permission of the government, this did not work at first. The staff walked out, and for weeks the paper published only wire-service stories (from Xinhua). Its website was taken down, and its name and some of its bylines became targets of the Internet censor machines. Inevitably, the *BN* staff were replaced with more tractable editors and writers, and an assimilated *Beijing News* was back in business within a year. Yet, some of the old journalistic spirit may survive. In 2008 *BN* was in trouble again, this time for publishing a photograph of the forbidden kind – recalling the ugliness of the suppression of the great Tiananmen protests in 1989. Most newspaper editors and writers these days receive warnings – more often implicit than explicit – to avoid coverage of earthquakes, floods, mine disasters and water crises. Such "natural" disasters usually involve some degree of official corruption or neglect of building codes, work safety or public hygiene provisions. At worst, news coverage can suggest direct government culpability; at best, it reminds the public of an ancient but still persisting connection between public welfare and government legitimacy.

The contemporary incidents discussed above follow a general paradigm that was established in China long before the eighteenth century, and has continued to shape China's modern transformation. All governments in China have dealt with rural protests, in most cases relating to taxes or to material abuses by county magistrates. In a tiny number of famous cases, these protests have led to rebellions large enough to cripple or destroy the ruling dynasty. The more usual conflicts grew to a size where they became noted by the state, resulting in predictable round of concessions, punishments and restoration of order. From early times, empires in China have endured and absorbed protests by élites as well as by farmers; in the Han empire, placards, poems and essays written by protesting students and officials were recognized as the genre of "impartial critique" (*qingyi*). Subsequent regimes regarded *qingyi* as a form of protected speech (though, like all protected speech, liable to be suspended on official whim), perhaps even useful for identifying officials whose reputation for greed or incompetence had compromised their effectiveness. In its small version, the paradigm of stimulus and response starts with the collective expression of public outrage against official cruelty, arrogance or corruption. It might be incited by the kind of official pettiness that resulted in the death of the moped rider in Taishan in 2008, or the similar pettiness that enraged a crowd at Xi'an, Shaanxi province, in 1630 to attack local officials and free Li Zicheng, who went on to lead one of the most devastating uprisings of the early modern period. An incident may, depending upon the economic and environmental circumstances and the deftness of local officials, swell into a large disturbance.

The government typically responds in two ways: repression and appeasement. Local officials or magnates will mobilize forces to quell the disorders if possible. If they fail, the central government will send troops; police and paramilitary officials will be instructed to avoid violence whenever possible. But before such forces arrive, the government (usually the central government) will begin the task of restoring its reputation. Studies and investigations will be promised. Based on popular complaints, miscreants (not uncommonly from the ranks of local officials, but the status can rise to as high as a former Supreme Court Chief Justice, who in November 2008 was arrested on charges of running a corruption network worth US $22 billion) will be identified and sent off for trial, and at least one scapegoat will be convicted, to be much noticed in the press. There will be promises of reduced taxes (a very ancient tactic, despite the Wen government's claim of novelty) and the offer of help with local problems. The rhetoric of benevolent government will be paraded before the public. Life will return to a more or less orderly condition.

This small version of the paradigm may be very small, as when the government made lip-syncing illegal after the Chinese (and international) public verbally expressed outrage over little Lin Miaoke's lip-syncing to the recorded voice of Yang Peiyi (whose round face and crooked teeth disqualified her from being presented to global television) in the Olympics entertainment in the summer of 2008. Or it may be medium sized, as when public anger over the suppression of news about tainted milk, deaths of miners, and poisoned medicines led the propaganda chief of the Politburo to decide that instant tailored publication of bad news was the correct remedy – "Let us use the method of providing news as the way to control news," he pronounced. Or, it may be very large, as it was in the case of the April 5, 1976 incident in which a demonstration in Tiananmen Square commemorating the death of Zhou Enlai led to both police suppression of the demonstrators and the purging of Deng Xiaoping (blamed for inciting the movement) from his party posts. In the second phase of the paradigm in this instance, to be described in chapter 14, the popular sentiments expressed were acknowledged, scapegoats were identified, and Deng Xiaoping rose higher than ever. In either case, it is possible to interpret the arc, long or short, of government reaction as being basically restorative. It recalls, in some ways, Lucien Bianco's assertion (following, in a general way, Marx) that "peasant" rebellions are conservative, seeking not a transformation of relations between state and society but the restoration of a balance perceived to have been successful for centuries at a time.

This small paradigm of arousal and pacification in the interplay between local organization and state coercion exists inside a much larger paradigm which has underlain the structure and functioning of the Chinese state for most, though not all, of the past two hundred years. Disorderly confrontations, or the threat of them, between the government and the people are much of the stuff of Chinese history. Local, rural communities have over the centuries developed structures, organizations, values and communications that have allowed them to deal with unexpected hardships as well as pressure from landed élites and from the state. Some historians, comparing the administrative structures of China's cities to those of Europe, have been skeptical that true urban communities of action have existed in China, but both history and the present suggest that contiguous communities within the cities have cohesion that approaches that of the countryside – while political and economic élites of the twentieth century have created new vectors of coherence and action that not only bind cities together but also link cities across national and global space. Just as the government has used coercive measures to prevent a destabilizing concentration of power and initiative at the community level and also in long-distance networks, so have local communities and networks used coercion to resist crushing pressure from the center.

Before the twentieth century, governments of China depended on a surface tension between state and society for their coherence. In the interplay of competing coercions and competing terrors, communities, families and individuals have found – in some periods of time – safety, comfort and creativity. In other periods, chaos has run rampant, though rarely to the degree that the local habits of order and support have entirely disappeared. Chinese history is not a history of despotism or unfettered authoritarianism, but one that has been sustained during long periods of peace and stability by the awareness of the limits on government power presented by a volatile and organized public, and the limits on public expression presented by a government equipped to violently suppress what it regards as threats. In the centuries of balanced intimidation between state and society, China has been overall peaceful and prosperous. When the power on one side or the other has grown excessive, revolution or effective fascism has resulted.

Government has floated upon the crust of social and economic self-sufficiency of the governed. Between state and society there has, for most periods of time, existed a gap in social, ideological and material space. No state before the twentieth century ever established a central educational system or a genuine police system. Instead, they created examination systems and domestic military occupations. Even the largest imperial governments in China (measured in ratio of officials to general population) never extended the floor of the state below the level of the county magistrate. Only a vanishingly small portion of the population ever saw an official person apart from the magistrate, who was seen either at a safe distance, or under very stressful circumstances. All governments in China depended upon this superficiality more or less; in the case of the last empire based in China, the Qing, it was more. The process of conquest in the seventeenth century had rested upon a strategy that avoided any obligation to engage with the majority of the population. When officials of the defunct Ming could be recruited to run their old departments, more or less as they had run them before, they were. When this was impossible, occupation authorities were given discretion to occupy and administer their territories as they saw fit, so long as such territories were pacified and taxed.

When the conquest was accomplished, administration changed only slowly. The financial strategy of the government in the late seventeenth century was one of frugality. Military conquest, which remained the prime government priority until the middle of the eighteenth century, was expensive and it occupied by far the greatest part of the government budget. Maintaining major routes of travel along roads, rivers and canals was a closely related project, and it also got a significant outlay. Education, public safety, food security and culture were not high state spending priorities. This was not because the emperors and their officials did not care about them. It was because the state used the mechanisms, long established in China, of mandates to achieve them. The state ran the examinations, which were the only avenue to government employment and a certain level of élite status. Passing the examinations was entirely the task of aspirants and their families, who spent enormous sums supporting their sons, sometimes for decades before success or, more likely, dismal failure. The state demanded that local élites look after the management of charitable hostels, grain reserves and security of the streets. Occasionally state inspectors would arrive to see that the tasks were being performed, and slackness could be punished severely. More often, local élites were left on their own to run their communities. Mismanagement, the state theory suggested, would become manifest in the outbreak of floods, famines, droughts, banditry, rebellion, witchcraft or miscarriage of legal cases that would become evident upon appeal to the central government. When problems arose, it was the first task of the local élites to solve them. They should disturb the state with ill reports only if they failed at that first task. And their punishment might be chilling.

The interplay between public intolerance of state intrusion and the state's search for wider and deeper power is a constitutional element of the Chinese polity from, at the latest, the seventeenth period to the present. It is not a unique dynamic, but certainly differs from the discourse and probably from the history of state and society interaction in Europe and North America. Social scientists have contributed many methods of describing and analyzing the relationship between Chinese state and society. Some of the elements are self-evident. "Benevolent government" (*renzheng*) as a value in Chinese society was rooted, among the traditional élites, in their reading of the Chinese classics and preparation for the civil service examinations. But it became generalized throughout the society in early modern times, as state lecturers and local organizations for moral improvement impressed the idea upon the semi-literate or illiterate. The state was to be regarded as legitimate to the extent that it looked after the material welfare of the people, restrained the powerful from preying upon the weak, and distributed justice through its system of local magistrates and their courts. For their part, the people were to respect the state as an integral part of the social hierarchy, superior to (but more distant than) parents and those playing the parental role in local life – landowners and local officials. This was, however, respect without dependence (a corollary to the attitude of the moral adult to his parents in the disseminated social philosophy). The state in the traditional context did not supply food, housing or water. These were created or managed at the local level. The ruler's "benevolence" consisted of keeping the state correct with Heaven, so that natural conditions would support happy human life; not interfering in the local community's ability to supply itself, nor taxing the community to the point of crippling its ability to thrive; and being ready to redistribute to it emergency supplies if natural disasters should occur. A surfeit of natural disasters was a very bad sign, in the public view: Heaven was out of balance, or punishing the people, because of the transgressions of the rulers. A great deal of the religious content of this value has eroded from modern Chinese discourse and belief. But enough survives to consistently inform a rhetoric of indignation or protest, casting economic, environmental and even military troubles as evidence of unjust, malign, and possibly illegitimate government.

For its part, the state in China has demonstrated no less interest in the famous monopolization of violence than any other state. But the definition of violence in the discourse of the traditional Chinese state was not easy. As a term in English "violence" is not a very good translation for the normal terms in the Chinese documents for description of armed robberies, riots or rebellions. Traditional reports described these phenomena as "disorders" (*luan*), along with other unlawful gatherings that involved no violence at all. The contemporary reflection of this state viewpoint is the use of "mass incidents" (*quntixing shibian*) and related shorthand (for instance, *naoshi*, "ruckus") in the PRC to describe all the episodes above, as well as peaceful gatherings protesting everything from water quality to suppression of the Falungong religious movement. The state's long-standing habit of not distinguishing fundamentally between disorder and violence means that it must forego the simple monopolization of violence in favor of enjoying hegemony in the maintenance of order. Because the definition of disorder is porous, the state has historically settled for leverage instead of monopoly, with one brief exception in the twentieth century.

The study of mass movements and protests, including rebellions, in China is very well developed, thanks to scholars such as Jean Chesneaux, Elizabeth Perry, Joseph Esherick, Lucien Bianco, Mark Selden, Susan Naquin, Ralph Thaxton, Jeffrey Wasserstrom and many others. In these critically important works, rebellion is often depicted as a punctuating event, a turn in which the people cast off, if only temporarily, the bonds that normally kept them docile. Local populations are seen as "resisting" central intrusion and oppression when the occasion arises, but not constituting an indispensable element in the governing process when doing so. The inherited view is heavily colored by tropes of feudal deference (whence the consensus that Chinese farmers are "peasants") and revolutionary iconoclasm. In the present narrative, rebellion and resistance are regarded as limited facets of an institutionalized local tension barrier, both supporting and limiting the state. Rebellion itself is not a major theme here. Rather the emphasis is the mutual understanding between state and society of the persistent threat of collective demonstration of dissatisfaction and the justification for it. More important, the element of organization in collective local action is viewed here as a way of linking contemporary China to its immediate past. Sectarian rebellions have been regarded as more potent than non-sectarian rebellions partly because a religious organization is first and foremost an organization. It has a hierarchy, it has a form of training and education, it has channels of communication, perhaps long-distance communication. Its roots lie in the fundamental patterns of local life in China before 1949 and share lineage with village labor systems, market rules and rhythms, collective self-defense, established criminal organizations, loan clubs and extended lineages. This sturdy fabric of local life was what the Qing empire expected to support itself upon.

But that required a sophisticated balancing act. The state attempted to rule by mandate (what we would now call unfunded mandates), by suasion, and when necessary by the application of precise violence. It had to guard constantly against three dangers inherent in the system. First was the development of partnerships, between local officials and local landowners or merchants, large enough and strong enough to threaten the state. Second was the emergence of locally based cliques whose tendrils might reach into the central government itself. Third was the development of resistance at the local level of a magnitude sufficient to overwhelm state credibility or power. The wise state, as envisaged by conventional political thinkers in China from the Han period on, rested lightly on the surface of local society – hierarchical, peaceful, efficient and resilient in crisis, benevolent toward the weak and demanding of the strong. But the tendency of successful local organizations to grow grander in size and in ambition was a constant danger to the imperial state, which fought back ruthlessly when threatened. The example, it was hoped, of terrible consequences for those straying outside their assigned roles would be sufficient to make the local organizations eager to impose limits and restraint upon themselves.

When the empire ended in 1912, the constitutional elements in the relationship between the central state (or state aspiring to centrality) and the localities persisted. Both the Nationalists and the Communists relied upon the principle in their way, but both also realized the terrible vulnerability of the state to hypertrophy of local power. The Nationalists failed to solve the conundrum, and the CCP entered into an inhospitable coexistence with it, from which the state deviated with tragic results between the middle 1950s and the middle 1970s. Though the contemporary Chinese state is gigantic in comparison to its predecessors, it is still too small and too uncoordinated to truly permeate the wide and very complex space of the PRC. Allowing the pivot to wobble, without letting it fall, continues to be the challenge for a state unable or unwilling to break its dependence upon the deep roots of local coherence and autonomy.

Further reading

The anecdotes here of popular protests, demonstrations, riots and uprisings come primarily from current information that is ubiquitous. The specifics used in this chapter come from:

- Tim Johnson's bus ride: May 9, 2008, "Taking the Slow Road in China," in *China Rises* blog: www.washingtonbureau.typepad.com/
- On coverage in Chinese of the Zhang Longping incident: www.club.qingdaonews.com/showAnnounce.php?topic_id=3859116&board_id=131
- The Xinhua editorial on the disorders in Dongzhou: "Protests and Riots on the Rise, Chinese State Media Says," *International Herald Tribune*, December 8, 2006.
- The case of the Fuda Property Development Company: Rowan Callick, September 8, 2008 in *The Australian*, "Investors Riot as Get-rich Scheme Fails in Hunan, 9 Held After Two Days of Unrest." *SCMP* Minnie Chan, September 6, 2008.
- The prosecutions of Wu Dianying and Wang Xiuying: "China's Totalitarian Games," by Jeff Jacoby, *Globe* columnist, August 24, 2008.
- The attacks in Qizilboy, Xinjiang: *Radio Free Asia*: "Chinese Police Killed, Wounded in New Xinjiang Clash."
- The difficulties of Chen Yunlin in Taiwan: Jonathan Adams, Saturday, November 15, 2008 5:49 a.m., "Strait Talk: So Near And Yet So Far," *Christian Science Monitor*.
- Interview with Ambassador James Sasser: "Besieged but Unbowed, Ambassador Is Hopeful on China," by Philp Shenon: online at www.nytimes.com/1999/08/30/us/public-lives-besieged-but-unbowed-ambassador-is-hopeful-on-china.html (accessed 08/21/09).
- On popular protests over the environment at Gaodong, Sichuan: China Digital Times (quoting Yale Environment 360), December 6, 2008, "In China's Mining Region, Villagers Stand Up to Pollution."
- Protests over administrative issues in Daye, Hubei: www.hrichina.org/public/contents/article?revision%5fid=36026&item%5fid=26823
- On police protests in Hunan and elsewhere: Xinhua: Police Employees Appeal for Better Pay in Central China," www.chinaview.cn 2008-12-04 00:41:34; *China Digital Times*, December 6, 2008, "First Strike Action by Police Officers Since the End of the Cultural Revolution in 1976."
- On popular reaction to the arrest, trial and execution of Yang Jia, there are numerous and continuing reports. For the specific incidents referred to here, see: "Chinese Defend Accused Police Killer," by Cara Anna, The Associated Press, Wednesday, August 27, 2008 1:21 p.m. © 2008. Last updated: October 17, 2008, 9:54:21 a.m., "Yang Jia Shanghai Police Murder Conviction Appeal Being Heard," by chinafreepress.org (translation). October 17, 2008, 10:52:16 a.m.: www.news.boxun.com/news/gb/china/2008/10/200810171512.shtml © 2008 by Boxun News. Eva Pils, "Yang Jia and China's Unpopular Criminal Justice System," in *China Rights Forum*, No. 1, 2009; paginated PDF at www.hrichina.org/public/PDFs/CRF.1.2009/CRF-2009-1_Pils.pdf
- On the overt government strategy for controlling the news: *The Times* (London), Jane Macartney, "Beijing Propaganda Chief Hatches Plan to Combat Age of Internet News," November 19, 2008.
- On the petition for the release of Ilham Tohti: Edward Wong, "Intellectuals Call for Release of Uighur Economist," in *New York Times* [online edition], July 14, 2009.
- On activist lawyers, see Teng Biao, "The Law on Trial in China," in *The Washington Post* [online], July 25, 2009: www.washingtonpost.com/wp-dyn/content/article/2009/07/24/AR2009072402940.html?referrer=emailarticle

Analysis of community in China has taken many forms. G. William Skinner framed much of the discussion. See especially G. William Skinner, ed., *The City in Late Imperial China* (1977). A pointed debate arose between Frederic Wakeman and William T. Rowe in the 1970s and 1980s. See especially Rowe, *Hankow: Conflict and Community* (1989) and Wakeman, "The Civil Society and Public Sphere Debate" (1993). The characterization of urban communities in this book is perhaps most compatible with the approach of Belsky, *Localities at the Center* (2005). For a broad but penetrating overview of the topic, see Xu, "Urban Communities, State, Spatial Order, and Modernity: Studies of Imperial and Republican Beijing in Perspective" (2008). Tsai, *Accountability without Democracy* (2007) has presented an important interpretation of community action in contemporary China (see also chapter 17 of this book).

For the major historical studies of "peasant" rebellions, uprisings and revolutionary movements in China in the early modern and modern periods, see Johnson, *Peasant Nationalism and Communist Power* (1962); Selden, *The Yenan Way in Revolutionary China* (1971); Chesneaux, *Peasant Revolt in China 1840–1949* (1973); Friedman, *Backward Toward Revolution* (1974); Naquin, *Millenarian Rebellion in China: The Eight Trigrams Uprising of 1813* (1976) and *Shantung Rebellion* (1981); Perry, *Rebels and Revolutionaries in North China, 1845–1945* (1980); Chen, *Making Revolution* (1986); Esherick, *The Origins of the Boxer Uprising* (1987); Thaxton, *China Turned Rightside Up* (1983), *Salt of the Earth* (1997), *Catastrophe and Contention in Rural China* (2008); Bianco, *Peasant Without the Party* (2004) – based on influential articles published over thirty years. For the related subject of "secret societies," see chapter 3. For a general background discussion of popular protest, see Wasserstrom and Perry, *Popular Protest and Political Culture in Modern China*.

Qingyi has been the subject of a significant amount of scholarship, almost all in reference to its use in nineteenth-century reform movements (see chapter 10). It has been variously translated as "public opinion" (Rankin and others), "moral censure" (Polacheck), and "pure counsel" or "disinterested counsel" (Bastid). Recently Alan Baumler posted a very engaging essay on Han period official protests at his website, "Frog in a Well" (June 1, 2009), which drew on Rafe de Crespigny's "Political Protest in Imperial China" (1975). See also Eastman, *Throne and Mandarins* (1967); Iriye, "Public Opinion and Foreign Policy" (1967); Rankin, "'Public Opinion' and Political Power" (1982); Whitbeck, "Kung Tzu-chen and the Redirection of Literati Commitment" (1983); Bastid, "Qingyi (Disinterested Counsel) and the Self-Strengthening Movement" (1988); Polacheck, *The Inner Opium War* (1992); Schrecker, *The Chinese Revolution in Historical Perspective* (2004).

2

Sources of Order Under the Qing Empire

IN 1804 THE Jiaqing emperor (r. 1796–1820) marked the end of the White Lotus Rebellion by receiving at court his greatest warrior, Eldemboo, who symbolically ended his role in the suppression of the uprisings by returning to the emperor his seal of office. The emperor, like many at his court, regarded the general as something of a curiosity. Eldemboo was a quiet man of gentle carriage, seen as modest in his unwillingness to seek attention and as honest in his apparent lack of interest in the riches or honors that had lately corrupted so many in the court's environs. But in battle Eldemboo was known to be as fierce as he was meek in domesticity. He had fought those who struck against the empire, from within or without, for well over thirty years – killing Burmese invaders of Yunnan in the 1760s, Muslim rebels in Gansu in the 1780s, secret society separatists in Taiwan in the 1780s, Gurkha invaders of Tibet in the early 1790s, Miao rebels at the confluence of Guizhou, Sichuan and Hunan provinces in 1795. When the Jiaqing emperor had gained actual power over the government in 1799 it appeared that corruption and incompetence had already lost the war against the White Lotus rebels. But Eldemboo was among the Manchu generals the new emperor charged with turning the war around. He pursued the rebel leaders ruthlessly but was kind to refugees, considerate to farmers and generous to those who abandoned the enemy cause. The emperor regarded the general as the kind of Manchu soldier his own late father, the Qianlong emperor (r. 1736–95), had idealized, if unfortunately not always preferred in practice: Eldemboo was honest without fault, reporting his failures and his successes to the government in equal measure. And, very unusually for a Manchu of his generation, Eldemboo neither spoke nor wrote Chinese. At 52 his service had worn hard on him. He died the next year.

Eldemboo came from relatively humble origins in the old northeastern homeland of the Manchus, but early in his career his merits had shot him up the ladder of the Eight Banners, the hereditary military population of the empire. He did a few things other than fight rebels or invaders taking advantage of trouble with rebels, but rebel fighting turned out to be his main assignment, and the source of all his honors. The first rule of Qing governance was that no official could rest on his laurels and, model though

Eldemboo was, he too felt the sting of imperial sanction when things did not go right. Before setting out against the White Lotus in 1797, he had already been raised to the highest civil honorary rank (*gong*), which historians in English works translate as "marquis." But when the court became impatient of waiting for him to sweep out a nest of rebels along the Yangtze River, he was broken down to a lower rank (*bo*, which is sometimes translated "earl"). He eventually achieved the task but the court still did not forgive him for his previous failures and took away even his lower rank, making him a commoner again. Apparently unimpressed by the court's fickleness, Eldemboo carried on, and his strategy of isolating the rebels from supporters in neighboring provinces was eventually credited with the imperial victory. In 1803 the court warmly restored his high rank – as it happened, virtually on the eve his death – and when he was dead he was given nearly every posthumous honor possible.

Eldemboo's reputation after death was connected to many complex issues. The Qing empire, though considered in the eighteenth century to be at peace, was never actually a peaceful place. In 1799 the court had been in crisis, and the country engulfed in a civil war. It was not the first large-scale internal war for the Qing, nor the first to raise doubts about the empire's survival. But it exposed the degree to which corruption, incompetence and complacency had undermined the Qing ability to keep its vast territories in order. Eldemboo, appearing as he did to represent the best of the virtues of the past, seemed to the Jiaqing emperor and his court to be the key to restoration of the imperial efficacy. As previous empires had attempted to inculcate in all Manchus and, if they could, in Chinese as well, Eldemboo lived frugally and worked his troops to get the most out of every ounce of silver spent. He considered force the primary means of keeping the peace, and did not hesitate to use it if more amicable means failed. The problem for the court was that Eldemboo died almost as the White Lotus Rebellion ended. There had never been a lot of officials – Manchu or Chinese – like him, and after he died there were none. Finding a few ideal ministers and generals was not going to be the key to fixing the empire's problems. Structural restoration, or structural innovation, would be essentials.

The Qing empire was born in chaos and then reborn in China, in more chaos. Their origins lay in an informal Jurchen commercial and military regime coalesced from the low-grade disorder of the Ming border province of Liaodong (the modern province of Liaoning, in the general area of southern Manchuria). The Jurchens had a complex history, including a brief empire and longer periods of political disunity. During the Ming period (1368–1644) they grew wealthy from trading horses, dogs, sable and fox pelts, pearls and pine nuts in the Ming markets, and also became agricultural (though they preferred to use captives – Jurchens captured in inter-village warfare, kidnapped Koreans and Chinese – to work the fields). Their population increased in the sixteenth century to the point that land wars among themselves, and between them and the Ming, were frequent. Out of the contests emerged a lineage based near the eastern perimeter of Liaodong. Later, they would be known by the lineage name of Aisin Gioro (the Golden Gioro, Gioro being an ancient Jurchen lineage name). In 1587 a scion of this lineage, Nurgaci, established a capital for himself and organized his followers and captives into units called "banners" (*niru*). In 1616 Nurgaci decided to reorganize the military units by which he ruled his population into the Eight Banners, to announce a new state – the Jin khanate – and to install himself as khan. Two years later he declared war on Ming. By 1621 he had seized much of Liaodong province,

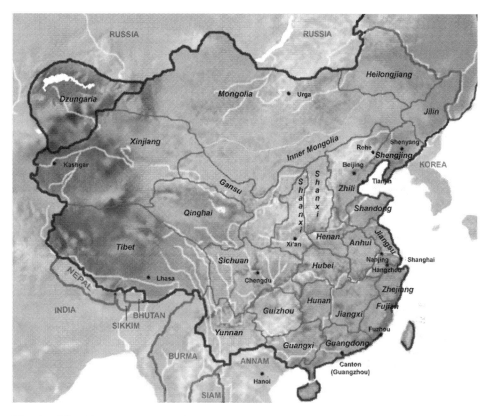

Map 1 The Qing Empire to *c.* 1860

including its capital at Shenyang. He took the city as his own capital and named it Mukden (in the Jurchen language, the equivalent in meaning to Shenyang). Thereafter his military campaigns to the west of the city continued, in an apparent attempt to extend his domain as far as the Great Wall of China. Nurgaci died in 1626 from wounds suffered in battle at Ningyuan, near the Great Wall.

Nurgaci's fourth son Hung Taiji soon established himself as successor. In the process Korea, a long-standing ally of Ming China, was forced by threat of invasion to acknowledge Jin as the dominant local power. Mongolia, on Hung Taiji's eastern frontier, was also being politically consolidated by Genghis Khan's direct descendant Lighdan Khaghan. Hung Taiji challenged Lighdan for control of northern Liaodong and the eastern edge of Mongolia, and in 1634 defeated him. The Jin khanate essentially absorbed the Great Khanship of Lighdan, absorbing those Mongol populations who had followed Lighdan and confiscating the objects and rituals by which Lighdan had legitimated himself as Great Khan of the Mongols. In 1636 Hung Taiji dramatically announced that he was now an emperor, and that he was founding a new empire, the Qing, of whom the foremost followers would now be called not Jurchens but "Manchus." Hung Taiji died in 1643, as his forces reached and threatened to overwhelm the Ming fortifications at the Great Wall.

After 1600 the Ming empire was critically inefficient in meeting the challenges that arose, both at its borders and in its central provinces. Political strife at the Ming court in Beijing over border policy was connected with competition between eunuch cliques and scholarly cliques, between networks of corruption and campaigns for reform, so that both border management and internal administration were paralyzed. In China the poverty of farmers and popular disaffection helped fuel two enormous uprisings. The rebel Zhang Xianzhong seized control of Sichuan province, the "breadbasket" of China, while the rebel Li Zicheng arose in western China and moved toward Beijing. In 1644 the Ming were squeezed by the eastward movement of Li's forces, and the westward press of the Qing empire. Li entered Beijing in April, and the last Ming emperor killed himself. Ming officials, both civil and military, chose various paths. Some followed the emperor in suicide, some clung loyally to the Ming cause and fled south, some resigned themselves to loss of the Ming and offered their services to Li Zicheng. Ming military commanders had few options but to attempt to enlist the new power to their east, the Qing empire of the Manchus. General Wu Sangui enabled the Qing forces to enter China through the Great Wall at Shanhai Pass. They quickly shattered the inchoate Shun dynasty and set out to capture and execute Li Zicheng and Zhang Xianzhong. But instead of restoring the Ming, they put Hung Taiji's young son on the throne in Beijing as the Shunzhi emperor. Qing commanders, leading growing throngs of former Ming soldiers and new recruits from north China, set about consolidating their hold north of the Yangtze River.

The Qing had on their side the willingness of hundreds of thousands of Chinese to join in the campaigns to eradicate Ming authority and restore order in all the provinces, and in general the conquest proceeded under the disciplined and incisive leadership of the Qing imperial armies, the Eight Banners. Nevertheless this was a knife-edge enterprise, and until nearly the end of the seventeenth century its outcome was not at all certain. China north of the Yangtze came rather quickly under Qing control, and with altogether less bloodshed than had been caused by the rebellion of Li Zicheng. But south of the Yangtze was a different experience. Urban resistance in the Yangtze delta, particularly in its extremely wealthy and culturally central cities, was intense. Extinguishing the disparate members of militant Ming restorationism took the Qing thirty years. The conquest left the urban elites profoundly mistrustful of the Qing court. Taiwan, which was a fulcrum of the pirate world reaching from Japan to the Philippines, became a launching point for the combined resistance of Ming loyalists and those struggling to retain local independence under the leadership of Zheng Chenggong. They made dangerous forays into the mainland province of Fujian and threatened stable Qing control there.

Under these pressures, the very early Qing empire in China conducted a great experiment in minimal central government. Absorbing north China, which swelled the ranks of the Qing military but seriously exceeded the grasp of its fledgling bureaucracy, had put the empire at the mercy of its Chinese supporters. In 1647 the Manchu aristocrats, who effectively controlled the government, decided to dispatch former Ming generals who had joined the Qing cause in the 1630s, as well as Wu Sangui – the high-ranking northeastern general who had facilitated the Qing entry into Beijing – to the south. Their commission was to destroy Ming loyalist holdouts in the region, and their compensation was the right to their own dominions in south China, acknowledging only the Qing court as their overlords. It took these super military governors of the south – in the English-language histories sometimes called "feudatories" or "satraps" – more than a decade to impose their rule upon their designated regions of the south, but by the late 1650s each had a regime in place, collecting taxes, maintaining armies, building palaces and keeping their own bureaucracies. Wu Sangui even conducted his own foreign policy, opening a trade route to Tibet and invading Burma to capture – and execute on his own command – one of the last resisting Ming princes. Through various bureaucratic manipulations Wu dominated not only the southern lands he ruled directly, but also the bureaucracies of the provinces of northwestern China.

In 1661 the first Qing emperor in China died prematurely, and a regency of Manchu aristocrats ensured that his third son Xuanye, then 8 years old, succeeded to the throne as the Kangxi emperor (r. 1662–1722). In the early 1670s the young Kangxi emperor threw off the power of his regents and, with the strong support of very powerful Manchu aristocrats, confronted the situation in the south. In the Qing bureaucracy there was rising alarm about the power of the southern governors, particularly Wu, who showed every sign of attempting to pass power to his son and establish an independent dynasty. The Kangxi emperor abolished one of the southern governorships in which a succession issue had arisen, and signaled to the others that their days as independent baronies were over. The "Rebellion of the Three Feudatories" followed in 1673 and raged until 1681. On the momentum of the destruction of the southern occupation regimes, the Kangxi emperor established control over all of Yunnan (which the Ming had thinly governed) and proceeded to crush the last vestiges of combined Ming loyalists and independent pirates on Taiwan, which in 1685 was for the first time incorporated into an empire based in China. The end of the southern occupation governments marked the end of the first Qing experiment in trading local independence for diminished central responsibility; in exigency the state had delegated almost total discretion to the southern super-governors, and had quickly seen the accretion of power to the point of secession. In the case of the war of 1673 to 1681, the state responded by destroying the local threat, but at the cost of a long and very risky campaign.

Qing society in the later seventeenth century recuperated slowly from the worst effects of continual war, from the late Ming rebellions of the 1630s to the resolution of the civil war of 1673–81. Society generally, and pockets in the Yangtze delta particularly, was growing wealthier, but the government was not. Imperial finances were continually overextended. The Banner populations distributed through the provinces as an occupation and policing force swelled as the rest of the population did, and the state was responsible for providing the salaries which were supposed to support entire Banner households. Government penury was also due to the costs of reconstruction. The Ming had not had the means or the time to repair damage wrought by the Li and Zhang rebellions, and now the additional damage of the conquest had to be mended as well. City walls, administrative offices, wells, dams, dikes, undredged rivers and canals, ruined systems and roads had to be attended to. Shrines to the dead had to be constructed. Sufficient government had to be provided to allow markets to function, travel to be moderately safe, lawsuits to be processed. There were probably additional problems created by the effects of the so-called "little ice age," with temperatures reaching an annual low in 1650. The stall in the agricultural recovery caused the government to attempt to compensate by encouraging farmers to migrate from inactive or underproductive tracts in central China to rich but underexploited lands in the Northeastern provinces (Manchuria); the policy would be reversed in 1688, when a convergence of economic developments and political pressures led the Kangxi court to forbid immigration to the Northeast by Chinese civilians. Modest taxes on agricultural yields and on the transport of products from place to place encouraged the resettlement and renewed exploitation of the valuable agricultural lands of central China destroyed in the rebellions and the conquest. In this way, the imperial government hoped to gain the benefits of a revived economy and improved political relations by foregoing a high tax to finance its continuing campaigns of expansion.

Originally the Qing had inherited from the Ming two tax bases, one founded on the percentage of males of working age (the head-tax, or *ding*) and the other based on the productivity of each surface unit (*mou*) of land. In 1711 the Kangxi emperor froze the head-tax, essentially making each county responsible for an inherited head-tax obligation, which it could meet by whatever means the magistrate contrived. Land taxes were supplemented by transport and commercial taxes. The court lived primarily off its monopolies in salt, iron, jade, the manufacture of textiles and porcelain, and customs receipts from the trading ports. Court revenue was also augmented in an incidental way by frequent gifts from officials of all levels, and by the occasional valuable gift (often a prize horse or an exotic mineral) coming through the embassy system. The government economy was expected to supply the salaries of officials and the government's portion of public works.

The number of Qing officials at any given time is not known with great precision, but it is clear that the number of Ming officials at the end of the former dynasty was not enlarged by the Qing. They had the same number of counties (about 1,500) in the Chinese provinces as the Ming had had, and therefore the same number of magistrates. The central bureaucracy and the inspectorates added the vast majority of Qing officials, who are thought not to have exceeded 23,000, and may have been closer to 15,000. The nineteenth-century figure was much the same, and compares to about 60,000 civil servants in Britain, about 80,000 in the late nineteenth-century USA (and the modern figure of about almost 11,000,000 modern government employees in the PRC). Of course, the disparities in numbers of bureaucrats do not indicate a similar ranking of the total volume of state business. The Qing had much more to do in the way of governing than the British government, but Qing and Russia contracted out most of the local work, and both tolerated a very fuzzy line between official and non-official status.

The Qing financial strategy which evolved in these years remained the style of government in much of the two centuries that followed. To the extent possible, the state attempted to control regulations and standards, but to shift financial responsibilities to the localities. For example, candidates for high office and magistrates were required to pass, or continually prepare to pass, the highest examination level (*jinshi*). The examination system was run by the state, with examinations normally administered at the highest level every three years. The costs of preparing for the examinations were borne solely by the degree candidates and their families. The costs of tutoring from a young age, devotion to studies to the exclusion of all remunerative work, traveling for study or sitting for the examinations, buying clothing suitable for mixing with scholars and officials, all strained the wealthy and excluded all others. Those on the economic littoral of examination viability could sometimes find wealthy sponsors to advance their expenses, which created client relationships with landowners or merchants that the aspiring officials would continue to service through their government

careers. Even elementary education for improvement of the labor force (by instruction in efficient planting and harvesting, new crop strains, fertilizing and other areas
of knowledge that changed in the seventeenth and eighteenth centuries) was supported by local landlords, lineage associations, or charitable foundations, and not the
state. The funding of the armed forces was a complex matter, but over time followed
the same principles, oddly enough. Historically the Eight Banners were the posses-
sion of the emperor, and were funded from his own treasury. It is clear that well into
the eighteenth century the imperial court was expected to supply the funds for banners and their garrison communities. However, after the conquest, the nature of the
imperial forces changed with the addition of very large numbers of professional
Chinese soldiers in the Green Standard armies and specialized provincial units.
Funding was sometimes ad hoc, taken from the imperial treasuries or from the government reserves, and these inconsistencies increased through the eighteenth and
early nineteenth centuries.

Outside the capital the reach of the state generally never went below the county
magistrate. At the furthest reach of imperial finances and communications, the magistrates were the capillaries of the state – they diffused imperial commandments and
legal presence while being infused with emoluments, companionship, collaboration
and occasionally the uxorial supplies of the local elites. In much earlier times, empires
had staffed the counties with not only magistrates but commissioners reporting
directly to the court on legal, military, economic and public welfare issues. The Ming
had whittled the system down to a single magistrate under normal circumstances, and
the Qing adopted the system more or less as they found it. In some counties a few
imperial inspectors appeared from time to time to make sure that public works were
being maintained. A separate system of inspectors looked after the grain reserve system, which bought grain when markets were low to support prices and create stores,
and released grain when prices were high to cap markets and sustain the poor. In times
of famine or military mobilization, local stores of good grain could be commandeered
by the state. But in general a magistrate had no steady oversight, and was left to deal
with his own problems, and generate his own revenue. He received a salary from the
imperial government, but it was designed to be insufficient for his real needs. Historians
now estimate that officials in the Ming and Qing period were paid a small fraction –
perhaps as small as 10 percent – of the value of salaries paid to officials in the Song
period (970–1279).

The magistrate was permitted to enjoy donations from powerful local families to
complete his personal and administrative finances. The Qing expectation was that the
official would see his salary as representing his absolute duty to pursue imperial
interests, but that local contributions would reflect the extent to which local interests were also part of the official's calculations. The empire survived on its partnership with landowners, and the line between the state and the "gentry" (land-owners
and officials-in-waiting – scholars who had succeeded at least at the provincial level
in the examinations and who were waiting at home for a position to open up somewhere) was not always clear. But the empire expected to have the advantage.
Corruption – that is, an excessive or grossly selfish exploitation of possibilities for
income outside the imperial salary – was a serious crime and, when prosecuted, led
to severe penalties ranging from 70 blows with a hollow bamboo rod to strangulation,
depending on the amount the official had amassed. In the Yongzheng period

(1723–35), temporary rises in official salaries of as much as 300 percent were unusual attempts to limit corruption by positive rather than negative means. For reasons to be examined in the next chapter, the reforms had no hope of changing patterns of corruption permanently. As for more general applications of the legal system, the Qing strategy was similar to that employed in other areas of government: The appeals process was the main instrument for monitoring the administration of justice. County magistrates investigated, tried and punished crimes. Defendants who thought they had been dealt an injustice and had the courage and connections to pursue it could appeal to the Board of Punishments (*xingbu*) for review. At that point, the central government troubled itself to run its eyes over the case. As a logical corollary of the government's strategy for administering the most justice with the least investment, the government kept the avenue to appeals comparatively open, and magistrates were circumspect about making mistakes that would expose their methods, malfeasance or misjudgments to the central government.

Magistrates, like the provincial governors above them, tended to try to handle local problems on their own, without requesting help from (and exposing failure to) the central government. They could sometimes look to a neighboring magistrate for emergency supplies of grain, silver or troops, but when possible they turned to the partnership they consolidated with local civil leaders. The expectation of the state was that actual order at the local level would be effected by the magistrates in cooperation with the gentry. In their early days the Qing had encountered the effectiveness of local gentry-led organization, since the resistance in the Yangtze delta that had stymied the Qing advance and wrought a terrible toll on the local population had been primarily led by the gentry. Once the country had been conquered, the Qing considered their erstwhile enemies to be among their greatest assets. As landowners and aspiring officials (or fathers or brothers of aspiring officials), the gentry could be expected to be a force for conservation of the present system. By mid-seventeenth century, certainly, the gentry had forged a profitable partnership with the state. Though much less than 1 percent of the population, they owned about 25 percent of the farmland. Imperial taxes on the land were modest, ranging from 5 to 8 percent of total agricultural income, and practices both legal and illegal (see chapter 3) assured that the income of the gentry was taxed at somewhere between half and one fifth the rate of common farmers. Comparatively low taxes and comparatively deferential tenants were a pleasant combination for the gentry. The Kangxi emperor in the seventeenth century and the Qianlong emperor in the eighteenth century made a point of personally visiting the Yangtze delta repeatedly to highlight the mutual benefits of the system. Feasting, face time, gifts and expressions of the appropriate virtues – benevolent government from the emperor, fidelity from the gentry – forged a bond between the empire and the wealthiest landowners which remained strong all through the nineteenth century. The Qing, however, seem never to have taken the relationship for granted. Even as they praised the wealthiest landowners for their loyalty to civilization and to the empire, they promulgated laws that they expected would prevent the gentry from ever becoming a threat to them.

The Qing habit was to make use of the gentry – and gentry wealth – for the continuous tasks of construction and maintenance. Early states and empires in China learned that the way to control flooding on the Yellow River was to continually dredge its bottom. The region's soils are famously loose, and unless the river's bottom is dredged silt will build up from the bottom and force water over the banks. Even with regular dredging, the river bed rises gradually over time, and compensating levees progressively raise the river higher and higher above the plains around it, so that the modern vulnerability to flood is much greater than the dangers of a thousand or two thousand years ago. Good farming practices, including the planting of trees and fallowing of fields, slow the rate of silt accumulation because they anchor the soil in place and minimize erosion. At some points most rivers used for navigation need to have their banks reinforced, to maintain sufficient water depth without letting it rise above banks. Dams were used in China from ancient times to keep levels high enough for navigation and also to run water wheels to operate looms in textile factories. In the late Ming, imperial engineers had begun to bring the opposing embankments of the river nearer each other in certain areas. By narrowing the river, they intended to speed up the current and keep silt moving toward the sea rather than laying on the bottom. Irrigation systems carried water from riverine sources to the fields or, in south China, the paddies.

In the Yangtze delta, thousands of lakes, both real and man-made, had to be maintained to keep their water sources unsullied and their perimeters well defined. And millions of agricultural acres had to be fed by working irrigation systems. Apart from natural waterways, canals – foremost but not only the Grand Canal running between the Yangtze delta and region north of the Yellow River – needed to be kept staffed and in good physical repair, to assure the flow of crops and goods between the Beijing region and the China's most commercialized agricultural district. These complex tasks were shared by large landowners, independent farmers, county and town associations, and received occasional aid from the central government. The empire had a department of public works which focussed its attention on the Yellow River and the Grand Canal; in the late eighteenth and early nineteenth centuries, the state lavished about 10 percent of its overall spending on waterworks. Nevertheless it mostly demanded that local gentry get the maintenance work done, and sent officials to offer advice or inspectors to make sure it happened. Failure to fulfill imperial expectations had serious consequences for one's fortune, if not for one's physical health. The first line of imperial defense against predation from below was to shackle the local leaders with the anxiety and the expense of water management.

Another tactic important to this strategy was the implementation of provincial quotas for the examinations. Provinces with less historical success in the examinations were encouraged with more generous quotas, and provinces that were renowned for success were hobbled with more meager allowances. The rhetoric of benevolent government allowed the court to portray such policies as the fruit of a justice-minded, effort-encouraging ruler. The real concern was not equality of opportunity but the thwarting of power cliques based on provincial ties. The Qing were obsessed with the idea that the Ming government had been destroyed from within by factional strife. They did not intend their small and thin government to be riven by factions, and they most especially did not intend to allow any one faction to overwhelm the state itself. Keeping the wealthy areas – especially but not limited to the Yangtze delta – from using their means to fill up the bureaucracy with hordes of brothers, cousins, brothers-in-law and schoolmates was the first step. A second was the assiduous continuation of strict rules of avoidance for magistrates that had been inherited from the Ming. Magistrates were not permitted to serve in their birth areas, or their ancestral areas, or areas connected to their in-laws – nor could they decide legal cases that involved anyone connected to them in these ways. A candidate for office was required to file extensive genealogical records to prove conclusively that he had no connections to his areas of possible appointment. Usually after three years, but after seven years at the most, a magistrate was transferred out and landed in a new county, often in a far-away province, where he had to start anew. For their part, the gentry were with the same frequency faced with the prospects of building up a new partnership with a stranger. The Qing had no objections to partnerships between the magistrate and the local gentry so long as it was a new, fragile and perpetually insecure one (mirroring the empire's own relationship with local elites). The partnerships should be only strong enough to get the tasks necessary for maintenance of water works, defense works, defense drills, surveillance, disaster control, quashing of disorder and tax collection done. It should never grow strong enough to become the basis of an independent political force, even on a small scale.

Using the same logic, the empire enacted novel laws in the eighteenth century to prevent landowners from driving a majority of laborers from tenancy into slavery. The Qing were no abolitionists, but were using a technique that went back to the days of their ancestor Hung Taiji. The Qing was in origin a slave state. Its general economic base at the time of its early expansion under Nurgaci and Hung Taiji was slave agricultural labor, and the Eight Banners were legally the military slaves of the Manchu aristocrats (later, of the emperors personally). The power of the emperorship had been built in large part by depriving aristocrats of their slaves and transferring them to the emperor. Hung Taiji had permanently limited the growth of power among Manchu aristocrats by forbidding them to hold large numbers of slaves or to abuse the slaves they had. In China, the Qing emperors of the seventeenth and eighteenth centuries were as vigilant against the accumulation of slave populations as their ancestors had been in Manchuria. Though the laws were uniform across the empire, there is reason to believe that the real target was the Yangtze delta, where the levers of high rents and low wages had moved huge numbers of farmers and tenants into effective (or, in some cases, legally contracted) slavery by the early eighteenth century. Qing legislation of the 1730s required that the free status of such individuals be restored, and that heavy penalties be imposed upon landowners who concealed the slavery of their workers or contrived to force more farmers toward debt and slavery.

Finally, the Qing, like most imperial orders in China before them, had an abhorrence of horizontal connections among civilians that could become the basis of factions or other vehicles for gaining political influence. Waves of reorganization of the Eight Banners had destroyed vestigial aristocratic influence over the military forces, and subsequently weakened the tradition of certain lineages controlling officer positions in the individual banners and banner companies. In the civilian realm, scholars and officials were kept wary of each other by means of the examination system, where the very steep incline toward success made educated and ambitious men perpetual rivals. Nevertheless the emperors were never satisfied that the combination of personal rivalries among and terrible punishments visited against the officials were sufficient to ensure that they would not conspire against the court. Secret networks of communications between the emperors and their personal spies existed from Nurgaci's time and were greatly elaborated by the Kangxi and Yongzheng emperors. By these means the emperors attempted to constantly verify the honesty and competence of reports given them by magistrates, governors, military commanders and even officials within their own courts, and to monitor officials at all levels for any tendency toward conspiracy. Too many favorable reviews of a colleague's work or too many unexplained social visits could raise imperial suspicions of factional intrigue. For their part, officials were watchful of attempts by landowners, artisans and especially merchants to make social or political combinations based on shared interests.

This wariness of organization among colleagues was in some tension with the state dependence on cohesion and self-dependence at the local level. How the contradictions were intended to be resolved may be illustrated by comparing the workings of the local *lijia*, or local registration and taxation unit, and the *baojia*, or local security unit. Both institutions had been inherited from the Ming. Each system encompassed sub-units that were normally arrayed in decimal fashion, with each level having ten sub-levels. In the cities the smallest units tended to correspond to the block residential complexes within the grid of streets; in the countryside the smallest units tended to correspond to individual villages. In the first part of the Qing period the *lijia* units and jurisdictions were larger than the *baojia* units, and all residents belonged to both – precluding a coincidence of *lijia* and *baojia* registrations that could have promoted identification with or independence of the units themselves. The *lijia* allowed the magistrate to continuously account for the population, publishing identities, births and deaths and organizing the assessment and collection of taxes. The *baojia* were security organizations with a double edge. On the one hand, they provided mutual security. They were sometimes bounded by high walls and gates locked on a strict schedule that prevented thefts and assaults by outsiders. On the other hand, they were mutual surveillance organizations, and were the basis of the empire's collective responsibility system in law. *Baojia* members were expected to inform their superiors, and eventually the magistrate, of any known intention to break the law by other members of the unit; if they were later revealed to have had knowledge and done nothing, they and their families would be punished as co-conspirators. All members of the unit were to post the names of all residents of their households on their doors, and to inform the authorities if they were absent for any time. Visitors to the unit, including residents of hotels and hostels, were also to be registered. Failure in any of these requirements would involve punishment of the relatives of a violator, and probably of other members of the *baojia* as well.

To work effectively, the *baojia* had to be intertwined with the kinship networks that were influential, to one degree or another, everywhere. Some very small villages were single-surname villages, where all the male lines had a single ancestor and wives were sought from other villages. More commonly communities were made up of set of lineages with marriage alliances repeated over several generations. In areas where wet rice was the predominant form of agriculture (primarily the south), collective work was essential to planting, maintaining and harvesting; the lineage was the most obvious way to organize the work and distribute the proceeds. In these areas it was common for lineages to own land – or land rights – together, which could produce complicated legal wrangling in later generations. In areas such as the north of China where there were more small holders working independently, lineages were still an essential line of connection. Gathering together to worship common ancestors or for weddings and funerals kept male relatives, in particular, in communication, and made an appeal to brothers or cousins for financial or material help that much easier.

Alternatively, lineages could become the basis of cult organizations, oriented toward either local gods or traditional Daoist spirits, competing with each other for the attention of the magistrates or for the donations of villages. When difficult personal circumstances, environmental deterioration, or disorders (see chapter 3) forced families or individuals to relocate, relatives of any degree were expected to provide aid at the new location. In extreme circumstances lineages might have to band together to physically defend themselves against petty criminals or avaricious neighbors. When disasters of any kind struck, the hierarchies of major and minor family lines, age and gender provided instance organization of command and communication patterns. In good times, lineages could band together to save money and make loans, to hire tutors for their children, to support widows and to aid members who had fallen on hard times. Wealthier lineages could pay to have their histories printed in the gazetteers that each county published periodically, and could pool their money to try to send a young male relative through the examination system. Those who experienced success with this could build on lineage connections, and expand them, to pull themselves further up the ladder of wealth and influence.

In China as in all traditional societies, lineage cohesion depended upon the effective control of women. Any women not affiliated with families or lineages were regarded as unfortunates, who would either work themselves to death on tiny farmplots of their own or disappear into the brothels of the cities. In the countryside, women were essential laborers in the fields, in the threshing houses, at the loom and in the mines. The importance of marriage links among lineages made it essential for the elders (usually but not always men) of a lineage to control any woman's marriage arrangements, and young girls were often affianced at very young ages to men of desirable lineages. Traditional values, often described in English-language scholarship as "Confucian," forbade women from seeking divorces except in very extreme circumstances, while men could divorce women much more easily. The same value system forbade widows from remarrying. Many women, as a consequence, spent their adult lives as the legal dependents of sons or brothers, unable to control property or make many decisions about their lives. The cultural value held to account for these practices is normally described as "filial piety," or self-sacrifice to the honor of parents and ancestors.

Many scholars have noted that filial piety has a precise fit with prescriptions for female behavior that would enhance the cohesion and the wealth-accumulation of extended lineages. The same might be said of the practice of foot-binding, a process which crippled the girls and women upon whom it was practiced. Though foot-binding is often discussed in connection with Confucianism, the fact is that Confucian influence – the social philosophy endorsing social hierarchies with educated men at the top and women at the bottom – has been widespread in East Asia from about 600 CE to the modern period, but foot-binding has never caught on outside China. It was introduced in China more than a thousand years after Confucius lived, at a time when long-distance commerce gave married women of the landed and mercantile classes important new responsibilities in the management of households and businesses. China was not the only society to increase social and legal restrictions of women as their role in economic transformation became indispensable. Foot-binding was an extreme method of restricting women's activities and choices, but an effective one. In the Qing, foot-binding was regarded as the peculiar practice of the Chinese civil elite. It was not practiced among Manchus, Mongols, Uighurs or the cultural minorities of central, southern and southwest China. Working families could generally not afford to bind the feet of their girls, since they could not dispense with their labor. This fact, however, made conspicuous foot-binding by those aspiring to marry upward a growing practice in the Qing; those families who did not succeed would often unbind the feet of young women, leaving them useful as laborers but in excruciating pain for the rest of their lives.

The state recognized the essential cohesion that lineages provided at the local level. Laws and legal precedents were carefully annotated to prevent the imposition of punishments that would leave dependents destitute or otherwise cause strong lineage organizations to disintegrate. When it had the opportunity it awarded virtuous lineages grants for small monuments of commemoration. But it was important that lineages and other forms of local organization not take on enough power to blunt the force of law or edict. The *baojia* system, with its collective responsibility underpinning, was perfectly formed to allow the state to use the lineage as a means of periodic coercion and prevent the lineage from becoming a power itself. The relatives of a convicted criminal were convicted along with him. If he was flogged they were flogged, if he was fined they were fined, if he was executed they were executed. The only way to escape the logic of belonging to a lineage on which the state was turning a hostile eye was to break the lineage bonds altogether and inform on prospective crimes or ferociously denounce not only the criminal but other members of the lineage. Through collective responsibility, the state – not merely the Qing state but empires in China back to the Han – hoped to make the strong filaments of lineage connection upon which the empire itself was suspended combust when exposed to heat.

The importance of *baojia* security regulation to the Qing – reflected in the fact that the empire eventually abolished the *lijia* in favor of unified administration under the *baojia* – is underscored by the evolution of systems of local defense as disorders of the sort of the White Lotus Rebellion and its successors became more frequent in the early nineteenth century. The state was not in a position to respond with the Eight Banners or even with the ancillary Green Standard Army (originally made up entirely of recruits from the old Ming armies, and later the professional military for Chinese with no connection to the Eight Banners) to internal uprisings. Moving Eight Banner or Green Standard units from province to province took weeks or months. Local riots, rebellions or outbreaks of large-scale banditry required a local response. The empire encouraged gentry to pursue their tradition of organizing, training and when necessary mobilizing their own forces drawn from local civilian residents. Using existing *baojia* units, local gentry instructed residents to repair village and city fortifications and lay in dry goods in case of siege. By the time the White Lotus Rebellion was in full swing, these militia units were commonly called *tuanlian* and had a life of their own outside the *baojia*. In the very early nineteenth century the court viewed the *tuanlian* as a necessary evil, to be relied upon in times of local war and disbanded or intensely monitored in times of local peace.

The desire of the empire to strike the right balance in places like the Yangtze delta between stable local self-governance and perpetual central vigilance against local accumulations of power was also at play in the empire's relationship with its peripheries. The early leaders of the Qing empire grasped the frequently-demonstrated principle that conquest nearly always requires more conquests, in order to secure newly expanded borders. Today's periphery is tomorrow's province, and today's conquered are tomorrow's agents of conquest. After the young Kangxi emperor had eradicated the destabilizing threats from south China and Taiwan in 1685, he turned his attention to Mongolia. He was aware that Mongolia had been a constant threat and expense to the Ming. He considered himself the rightful heir of Genghis Khan, owing primarily to his grandfather Hung Taiji's victory over Lighdan and assumption of the legitimate heritage of the Great Khans. For both strategic and ideological reasons, the Kangxi emperor intended to control Mongolia. The most populous portion of central Mongolia, the Khalkha territories in the vicinity of present-day Ulan Baatur, had some history of partial submission to the Qing and were largely agreeable to the emperor's demands. But an ambitious leader in western Mongolia, Galdan, objected. He harried Khalkha to pressure their leaders to turn their submission from the Qing to him, and when that did not work his forces went to war against the Qing. The Kangxi emperor personally led the Eight Banners against Galdan, in a series of campaigns during the 1690s. They concluded with Galdan's death as a fugitive in Siberia in 1697.

The Qing hold over Mongolia was necessary not only to spare the empire the constant worries over possible Mongol attacks, but also as a buffer against the Russian empire. Under Peter the Great, Russia was becoming more aggressive in the east, attempting to establish a foothold in the Amur River region (which the Qing considered part of the Manchu homeland) and to control the coast of northeast Asia. The early Qing emperors had retained control of the north Pacific coast (now the Russian Maritime Province) despite repeated Russia attempts to settle parts of it. The Kangxi emperor realized that central Mongolia could not be securely held without controlling western Mongolia (called during the late seventeenth century and eighteenth century "Dzungaria"), Tibet and at least part of Turkestan. Across Dzungaria and Eastern Turkestan ran a spectrum of Muslim religious and political alliances. At the same time, between Tibet and Mongolia stretched a century and a half of shared belief in Tibetan Buddhism and the authority of the Tibetan clergy. The areas were also part of a single geographical unit – high and arid, sitting on what is basically the extended Tibetan Plateau and its basins, circumscribed by the Gobi on the east, the Altai Mountains on the north, the Kunlun and Karakoram Mountains on the west, the Himalayas on the south, and on the east China and Burma, as the Yellow River, the Yangtze and the Mekong all diverge from their nearby origins in the Tibetan highlands. The emperor stabilized the frontier with Russia (and neutralized a Russian military threat) with the Treat of Nerchinsk in 1689. He spent the ensuing decades until his death in 1722 securing the Qing hold over what is now Tibet and Qinghai province. Dzungaria was left in limbo.

The work of completing Qing dominion over the west fell to the Kangxi emperor's grandson Hongli, who in 1736 became the Qianlong emperor. In 1745 the Qianlong emperor reinitiated the conquest of Dzungaria, and Qing incursions quickly spread to eastern Turkestan which the Dzungars had ruled and to which they could flee. The small city-states of eastern Turkestan were destroyed in the process, and the Qing instituted military rule from the city of Ili, aided on the ground by Sufi leaders. Resistance by the Uighurs was fierce, but by 1760 Qing control of the region was firm. The emperor's officials took to referring to it as the "New Frontier" (*ice jecen*, *xinjiang*). It became part of the empire – along with nearby Gansu province, Tibet and parts of Sichuan – that was put under a special military administration. This was an expensive operation, forcibly occupying the continually resisting cities of the New Frontier and suppressing rebellions – such as those in Jinchuan where Eldemboo got his start – which sporadically arose in areas where Tibetans and other minorities of the southwest lived under martial law.

The extension of special military districts in southwest China coincided with state assimilation policies. The Qing empire advocated the assimilation of cultural groups who had been resident in south and southwest China at the time of the conquest. This was a great contrast to the policy toward Manchus, Mongols and some other groups who had been fundamental to the Qing conquest; in those cases, the court insisted that these groups remain culturally distinct, in order to maintain their identities as conquerors and occupiers in China. But when peoples were likely to rebel because of a sense of displacement or economic disadvantage, the state tended to try to weaken and if possible destroy their sense of cultural separateness. At times the empire was aggressive about this, in other periods less so. During the Qing period, southwest China in particular was dotted with indigenous groups surrounded on all sides by Chinese farmers. The government plan was to assimilate them by teaching them to speak Chinese, and putting them to work at farming. Families were also reformed. Some of the local cultures were matrilineal, some did not recognize the nuclear family with three generations that the government liked, many pursued livelihoods in which property made little sense. The family pattern the government approved was one it considered "Confucian" – two, or ideally three, generations living together with all authority monopolized by the oldest male, and perhaps his oldest son.

Finally, the imperial government insisted on loose conformity to certain religious practices. Proper religion for Chinese, in the government's view, was ancestor worship as prescribed by the followers of Confucius, with veneration of the occasional official, or traditional hero, or city god thrown in. Religions – like those of the southwest – that featured animistic elements were regarded as dangerous superstitions. Shamanistic practices, particularly those involving dancing, were seen by the state as witchcraft (and cross-dressing was strictly prohibited, not least because the Qing knew that a shaman's robe could pass as a woman's dress). The Qing imperial court feared witchcraft and punished it very severely. The solution to all these problems, imperial bureaucrats considered, was complete destruction of the cultures of the southwest (and any remnants that remained in other parts of China), and assimilation of the peoples into the general Chinese population.

The Qianlong emperor was aware that his rapid expansion of the empire in the middle eighteenth century was inconsistent with the counsel of his grandfather, the Kangxi emperor, to be thrifty in the costs of war and occupation, and to so seek only necessary expansion and nothing more. It is possible that his construction of the so-called Confucian temple at the imperial retreat at Chengde (Jehol) was intended as a signal that he now intended to give up conquest and focus on civil pursuits. On the eve of the expected arrival of the Banchen Lama (the cadet lama branch after the Dalai Lamas) in 1780, the emperor embellished a written commentary on a passage from Confucius' *Analects* to ostentatiously characterize his relative abstemiousness as a conqueror. He first recalled writings in which his grandfather had railed against the tendency of the powerful to become greedy and destroy their regimes through the pursuit of unneeded conquests; he summarized the earlier emperor's contempt for this as "overdeveloping one's army at the expense of the people." As for himself, the Qianlong emperor protested that his conquests, however vast, were only what was necessary. Yes, he had taken Dzungaria and eastern Turkestan, and suppressed the Tibetans of Jinchuan in Sichuan province, but "I did not dare to depend upon my army's strength or my generals' plans [instead of Heaven's favor], and I did not over-develop the army for my selfish desire." Despite his intentions, the Qianlong emperor's military mobilizations, and the concomitant hemorrhages from his treasury, were not over.

Though his military expenditures far overshadowed those of his father and grandfather, the military alone was not the only object of the emperor's extravagance. He funded huge cultural projects such as the Four Treasuries (*siku quanshu* – a republishing of all the worthy literature his officials could acquire throughout the realm); thorough revisions of all the imperial histories from the Tang to the Ming, with special attention given the Liao, Jin and Yuan histories to which the Qing felt themselves connected; the building of seven libraries throughout the empire (four in the Yangtze delta) to house the newly published collections and make them available to local scholars; renovations of the pavilions and gardens at many of the empire's scenic spots (not a few in the Yangtze delta), as well as the Qing summer retreat at Chengde; and seed money for charitable housing and schools in areas where he wished to shame the gentry into giving more. Many of these enterprises had a dark side that was also not cheap. The Four Treasuries, for instance, was not merely a project to revitalize China's literary heritage, but was also a literary inquisition. As the worthy bits of writing were discovered and praised, the poorly written and the seditious were identified and their authors punished – posthumously or in life. Some authors who were found to have written less than desirable historical or political commentaries – or suspected of it, since the writing system allows certain ambiguities that the eye of the beholder may interpret as innocuous or treasonous – were sentenced to writing self-denunciations and publishing them at their own expense. At least one author, the tragic Zeng Jing, was sentenced for his efforts to death by slicing. These investigations were also expensive.

In the last decades of the Qianlong emperor's life, however, the normal if lavish expenditures of the throne were extended by a growing net of corruption, which cumulatively dealt a blow to the empire from which it never recovered. In the 1770s the emperor had developed trust in a Manchu official named Heshen. In basic outline Heshen's background resembled that of Eldemboo who would come a couple decades later. He was from a moderately distinguished but not wealthy lineage in Manchuria, and became an imperial bodyguard. He drew the emperor's attention, and began to assume more and more administrative duties as the emperor aged. Heshen developed a clique of the sort so intensely feared by earlier Qing emperors. For his partners he chose high ranking military officials, mostly Manchus, and a few allies in the Board of War. They used campaigns against the uprisings in the border areas, whether Xinjiang, Yunnan, Guizhou or Taiwan, as the pretext for draining huge sums from the imperial treasury. The network grew to be empire-wide, and operated almost in the open. Officials who attempted to prosecute Heshen were accused by him of corruption and usually convicted on the charges. When the emperor died in 1799, Heshen's estate (now a popular tourist spot in Beijing) was raided, and discovered to be bulging not only with incredible wealth in gold, furs, silks, jade and ivory, but more silver than was left in the imperial treasury. The new Jiaqing emperor allowed Heshen to hang himself, and began to attempt prosecutions of Heshen's collaborators, hoping to trace and reclaim some of the missing money. The network protected itself well, however, and the losses to the government were never recouped. In the meantime, the wars that had been neglected by the military commanders while they siphoned off the funds appropriated for the campaigns had to be picked up and continued by soldiers such as Eldemboo.

The inability of the Qing court to recover from the predations of late Qianlong corruption has led to an impression among some students of Qing history that China as a society must have become progressively impoverished over the eighteenth century, and markedly poorer in the early nineteenth century than it was half a century earlier. Recent research suggests that this is not so. In the seventeenth century the sheer size of the Chinese economy and the accumulation of wealth in its great ports made it a necessary part of the continued advancement of Korea and Japan. By this time, Europeans, too, worked assiduously to insert themselves into the China trade and the Asian network to which it was central. They were not successful in finding a market for European goods (apart from guns), but many European middlemen enriched themselves by handling the nascent trade of porcelain, silk and fans to Europe. Chinese porcelain factories, most of which were under imperial control, readily accepted European orders for custom designs on porcelain or silk. In the early 1600s, Spanish discoveries of silver in Central America had made Mexican dollars the basis of international trade. The empire already had an ample supply of silver from Yunnan province. The additional silver flooding into China in exchange for goods sent to Europe began to seriously distort the Chinese bimetallic system (in which copper coins were supposed to have a fixed ratio to silver). The poor were put under serious pressure. They normally held copper (when they had any money at all), but were forced to pay rents and taxes at the value of silver. Since silver was deflated by the influx of foreign payments, the amount of copper necessary to meet the value of the demanded payments rose sharply. The Ming government had been aware of the distorting influence of silver surpluses and attempted to control the gyrating economy by limiting access to Chinese markets by foreigners. Koreans, Japanese, Portuguese, Spaniards and Netherlanders were permitted to trade only at certain ports, and only after presentation of passes. The passes quickly became the object of a black market (dominated by the Japanese and a Chinese-Japanese demi-monde based in Taiwan), and piracy became serious enough to ruin the coastal trade in some areas. Distractions in Mongolia, Manchuria and elsewhere prevented the Ming from finding a response to the problem of conserving its wealth in the face of rapidly advancing commercial technologies in neighboring countries. When power in China passed to the Qing empire, these problems remained.

Like the Ming, the Qing viewed foreign relations and foreign trade as two sides of the same coin (as it were). The Ming had used an elaborate form of the embassy system developed in earlier times to regulate, and sometimes manipulate, foreign contact, both economic and cultural. This system, often called in historical scholarship the "tribute system" (close to the Chinese term, *zhigong*) was actually an embassy system. Tribute was hardly the point, since tribute to the Qing court was a universal practice by cultural groups residing inside the empire, by officials of the empire, and of course by visitors from abroad. Rather, the point of the embassy system was that foreign countries would express a willingness to communicate with and trade with China by acknowledging the emperor based in China as a unique, supreme "son of heaven." Foreign rulers who made this acknowledgement in no way surrendered their sovereignty or their trade policy independence, but did become part of a loose network of countries that traded with China and maintained either military neutrality or alliance with China. The Qing retained not only the Ming embassy system but the general ranking of traditional embassy states. Korea stood highest (and had the most frequent embassies), Liuqiu (now part of Okinawa) was second, Annam (the ancestor state of Vietnam) was third, and other states such as Thailand, Burma, the ancestor states of Cambodia, Laos, Brunei, small states of Indonesia, and others throughout Southeast Asia and Central Asia retained their status. Like the Ming, the Qing occasionally intervened militarily in the affairs of embassy states that were also on its borders. The war against Burma (an unenthusiastic and often neglectful embassy state) that had seen Eldemboo dispatched to Yunnan was ignited when Burma attacked Thailand in 1767 and attempted to assert military control over territories that the Qing considered inside their boundaries; in 1769 the Qing declared victory and Burma continued its embassies. In 1789 the Qing tried to interfere in a dynastic transition in Annam, but were quickly repulsed. Generally the Qing distinguished clearly between their continuation of the Ming embassy system and their own methods of dealing with the border and foreign groups they considered to be strategic threats. Some Mongols retained embassy status, and exchanged gifts with the Qing court on an annual basis. But Mongolia once it was conquered by the Qing was administered through a separate government within the empire, the Department of Frontier Administration *(lifan yuan)*.

This government had originated well before the conquest of China, in 1636, when Hung Taiji absorbed the government of Lighdan and proceeded to create the Qing empire. Over time it took on responsibility not only for managing communications with Mongol groups (whether subordinated to the Qing or visiting as foreign embassies) but also linking to the administrative offices of the Dalai Lama and the Banchen Lama in Tibet. The Qing, like the Ming, allowed traditional village and lineage headmen of the Tibetan, Miao (the modern Hmong), Yao and other groups in Yunnan, Guizhou and Sichuan to act as local officials of the empire, preserving some degree of traditional culture and social structure; the Department of Frontier Administration was also the coordinating body for the governing of those areas. The Frontier Administration also had important economic functions. It regulated trade with Mongolia and Xinjiang, but more important was the fact that its jurisdiction mapped the economic heart of the Qing empire – mineral resources critical to military expansion, and enriching to the Qing court. Iron, coal, silver and gold from Mongolia and Manchuria, jade and copper from Xinjiang, copper and silver from Yunnan were largely mediated through the military detachments connected to the Frontier Administration. Finally, the Department of Frontier Administration was the venue for handling communications with the Russian empire. The Treaty of Nerchinsk and the Treaty of Khiakta (1729) which formed the matrix for the complex and lucrative trade across the northern border, marked the border itself, and established all rules for the movement of people across the borders were all managed through the Department of Frontier Administration. Its administrative language was Manchu, it drew up genuine treaties with foreign powers, it used the language of diplomatic equality when necessary and it was a much older part of the Qing imperial structure than was the Ming embassy system incorporated later.

When Europeans arrived in China, whether in the late Ming or the early Qing, many were nonplussed to discover that they were expected to enlist as representatives of embassy states and to perform the rituals that ambassadors normally performed – including the "three kneelings and nine head-knockings," the kowtow. Early Dutch traders arriving in the late Ming decided to do it, and got the Netherlands signed up as a Ming embassy state, and Portuguese merchants signed up Portugal. Jesuits coming to the Ming after 1600 did it, and so the Vatican appears on the list of Ming embassy states. The Qing carried over the status of these entities to its own embassy lists. British private merchants arriving at the port of Canton (Guangzhou) from their colonial ports of Singapore or Bombay (Mumbai) refused to be regarded as representatives of the British government. Some among them attempted to trade illegally at ports other than Canton, causing Qing trade officials to repeat and underscore their intention to enforce the restrictions on trade cities with the creation of what is often called the "Canton system." From the Qing point of view, the system was nothing new. Like the Ming, the Qing regulated foreign trade. Embassy states given permission to trade in China – or treaty states, such the Russian empire – were restricted to certain points of entry.

Two very significant facts figured in this scheme. First, the Qing like the Ming before them had a problem with piracy. Though the Kangxi emperor had destroyed part of the pirate network when he conquered Taiwan, the network as a whole had quickly revived. Japanese and Filipino pirates and smugglers, in league with Taiwanese and Chinese colleagues, ran silver, porcelain, tea, silk and women up and down the Pacific coast. The Qing claimed Taiwan but only controlled a few urban centers around present-day Tainan. The rest of the island was as open to pirates as it had been in Ming times. Fishermen and residents of the coasts were frequently set upon by pirates who kidnapped them, stole their ships and goods, or burnt the villages if the residents refused them shelter or food. One way the Qing dealt with the problem was by outlawing all coastal trade except for the designated ports, clearing the way for magistrates who might be brave enough to charge pirates all with smuggling, a capital crime. Second, the revenue from foreign trade went straight to the imperial court's own treasury. The Qing court, perpetually seeking funds but looking with new fervor for money during the distressed times of the late eighteenth century, had no intention of allowing a critical revenue stream to be lost by disseminating trade to innumerable unregulated ports.

As part of the system, Japan traded at the port of Zhapu, near the mouth of the Yangtze River; Russia traded at Nerchinsk on the Mongolia border; Central Asian states at Kashgar in Turkestan. In general the point of trade was determined by the general geographic direction from which foreign traders approached. During the eighteenth century, all merchants originating in Europe approached China from the South China Sea, where the largest port was Canton. As a consequence, the city of Canton was the designated port for Europeans, who in light of this were called *yangren*, or "people from over the [South China] Sea." Before the British arrived, European merchants who traded at Canton resided off the Chinese mainland, on the island of Macao (which Portugal claimed as a colony in 1510 with no remark from the Ming empire, nor later from the Qing). Early British traders who arrived and began to understand the conditions were associated with the East India Company, a firm chartered by and partly invested in by the British Crown, but mostly owned by private merchants. They refused to represent themselves as ambassadors or to do the kowtow, but requested the right to trade and reside at Canton. In the late eighteenth century local officials at Canton agreed to allow British and some other European merchants to reside in a special compound in the city, and allowed British ships to dock at Canton. From the outset, the East India Company shareholders grumbled about what they considered a discriminatory system. They not only resented the fact that they were legally permitted to trade only at Canton, but they lived in fear of the fact that their merchants at Canton – the merchants called "factors," and their residence called the "factory"– were subject to Qing law. The British knew little about the law, except that it cost the life of a British sailor in 1784 who fired a signal cannon and accidentally killed a Chinese fisherman close by. The British had surrendered the sailor to Qing authorities believing that the incident would be treated as accidental manslaughter. In fact the sailor was tried for murder and strangled. British politicians as well as the East India Company had sworn that no more British nationals would be handed over to Qing justice. But the provisions of the Canton system continued to require it if another incident should occur.

The product moved from China to Britain by the East India Company was tea. In the previous century Dutch and Portuguese traders had innovated with large-scale imports into Europe. It became immensely popular by the very early eighteenth century. The British government had at first opposed the beverage and a ban on it nurtured a huge network of smuggling that encompassed Asia, Europe and North America. Later the British government legalized tea but imposed so high a tax that smuggling remained healthy. Only in the late eighteenth century did the British government reduce the tea tax to a level that ended tea smuggling. Despite the high cost of legal tea in Britain and North America, demand for the product was such that by the 1770s Britain was running a deeply negative balance of trade with China, probably aggravated by the fact that standard British gold bullion had to first be traded for silver in Europe before being sent to China. While the British government was alarmed, the East India Company was not. They profited from the trade regardless whether it went from China to Britain or Britain to China. This was only one aspect of the difficulties arising between the British government and the East India Company. By 1790 the British government had calculated that the best way to deal with the East India Company was to break up its monopoly on the China trade. But among British merchants only the East India Company had permission to trade in China. Britain would have to establish a trade treaty with the Qing empire that would assure open competition among British sea merchants. The government concocted the idea of sending an emissary to the Qing to negotiate such an agreement. After some discussion the government settled upon the Irish aristocrat George Macartney to lead the mission, and he departed for China in 1792.

The Macartney mission, as it is usually called, is an extremely well-known episode in the history of relations between China and Europe. During his roughly two years of sailing to China, staying there hoping to open negotiations, and sailing back without success, Macartney became the symbol of reasonable diplomacy, rational trade practices and European civility treated roughly, rudely and ignorantly by an arrogant "China." This assessment persists in some modern histories of the period. All historians recognize the folly of British diplomats setting out for a country with an entourage in which nobody at all knew the language of the country to which they were going. During the months of travel to China Macartney's colleague George Staunton arranged for his 10-year-old son, called Thomas, to learn Chinese from Manchu and Chinese Jesuits who boarded the English ships in Rome. Though the embassy system of China was not strictly diplomatic, it was as demanding of linguistic precision and courtliness as the European system was, and Thomas' child-like Chinese neither impressed the Qing authorities nor freed the British of the need to hire local translators. Upon arriving in China and finding that his initial attempts to connect to Qing officials were rejected, Macartney was puzzled and then outraged that there was no way to fix the problem except to have Britain enrolled as an embassy state of the Qing, including performance of the kowtow. Macartney had no intention of making kowtow. Things stood at an impasse for months while he continued to seek help from Chinese merchants, Qing officials, European Jesuits and European merchants already trading in China. Nearly all told him the same thing: To drop his quest and return home. Nevertheless, Macartney achieved a breakthrough of sorts when he managed to have a letter from George III delivered to the Qing court, and got a note authored by the Qianlong emperor in exchange. An original of the letter has never been found in the British archives, and it is believed that nobody in Britain ever saw any version of it except the rather florid anonymous translation that is well known today.

Macartney eventually returned to Britain to face not only government anger over his failure to achieve a trade agreement with the Qing empire, but also suspicions that he had disgraced the country by actually performing the kowtow, which he continued to deny. The British government, and many historians, would insist for centuries after that the Macartney debacle was caused primarily by the arrogant "Chinese" wish to remain aloof from the realities and morality of international law and free trade. Historians and anthropologists have puzzled over the irrational complacency of an empire that would spurn an invitation to profitable trade and draw down upon its head the wrath of a military power able to do it very grievous harm. But the facts suggest that the Qing position was not only economically rational but necessary to the continued stability between central government and locality. In the letter delivered to the British government by Macartney, the workings of the trade system were explained in patient detail. The emperor cautioned the British against thinking that the strictures of the trade system were directed at them or at Europeans particularly. The British request to establish an ambassador at Beijing was politely declined with the explanation that there were no resident ambassadors but only periodic embassies; foreigners resident in Beijing, such as the Jesuits, were forbidden to leave. Surely, the emperor reasoned, there would no advantage to Britain to establish an ambassador under such conditions. More important, the trade matters that the British were concerned about all arose at Canton. The emperor pointed out that Canton was 2,000 miles from the capital, and an ambassador could hardly manage trade issues from such a distance. As for lifting restrictions on the movement of foreigners in China, the emperor responded that previous British protests against the imposition of Qing legal punishments upon them had resulted from conflicts between Chinese and foreigners. The way to avoid conflicts and their legal consequences, he suggested, was to avoid contact between Chinese and foreigners.

Fundamentally the emperor attempted to impress upon Macartney that the latter had confused the center and the locality. Trade at Canton was a matter for Canton and its officials. There were no answers to trade problems in Beijing. A decision by the central government to expand trade and expand the scope of foreign residency would expose local populations and officials to hosts of problems – from increased piracy to petty conflicts that could lead to tragic circumstances – that they would be unable to manage. Though the letter is full of oblique references to the practical constraints of the empire in considering the British requests, the largest of considerations was left implicit. The Qing government had never had a method of policing coastal ports, and had no intention of developing one. Pirates and smugglers were the concern of provincial and county officials and their gentry partners. The most the central government had ever done for these localities was to not increase their problems deliberately. From that perspective, the relationship with the East India Company was a desirable one, since the company itself suppressed smugglers and pirates whom it saw as competitors. Opening the coasts to motley British traders would bring a cascade of enforcement issues to the coastal communities, and this had never been Qing policy. Finally, the court left unstated its own dependence upon a tightly regulated and closely taxed foreign trade. Its official in Canton, after all, was called the *hubu* ("hoppo") because he reported directly to the imperial revenue department of the same name. He was the acknowledged face of the Qing empire on the ground, and exactly like a magistrate he had the option to partner and negotiate with local actors. The Qing were puzzled that the British could not understand that entering into a mutually advantageous partnership with the *hubu* was the logical course for them. Asking the court to strangle its own sources of cash and evaporate the thin edge of local order in the coastal communities for the purpose of correcting the trade balance of a very, very far away country was a doomed mission from the start.

This was one of those episodes of the last decades of the eighteenth century in which order and disorder changed places. In this case, the Qianlong emperor's attempt to maintain the order of the trade and revenue system while preserving the balance of civil control along the coasts was part of a dynamic actually galvanizing new sources of disorder. The British stopped smuggling tea into Europe and North America and started smuggling opium, the only product they had found a way to make a profit on, into China. British politicians and opinion-makers started to clamor more stridently for a diplomatic and trade opening to China, whether by suasion or by force. In a parallel development, ostensible attempts to quash uprisings in various border areas of China spawned the crippling corruption of the Heshen network, and because of the way the network obstructed actual military mobilization, the uprisings only became more frequent, larger and more widespread. By the time the Qianlong emperor died in February of 1799, tides of order and disorder washed against each other, with disorder advancing its margin at each round.

Further reading

On the origins of the Qing, early history of the Eight Banners and history of the Qing court, see Spence, *Ts'ao Yin and the K'ang-hsi Emperor* (1966); Kahn, *Monarchy in the Emperor's Eyes* (1971); Huang, *Autocracy at Work* (1974); Wu, *Passage to Power* (1979); Wakeman, *The Great Enterprise* (1985); Bartlett, *Monarchs and Ministers* (1991); Crossley, *A Translucent Mirror* (1999); Elliot, *The Manchu Way* (2001).

The quotation from the Qianlong emperor's *Analects* comments at Chengde is taken from Joseph Adler, "The Qianlong Emperor and the Confucian 'Temple of Culture'," though the interpolation "instead of Heaven's favor" is my own. For recent histories of the Qing conquests and competition against the Russian empire in Manchuria, Mongolia and eastern Turkestan, as well as Qing wars of conquest, see Mancall, *Russia and China* (1971); Bergholz, *The Partition of the Steppe* (1993); Millward, *Beyond the Pass* (1998); Elleman, *Modern Chinese Warfare* (2001). The best narrative in English of the Qing campaigns against Galdan and then the Dzungars is Perdue, *China Marches West* (2005).

An excellent overview of the middle Qing period in China is Naquin and Rawski, *Chinese Society in the Eighteenth Century* (1989). For more on the workings of civil administration and finance, see Chang, *The Income of the Chinese Gentry* (1962), Wang, *Land Taxation in Imperial China, 1750–1911* (1973), Zelin, *The Magistrate's Tael* (1984), Chao, *Man and Land in Chinese History* (1986), Bernhardt and Huang, *Civil Law in Qing and Republican China* (1994). On the Qing court, see Rawski, *The Last Emperors* (1998).

On the forms and necessity for local organization, see, among many excellent studies, Kuhn, *Rebellion and its Enemies* (1970); Perdue, *Exhausting the Earth* (1987); Elman, *Classicism, Politics and Kinship* (1990); Will *et al.*, *Nourish the People* (1991); Naquin, *Peking* (2000); Szonyi, *Practicing Kinship* (2002). On management of border and cultural problems in the Qing period, see Rowe, *Saving the World* (2001); Lee, *The Political Economy of a Frontier* (2004), Giersch, *Asian Borderlands* (2006), Herman, *Amid the Clouds and Mist* (2007). On the suppression of witchcraft, see Kuhn, *Soulstealers* (1990).

The Macartney mission is very amply documented and analyzed. For work heavily drawn from original sources, see Peyrefitte, *The Immobile Empire* (1992) and for an analysis of the event see Hevia, *Cherishing Men from Afar* (1995). The treatment here and continuing through the next chapters of the Macartney episode is an expansion of the relevant passages in Crossley, *The Manchus* (1997). A perplexing but influential volume is Fairbank, *The Chinese World Order* (1968). At the time of publication, reviewers noted that Fairbank's opening essay describing a hierarchy of relations in the "tribute system" (as he called it) and rigidly ritual relations between embassy states ("tributaries") and China was not actually supported by the content of most of the essays included in the book. The volume remains valuable for the essays themselves, and the introduction remains a valuable example of a period style in China studies.

On China's role in the global economy during the late Ming and earlier Qing, see Frank, *ReOrient* (1998); Wong, *China Transformed* (1998); Pomeranz, *The Great Divergence* (2000).

3

Sources of Disorder Under the Qing Empire

"CORPSE DRIVERS" WERE the subject of an ancient Chinese legend. It was said that these corpse drivers understood the esoteric arts of binding together the ankles, knees and wrists of the corpse in order to force it to stand upright. When poor people died far away from their ancestral homes, corpse drivers would be engaged to come in the night, bind up the corpse and join it with a herd of other corpses to be driven to their home villages. Then, using a long stick, the drivers knew how to prod the corpses so that they would hop forward. Corpse drivers were evidently patient people, who spent countless nights (they hid during the day) poking their charges one step at a time over hundreds or even thousands of miles. Finally each corpse would be delivered to its kin, who would prepare it for a proper burial and provide it with the numerous rituals that would preserve its memory for generations. Whatever its other purposes, however, the corpse driver legend spectacularly captures several major features of the social and cultural landscape of China, two or three centuries ago. It encompasses major changes in population growth, economic stratification and environmental conditions. But it also illuminates a continuity in Chinese life that controlled the lives of individuals as stringently as the ropes of the corpse drivers bound their helpless clients' limbs. The socially marginal in China, whether distanced by poverty, cultural identity or political views from the majority, must either band together to protect their interests, or live as hopping corpses prodded by the state or by the rich.

The characteristic thinness of the Qing local presence could become a destabilizing factor when combined with mismatches between population density and the depth of local resources. Most historians have believed that population is an important factor in economic development – and decline. The issues of population growth, economic development, migration and emigration are related, but in complex ways. Between about 1650 and 1800 the population of China approximately doubled, from about 150,000,000 to about 300,000,000, and the geographic expanse of the empire also doubled. This is now a commonly encountered statement, but must be scrutinized rather closely in order to make sense. First of all, take China's population in Qing times, in modern times, and in fact in early times (say, the Han empire of 2,000 years ago); this has always represented roughly 20–30 percent of the total human population. China's "population booms" of the Ming and Qing periods and of the early twentieth century are actually reflections of burgeonings of the total human population. The area around the Yellow River in north China, which was the locus of the earliest Chinese cultural and political centers, is one of about a half dozen (the number varies depending on interpretations by anthropologists, archeologists and historians) places of early, independent agricultural development. Five to ten thousand years ago, north China joined a few other places on the globe as an independent cradle of agriculture. Within a thousand years after the establishment of agriculture, the population densities in these places had risen dramatically, with complexly stratified societies, writing and outward expansion of the cultural systems following. Most of these areas have remained agriculturally oriented and densely populated to this day. But only China fully encompasses an ancient agricultural zone within its boundaries. The Indian agricultural cradle is divided among India, Pakistan and Bangladesh; the central American, among Mexico, Guatemala and Honduras; the Southeast Asian, among Thailand, Cambodia and Laos, and so on. Only China retains the size and historical geography to consistently represent the general contour of human demographic development. When the Chinese population grew dramatically in the fourteenth, eighteenth and twentieth centuries, it paralleled global rates of growth in the same periods. This pattern was attenuated at the end of the twentieth century, by means to be explored later.

During the Yuan period of Mongol occupation in the thirteenth and early fourteenth centuries, predatory taxation, social violence and disease were probably among the factors driving the population as low as 60,000,000 or 70,000,000, from a high of more than 100,000,000 in the previous century. The rebound in the Ming period from this population drop was marked, and by the year 1500 the population of China may have been as large as 150,000,000. When increases this steep occur, abandoned or under-exploited agricultural lands are brought to efficiency. New crops or improved strains of old crops are used, tilling and planting of the soil may be partly mechanized and in any event is done with very little waste, and means of transporting agricultural goods to the cities are improved. Land reclamation, achieved either by filling in wetlands or terracing the side of mountains, expands the amount of tillage. All these things happened in Ming China, particularly before 1500. But a population boom produces subsequent booms, and the point of profitable exploitation of the land may be surpassed. When this happens, land that had previously been given over to the production of specialized crops must eventually be used to produce staple crops, with a much lower return. The decreased profitability of farming and the increased labor supply may inhibit mechanization of farming. The surpluses that farming had previously produced – much of which may have actually been invested in urban commerce or development – decrease or disappear, and the economy goes into decline. In theory, this decline will in itself put a brake on population growth, and the ratio between population and resources may come back into line.

The exact point at which population growth suppresses economic development is murky. Societies have all kinds of ways of dealing with shortfalls and even structural crises. Some societies endure under intense pressures of population, while others collapse in the face of what might appear a minor challenge. In many cases, the situation in the cities and the situations in the countryside may be very different, depending on the ways in which they are connected. And there are many instances in which the behaviors which Thomas Malthus called "rational" affect the outcome. Malthus proposed that some societies – he meant northern Europe and Britain – had learned to control the degree of population growth in light of present and expected economic development. According to him, they understood that population could outstrip resources and inhibit economic development, and so attempted to rationalize population growth by use of late marriage, procreative discipline and, in extreme cases, infanticide. In Malthus' view, China was an example of irrational population growth – the Chinese did nothing to prevent their population outpacing their ability to either feed themselves or generate enough surplus to stimulate the economy. Only the intervention of natural or man-made disasters caused the periodic starvation that limited the Chinese population.

Recent research by historians of China demonstrates that Malthus' theories account for very little of China's population dynamics. The extent to which the behavior of a majority of Chinese in the fifteenth or the eighteenth century can be characterized as "rational" depends upon consideration of factors to which Malthus paid limited attention. In these times, China had a high infant mortality rate and an extremely high proportion of the population involved in agriculture. For such a society, it is rational to seek as many births as possible, and large families can be an assurance of sufficient labor as well as support through hard times. Nevertheless, it was clearly not the case that there was no upper limit on the desired family size. Methods of birth control were well developed, it was common for children from impoverished families to be raised by wealthier relatives and, in extremity, families practiced infanticide (usually female). It is not a question of whether or not Chinese had the means or the rational understanding to control population, but what expectations they were working with when exercising that control.

The magistrates on whom the Qing depended for their information about local conditions were unreliable actors in many respects. At the end of the eighteenth century, when the population of Qing China had doubled, the number of magistrates had remained effectively the same. The complexity of the magistrate's job expanded in at least the same proportion. Despite the severe Qing sanctions against corruption (see chapter 2), the state was very limited in its ability to pursue prosecutions. Historians estimate that for the entire Qianlong period there were no more than 400 corruption cases tried, which works out to about eight cases a year. A magistrate weighing the advantages of pursuing or not pursuing corruption might logically conclude that the risk was reasonable. Sociologists studying the problem in the Qing period suggest that the portion of a magistrate's income derived from corrupt practices (gifts from landowners in exchange for lower tax assessments or collections, payments from innocent residents threatened with false prosecution, payments from criminals in exchange for not reporting or prosecuting their crimes, bribes from all manner of people whose cases were being tried in the magistrate's court) as compared to his state salary ranged from about 14:1 for the eighteenth century (when the official salaries were hugely supplemented to discourage corruption) to 22:1 for the nineteenth century. Men whose families had spent deeply for many years to pay the expenses of the examinations may have felt that the opportunity to rake in cash from corrupt practices was the main goal of getting an appointment in the first place. The partnership between the magistrates and the gentry that the Qing had encouraged was more profound and material than the government may have intended. Since the gentry were overwhelmingly the primary source of income for magistrates, the actual income of magistrates tended to mirror that of the gentry, effectively making the officials landowners themselves. While agricultural output continued to increase through the eighteenth century and into very early nineteenth century, the real incomes of the farming population remained flat through the late Ming and Qing. The benefits of increased production and commercialization appear to have gone to the gentry and indirectly to the magistrates, so that 22 percent of all profit from agriculture went to less than half of one percent of the population. Farmers and laborers felt the immediate sting of the situation at tax time, when corrupt magistrates tended to pad the farmers' assessments to make up for the amount that had been deducted from gentry obligations. Beginning in the eighteenth century, when the Qing court attempted to ameliorate the corruption of the magistrates with a huge increase in their salaries, it also attempted to take the edge off popular anger by occasionally lowering the land tax, later adding tax amnesties for those who owed taxes they could not pay. It was not a tool the lean government dared use often, but it was understood by the policy advisors to be, in harsh times, a necessary buffer against widespread disorder.

The potentially explosive dynamics of dislocated populations, competition among groups cohering along lines of local place, kinship, culture and organized mutual aid and resistance are usually examined by historians in combination with other pressures of the early nineteenth century. Foremost, perhaps, is population pressure. Official practices must always be considered when assessing the population and putting it into the context of available support. The precise population of China at any time – including the present – is, like all population figures, a matter of a guess. This is not because of a lack of documentation. Most historians are impressed by the fact that as early as two thousand years ago empires based in China began to keep centralized population records. Population records are kept by governments for purposes of taxation and military conscription, both of which were well established in China at an early period. But there was no independent department for the census. It was run by local officials reporting to the central department of revenue. We now know that many factors caused local officials to distort these figures. An official who was sending in a tax amount lower than expected – perhaps to lessen the tax burden on his wealthy local patrons – could best explain the deficit by claiming a lower rate of population in that year. But it would be difficult for any official to make such a claim many years running, since the factors that would suppress population growth – flood, famine, rebellion, disease – would reflect poorly upon the official's performance and trigger an unwanted inquiry. On the other hand, before the early eighteenth century few officials had an incentive to inflate the population figures, since that would have inflated the amount of tax they were expected to collect. After the freezing of the head-tax in 1711, increases in population did not automatically require increases in taxes collected (though land continued to be taxed on its ascribed productivity). We know that after this time officials tended to systematically and marginally increase the reported populations in their counties. Whether these artificial increments (inadvertently) coincided with increases in population is simply not known with precision. Population increase could have been greater, less, or there could in some years have been a decrease. What is certainly known is that in the later eighteenth and early nineteenth centuries a large number of officials were not taking a precise census, but were automatically increasing the numbers of the previous census. Though this probably does not seriously alter the general statement that China's population roughly doubled between 1650 and 1800, it does mean we will never have exact data on the details of this increase. The general contours are clear, but while precision can be represented in our statistics we cannot assure that our statistics are an exact representation of fact.

When locally concentrated population pressures became overwhelming, the only choice for millions in eighteenth-century China was to leave. Separation from the systems of order and support that existed at home could be wrenching, even if conditions had eroded organization to a minimum. Employment, housing, marriage and the ability to pay taxes were all likely to hang upon finding and exploiting kinship connections in the new place. Fears of dying away from home, of being unburied and unworshiped by the lineage, were real. The return of the dead was a living value, though it remained only an ideal for the millions of people who could never dream of affording it. Nevertheless it left its mark on the environment. As the population increased in the eighteenth century, the forests disappeared. When wood was no longer available for building houses, brick was used. But the other great consumer of the forests was the need for coffins in which to encase the burgeoning numbers of dead. The wealthy continued to buy expensive wood for coffins, and to pay for the transport on expensive carts to their ancestral places for burial. The Qing government encouraged the retention of ancestral affiliations in migrants, to the extent that it required individuals to retain the legal registration of their ancestors. Thus in the eighteenth century a massive portion of the population of China was legally registered as native to towns or cities they had never seen, and that possibly their fathers or grandfathers had never seen. The reasons for this are unclear. It was partly a matter of bureaucratic conservatism, an echo of the millennia-old government fear of uncontrolled migration. But it was also an acknowledgment of the continuing profundity of ancestral attachments in the life structures of Chinese, even in an age of massive transfers.

Choices about where to move were often dictated by considerations of whether anybody from the home region had moved to the new place previously. Virtually all migrants attempted to recreate the basic structures of native regions in the areas to which they relocated. This could create tensions in the new home, and when these new tensions exacerbated existing problems, the results could be explosive. The Qing state, like the Ming before it, did everything possible to construct hurdles that made migration the very last resort, not only because of the possibility of increasing social tensions but also because every individual missing from his home was also missing from the tax rolls. All Qing subjects were registered in their ancestral localities unless legally transferred elsewhere. It was illegal to leave that locality without official permission, which was generally given only to officials, soldiers and merchants whose work required them to travel. *Baojia* rules were used to ascertain that individuals really were at home, or had permission to be absent. The penalties for absconding included flogging and fines heavy enough to permanently impoverish most families; those who impersonated somebody else in order to avoid prosecution (also not a rare crime) faced even more severe penalties.

Nevertheless, illegal migration was common. Though the state had done all it could to impede migration and had minimized frivolous transfers, the evidence is that at any particular time after the conquest and before the death of the Qianlong emperor, many hundreds of thousands of people were out of their legal domains. The problem affected the banner populations in the garrisons everywhere in the empire too, as richly attested by the monthly tally of how many bannermen, often with their families, had absconded. This "floating population" (*liumin* – still the modern term for illegal internal migrants, very many of whom are homeless) was likely to fluctuate with conditions, and different regions attracted the floating at different times. As the wealth of the Yangtze delta and the Pearl River delta in Guangdong began to develop six hundred years ago, people from various parts of China flocked there, attracted by urban life and by the comparatively high wages on the agricultural estates. Southeast China and Fujian province in particular suffered from extreme population density in Ming times, which could be alleviated with illegal emigration of various sorts. This began with the repopulation of Sichuan and southern Shaanxi in the later seventeenth century, when settlers from Fujian and Guangdong left their cramped districts for the fertile and disused lands of the interior. The population movements intensified as the empire expanded in the eighteenth century. Sometimes the geography of migration was intertwined with environmental change, including not only deforestation but the introduction of fresh crops that attracted new settlers. The Ming, with their population bulge, had made limited use of new crops to permit lands unsuitable to rice or grain to be used. The Qing, in the midst of their larger bulge, were far more active in the importation and application of new crops. The one which most dramatically changed the landscape was corn from the Americas. Lands that would otherwise have been abandoned or at least fallowed for periods were put to uninterrupted use, and for a time in the eighteenth century agricultural booms in remote areas were stimulated by the introduction of corn, which aided in the opening of new farmlands in Sichuan, Yunnan, Guizhou, Shaanxi, Gansu and Mongolia.

As in Ming times, the overwhelmed eastern coasts sent large numbers of sailors, merchants or aspiring farmers to various parts of Southeast Asia. Many went to Taiwan, where they were welcomed by the few Dutch officials in residence. Others went south to modern-day Vietnam, Malaysia and the Philippines. The Ming and the Qing regimes were adamantly opposed to external migration, since unlike internal migrants who might be caught and returned to the tax rolls, emigrés were lost forever. Nevertheless, the steady stream of Fukienese- and Cantonese-speaking emigrants to Asia, various parts of the Indian Ocean including Madagascar, and eventually the Pacific did not cease.

Massive migration changed the urban as well as the rural environments. Many uprooted people landed in the cities. Others who intended to farm or start small businesses found it necessary to join a provincial association (*huiguan*); an establishment in their new city of residence that was created by earlier immigrants from their own region. There they could speak their own language (which might not be intelligible to the majority), make connections necessary for jobs, housing and credit, find a social life and perhaps a wife. Attachment to a provincial association could make the difference for a migrant between a roof and no roof, between eating and starvation. No migrant would knowingly head for a city he did not believe had a provincial guild to which he could attach himself. But then the great cities had hundreds of provincial associations (*huiguan*), and nearly anyone could find some kind of connection for himself on arrival. Merely making connections did not mean finding a fortune, and it appears that most migration in eighteenth-century China was a result of despair, not optimism. Family and village relationships were vital to the survival of all but the wealthy. One would only attenuate them by migration if no realistic alternative existed. Once migration had occurred, the recreation of the links was vital. This often meant recreating social hierarchies in the distant locations. Those coming to the new region with some of the wealth of their families bought lands or businesses and assumed roles as patrons in the provincial associations. Those coming from poverty brought nothing but their bodies.

Environmental deterioration is part of the equation of how well a population, even a very large one, is supported by its resources. In the nineteenth century, the court in Beijing was acutely aware of the need to maintain the Yellow River. In 1494 the Yellow River had become so silted and the water levels so high that the river had changed course (see chapter 9), resulting in hundreds of thousands of deaths. The change, of course, had also wreaked economic havoc. Farms previously fed by the river were left dry, farms previously remote from the river were flooded and destroyed, and farmers had fled elsewhere either to avoid the flood itself or the resulting unemployment. Historians and geologists believe that by 1800 all the land that could possibly be farmed in the Yellow River was being farmed, meaning that trees had been removed from all arable land and that there was little or no opportunity to leave land fallow for a year. Neglect of the river's dredging and embankments occurred in the early nineteenth century at the same time that other changes made the health of the river even more critical. In many parts of the Yellow River basin, farming had been revived by farmers beginning to grow corn. Lands that had been over-farmed for wheat, barley or sorghum and appeared to be depleted could be profitably used to grow corn, since its roots penetrate far deeper into the ground to find nitrogen. Migrants came from parts of southern China to work in the active fields of the Yellow River basin, and in the later 1700s the area was growing in population and in wealth. But growing corn intensely without letting the land recoup its nutrients only exhausted the soil to the depth of six feet instead of one foot. Equally important, the increasing population demanded more natural resources, particularly wood, for housing, for heat, and for coffins when they died. By the middle eighteenth century, not only the Yellow River basin but most of China was deforested. As the land became disused, neglected and bare – both of trees and of crops – erosion increased, and so did the rate of silting of the Yellow River. The price of wood went up. The wealthy sought imports of exotic timber from Southeast Asia and Taiwan for their furniture and their coffins, switched from charcoal to coal for their heat. The poor built houses from brick, sat on their earthen floors, burned animal dung for heat and dreamed of corpse drivers to take their uncoffined bodies home.

Not all regions of China were subjected to the boom-and-bust cycle associated with corn in the early nineteenth century. Those residing in densely populated but progressively poorer areas had difficult choices to make regarding migration or criminal employment. In many parts of China, however, effective farming and growing income from trade continued into the nineteenth century. The poverty of provinces such as Shaanxi, Shandong and Anhui, for instance, was matched by the continued prosperity of Zhejiang, Jiangxi, Fujian and Guangdong. Indeed many historians believe that in as late as the year 1800 the standard of living in the Yangtze delta was comparable in most respects to that of industrializing Europe in the same period. As a consequence migration that had decades earlier been going north began to go south and east again.

Migrants were all outside the law, and many found it less terrifying than the Qing had intended it to be to engage in other illegal acts, sometimes necessary to survive. Prostitutes (male and female) and managers of prostitutes worked not only the cities, where they could amass fortunes, but also in the more modest countryside. In newly-opened regions of the west or in areas where agricultural labor was still short in the Yangtze delta, slave brokers could supply the needed backs – many of them migrants with no resources to get themselves into a better situation. Human smugglers also worked in the opposite direction, taking heavy fees to shift the unemployed and hopeless onto boats carrying them from Fujian across the seas. Fit and ruthless young men could join extortion gangs or pirate fleets, indeed many alternated between piracy and farming as opportunity dictated. Others could join smugglers, perhaps not even far from home. The Qing trade system tended to create many categories of profitable illegal activity, and Chinese smugglers were willing to join with European, Japanese or Filipino operators to get cheap (that is, stolen or pilfered) tea, silk and ceramics out of China, and to smuggle silver or slaves in.

Like social organizations in the legitimate world, criminal gangs – whether extortionists, pimps or smugglers – were sustained by stable structures. Partnerships with landowners or officials were sometimes practical. Gangs could lend muscle at tax or rent collection time, and could be of help in diminishing the power of other gangs. Magistrates seeking particularly heinous offenders, such as murderers or rapists, could sometimes turn to the gangs for information or help in an arrest, in return for various favors. Kinship was also important, as some organizations were dominated by certain lineages, and relatives tended to join gangs where other relatives could protect them or cooperate with them. The gangs went wherever the Chinese went, offering a crude structure to the Chinese communities of laborers and shopkeepers springing up throughout Taiwan, Southeast Asia, Central Asia and Mongolia. Criminal gangs and "secret societies" often shared information, membership and history, so that most historians of modern China had difficulty making a meaningful distinction between them.

The most venerable secret societies, such as that connected to the White Lotus sect, believed that their predecessors had banded together to oppose the Mongol conquest of China in the thirteenth century, employing secret organizations and communications and illegal study of the martial arts. In the Ming period, White Lotus cells saw themselves as champions of justice. They would vandalize or harass landlords or even magistrates, collect money for members in distress, distribute grain to the poor and guarantee each other's safety on the roads. In the case of the White Lotus, there were also meetings for religious indoctrination and practice of meditation techniques. The White Lotus was the symbol of the Buddhist idea of the perfect world to come, after the present world of corruption and injustice has been swept away. This general millenarian idea was not unique to Buddhism. Daoist folk beliefs also supported it and had been an inspiration in rebellions since the Han era. By late Ming times, White Lotus adherents combined Buddhist and Daoist ideas with practices from folk religion. There is evidence that they may have practiced some forms of sexual equality, allowing women to lead units within the society and join battles against the authorities. In the Qing, societies associating themselves with the White Lotus claimed to be fighting against the usurpation of the government by the Manchus, against the inherent injustices of Confucian elitism and against the wanton injustices of corrupt magistrates.

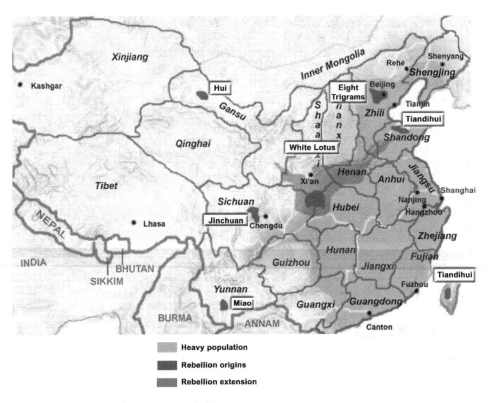

Map 2 Qianlong and Jiaqing era rebellions

In the late eighteenth century, Qing officials and soldiers were wary of the activities of secret societies and religious sects throughout the country. The White Lotus was regarded as a constant threat, but the empire also took serious note of a rebellion in Taiwan in 1782. Rival kinship federations who had immigrated from Fujian to Taiwan became embroiled in an outbreak of violence after a member of one gang was executed by the authorities for gambling and murder, and members of the other gang joined the authorities in hunting down and arresting his confederates. The persecuted faction rose in rebellion, occupied settlements all over Taiwan and declared a new dynasty.

The speed with which accused gamblers and smugglers had turned themselves into an organized rebellion with pretensions to statehood was explained by their affiliation with a secret society, the Tiandihui (Heaven and Earth Society). Many scholars today trace the origins of the Tiandihui to migrant populations seeking security and enough leverage to gain minimal employment in some of the most competitive economic regions of China; others claim it originated as a remnant of Ming resistance against the Qing invasion. Qing officials and soldiers, with decisive aid from local leaders and tens of thousands of civilians, managed to quash the rebellion in 1788. But the Qing court remained aware the Tiandihui survived. Whatever its origin, the government understood that Tiandihui was a loose organization, possibly without a head, but with tendrils reaching rapidly through the populations of migrants, homeless, itinerant laborers and ferry-pullers, stevedores, textile and porcelain workers. They had a belief system that combined millenarian idealism with potent sorcery, and they provided services and organization that compensated for the sagging structures of civil order in many areas of China – not only weakly administered border areas, but internal frontiers where economic stress and collapse of agriculture had eaten away at the thin strands of official control. As the government and some traditional landowners lost the economic edge, Tiandihui and similar organizations began to gain it through extortion and smuggling. Suppression of Tiandihui uprisings did not eradicate operations of the secret society, which melded its activities into pirate networks linking Taiwan and Vietnam, ran gambling schemes throughout rural China, and eventually became involved in smuggling of illegal migrants into Manchuria, Mongolia and other areas.

Cultural elements apart from kinship contributed to the cohesion of local groups, whether legal or illegal. Though the Qing court made extensive efforts to eradicate what it regarded as destabilizing cultural differences, the fact was that cultural differences were actually normal, and the standardized culture the court promoted was observed primarily by the gentry and imperial officials. Chinese is not a single language but a family of languages that were spoken in different corners of China, and each of the languages had many dialects, some specific to individual villages. Along with the vast linguistic spectrum of what was "Chinese" went differences in worship and religious conceptions, different preferences or taboos on food and dress. Reliance upon common beliefs and practices when dealing with stress was as urgent a matter as relying upon kinship ties if they could be found. Internal migration caused groups from different parts of China to compete for resources, whether access to water or access to jobs. Tensions could sharpen cultural differences that would otherwise be negligible, a dynamic vividly demonstrated in the Taiwan rebellion of 1782–8. The "Hakka" (*kejia*); for instance, are sometimes regarded as a classic cultural minority in China, but they are originally from north China, like all other Chinese speakers. When they arrived in the south, those who arrived earlier regarded them as different. The Hakkas relied upon themselves, and retained many of what had once been their local customs. Over time, they tended to settle into the less desirable jobs and live on the less desirable land, causing them to appear to the observer – whether a Qing official or a visiting foreigner – as yet another disadvantaged and disgruntled minority, not greatly different from the Miao, Yao, Lolo, Dai, and other groups living in pockets of Guangdong, Guangxi, Guizhou, Yunnan and Sichuan.

Degrees up on the scale of cultural difference were the groups distinguished by history, language and religion from any recognizable group of Chinese. The Qing Eight Banner forces – with their subdivisions of Manchu, Mongol and Chinese-martial – were in theory elevated over the general population by their status as conquerors and occupiers. The court attempted to encourage them to remain separate from the general population by requiring them to be literate in Manchu or Mongolian, to practice military skills of horsemanship and archery, to live in the compounds built for them (or merely appropriated) in the seventeenth century and to marry only among the banner families. Soon after the conquest, however, the court discovered what it considered annoying – and then alarming – evidence of cultural disorder among the bannermen. They were learning the local dialects and forgetting their ancestral language. Many grew tired of waiting for military appointments in the banners (which became progressively scarcer after 1685) and illegally contrived new occupations for themselves – as actors and acrobats, singers, food stand owners, and eventually as laborers and beggars – when they could not live on the stipends from the court. In its usual fashion, the imperial government urged commanders of the banner garrisons to use their ingenuity to meet budget shortfalls. The commanders sold the garrison lands intended for grazing the horses, then sold the horses, in order to meet expenses for food, paper and ink. They refrained from buying ammunition for their cannon and cancelled drills. The court concentrated on maintenance of a small number of élite, well-equipped units, such as Eldemboo's, to dispatch to trouble spots. It otherwise relied on local army units and militia to keep the peace. In the early eighteenth century the court gave sporadic attention to the problems of banner livelihood. Many low-ranking bannermen despaired of being able to survive on the salaries, even when they were paid. Special disbursements were made infrequently to try to catch up with outstanding salary payments. In the middle eighteenth century the court suspended the legal penalties on bannermen who lived outside the garrison (and by implication lived by non-military, private work). Bannermen and their families who seemed to have nothing to do were first enticed, then forcibly transferred to state farms in Manchuria, from which many – or most – promptly escaped. Their tendency, when leaving the garrisons, was to seek employment in the civilian economy and to marry Chinese if they pleased.

Far more resilient in maintaining their identities were Muslim groups in the empire. Qing Muslims were broadly distinguished between Chinese Muslims and Turkestani Muslims. Since the tenth century China had had many Muslim communities in its large coastal cities, as well as Beijing. These communities, commonly called the "Hui," were populous and prosperous by the Ming period, though there were pockets of Muslims in southwest China who were economically marginal. Their relationship with the state was various. The Ming often sponsored mosques and made other gifts to prominent Muslim communities, mostly in the interest of facilitating trade with or competing for favor against rulers of Central Asia. The Qing were more querulous in their attitudes toward the Hui. In the eighteenth century, when the court of the Qianlong emperor was most extravagant in its pretensions to impartially dominate and patronize many of the world's civilizations (including Christian Europe, represented by the Jesuits at the Qianlong court), Islam remained indigestible. Muslim communities could not accept the Qing emperor as a moral authority. For their part, the Qing emperors could not insist that the Hui assimilate like the populations of southeast China, for the Hui gave every evidence of literate civilization and long history, and many individual Hui were accomplished scholars. The court's solution was to attract as many Hui officials as possible, while making it clear that Muslims in general were not to be trusted, and Muslims as individuals would do well to make themselves as inconspicuous as possible.

About a third of the Muslims in the Qing empire by the end of the eighteenth century were in western Mongolia and eastern Turkestan. It had been nearly a thousand years since any part of Turkestan had been governed by an empire based in China. Historically eastern Turkestan and western Mongolia had been under the control of small states based in the oasis cities or run by leaders of nomadic bands. Civil administration had been largely in the hands of Muslim clerics. The communities ranged from Mongolian to Turkic to Tibetan in culture. In Turkestan itself, the Turkic groups were various, including Turkestani, Kazakh, Kirghiz, Uzbek, and smaller groups, as well as many Hui merchants and farmers, Mongols, Tibetans and Tajiks. Most could speak the Turkestani trade language that is today known as "Uighur." After the conquest of eastern Turkestan and the Qing designation of it as Xinjiang, the empire considered the region a hostile, occupied frontier. They saw all Muslim residents of Xinjiang as rebellious, treacherous and violent unless restrained. Qing officials assiduously sifted through the local headmen to find those who would be willing clients, and rewarded them with embassy rights, titles, stipends and other honors. As it had done in its infancy in Manchuria, as it did in Mongolia, China and the southwestern borders, the Qing preferred to have the locals rule the locals whenever possible. The result was a small number of wealthy and influential Turkestani factota, surrounded by a suspicious, resisting Turkestani majority, well organized through its Muslim congregations and trade organizations.

The general picture of employment for local populations that had either increased naturally or been augmented by migrants was complex. From the seventeenth forward, industry offered survival wages and minimal housing to millions. Mining (often done by convicts, but also by more or less voluntary labor) in Manchuria, Xinjiang and Mongolia demanded increasing labor. Rising mining in the eighteenth century demanded more and more smelting operations to produce military weapons, cooking pots and tools. Labor demands were also very high in the porcelain factories of the Yangtze delta, which in the seventeenth century were already huge, employing tens of thousands of laborers at a single facility, working long mass production lines, firing and loading the kilns. Textile factories were equally large, employing both men and women in endless shifts. Though these industries were dominated by government monopolies (like salt mining and processing), they are known to have devoured both legal (including convict) and illegal labor when their needs were high. In the cities, migrants could find work as nightsoil carriers, taking human sludge to be buried and composted outside the city limits. They could carry sedan chairs laden with men unwilling to walk or foot-bound women unable to. They could offer to trim beards and hair in the street. They could do the most menial work in the restaurants, tea houses and brothels (the better jobs would be given to the proprietor's relatives). If nothing else worked out, they could sell themselves or their dependents into effective slavery or prostitution.

Issues of wages, work conditions and housing were frequent causes of friction and even disorder in the late Ming and early Qing periods. Ming farmers frequently protested high rents, frequently resulting in damage to the landowner's property and the arrest and execution of those regarded as fomenters of protest. Ming workers in the porcelain factories frequently sat down or rioted to protest their miserable working conditions; in 1601 workers made their points by throwing themselves into the kilns at the imperial factories at Jingdezhen. After their conquest of Qing was complete and their bannermen distributed to the provinces, the Qing were dismayed to find that they had to suppress not only the disorders arising from local Chinese complaints but also demonstrations and rioting by the bannermen themselves – they protested poor housing assignments in south China, they protested what were perceived as inequities in land allotments given to different groups within the banners, they protested, almost continually, the shortages of pay that the empire frequently used to balance its budgets.

The effects of population weight, particularly in the decreasing profitability of agriculture, can be discerned in the very late Ming period. There was a shift away from cash crops such as mulberry trees and toward rice in the south, millet and barley in the north. This shift was demanded by the market, but the return from farming declined. At the same time, there was a fall in real productivity per acre and this has not been entirely explained. The rural immiseration of the very late Ming is clearly reflected in this picture of a gradual shift away from commercial, mechanized agriculture to subsistence farming. Though Qing attempts to restore the agricultural economy in the decade after suppression of the Zhang and Li rebellions and conquest of north China were hindered by infelicitous climate change, by the end of the seventeenth century farming had resumed in the most devastated areas and movement of products over improved roads had increased. What the early Qing economy did not bring to the countryside, however, was technological change of the sort that had stimulated the economy in early Ming times, and was in the seventeenth century bringing economic advances to other places in East Asia, as well as northern Europe. Historians speculate that a generous labor supply removed the need for mechanization of many tasks. Others have added that deforestation in the eighteenth century and the neglect of water works in early nineteenth century created an energy crisis in the early Qing period. The necessity to use coal instead of wood for firing kilns or smelting operations meant that fuel needed to be expensively transported from faraway mining sites, while slow or diverted rivers were unable to power water wheels. Declining profit margins for small farmers diminished the use of oxen in farming. Farmers and shop owners coped with declining profits or increasing market opportunities by working themselves and their families harder, rather than seeking more profitable crops or hiring more workers. The result was continuing and in some cases increasing productivity without increasing wealth. Such processes created plateaus in development – an economy that cannot create new jobs or enterprises to cope with a population that continues to expand.

In early modern Chinese history, there is a vivid pattern of diminished margins for profitability, especially in agriculture, occurring prior to the outbreak of large rebellions. During the late Ming, when a constrained agricultural economy coincided with rising complaints about official corruption, the state was challenged by – and eventually destroyed by – two huge rural rebellions. The earlier, led by Zhang Xianzhong, began amidst the turmoil of famine and small rebellions against corrupt government in 1628–30; he established a capital for himself at Chengdu in Sichuan province and declared his state the Daxi ("Great West"). Zhang's war-making and regime-building went on intermittently until his death in 1647. Zhang's forces killed hundreds of thousands but did not succeed in toppling the Ming. That accomplishment fell to his rival rebel, Li Zicheng, who came from the same famine-wracked section of northwest China. In 1630 Li was shackled for failure to pay his debts. When a soldier offered him water, the local magistrate knocked the water away and had the soldier beaten. A crowd of onlookers set upon the magistrate and freed Li, who fled to the mountains. In the ensuing years he built up an army of hundreds of thousands and fought his way to Beijing. In April of 1644 Li's army entered Beijing, the last Ming emperor committed suicide, and Li announced the new dynasty of Shun ("Obedience [to the will of Heaven]").

For the Qing, the processes of dislodging Li from Beijing, wiping out the last vestiges of his rebellion, and ending the Ming were actually all one process. As discussed in chapter 2, the Qing were so extended in their efforts to keep their vastly enlarged military forces organized that they were forced to be somewhat perfunctory in the establishment of civil governments both in the conquered north and in the unconquered by neutralized south. The first century of the empire was marked not only by large and generally well-organized campaigns to extend the empire to Taiwan, Yunnan, Mongolia, Xinjiang and Tibet but also quell small uprisings throughout the empire. Some rebellions were the final cry of resistance to the conquest, others – for instance, among hereditary leaders in Mongolia – were attempts to exploit the distractions of the court to regain local autonomy. The Kangxi emperor's grand sweep of pacifying south China, Taiwan and Mongolia ended a critical stage of conquest, and the end of these campaigns coincided with a distinct period of rural and urban prosperity in the early eighteenth century. During the middle eighteenth century, the court was troubled mainly by the Tibetan rebels of Jinchuan in Sichuan province, who were attempting to throw off Qing rule. In two brief wars, one in the 1740s and one in the 1770s, the Qianlong court achieved only tenuous victories. Yet the campaigns were the most expensive in which the empire engaged. Though the conquest of Xinjiang that ended in 1755 and its subsequent occupation cost the empire much more than it ever gained from the colony, the Qianlong emperor estimated that the Jinchuan wars cost twice the conquest of Xinjiang. His estimate, of course, did not delineate the magnification of those expenses by the corrupt military clique run by Heshen, of which the emperor may never have been fully aware.

The tendency of the late Qianlong authorities was to suppress rebellions with a show of violence, then pass the peacekeeping task to local powers and move quickly on to the next trouble spot. This pattern may have been encouraging to groups such as White Lotus adherents and Tiandihui affiliates who had the structure and resources to maintain their resistance for long periods of time. In 1774 a sect connected with the White Lotus seized several large towns in Shandong province before local government forces could be sent against them. When the opposing forces engaged, the imperial troops were scattered by the rebels. Such incidents quickly convinced sect and secret society followers that their practice of martial arts and esoteric medical regimens, in combination with their divine inspiration, meant that they would eventually prevail over the empire. In the case of the Shandong rebellion, in a matter of months the government transferred enough troops from neighboring provinces (and at least 7,000 bannermen from as far as Jilin province in Manchuria) to end the uprising and martyr its leaders. But the imperial response had been slow enough to suggest that a quicker and larger rebellion might succeed in ending Qing rule in China.

Even as the Shandong rebels were being suppressed, other White Lotus followers were heading toward revolt. A group of White Lotus adherents province were making money by selling amulets and potions to villagers in Hunan. When magistrates attempted to interfere with the trade, sometimes by demanding a share of the profits, the White Lotus peddlers tried to fight back by putting a spell on the more vexing officials. The leader of the sect was banished for his actions, but his followers decided that defending their trade and their faith would require more organization, solicitations of money from sympathizers and more martial arts practice. In 1793 magistrates ordered the arrest of local sect leaders, and when they could not be found, the officials simply arrested random residents and threatened to arrest more if extortion payments were not made. White Lotus believers and non-believers alike rose in rebellion in 1795, waving banners with the slogan "officials have forced the people to rebel";

in their reports to the throne, officials estimated that only one in ten rebels had any religious motivation. Magistrates and governors followed their usual tendency to try to deal with local problems before the news could be known in Beijing. The Qing court heard of the uprising only after it had spread outside the control of Hunan magistrates, and then beyond the capacities of the governor of Hunan to stem its spread. The Qianlong emperor fatally put responsibility for suppressing the rebellion into the hands of Heshen, whose clique had already prolonged the Jinchuan campaigns (and others, such as against the Miao in Guizhou in the middle 1790s) in order to drain the treasury.

The White Lotus network of communications quickly spread the revolt to Henan and Sichuan provinces, and eventually to more distant Shaanxi. They gathered tens of thousands of fighters at their extemporized capital at Xiangyang, in Hubei (once used as a base by the late Ming rebel Li Zicheng, and famous for its doomed resistance to the Mongol invasion in the thirteenth century). Though generals dispatched to the front told the court that the rebellion was contained in Hunan, the rebels themselves knew the facts, which were that they were holding their own against the Qing forces in almost all theaters. Even when the Qing shut down violence in certain locations, the rebels quickly located elsewhere and coordinated with other White Lotus units. Commanders of the Qing forces who were actually determined to defeat the rebels were in a difficult position, since they could not request additional forces or resources from the court without admitting that they were not actually succeeding in the field. They eventually turned the tide against the rebels by relying on gentry leaders in Hunan, Hubei and Shaanxi, who with their *tuanlian* forces managed to pacify and hold those provinces.

Early in 1799 the White Lotus rebels were largely defeated, but Qing militarists were reluctant to end the war. Eight Banner forces were still being led about to locations where rebels had either never been or had already vacated, and reports continued to flow to the court requesting more requisitions to fight remnants of the insurrection. In an attempt to sever the influence of the old, corrupt military leaders, the emperor put the war in the hands of a group of Manchu soldiers (including Eldemboo) who had weak or no connections with Heshen (see chapter 2). They continued the policy of relying on gentry militia, supplemented when possible by Eight Banner or other imperial troops. Eldemboo himself concentrated on keeping the rebels on the run in the highlands and other inhospitable areas, working with the gentry on an innovative strategy to basically lock the rebels out of the populous and well-supplied towns. In 1804 the last rebel holdouts were seized, and the emperor announced that the war was concluded – more a measure to fight high level corruption by cutting off the spigot of war appropriations than a meaningful strategic statement, since small outbreaks of White Lotus and Tiandihui armed resistance continued for some years. And while his father had been astounded at the cost of the Jinchuan wars, the Jiaqing emperor was looking at the greatest expense to date of any Qing military operation -perhaps as high as 120,000,000 ounces of silver, at least 25 percent higher than the Jinchuan wars expenditures.

It was not the end of the White Lotus movement or of other popular rebellions. The Yangtze basin, the highest priority for the state in its pursuit of economic security, was pacified, but offshoots of the White Lotus ideology survived in north China. Tiandihui branches, now largely specialized in criminal activities, were more widespread than ever. As evidence of Qing military weakness increased, local secret societies and no doubt many individual farmers and laborers felt not only emboldened but confirmed in their belief that the Qing regime, and along with it the current order of the world, must be dying. One of the boldest was the "Eight Trigrams," or Heavenly Principle (Tianli) uprising. Sometime in late 1812 two leaders of the sect conceived of a plot to seize control of Shandong and Zhili provinces in October of 1813, after which they would assassinate the Jiaqing emperor. They set up an elaborate organization of communications and military deployment, which they called the Eight Trigrams. They infiltrated the population of eunuch officials inside the imperial city, and convinced so many people in Beijing that their uprising would succeed that those who wished to be on the good side of the new regime prepared to affix white banners to their doors on the day of the seizure of the capital. Qing officials discovered a cell of the organization and captured one of the Eight Trigrams leaders, whom they planned to torture. But sympathizers broke into the magistrate's offices and freed the rebel. They then initiated the local uprising in Shandong. In the meantime their co-conspirators in Zhili found out that the Jiaqing emperor would be away from the capital in early October, and planned to ambush his entourage on his way back to the capital. They followed the emperor to the gates of the imperial city, then were surreptitiously admitted to the inner sanctum by their eunuch compatriots. Eight Banner soldiers and even the prince Minning who would one day be the Daoguang emperor disarmed the rebels and arrested them, after which they were executed. Manchu generals were dispatched to the environs of Beijing to scour out the last of the Eight Trigrams units and supporters, eventually executing 20,000 people. Defeat of the Eight Trigrams rebels and furious pursuit of their sympathizers seemed to quell ideological rebellion in the empire for some time, though disorders in cultural minority areas of Sichuan, Yunnan and Xinjiang continued to erupt every few years.

During the second decade of the nineteenth century, the Qing court under the Jiaqing emperor attempted in ways tried by his predecessors in the eighteenth century to deal with the problems of a stumbling domestic trade network, a weakening agricultural sector, and widespread disaffection threatening social disorders small and large. For the first few years of his reign the emperor supplied funds for river management to the extent he could, and attempted to improvise relief works for the Eight Banners. To raise funds, he increased the sale of offices and ranks, and he maintained a high tariff on the European trade at Canton, the source of about 80 percent of his income. He also became obsessed with personal frugality, eschewing any lavish court displays and any significant expenditure on his own clothing and housing. Like his father, he frequently invoked the aphorisms of his imperial predecessors on the evils of profligate spending. This time it had the ring of sincerity. But at nearly every turn, the emperor seemed to be defeated by mechanisms in place before his ascension to the throne, which sometimes inverted the intended effect of his policies. Extractions from the tariffs on foreign trade brought complaints from Britain in particular, which in 1816 resumed its campaign to open the China trade to competition. Only a small portion of the imperial appropriations for river management actually were applied to that task; most disappeared into the pockets of officials. During the Jiaqing reign the Yellow River flooded at least seventeen times. Increasing the sale of offices, which brought immediate revenue to the court (and had been used in the past in times of war), only made the problems of corruption worse, since officials who had purchased

their offices felt entitled to recoup the expense through graft. The emperor's pronouncements on thrift were maliciously quoted by his detractors, giving the popular
impression of a miser who was indifferent to commoners' troubles.

Unsure how to gain leverage against the problems rising on all sides, the emperor
became convinced that Christianity was a major factor in social disorder. Jesuits had
been active in China since the arrival of Matteo Ricci in 1600. The Qing imperial
lineage, unlike the Ming, never converted to Catholicism, but the early emperors
were neutral on conversion of others (including members of the maternal family of
the Kangxi emperor); permitted the building of four large cathedrals in Beijing. The
court employed Jesuits as cartographers, tutors in mathematics and astronomy, engineers, architects, illustrators of the campaigns of conquest, and portrait painters. After
the death of the Kangxi emperor the Qing court outlawed further conversions, and
Jesuits provided only technical functions (including drafting and architecture) at the
Qianlong court. Nevertheless, by the time the Jiaqing emperor took power there
were probably about 300,000 Catholics in China, and nearly half the priests were
Chinese. In one of the few policies in which he directly reversed his father, the Jiaqing
emperor set about eradication of Roman Catholicism and persecution of Catholics. In
1805 the court outlawed further conversions, forbade foreigners to learn Chinese or
Manchu, and undertook prosecution of Catholics that continued through the Jiaqing
reign. The religion was not in fact eradicated, despite execution of adherents and the
banishment of others to Xinjiang as slaves in the mines. The emperor accomplished
little more than a marginal increase in the popular ill-will and new suspicions of the
empire from European governments that had previously been friendly.

The Jiaqing emperor's training and personality made him a weak contrast to his
father at the same age. As a child he had shown unusual intelligence and a strong
scholarly bent. His father secretly named him heir apparent in 1773, but the designation was kept so secret that the prince's education, travel, and personal contact with
his father were kept identical to those of his nine brothers, four of whom were older
than he. The result that he was unprepared for the throne even at the relatively
advanced age at which he achieved it, and the unusual circumstances of his father's
abdication did not permit him to gain any real experience even after he became
emperor. The relative indifference of officials and foreign emissaries to his instructions
frequently angered him, but his anger rarely had any effect other than to make him
eager afterwards to regain good will. His frustration with policy often led him to
return again to his scholarly interests. He wrote a great deal about history, manners,
travel and literature, though the works are usually ignored by historians focused on
Jiaqing policy failures. The emperor may have agreed with this assessment; toward the
end of his life he told his officials to stop submitting the traditional "as intended, so
done" (*ruyi*) wands as gifts, since it depressed the emperor to look on them and consider their name. The Jiaqing emperor died relatively early (aged 60) and suddenly,
during a trip to the imperial retreat at Chengde in September of 1820.

Great hope was placed in Yongyan's second son, Minning, when he became the
Daoguang emperor on Lunar New Year's Day, 1821. Like his father, Minning was a
scholar by inclination and, like his father, he was secretly designated heir apparent.
But by the time he became emperor he also had a dashing side to his public profile,
owing to his killing an Eight Trigrams rebel and wounding another with a musket in
1813. He was tested by rebels again in the 1820s, when a rebellion broke out in

Xinjiang. The local Manchu military commander aroused the ill will of Turkestanis at Kashgar, inspiring Jehangir (the exiled grandson of a local magnate who had been displaced by the Qing conquest in 1755) to conceive the idea of taking the city and establishing himself as its new ruler. He did not make it into the city, but managed to maintain his encampment not far away. The emperor was informed that poor management in Xinjiang had led to public disorder, and he ostentatiously had the local commander removed and punished. He also sent one of his most trusted Mongol commanders to Xinjiang to try to reform the situation there and quiet things down. Jehangir struck again, with a coalition of Kirghiz, Turkestanis and other local peoples outraged by the excessive violence practiced by Qing troops and the restrictive trade policies imposed by the new commissioners. This time the authorities were able to muster banner troops in relatively short order and dispel Jehangir's forces. In the aftermath the emperor expressed great dissatisfaction about two facts: one, the new officials sent in suggested that the best way to restore peace was to appoint a local Turkestani as a kind of magistrate of Kashgar and, two, Jehangir had escaped. The emperor insisted that the military commanders in Xinjiang become not more flexible but more harsh, and insisted that Jehangir be apprehended. The rebel was captured in 1828 and brought to Beijing, presented in a humiliating ritual and then killed by dismemberment. It was the last time the Qing ever imposed this particularly brutal death; it also marked the height of Daoguang-era ferocity in campaigns to suppress rebellion in Xinjiang. Jehangir's brother and others of his relatives continued to hold trade cities in defiance of Qing commands. In 1835 the Qing accepted a treaty whose terms were practically dictated by the nearby khanate of Kokand, permitting trade representatives of the khanate to reside in parts of Xinjiang exempt from Qing regulation, and fixing a very low tariff on Kokandian goods. The empire hoped that the treaty would simplify its maintenance of order in Xinjiang by eliminating Kokand as a source of aggression and interference.

Apart from the capture and execution of Jehangir, the Daoguang emperor was not particularly given to authoritarianism or ruthlessness. He had a contrasting quality that is now of great interest to historians who compare this phase of the Qing empire to similar passages in the Ottoman and Russian empires: The emperor had a very strong consultative tendency. He faced many of the same crises as his father, including flooding of the unmaintained Yellow River, regional rebellion, corruption among his officials, and British dissatisfaction with trade rules. But he also faced new crises, particularly deterioration of the Grand Canal, instability in silver prices, and the spread of opium addiction. In each case, he instituted a period of investigation by his officials to supply him with full information on the problem, followed by an invitation to officials to debate proper policy courses (*qingyi*, see chapter 1). The information gathered was good, the debates were searching, often systematic, and produced results that still interest modern scholars.

Before the outbreak of the Opium War between the Qing and Britain in 1839, the Daoguang court was faced with three great policy questions. The Grand Canal – which in addition to its normal function of bringing grain and other tribute from the south to the north to feed the huge population around Beijing had recently been critical in supplying the grain given to the homeless and starving – had ceased to function. In order to bring grain from the Yangtze delta all the way to Beijing, the canal had to actually traverse the Yellow River. A dam that controlled the water supply which sustained this delicate juncture collapsed in 1824, and the court had to decide whether to repair it or change to shipping the grain by sea. Advances in shipbuilding technologies since the canal had been rebuilt in the Ming period meant it was no longer dangerous to send grain directly from the Yangtze delta to Tianjin (effectively the port of Beijing), and the emperor insisted that the change be made. It was a controversial decision, however. Merchants who outfitted the ships and ran the new lanes were rewarded by the court, but they were very small in number compared to the merchants already invested in the Grand Canal – not only the goods that traveled it, but the shops, hotels, depots and brothels that lined it for hundreds of miles, not to mention the huge population of laborers who depended upon the canal for a living. The emperor was pressured to agree to restore the canal at the earliest possible time, and by 1826 the court was attempting to repair the complex waterworks and machinery of facility that was, outside the calculations of those who already were invested in it, obsolete. For the ensuing decades the court continued to switch policy between abandoning the canal and attempting to restore it, the debate perpetually swinging between the practicality of sea transport and the profitability of the canal's ancillary industries.

The other two great problems were intertwined. One was the destabilizing effects of the changing real value of silver. China's trade imbalance turned negative in 1826, and from 1828 to 1836 China lost 38,000,000 ounces of silver. Commercialization of the economy from Ming times forward, the mining of large amounts of silver in Yunnan and Xinjiang, and the influx of silver payments from Europe (and Britain in particular) for tea in the late eighteenth century had wrenched the rural economy. Ming and Qing China had used a bimetallic currency system, with a fixed ratio of 1:100 between copper (or brass, depending on the coinage) and silver. Tax payments (and by extension most land transactions and rent) were calculated in silver and copper was used by most people for the daily purchases. As the real value of silver dropped in the eighteenth century, the cost of things purchased with copper radically inflated. Farmers attempting to convert copper to their silver tax obligations paid about twice as much in the early 1800s as they had twenty years before; peasants needing to convert grain to silver were squeezed even more. At the turn of the nineteenth century, the flow of silver into China reversed as a result of the increase of opium smuggling. In the Jiaqing period, shrinkage of supplies of silver, as well as many regional variations in market value and in supply, demanded for the first time a requirement that the state mint silver coins in order to make the value of a basic unit of silver exact (previously silver had been exchanged in lumps cut by silver vendors or by magistrates, resulting in inexact valuation). The model chosen for the coin was the so-called "Mexican dollar" (the Carolus) which was also an international standard accepted in most commercially-connected parts of the world.

In the Daoguang period, scholars and bureaucrats realized that the silver problems had continued to worsen. In 1825 the censors informed Emperor Daoguang that in the past five years China's favorable trade balance had become a major deficit as silver went to the British for opium from India. The opium trade, regional variations in circulation and valuation of silver, copper and brass coins, and corruption clearly all had an effect, but the court sought consultation primarily on possible remedies. By 1838 the exchange rate had increased from 1:1,000 to 1:1,650 copper cash. The copper mines of Yunnan were being depleted, and the government debased the copper coins such that during Daoguang's reign the rate would reach 2,700. The value of goods traded at market was falling, but tax obligations remained high, plunging many farmers who had been struggling for years below the survival threshold. In the early 1820s, these factors combined with environmental and climate mishaps to create a huge increase in the "floating population," who left their lands in various parts of north China to flee to Beijing and to Manchuria. Difficult harvests in the eastern Yangtze provinces in the 1830s contributed to the outbreak of grain riots, but a deeper cause was the maldistribution of the population. Officials also blamed the rich, who hoarded grain. The Daoguang court laid out massive expenditures from tax revenues and from the imperial treasury to deploy peacekeeping forces and to feed and shelter refugees. The government could not get control of the value of either the silver or the copper currencies, because it had not taken out of circulation the private and locally minted coins, foreign imports, and even coins produced in the Ming period. Advice of many sorts poured in, including a radical plan to introduce government-issued paper money as the only legal tender. In the end, the court rejected solutions that would have required massive (and expensive) government intervention, tending to look at traditional concepts of quantity and value. As an immediate aid to farmers, the court attempted to release grain from the imperial stores (including those reserved for the Eight Banners) but the side effects were to lower the price of grain further for farmers still trying to sell, and to open opportunities for merchants and corrupt officials to buy and hoard the grain for sale at a more profitable time. The most direct aid the government could provide, apart from distributions of grain directly to the starving, was lessening its tax demands. In 1835 the Daoguang court forgave all outstanding taxes back to 1830. At the same time, it lightened the taxes on trade going into and out of Xinjiang. Lives were saved and in some areas tempers were cooled, but the government was gradually sacrificing its ability to maintain infrastructure, to deploy forces to control or block immigration to areas that could not tolerate an increase, and even to control the smuggling it saw as the root of its monetary problems.

Tied to the currency issues was the new social problem of opium trade and addiction. The Qing court had always opposed the use of opium for anything other than medical uses. In the early Qing centuries the problems of opium and tobacco had been related, as the court opposed both the smoking of tobacco (by commoners) and the weak mixture of opium and tobacco known as *madak*, which the government outlawed in 1729. But in the late eighteenth century a fairly sudden abundance of opium made smoking the narcotic by itself popular in many circles. In 1799 the court had reiterated its ban on opium use and also on importation. By that time, the British East India Company was already heavily involved in smuggling opium into China. The amount is believed to have increased from about 27,000 lb per year at the time of the prohibition of 1729 to 540,000 lb in 1790, 675,000 lb in 1820, and 2,200,000 lb in 1830. The trade not only vastly enriched many members of the East India company but also stimulated the growth of Chinese smuggling syndicates throughout south China – most grafted onto the organizational framework of the Tiandihui cells.

In the debates regarding the cause of silver instability, the view that won the day was that the opium trade was primarily responsible for the decline in the supply of silver. For years the emperor and his advisors had been aware of the fact that opium smuggling was undermining local trade on the southern coast, debilitating addicts (who were mostly wealthy); and draining silver. The emperor was determined to understand the issue more exactly, and in 1831 ordered that officials from all over the country inform the court of the methods of distribution and sale in their localities. From Guangdong, Fujian, Sichuan, Zhejiang, Hubei, Hunan, Yunnan, Guizhou and other provinces came convincing reports of vigorous underground traffic and huge fortunes amassed by vendors. Local magistrates were reported to be blackmailing known users within their jurisdictions, and padding their tax collections with payments from sellers and growers hoping to avoid exposure to higher authorities. The wealthy were spending their silver fortunes (most of which found their way outside the country) on the drug. Soldiers were found to be unfit for duty because of the debilities caused by their addiction. Manchu noblemen and court eunuchs bought, sold and used the drug together. The numbers of users and addicts were unknown, but an estimate later in the decade put the number at 1 percent of the population. Considering that at this time opium use was not common among farmers, the indication was that the official population was very heavily involved. A foreign estimate of 1836 put the number at 12,500,000. The emperor's own officials advised that the magistrate or governor who did not smoke opium was an exception.

A debate at the capital ensued over the possible suspension of prosecution against smokers or purchasers in order to concentrate effort upon the seizure of primary distributors and their suppliers; in addition, it was suggested, the government could assuage some of its own troubles by legalizing and taxing opium. As in others of the policy debates invited by the Daoguang court, opinion seemed to divide between one side advocating quick but expensive government intervention, while the other proposed minimal government involvement and expenditure. Though the Daoguang emperor often appeared personally inclined toward aggressive action on fiscal, infrastructural or social issues, he was frequently convinced in the end that that the financial circumstances of the state required that the government intervene only minimally and buy time to find better options. With opium, however, the emperor followed his own instincts for rapid, comprehensive action. At the height of the opium debate, in 1838, he turned to Lin Zexu, the governor-general of Hunan and Hubei provinces. Lin not only agreed in the debates with those who advocated strict prosecution of all those involved in the trade and stern rehabilitation of addicts, he was already enacting such policies in the provinces under his supervision. He pointed out that in addition to the primary evils of the drug, its attendant evils more widespread and more violent crime, while the concentration of wealth in the hands of unscrupulous and disrespectful merchants threatened the moral foundations of society. His advice to the court was that no matter how high the cost, failure to eradicate opium and the opium trade would lead to comprehensive disaster for the empire within a short time. Many officials, both Manchu and Chinese, attempted to dissuade the emperor from a radical approach. He concluded, however, that most of them were either addicts or had been corrupted by the opium smugglers. He explicitly rejected the option of legalizing and taxing the drug, stating that although it might bring in needed revenue, it would be a betrayal of the people. He entrusted Lin Zexu with full powers to do whatever necessary to end the opium trade and destroy all the opium already in the country. Lin gave up his lofty post of governor-general, and set out for Canton to do the emperor's will. After decades of disorder and indecision, Lin thought the emperor had decided to put the vessels of government upright again, by smashing the independent local power of the opium merchants and imposing imperial control.

Further reading

In modern Chinese culture, hopping corpses (*jiangshi*) have somehow taken on vampire characteristics, which is the basic idea in a series of hopping corpse films of the 1980s; the transformation seems to owe something to *Legend of the Seven Golden Vampires* (Hammer films, 1974 – in which Peter Cushing played vampire hunter Lawrence van Helsing). The traditional legends had no vampire theme and so seem only loosely connected to the current fashion. The theme, in its traditional form, has come back recently in Liao Yiwu, *The Corpse Walker* (2008).

On economic and technological trends since 1600, see Elvin, *The Pattern of the Chinese Past* (1973); von Glahn, *Fountain of Fortune* (1996); Wong, *China Transformed* (1998); Frank, *ReOrient* (1998); Pomeranz, *The Great Divergence*, (2000); Allen, "Real Wages in Europe and Asia" (2005); Perdue, *China Marches West* (2005); Lin, *China Upside Down* (2006). On government policy debates, see Kuo, *A Critical Study of the First Anglo-Chinese War with Documents* (1935); Polachek, *The Inner Opium War* (1992); and Lin, above. On China's population history, see Ho, *Studies on the Population of China, 1368–1953* (1959) and Lee and Feng, *One Quarter of Humanity* (1999).

For issues of migration, environment and environmental crises, see Wong, "Food Riots in the Qing Dynasty" (1982); Leonard, *Controlling from Afar* (1996); Leong, *Migration and Ethnicity in Chinese History* (1997); Elvin and Liu, *Sediments of Time* (1998); Marks, *Tigers, Rice, Silk and Silt* (1998); Szonyi, *Practicing Kinship* (2002); Miles, *Celebrating the Yan Fu Shrine* (2004); Belsky, *Localities at the Center* (2005); Elvin, *The Retreat of the Elephants* (2006); Li, *Fighting Famine in North China* (2007). On the White Lotus, Eight Trigram and other uprisings, see Perry, "Worshipers and Warriors" (1976); Naquin, *Millenarian Rebellion in China* (1976); Antony and Leonard, eds., *Dragons, Tigers and Dogs* (2002); Dai, "Yingyong Shengxi" (2005).

On bureaucratic corruption and crisis-handling, see Zelin, *The Magistrate's Tael* (1984); Leonard, *Controlling from Afar* (1996); Ni and Pham, "High Corruption Income in Ming and Qing China" (2006). Comments here on inflation of population figures are based on Skinner, "Sichuan's Population in the Nineteenth Century" (1987).

On troubles in early-nineteenth-century Xinjiang, see Fletcher, "The Heyday of the Ch'ing Order in Mongolia, Sinkiang and Tibet" (1978); Millward, *Beyond the Pass* (1998); Elleman, *Modern Chinese Warfare* (2001). On cultural differences and identities in early modern and modern China, see Dreyer, *China's Forty Millions* (1976); Lipman, *Familiar Strangers* (1997); Crossley, Siu and Sutton, *Empire at the Margins* (2006).

Most narratives, including this one, of the rise of importation into China rely upon the details from *The China Yearbook* for 1916. On crime, rebellion and corruption in the early nineteenth century, see Spence, "Opium Smoking in Ch'ing China" (1975); Lipman and Harrell, *Violence in China* (1990); Ownby and Heidhues, *Secret Societies Reconsidered* (1993); Murray, *The Origins of the Tiandihui* (1994); Antony, *Like Froth Floating on the Sea* (2003); Dikötter, Laamann and Zhou, *Narcotic Culture* (2004); Ni and Pham, above; Zheng, *The Social Life of Opium in China* (2005); Rowe, *Crimson Rain* (2007).

4

Essay
Strategic Borders

Historians writing in English often refer to "China proper," which roughly corresponds to what historians writing in Chinese used to call *guannei*, the "land within the passes" – usually taken as a reference to the Shanhai Pass at the eastern end of the Great Wall and the Jiayu Pass at its western. China proper could not include the three northeastern provinces ("Manchuria," but usually called by contemporary writers "the Northeast"), nor Inner Mongolia, nor Xinjiang, nor Tibet, nor Yunnan, nor Taiwan. It does, however, encompass territories that for the past two thousand years have consistently been claimed – and often governed in fact – by states based in China, using Chinese as a written medium, and using laws derived by some means or other from Chinese tradition or consensus to rule. China proper is the region historians see as more or less uniformly (at least for the past 1,500 years) dominated by a Chinese-speaking, farming population. It is the space of reference for Chinese culture and history.

Despite that, the contours of unified states based in China have changed dramatically, sometimes from century to century. The Tang ruled all of China proper, as well as much of Manchuria, and Central Asia as far as modern Afghanistan. The Song, however, ruled only China proper and for the last decades of their history only about two-thirds of that. Yuan added the Northeast, Siberia, Mongolia, and Yunnan. Ming retained Yunnan and part of the Northeast but lost Siberia and Mongolia. The Qing added the rest of the Northeast to the Pacific Coast, all of Mongolia, eastern Turkestan (later Xinjiang), and Taiwan. The PRC retains the Northeast as far as the Amur River, Inner Mongolia, and Xinjiang, but not Mongolia or Taiwan.

Beyond China proper, the acquisition and occupation of border territories appear to be driven almost exclusively by strategic concerns. The Northeast, for instance, was twentieth-century China's industrial cradle and an essential source of grain, coal and iron. Both Russia and Japan strenuously attempted to take it from the Qing (Russia succeeded in acquiring the Pacific Coast), and during the Republican era China's fragmentation allowed Japan to make the Northeast its highway into north China. After the founding of the PRC, the government watched Northeastern governors closely for signs of lack of loyalty, or in inclination to declare independence. Though the Northeast is now firmly under the control of the central government, it

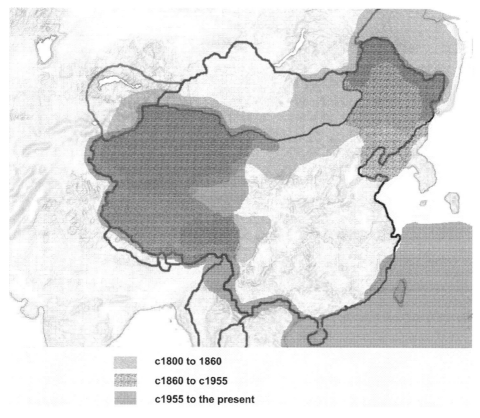

c1800 to 1860
c1860 to c1955
c1955 to the present

Map 3   Changing strategic borders. Persisting regions of strategic concern, by period

is still a security concern. Its industries are often venues of large-scale conflict between workers and state management. And its increasing population in contrast to the thin population of the Russian Far East is believed to inspire fear in Russian strategic planners that may lead to an increase of Russian military patrols along the Northeastern borders.

Though China "within the passes" does not strictly include the present area of Inner Mongolia, for instance, the region around modern-day "Hohhot" has been economically connected to China since Han times. Its relatively dense population, developed commerce and proximity to north China makes it a dangerous territory for a state based in China to not control (as the Ming empire learned after repeated military catastrophes). As a result, most states based in China have extended their strategic boundaries beyond the Great Wall, to include modern-day Inner Mongolia. The territory of present day Mongolia, in contrast, has always been economically complementary to China, sparsely populated and difficult to travel apart from a few central roads. Controlling it from China is a challenge that only the Yuan and Qing accomplished, and in the Qing case it took half a century and a huge investment to achieve; even before the Qing empire was dissolved, Mongolian leaders declared independence, and Mongolia is an independent republic today. During the Republican era in China, Inner Mongolia warlords were often critical players in defense against Japan

and against communist infiltration (see chapter 13). Several Inner Mongolia communists were prominent in the revolution and in the early PRC. But since the Cultural
Revolution, evidence of nationalist movements in Inner Mongolia are frequent (at
present there is even a small neo-Nazi nationalist movement). Despite its intense historical ties with China, Inner Mongolia also enjoys a renewed sense of identification
with post-communist, developing Mongolia.

Before modern transport, western Mongolia, eastern Turkestan, Gansu, Tibet,
Yunnan and southwest China constituted a spectrum of cultural exchange and population movement, creating havens for bandits or rebels, and a danger of perpetual
destabilization from rival empires. In the Ming period, Central Asia and Mongolia
were both fragmented, and the western frontiers were not considered a pressing concern. In the early Qing, however, the Russian empire was pushing into Central Asia
and across Siberia, and the Qing emperors determined to conquer and control
Mongolia, eastern Turkestan and Tibet in order to harden their western frontiers,
quash rebellions and defend against encroachment.

The Qing began the relatively dense military occupation of Xinjiang that allowed
them to successfully repel Russian advances in the nineteenth century and extend
absolute authority to Xinjiang by making it a province in 1884. A heavy military presence in Xinjiang continues today, often reinforced by the peculiar institution of the
bingtuan (The Xinjiang Production and Construction Corps). It was originally created in the early PRC to employ military veterans in the economic development of
Xinjiang. In agriculture and in industry, the *bingtuan* has brought Xinjiang revenue
through the "export" of Xinjiang products to the rest of China. But it has also intensified differences between Han (many of whom have immigrated due to *bingtuan*
policies) and the Uighurs, very few of whom are employed by the *bingtuan* or enjoy
its relatively high wages. Since the independence of the Central Asian republics –
particularly Uzbekistan and Kazakhstan – the PRC has been particularly wary of
cooperation across the border by the Uighurs, whether the cause is smuggling or the
importation of nationalist or Islamic radical ideology. The *bingtuan*'s administration
was moved in 1990 from the Ministry of Agriculture to the State Council, partly
because of general sensitivity to the increasing importance of Xinjiang both as an asset
(a transit area for oil imports from Central Asia, a developing area of agriculture and
mining) and as a liability (a defensive front against aggression from Russia or
Kazakhstan, a defense against foreign observation of military research centers in
nearby Qinghai, a possible soft spot for organizing by Muslim insurgents).

Tibet and the rest of the Himalayan highlands have historically shielded west and
southwest China from India, Burma, or – in the nineteenth century – the British
empire. The Qing became convinced of the need to militarily occupy Lhasa when they
feared that Tibetan rulers could combine with Mongols, Uighurs or other local resisting populations to undermine Qing authority. In much earlier centuries, Tibet had
been a collection of independent countries, and in the days of the Tang empire had
been a powerful rival empire. Internal changes, however, and the Mongol conquest
had begun a pattern of connections with – and, in the Qing case, subordination to –
states based in China. Like other western territories except for Xinjiang, the Qing
permitted local administrators a great deal of discretion. The Dalai Lama had his own
government and collected his own taxes but he was not free to transfer his loyalty to
an outside power. The Republican government tried for a time to impose similar

restrictions on Tibet, but was distracted by other issues and could not enforce them. The PRC occupied Tibet in 1950 and signed an agreement with the Dalai Lama securing Tibet's affiliation with the PRC. The decade was disturbed by local uprisings against Chinese rule, many of them fomented or aided by the American Central Intelligence Agency. In 1959 a massive uprising resulted in direct military occupation by the PRC and the exile of the Dalai Lama to India. Though Tibetan sovereignty as a legal and ethical issue remains a matter of global debate, the PRC's strategic interests in Tibet are indissoluble. Tibet is the source of most Chinese water, and it is the PRC bulwark against encroachment by India.

Though Yunnan is not generally acknowledged by the foreign press as a border territory in the same sense as Xinjiang or Tibet, it has a distinct history. It was an independent country for centuries before the Mongols made it part of the Yuan empire, and Ming control over the area was loose. Yunnan has a deeply diverse population, including not only descendants of the ancient settlers –Yi, Zhuang, Miao, Dai and others – but also descendants of medieval Mongol occupiers, of Muslim merchants and soldiers, of Vietnamese and Chinese settlers. The Qing governed the region with great difficulty, rarely disrupting its lively smuggling economy. In the Republican era the province was nominally connected to the Chiang Kaishek government, but was in fact divided up among independent warlords. The PRC has concentrated on developing Yunnan's historical pre-eminence in mining, particularly copper (see chapter 15). The province is one of China's poorest, and the PRC has clearly not been successful in establishing firm control over the region's traditional involvement in the smuggling of drugs and people, with the consequence that today Yunnan is one of the regions of China most seriously affected by HIV/AIDS (see chapter 16), and one of the most difficult in which to administer medical care.

As the above discussion suggests, historical China's strategic concerns were almost exclusively on its inland borders, and virtually never included its long coastline. Until the Opium War in 1839, China never experienced a foreign assault from the sea. Only in the later nineteenth century did China's rulers begin to weave the coasts and the surrounding seas into its military planning. The PRC has made a spectacular departure from the historical pattern by pursuing a very ambitious plan of both coat and long-distance naval development. This has brought Taiwan front and center as a strategic concern. During periods of intense talk of formal independence in Taiwan, the PRC bristles both rhetorically and militarily. As the USA gradually decreases its naval presence in the South China Sea, the PRC increases its presence and its surveillance. A hostile Taiwan – especially if backed by the USA or Japan – would be a serious strategic vulnerability to the PRC, which would have to be either absorbed or eradicated. In times of peace PRC leaders may rely upon nationalist rhetoric to keep up popular interest in the Taiwan issue, but in the final analysis strategic concerns will govern the PRC approach to Taiwan, as with all other PRC borderlands.

Further reading

Wiemer, "The Economy of Xinjiang" (2004); Perdue, *China Marches West* (2005); Crossley, Siu and Sutton, *Empire at the Margins* (2006); Giersch, *Asian Borderlands* (2006); Andrade, *How Taiwan Became Chinese* (2007).

5

Qing and the World

THOMAS STAUNTON, THE child translator who had tried his best to help his father George Staunton and the British emissary George Macartney break the ice with Qing officials in 1792, spent most of the years following that debacle in the Portuguese colony of Macao and in the Qing trade port at Canton. He was in his late teens when he became a clerk with the British East India Company (BEIC). Before he was 30 Staunton had began to undertake translation of modern medical texts from English into Chinese. In 1816, he was recruited as translator, guide and assistant to William Pitt Amherst's mission to China. Staunton returned to England shortly afterward, his first return to the country since he was a young boy. He became a member of Parliament from southeast England and a member of the Select Committee on the BEIC (responsible for investigation and reporting on BEIC's finances and practices). In 1823 he founded the Royal Asiatic Society with Henry Thomas Colebrooke. Staunton's scholarly accomplishments were substantial and were strongly marked by the experiences of his youth. He translated portions of the Qing legal code that had so astonished and terrified British officials of the Qianlong period, and his translation is still used by students today. For these reasons as well as, it appears, religious reasons, he was outspoken in Parliament and in the press against opium smuggling to China. But he was also sternly uncompromising in his position that the Qing empire must deal with Britain on British terms, and allow British representatives to negotiate a new trade system. Staunton's opinions as an eloquent and informed advisor on China shaped both British policy and public opinion until his death in 1859.

Once again, Britain was attempting direct communication, on its own terms, with the Qing empire for purposes of opening China to competitive trade. The British government was well aware that opium smuggling into China by merchants belonging to the BEIC had reversed the flow of silver, giving Britain (or at least merchants based in Britain) an edge. But the BEIC was becoming a bigger problem than ever in British politics and society. It practically had its own country in India, and its monopolies on various products from East Asia, Indonesia, Malaya and India gave it wealth and power that threatened the independence of policy making by the British government.

The mercantilist combination between the crown and the company had been blamed in many quarters for loss of American colonies. The monopolies of the BEIC, on tea and other products, were distorting prices and wages at home. The courts were peppered with lawsuits against the BEIC, claiming wages, compensation for injuries and compensation to families for deaths. And when Parliament discussed ending the BEIC's monopoly, bribes flowed to politicians to sap the government's will. Breaking the BEIC's monopoly over the China trade would not only create competition that would restore health to British prices and clean up Parliament, but it would give the government rein to tax the profits of private merchants at a commensurate rate. In 1816 William Amherst was appointed an "ambassador extraordinary" from Britain to the Qing empire. His plan, like Macartney's, was to arrive in Beijing and begin conversation with officials representing the court. He picked up Staunton in Hongkong, and during the trip northward along the coast was lectured by the young China expert on the necessity of making no compromises with Qing protocol, most of all, the kowtow. When the entourage made land south of Tianjin, Amherst was sternly informed that the way to join the Qing trade network was to perform the kowtow, after which all things were possible. Unlike Macartney, Amherst did not linger. With the leisure his disappointment afforded he sailed to Korea and then turned south and west to return home, dropping Staunton in Hongkong and then running his ship aground in Indonesia.

Issues remaining unresolved from the Macartney and Amherst episodes converged with others to eventually bring calamity upon the Qing. The Opium War (1839–42) between the British empire and the Qing empire and its conclusion in the Treaties of Nanking and of the Bogue were, together, a milestone in global history and remain a landmark of studies of modern Chinese history. Interpretations have veered between extremes. Earlier views emphasized that the Qing empire had not on its own developed institutions for dealing either with international diplomacy or international trade, and were unwilling to do so when presented with the pleas of Britain, making a military confrontation between Britain and Qing inevitable. The origins of this view seem to lay with nineteenth-century European opinion-makers, including de Tocqueville and Marx, who thought that China, like other ancient Asian empires, was not capable of changing its institutions or culture unless forced to do so by outside powers. At the other pole are views that have taken hold since the 1970s. Based on research on the history of opium traffic in the eighteenth, nineteenth and twentieth centuries, recent historians see the financial and political weight of the opium trade as overwhelming the ability of any government to make decisions in the rational interest of its own people. The war, from this point of view, was an inevitability so long as Qing laws and Qing officials remained impediments to a growing and still hungry international opium network. Imperialist domination and opium purveying were two sides of the same coin. Yet a third line of argument is that the British empire, as the sole superpower of the middle and late nineteenth century, was destined to bring its overwhelming military force to China, and to use that force to construct an imperialistic relationship that would subject China to British economic will for a century. None of these views is lacking in evidence or in logic. There are, however, nuances in the origins of the war and in the Treaty of Nanking that deserve to be considered.

From the British side, the events directly leading to the war begin with abolition of the BEIC's monopoly on the China trade in 1834 and the failure to install a British trade superintendency at Canton. The Palmerston government sent the Scottish nobleman William Napier to Canton as its new commissioner of trade after the British government removed the BEIC's monopoly. The Qing system required foreign merchants to go through compradors, or intermediaries, in all communications with officials. Compradors were to arrange housing, servants, supplies, credit and translation for the merchants. Foreign merchants who for any reason needed information from or to make a request of a Qing official were instead to invoke a comprador as an intermediary, and instructions from the Qing officials were conveyed to foreign merchants by the compradors. Napier's idea was that as a new sort of official he should establish new sorts of communications, despite the fact that his instructions from the British government were to conform to Chinese procedures (short of the kowtow). He attempted to send a letter directly to the Guangdong provincial governor introducing himself and his functions. The officials not only refused Napier's letter, but pointed out that since he had not had permission to come ashore at Canton or otherwise undergone the entry processes for foreign merchants he was in violation of the law. The governor stopped trade going in and out of Canton until Napier would take himself out of the city. Napier went to Macao where he died, within weeks, and was buried. Back in Britain, government and public opinion held him responsible for going ashore in the middle of the night and attempting to intrude himself into venues where he had no diplomatic standing. The Chinese government, members of Parliament argued, had been reasonable in refusing Napier's awkward demands and overbearing approach.

The situation at Canton was very complex. As a trade port it had more Qing officials than was usual, but they were at some distance from – and often in tension with – the majority of the population. British, American, Dutch, French and other foreign merchants were required to stay in their walled residences and be totally segregated from the general populations. The merchants were forbidden by law to bring their families to China, but with the connivance of the compradors they often maintained Chinese mistresses and children in the city as an open secret. The foreign population slowly began to include missionaries (despite the Jiaqing emperor's determination to eradicate the religion) and proselytizing doctors, most famous among them, Peter Parker, who established a hospital at Canton in 1835 that treated foreign and Chinese patients. By the middle 1830s both Chinese-speaking foreign missionaries and native Chinese converts were active in spreading their message to the residents of Canton.

The compradors were close in outlook to the foreign merchants. Qing officials had been inculcated with the traditional philosophy that merchants were parasites on society, and the officials were high-handed with all Canton's businessmen, whether Chinese or foreign. Indeed they were harder on the Chinese merchants, since the compradors were required to take responsibility for any crimes, insults or debts attributed to their foreign charges. As the empire began to gasp for cash in the very late eighteenth century, it learned to look to the Chinese merchants of Canton as a fresh resource. They were ordered to contribute 600,000 ounces of silver to the campaigns against the White Lotus and Tiandihui rebels, and the same amount twenty years later to fight Jehangir in Xinjiang. It seems that they gave a total of nearly 2,000,000 ounces of silver for river maintenance during the Jiaqing period.

They could afford it. As wealthy as the BEIC merchants became, so did the compradors. They were permitted to double the tax assessments on their foreign partners, collect it, and keep half for themselves. A number of them also engaged with foreign merchants to cheat the Qing government of revenue through smuggling. Compradors were required to maintain warehouses, docks, banks and language tutoring programs as necessary to their legal functions. It was only another step for them to become partners in the concealment of illegal products from Qing military officials or hoards of cash from tax inspectors, whether Qing or European. The business also required connections to vast criminal organizations within China, and the compradors were the natural link. Throughout south China, river networks were travelled and controlled by gangs of smugglers (*yaokou*), including farmers and artisans who abandoned their previous livings for quick profits in opium.

The compradors were organized into firms (*hang*, which because of its Cantonese pronunciation became the English word "hong"). Many were run by extended families; the British and other merchants at Canton called the firms by the name of the comprador who headed it. The Fujianese family Wu were called "Howqua." They were the premier compradors, not only providing the usual comprehensive services to private merchants but also having an imperial patent to exclusively provide silk and porcelain from the imperial factories. In 1834, when Napier tried to break up the cozy relationship of compradors and foreign traders in the city, the current head of the family firm, Wu Bingjian, was estimated by accountants of the BEIC to be worth more than 6,000,000 pounds sterling. This was approximately equal to the combined wealth of the six most senior members of the Rothschild family put together, and in modern terms would be about 300,000,000 pounds, or nearly 600,000,000 dollars (USD). Wu is believed to have been the richest individual merchant in the world. He was entirely self-made, starting from straitened circumstances, and had a personal history of being insulted and disadvantaged by Qing trade officials overseeing the comprador firms in Canton. His association was highly coveted by British and American merchants, but he seemed to favor the Americans. A story told among both the Chinese and the American merchants of Canton stated that Wu had learned of an American merchant from Boston who had incurred over 70,000 dollars of debt that he could not repay, and as a consequence he dared not return to Boston. Wu heard of the situation, and had his servants deliver enough money to the merchant to make up the debt; when the American tried to indicate his intention to repay by presenting Wu with a receipt, Wu tore the up the paper and declared the slate clean. Several American trading families, mostly based in Massachusetts, had portraits of Wu in their parlors. The A.A. Low Brothers shipping firm named one of their clippers *Houqua* in his honor. In 1826 Wu retired from the firm, but his eldest son, the third Howqua, was soon convicted by the authorities of improprieties and Wu deprived his son of access to his fortune. Instead, he eventually entrusted it to the American firm of Russell & Company, which in time diverted it to industrial facilities in New England and into American foundations, including Yale University.

By the time of Napier's arrival in Canton in 1834, Americans had begun to eat into the British opium profits. For decades the BEIC had enjoyed a monopoly on opium as it did on tea. Opium grown in India was loaded at Calcutta into ships whose registry was disguised in order to drop the drug along the China coast. Americans began to send their own tea ships to China in 1784, and soon afterward gained access to their own opium supplies, from Turkey. Incidents in 1805, 1806 and 1818 made clear to the BEIC (and to the Qing authorities) that the Americans were using all the same

1. Wu Bingjian, *c.* 1830, painted in his office overlooking the Canton docks. (Unidentified Chinese artist after George Chinnery. M23228. Photograph courtesy of the Peabody Essex Museum.)

techniques as the company itself – piracy, extortion, double-crossing, and theft – to pry open a slot for themselves in the business. The market share commanded by the Americans was minor but not negligible, since in 1823 they are known to have brought well over a tenth the amount of opium to China that Britain brought. The importations of Turkish opium were sufficient to set off a price war, taking something off the marginal unit profit for British and American traders but vastly increasing the volume of sales, as poorer and poorer people in China discovered they could now buy the drug.

John Francis Davis succeeded Napier as trade superintendent, but Qing officials still refused to acknowledge his official standing. British merchants who had expected the trade superintendent to be able to provide them administrative and legal assistance after the BEIC could no longer do so considered themselves victims of the Qing position, and began to demand that the British government become aggressive in forcing China to pay compensation to traders whose business was impeded. The response of the government of J.H. Temple (Lord Palmerston) was to promote a British naval officer already in Canton, Captain Charles Elliot, to superintendent.

The British government was well aware that attempting to closely administer a China trade policy from London was hopeless. Correspondence between London and Canton took between two and three months each way, and any British representative in Canton would have to make his own decisions, based only on a general outline of principles from the British government. Those principles were protection of British subjects and their property, refusal to engage in behaviors (or written forms) that would appear to humble Britain, and to ensure that trade be as free as possible. For its part, the Qing court had dispatched Lin Zexu to confront not merely foreign importers of opium, but the entire Canton merchant community. Lin and Elliot were both too far from their sovereigns to receive detailed instructions. They would face their governments only after they had made decisions that, in the summer and early autumn of 1839, would change everything.

At the time, opium was the most profitable product on earth, and global networks of production and distribution ranged out of the control of any individual government. Despite long tirades in Parliament against the moral evils of the opium trade, most in Britain were aware that the ruinous trade imbalance with China (see chapter 3) had reversed solely due to opium sales from British India to China. In China and throughout many other parts of the world, many involved in the trade were outright criminals, others were ostensibly respectable individuals such as the members of the BEIC, leaders of British and American banking and industry, or the Chinese landowners and officials who aided the trade in various ways. When the Daoguang emperor commissioned Lin Zexu to eradicate the opium trade, the former was well aware – and said many times – that the nature of man was to be greedy and ruthless, and that only a forceful application of law could cure the opium illness. The emperor also knew that before he sent Lin to Canton the empire's laws against opium – which had never been softened in almost a century and a half – had never been successfully enforced. Both corruption and the overwhelming size of the empire had made the task impossible. On his side, Charles Elliot was also morally opposed to opium, as many in Britain were. After Napier's failure in 1834 the British government was well aware that the Qing government's policy was to ban the opium trade totally, and members of Parliament were frank that all standards of international law – the standards some were claiming the Qing were fatally ignoring – were on the side of the Qing. In numerous debates in Parliament, and many more in the British press, the opinion was almost universally held that international law supported any state wishing to criminalize immoral activity, and that any state that knowingly subverted the laws of another state was in the wrong.

The debates at the Qing court over how to handle the opium problem were tempered not only by moral certainty but also by an assessment of Britain's position that was very nearly correct. Though Britain was the world's only superpower after its defeat of Napoleonic France, it was a busy superpower with recent, ongoing or impending military actions in western Europe, eastern Europe, the Mediterranean and the Middle East. The abolitionists in Beijing thought it very unlikely that Britain

would try to conduct a war ten thousand miles from its shores in order to wrest powers that nothing in international law or morality said it should have. And as of 1836
or 1837 that was indeed more or less the opinion of the Palmerston government too.
The clamoring of British traders for military intervention to get what they wanted in
Canton still sounded like the BEIC lobbying to the British government, and the private interests of the merchants were dismissed by Palmerston as beneath the high
mission of the British empire. On the other hand, Palmerston himself had no ability
to stop the opium traders from engaging in the activities that were causing friction
between Britain and Qing. Before Lin was sent to Canton, the British superintendent
in Canton received a letter saying that the Qing government had resolved to smash
the opium trade and that the merchants were advised to put themselves in order.
Once Lin arrived in 1838, he hired inspectors and enforcers who quickly rounded up
a large number of addicts and opium pipes, executed 400–500 accused smugglers and
burned their boats, and intercepted about 35,000 pounds of opium; Elliot reported
to London that Lin's actions had destroyed much of the infrastructure of the Canton
trade, not least by raising the price of opium six times its previous price and destroying
the market. Lin decided to use the Canton merchant community against itself; he put
Wu Bingjian's second son – the current Howqua Wu Chongyue – and a colleague
under arrest. If they could not persuade the foreign merchants to surrender the man
Lin thought the most malign of the opium traders, Lancelot Dent, they were to be
executed. To make matters much worse, Qing officials claimed that British sailors had
beaten a Chinese fisherman to death on the coast east of Canton. As Elliot assumed
his powers as superintendent, he was faced both with the demand from Qing officials
that he hand over the British sailors who were responsible, and with a demand from
Lin that he surrender all opium in Canton and that the traders sign bonds promising
to never again transport opium to China.

A small number of British captains agreed to sign the bonds, only to find that they
were quickly shelled by other British vessels owned by both private traders and by the
BEIC. When Elliot hesitated to surrender either the opium or Dent, Lin blockaded
the port at Canton (the same tactic used earlier to force Napier to withdraw). The
roughly two hundred foreign merchants and their households in the city were walled
up in their compound. Lin wrote a much-quoted letter to Queen Victoria on the
immorality of the opium trade, imploring her to stop the internationally-recognized
crimes. The letter showed Lin's usual habit of research and precision; he had con-
sulted a friend of his who was an expert on European geography, and had also been
briefed on standard European reference works on international law. Elliot offered
Lin about 200,000 pounds of opium, but Lin rejected the offer because his inspectors knew the total was about ten times as high. The foreign merchants met together
with Howqua and one of his colleagues several times, attempting to work out a
scheme to save Dent and themselves. After about six weeks Elliot convinced the
traders to surrender their 2.6 million pounds of opium to him, for compensation.
Elliot then turned the opium, which was now the property of the British government, over to Lin. The blockade of the factories and of the port was lifted, but
Lin banished the foreign merchants, who had no choice but to repair to Macao. Lin
prayed to Heaven for protection of the fish in the harbor, had his workmen pour the
opium into long trenches, burn it, and sluice the ashes into the sea, an operation that
took three weeks.

Elliot's report of the destruction of crown property and banishment of British traders to a Portuguese colony reached the government months later, and still Palmerston was reluctant to declare war. But some members of Parliament argued that since the Qing had not enforced their anti-opium laws before Lin, they had no right to expect that anybody else would respect those laws now. The opium trade, they argued, was actually unstoppable, whether by Qing or by Britain. It was a lost cause, and the government must now take steps to guarantee its diplomatic and legal rights without respect to the opium trade. Though the British sailors who may have been responsible for the death of the Chinese fisherman were safely in Britain, at any time Qing authorities might make another demand that the suspects be handed over. And now the honor of the British government was at stake, since property belonging to the queen had been destroyed at the order of a single Qing official. Whatever possibility there had been, the politicians and editorialists argued, for a negotiated solution to the opium problem had been shattered by Lin's uncompromising approach. At the peak of the debate, newspapers carried false reports that Lin had poisoned the wells of the foreign compound at Canton.

At length the importuning of the merchants, together with rising British public opinion in favor of war, moved Palmerston to authorize Elliot to demand reparations from the Qing. When British ships at last arrived in the harbor of Hongkong, Elliot was still hoping for a concession from the Qing authorities, but he was pessimistic that war could be avoided once British ships and marines were on hand. In September a banner officer attempted to board one of the British ships to search for the British sailors whom the Qing were still seeking. A chance encounter with a bonded British vessel headed for Canton induced the British ships to fire warning shots, to which the Qing ships responded with cannon fire. When the news reached London, it struck many, including Thomas Staunton, as grim. Some noted that the last time the Qing had fought a foreign war they had defeated the Gurkhas – the fiercest fighters the British had encountered. William Gladstone denounced the war as immoral and led a fight in Parliament, only narrowly defeated, to abort it. Robert Peel, after talking with Staunton, remarked that Britain was "on the eve of hostilities with a country ... which, in point of population, exceeded all that of the continental countries of Europe; nay, at this moment, we might actually have entered into hostilities with a nation comprising a population of 350,000,000 inhabitants, very little short, in fact, of one third of the whole of the human race."

Elliot initiated warfare against the Qing and requested permission from the foreign office to demand that the Qing cede the Zhoushan Islands, near the mouth of the Yangtze River, to Britain. But British attempts to occupy the islands were frustrated by local resistance, anticipatory placement of a flotilla of Qing war junks, and a local disease (possibly dysentery) that decimated their troops once they fought their way to shore. Nevertheless, British ships had encountered little real challenge from coastal defenses. The Qing had cannon along the coast to discourage pirates, but they were unable to swivel the guns to make accurate shots or reach vessels that were not actually close to shore. The British, on the other hand, could bombard Qing fortifications accurately from a safe distance out on the water. Land engagements were infrequent, partly because the British faced more challenges there. Even though Qing losses ran a minimum of twenty to one compared to British losses, the British were often demoralized by fierce, if hopeless, resistance of bannermen and civilian defenders in land encounters.

Elliot first tried to end hostilities by engaging the Qing in negotiation in July of 1840, when he hoped to deliver letters inviting the Qing to discuss terms. The letters were never accepted, and as far as Elliot could see he was having the same problem as Napier, Amherst and Macartney – he simply could not find a way to meet face to face with his counterparts in China. In all likelihood the response of the Qing was much more complex. The Daoguang emperor had known when he sent Lin to Canton that there was a risk of war, but he and his advisors considered it small. They were shocked by the British decision to bring warships into their waters. Advisors to the Qing court were split as to the best next step. Some, particularly the Manchu official Mujangga, demanded that Lin be punished and that the court mollify the British by claiming Lin had exceeded his mandate (the court did in fact fire Lin from his post as commissioner, and a few weeks later sent him into exile in Xinjiang). Others urged that the court be calm and slow in response – the British force was not large and they would eventually run out of provisions. In the view of the latter group, the arrival of the British belligerents was not a larger or substantially different problem from that of the pirates who at times ravaged the entire coast. Informants who had observed British ships at Canton, Macao and Singapore for decades thought that the British ships were too deep-draughting to be able to navigate China's rivers, and so the problem was necessarily limited to the coasts. This information was only slightly out of date. In 1839 the *Nemesis* was completed for the BEIC as a novel vessel designed for opium smuggling. It was made of iron, equipped with long guns, and draughted only 5 or 6 feet into the water, making navigation of China's large rivers easy. In January of 1841 *Nemesis* appeared in China as a ship of war, landing 600 Indian marines at the Quanbi forts east of Canton, providing enough of a shock to the Qing officials that one of them, the Manchu Qishan, sat down with Elliot to outline terms for ending the war.

The elements of the agreement included the cession in perpetuity of Hongkong Island (then rocky and sparsely populated) near the mouth of the Pearl River; reopening of Canton to foreign trade; payment of $6,000,000 (Mexican) in reparations; making good the debts of Canton merchants to the British traders; and allowing equal diplomatic intercourse between the British government and the Qing court. Qishan was evidently afraid to report the terms to the court. But in late February the emperor learned of what Qishan had done and ordered him dragged to Beijing in chains, and sentenced to death – then commuted to banishment to Xinjiang. The emperor was shocked at the nature and magnitude of the British demands, and refused to accept them. Nevertheless, with British bombardment of the southern coast continuing, the court sent three senior officials, all bannermen, to Canton to meet with Elliot. The trio was handicapped by age, lack of information and opium addiction, and Elliot found them impossible to deal with. Months went by and Elliot decided to press the war to a conclusion. The *Nemesis* destroyed nearly an entire Qing squadron of war junks as well as a number of gun batteries on the land in May of 1841, and then proceeded up the coast to the mouth of the Yangtze. When the Qing court learned that the British fleet had blocked the Grand Canal, obstructed boat traffic on the Yangtze and was heading for the historic city of Nanjing, they agreed to negotiate an ending to the war and sent a Manchu official, Qiying, to represent them.

Narratives of the Opium War written in the twentieth century have emphasized the one-sidedness of the conflict. The British empire had defeated the last of its great rivals for dominance of the seas, France, in 1815, and thereafter enjoyed an assurance of victory in nearly all its struggles. Only Russia, the Ottoman empire and the Qing empire remained as possible opponents of the British navy. Of those three, the Qing was the first to be engaged, and from that conflict, Russia and the Ottoman empire would learn lessons. The Qing had no precedent for the conflict other than the one that came to their minds, piracy. Their historical approach to large outbreaks of piracy had been defense (with substantial cannon emplacements and local boat patrols) and avoidance, including the occasional evacuation of the coasts until the pirates had no reason to stay and went away. This did not mean that the empire's habit was to avoid conflict when invaded. On the contrary, its overland policies against Mongols, against Russia, against Turkestan and against Nepal had been ferocious. But no substantial threat had come from the sea since the Japanese invasion of Korea in the late sixteenth century. Moreover, the Qing were experienced and precise in their calculations of the cost and tribulations of long-distance mobilization. They expected British assaults to be brief and easily deflected. Failure to anticipate creation of the *Nemesis* was hardly surprising, given the fact that the BEIC completed it only at the moment that the war broke out, and even officials of the British navy were surprised at some of its capabilities. Overall, the Qing made specific, not general, miscalculations regarding the magnitude of the British threat, which is probably a large explanation for their reluctance to negotiate with Elliot. They thought that defense and avoidance would eventually starve the British effort, and that unretractable concessions would not be necessary.

At the time of the war, British commanders of the land forces reported that Qing resistance in land engagements was formidable. Peel's comments on engaging a third of humanity in war were prescient with respect to British experience on the land. There, the British encountered the combined coordination of local militia, local bannermen, and spontaneous village defense that had ended the White Lotus and Eight Trigram rebellions and throttled many uprisings and criminal enterprises before they became the major threats. Repeatedly British officers reported substantial resistance coming from apparently unarmed civilians, as well as inadequately armed bannermen. The numbers and the coordination were effective. Chinese historical romantics have vastly exaggerated the British casualties at Sanyuanli outside of Canton in 1841, for instance, but the loss of about a dozen marines there shook the British tacticians, who were accustomed to attacking from a relatively safe distance at sea. At Humen, at Zhapu (where bannermen took the brunt of the attack), at Zhenjiang, and other locations British officers reported daunting resistance and haunting courage demonstrated by the defenders. A longer war, and one conducted on land, would have involved very different parameters of victory and defeat.

While military historians may continue to debate the imponderables of the war itself, it is the Treaties of Nanking and the Bogue that constitute the key to the historical significance of events, and this would be true of later engagements between the Qing empire and its foreign opponents in the nineteenth century – Britain and France in 1858, France in 1884 and Japan in 1895. The provisions of the later treaties were patented in the Treaty of Nanking, which was signed by Henry Pottinger for Britain and Qiying for the Qing empire in 1842. While Britain may have entered the Opium War tentatively, it pursued its terms of settlement aggressively. British demands when finally accepted by the Qing under a catastrophic threat dwarfed the original draft agreed by Elliot and Qishan at Quanbi. It was a list of the long-standing wishes of British merchants at Canton and of concerns issuing from the British government's long struggle with the BEIC. It demanded friendship between the Qing emperor and the British sovereign and equality in all communications, abolishment of the requirement that hong merchants be intermediaries between British merchants and diplomats and Qing officials, freedom of British merchants to engage in commercial activities not only at Canton but also at Xiamen, Fuzhou, Ningbo and Shanghai, with a British trade superintendent in each. The island of Hongkong was ceded to Britain in perpetuity. Chinese subjects who were regarded as having collaborated with British merchants, soldiers, sailors or diplomats for any reason were to be given amnesty. Tariffs at the point of import were to be modest (a codicil effectively set it at 5 percent), published and respected, and British goods taken into the interior by Chinese merchants were not to be subject to any additional tax.

The cession of Hongkong island proved to be a pivotal moment in the history of global trade and migration. After 1841, trade of opium in and out of the new colony was legal. Commercial firms bid on the right to monopolize the trade, and the colonial government taxed sales of the product. The cosmopolitan (or what some historians today would term "creole") qualities of the old Canton community before the onslaught of Lin Zexu were recreated in Hongkong, where British and Chinese merchants competed for market share and export rights to all products, but particularly opium. Over time the Chinese firms, drawing upon the profound investment resources still available to them in China, pushed the British firms aside. By the end of the nineteenth century Chinese firms from Singapore, where the system of opium monopolization had started earlier and always been larger in volume, bought out the major competitors in Hongkong. The integration of the Hongkong-Singapore opium export trade with developing global steamship routes took the product to Australia, Hawaii and California by the end of the century. If anything, British victory in the Opium War only increased the depth of British – both government and private – investment in opium. But in any case the war itself, and the acquisition of Hongkong, could not be separated from the peculiar qualities of the drug as an international commodity.

The treaty also specified sums of silver which the Qing empire was to pay to Britain. Some was compensation for damages incurred before or during the war: a total of 3,000,000 dollars (Mexican) for debts which British merchants said they were owed by Canton merchants; 6,000,000 for destroyed opium. Delay in paying these amounts would incur a 5 percent per annum interest penalty. An additional 12,000,000 dollars was levied in compensation for British expenses in mobilizing its navy and marines – the treaty specified that this total would be lessened by the value of goods "looted" (a neologism that comes to us from the Opium War) by British troops during the war and occupation. The Qing government, of course, was unable to pay the total $21,000,000 demanded, which it translated into its currency as 300,000,000 ounces of silver. Its recourse was to demand that the merchants of Canton, whom it blamed for the conflict, provide the money. Wu Bingjian, who was near death, paid a third of the amount himself. The Qing made a down-payment on its outstanding obligations, though it had no choice but to suffer the mounting interest caused by being in default on the remainder.

The next year, in the Treaty of the Bogue (Humen), the British government added extraterritoriality and a most-favored-nation clause to its treaty relations with the Qing empire. The first of these provisions excused British residents in China from being subject to Qing law inside their allotted space, removing from British life in China the terror of what appeared to be arbitrary and draconian sanctions. Historically such concessions had been extraordinary, enjoyed by a small number of European merchants quartered within the Ottoman empire in the late Middle Ages. Most of the early nineteenth-century world was in agreement that respecting law was civilized; the British Parliament's argument was that China was only half civilized, and therefore its law did not meet the criteria for universal legitimacy. The second provision, most-favored-nation, was the real engine for the construction of a system that virtually required that all Britain's rivals in the world rush to China to demand economic and political privileges. In practice, most-favored-nation meant that the Qing had no ability to limit any treaty privilege to any individual signatory; all who subsequently signed treaties with the Qing would automatically gain the benefits of the Treaties of Nanking and the Bogue, and Britain would gain any new privileges introduced by subsequent signatories. For their part, the Qing did not resist the most-favored-nation clause. It superficially resembled historical practices by which the Qing had distributed ranks, money, and favors among competing groups in Mongolia, Turkestan and Southeast Asia in order to keep them divided and tractable. In some ancient Chinese and historical texts it was referred to by the shorthand of *yiyizhiyi*, "using the barbarians to control the barbarians." Rationalizations offered by Qing officials in the aftermath of the treaties with Britain, however, were just that. All terms of the treaties had been unilaterally proposed by Britain, and the empire accepted them under duress. The British relaxed their control over the Grand Canal, the Yangtze River and the Zhoushan Islands only when they received promises from the Qing to comply. The Qing court understood that resisting British demands would bring back British interference in commerce on the Yangtze, and possibly a new war. Their strategy for dealing with demands they could not meet did not involve rejecting British demands or modifying them, and would become clear only in the ensuing decade.

Though neither the Qing nor the British commented on it at the time, the Nanking/Bogue treaties were the critical point in the transformation of concepts of sovereignty in eastern Eurasia. The traditional Chinese methods of relating to outside rulers had never before been based upon a notion of absolute sovereignty, an idea that informed European theory and practice of diplomacy. Outside of Europe and its developing colonial systems, graduated sovereignty was a more common method of negotiating inter-state relations. The Qing, as described in chapter 2, were not limited to the traditional Chinese channels of communications with foreign states, and in the case of Russia famously used a different government venue, the Frontier Administration, to produce treaties ostensibly between equals. But within the Frontier Administration the concept of absolute sovereignty was also unknown. Regions under Qing military domination or indirect governance were managed through the Frontier Administration without concern that their formal incorporation into the civil government might leave them in an ambiguous state of suzerainty rather than sovereignty. As the Qing empire was moved gradually toward an acceptance of a dichotomy between absolute sovereignty and absolute dependence, its relations with Korea, Annam and Russia were profoundly transformed. In response to the same stimuli, the internal configuration of the Qing empire was also transformed, as the ambiguities in the status of Xinjiang and Taiwan were ultimately resolved by their creation as provinces of the Qing empire in the middle 1880s. Both losses of territory and formal incorporation of previous dependencies reflected the progressive accommodation of the Qing empire to the practices of absolute sovereignty.

The transformative terms of the Nanking and Bogue treaties obliged nations who did not relish a British monopolization of all trade with China to wrest their own treaties from the Qing. France was first, concluding its Treaty of Whampoa (Huangpu) in October of 1844, and the USA arrived to sign the Treaty of Wanghia (Wangxia) a month later. In 1847, the Swedish-Norwegian Union concluded the Treaty of Canton. The empire entrusted the negotiation and processing of all the treaties to Qiying, who was enduring and would continue to endure the enmity of important court factions for playing the role of the imperial concessions specialist. All the foreign signatories enlarged their privileges as the treaty system developed. The French treaty required that Christianity be legalized, and that missionaries be permitted to travel in China. The American treaty added the right of foreigners to buy land, build and learn Chinese.

Many at the Qing court regarded the increasing number of disadvantageous agreements with Europe and the USA as ominous, but the court was occupied by crises it saw as much bigger. Problems that had forced the closing the Grand Canal twenty years before rebounded in the 1840s. Though the revolt of Jehangir had been suppressed in 1828, Xinjiang remained restive, and in 1847 a rebellion based at Kashgar required a major mobilization of the banner forces to suppress. The emperor remained primarily occupied with the fiscal problems that had been on his mind before the British had arrived (see chapter 3). Both to simplify policy challenges and to insulate the imperial treasury to the extent possible, the emperor tasked Qiying with finding the money needed to pay the British, mostly by means of extractions from select Manchu aristocrats, coastal merchants and a few wealthy enclaves in the Yangtze delta. Some of the privileges demanded by the nations at Canton and the other treaty ports were realized; others – including the complete opening of the ports to competition among the merchants of the treaty nations – were delayed without explanation. In 1848 the new governor of Guangdong province, Ye Mingchen, directly refused to allow British residents of Canton to choose their place of residence in the city. The court appreciated his initiative and, evidently, his confidence; in 1852 it would make Ye a kind of commissioner for all dealings with the signatory nations, displacing the too-agreeable Qiying. In 1850 the court was dealing with the death of the Daoguang emperor and transition to the rule of a young and inexperienced Yizhu as the Xianfeng emperor, at the same time entering into its greatest and perhaps most fateful challenge, against the Taiping rebels (see chapter 7). Further inquiries or demands from the treaty powers could not penetrate the court's focus on its internal crises, as Britain discovered in 1854 when it attempted unsuccessfully to engage the Qing government in revising the terms of the Treaty of Nanking to include explicit legalization of opium.

For their part, Britain, France and the USA in particular were intrigued by the possibilities that the Taiping rebellion offered. Early reports portrayed the Taipings as being Christians with connections to American protestants in Canton. The rapidity with which the movement spread from Guangxi province to the Qing economic center in the Yangtze basin panicked the Qing and startled the foreign powers into speculation that the Taiping movement could mean the end of the Qing empire. After the Taipings had established a separate capital and government for themselves at

Nanjing in 1853, appraisals by British consul in Shanghai, Rutherford Alcock, supported recognizing the Taipings as a legitimate state. But British and American envoys to the Taipings sent back pessimistic and sometimes shocking assessments of the Taiping leaders, whom they now regarded as sunk in delusion, indolence and immorality. The treaty powers had a dilemma. They were not sure the Qing empire could survive the deepening destruction of the Taiping War, but the Taiping government gave no evidence of being competent or trustworthy partners. Despite their growing consensus that the Taipings were not in fact a viable alternative government, British and American officials from time to time raised the issue of recognition in attempts to pressure the Qing government to acknowledge demands that the treaties of the 1840s be fully implemented. By 1856, the foreign signatories had still not endorsed either side in the civil war.

The British had a chance to clarify their ambivalence in 1856, when a clash between Ye Mingchen's officials and the crew of a rented ship flying under the British flag, the *Arrow*, started another war, and France quickly joined on the British side. This time European sea and land forces were on the scene briskly. They kidnapped Ye Mingchen and sent him off to Calcutta (where he soon died), then headed straight for the capital. Qing officials had no wish to add a major military engagement with Britain and France to its troubles, and quickly signed the Treaties of Tientsin with Britain, France, the USA and Russia in 1858. But when the emperor refused to sign the treaties Britain and France realized that the Qing intended to ignore or renege on the treaties. As their representatives travelled to Beijing to attempt to discuss the matter they were fired on and dispersed by troops of the Qing general Sengge Renchin. The foreign forces regrouped and had some luck after the accidental explosion of the Qing arsenal and gun battery at Dagu on the Tianjin coast. In 1860 their combined forces of about 20,000 men entered Beijing. James Bruce (Lord Elgin), who was charged with coordination of the British military and diplomatic fronts in China, ordered destruction of the ornate European-style follies and gardens of the Summer Palace (*Yuanming yuan*) built by the Qianlong emperor and sacking of the adjacent palaces after he received first-hand reports of the torture and execution of British and French prisoners. The Xianfeng emperor talked briefly of taking charge of the banner troops and driving the foreign allies out of the capital. His fantasy of fighting off the allied armies soon faded and he was advised to leave the capital for the relative safety of the summer retreat at Chengde. The imperial entourage hastened off anyway, leaving both Manchu and Chinese officials to deal with the foreign occupation and subsequent negotiations.

One outstanding official, Wenxiang, had advised against the emperor abandoning the capital. He had distinguished himself earlier for making a stand in the capital while it was under threat from the Taipings, and urged the emperor to stay in Beijing and meet the invaders to resolve the dispute. Though a Manchu bannerman, Wenxiang was an accomplished literatus who had achieved the highest examination degree at the age of 27, and thereafter had risen quickly in the imperial bureaucracy. He was known for honesty, extreme competence and a disdain for wealth and extravagance. The preference of many British and European envoys for Manchus, and the idea that Manchus were similar to Europeans in a way that Chinese were not, was probably inspired by their experience with Wenxiang. Thomas Wade waxed poetic about him, claiming he had "never encountered a more powerful intellect." Wenxiang was not unique among either Manchus or Chinese of the time for his flexibility, ingenuity,

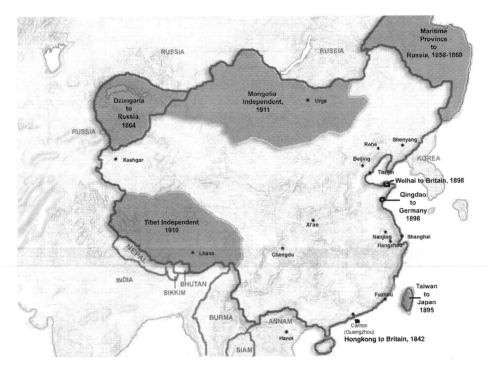

Map 4   Qing territorial losses

practicality and ethics. He had colleagues who worked very hard, particularly between 1860 and 1880, to respond to the shock of the Beijing invasion of 1860 by creating institutions to allow the empire to speak in the language of international law and practice. His expressed hope was to learn defenses by studying the medium of attack. More concretely, he hoped to renegotiate the coercive terms of the network of treaties in which the empire was becoming more deeply ensnared.

Yixin (the emperor's brother, Prince Gong), Wenxiang and their colleagues oversaw negotiation and then ratification of not only the treaties drawn up hastily in 1858 but an additional treaty of 1860. The Treaties of Tientsin permitted the signatories (Britain, France, Russia and the USA) to have full legations stationed in Beijing. Ten additional treaty ports were added, including Danshui (very close to modern Taipei, Taiwan) and the great historical center of Nanjing. Foreign ships were permitted to navigate the length of the Yangtze. Foreigners of the signatory nations were granted complete freedom of travel, for any purpose, to the interior of China. The Qing government was to establish institutions of diplomatic communication with the signatories, and to abolish derogatory terms for foreigners from its official lexicon. The opium trade was made legal. And the Qing government was to pay Britain and France each an additional indemnity of 2,000,000 ounces of silver (about 180,000 Spanish dollars). In the Convention of Peking signed at the time of the ratification of the Tientsin treaties, the Qing government ceded to Britain, in perpetuity, the tip of the small peninsula facing Hongkong, and an additional small island near Hongkong. A new indemnity of roughly 16,000,000 ounces of silver was added to the Qing obligations to Britain.

The Tientsin Treaties and most of the provisions of the Convention of Peking were elaborations, if extreme ones, on elements already present in the Treaty of Nanking and its imitators of the 1840s. It was another treaty, the Treaty of Aigun, signed with Russia, that marked a change as profound as that represented by the Treaty of Nanking. The Qing and Russian empires had for centuries been rivals for control of Turkestan, trading routes through Mongolia, and the Amur River basin. In its infancy the Qing empire had struggled against Russian vanguard units based at Fort Kumarsky for control of the Amur, and the Qing had won. In the eighteenth century the Qing had been vigilant against Russian interference in its developing relations with the Khalka Mongols and its struggles to control western Mongolia and eastern Turkestan. Russian rulers had recognized that the Qing had the advantage of proximity and numbers in these struggles, and competed only enough to get the Qing to establish terms for boundary administration and trade in the treaties of Nerchinsk in 1689 and Khiakta in 1727. Russia continued its eastward advance through Kamchatka into Alaska without violating the boundaries that the Qing sternly enforced. Russian advances through Kazakhstan stalled at the edges of the Qing military domain in Turkestan.

In the nineteenth century, Russia was more eager to make itself a presence in the north Pacific, as British and then American vessels began to investigate Japanese waters and to ponder the rich resources of Siberia. In the 1850s Russian troops again tried their luck at broaching Heilongjiang province, but were beaten back by Qing bannermen. At the other end of the Qing empire, Russia made an early advance in establishing a presence at Ili (modern Yili Kazakh Autonomous District), in Xinjiang, by requesting and receiving the Treaty of Kuldja in 1851. It was a direct descendant of the Treaty of Kokand (chapter 3), which permitted Russians to trade at Ili, keep warehouses and hostels, and have resident Russian trade inspectors during the part of the year when trade was active. But the large scale assault on Beijing by Britain and France from 1858 to 1860 finally gave Russia the chance to transform itself from a rival empire of equal status to an imperialist able to impose unequal terms on the Qing. Directing Russian diplomatic and espionage efforts in Beijing was Nicholai Pavlovich Ignatiev, not yet 30 years old, but a wily agent for his country in efforts to outflank Britain in the competition for dominance in Central Asia, and particularly in Turkestan. Russian troops joined the British, French and Americans in the occupation of Beijing and in the consequent round of treaty negotiations insisted that the Qing cede a million square kilometers of its easternmost lands to Russia. Lands east and north of the Amur were given to Russia outright, some Manchu villagers north of the Amur were to be governed by Qing officials even though they were now to live in Russian lands, a small portion of land east of the Amur River was to be under joint Qing and Russia administration. When these terms were first produced in 1858 even the disinterested Xianfeng emperor recoiled in horror. The Manchus claimed Changbaishan, only slightly to the west of the Amur, as their ancestral and sacred ground; the lands to the east were the historical range of the Jurchens and their modern descendants, the Manchus, Ewenks, Nanai, Orochens and others. It took the occupation of Beijing for the court to be willing to ratify the extraordinary Russian land terms. Before the ink was dry, Russians were moving into their new Maritime Province, establishing Vladivostok, Ussuriysk and other settlements, and planning a naval station to make themselves a presence in the north Pacific.

The agreements of 1858 to 1860 also transformed some aspects of relations between Britain and the Qing. The British had already had small skirmishes with the Taipings at Shanghai and elsewhere in the Yangtze delta, and they understood the threat that the Taiping capital at Nanjing posed for the Qing empire. Before the Convention of Peking was signed, British commanders were bringing ships, marines and soldiers to the Yangtze to defend Shanghai and other treaty ports in the area. France was determined to keep pace with Britain, and also sent troops. Russia, which had no installations in the Yangtze region to defend, offered in 1860 to bombard the Taiping capital at Nanjing on behalf of the Qing government. In 1860 the mercenary band of the American Frederick Townsend Ward, already based in Shanghai, began joining with imperial forces to combat the Taipings in the region. The British and French forces which had come to invade Beijing were soon deployed in the imperial cause, often in combination with the newly-restructured provincial forces and portions of the Eight Banner armies. When the Taipings were defeated in 1864, Britain and France were quick to claim that their contribution to restoring the Qing had been indispensable.

The first projects of Yixin and Wenxiang were an office of foreign affairs and a language school for Qing diplomatic personnel. The foreign affairs office, the Zongli Yamen, was created in 1861 partly in response to the demand in the Treaties of Tientsin that the empire come up with terminology for foreigners and foreign communications that the signatories did not find offensive. The enterprises were at first, and for at least a decade, largely a Manchu institution. All of the original directors were Manchus, and most of the students at the language school (*Tongwen guan*) were bannermen (though its president was the American missionary, W.A.P. Martin). Employment for bannermen had been a problem for nearly a century, and the Zongli Yamen and the language school were the first fresh opportunities for scholarly Manchus to appear in that time. Their first customer was Count Friedrich Albrecht zu Eulenberg, who arrived with his diplomatic expedition in June of 1861 demanding terms modeled on the Treaties of Tientsin for not only Prussia but the entire Zollverein (German Customs Union). The circumstances were the sort that in earlier times would have stymied a European new-comer – the Xianfeng emperor had never returned from his retreat to Chengde and was unable to ratify any formal agreements (he died there in August, see chapter 7). Nevertheless, the Zongli Yamen completed the treaty, got it signed by the new Tongzhi emperor, and sent Eulenberg away with an agreement that Yixin and Wenxiang hoped would forestall Prussia from deciding to bring its gunboats to China. Their next new applicants were Portugal and the Netherlands, both among the ancient embassy states of the Ming and Qing, now arriving to turn themselves into signatories of the new species of "commerce and navigation" treaties. Denmark signed up in 1863. Spain concluded its own Tientsin-style agreement in 1864. Then came Belgium, which had been using Britons in Canton to represent its commercial interests in China for decades. Now they saw that Beijing was the new center of negotiation, and they concluded a treaty, also based on the Tientsin treaties, in 1865. Freshly-unified Italy signed up in 1865. The round was finished with Austria in 1869.

By the end of this second round of treaty concessions, two dozen cities throughout the empire had been designated treaty ports. Most large cities on the Yangtze had been claimed by one or another of the European powers, as well as the major seaports of Fujian and Guangdong provinces. Two cities on Taiwan had been designated, and Tianjin was claimed by all the signatories except Spain. The treaty powers also all established legations in Beijing. The area set aside for them in the southeastern part of the "southern" or "Chinese" part of the city was separate from but not far from the Imperial City (inside which was the Forbidden City). Tiananmen – then a flat paved area outside the south entrance of the Forbidden City, atop which were wooden and brick buildings used as bureaucratic offices, restaurants and kiosks – was a short walk north and west. Directly west of the legations were several major Qing administrative centers. The neighborhood had always been associated with officialdom; for centuries the Hanlin Academy, the acme of imperial bureaucratic achievement, had been based there. Many of the legations were estates sold by impoverished Manchu aristocrats, with high walls and stout gates, inside which were rambling mansions surrounded by courtyards and gardens. The quarter was known as a quiet, leafy enclave in a city that was otherwise loud, dusty and overbuilt. The British legation was largest and most elegant, and the Belgian legation was the smallest. During the first decades after 1860 the streets of the neighborhood, which was soon known as the Legation Quarter, changed little. In time a large cathedral was added, and a railway station near the city's south gate became the main means of arrival and departure for residents of and visitors to the legations.

Acquisition by the foreign powers of the right to use the Yangtze River greatly expanded the role of one of their innovative and very peculiar institutions. In the 1850s the signatories considered that, as they were now creditors of the Qing government, they might do something about the imperial history of relatively light taxation, encumbered by the diversions of corruption and smuggling, that could not contribute to efficient payment of obligations. The distractions and destruction of the Taiping War had also impeded the ability of the Qing government to replenish its revenues through the thorough collection of taxes. In 1854 the signatories, led by Britain, created the Imperial Maritime Customs Service, undertaking on their own to collect the taxes due to the court from the foreign trade – after deducting a large portion for amortization of Qing indemnity and interest debts. The service was headed by an Inspector General, and in 1863 Robert Hart took up the post. He had been in China since 1854 and was fluent in Chinese. In the aftermath of the Convention of Peking and creation of the Zongli Yamen, Hart worked closely with Yixin, Wenxiang and others of the high-ranking officials who had taken responsibility for dealing with the signatory powers. Hart brought the service directly under the command of the imperial government, and reported to the court as one of its officials. His definition of his mission as one serving the Qing and not Britain was clearly demonstrated in 1885 when he declined an appointment as British ambassador because it would conflict with his determination to represent the Qing government and its interests. He stayed in China, and at the helm of the IMCS, until retiring in 1907. Like many foreign merchants and diplomats in China, Hart had a Chinese common law wife and three sons, the latter all sent to Britain for their education.

Hart was an exemplar of a group of foreign men who put themselves in the service of the Qing government after the Taiping War. The Qing were readily able to fit this kind of service into their worldview and their rewards system. For centuries they had integrated Manchus, Mongols, Chinese of various backgrounds, Muslims, Tibetans, Miao, Yao, Jesuits and others into their world of conquest and administration.

Frederick Townsend Ward, when he was killed fighting the Taipings, was buried with the full honors (and part of the costume) of a Manchu nobleman; W.A.P. Martin was awarded the status of high civilian official for his service to the Qing government. Chinese-speaking foreigners such as Hart, Wade and Martin hardly stretched the contours of a Qing system that had already proved itself elastic. The American Anson Burlingame was a more difficult fit. He came to China as a mature man, speaking no Chinese and with very little foreign experience when Abraham Lincoln appointed him ambassador in 1861. After Lincoln's death, Burlingame felt free to switch roles and undertook a new career as an ambassador-at-large for the Qing empire. In that capacity he led a delegation to Washington in 1867 that included Chinese Qing officials and degree candidates as well as French and English secretaries to negotiate on behalf of the empire.

The result was the so-called Burlingame Treaty of 1868, the only diplomatic document of the time that was shaped around the interests of and the desires of the Qing government, and by virtue of this it threatened to put the USA outside the consortium created by the one-sided treaties of the 1840s and late 1850s. It gave the empire the right to appoint trade officials at designated ports in the USA who would have the same powers as American trade consuls in Chinese ports, and it granted the empire most-favored-nation status with the USA. It incidentally established a slot for the Qing in the protocol symbols of the time, since when fêting Burlingame it was required that the assembly honor a Qing flag (derived from the battle flags used in the war against the Taipings) and a Qing national anthem. For a dozen years the Burlingame treaty stood equal to the treaties of Wanghia and Tientsin as a pillar of relations between the Qing empire and the Unites States. When addressing a state banquet (including Theodore Roosevelt) in New York City in June of 1868, Burlingame argued vigorously against what he called the "tyrannical school" in American opinion – merchants, industrialists and politicians who wished to change China by force. Instead, Burlingame insisted that the Chinese should have equality with America in personal rights and in national rights. He described China as egalitarian, a place where "the power goes from the people into practical government." He denounced as un-Christian, undemocratic and brutal any policies that would further compromise the neutrality of Chinese waters or the integrity of Qing territory. In a short time, Burlingame established a groundwork for the amelioration of the effects of the coercive treaties forced on China by the USA and other countries.

Hart and Burlingame were the foremost of the foreign participants in the efforts at reconstruction and reform that followed the end of the Taiping War. The war was more destructive than any war, anywhere, before it. But after 1861 a certain optimism and vigor set in. The death of the impossibly withdrawn and ineffective Xianfeng emperor in 1861 had brought his son Zaichun, only 6 years old at the time, to the throne as the Tongzhi ("Ruling Together") emperor (see chapter 7). Regents for the young emperor, including the boy's mother Xiaoqin, were supportive of policy initiatives from a remarkable group of civil governors who had emerged as the chief strategists in the defeat of the Taipings and in the massive reconstruction efforts afterward. Among their programs for revival and reform, these governors had decided to send talented young Chinese men not through the traditional examination system exclusively, but also to American preparatory schools, where they would gain a grounding in mathematics, physics, chemistry, medicine and engineering. Those students followed the example of Rong Hong (Yung Wing), who was graduated from Yale in 1854 with top prizes in English and subsequently became an important agent for acquisition of American technology and development of educational programs. The reforming governors openly talked of a Tongzhi "restoration," merging a traditional political ideal with a plan to meet the challenges posed by modern trade and modern navies. Viewed together with Yixin, Wenxiang, Baoyun and others, foreign observers of the late 1860s and early 1870s felt that the talent pool for reshaping a government and a political culture in China was a cause for enthusiasm. Perhaps most convincing, China continued to be a money machine. Between 1861 and 1868 foreign trade with China had risen in value from 82,000,000 (USD) to 300,000,000, and it was continuing to grow. In theory, there would be ample resources for the Qing to revive the rural sector, industrialize its factories, build a modern army and navy, and establish a new education system. To Burlingame and many others, profound changes in Qing government, and as a consequence profound changes in China's relations with the world, were imminent. These hopes, however, were dimmed with the passing of each decade after 1870.

Neither the Qing nor the foreign governments were successful at making the presence of large Christian establishments, particularly Roman Catholic orphanages and schools, palatable to the Chinese public. Western medicine under Christian auspices (as practiced at Peter Parker's hospital in Canton), Christian ideas as filtered through the trauma of the Taiping movement, and rumors that Christian orphanages were buying and selling Chinese children or using them for sacrifices, threw a dark reputation over Christianity in general. With the elaboration of the residence and travel privileges of missionaries accrued through the series of treaties, popular exposure to and resentment of the missionaries increased. Old stories of alleged secret Christian atrocities against Chinese children were gathered together and published in 1862 by unhappy Chinese gentry, claiming among other things that when missionaries gathered together with the body of a recently deceased Chinese convert, ostensibly to pray, they were actually there to extract the eyes and heart, which they used in alchemical tricks. At Yangzhou (a new treaty port) in 1868 an enraged mob of thousands surrounded British missionary headquarters. The families escaped to another missionary settlement, and when word of their ordeal reached Rutherford Alcock, the British Consul at Shanghai, he sent British gunboats toward Nanjing to demand reparations. Governor Zeng Guofan (see chapter 7) took control of the situation immediately, issuing public statements assuring the British of the right to travel and live in the interior, and condemning the attack. When the British government learned of Alcock's dispatch of gunboats, he was quickly reprimanded. Both the British press and Parliament expressed frustration with the missionaries, who were now being attacked by enraged mobs not only in China but also in Japan and Korea. The British government considered the missionaries a menace to smooth relations between Qing and Britain, always ready as they seemed to be to trample on local custom and risk their lives in proselytizing.

A further incident happened in Tianjin in 1870. The usual lurid rumors about Christian crimes against children had been circulating. The local magistrate started arresting Chinese converts and attempting to extract confessions from them. Announcement of a conviction based on the forced confessions caused a riot outside the local Catholic church, which brought both Chonghou – the Manchu official who was the regional representative of Zeng Guofan's administration – and the French consul M-H.V. Fontanier to the local magistrate's office. In his outrage Fontanier pulled a pistol and fired a shot that missed Chonghou, then began to rampage through the premises, smashing ceramics and furniture. Finally he stormed into the street, where he caught sight of the magistrate and fired his pistol again. The magistrate's servant was killed, and the gathered crowd immediately set upon Fontanier, beating both him and his assistant to death. The entire neighborhood was engulfed in days of rioting in which more than 30 Chinese Christians and 21 foreigners were killed. The French government sent gunboats toward Nanjing, and Zeng Guofan once again quickly moved to mollify the foreign governments. Tianjin was his own base of operations, so he met personally with the French representatives.

The Tianjin riots and the aftermath proved to be a knife in the side of cooperation between the Qing and the foreign powers. Zeng Guofan and his colleagues of the Zongli Yamen, including Prince Gong, faced their foreign colleagues as enemies for the first time in a decade. Zeng, who was terminally ill, felt so exposed in his home city during his confrontations with the French that he ordered another governor, Li Hongzhang, to bring troops to the city for his protection. Zeng managed to end the incident by promising reparations (400,000 ounces of silver) to France, exiling the magistrate, executing dozens of accused rioters, and reiterating the legality of French settlements and of Christian proselytizing. He also dispatched Chonghou to France to apologize personally to the provisional president of the French republic.

Sharp rejection of Zeng's appeasement of the foreigners arose from his colleagues. Foremost among them was Zhang Zhidong, at that time an academician, who pointed out that France had just attempted a brutal assault on Korea after the murder of French missionaries there. Not only was there no moral reason to reward French aggression, he argued, there was no practical reason – the French invasion of Korea had failed, and French missionary activity in Korea had been suspended. Zeng Guofan, covered in glory his entire adult life, was in his final months the object of criticism by his colleagues who accused him of inviting continued foreign encroachment by being too eager to quell foreign anger – whether that anger was real or staged for purposes of extracting more concessions. For their part, Zeng and Li contended that the benefits of good relations with the foreign powers for China's educational and military reforms, industrialization and economic recovery outweighed the cost of occasional reparations and embarrassment. Moreover, the treaty ports and the coast were not where China was meeting its real strategic challenge. That was in Xinjiang, where the young military chief Yakub Beg (see chapter 7) had used his base at Kokand to attack and in some cases seize cities that had been under Qing occupation. In the decade after 1863 Yakub consolidated his leadership over several different Muslim rebellions in the region and created a capital at Kashgar. The Ottoman empire recognized his state in 1873, as well as that of a separate Muslim uprising in Yunnan province (see chapter 7). In 1873 Britain sent an expedition to Kashgar to assess the prospects of cooperation with Yakub, and the next year signed a trade agreement with him. Russia assumed that the Qing were too distracted to deal with Yakub on their own, and they moved troops into Ili in 1871 to prevent the Muslim rebels from moving westward into Russian territories. Yakub sought Russian recognition of his state; Russia first equivocated, but a year later agreed.

In the aftermath of the Tientsin Massacre and the Russian incursion into Xinjiang, the Qing court began to distrust the foreign powers to whom it was indebted, and who until lately had been its apparent supporters in military modernization. The programs for industrialization of the Qing army and the new navy (see chapter 7) of the late 1870s and 1880s drew heavily upon these resources. These more focused plans for intensification of Qing military effectiveness coincided with the succession to the throne of Zaitian, the Guangxu emperor, in 1875. The new reign period was marked by the emergence into the highest policy circles of new advisors, foremost among the Zhang Zhidong and Zuo Zongtang, who both urged that the new military forces be deployed to bolster Qing defenses against further encroachments, particularly by Russia and France, as well as to firm up resistance to encroachments in Yunnan by Burma. Zuo had served as governor-general of Shanxi and Gansu province during the 1860s, and had become an experienced suppressor of Muslim rebellions in those areas through employment of modern military units. Soon after the beginning of the Guangxu reign he was directed by the court to move against Yakub Beg. Britain suggested to the Qing government that there might be a way for Yakub to conduct his autonomous state peacefully within the Qing boundaries, a suggestion that Zuo indignantly rejected. He took Kashgar in 1877, Yakub Beg died in unclear circumstances, and Qing troops reoccupied all of Xinjiang except for the areas taken by Russia. Since Russia had earlier claimed that it was occupying Xinjiang territories only to prevent expansion of the territories of Yakub, the Qing court reclaimed the territories by sending Chonghou to St. Petersburg. In the Treaty of Livadia, Chonghou achieved only partial remission of the held territories, and in addition agreed that the empire would pay Russia a 5 million ruble indemnity and grant an expansion of Russian trade privileges.

Reaction at the Qing court to the treaty demonstrated the degree to which attitudes toward the treaties in general had changed. Where the departed Zeng Guofan and Wenxiang had viewed the treaties as ways to buy time and access resources, Zuo Zongtang and Zhang Zhidong viewed them as acts of aggression that the empire no longer needed to accept. When news of the Livadia terms – and the report that Chonghou had signed the treaty himself in October of 1879 – reached Beijing, reaction from the new hardliners was sharp. Zhang demanded that Chonghou be executed, and Zuo was ready to take his troops to war against Russia. Chonghou, who had already had a special suit of prison clothes made, was arrested and deprived of all his titles. Despite its rivalry with Russia in Turkestan, Britain joined with the USA to protest both the treatment of Chonghou and the aggressive Qing stance against Russia. Thomas Wade was instructed by the British government to deliver the joint note of protest. He made his reluctance to do so known to his government, but complied. The response from his old colleagues at the Zongli Yamen astonished him. The concerns of Britain and the USA were dismissed absolutely, and the Zongli Yamen further demanded that the trade treaties all be revised, including abrogation of extraterritoriality and Christian proselytizing, before any foreign comment on Qing policy would be considered. Commentary in Britain and the USA warned that the Qing were overplaying their hand, and that war against Russia would be foolhardy. But at the time, as a century before, the Russian military was still thinly deployed on the Qing perimeters, and Zuo's threat to fight them in Xinjiang had the desired effect. Russia agreed to receive Zeng Jize, son of the late Zeng Guofan, as the new negotiator in St. Petersburg. In 1881 the Treaty of St. Petersburg restored all Russian holdings in Xinjiang to the Qing, without indemnities or major revisions of the standing trade regulations. Russian officials, with the backing of Britain, did ask for release of Chonghou, and the Qing court agreed. In 1884, the Qing empire translated its domination of eastern Turkestan into internationally legible terms by creating the province of Xinjiang.

Successful assertion of military power and diplomatic acuity against Russia had a dramatically reinforcing effect upon the emerging party of Zhang and Zuo at the court. The willingness of Britain to side with Yakub Beg, and then with Russia, against the Qing inspired deep cynicism at the court regarding the goodwill of Britain. At roughly the same period, in 1882, the USA passed the Chinese Exclusion Act, essentially eradicating all the provisions of the Burlingame Treaty. Foreign representatives were complaining that while trade in and out of the Chinese ports remained brisk, it also remained one-sided, since foreign merchants had not yet found a product that they could successfully sell in China. Even opium, now legal, was being grown in China by Chinese, and the domestic product could outsell the foreign import. The Qing court considered that it was now on its own, but the advisors to the young emperor and his regents thought they had progressed sufficiently in military strength and organization to be able to fend for themselves. The reforms of Zeng Guofan had inspired a "self-strengthening movement" (see chapter 7) that had not only brought European and American weapons, dress and organization to part of the Qing land forces, but had also grown to include industrial arsenals at Shanghai, Tianjin and Nanjing and the beginnings of a modern navy. Germany, then the leading producer of armored naval destoyers, was building ships for the Qing in their own shipyards. The effect of these ambitious modernization programs, partly financed by foreign governments and often advised by foreign advisors, was to give the Qing imperial advisors, particularly Yixin and Yihuan (Prince Chun), confidence to begin resisting foreign attempts to encroach upon Qing territory or further erode Qing legal sovereignty. When France challenged Qing border integrity as well as the empire's traditional influence over Annam (the ancestor state of Vietnam) in 1884, a group of Qing military leaders were ready to respond with force.

In the 1860s France had seized a portion of central Annam, declaring it the colony of "Cochinchina." At the time the Qing court was preoccupied with the Taiping War and many internal cares, and could neither protest nor resist French invasion of its traditional embassy state. The French, however, came to realize that for their holding and their trade routes in Annam to be secure, they would have to deal with the complex world of independent smuggling and bandit communities that braided the interface of northern Annam and the Qing empire's Yunnan province. The region was regarded by the Qing as nearly ungovernable, and was vulnerable to attempted secession by aspiring outlaw states, as happened in 1873 with the Panthays (see chapter 7). In 1882 the French sent an expedition toward Hanoi in northern Annam in an attempt to root out local banditry which threatened French trade in the area. Annamese authorities relied not only on their own resources but also upon mercenaries. Many of the mercenaries were from the outlaw communities of China's southwestern border zones, and they succeeded in fending off the French attack. The events drew the attention of the Qing court. They moved troops into northern Annam (the Tonkin region) in 1882, and the French representative agreed to recognize both French and

Qing spheres of influence in Tonkin. The French government was not willing to honor the agreement, but was also hesitant to go to war against the Qing empire. French military commanders felt, in the circumstances, that provocation against Qing military installations in northern Annam might force a renegotiation.

When the provocations came, the Qing used not only their own forces, but all the mercenaries they could attract from the border zone, and turned back attempted French advances. The French expanded their holdings in central Annam and called for talks in Shanghai in 1883 to persuade the Qing to withdraw their regular forces and the mercenaries. Zeng Jize, then representing the Qing government in Paris, suggested to the Qing court that France was unlikely to engage in full-scale war. On the basis of these assurances the Qing refused to compromise on Annam, and also launched a popular propaganda campaign against France that inspired several riots in Shanghai and in Canton, bringing French gunboats into Canton harbor (which inspired yet more riots). During the last days of 1883 the French government authorized a full-scale attack in Annam. The land engagements went against the Qing, and Li Hongzhang on behalf of the Qing government initiated negotiations with France.

Li considered the war an unnecessary distraction and expense for the empire, and agreed to terms that, predictably, Zhang Zhidong and his supporters rejected. The terms included a greatly expanded norther border for Cochinchina and new privileges for France in its China trade. More to the fury of Zhang, Li had permitted the seal awarded to the king of Annam by the Daoguang emperor to be melted in his presence, symbolically renouncing the Chinese relationship with one of its most ancient embassy states. The reaction at court caused Li to hesitate in withdrawing Qing forces from the regions granted to France, and in 1884 France sent a fleet to attack the Qing naval center at Fuzhou, then under Zhang Zhidong's own command. The Qing squadron patrolling the home waters was obliterated, and the French fleet moved on to Taiwan, where the Qing defense was more formidable. Nevertheless the French succeeded in blockading both Taiwan and the mouth of the Yangtze. The Qing did not deploy ships from its naval base at Shanghai, nor from the large shipyards and foundries under Li Hongzhang's control at Tianjin. With Qing naval power neutralized, France redoubled its efforts in the land war in Annam. In June of 1885, the Qing and France signed a treaty requiring French withdrawal from Taiwan and other islands off the China coast, while the Qing withdrew all forces from Annam. France went on to conduct a similar war against Thailand that eventually brought Laos and then Cambodia into its newly consolidated Indochina colony in 1887. The Qing consolidated its hold over Taiwan by creating the island a separate province in 1885.

The effects of the war against France were far-reaching. The rift between the accommodationist party led by Li Hongzhang and the rejectionist party led by Zhang Zhidong deepened. The Qing had been a considerable obstacle to French ambitions in mainland Southeast Asia for a time, but lack of a central command to coordinate naval forces as well as the means to push the ground war in Annam to the desired conclusion were ominous developments. The expense and educational diversions needed to create a technologically advanced navy had not had the effect that the court had hoped. Defeat by France was quickly made into a public issue by Qing officials, who denounced French assaults on Canton and Fuzhou, and the invasion of

Taiwan. Antiforeign riots swept coastal cities, as well as the British colony of Hongkong. Overall the effect of the war was to harden the attitudes of many advisors to the Qing court regarding foreign motives. It is probable that, had it not been for one factor, an open break between the empire and the signatory nations could have occurred.

The factor preventing this was Japan. In 1868 a group of relatively young, well-educated, ambitious young men had overthrown the Tokugawa shogun and established a new government, with themselves as its leaders. The young Meiji emperor was the figurehead of the government, and in some ways a member of the ruling clique. The group set up a program of industrialization of the military, modernization of the educational system and restructuring of the financial system. Their intention to bring Japan into the stratum of global sea powers was implied at first, and later explicit. As soon as the new government was established in 1868, it sent a small naval expedition to Korea, to impose upon Korea the sort of unequal treaty that European nations and the USA had already imposed upon the Qing empire (and which the United States had imposed upon Japan itself). In subsequent years emerging Japanese industrial firms began to look to Korea for needed coal, iron, wheat, and labor. The same expansionists who had argued for an aggressive stance toward Korea also proposed that Japan force the king of the Liuqiu Islands (now part of Okinawa) to renounce Liuqiu's traditional status as an embassy state of China and make him acknowledge Japan as hegemon. In 1871 sailors from Liuqiu were shipwrecked on Taiwan and then killed by Taiwan natives. Japan demanded reparations from the Qing, which would have meant that the Qing recognized Japan as custodian of the Liuqiu Islands. When the Qing failed to respond, Japan announced that it had annexed Liuqiu (henceforth Ryûkyû) and a few thousand Japanese marines landed on Taiwan. The Qing finally paid the demanded reparations and accepted the implications of the payment. In 1876, Japan felt secure enough in its military power and international standing to impose its own unequal Treaty of Kanghwa (Ganghwa) on Korea, which required the Korean court to renounce its status as a Qing embassy state.

Japanese strategists continued to argue that both Korea and Taiwan would ultimately have to come under Japanese control if Japan was to compete as a sea power. The Japanese embarked upon an ambitious naval program intended to surpass similar programs of the Qing empire. In 1882, anti-Japanese riots in Korea created the opportunity for Japan to send its marines to Seoul for the first time. In 1884 more riots in Korea threatened foreign missionaries. Japan sent in marines to restore order and briefly overthrew the Korean monarchy, putting a reformist faction in power. Qing forces under the command of Li Hongzhang's follower Yuan Shikai (see chapter 7) attacked Seoul and violently dislodged the new government, restoring the Korean king to the throne. In 1885 Qing and Japan addressed their tensions in Korea with the Convention of Tientsin, in which both sides appeared to promise to remove their military forces from Korea and not to send them back without mutual consent. In the aftermath, Japanese officials and educators, sometimes with the support of Americans in Korea, promoted a style of Korean nationalism that was directed against traditional Chinese culture. The result was a reputation for the Qing in Korea –and abroad– as an obscurantist, reactionary, arrogant and ruthless regional bully. Opinion in the USA, in particular, praised Japan as the champion of progress in East Asia, and as a healthy model for aspiring nationalists in Korea.

In Beijing, advisors to the Guangxu emperor were alarmed that loss of Qing authority in Korea was now intertwined with the rise of Japan as an expansionist sea power that would certainly challenge Qing authority over Korea, Taiwan, and perhaps even portions of the Chinese coast. The Qing loss to France clearly inspired Japan to greater boldness. In 1893 the Korean nationalist Kim Ok-kyun was murdered and dismembered while in Shanghai, and international suspicion quickly fell upon Yuan Shikai. The Japanese press, in particular, expressed outrage that the Qing government would use such grisly tactics to intimidate Korean progressives whom the Japanese were cultivating. In 1894, adherents of the Donghak nativist religion in Korea began to riot in Seoul, and King Gojong of Korea asked Li Hongzhang to send troops to restore order. When about 3,000 Qing troops arrived in Seoul, the Japanese cited the Convention of Tientsin and sent in about 8,000 troops of their own. The Donghak disorders were suppressed within weeks, and the Qing government announced it would withdraw its forces from Korea as soon as the Japanese government did the same. But Japan kept sending more troops to Korea. In July of 1894 they arrested Gojong and installed a new government of young modernizers. This group explicitly rejected all relations, formal or informal, between Korea and the Qing empire, and invited the Japanese army to expel the Qing troops. Instead, Li Hongzhang decided to increase his troops in Korea by using a contracted British ship. The ship was blocked by Japanese cruisers, while Japanese troops battled Qing soldiers in northern Korea. The two countries declared war in August of 1894. After more than a month of fighting the Qing forces in Korea were virtually annihilated by the far more numerous Japanese. Soon after, the northern fleet of the Qing navy engaged the Japanese navy at the mouth of the Yalu River. The Japanese fleet destroyed 8 out of 10 of the Qing ships, some of which had been supplied by corrupt military officials with rice instead of ammunition. Japanese ground forces moved north of the Yalu into the Qing Northeast, and began to march overland toward the critical Qing port of Lüshun (Dairen, Port Arthur). In November they seized the port.

In the final stages of the war, Japanese ships and marines circumscribed the range of the Qing navy by controlling the eastern tip of Shandong province and Taiwan. In April of 1895 Li Hongzhang represented the Qing government in signing the Treaty of Shimonoseki with Japan. The immediate impact of the treaty was impressive. Qing was to grant both Taiwan and the Liaodong peninsula, where Lüshun was located, to Japan; to allow Japanese ships to navigate the Yangtze River; to allow Japanese industrialists to build and operate their own factories in China; and to pay to Japan 340,000,000 ounces of silver. The previous signatory nations were shocked at the terms. Li Hongzhang returned to his lodgings in Tokyo without signing the treaty, and was shot in the street by a Japanese military supporter. Negotiations were suspended for more than a month while Li was being treated, and in the interval public opinion both internationally and in Japan turned against the Japanese demands. Russia, whose own interests in the Qing Northeast were threatened by the terms of Shimonoseki, convinced Germany and France (the Tripartite Powers) to join it in threatening war against Japan unless the Liaodong peninsula was returned to the Qing empire. When negotiations resumed Japan agreed to the demands of the Tripartite powers, accepted an indemnity of 200,000,000 ounces of silver, and an additional 30,000,000 ounces of silver for relinquishing the Liaodong peninsula. In October, Japanese troops, convinced that Gojong's queen Myeongseong (Queen Min) was conniving with Russia to frustrate Japanese ambitions in Korea and Manchuria, broke into the royal compound in Seoul, hacked off her hands, stabbed her to death, and then burnt her body on the grounds. The money paid Japan as part of the Shimonoseki and Tripartite agreements represented about a third of the Qing treasury at the time, and was more than six times the annual income of the Japanese government.

The long-term impact of the Treaty of Shimonoseki was the unraveling of the structure of commercial, diplomatic and strategic dynamics of the relationship between the Qing empire and the signatory powers, reaching back to 1842. At Shimonoseki Japan demanded that the role of the Chinese comprador class as necessary partners of the foreign merchants be discontinued, and that China become a field for cheap manufacturing. Where European and American merchants had failed to find a way to profit from the China trade by selling items to Chinese customers, Japan had figured out a way to profit from China by employing the Chinese as laborers. Japan had introduced, for the first time, the concept of massive territorial concessions from China, a move that threatened the interests of all the signatories, particularly Russia. Li Hongzhang, eager to exploit Russia's resentment over Japan's attempted seizure of part of the Liaodong peninsula, set out in the spring of 1896 for Moscow. In June he signed a treaty awarding Russia profound rights of industrial development and military occupation in the Northeast, expecting that this would create a block to further Japanese encroachment there. In the ensuing years, Japan was able to settle most of its debt, finance continued industrialization, expand its educational programs, and renegotiate its one unequal treaty with the USA in 1911, all due directly or indirectly to the massive infusion of cash from the Qing government after 1895. The framework for a wider and in some ways more decisive war had been established, Japan's development as an imperialist power had been accelerated, and the stunting of Qing domestic and foreign reform became all but inevitable.

Further reading

On the wealth of Wu Bingjian, see Hunter, *The Fan Kwae at Canton* (1965 [1882]) (p. 56) and Hummel, *Eminent Chinese of the Ch'ing Period* (1943–4, p. 877). Converting 26,000,000 Spanish dollars can be done by using an 1856 conversion rate found in S. Wells Williams, *A Chinese Commercial Guide*: 1,000 Spanish dollars = 720 *taels* (ounces), 1 *tael* = 6s 8d. One pound sterling = 20 shillings = 240 pennies. So, 26,000,000 Spanish dollars = 18,720,000 *taels* = 112,320,000 shillings (s) and 149,760,000 pennies (d), or 6,240,000 pounds. Morse, *Chronicles of the East India Company* (Vol. IV) lists Wu Bingjian's fortune as "upwards of six million pounds" in 1834 (p. 348). Ferguson, *The House of Rothschild* (1999), lists the fortune of the Rothschild family as 6,007,700 pounds in 1836 (p. 269, Table 10a). Using a price index table for the relative value of sterling found in Mayhew, *Sterling: The Rise and Fall of a Currency* (1999), Wu Bingjian's holdings in 1834 can be given an approximate worth for the 1990s. In Appendix 1 (p. 281 of *Sterling*), the value of sterling in the 1990s is given as approximately 50.8 times what it was in the 1830s. Using this multiplier, Wu Bingjian's 6,240,000 pounds in 1834 becomes 318,240,000 pounds in the 1990s. Comparing Wu Bingjian's fortune to that of the Qing treasury in 1841: In 1841, the total revenue (gross) of the Imperial government is listed as 38,598,000 taels on p. 195 of Ch'en's *State Economic Policies of the Ch'ing Government, 1840–1895* (1972). This converts to 12,716,000 pounds, about double Wu's fortune in 1834.

On the Canton merchant community and foreign trade, see Williams, *A Chinese Commercial Guide* (1856); Forbes, *Personal Reminiscences* (1978); Hunter, *The Fan Kwae at Canton Before Treaty Days* (1882); Low, *Some Recollections of Captain Charles P. Low* (1905); Fairbank, *Trade and Diplomacy on the China Coast* (1963); Chang, *Commissioner Lin and the Opium War* (1964); Garrett, *Heaven is High and the Emperor Far Away* (2002).

On opium as an import to China, see the early chapters of Chang, above; Trocki, *Opium, Empire and the Global Political Economy* (1999); Brook and Wakabayashi, *Opium Regimes* (2000); Bello, *Opium and the Limits of Empire* (2005). The role of opium in the development of Hongkong has been traced in Munn, "Hong Kong Opium Revenue" (2000); McMahon, *The Fall of the God of Money* (2002). On opium as a domestic issue in the nineteenth-century Qing empire, see the reading recommendations for chapter 7 of this book ("Visionaries").

On the Opium War, the Arrow (Second Opium) War, the unequal treaty system and various aspects of imperialism in China, see Tuck, Pritchard and Morse, *Britain and the China Trade* (1926); Waley, *The Opium War through Chinese Eyes* (1959); Cohen, *China and Christianity* (1963); Chang, above; Iriye, *Across the Pacific* (1967); Beeching, *The Chinese Opium Wars* (1975); Fay, *The Opium War* (1975); Inglis, *The Opium War* (1976); Fletcher, "The Heyday of the Ch'ing Order in Mongolia, Sinkiang and Tibet" (1978); Graham, *The China Station* (1978); Wong, *Deadly Dreams* (2002); Hevia, *English Lessons* (2003); Liu, *The Clash of Empires* (2004); Hanes and Sanello, *The Opium Wars* (2004); Wang, *China's Unequal Treaties* (2005); Austin, *China's Millions* (2007). Members of Parliament commenting on the Opium War of 1839 to 1842 come from Hansard (transcripts of Parliamentary debates), 9 April 1840, "War with China – Adjourned Debate," H.C. Deb. vol. 53 cols. 844–950 (9 April 1840).

On the evolution of Japanese imperialism in China and the origins of the conflict between Qing and Japan over Korea, see Conroy, *The Japanese Seizure of Korea* (1960); Rawlinson, *China's Struggle for Naval Development, 1839–1895* (1967); Auslin, *Negotiating with Imperialism* (2006); Paine, *The Sino-Japanese War of 1894–1895* (2003); Larsen, *Qing Imperialism and Choson Korea* (2008).

6

Essay
Rebel Heroines

SCHOLARS OF WOMEN'S history in China eager to find models of powerful, competent, influential women have been attracted to the hints in the records that the Taiping leader Hong Xiuquan (see chapter 7) may have had a sister named Xuanjiao. The fact that she came to prominence in the Taiping era is suggestive, since Taiping law and religious belief overtly supported the equality of women. But visitors to Nanjing in the 1850s noted that equality was often neglected in practice. Hong Xiuquan himself wrote in a poem:

> Women in the rear palaces should not try to leave;
> if they should try to leave it would be like hens trying to crow.
> The duty of the palace women is to attend to the needs of their husbands;
> And it is arranged by Heaven that they are not to learn of the affairs outside.

Hong's sentiments have appeared ironic in light of the fact that his own sister Hong Xuanjiao was one of the most famous and valiant women generals in the Taiping armies, with one of her most celebrated victories occurring at "Crowing Cock Mountain" (Jinjiling) in Guangdong province. Xuanjiao's battle persona made its own impression on Chinese culture, almost distinct from that of the Taipings themselves. Her loose silk garments gave the illusion that she was flying into battle, and a popular poem of the Taiping era celebrated her victory at Niubailing in Guangdong province:

> Women able to follow Hong Xuanjiao
> able to use firearms, do sword play;
> at Niu Bai Ling, Hong Xuanjiao prepared
> her defences, throwing the enemy
> with broken backs down the hillside.

Hong Xuanjiao became the subject of operas and plays of the Republican period, when Taiping heroes were often used as mouthpieces for social and political criticism covertly aimed at the Nationalist party. In 1962 she was the subject of a Cantonese movie, and she is a stock character in more recent films based on Taiping history.

The first mention of Xuanjiao as a historical person was in a compilation of 1906, called *Biographies from Our Nation's Female World* (*zuquo funujieweiren zhuan*). There, Hong Xuanjiao was described as a younger sister of Hong Xiuquan who later married Xiao Chaogui (who became "West King" at the Taiping court). Before the age of 30 Hong Xuanjiao was an expert in the martial arts and in fencing, and in the Taiping campaigns she led her own army of several hundred women, brandishing two swords, often attacking from horseback.

But recent research has cast doubt on the historicity of Hong Xuanjiao. The Taipings had no opportunity to write their own history or preserve their historical records, so most of what we know of Taiping biography comes from missionaries who taught the Taipings, British and American diplomats who visited them, the testimony of captive Taipings, or Qing generals who fought them. Historians have occasionally supplemented this information with folk traditions from Guangdong and Guangxi, and from "wild histories" (*yeshi*) combining rumor and recollection with documented fact. The report of 1906 was based to a large extent on such informal sources.

Formal histories of the Taipings make clear that Hong Xiuquan had no younger sister (and so was not really Xiao Chaogui's brother-in-law). It is likely that outsiders got the idea that she was Hong Xiuquan's younger sister because the wives and concubines of the subordinate kings at the Taiping court may have been referred to as "younger sisters" of Hong Xiuquan. Xiao Chaoqui's wife was born with the surname Wang (or, in some reports, Huang), and later changed it to Yang. Her personal name seems to have been Yunjiao, but it was later changed to Xuanjiao, perhaps because of dialectal pronunciations and confusion. Folk histories later gave her the surname "Hong" in honor of Hong Xiuquan. After Xiao was killed in 1852, his wife came under the protection of Yang Xiuqing, who was killed in the political crisis in Nanjing of 1856 (see chapter 7). It appears that "Hong Xuanjiao" died in the same series of events, possibly during the assassination of Yang Xiuqing.

Despite the fact that Hong Xuanjiao was not surnamed Hong and was not Hong Xiuquan's younger sister, much of the tradition that has come down relating to her has a factual basis, possibly connected more to her contemporary women than to Hong Xuanjiao herself. There were certainly women generals with female armies, whom the Qing generals referred to as "savage big-foots," since the Taipings did not bind women's feet. These female generals were active not only among the Taipings but also among the Nian and the Small Sword Society (where an attested woman general, Zhou Xiuying, was prominent). Many of their histories may be amalgamated in the stories of Hong Xuanjiao that continue to live in contemporary culture.

Further reading

Croll, *Feminism and Socialism in China* (1978), pp. 40–1, and Internet forum commentary by contemporary Chinese historians.

7

Visionaries

WHEN FIRST RETURNING to China in 1854, Yung Wing (Rong Hong) had been focused on Christianity. It was the religion of his sponsors in the USA, he was himself a convert, and in the aftermath of the treaties of the late 1840s Christian missionaries traveling the interior were in need of reliable translators. After a few years Yung switched his professional activities to commerce, and by 1859 was employed by a large tea exporting firm. In that year he decided to accept an invitation, arranged by another Christian friend, to visit the city of Nanjing, then the capital of the Heavenly Kingdom of Great Peace (*Taiping tianguo*). This remarkable movement, to some degree inspired by Christian beliefs, had carved out a separate domain for itself in the central Yangtze valley, cutting through the most vital trade circuits, wealthiest agricultural sectors and more commercially vibrant cities of the Qing empire. In Nanjing, Yung was welcomed by Hong Ren'gan, the cousin of the Taiping leader, Hong Xiuquan. Hong Ren'gan himself had only recently arrived in Nanjing, after years of attempting to negotiate the bureaucratic and military obstacles to his travel first from Shanghai and then from Hongkong. In Hong, Yung Wing saw a young man only a few years older than himself, also educated by Christians, who had also lived for a time outside the empire. Yung stayed only briefly and exchanged ideas with Hong. For Yung, the creation of a rebel state meant a chance to instantly bring to China modern education, an industrialized army and navy, and an American-style banking and currency system. He was not sure, however, that he had swung Hong over to his point of view. In time, he would learn that his ideas and Hong's were closer than he had imagined.

Yung returned from his brief visit to Nanjing to his commercial work in Shanghai. In 1863, he received an invitation to visit Anqing in Anhui province, about 300 miles west of Shanghai, which he had to reach in a small boat. There he was ushered into the operational headquarters of Zeng Guofan. In two separate meetings, Zeng questioned Yung on his recommendations for improving things in China. Tens of millions had been killed in the past decade in a civil war that was not concluded, and many more were dislocated or homeless. Vast stretches of farmland had been ruined and abandoned. Shanghai and other cities in the Yangtze basin had been assaulted or occupied, sacked by one side of the conflict, or perhaps both. Muslims rebels with deep communal and economic roots were occupying parts of Xinjiang, Gansu and Yunnan. Smaller rebellions had broken out in other areas, where government troops had sometimes been taken away to meet the Taiping threat. The Yellow River had changed course in 1855, killing hundreds of thousands and ruining the livelihoods of millions. Opium addiction was spreading through south and central China at an unprecedented rate. A war with Britain and France had broken out in 1856; in 1860, those two countries, aided by Russia, had invaded Beijing and begun dictating a new round of predatory treaties. As a result, a huge chunk of the empire's northeast had been broken off and taken by Russia. The Qing government was bankrupt, and still hopelessly in debt to the European signatory powers. But Yung Wing's answer to Zeng's question was crisp: Machine tools. Zeng nodded, and ordered Yung to acquire machine tools from abroad and establish a machine shop near Shanghai. The next year a division of Zeng's forces broke the Taiping defenses at Nanjing, and arrested and executed Hong Ren'gan along with the other Taiping leaders in residence. Yung Wing's machine shop became, before the end of the decade, the great Jiangnan Arsenal.

By the time that Yung Wing died in 1912 he may have wondered which of his interviews with Hong Ren'gan and Zeng Guofan had really done any good. The prospect of a revolutionary remaking of Chinese society offered by the Heavenly Kingdom of Great Peace had captured Yung's imagination as it had the imagination of many Chinese – and many foreign observers – in the early 1850s. The ideas that Yung had proposed for reshaping institutions, culture and foreign policy were broad and bold (as well as vague). But by 1863 the Taipings were collapsing from the inside, while a combination of Qing and foreign troops pressed them from without. The survival of the Qing empire as a nominal entity was no longer in doubt. The best Yung could offer then was s single, concrete solution, a solution that would cement China's fortunes to the achievements and the goodwill of Europe and the USA for decades at a minimum. His vision of a strong, practical government standing up militarily and economically, thanks to machine tools, may have seemed exhilarating, too. But within decades even the most modest goals of reformers such as Yung would be in shards. By the end of the century, Yung was a fugitive from the Qing with a huge price on his head, and had become an illegal recluse in the USA, which had revoked the citizenship he had gained in 1852 and banned him from regaining a legal home.

From the White Lotus uprising on, the Qing territories had been plagued by continuous revolts of small and large scale, but they were not all of a kind. Some were networked uprisings, loosely affiliated over long distances, focused on harassing Qing officials and protecting local crime networks. Others were rebel kingdoms, controlling amalgamated territories from a center, nurturing ideologies and pretending to statehood. The more dangerous, widespread and stable rebel kingdoms had a religious base or at least a religious reinforcement. The Taiping phenomenon had so many remarkable characteristics that historians have called it a "movement," or even, as in the cases of Jen Yu-wen and Immanuel Hsü, a "revolution." For a century after the kingdom was suppressed, historians would trace the inspiration for great public upheavals, in which they would include the Communist Revolution of 1949, to the Taipings. While the Taipings were indeed unusual, they shared enough traits with other rebel kingdoms – notably the Panthays of Yunnan in the 1870s – to constitute a distinct phenomenon. They tell much both about the level of alienation in the Qing empire and the level of creativity and inspiration emerging from local organization.

Taiping origins had many sources. First there were the economic troubles of the interior of Guangdong and Guangxi provinces in the 1840s. The region around the Pearl River and its tributaries to the west is known to have been affected by both opium addiction and the opium trade well before 1820. Addiction spread from Canton toward the interior via the rivers, while criminal syndicates battening off the spreading addiction began to involve residents of virtually every large village. Young men who could connect with the opium smuggling networks frequently abandoned farming, fishing or other essential but less remunerative occupations. Criminal gangs began to control vast stretches of the countryside, as well as the lives of the farming and trading populations. The price war of the 1820s caused by American competition with British opium stressed the income of the criminal syndicates, who diversified their enterprises to prostitution, gambling, human smuggling to the cities and blackmail.

Qing control of the Guangdong coast was compromised by the Treaty of Nanking and subsequent agreements. Opium importation was eventually legalized, so that Qing officials had no reason to be on the lookout for coastal smugglers. Taxes on the trade were collected after 1854 by the Imperial Maritime Customs Service (see chapter 5). The British navy undertook to patrol the Guangdong coasts to quash piracy when it interfered with British trade in the aftermath of the loss of the British East India Company's monopoly (see chapter 5); the Qing was spared primary responsibility for fending off raiders and smugglers. Chinese fisherman made private contracts with British ships, both naval and private, for protection. The ungoverned zone between central Guangxi and the borders with Annam and Burma that had so perturbed French colonialists (see chapter 5) was basically given over by the Qing authorities to the control of gangs running drugs, women and weapons between China and Southeast Asia. As eradication of a global slave trade raised the demand for indentured servants, the over-populated coasts of southern China became the source for laborers. Gangs in Guangdong smuggled both the willing and the unwilling through Canton and Hongkong to Australia, Indonesia, Hawaii, California, Latin America and the Caribbean. These developments contributed to loosening civil control of Canton itself. Canton officials made only casual efforts to suppress riots sparked by fears of forced labor abductions and anger over British attempts to settle in Chinese neighborhoods. British merchants shifted their trade from Canton to Shanghai, where it was easier to work with the local officials and the population was regarded as less volatile. The loss of trade contributed to the downward economic spiral in Canton and in Guangdong province generally.

Social malaise in the countryside due to these economic changes was intensified by what historians often characterize as "ethnic" rivalries. The group called "Hakka" (*kejia*) were often in competition with the "local" (*bendi*) population of Cantonese speakers for land, crop sales, water access and, in some cases, mining rights. The majority were often contemptuous of the Hakkas, whose women's feet were unbound and regarded as uncouthly large. For Hakkas, extended lineages and village organizations were essential to safety and livelihood. In Guangxi, to the west, the indigenous Miao were also inclined toward the use of gang organizations to protect their land

and fishing rights, and to prevent predation by criminals, by Hakkas and by the local population. The Tiandihui also had local branches, combining a forbidden pro-Ming and anti-Qing ideology with their usual criminal pursuits of smuggling goods and humans.

The local organizations, whether overt or covert, were agitated by the rampant spread of Christian preaching and Christian institutions, the second proximate source of the Taiping rebellion. After 1844 Christians had the right to travel and teach in China again. In Canton, the American Baptist Issachar Jacox Roberts had started up a one-man religious crusade. Roberts was born in Tennessee in 1802 and was an ordained minister by the time he was 26 years old. By 1837 he had saved or solicited enough money to create the Roberts Fund and China Mission Society, whose first project was working with lepers in Macao. In 1841 he joined the Baptist Mission, which allowed him to return to full-time preaching. His relations with the Baptist establishment were evidently stormy. He switched sectarian connections at least once and by 1852 had split with Baptists entirely. Till he left China in 1866 Roberts was an independent preacher, evidently more reliant on his own congregation, both Chinese and foreign, than on international Christian organizations. His devotion to his calling eventually cost him his life; he died of leprosy in 1871, in Illinois.

Roberts' personality and fiery preaching both had an impact on China's future. His fanaticism allowed him to make extraordinary inroads among the Chinese population in and around Canton and also estranged him from friends and family. In Canton his teaching was facilitated by the availability of Liang Afa's translations of short Bible summaries, excerpts and lessons into Chinese, probably written under the tutelage of Robert Morrison, who had arrived in Canton in 1834 as the first Protestant missionary, and eventually translated the whole Bible into Chinese. In early 1836, a Hakka native of Guangdong, Hong Xiuquan, received Liang's tracts. Hong came from a family of farmers who had pooled their resources to put him through the examination system. The young man toiled desperately, hoping that success in the examinations and an official appointment would repay his family's sacrifice many times over. He went to live in Canton to prepare for the provincial-level examinations, and supported himself as a private tutor while studying. In 1837 Hong failed the examination, and he shortly fell ill. According to his later testimony, he experienced visions in which he met an elderly man who exhorted him to rid the world of demons, and a middle-aged man who taught him about morality. Hong continued to tutor, but also began to work as a fortune-teller. He convinced his younger cousin Hong Ren'gan, also an aspiring but frustrated scholar, and childhood friend Feng Yunshan to form a religious alliance, built on the belief that Hong Xiuquan's dream visitors had been God and Jesus, and both had given him guidance on rebuilding the world. The three men preached against the traditional local gods in their home village, and may have attempted to destroy shrines. They and their followers were chased out of the village and ultimately out of Guangdong province, and fled to the lawless fringe in Guangxi province, to the west. There they continued preaching and converting, while selling pens, ink and other household goods. In 1846 Hong left his followers behind to return to Canton.

Rumors of Hong's visions circulated among the educated and the Christian in Canton, and in 1847 Hong and Roberts met face to face. Roberts felt he had found a fitting disciple, and for some months the two were engaged in intense study of the

Bible, with the goal of baptizing Hong Xiuquan. The testimony of other missionaries suggested that Hong gave up his baptismal goals when he discovered that he could gain no financial support by becoming a Christian (possibly the report of another convert deliberately derailing Hong's reputation in Roberts' eyes). In any event, Hong's visions as they were transmitted to his family and childhood friends would not have passed Christian doctrinal standards. He now interpreted the messages to mean that he was a new prophet, the younger brother of Jesus. God had commissioned him to lead armies and a government to eradicate the world of Satan's agents, the Manchus. Hong returned to Guangxi, to continue to build upon his own beliefs and his own congregation, the Society of God-Worshippers.

The sect attracted the attention of the area's secret societies and mutual-protection alliances (not always easy to distinguish), whose functions were greatly enlarged in an area where the Qing had all but forsaken formal government. Famines in Guangxi between 1847 and 1849 also brought refugees into the God-Worshippers' ranks. By 1850, Hong's group of most trusted followers included businessmen who knew how to negotiate with local warlords and distant Qing officials, pirate captains, smuggling bosses and mercenaries. All professed fervent belief in Hong's visions, and some were truly devout; others were there to exploit Hong's extraordinary ability to attract and organize a community with unprecedented military and economic potential.

Hong conducted outdoor meetings that very strongly resembled the tent revivals of the Baptists he had attended with Roberts. Farmers from miles around flocked to the events, either out of boredom or conviction. Hakkas and Miao particularly identified with Hong's message of liberating the oppressed, and most of the gathered saw something appealing in Hong's denunciation of the Manchus, whose government was each year suffering more humiliations at the hands of European or American navies and diplomats. Tiandihui and other secret societies saw a theme of Ming restorationism in Hong's vision. Those who were unmoved by Hong's religious or political message were often intrigued by reports that Hong and his followers were acquiring magic powers, including flight, spirit communication and supernatural healing.

The local Guangxi magistrate and his colleagues in neighboring counties were worried about the God Worshippers. They were aware of the seditious message, and in principle opposed to mass gatherings. But Hong's events were not unruly, and no magistrate had the time or resources to go looking for trouble. The officials hesitated to report the events to higher authorities, preferring to consult among themselves about the level of risk and possible remedies. It was not until 1850 that the size of the meetings, now on the order of ten thousand, and Hong's overt denunciation of the state moved the governor of the province to ask the empire to send in banner troops to break up the throng. Hong and his commanders not only intensely exhorted the followers to unite against the empire's forces, but also seized all private property from among wealthier believers, promising to distribute it to all the believers when the battle was done. Hong's followers handily beat off the government troops. The rebellion had begun. Hong Xiuquan sent news to his cousin Hong Ren'gan in Canton to hurry to join the rebellion in Guangxi. Ren'gan made several attempts to do so, but was repeatedly frustrated by the local police, who eventually succeeded in arresting him. He escaped and fled to Hongkong for safety.

Hong's followers moved very swiftly to expand their control over local villages, mostly by virtue of the community organization that Hong had earlier imposed.

By 1850 he was no longer merely summoning large crowds for prayer meetings. His followers had settled in communities in Jintian, which they reorganized around their principles. Hong had a Christian fundamentalist's suspicion of sexual relations. Among his followers, men and women were strictly separated outside the household. In their separation, the sexes were ostensibly equal. They performed the same labor in the fields, drilled in their own military units, had their own evening prayer and study meetings, and had the same access to everything except, evidently, high political office. That was largely the preserve of Hong's close male relatives and childhood friends.

The Taiping base, by 1850, already had the hierarchy, the lateral cohesion and the specialization of a thriving community. The ad hoc abolition of private property became institutionalized afterward, giving Hong and his followers total control over rewards in the community, and appealing to the egalitarian sentiments of poor local followers and Miao allies. In the aftermath of the defeat of government troops and rapid control by the God-Worshippers of a chunk of Guangxi, Hong formed a state. It was to be called the Heavenly Kingdom of Great Peace (*Taiping tianguo*); and he was the Heavenly King (*Tian wang*). His highest-ranking and most trusted commanders were made sub-kings (named for the four directions), his greatest soldier Shi Dakai, who turned 20 in 1851, was made an "assistant king," and other followers were named as ministers, generals and secretaries.

Government troops attempted to encircle the Taipings in Guangxi but failed; instead the Qing commanders presented to the emperor in Beijing, for execution, a man surnamed Hong, from Guangxi, whom they insisted was the "King of Heavenly Virtue" (*Tiande wang*); the real Taipings proceeded by boat and cart toward Hunan province in central China, bordering the Yangtze River. Hong's childhood friend and loyal follower Feng Yunshan was killed in a skirmish with government troops in 1852. In Hunan the Taipings were joined by enthusiastic secret societies and bandit gangs, eager to throw in their lot with the apparently unstoppable rebels. The Taiping commanders felt confident enough to attempt to seize the provincial capital, Changsha, but its defenses held. In view of the city's defenders, Hong was saluted by his throng with thundering imperial salutations of *wansui* ("bonzai, 10,000 years") and Hong declaimed that they had received the seal of state from God. With weapons gathered from the defeated government troops, Taiping armies moved northward and eastward, overwhelming villages and conscripting the residents. By the time winter settled in, they had seized and were occupying the Yangtze River port of Wuchang. A half million Taiping soldiers and their families continued eastward along the river, seizing cities in Anhui province in early 1853. In March they entered Nanjing, and then spent the ensuing months occupying as much of the surrounding settlements as was necessary to make themselves secure.

The same period, 1850–3, was a time of transition and confusion for the Qing court. In 1850, just as the court was receiving news of the defeat of the troops sent to disperse Hong's followers in Guangxi, the capital was mourning the Daoguang emperor, who had died at the age of 52. Despite the Qing losses to Britain and the other signatory states, the emperor was beloved by the public and respected both by Qing and by foreign officials. His consultative and reforming government had been hobbled by profound financial crises and insuperable challenges of long-distance communications. But there were few problems that he was ignorant of or indifferent to, and many that his officials and volunteer scholars had investigated in a thorough and

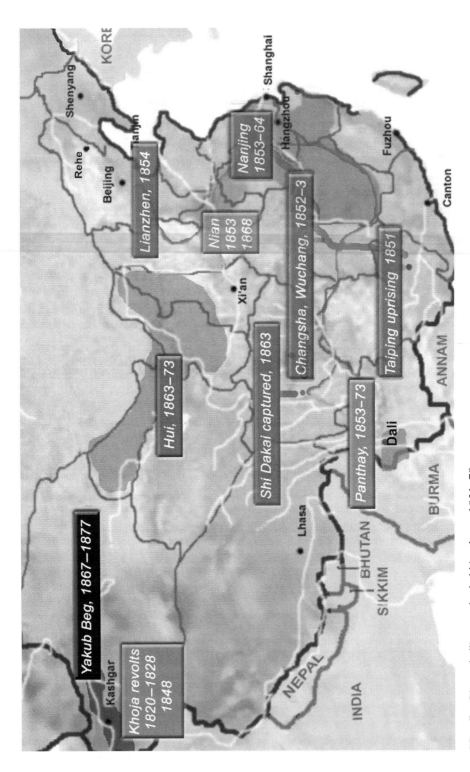

Map 5 Qing rebellions and rebel kingdoms, 1821–78

objective fashion. The distractions of the Opium War, the subsequent demands for treaties by France and the US, a huge flood of the Yellow River in 1846 and the Kashgar rebellion in 1847 completely consumed the emperor's last years. Restoration work on the Grand Canal was abandoned in 1849, throwing laborers and merchants in the economic depression the emperor had tried to avoid 20 years before, and seeding ground for recruiting by criminal organizations. Counting the unpaid indemnities from the first round of treaties of the 1840s, government obligations were ten times the government income at the time of the emperor's death.

The new emperor, 19-year-old Yizhu, ascended the throne as the Xianfeng emperor. He considered the deliberation and moderation of the Daoguang court to have been a disaster. He was attracted to the stories of stubborn provincial governors who defied the provisions of the unequal treaties. He distrusted élite Manchus whom he saw as representative of the failed Eight Banner military establishment, and demanded that wealthy Manchus contribute heavily to the imperial treasury. Though Lin Zexu had been exiled by the court for his role in provoking the war with Britain in 1839, he had been recalled by the Daoguang emperor and put into service in various provincial offices in the late 1840s. The Xianfeng emperor dismissed Mujangga, who had been the primary critic of Lin, and formed the idea of making Lin the governor of Guangxi province, where the God-Worshippers were gobbling up villages. Unfortunately Lin died suddenly on his way to put down the rebellion. The court was uncertain how to deal with the threat through a year and more of discouraging reports. But eventually the emperor turned to, ironically, Mujangga's favorite civil official, Zeng Guofan. In 1852 Zeng was in the middle of a three-year mourning period for his mother when the court ordered him to report for duty in the war against the Taipings. In consultation with other court officials, Zeng concluded that the successful defense of Changsha had been the key. Local gentry, with their drilled militia of local residents, had maintained the defenses and the supplies while fending off the Taiping attacks. Zeng headed to Hunan to begin to recruit these experienced local militiamen for a new Hunan Army (Xiangjun). Local gentry had been ordered by the court to supply money for Zeng's program, but he had to cajole them himself. He began organizing means of getting them weapons and uniforms. Even in their early days of organization and training he kept them busy fighting local bandit groups and smugglers, not only for experience but to quash the resources the Taipings tended to draw upon to extend their own forces. High-ranking banner commanders and many court strategists denounced Zeng for delays and distractions while the Taipings continued to defeat regular government troops.

Zeng's first victory against the Taipings in Hunan in early 1853 changed opinions. He was made controller of the finances of Hunan and Hubei, in which position he adapted a technique already being used to finance local defense in the Yangtze delta, the *lijin*. This tax was imposed on local trade and used exclusively for local defense, bypassing the imperial treasury. Under Zeng, it was generalized to the provincial level and provided resources for the other provincial armies. Zeng also worked with other officials to organize a fleet of boats to prevent the Taipings from controlling the Yangtze River. The emperor and his advisors authorized volunteers from the Eight Banner Manchu and Mongol units, particularly cavalry, to coordinate with Zeng and other civilian officials to form novel composite armies, combining the local strengths of the Hunan militia with the ability of the cavalry to make concentrated, long-distance strikes.

The brutality of the war was evident in the fate of cities on the eastern Yangtze River. During the first Taiping attacks in 1852, cities such as Jiujiang and Wuchang were sacked and occupied. In such circumstances, the government surrounded the cities, attempting to cut off supplies to the Taiping armies inside (who numbered in the hundreds of thousands). Atrocities by occupiers were coupled with deprivation imposed by the defenders. After weeks the Taipings left the cities and continued eastward toward Nanjing. The defenders then entered and sacked the cities. Rape, murder and pillage are amply attested in both local and foreign testimony. The Taipings, once settled in Nanjing, needed to periodically attempt to reassert control over a certain number of Yangtze communities in order to prevent themselves being surrounded and starved in Nanjing. An independent band of rebels called the Small Sword Society declared solidarity with the Taipings and briefly seized control of Shanghai in very early 1855 before being ousted by mercenaries hired by the foreigners in Shanghai. The Taipings thereafter ranged westward again. Wuchang, in addition to its neighbor communities, was subjected to new rounds of attack, occupation and counterattack through 1854, 1855 and 1856; in Jiujiang, the same traumas continued until 1858. Zeng himself was attempting to defeat Taiping advances by boat in several of the major lakes that feed from the Yangtze. He lost a major encounter with the Taipings in 1854, but afterward became adept at planning naval as well as ground warfare. Though he faced the greatest Taiping general, Shi Dakai, and a massive rebel army in these Yangtze encounters, Zeng and his combined army, the Southern Grand Battalion, had the Taipings bottled up inside Nanjing by late 1856. The Northern Grand Battalion was being readied to prevent a Taiping push north of the Yangtze.

As Zeng and his colleagues were halting the Taiping advances and attempting to root out support for the rebels in the middle 1850s, the court was struck by simultaneous crises. Though the Taipings were the largest and most frightening rebel movement, they were not the only one. In northern China, a group of free-roaming horse rebels under the leadership of Zhang Luoxing, called the Nian, had been leading Qing authorities on a chase, raiding village grain stores and silver caches since 1851. Nian methods of organizing and communications suggested that the history of White Lotus rebel cells in the north China region – particularly the Huai River basin – had contributed a lasting infrastructure of illegal and insurrectionary movements to the region. It appears that the sophistication of Nian organization was partly a legacy of the suppression of the White Lotus Rebellion; militiamen mobilized to fight the rebels returned home with both military and organizational skills, both of which they readily put to use when famine or financial distress drove them to the other side of the law. The Nian had their own "banner" military organization (the units of which were called *nian*) that may have been inherited from the White Lotus, as were the Nian's emblematic red turbans and Eight Trigram flags. Like both the White Lotus and the Taipings, the Nian used women in their military, sometimes (for White Lotus and Nian) as unit commanders. But the religious legacy was primarily organizational. The Nian rebels had no formal ideology and only one evident goal, captured in their slogan, "kill the rich and aid the poor." When the Nian learned that the Taipings had seized Nanjing and established a capital there, they sought an alliance. Hong Xiuquan gave the Nian leader a title, and in ensuing years the Nian and the Taipings were occasionally able to cooperate in keeping the Qing fighting a two-front war in eastern China. Fortunately for the Qing, the Taiping leaders' insistence on their divine mission prevented full coordination with secular but equally ambitious rebels.

By 1853, as the Taiping armies began to sweep eastward along the Yangtze, Beijing residents feared that the Taipings would turn north toward the capital, in fulfillment of Hong Xiuquan's vow to destroy the "nest" of Satan's demons. Many of the highest-ranking officials of court panicked, recommending that the Xianfeng emperor be taken away to safety in Chengde, and making provisions to have their own families escorted to safety in the Northeast. In time the panic passed, but to many officials it was clear that the Xianfeng emperor, then in his early twenties, was unsteady in his judgments, jumping at alarming reports and easily misled by overconfident presentations. The court quickly delegated responsibility for dealing with the Taipings to Zeng Guofan and his fellow Hunanese official Hu Linyi. Whenever possible the emperor also shifted responsibility for administrative decisions to his younger half-brothers Yixin (Prince Gong) and Yihuan (Prince Chun); in the middle 1850s he also began to depend upon the company of his young concubine, Xiaoqin. As a boy, Yizhu had been married to a girl from a distinguished Manchu lineage who died in 1849. After his accession to the emperorship in 1850 he married again, but he and the empress never had a child. The concubine Xiaoqin was the daughter of a Manchu official whom the emperor dismissed in 1853 for deserting his post in Anhui as the Taipings advanced; nevertheless, she was promoted in rank (meaning, the frequency of her sexual contact with the emperor) in 1854, and in 1856 gave birth to the emperor's only son who would survive past infancy. Xiaoqin was literate, and the emperor sometimes let her read state papers and discuss pending decisions.

In 1855, in the midst of some of the darkest days of fighting against the Taipings and the Nian, as tensions with the British and French escalated, perhaps the most staggering single blow of the Xianfeng reign struck when the Yellow River changed course. The last great flood of the river had been in 1846, when hundreds of thousands had been killed and millions displaced. But the river largely stayed in the bed it had inhabited since 1194, cutting south of Shandong peninsula and joining the sea only slightly north of the mouth of the Yangtze. In 1855, the river rejected the southern route entirely, leaving its bed east of Zhengzhou and cutting north of the Shandong peninsula, emptying into the Bohai Sea for the first time in nearly a thousand years. The Ji River, on which the ancient Shandong provincial city of Jinan once fronted, was completely suffused by the Yellow River (on which the docks of Jinan now stand). The river flooded the Grand Canal about half way between Nanjing and Tianjin. During the months of the river's transition, millions died in flooding, and in subsequent months millions more were at risk from famine and disease. Until 1889 (the year of another disastrous flood of the river) the river channel remained unstable, since the new course was not banked and the river freely wandered from its course during the rainy seasons. Shandong, Zhili and Anhui provinces were as a consequence plunged into economic and social misery, in which local protection organizations both provided critically needed aid and exploited that need to enhance their standing and influence. The Nian and the Tiandihui, in particular, competed with government officials to provide for refugees as they could, and to gain recruits.

In the years before 1853 the swift expansion of the Taiping domain was fueled at least in part by popular disgust with the Qing government and its representatives, combined with coercive measures imposed upon populations already subordinated. Foreign testimony vividly described the local populations of Zhejiang and Jiangsu being so terrified by reports of the predations of imperial troops that they fled the arrival of loyalist forces and flocked to the Taipings. At its most fully developed point, the Taiping regime demanded enrollment of every individual in work details and military training squads. Confiscated land was classified according to its productivity, and distributed to all members of the kingdom, male and female, according to age. Those over the age of 15 received a smaller portion of excellent land or a larger portion of inferior land, and household members under 15 received a half portion each. The land was entrusted to the individual to be worked; he or she could use the proceeds from the land for sustenance, but not for profit. All surpluses were gathered in state warehouses, to be used as the Taiping leaders saw fit. How practical the system could have been if implemented widely was never known, since constant warfare on all fronts and turmoil in the capital hindered its applications outside a few small areas.

Some landowners, farmers, and foreigners entertained the possibility, between 1850 and 1856, that the Taipings presented the possibility of modern and competent government. But Hong's religious visions offered few clues for conduct of the state, and the Taiping leaders rejected the imperial forms of government in China absolutely. They claimed to take their basic theory of government from the Chinese classic the *Rites of Zhou* (*Zhouli*), which predated the creation of the first empire in China in 221 BCE. Confucius had claimed, in the fifth century BCE, the *Rites of Zhou* as his own guide to good government. It specified decentralization of administration (in the original context, aristocrats governed local life); egalitarianism in village life, and the pursuit of the material welfare of the people as the highest goal of the state. As with many aspects of the Taiping phenomenon, the gap between what was claimed and what was practiced could be wide. The policies of the Taipings called for centralized government, in which religious indoctrination, work and military training wholly encompassed the life of every individual.

Taiping government was staffed by officials, selected through an examination system, but one very different from that used by the Qing. The simpler language used in Taiping religious publications was also used in the examinations, and the examinations themselves were based on the religious texts. A much wider variety of social, economic and gender backgrounds was swept into Taiping government than had ever been tolerated by the Qing. Indeed, most candidates for the examinations passed, which not only kept the Taiping government well staffed but thrilled a populace conditioned to believe that the privilege of government service should be limited to much less than one tenth of 1 percent of the male population. To support universal education and the cultivation of religious instructors and officials, the Taiping government supported an energetic publishing program, producing religious texts and instructional manuals for free distribution to the population.

The Taiping armies were inspired by the Ming policies intended to make the armies economically independent and socially malleable. The armies were derived from the work units consisting of 25 farming families. Each unit was responsible for its own religious training, security, food rationing, settlement of disputes, and legitimation of marriages. Leaders of the farming units were also trained as military officers, and drilled their farmers in much the same manner that gentry landowners under the Qing drilled their farmers at the time. Smaller units were consolidated into larger ones, under higher officers, in a pyramidal pattern that culminated in an army of 10,000 families along with their officers. There were many women among the officers, and at least one whole unit – supposedly commanded by Hong Xiuquan's sister Hong Xuanjiao (see chapter 6) – that was composed entirely of women.

Taiping subjects were all required to convert to the Taiping religion, and to read the Bible along with additional teachings written by Hong Xiuquan. Children read a primer reminiscent of a traditional Chinese primer but revised to carry Hong's message of God the creator and his commandments. Taiping indoctrination materials were consciously written to be read by marginally literate farmers, using a restricted vocabulary and punctuated sentences. Traditional ancestor worship was forbidden, and traditional temples in Taiping-ruled areas were destroyed or made unrecognizable after being converted for Taiping uses. In its essentials Taipingism was not very different from Mormonism (to which Roberts compared it). Hong proposed that Christianity as Roberts preached it was only a transitional state in ongoing revelation of the divine will, and that Hong Xiuquan was the prophet sent to bring the final message to men. That message was a command to continue the battle between the godly and the satanic forces on earth, paving the way for the final revelation of God's kingdom. But a living messenger from God, especially when surrounded by competing messengers, meant that God's message was liable to be revised without notice. In particular, descriptions of the Taiping paradise seemed to mutate in response to conditions of the rebellion. In the beginning, the paradise was ethereal, unachieved and unlimited. After Nanjing became the center of Taiping earthly kingdom, paradise began to take on material shape, and to be subject to limits and space and time. In the late stages of Hong Xiuquan's isolation from political life and military affairs, paradise became inward, personal and unique to each individual.

The testimony on how many of the newly-conquered after 1852 were convinced – immediately or over time – by the Taiping religious vision is very unclear. The main obstacle to Taiping progress in the early years of government paralysis and local unpreparedness was the resistance of individuals to the loss of family, property and such personal discretion as a hard-pressed farmer could manage in south-central China in 1850. That obstacle the Taipings overcame with threats of execution, and the psychological reinforcement provided by the fanaticism of tens of thousands of fervent believers. Religious conversion was mandatory; refusal meant execution. The prohibition on private property permitted all seized goods to become state property, to be used by the farming units as needed, without the a bureaucracy redistributing goods or adjudicating ownership. The decimal military organization made the addition of new forces relatively orderly. Since many newly-absorbed populations were already organized as *baojia* or *tuanlian* self-defense units, the work of plugging them into the Taiping organizational grid was relatively simple. Whether leaders or followers, Taiping identity was imprinted on the body. Men were forced to wear their hair long all over the head, in opposition to the Qing requirement of a shaven scalp in front and a long queue in back, and women were required to avoid foot-binding and unbind their feet if already bound (incurring excruciating and permanent pain); Taiping adherents or captives who were tempted to surrender to the authorities were given pause by the widely circulated reports of the brutal and summary beheadings of individuals who showed the physical signs of subordination to the Heavenly Kingdom of Great Peace.

The provincial armies stopped the Taipings at the Yangtze in 1853, and during the middle 1850s they struggled to keep the forces of the astonishingly capable Taiping generals Shi Dakai, Li Xiucheng and Chen Yucheng out of Anhui. They were joined in these campaigns during the middle 1850s by the innovative composite armies of the Northern (*jiangbei*) and Southern (*jiangnan*) Grand Battalions (*daying*), composed of volunteer Banner cavalrymen, seconded units of the Green Standard armies, recruited mercenaries, civil officials who acted as quartermasters, and the local militia. Li Xiucheng and Shi Dakai, when engaging the Qing forces at the Yangtze in the middle 1850s, had commanded forces totally 700,000 or 800,000. Zeng's Hunan Army alone had 120,000 men in it by the late 1850s. By 1858 Li Hongzhang, an aide to the Manchu governor of Anhui, left his post to follow Zeng's example, forming his own army of Anhui mercenaries (Huaijun). Zeng's organization of "tent government" (*mufu*) – a mobile office, with personal secretaries, household servants, military aids and regular attendance by high-ranking officers – became replicated in the new armies of Li and others. Within months Li's army approached the size of Zeng's Hunan army in size, and each of the Grand Battalions numbered almost 500,000. Among the Taiping commanders, Shi Dakai understood the importance of destroying the Grand Battalions and retaking control of the Yangtze, but the Taiping generals never succeeded in coordinating a total campaign. For the remainder of the war the Grand Battalions remained seriously challenged (especially south of the Yangtze) by the Taipings, but never broken. On their southeast, the Taipings never succeeded in pushing all the way to Shanghai. In 1853–4, when the Small Swords seized Shanghai and declared solidarity with the Taipings, Hong Xiuquan's government did not respond with enthusiasm, and Hong Ren'gan failed to make himself credible to the Small Swords as a Taiping emissary. Within months the Small Swords were eradicated by the mixed local and foreign mercenary force hired by Shanghai merchants.

British officials sent Thomas Taylor Meadows, who was fluent in Chinese, to the Nanjing to give an assessment of the Taipings. There he encountered, along with the Taiping officials who greeted him, the Englishman August Lindley, who with his wife Mary had joined the Taiping military forces; Lindley himself became a naval advisor and may have been instrumental in defeats of Zeng Guofan's forces, while Mary was a sniper. Meadows was sanguine, mostly because he thought the Taipings were doing remarkably well at guiding the population toward a sinless life, and he reported in some depth on humane Taiping treatment of prisoners, the wounded, and the displaced. In the poverty-plagued countryside, the Taiping policy of seizing private property and distributing it to the poor appeared to Meadows as a demonstrable aspect of the Taiping appeal to a population desperate to escape Qing demands for tax payments and obligatory labor (*corvée*). He was uneasy mainly about the Taiping conviction that the Heavenly King, and perhaps others among the Taiping rulers, could receive divine messages. British officials reading the reports thought that Meadows might have been swept away by Christian sympathy and imaginary solidarity with the rebels, and decided to wait as long as possible before making any decision about aiding or opposing the Qing state in its struggle against the Taipings. But if the Taipings were some day to rule all of China, the British thought, as of 1854, that they could both defend themselves against it and possibly enter into productive relations with it.

At the Taiping capital in Nanjing, 1856 was a critical year. The longevity, and perhaps much of the appeal, of the Taiping rebellion rested not with Hong Xiuquan but with his followers, particularly the generals Shi Dakai and Li Xiucheng. Both were genuinely popular figures. They were visibly concerned to limit casualties among the farmers during their battles and their supply forays, and they took measures to look after the needs of the wounded, sick and homeless. Perhaps more important to their appeal was the fact that they were not evidently mad. Hong Xiuquan had always shown qualities that believers found visionary and skeptics found best explained by serious, if episodic, mental illness. In Nanjing, Hong Xiuquan was not frequently seen in public, but news of his fits and visions spread widely, as did rumors (never substantiated) that he was addicted to opium. Daily affairs of the kingdom were administered by Yang Xiuqing (King of the East). By 1856 Yang was clearly attempting to displace Hong, partly by evincing his own visions and messages. As removed from daily affairs as Hong appeared to be, he was aware enough of the drifting political situation to have Yang assassinated in 1856. Shi Dakai, who had intended to help arrest Yang, criticized the assassin for the excessive bloodshed in Yang's murder, after which Shi's family was murdered and Shi himself narrowly escaped. Before long Hong became suspicious of Yang's successor, and had had him killed as well. Thereafter, Hong Xiuquan relied on his brothers Hong Renfa and Hong Renda to conduct the affairs of state. By the end of 1856, the kingdom's leading administrative talents had been eliminated, and Hong seemed to spend most of his time waiting in his palace for news from the battle fronts in Zhejiang, Fujian and Jiangxi. Shi Dakai undertook administrative duties briefly, but soon realized that it was impossible to avoid the suspicion of Hong Xiuquan and its fatal consequences.

Though Hong Xiuquan himself appeared indifferent to foreign issues, others of his followers, and particularly Hong Ren'gan, argued in the early 1860s that recognition of the Heavenly Kingdom would provide not only possible material aid (or at least prevent the supply of such aid to the Qing), but would establish the Taiping government as a legitimate source of law, military deployment and revenue collection. He was supported in this view by letters sent secretly to the Taiping capital by the extraordinary Wang Tao (see chapter 10), who had been working with English-speaking missionaries since 1848. Wang suggested ways of defeating Zeng Guofan and predicted that Britain and the USA would join the Taipings to defeat the Qing. But foreign merchants, especially those based in Shanghai and suffering repeated threats of Taiping invasion, were unimpressed by favorable reports raising hopes of a new Taiping national state in China. They saw the Taiping disruption of trade on the Yangtze together with the Taiping hatred of commerce and usury (Taiping subjects suspected of smuggling or facilitating commerce were executed) as evidence that the Qing, whatever their faults, were far more attractive as the rulers of China than the Taipings would be. Before the outbreak of the Arrow War in 1856 (see chapter 5), British policy makers discussed the possibility that the division of the country between the Qing and the Taipings might pertain indefinitely. Only the end of the Arrow War in 1858 followed by the Treaties of Tientsin changed the perspective of the British, who were now firm partners with the Qing. The USA, however, appeared to Hong Ren'gan as a possible ally, and in many ways a kindred nation to Taiping China.

During these years the late 1850s Hong Ren'gan was still trying to get to Nanjing. When the Taiping rebellion had broken out in 1850 Ren'gan had been in Canton and had been unable to break through the imperial cordon to join his fellow believers in Guangxi. Soon he was himself a fugitive from officials in Canton, and fled to Hongkong and the protection of British rule. There he studied Christianity, giving the missionary Theodore Hamberg a recitation of the beliefs of the Taipings that became part of a standard source for study of the religion and the rebellion. In 1854 Ren'gan went to Shanghai during the Small Sword Rebellion, but quickly returned to Hongkong when he could not persuade the Small Sword leaders of the authenticity of his relationship to Hong Xiuquan. In Hongkong, Ren'gan connected again with the Baptist community, who in 1858 donated funds to allow him to get to Nanjing, where he arrived in April of 1859. Ren'gan was made prime minister and began to attempt the reform and revival of the government. But the deep political divisions at the capital made Ren'gan's goals impossible to achieve. His sudden arrival and appointment as prime minister aroused the resentment of the generals, foremost Li Xiucheng. To create a political base for himself, Ren'gan promoted many, perhaps nearly three thousand, minor officials to the high rank of "king" (*wang*), which by default caused bureaucratic appointments to become his overriding preoccupation. He produced a written plan for reform that in its basic outlines resembled the ideas that he and Yung Wing had discussed. It proposed a two-pronged approach to restoring the kingdom's fortunes. First, there should be a rapprochement with the Chinese gentry through an accommodation of traditional ancestor worship and permitting classically-trained scholars to become Taiping officials. Second, the Taipings should actively seek a partnership with the Christian nations, inviting foreign capital and advisors to create a road system, a banking system, new mining industries and special measures for the export of Taiping agricultural products. Hong Xiuquan summarily rejected all of his cousin's proposals.

Ren'gan put hope in the arrival of Issachar Roberts in 1861. Roberts was, after all, a proximate inspiration for the entire movement. His preaching style, his open air revivals, the organization of his own church in Canton and many of his own religious pamphlets had been the model on which the Taipings had based much of their ritual, practice, social organization and religious ideology. In the early years of the Taiping push toward the Yangtze, Roberts had tried to leave Canton to travel to the Taiping encampments. He had not received permission for this from the British colonial authorities, who would have been responsible for protecting him, and when he ignored their commands and set out for Nanjing anyway, Qing forces blocked him at the Yangtze and sent him back to Shanghai. In the middle 1850s, Roberts' wife became ill and the family returned to the USA for a time, where Roberts attempted to sell publications describing the ideas and the history of the Taipings. But Roberts was back in China less than two years later, still determined to get to Nanjing.

In 1860 the Taiping forces lost ground in the west but gained in the east, moving closer to Shanghai. Li Xiucheng sent an invitation to Roberts to meet him in Suzhou, close to Shanghai. Taiping guards conducted Roberts to Nanjing, where he became the guest of Hong Ren'gan. Problems began immediately. When Roberts was finally reunited with Hong Xiuquan, he broke Taiping etiquette by sternly refusing to kneel before the Heavenly King. In conversation afterward, Hong attempted to convert Roberts to Taipingism, proposed making him a "king" and offered him three wives. Roberts refused everything, but did agree to stay on in Nanjing for a time to help Hong Ren'gan establish relations with foreign powers. Roberts found much to approve of in Taiping belief and practice. The Taipings worshipped on Sunday, observed rules close to the ten commandments and forbade opium use. But Roberts continually demanded that Hong Xiuquan defend the apparent tenets of the Taiping religion: That certain Taiping leaders had healing gifts, that the Taiping religious leaders collectively were a holy "quarternity," that Hong Xiuquan was a literal son of God, that the Taiping project was to establish heaven on earth. Roberts thought briefly of importing his own army of missionaries from Shanghai to convert the Taipings to Christianity. But by then the Taipings themselves felt that Roberts had exhausted their hospitality. Roberts fled for his own safety in January of 1862. After returning to Shanghai, his assessment of his former pupil was ferocious: "Hong [Xiuquan] was a crazy man, entirely unfit to rule ... He is violent in his temper, and lets his wrath fall heavily upon his people ... ordering such instantly murdered without judge or jury."

Shi Dakai's impressions may have been much the same. When he joined the Taipings, Shi had been one of the youngest and most earnest followers, and he had risen rapidly to the highest ranks due to his military and administrative talents. He was, however, a critic of the harshest measures of the Taiping troops and of the murderous turn at the top of Taiping politics. In 1862 he arrived at the conclusion that the Taiping religion could not survive the eccentricities of Hong Xiuquan's behavior and the strategic error of remaining in Nanjing. He attempted to lead his troops westward into Sichuan, toward a frontier where he thought he could find a new sphere for propagation of Taiping beliefs. He corresponded several times with Zeng Guofan, professing his admiration for the governor-general and entreating him to abandon the Qing cause. In 1863, Shi and his forces were surrounded by local militia in Sichuan and their supplies cut off, Shi thought that if they all surrendered to the Qing their lives would be spared. He ordered his followers to capitulate, but he himself was arrested, given a very brief arraignment and summarily executed. The verdict on Shi among Chinese historians and partisans of the Taiping in the century and a half since his death has hardly been more kind; he has been condemned as a traitor to the Taipings, and perhaps the cause of their downfall.

The Shanghai defense force under the command of Frederick Townsend Ward continued to grow as the Taipings continued periodically to threaten Shanghai. After the war against Britain and France was concluded with the Treaty of Peking in 1860, Ward's private army was recruited by Li Hongzhang to join the imperial side as the "Ever Victorious Army" (*Changsheng jun*); Commanded by Ward and Li Hengsong, the EVA was deployed at various points in the eastern Yangtze delta. In 1862 Ward was killed in battle in Zhejiang province. He was briefly succeeded by Henry Burgevine, and in 1863 the British adventurer Charles Gordon assumed command of the EVA. Together with the weaponry brought by the tens of thousands of French and British soldiers in order to fight the Taipings after 1860, the EVA contributed to dramatic changes in the technological base of the Taiping War. Rifles, revolvers, grenades, wheel-mounted machine guns and trench defense-works were rapidly disseminated to segments of the imperial forces; the same weapons were quickly captured by and the techniques learned by the Taipings. Partly as a consequence of the participation by foreign soldiers and mercenaries, the last four years of the Taiping War more deadly than the ten years preceding.

Following Shi Dakai's death in 1863, there were massive defections of Taiping military leaders to the Qing forces. Within months, only Li Xiucheng remained of the great military talents who had given the Taiping movement its successes. Li assumed the role of the last lion of the Taiping rebel kingdom. During 1861 his military tactics forestalled Qing and international attempts to crash the Taiping lines in Anhui, Zhejiang and Jiangsu, but in 1862 the imperial forces permanently regained control of the strategically critical city of Anqing, Anhui. Li Xiucheng turned his attention to Shanghai, attempting several times to take the city in 1862. He was repulsed by the Eva Victorious Army (though Ward was killed), but he defeated Li Hongzhang's armies several times in the city. At length Li Xiucheng responded to the repeated orders of Hong Xiuquan to return to Nanjing, which was under assault by armies led by Zeng Guofan's younger brother. Li Xiucheng forced the imperial armies to lift the siege of Nanjing and chased them across the Yangtze. He realized that the Taipings could not hold Hangzhou and other cities of the Yangtze delta, and recommended to Hong Xiuquan that the Taiping leaders and as many followers as possible leave Nanjing and return to the relative safety of their original base in Guangxi. Hong refused and, as Li feared, the imperial forces gradually ate away at the Taiping holdings on all sides of Nanjing.

When Li Xiucheng returned to Nanjing in 1864, it was clear that the end of the Heavenly Kingdom was in sight. The population was starving by this time, partly because Hong Xiuquan had refused to provision the city as the imperial troops advanced. In June Hong committed suicide, declaring his 9-year-old son as successor and Hong Ren'gan as regent. The imperial troops broke into the city at the end of the month. The mass of people fled into the countryside, while hundreds of Taiping officials drowned, poisoned or hanged themselves. Imperial forces swept through the government compound and found Hong's corpse wrapped in yellow silk, placed in a culvert. The jade seal of the Heavenly King (the one Hong had brandished outside the city walls of Changsha) was delivered to Zeng Guofan, who later presented it to the Qing court. Li Xiucheng, with Hong Xiuquan's heir, Hong Ren'gan and with what was left of the Taiping treasure hoard, attempted to escape. Outside the city walls the group dispersed. Li ended up on foot in a local village and when the villagers began to quarrel over distribution of the Taiping treasures he carried, local officials investigated and discovered him in hiding. He was eventually taken to Zeng Guofan, who had arrived in Nanjing. Zeng demanded that Li write an account of the Taiping movement and his role in it, a document that is today an essential source for the study of Taiping history. When Li had completed it, Zeng deleted more than a quarter of it, then had Li executed. Hong Ren'gan and the young Heavenly King made it to Jiangxi, but were run to ground in the highlands. Hong Ren'gan was identified through a legal inquiry and executed in November of 1864. Remnants of Hong's party continued to fight the Qing and actually held the town of Jiaying, in Guangdong province, until 1866. Most were killed when the town finally fell to imperial troops, but some escaped to the borderlands between China and Annam, and their descendants remembered their history into the twentieth century.

The Taiping War was the most destructive war in human history to that time, and in the twentieth century only the Second World War appears to have surpassed it. It may also have been the most significant war of the war-torn nineteenth century. The economic heartland of the Qing empire was destroyed. Farmers had fled the Taiping advance, then fled the advance of imperial troops and what was once productive acreage lay uncultivated and unirrigated. The cities of Nanjing and Hangzhou had been scenes of slaughter and starvation, and whole neighborhoods had been leveled by cannon fire or disassembled by desperate residents seeking fuel. With agricultural productivity impeded, hundreds of thousands of refugees smothered Shanghai. International relief organizations attempted to provide food and shelter, and Zeng Guofan instructed his own troops to make protection and pacification of the refugees a high priority. It would be decades before any kind of definitive assessment of the damage done in the war could be approached. In all it appeared that a minimum of 20 million had perished from the primary or secondary effects of war, and the figure might have been twice as high as that. With critical sectors of agriculture inoperable, an unprecedented number of refugees and migrants, as well as the destruction of academies, government offices, libraries, orphanages, market places and millions of private homes throughout Zhejiang, Jiangsu, Fujian, Anhui, Hunan and Guangdong, the challenges of the reconstruction appeared overwhelming. In some ways the difficulties of Zhejiang were the most daunting. During the last four years of the war the conquests and re-conquests in the province had been intense. The city of Hangzhou had more than doubled in size with refugees, who had been reduced to eating leather and wood, and possibly the bodies of the dead, during the bleakest months of Taiping attempts to wait out the imperial forces. Towns in the Zhejiang countryside reported peddlers selling cups of blood to the starving.

The central government could do little to improve affairs in the Yangtze delta, or much of southern China. During 1861 the court had been seized by another succession crisis. The Xianfeng emperor died in 1861, after suffering debilitating depression and withdrawal for over a year. During that time, the Manchu official Sushun (a member of the imperial lineage) had undertaken most of the administrative tasks, and at the emperor's death Sushun and two relatives assumed the roles of regents for the new Tongzhi emperor, Zaichun, then aged 5. However, Zaichun's mother, Xiaoqin, and the empress dowager Xiaozhen banded together with the emperor's uncles Yixin (Prince Gong) and Yihuan (Prince Chun) to depose the regents. They accused Sushun of treason, partly because he allegedly forged the document of succession that created the regency in the first place. He was publicly beheaded and his political allies all purged from government. In the aftermath, the new regents monopolized the power to form and promulgate edicts. They rejected an earlier suggested reign title and chose Tongzhi ("ruling together") in honor of the two empresses – Xiaozhen, the wife of the late Xianfeng emperor, and Xiaoqin, his highest ranking concubine and mother of the present emperor. The young emperor was to spend most of his time with his tutors, including the great scholar Weng Tonghe, and leave the business of government to his regents.

Perhaps the most significant effect of the Taiping War was that suppression of the Taipings and the accession of the regents radically transformed the face and function of government, to such a degree that the Qing imperial government – though not the empire itself – may be said to have been the last casualty of the war. The regents were active in the early 1860s in creating new institutions and reforming a few of the old ones, even as wars continued against the Nian rebels in north China and new wars started against rebels in the southwest and in Xinjiang. Yixin and a group around him created the Zongli Yamen (Foreign Office) and the Foreign Language College (*Tongwen guan*) attached to it. They worked to cultivate communications with the new ambassadors sent from Russia, Japan, Britain, France and the United States. Beyond that, the regents were primarily concerned with the distribution of funds collected through taxation of those portions of the country where agriculture and trade were still viable, and through still healthy income from the treaty ports. Demands on the funds, in the 1860s and early 1870s, were overwhelming. The court's small grants for modernization of the military, development of shipyards and weapons factories and support of the Zongli Yamen competed with more traditional demands to support the Eight Banners, continue the examination system, pay the salaries of officials and provide rewards for the families of the dead and wounded (on the imperial side). There were also the costs of building a political constituency to consider, as the regents attempted to buy loyalty with emoluments. The Tongzhi period was marked by an uneasy suspension of open disagreements between the regents and the civil governors who had gained unprecedented powers during suppression of the Taipings and between all Qing officials and the foreign contacts. However, the deaths of Zeng Guofan and Wenxiang, followed by the death of the young, childless Tongzhi emperor in 1874, allowed for deeper divisions – both between Qing rivals and between Qing officials and the foreign powers.

Many historians have focused on the decade of the 1860s as the fatal period in which Xiaoqin, later to be known as the Empress Dowager Cixi, established herself as the dominant political manipulator at the court, starting or ending subsequent efforts at reform. But the decade of the 1860s actually marked the period in which political and economic initiative swung permanently away from the Qing court. Distinct local bases combining political, economic and military policy emerged at Tianjin in north China, at Shanghai and at Fuzhou in south China. This devolution and regionalization of power profoundly altered the political structure of the late Qing empire, and created the matrix that would control the fortunes of the state that would succeed the Qing. As colorful and as damaging as the manipulations of the Empress Dowager would prove, they are not central to the history of the Qing empire between 1860 and 1912. The continuation of the empire until the abdication of its last emperor in 1912 is nominal. Far more central to the course of history was the logistically necessary emergence of regional power structures. The largest, richest and most influential of them was the so-called Northern (Beiyang) Intendancy. And the post-Taiping civil rulers of the Qing proved to be as visionary as the Taipings had been. Though the Taipings had not succeeded in creating a rebel state within the empire, the process of suppressing them generated a new regional state within the empire that was much more deadly to the imperial court.

The requirement that the court not only allow local forces to take the lead in the fight against the Taipings, but also permit discretion in the organization of financial and military resources, led directly to the assumption of enormous power by Zeng Guofan, Li Hongzhang, Feng Guifen, Zuo Zongtang and other Chinese civilian officials who even a decade before could not have dreamed of occupying the military command center of the empire. Many banner colleagues, from the civil officials Wenxiang and Chonghou to the soldiers Sengge Renchin, Tacibu, Duolunga, Hualianbu and others, worked hard alongside and under the command of these civilians during the war, like Wenxiang, who survived the war and continued to cooperate with Zeng and his fellow officials to deal with problems of reconstruction. Though many provinces became leaders of social and economic reform as well as industrialization, in the decades after the end of the Taiping War, they all operated within a polarized field of authority, with the Beiyang Intendancy at Tianjin becoming the stronger pole, and the Nanyang Intendancy at Fuzhou the weaker.

In 1864 Zeng Guofan outshone all other officials for talent, fortitude, perseverance, integrity and loyalty to the Qing court. He alone, or he and his colleagues, might have simply displaced the Qing and initiated a new state, but the possibility seemed absent from his mental landscape. Zeng consciously modeled himself after the ancient Duke of Zhou, the militarily powerful uncle of the Zhou king, who assiduously protected his nephew as the legitimate ruler instead of overthrowing him. The culture war between the Qing and the Taipings had caused officials such as Zeng to become more archly and more ardently champions of a newly codified "Confucian" order. Revitalization of the traditional hierarchies of father over son, ruler over subject, man over woman, scholar over the unschooled, civil over military, was regarded as critically important in a society beset by chaos, desperation, rootlessness and anger. In reconstruction, Zeng emphasized the rebuilding of libraries and the reprinting of millions of lost books as tasks as central as food, shelter and markets. To him, protection of these hierarchies and the social order to which they were essential had been the entire meaning of the war. At heart Zeng was a scholar and a philosopher, and he couched his arguments for industrialization and scientific education in what passed as a Confucian formulation, a dichotomy between "essence" and "function." The essence was the values that he and his colleagues had struggled to preserve against the Taipings, while the "function" was the technologies of Europe and the USA that would be mastered in order to protect the essence. Like his contemporary Wenxiang, Zeng's interest in foreign learning was frankly limited to its uses for protecting and if possible reviving the power of the empire. During his lifetime his initiatives, many of which were self-consciously progressive, were routinely given the imprimatur of the Tongzhi and later the Guangxu emperors, usually after they had been approved by Xiaoqin. It is impossible to know whether the court could have survived repeated refusals to sign off on Zeng's programs. The occasion did not arise.

Zeng Guofan, Li Hongzhang, Zuo Zongtang and other governors did not disband their armies at the end of the Taiping War, though the matter came under discussion. Zeng's argument was that disbanding the armies would deprive him of the means to keep the peace while society was still in turmoil and distress, while the demobilized soldiers would dramatically increase the numbers of the unemployed and displaced. Of more immediate importance, the end of the Taiping War did not mean the end of the empire's battle against rebels and rebel kingdoms. The Nian cavalries were still active in north China, and in fact gaining ground against Qing infantries when they killed Sengge Renchin in an ambush in 1865. Li Hongzhang and Zuo Zongtang brought in artillery units freed by the defeat of the Taipings in the south, but it took three years for the heavy Qing units, backed by the EVA, to finally break the Nian organizations. Zuo then moved west to Gansu province, where Chinese Muslims (Hui) under the Sufi leadership of Ma Hualong had seized the city of Jinjibao in 1862. Nearby Shaanxi province was also disturbed by conflicts between Muslim groups and local officials. Zuo set up a headquarters for himself at Lanzhou in Gansu province (and a printing office at Xi'an in Shaanxi), and began to impose military government on both Shaanxi and Gansu. Ma's group at Jinjibao was well provisioned and well armed, and managed to resist Zuo's assaults upon their stronghold until 1871, when Ma was captured and executed.

Zuo was now committed to permanent suppression of Muslim rebels and rebel states in the northwest. He transferred a portion of his troops to Xinjiang, which had been an important point of supply and refuge for the rebels in Gansu. Supplies were a continuous source of strain, and Zuo was careful to assure that his soldiers worked to revive or open new farmlands, to avoid encroaching on the delicate supplies of the existing garrison. Zuo tried to break the widespread cultivation of opium, encouraging local farmers to produce staples for his troops instead, and using his printing offices to produce friendly messages for distribution to the locals. His charm offensive, however, was competing with those of both the Russians – who actually brought grain to the hungry region – and Yakub Beg, who had assassinated a hated local despot and established a Muslim capital for himself in Kashgar. Zuo, ignoring advice from Li Hongzhang to direct his energies elsewhere, was determined to root out Yakub's growing state. He amassed a composite army and the necessary supplies, and set out for Kashgar. By 1878 Yakub had been defeated and all of Turkestan was firmly in Zuo's grip. The event began the years of diplomatic debate with Russia that ended in total Qing control of the region and its incorporation into the empire as the province of Xinjiang in 1884.

At the same time that Zuo was engrossed in suppressing unquiet Muslims in Shaanxi, Gansu and Xinjiang, a very different rebel state, also Muslim, was established in Yunnan. The province, and particularly the southern border with Burma, had been dominated by smuggling gangs, secret societies and local militarists for a century. It was culturally complex, settled both by indigenous populations of Miao, Yao, Tibetans and Shan, and by the semi-migrant Muslims of Chinese ancestry, the *pangse* or *haw*, called by British observers the "Panthay". In 1855 Qing officials were attacked by a crowd of the discontented, including not only Muslims but miners disgusted at their brutal working conditions, traders opposed to high taxes and others attracted to the action. Qing hesitation in quelling the disturbance allowed the group to become better organized under the leadership of the Panthay Muslim Du Wenxiu. In less than a year Du assembled a standing army that fought a sustained war against local militia groups. Other Muslims also formed armies that more or less coordinated with Du, and in 1863 one of them assassinated the Qing governor-general of Yunnan and Guizhou. Local militia leader Cen Yuying succeeded in eliminating a portion of the Muslim rebel leaders afterward, but Du Wenxiu himself remained strong and dug in at the city of Dali. Cen was able to consolidate enough militia force under himself that the two armies remained in a virtual standoff for some years. Du announced that his state would be called the *Pingnan guo*, or Kingdom of the Pacified South. Though he was an orthodox Muslim who styled himself a "sultan," Du carefully cultivated a public message (conveyed in preaching and in print) of solidarity with the local Chinese; all should unite, Du exhorted, against the Qing. His overriding vision was of a distinct regional state able to protect local interests against the Qing, against Annam, against Burma, and against both Britain and France.

By the late 1860s the empire was able to redirect more military resources to Yunnan, which it put under the command of Cen Yuying. Du realized by 1871 that his position was dire. He sought and gained recognition from the Ottoman empire, which nevertheless sent him no material aid. He knew that Britain was interested in possible trade arrangements between Burma and Dali, and so he sent a diplomatic mission to London; it made an impression (and has sustained numerous historical footnotes), but yielded no results, because while the group was in London Qing troops overran Dali and Du Wenxiu was captured and beheaded. The Qing militia scoured the countryside, killing a reported million Muslims or other suspected supporters of the Pingnan kingdom, and driving tens of thousands into Burma. Cen Yuying remained a quasi-independent power in Yunnan until the embarrassment of the murder of a British traveler in the area in 1875 (leading to the Chefoo Convention of 1876 and more penalties for the empire).

Overwhelming and continuous pressures of local reconstruction and recovery, as well as large, well-organized, stable local rebel states, created a centrifugal force preventing the Qing court from regaining the initiative, regardless of the talent and determination, or lack of both, it might have manifested. As in the case of suppressing the Taipings, battling Muslims in the northwest and southwest accelerated in the decentralization of military command and resources. A man of marginal qualifications and exclusively local experience such as Cen Yuying could rise to a virtual governorship of a huge province due to the continuing pressures of revolt, while Zuo Zongtang was almost a force unto himself during his campaigns in Shaanxi, Gansu and Xinjiang. At Tianjin, Zeng Guofan either built the facilities to modernize the huge army now under his control, the communications systems and education, or he organized command centers to oversee such programs elsewhere in the territories under the purview of the Beiyang Intendancy. Keeping the regional armies intact meant keeping the distinctive *lijin* tax, through which Zeng collected and dispensed his own revenues according to his own priorities. He ran his own arsenals at Tianjin and Shanghai, where he was able to manufacture his own weapons. Attached to the facility at Tianjin was a new military college. Recruits were sometimes sent abroad to study military history, chemistry, physics and engineering, and increasingly the college was staffed by young men freshly returned from military science programs in France, Britain and the United States.

Since the distributive functions – modest though they were – that had been traditional to the empire were all but destroyed by the Taiping War, the economic foundations of Zeng and others of the provincial governors were by definition local. Provinces whose wealth was exclusively, or nearly so, derived from agriculture might be swamped by the problems of war recovery, as in Jiangxi, Anhui and Jiangsu, or environmental disasters, as in Shandong. But provinces with large coastal trade cities could generate significant revenue for the regional government. Rural Zhejiang, for instance, and many of Zhejiang's cities had been profoundly damaged in the war, but the nearby city of Shanghai continuously generated wealth during the war and after. The transfer of gravity of foreign trade from Canton to Shanghai during the middle and late nineteenth century accounted for much of the income. Despite the privileges supposedly granted the foreign powers in the unequal treaties, many Chinese products continued to dominate the domestic and the international markets. Though textiles was one of Britain's leading exports, British cotton goods never accounted for more than 10 percent of Chinese domestic market at any point in the nineteenth century. Chinese silk continued to nearly monopolize the foreign market, a source of frustration to Japanese industrialists hoping to compete in the silk trade. In the late nineteenth century, industrially-produced foreign yarn began to become significant as an import in China, but the result seems to have been to stimulate the growth of Chinese weaving factories, leaving Chinese-finished goods as the main domestic product and a profitable export. Tea, ceramics, carpets and furniture from China continued to enrich import-export firms in the coastal cities. A new, and newly-legal, export had also become important: Chinese contract laborers to Southeast Asia, the Pacific, and North and South America. During the latter half of the nineteenth century, as many as two million laborers were legally sent abroad to perform work on railroads, mining projects, plantations and docks. The human smuggling that had once been channeled through Hongkong and the southwest borders, beyond the reach of imperial tax collectors, was now legal and taxable. The coastal income base grew rapidly, at the expense of the court. Importation of Chinese contract labor was banned by the USA and Britain in the later nineteenth century, but continued to expand into the Caribbean and Latin America. Modern scholars estimate that the ranks of apparently legal laborers – "coolies" – were at least 25 percent abducted, mixing the illegally-obtained with the legally-induced in an ostensibly legal labor network.

Zeng Guofan nominally oversaw a new arsenal at Jiangnan (the descendant of the machine shop that Yung Wing had suggested to Zeng at Anqing in 1863) in addition to the arsenal at Tianjin, though it was managed by Li Hongzhang and, most directly, Feng Guifen. Zeng's command structures were heavily dominated by men from his home province of Hunan (see chapter 8). Zeng died in 1872, and his closest aide died soon after. Li Hongzhang succeeded to Zeng's position as Beiyang Intendant, and men from Zeng's Hunan group were eventually appointed by the court to governorships, sometimes well outside the conventional domain of the Beiyang Intendancy. After the death of Zeng, his coterie quickly began to show fracture between a centrist group organized around Li Hongzhang, and a dissident group among whom Zuo Zongtang and Zhang Zhidong were prominent.

Like Zeng Guofan, Li Hongzhang was more inclined to collaboration and compromise than to rugged independence. Zeng had found this approach necessary to coordinating the diverse resources and interests needed to defeat the Taipings. He had never enriched himself (in fact he spent his last years fretting over the debts of his family and his inability to cleanse them); and whatever his compromises in practice his advocacy of high ideals of loyalty to civilization never flagged. Li, on the other hand, during his long career from the 1850s to his death in 1901 tended toward an amalgamation of his own financial interests and influence with policies for industrialization and reform that he hoped to generalize throughout the Beiyang Intendancy and ultimately throughout the empire. His personalization of the intendancy and its command structures worsened the parochialism of many of the economic and trade policies, the foreign policy decisions and the military deployments of the late nineteenth century. Normal irritations among the competing local governors were aggravated by Li's preference for his old Huai Army colleagues – from Anhui – over Zeng's Hunan group. Zuo Zongtang and Zhang Zhidong began, as early as the late 1870s, to criticize Li Hongzhang for his reluctance to use military force to forestall foreign encroachment upon Qing territories. Because the Qing had a permanent garrison in Xinjiang, Zuo argued that the empire had a realistic hope of asserting itself there to thwart repeated Muslim attempts to establish zones of political independence, and against the attempts of Russia to pursue its own trade and political goals in Xinjiang. The Yakub Beg rebellion and attendant issues with Russia proved Zuo's point. It was nevertheless true that Li Hongzhang saw Xinjiang – in contrast to Korea – as very far removed from his personal plans for regional political domination and reform. It was also true that Li foresaw the end of an era in which the Qing empire (or China particularly) measured its might in square miles of regional dominance instead of the wealth and power that could be achieved through military industrialization and scientific education. Zuo died in 1885, but in the same year the dispute between Li and Zhang Zhidong became more heated.

In that year Zhang attempted to deploy his ships and marines based at Fuzhou against France, to prevent further colonization of Annam and possible French encroachment upon Taiwan and other parts of the southern coast (see chapter 5). Again, Li saw the fight as outside his personal sphere of interest, and declined to expend the resources of the Beiyang Intendancy to support Zhang. Ten years later Zhang returned the insult when Li's navy needed support against Japan and did not receive it. Li and Zhang were both self-described modernizers and "self-strengtheners," whose personal estrangement fueled rapid development of their bases at Tianjin, Shanghai, Fuzhou and Canton. Both intendancies controlled revenue-generating ports of high-volume foreign trade, which they used for their respective programs of industrial and educational reform. But the empire's territories as a whole remained mired in agricultural stagnation due to the failure to manage effectively recovery from the devastation of the Taiping War; due to environmental distress as a result of failure to properly dredge or embank the new course of the Yellow River; and due to domestic market contraction, in the interior as a result of rutted and blasted roads or ruined docks and warehouses necessary to move agricultural products from one part of the country to the other. Indeed, some regional governors actively worked against reintegrating a national trade network, since the transport taxes on farmers were a heavy burden, and some governors felt that it was better to see grain sold cheaply in local markets rather than see it transported to Beijing or other areas always in need of imported food.

The divisions between Li and Zhang in the 1880s and 1890s were not bounded by geographic lines. Zhang served briefly, but with great distinction, as governor of Shanxi province, on Li's northern Zhili border, and later sponsored intense industrial development in Hankou and Wuchang, on the Yangtze, not far to the east of Li's developing enterprises in Shanghai. They were both also connected to factions at the court in Beijing. The court still retained control over revenues from the coastal trade and internal taxation, and Li and Zhang both lobbied regularly for grants for their separate projects. Weng Tonghe, who became overseer of the imperial treasury in 1886, disliked Zhang, apparently because he originated from Zhili, in the north, and Weng favored officials originating, like himself and Li Hongzhang, from the Yangtze region and the south. Zhang, however, had persuaded the imperial princes of the value of his specific plans for modernization of the navies and shipyards, and the princes prevented Weng from strangling Zhang's portion of the budget.

The Li and Zhang rivalry also seems to been reflected in divisions arising among the Guangxu regents. Yihuan died in 1891, but in the decade before his death considered himself champion of the development of an imperial admiralty, with himself as its chief minister. With the approval of Xiaoqin, Yihuan created the new naval department in 1885, following Zhang's defeat by France. Yihuan realized that the failure to coordinate the northern and southern resources under a single command was the source of the defeat, and his hope was to work with both Li Hongzhang and with Zhang Zhidong to build and deploy advanced ships. For a few years things went reasonably well in his hopes to engage both intendants in a national plan. But in the late 1880s his health began to fail, and with it the will and the wits to oppose Xiaoqin. When the empress dowager learned that funds were accumulating for development of a new navy, she demanded in 1891 that Yihuan assign the money to her, for development of a new imperial retreat and opera house at the Haidian Summer Palace (*Yihe dian*). Yihuan, only weeks before his death, agreed and Xiaoqin proceeded to spend the

2.   Two veterans of transformative civil wars met in Tianjin in 1879: Ulysses S. Grant, two years after finishing his presidency, and Li Hongzhang, then "Viceroy" of the Qing empire.

naval funds on kiosks, follies, the opera house, artificial lakes and the infamous marble boat that now stand at this tourist attraction.

The year of Yihuan's death was also the year that the Guangxu emperor attempted to assert personal rule. Though he married a young empress of Xiaoqin's choice in 1889, by 1891 he had put her aside in favor of a consort he preferred. He began to distance himself from the eunuch companions assigned to him by the empress dowager. Xiaoqin, perhaps sensing that she would need greater leverage to keep the emperor under control, made a point of integrating the leadership of the Beiyang Intendancy into her own court faction. Li Hongzhang was the proxy for the emperor and for the empress dowager (who received her own greetings in some correspondence from European capitals) in negotiations with foreign powers; in some foreign venues, such as Korea, the interests of the court and of the intendancy were identical. But the solidarity between the court and the intendancy was a thin veneer over the roiling, and worsening, tensions and rivalries developing in the areas of finance and industry that it attempted to contain. In coming years, only one part of the contrived chimera with the body of the intendancy and the head of the court could survive; the other would atrophy or be amputated.

The weaknesses of the Qing empire after the Opium War inspired visionaries from various quarters to attempt to build their own societies in their localities. In the wreckage resulting from the campaigns of Hong Xiuquan, Yakub Beg, Du Wenxiu and others, new visionaries took their turn. Xiaoqin and Yixin aimed at restoring the glory of the Qing empire. Others hoped to use the shell of the empire to nurture a new society. Zeng Guofan and his contemporaries saw it based on ancient Confucian rectitude backed up with heavy weapons; Yung Wing saw it based on Christianity and machine tools; Li Hongzhang saw a pragmatic and profitable regime, headed by men whose privileges derived from their superior determination, using military force and communications technologies to bend the directionless and defenseless toward a new age in which East Asia would be in the grip of ruthless powers, both local and foreign. By the end of the nineteenth century, the revenues and the political resources of China were being systematically split between the Qing court and the several centers that emerged from the destruction of the Taiping regime. Rebel kingdoms had given way to regionalist governments, only steps short of finding their own language of sovereignty. In ways direct and indirect, all the nineteenth-century experiments in regimes drawing organization, economy and in some cases ideology from local circumstances contributed to similar experiments in the twentieth century, one of them resulting in the creation of the modern Chinese state.

Further reading

I first encountered Yung Wing's proposals to the Taipings in Cheng and Lestz, *The Search for Modern China* (1999); but see additional context and details in Yung, *My Life in China and America* (1909) and Rhoads, "In The Shadow Of Yung Wing" (2005).

On the Taiping War, see: Lindley, *Ti-ping Tien-kwo* (1866); Hail, *Tseng Kuo-fan and the Taiping Rebellion* (1927); Cohen, *China and Christianity* (1963); Teng, "Reverend Issachar Jacox Roberts and the Taiping Rebellion" (1963); Teng, "Hung Jen-kan, Prime Minister of the Taiping Kingdom" (1970–71); Michael, *The Taiping Rebellion* (1971), Teng, *The Taiping Rebellion and the Western Powers* (1971); Jen, *The Taiping Revolutionary Movement* (1973); Curwen, *The Deposition of Li Hsiu-ch'eng* (1977); Withers, "The Heavenly Capital" (1983); Carr, *The Devil Soldier* (1995); Spence, *God's Chinese Son: The Taiping Heavenly Kingdom of Hong Xiuquan* (1996); Schoppa, *Song Full of Tears* (2002); Reilly, *The Taiping Heavenly Kingdom* (2004).

On consolidation of the court clique and the emergence of the provincial governors, see: Feuerwerker, *China's Early Industrialization* (1958); Spector, *Li Hung-chang and the Huai Army* (1964); Folsom, *Friends, Guests and Colleagues* (1968); Liu, "The Confucian as Patriot and Pragmatist" (1970); Kwong, "Imperial Authority in Crisis" (1983); Chu and Liu, eds., *Li Hung-chang and China's Early Modernization* (1994); Guo and He, "Reimagining the Chinese Nation" (1999); McMahon, "The Yuelu Academy" (2005); Platt, *Provincial Patriots* (2007); Li, *A History of the Modern Chinese Army* (2007).

On post-war local recovery efforts, see: Rawlinson, *China's Struggle for Naval Development, 1839–1895* (1967); Feuerwerker, *The Chinese Economy* (1969); Li, *China's Silk Trade* (1981); Esherick and Rankin, eds., *Chinese Local Elites* (1990); Szonyi, "The Illusion of Standardizing the Gods" (1997); McMahon, *The Fall of the God of Money* (2002); Lin, *China Upside Down* (2006); Platt, above; Li, *Fighting Famine in North China* (2007). On emigration in post-war conditions, see: Wang, *The Chinese Overseas* (2002); Parreñas and Siu, *Asian Diasporas* (2007); Beng, Storey and Zimmerman, eds., *Chinese Overseas* (2007); Kuhn, *Chinese Among Others* (2008); McKeown, *Melancholy Order* (2008).

8

Essay
Hunan Takes the Lead

In the nineteenth century, Qing strictures on the development of provincial power (see chapter 2) were weakened by state insolvency, rising local disorders and civil war. The élites of a few provinces rose to national leadership, and in some instances their connections created new platforms for the development and implementation of policies on an empire-wide scale. Hunan province was the preeminent province in the provision of the post-Taiping élite.

Hunan's boundaries generally corresponded to the area of the ancient state of Chu, a culturally distinct state. By imperial times the area of modern Hunan had come to be dominated by Chinese-speaking farmers, and the Miao, Yao, Tujia and other peoples who had earlier lived there were driven south and west toward Guangxi. With the incorporation of the Yangtze River into the central economic patterns of medieval China, Hunan became a critically important agricultural center and its Xiang River became a commercially essential tributary of the Yangtze. Cities along the Xiang became centers of trade and learning, and the province became famous for painting and poetry. In the seventeenth century, Wang Fuzhi was a leading intellectual from Hunan; he rejected the idealistic "neo-Confucian" philosophy of the Song period, arguing that material factors are the determinative forces in historical change. Wang refused to work as an official under the Qing, since he regarded the Manchus as barbaric and a mortal threat to the survival of civilization. His few works that were published and became known to the Qing empire were banned, but local scholars continued to be aware of and to revere his ideas.

Hunan scholars were distinguished in the early nineteenth century for their interest in pressing policy issues. Many were graduates of the Yuelu Academy in the provincial capital of Changsha. The academy had been a scholarly center since the Song period, and was an ancestor of the modern Hunan University. From early times the academy was famous for encouraging an interest in practical issues, and in the 1830s it added scientific studies to its curriculum. The Yuelu scholar Wei Yuan argued, along with the Fujianese scholar Lin Zexu, that the Opium War had demonstrated that the Qing empire should assiduously learn about European weapons, ships and communications in order to defend against further European attacks. The academy continued for the rest of the nineteenth century to encourage its students and graduates to be open-minded with respect to science, technology and political change.

Zeng Guofan, a native of Hunan, came from a family of scholarly dedication but very limited means. He successfully completed the highest level of the examinations in 1838, when he was only 27 years old, and entered several departments of the central bureaucracy, where he gained a reputation for unusual wisdom and great honesty. When the Taipings reached Hunan, Zeng responded to an imperial command to organize a provincial militia, which was called the Xiang Army (after the Xiang River) (see chapter 7). When he became the Northern Intendant and moved his headquarters to Tianjin, Zeng continued to develop the basic patterns of military reform, a more efficient civil bureaucracy, and technological advancement that he had first explored in the Xiang Army. Under Zeng's influence, men from Hunan – many of them former students at Yuelu Academy – became hugely influential in the late Qing period. Zeng's younger brother Zeng Guoquan, Liu Rong, Liu Changyou, Liu Kunyi, Zuo Zongtang, Luo Zenan, Hu Linyi, Guo Songtao and Li Xubin were outstanding military strategists and administrators in the war against the Taipings, and those who survived the war went on to distinguished careers. Zeng Guoquan was governor-general of the provinces of the eastern Yangtze delta (eventually succeeded by Liu Kunyi); Guo Songtao was a governor of Guangdong, Liu Changyou became governor of Guangdong and Guangxi. Zeng also made a point of reviving the works of Wang Fuzhi, as a model of patriotic thinking. Many of the Hunan men, such as Zuo Zongtang, tended toward refusing capitulation to foreign powers in trade and military matters, and taking a hard line with domestic disorders. For this reason among others several historians have attributed to late-nineteenth-century Hunan political leaders an early "sense of nationalism."

At the end of the Qing and into the twentieth century, Hunan men and women continued to be prominent in reform and revolutionary movements, and Yuelu Academy attracted revolutionary leaders such as Liang Qichao as guest lecturers. Chen Baozhen, the governor of Hunan province from 1895 to 1897, put the ideas of self-strengthening and government reform – both of which were strongly advocated by teachers and speakers at the Yuelu Academy – into practice; he became so publicly identified with the reform movement that he was dismissed from his governorship when the Hundred Days movement was suppressed in 1898. Tan Sitong, an intellectual syncretist combining Buddhism and Confucianism, was executed in 1898 for his part in the Hundred Days Reforms (see chapter 10). Cai E and Tang Caichang, both Yuelu students, joined the revolutionary movements after the failure of the Hundred Days Reforms, leading uprisings and organizing underground revolutionary cells, leading to Tang's death in 1901. After the Revolution of 1911/12, Cai helped defeat Yuan Shikai's attempt to make himself emperor, but Cai died shortly afterward of natural causes.

In 1917 Zeng Guofan's great-grandson and great-granddaughter returned to Hunan from study abroad to found the Yifang School for Girls at Changsha; it was not the first school providing modern education for Chinese girls, but it quickly became one of the most prominent. Not long afterward, Mao Zedong, another Hunan native, was on his way to Beijing, where he would eventually help found the Chinese Communist Party. His report on the Autumn Harvest Uprising – a Hunan farmers' movement of 1927 – defined his ideological position in contradiction to the orthodox line promulgated by the Comintern. But until 1966 Mao would be in intermittent rivalry with another Changsha native, Liu Shaoqi, for control of the party and the government. Hunan's contrarian tradition continued into the twenty-first century with native son Zhu Rongji, who adhered to the Zhou Enlai/Deng Xiaoping line of pragmatism and reform before his retirement in 2003.

Further reading

See Zeng Baosun, *Confucian Feminist* (2002); Schoppa, *Song Full of Tears* (2002); McMahon, "The Yuelu Academy and Hunan's Nineteenth-Century Turn Toward Statecraft" (2005); Platt, *Provincial Patriots* (2007).

9
Essay
Water

WATER MANAGEMENT HAS been a concern of governments in China since the earliest times. Inhibiting floods and making sure that irrigation systems were fed was critical, and use of waterways to transport goods was essential to the economy in early modern and modern times. Floods, water shortages and the condition of the Grand Canal were the primary concerns before the twentieth century. Since then, pollution, soil salinity and the effects of diversion have been added to water concerns. Modern analysts of China's water situation consider problems of supply and quality to be among the most severe of the many environmental problems that the country faces.

China's major rivers – the Yellow River and the Yangtze – both originate on or on the shoulders of the Tibetan Plateau (as do the Mekong, Irawaddy, Salween, Brahmaputra and Indus Rivers). This is one of many reasons why control of Tibet is regarded by the modern Chinese government as a strategic necessity. Modern technology allows even very large rivers to be diverted or dammed to produce electricity or drinking water reserves. The PRC is considering damming the Brahmaputra (in China known by its Tibetan name, the Yarlung Zangbo) for such purposes, which would deprive much of northern India of a main water supply.

The Yellow River runs through the famous loess soil of north China, a loose, light soil that is vulnerable to erosion. For millennia residents of the Yellow River basin have banked the river and its tributaries to keep the flow of the waters swift enough to wash the sediment out to sea. But deposits of the sediment at the mouth of the river have impeded the flow. The river has been dredged to pull the sediment mechanically toward the sea. Banking and dredging have raised the river bed high above its natural depth, so that over time the risk of flood increases. Since 1800, the river has changed its course in a major way three times. In 1855, after decades of neglect, the river abandoned its southern course and flowed north, into the Gulf of Bohai. In 1938, Chinese armies bombed the river's levees in an attempt to impede the advance of Japanese invaders; the river turned south again, this time flowing in multiple streams toward the Yangtze. In 1947 the levee was rebuilt, and the Yellow River flowed north again, as it does today, through northern Shandong to the Gulf of Bohai. Each change of the river course has resulted in high death tolls from flooding, as well as droughts for areas deprived of the river's water. In addition, the Grand Canal was usually disrupted when the river flooded some locks and emptied others.

Chinese migrations from northern China southward during the centuries between 200 BCE and about 1200 CE brought the Yangtze River to the center of subsequent economic development. It is China's longest river, which has inspired its normal name in modern Chinese (Chang Jiang). Unlike the Yellow River, the Yangtze runs through mountainous terrain, and is richly reinforced by lakes along its course. Its depths would have permitted navigation further westward than the Yellow River, but the Yangtze is narrow at some points and tumultuous. Before the nineteenth century the pace of the river and its many tributaries allowed mills and foundries in the Yangtze basin to be powered by waterwheels or escapements. Its full commercial exploitation was rapidly advanced in the nineteenth century by foreign steamships, which were more suitable for countering the currents and steering around the river's obstacles than traditional boats had been.

The upper (western) reaches of the Yangtze have seen very steep increases in population during the twentieth century – partly due to westward migration during World War II, partly due to the improvements in travel and communications technology, and partly due to the agricultural and commercial development of China's southwest region. The vicinity of Chongqing is today the world's densest region of urban development, with almost 32 million people. Beginning with Sun Yatsen, China's leaders have planned to dam the Yangtze in the vicinity of the Three Gorges (formerly a very famous scenic spot near Yichang in Hubei province) in order to provide water and

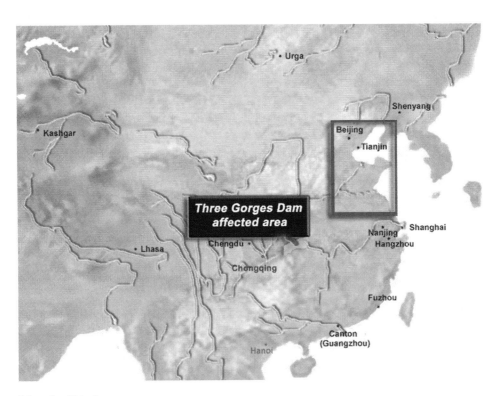

Map 6   China's waterways

electricity for the Chongqing region. This long-term strategy was realized only in 2006, when construction of the dam was completed (the world's largest hydro-electric dam, and one of the largest public works projects in history). The total cost of the project was just under US$40 billion and something over 1.25 million residents were displaced to make way for the catchment; more will be relocated in future to assure the safety of the region.

PRC officials hope that the dam will improve flood and drought prevention in southwest China. The new source of hydro-electric energy is expected to lessen the need for mining, which should in turn slow deforestation, water pollution, air pollution and greenhouse gas emissions. But like all huge dams, the Three Gorges dam poses the possibility of making extinct several species of birds and fish; it may produce silting of the Yangtze River (primarily through reduction of water flow), and will certainly raise the salinity of the soil in the region, interfering with agriculture. A failure of the dam would bring unprecedented catastrophe. In addition, the practice of water diversion – which the Three Gorges Dam and its nearby companion, the Gezhouba Dam, represent on a gigantic scale – has now threatened many of China's most important rivers. Nevertheless diversion is a necessity in a country where water is very unevenly distributed. The northern PRC has about a third of the nation's population, but well under one tenth of the surface water. As desertification in northern Asia generally is affecting these areas, available water is disappearing. For irrigation, drinking water and energy generation, local governments have been permitted to drain off the greater volume of many rivers. Some substantial rivers have already run dry (or are dry for certain seasons), and environmental analysts fear that the Yellow River itself may in danger of depletion. In combination with pollution which has ruined many sources of drinking water, these practices threaten to catalyze a water crisis in China of a scale and severity that would be unique in the world. In contemporary times as in the past, China's well-being depends upon acute management of its delicate waterways.

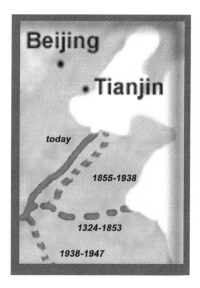

Map 7 The changing Yellow River

Further reading

See Chetham, *Before the Deluge:* (2002); Xu, "Growth of the Yellow River Delta over the Past 800 Years" (2003); Economy, *The River Runs Black* (2005); Li, *Fighting Famine in North China* (2007); Pomeranz, "The Great Himalayan Watershed" (2009).

10
Beiyang Ascendancy

CHINESE TRADITION CLAIMED that the ghosts of men who had been eaten by tigers were doomed to forever call out to fresh men, luring them into the forest for the tigers to eat. In the last years of the nineteenth century, activists opposing Chinese indebtedness to foreign firms and foreign governments applied the term "a man eaten by tigers" to Li Hongzhang. The Beiyang Intendant, now called by foreign observers the "Viceroy," advocated incurring foreign debts in order to build railroads, arsenals and communications enterprises. But a rising movement, made up variously of Chinese and overseas Chinese merchants, students of all ages, journalists, workers and farmers, opposed the position of Li and other governors. They argued, instead, that Chinese companies should finance the new enterprises, and that foreign industries – foremost the railroads – already owned wholly or in part by European, American or Japanese investors should be made legally the property of the Qing government. Li died in 1901, and his successors in the Beiyang Intendancy and its related governorships would have to continue the campaign to keep the Chinese public from controlling the development agenda of and garnering any profits from the railroads. The conflict between public control and imperial survival deepened and widened between 1898 and 1912. It gathered into itself related issues of foreign encroachment, public participation in political discussion, public education and public expression. After 1911, the sudden absence of the state atop what were now very large local and regional organizations with complex functions, dominated but not legitimately controlled by the remnants of the Beiyang Intendancy, plunged China into decades of political turmoil, while its neighbors in Mongolia, Xinjiang and Tibet enjoyed some fleeting autonomy. The path toward reconstructing a state to unify the furthering parts of the country would be long, culturally transforming and often very bloody.

News of the provisions of the Treaty of Shimonoseki, and of Li Hongzhang being shot by a Japanese fanatic on his way to sign the final accords, traveled quickly through the cities of China. The unprecedented speed with which information and opinion now flooded the cities, particularly the treaty ports, was due primarily to newspapers, journals and the development of public speaking venues. Newspapers seem to have first appeared in China in 1845, when the *China Mail* began publishing in English in Hongkong. Five years later the predecessor of the *North China Herald* began printing in Shanghai. Other treaty ports followed suit, and by the end of the Taiping War the English-speaking communities on the China coast were normally well and speedily informed of developments. Editorials were a prominent feature in these newspapers, and were a potent force in an environment in which British sentiment regarding China, the Chinese and Chinese development could have severe consequences. By the early 1870s in Shanghai, British editor Ernest Major had set up a publishing house to produce a Chinese-language newspaper, *Shenbao*, with stories and editorials written by both Chinese and foreigners. Soon after the paper starting printing, Xiaoqin sent messengers to arrange with Major to have a court-produced paper, *Jingbao* (Peking Gazette), printed inside each issue of *Shenbao*. Editorials in the newspaper often criticized the views of the court gazette they were published beside. Residents of Shanghai sent both poetry and opinion letters to the editors, and the newspapers became not only influential bur very profitable. The domain of safety for the production of newspapers in both Chinese and in English expanded as the number of treaty ports multiplied, so that by the height of the Railroad Rights Recovery movement in 1909–11, English and Chinese newspapers were being published in treaty ports as widely spaced as Beijing, Tianjin, Shanghai, Hangzhou, Canton, Fuzhou, Changsha, Chengdu and Hankou.

For reasons to be explored below, literacy in China became not only a more widespread phenomenon in late nineteenth-century China but a fundamentally different phenomenon. In the eighteenth century, literacy was primarily reserved for scholars, bureaucrats and writers (the latter including women of some wealthy families) who could read the philosophical classics, histories and medieval poetry, and write elegantly in the formal language. Estimates of this kind of skill in China before 1800 have never ranged much higher than 1 or 2 percent. Merchants had always had the ability to handle practical correspondence, bookkeeping and infrequent ritual confrontations with local officials. This style of literacy much more resembles the kind of increasing knowledge of the Chinese printed language that became widespread in the cities of China in the later nineteenth century. The roots of the change were filaments of the work of Protestant missionaries (foreign and Chinese), who translated the Bible into vernacular Chinese for purposes of preaching, but also ran schools to educate children and adults to the level of being able to read Bible passages. They were also connected to the spread of internationally-oriented trade in the Chinese cities, in which contracts, memoranda and timetables needed to be shared with a very wide variety of employees,. Popular literacy was reinforced by the increasing availability of popular fiction in the middle nineteenth century. Traditionally performed stories – either as drum songs or as opera – were redacted to print, and romances of martial arts masters righting wrongs over the sweep of Chinese history became very profitable.

The journalist, translator and short story writer Wang Tao was exemplary of the new life possible for literati in the age of rising literacy. As early as 1848 he was familiar with the publishing ventures in Shanghai of the London Missionary Society, and aided them producing a Chinese translation of the New Testament. His English became good enough that he proceeded to translate scientific, engineering and legal texts for popular consumption. When a letter of support he wrote to the Taipings was discovered in 1862 (see chapter 7), he boarded a ship owned by Howqua's firm for

Hongkong and went from there to Britain, where he lived, translated, wrote and lectured until he returned to Hongkong in 1872. He quickly translated into Chinese a work on French history and a military history of the Franco-Prussian War, which became favored reading of Li Hongzhang. At the same time he purchased the printing works of the English missionaries in Hongkong and founded the China General Publishing Company (*Zhonghua yinwu zongju*). In 1874 Wang began to publish a Chinese newspaper, which featured his own editorials calling for China to take up the science, industrial transformation and parliamentary system of Britain. He became a celebrity in Japan, which he first visited in 1879. In 1884, Li Hongzhang promised to smooth all obstacles to get Wang resettled in China. Wang returned to Shanghai that year, founded a new newspaper and remained active in publishing, writing and educating until he died in 1897. He was supremely successful and eerily prescient in his opinions, but he was not unique as a Chinese writer who found fame and fortune in the new niches of publishing and travel that opened up in the Chinese cities of the late nineteenth century. Shanghai's first large printing establishment, Commercial Press (Shangwu), was not established until 1897, but before that smaller, very profitable enterprises in Shanghai, Hangzhou and Canton were churning out newspapers, opinion journals and fiction.

Popular literacy is a phenomenon of mutually reinforcing parts, with a rising range of reading contributing to a rising rate of preparation to read, and vice versa. By the 1890s, the functional literacy rate for China as a whole was probably close to 50 percent for men, and it is possible that one woman in ten knew how to read. Reading incentives and tastes were also influenced by the growing number of private academies, elementary schools and colleges (many of them affiliated in one way or another with Christian missionary activities). Before 1896 these schools were very small in number, but after 1896 the growing passion for inculcating new political ideas in the population at large led to nightly and weekly lecture programs at these institutes, to which farmers and workers were invited. Those with no or weak literacy were in this way alerted to the latest news, usually strongly spiked with the opinion of the speaker delivering it. The result was that the treaty port cities and their hinterlands more or less defined a zone, at the end of the nineteenth century, in which information moved with speed and detail that had never before been possible in China. It is also of critical importance that in parts of each of these cities European and American notions of freedom of speech applied in a general way. Chinese wishing to say and write things that the Qing court did not like were nevertheless able to publish and distribute their views.

News of Japan's demands in the draft Treaty of Shimonoseki was known before the demands were repudiated by the Tripartite Intervention (see chapter 5). Government and popular outrage at its terms began in May, as reports of the final stipulations were confirmed. High-ranking officials, previously trusted by the court, criticized Li Hongzhang for not resisting Japan's extraordinary demands more strenuously. Xiaoqin feared that news of such criticism would quickly leak out and the government would be further discredited; she sent involved officials home and ordered their reports to be destroyed. While the court attempted to put the best face on the treaty, Beijing was flooded with protest gatherings by scholars who were in the city for the 1895 sitting of the capital and palace examinations. These younger scholars, regarded as the acme of Chinese intellect, became personally visible and verbally audible in the denunciation of Japan's aggression and of Li's capitulation. They immediately organized societies (*hui*) which managed the production of manifestos and the coordination of demonstrations. They used the traditional gesture of petition to put their written complaints and suggestions into the hands of palace officials who opened the gates of the Forbidden City enough to step out and receive the scrolls.

The intellectual guide of the student movement in 1895 was Kang Youwei, who successfully passed the examinations that year. Unlike some of his fellows, Kang eschewed angry or threatening rhetoric in favor of urging the Guangxu emperor personally to lead China to a renaissance, perhaps of the sort that Japan seemed to have achieved under its Meiji emperor and his group of advisors and ministers. Kang's ideas of Confucian transformation (see chapter 11) clearly appealed to a very diverse group of disappointed and near despairing young men. Among them was Tan Sitong, a young Hunanese of a slightly mystical bent who was nevertheless attempting to fulfill his father's hope that he would become an imperial bureaucrat, and Liang Qichao, a Cantonese academic prodigy who nevertheless failed the examinations in 1895 for the second time and was looking for a new path not only for China but for himself. Kang's followers dressed in traditional robes and wore queues. All, in 1895, adhered to traditional methods of protest. But their thoughts and their ambitions were transforming them from the inside out.

Liang and Tan both stayed on in Beijing after the fever of the public demonstrations had passed. Kang Youwei returned to his previous work of social reform in Guangdong province. For years he had argued against foot-binding for women, and taught a critical approach to Confucianism that threatened the interests of both established scholars and the purveyors of state rhetoric based on Confucian platitudes. As early as 1888 he was already participating in the growing young literati practice of sending unsolicited reform proposals to the court, in emulation of traditional "impartial opinion," or *qingyi*. He and Liang Qichao worked together in 1891 to publish an extended attack on Confucian orthodoxy, and in the following years they founded a Self-Strengthening Society, publishing their own newspaper and running their own lecture series. After the convergence of the capital examinations and news of the Treaty of Shimonoseki made Beijing the center of national protests in 1895, Kang and his organizations transferred their operations to the capital, where their reputation was already known among thousands of young scholars. When Kang presented his "Ten Thousand Word Petition" to the court in May of 1895, it had the written endorsement of hundreds of these scholars, and thousands gathered to see it carried into the Forbidden City. Qing authorities arrested and detained a number of the demonstrators and pronounced Kang's Self-Strengthening Society illegal. Kang returned to Guangdong, Liang went to Shanghai where there was a branch of the Self-Strengthening Society that the Qing could not interfere with, and Tan Sitong took up a quasi-bureaucratic post at Nanjing, where he remained in contact with Liang and started his own press to print – in collaboration with the Welsh missionary Timothy Richard – Buddhist liturgies, hagiographies and essays. In 1897 Tan became an assistant to the remarkable Chen Baozhen (see chapter 8), governor of Tan's home province of Hunan, who in the mode of Zeng Guofan hoped to make Hunan a model province for modern elementary for boys and girls, technical secondary education and a streamlined government that would promote its own railways, wireless communications, police force, steamship lines and hospitals. Tan started a local reform society, and also an "Academy of Current Affairs" (*Shiwu xuetang*), founded by a graduate of the Yuelu Academy (see chapter 8). Liang Qichao was a favorite guest speaker, frequently delivering fiery denunciations of the Qing court and of the Manchus as a people.

Repercussions of the Treaty of Shimonoseki continued. Germany, following up on its intervention to prevent Japan from acquiring the Lushun peninsula, demanded that the Qing lease Qingdao on the Shandong peninsula to them (the better to keep an eye on Japanese expansion). Britain demanded similar privileges at Weihai, also on the Shandong coast, in 1898, and Germany then demanded that Qingdao be granted to them as a colony. The Qing court gave Russia railway rights in the Northeast in 1896, and Russia forcibly appropriated Port Arthur (Dairen) on the Liaodong peninsula in 1898. Kang, buoyed by deepening discontent of his correspondents and their scholarly reform societies all across the empire, continued to send reform proposals to the court. At length the Guangxu emperor, disgusted at the deteriorating position of the empire's relationship with the foreign powers and eager to shape his own rule, decided to take what steps he could. In 1896 he founded an imperial university, the ancestor of the current Peking University (*Beijing daxue*). It emphasized employment of young scholars, both Chinese and Manchu, who had been to Japan and could come back and lecture on modernization. Now the emperor invited Kang and his colleagues to court. After an interview, the emperor gave Kang an appointment in the Zongli Yamen, and Tan Sitong was given an appointment in the Grand Council (before the Taiping War, the highest-ranking policy body in the Qing empire). Kang Youwei's younger brother, along with a handful of reformist writers and teachers from Sichuan and Fujian, were also appointed to modest bureaucratic berths. At the suggestion of Kang Youwei, the emperor began to issue edicts requiring reforms. Manchu aristocrats were to lose their stipends, the Eight Banners were to be guided into civilian life and the garrisons were to be shut down. A new military in the style of Li Hongzhang's Beiyang Army would be created, as would new military schools. Universities would be founded, emphasizing the study of science and engineering. Agriculture would be reformed, with regulation of rents and labor practices as well as instruction of farmers in new agricultural techniques. An alliance with Britain and Japan (who were forming an alliance with each other) would be concluded for purposes of halting the Russian progress into the Northeast.

In essence the plan was not radical. Its roots reached back to the policy discussions of the Daoguang period, and echoed the armament suggestions of Lin Zexu, the reform plans of Yung Wing and Hong Ren'gan in 1859, and popular opinions such as those of Wang Tao. Nevertheless, it struck directly at the wealth and the status of Xiaoqin and her supporters at court and in the Eight Banner garrisons across the country. In September of 1898 the emperor sent a note to Kang Youwei suggesting that his life was in imminent danger. Kang went to visit Yuan Shikai, the highest-ranking lieutenant of Li Hongzhang in the Beiyang Intendancy, the commander of the Beiyang Army, and the recipient of some honorary ranks in the Guangxu reform plans due to his advocacy of and mastery of modern military matters. Yuan evidently said reassuring things to Kang, but when Kang was gone Yuan went straight to the Manchu general Ronglu, whom Xiaoqin had recently appointed as commander of military forces in the Beijing vicinity. Ronglu consolidated a special unit from his provincial forces and from the Beiyang Army, and proceeded to arrest the emperor and all the reformers. On September 22, Xiaoqin canceled all the reform edicts, and condemned the reform advisors to death. By means still not known, Kang Youwei and Liang Qichao escaped arrest or were released, and rushed to Shanghai, then on to Tokyo, for safety. All the other high-ranking appointees, including Tan Sitong and Kang Youwei's younger brother Kang Kuangren, were beheaded. For good measure, Chen Baozhen was dismissed as governor of Hunan, and died two years later. Yung Wing, who had publicly supported the efforts of the emperor's reform group, was declared a wanted man by the court; he followed Kang Youwei and Liang Qichao to Shanghai, then boarded a steamer for Hongkong where he applied to return to the USA. The Chinese Exclusion Act of 1882 passed by the American Congress made Yung's citizenship of 1852 invalid, but he eventually returned illegally to the USA and lived in obscurity till his death in 1912. The Guangxu emperor remained a virtual prisoner of Xiaoqin for the rest of his life, and was confined for long periods to an island in the middle of the artificial lake that she had constructed at the Haidian Summer Palace.

In suppressing the flow of paper from the emperor and his reformers, Xiaoqin had done nothing to deal with the practical and, now, political problems caused by the unbridled expansion of foreign railroad construction. The lines were managed by foreigners residing in China and guarded by foreign troops. Li Hongzhang and Xiaoqin shared the view that agreeing to foreign demands for railway concessions was better than dealing with the military onslaught that would certainly follow if the demands were rejected. They were aware that the public outcry against the railroads was multifaceted. Scholars and journalists saw the concessions as humiliating, as a diversion of profit away from Chinese entrepreneurs, and as a strategic liability, since railroads were often used for troop transport and conveyed an advantage on whomever controlled them. But farmers and farm laborers were also outraged. Their lands were appropriated for railroad construction and their communities were cut into pieces by the long and unbroken lines. Cart-pullers and donkeys, women going to market or children visiting relatives were killed on the tracks as they tried to follow their customary routes. The noise of the trains was nerve-racking, and it was believed that the crops within a certain distance of the tracks were poisoned. The trains were seen as malevolent giants, doing nothing for the locals and only enriching foreigners who had no right to be there in the first place.

In Shandong, the German missionary presence increased sharply after 1896. The material intrusion of the railroads, churches and schools so resented in other parts of China stung the intensely rural portions of the province. Almost immediately, traditional social organizations, including old believers in the White Lotus folk religion, village mutual aid groups and secret societies were agitated, and the governor reported to Beijing on anti-foreign riots. But officials sent to Beijing to observe and dissolve the rebellion were sympathetic to its anti-foreign rage, and worked with leaders to change the slogans of the rebellion from hatred of the Qing to support of the Qing against the foreign powers. With this orientation, the uprisings continued to spread. The rebels at first called themselves the "Harmonious Fists" (*yihe quan*) – a reference to their origins in martial arts societies – and for this reason foreigners referred to them as the Boxers. They later, perhaps at the suggestion of supportive officials, changed it to the "Harmonious Team" (*yihe tuan*). Because the Boxer movement depended upon traditional and independent social organizations, it was impossible to end it by arresting its leaders. Provincial officials did comparatively little to inhibit the spread of the Boxers. Foreign diplomats and missionaries complained bitterly of this to the court, which made a show of dismissing pro-Boxer officials and sent Yuan Shikai with his Beiyang Army units to Shandong to quash the uprising. Instead it spread toward Beijing, with soldiers sent to fight the Boxers instead joining them in vandalizing railroads, cable lines and foreign institutions. Chinese Christians were attacked and killed.

At court, a debate raged. Yuan Shikai demanded that the court publicly denounce the Boxers and their violence, but many closest to Xiaoqin, including her chief eunuch, thought the Boxers represented righteous public wrath and could be useful in discouraging foreigners from staying in China, or at least from spreading their religion. The Manchu general Ronglu sided with Yuan Shikai, and they attempted to coordinate with other governors of the north to have Beijing surrounded by troops to prevent the Boxers entering the city. But Dong Fuxiang, the governor of Shanxi (and formerly a Muslim rebel until arrested by Zuo Zongtang), broke ranks. His troops killed a junior official in the Japanese embassy and may have opened the city to the Boxers. In April of 1900 the Boxers burst into Beijing. In June the German diplomat Clemens von Ketteler was shot and killed in the streets of the capital. The Qing court blamed the Boxers, foreign diplomats blamed the Qing government (though evidence suggests the assassination was committed by a bannermen, perhaps accidentally). The act set off a panic among foreign residents, and foreign governments quickly began threatening to invade Beijing.

Officials acting for Li Hongzhang immediately commanded regional governors to take responsibility for protecting foreigners in their provinces. In Beijing, imperial officials acted as ostensible intermediaries between the Boxers and the foreigners, who after von Ketteler's death were barricaded in their embassies (many had gathered at the large British embassy, which during the siege was defended by Japanese marines). Foreign troops in China attempted to get to Beijing, but were blocked by Boxers and forced to return to the coast. Only in August did foreign forces, in total about 20,000, reach Beijing. American, British, French, Russian, Japanese, Italian, German and Austro-Hungarian troops arrived and dispersed the Boxers from the embassy quarter. Foreign observers noted that the destruction in the city due to the military occupation was profound. The Japanese stabled their horses in the Temple of Heaven, an ancient landmark. British and American soldiers were ordered to refrain from looting, but others sacked the Forbidden City and the wealthier quarters of the city. Cannon were used to turn neighborhoods to rubble; rape and murder were widely reported. Ronglu had made sure that Xiaoqin was not in the city; with the Guangxu emperor in her custody, she had gone to the interior city of Xi'an in Shaanxi province. Boxers who were not killed outright melted into the countryside, returning to the same secret societies and village organizations that had generated the uprising. With Xiaoqin and her clique departed or discredited, Li Hongzhang, Yuan Shikai and the foreign powers were free to craft an agreement for reparations and reconstruction of the imperial government. Negotiations continued until September of 1901, with Li Hongzhang signing for the Qing government, only two months before his death.

The agreement with Russia, Germany, France, Britain, Japan and the USA was extraordinary. In total, the Qing were to pay 450,000,000 ounces of silver, over 39 years, to these countries (a third went to Russia and a fifth to Germany, with declining fractions to the other signatories, the smallest to the USA). In the background, the USA was anxiously circulating the so-called "Open Door Notes," designed to prevent the seizure of Chinese territory by European powers, or by Japan. Russia, however, had increased its troop strength in the Northeast during the Beijing occupation, and showed no signs of withdrawing; in 1903 Russian railway operations in the Northeast opened for business. The USA used its share of the indemnity to establish an educational fund for Chinese youth visiting the USA (they were still forbidden to immigrate there, however), created a special English academy in Beijing to prepare students for the program and permitted books on science and technology to be reprinted in China without copyright. Conditions were set for Xiaoqin and the emperor to return to Beijing. She was to publicly renounce opposition to government reform and condemn anti-foreignism. She was to begin transforming the empire into a constitutional monarchy. In return, she would not be prosecuted, unlike the ten imperial kinsmen who had been executed for having encouraged the Boxer rampage. Zhang Zhidong and Liu Kunyi, both of whom had been active in protecting foreigners and helping to suppress the rebellion, took the lead in coaching Xiaoqin on how to respond to the foreign demands, and by late 1901 she was issuing decrees, from the wilderness, promising broad reforms. In January of 1902 the imperial entourage returned to Beijing. Once back in the capital, Xiaoqin was extravagantly hospitable to foreigners and their wives, sponsoring fêtes and making public pronouncements on the great benefits the generous foreigners had brought to China. She repeatedly affirmed her wish to introduce a constitution, and in 1905 sent a group of her ministers abroad to Japan, the USA, Germany, Russia, Italy, Britain and France to learn about constitutional and parliamentary government.

After the events of 1898–1901, the stratum of officials and literati oriented toward liberal reform was all but destroyed, and biographies of young men and women of the time demonstrate how liberalism died. Some Chinese and Manchu reformists on the staff of the Imperial University had been arrested and executed by the forces of Ronglu and Dong Fuxiang; others had committed suicide as first the Boxers and then the allied foreign forces had overrun the city. Sympathizers who survived and intended to remain vocal moved toward Shanghai, Hongkong, Tokyo, London and the USA to save their lives. Tang Caichang, one of the few advocates for constitutional monarchy still living in China, attempted a small uprising in Shanghai, but was arrested and executed on the orders of Zhang Zhidong. Those willing to muzzle their opinions were regarded with suspicion by the remaining nationalists (see chapter 11) now tending toward revolutionary passion.

Radicalism and terrorism grew in the vacuum left by liberal reformers and fed off the determination of Qing authorities to suppress nationalism with new severity. Shen Jin, a fellow Hunanese and Hundred Days supporter of Tang Caichang, had fled to Japan in 1898, but returned to support the Boxers; after surviving the suppression of the Boxers, he joined riots against Russian railroads in 1903, and was shortly beaten to death by militia of the Beiyang Intendancy. Zou Rong was the son of a merchant family in Chongqing who was sent to school in Shanghai and Japan. While still a teenager abroad he became convinced that violent overthrow of the Qing government was necessary, and he attempted direct action by attacking a Qing educational attendant in Tokyo. Zou escaped arrest and next surfaced in Shanghai, where he found a publisher for his virulent tract, *The Revolutionary Army* (*Geming jun*), that called for war against the Manchu race, assassination of the Guangxu emperor, repudiation of Zeng Guofan, Li Hongzhang and others who had suppressed the Taipings, and creation of a republic ruled by and for Chinese. In Shanghai, the radical opinion journal *Subao* published a favorable review of *The Revolutionary Army*. The Qing government, then in the glow of the post-Boxer reconciliation with the foreign powers, appealed to the British administration in Shanghai to stop condoning such publications, and demanded that *Subao* writers, as well as Zou Rong, be arrested and tried for treason. The British cooperated and arrested the group, but the beating to death in Beijing of Shen Jin caused the British government to decide to keep the radicals in its own prisons rather than surrender them to the Qing. Zou died in prison in 1905 at the age of 20, becoming a martyr to the revolutionary cause.

At the same time, the Japanese government agreed to curb organizing among radical Chinese students in the country; Zou Rong's friend Chen Tianhua drowned himself in Tokyo in 1905, protesting the turn in Japanese policy. And, in the same year, Wu Yue, a student at a new military academy outside Beijing and a friend of Chen Tianhua, attempted to assassinate the group sent abroad by Xiaoqin to study constitutions; he blew himself up instead, and the grisly photos of his corpse triumphantly displayed by Qing officials created yet another martyr to the cause. Huang Xing, also a friend of Chen Tianhua from Hunan, had already fled to Japan after the collapse of the Hundred Days Reforms and joined revolutionary groups in Tokyo. Within a few years, he had returned to China to organize violent action against the government and its officials. In 1906, outbreaks of violence across the country among armed militia groups or recruits of the New Army units created by governors associated with the Beiyang Intendancy were suppressed with difficulty. Manchu garrison commanders were assassinated by bombers and snipers. Court officials and military authorities were alert to conspiracies and they rounded up military cadets in droves for interrogation, questioning them about their connections to possible conspirators. Few revolutionaries were identified, but alienation and outrage spread through the ranks of the military.

Radical tendencies in the political movements were accelerated by the death of the Guangxu emperor in 1908, which made untenable the arguments of constitutional monarchists such as Liang Qichao, the last survivors of late nineteenth-century liberal reformism. The emperor died barely 24 hours before Xiaoqin herself (and it is now believed that the emperor was poisoned at Xiaoqin's instruction). Elder male members of the imperial lineage selected the child Puyi (a cousin of the late emperor), born in 1906, as the new emperor. His father, the late emperor's wife, and several male members of the imperial lineage, were to serve as regents. Puyi's father, Prince Chun, attempted to take control of the government and particularly its treasury, hoping to curtail the power of the Beiying Intendancy by persuading Yuan Shikai to retire from his official government posts. The Qing government and the Beiyang Intendancy were briefly in a death struggle. But the international movement for constitutional monarchy in China went silent, unable to draw inspiration from the child emperor. From the time that Puyi was put on the throne, the government outside the immediate precincts of the Forbidden City was under the domination of Yuan Shikai and the Beiyang Intendancy. While revolutionary forces directed their words and weapons against the shadow play of the "Qing," Yuan and his lieutenants continued to build a military, bureaucratic and financial order that would be little affected by the tide of revolution.

Though Xiaoqin had continued to give her approval to new legislation until her death in 1908, she never regained control over the government after returning to the capital in 1902. Nor did Yuan Shikai and the Beiyang Intendancy dictate policy. Other governors with armies and industries came to the fore. Zhang Zhidong in particular finally achieved the level of national influence he had been attempting to wrest from Li Hongzhang for decades. Unlike Li, Zhang had actual practical experience with industries. He created the Han Ye Ping iron and steel plants in Hanyang, Hubei, designed the route of the railroad from Beijing to Hankou, and at the time of his death in 1909 he was still struggling to put together foreign financing for a railroad from Hankou to Canton. Zhang's other great preoccupation besides heavy industry was education. In 1904 he had himself placed in charge of a plan for universal education reform, based upon the universal military conscription plan used in Japan; in 1907 Zhang was made head of a Ministry of Education, largely ceremonial due to his advanced age. Other governors also considered themselves free under the post-Boxer terms of government to pursue their favored programs for local reform. Care and reform of opium addicts, education of women, promotion of adult literacy, sending of students abroad (particularly to Japan) to study, maintenance and repair of roads and irrigation systems were high on the list of many of the reform governor's projects. From 1907 to 1911, during the Qing era of "new policies," reform programs empowering governors to pursue social reform and local industrialization were plentiful. They showed the stamp not only of Zhang Zhidong, but of other governors who followed his model, including Sheng Xuanhuai and Zhao Erxun. The traditional examination system was ended in 1905, meaning that the examinations held the previous year, 1904, were the last ever conducted. In 1905 the Zongli Yamen was abolished, a new Foreign Ministry created, and a new central bureau of statistics was initiated.

In the provinces and in some cities, merchant associations were authorized, permitting wealthy industrialists and entrepreneurs to hold public meetings, publish newspapers and sponsor trade schools and overseas study programs. In most localities, the appearance of new, legal organizations inspired the creation of others, so that trade associations were quickly joined by groups advocating social reform. The most expansive plan called for the creation of "assemblies" at the local (1908), provincial (1909) and national (1910) levels. Only the local and provincial assemblies were realized, and not in all provinces. These assemblies had no legislative function, but were grand debating clubs. The government's goal appears to have been to create a venue for airing of opinions and release of political pressure, while at the same time educating the population on the mechanisms of political discourse. However, the gentry who dominated provincial assemblies were increasingly hostile to the Qing court. They not only assembled to discuss local or provincial affairs, but often also ran newspapers and lecture series that hosted fairly radical speech. When the discussion meetings did not turn into a means of influencing law or policy, frustration grew among the politically involved class, and the assemblies became one of many new dimensions from which oppositional organizations could emerge.

While the court (after 1902, very much under the guidance of Zhang Zhidong) and the Beiyang Intendancy were still the most prominent institutional peaks, changes in economy and in society in the late nineteenth century created new fields of interest and activism. Despite the huge devastation of the middle nineteenth-century civil war, rebellions, and foreign invasions, the overall trend in the Chinese economy, especially before and after the Taiping War, was toward growth. The court's ability to tax the proceeds was limited by the artificially low tariffs imposed by the treaties, and its ability to tax domestic trade was limited by the authorization of the *lijin*. Though in theory the *lijin* was only a supplemental tax that produced money for local use without necessarily interfering in central taxation, it in fact provoked smuggling and barter that continued to cut into the court's income from legal trade. By the end of the nineteenth century, many areas touched by the Taiping War had still not been redeveloped. The extent of the damage was so great that the possibilities for reconstruction and growth could not be exhausted in the central and eastern Yangtze delta. Speculators bought land cheaply, large landowners and factory owners found cheap labor, new migrants created markets for basic as well as manufactured goods, and secondary industries of housing, dry goods, banking and transportation flourished. Many rural areas of the interior remained wracked by famine, drought, flood and disorder to the end of the nineteenth century. But most urban areas, and the countryside connected to them by working market systems, were generating and circulating wealth.

British frustration at not finding a profitable export to China was eased in the early twentieth century by focus on a new and addictive product: cigarettes. Europeans had brought tobacco to Asia, from North America, in the sixteenth century, and Qing law had prohibited smoking by commoners and slaves since the empire's earliest history. Nevertheless, by the early nineteenth century, pipe smoking was common among both genders and all ages, and in the eighteenth century the use of snuff – which was not smoking and therefore was legal – was so widespread among the wealthy that the Qianlong emperor collected snuff bottles and imperial factories made a profit on the production of snuff bottles for both domestic and foreign purchase. Lightly-governed areas of China, especially the southwest, grew tobacco and smuggled pipe tobacco to many areas – including Burma, which had banned all smoking in 1729. The foreign treaties of the middle nineteenth century (see chapter 5) had stipulated that tobacco and cigarettes would be among the many products that would be legal to import, but the expense of cigarettes kept the market very small. Near the end of the century, however, new methods of producing cheaper cigarettes lowered the price, and by 1900 foreign cigarettes were being sold in large cities and in small villages. Chinese tobacco farmers had also begun to supply foreign manufacturers, further dropping prices and laying the foundation for the domestic production of cigarettes. In 1902 the leading cigarette producers of Britain and the USA decided to stop competing against each other and to band together to dominate their own and foreign markets.. The new conglomerate, British-American Tobacco Company (BAT) – two-thirds of which was owned by James Buchanan Duke, who endowed Duke University – opened its first formal sale and distribution center in Shanghai in 1903. Its combination of the existing legal import privileges of both its predecessors, its low prices, and the initiation in 1905 of a historic advertising campaign, made BAT one of the first true multinational corporations, and established the dynamics by which Chinese tobacco producers would begin to reap large profits in the early twentieth century.

The development of tobacco from a foreign import to a profitable domestic product followed the general pattern already established by opium. At the time of the legalization of opium in 1858, approximately eight million pounds of opium a year was entering China. But the criminal organizations within China were already figuring out that poppies grew well in Sichuan and Yunnan, where state control was very weak. While importation was legal, domestic distribution remained in a gray area, so merchants involved in the trade were heavily dependent upon organizations already organized for, and skilled at, marginally legal or illegal enterprises. The Tiandihui and its many offshoots rapidly expanded their wealth and influence, not only in seminal trade cities of Shanghai, Canton and Tianjin, but also in the countryside. These producers realized that profits could be amplified by exporting Chinese opium to Southeast Asia. They were able to combine this trade with already existing networks for the export of human beings. Chinese trade firms and criminal syndicates alike linked San Francisco, Vancouver, Honolulu, Hongkong, Macao, Singapore, Penang, Manila and other parts of Southeast Asia into a network that worked well to transport a great variety of commodities: opium, indentured servants and prostitutes, cheap silk and tea.

The man known to later history as "Charlie Soong" was exemplary of the forces reaching from the expanding Chinese economy of the later nineteenth century toward a social transformation in the early twentieth. Soong's real name was Han Jiaozhun, and he was a native of Hainan Island. Six hundred years before his birth the island had been a hub of trade in the Indian Ocean. But in the late Qing period Hainan (still a district administered by Guangdong province) was a political and cultural backwater, dominated by the pirate networks running opium, tobacco, humans and weapons between south China and Southeast Asia, and operating gambling and prostitution rings. Soong began working in commercial shipping, and spent about eight years in the United States being trained as a Christian missionary. In 1886 he returned to China, finding a way both to work as a missionary and to join an anti-Qing secret society. By 1892 Soong was a publisher in Shanghai, starting with Chinese bibles and branching out into more popular fare. In 1894 he encountered young Sun Yatsen (see below), who was then turning toward his revolutionary organizing (which was largely dependent upon the sort of secret societies to which Soong belonged). Later, from Tokyo, Sun recruited Soong in Shanghai as one of his major financial backers of the League of Alliances. The flow from secret societies and Christian proselytizing to legal and illegal trade profits to revolutionary financing involved thousands of merchants besides Charlie Soong, but his family became central to China's political fortunes for decades.

By the beginning of the twentieth century, these economic developments had produced two trends that were critical in the movement to end the Qing empire. First was the accumulation of wealth in the merchant classes, particularly of the coastal cities, that after 1896 was poured into the funding of associations that opposed the Qing government. Second was the increasing importance of the ability to find employment for Chinese laborers and their managers in overseas venues. Any revolutionary would of necessity need to chase money and grow credibility in the USA and Southeast Asia. In sum, by working below the Qing government level in the localities, and outside Qing jurisdiction in the treaty ports and abroad, revolutionaries could gradually surround and strangle the last vestiges of formal Qing rule.

The year 1905 saw not only bolder moves against the Qing by a radical revolutionary fringe, but also the defeat of the Russian armies and navy of the Pacific by Japan, in the Russo-Japanese War. The effects in China were galvanizing. Students and young professionals, including many military officers, who had gone to Japan for education after 1895 felt vindicated in their argument that Meiji Japan – an Asian industrialized

3. This photograph is assumed to have been taken in the USA in 1907, when Kang Youwei made one of several visits to speak on labor immigration and Chinese nationalism. He is shown with his daughter Kang Tongbi, level with him on his right, who was a student at Barnard College.

constitutional monarchy with an aggressive navy – was the model for China to follow in casting off the woes of the past. At the same time, Japan now took Russia's place in the Northeast, including control of the railroads and mines that Russia had developed since 1901. The Qing government acquiesced in creation of the Southern Manchurian Railway Company, which would grow in a short time to be a huge industrial combine with its own army and its own intelligence department. Journalists such as Yan Fu and Wang Tao (see chapter 11) argued to their readers in local merchant associations and the local assemblies that the best way to equalize the relationship between China and the foreign powers was to use the ample wealth of the Chinese urban sector to buy out the foreign hold over industry, commerce, transport and the government itself – and with this new encroachment by Japan the issue became all the more urgent.

   The effectiveness of the idea was vividly demonstrated during the American boycott of 1905. The USA and China had signed a treaty in 1880 that was in essence an affirmation of the Burlingame Treaty of 1868 (see chapter 5), and provided that Chinese who were not explicitly excluded from the USA had the same travel and residence rights in that country as Americans had in China. In 1882, however, the American

Congress passed the Chinese Exclusion Act, regarded by the Qing government as contradictory to the treaty of 1880. In 1904 the treaty of 1880 was up for renewal but was rejected by the Congress, making the Exclusion Act the total and permanent authority on the question. In the Chinese cities, the Act was seen not only as insulting but as a threat to Chinese economic security, since a portion of both urban and working people in south China, particularly, depended for sustenance upon periodic sojourns of male members of their families as contract workers in the USA. Chinese merchants in Shanghai, Nanjing, Hangzhou, Canton and other cities paid for meeting halls, publications, and travel expenses to organize a boycott of all goods and services of American companies. Their tracts argued that Chinese were only seeking jobs in the USA because cheap American imports, protected by the treaty tariffs, had put Chinese laborers out of work. They were careful to denounce violence against Americans, particularly after five missionaries were killed in a riot in Guangdong province. The Qing government was equally cautious, and took a neutral stance, claiming it was unable to suppress the movement, but also not overtly encouraging enmity toward the USA. The American government condemnation of the boycott was strong, including the dispatch of a fleet of warships to Shanghai. The two governments shortly came to terms: The USA would welcome Chinese as visiting students, tourists or lecturers, without permitting them to settle or work, and the American China Development Company would relinquish rights to the Hankou-Canton Railway line.

Organizations – from chambers of commerce and workers' associations to Kang Youwei's "Society for Protection of the Emperor" – behind the boycott continued their activities, raising an anti-Japanese boycott in 1908 after the Japanese government demanded that the Qing apologize for stopping and boarding a Japanese steamer (that was, ironically, smuggling arms into Guangdong province to support anti-Qing insurrections). The integration of popular political action in China with activism among Chinese workers and students abroad (see below) created a new political dynamic that challenged, simultaneously, the Qing government, the Beiyang Intendancy and foreign firms (particularly American or Japanese). The process had also demonstrated the magnitude and the importance of merchants as a political force. While nothing much was done for Chinese laborers who wanted or needed to work in the USA, the activist organizations formed and funded by merchants, gentry, journalists and intellectuals remained in place. Before 1898 many merchant associations had contributed to the sort of associations for the study of constitutional monarchy and social reform that Kang Youwei was noted for. After the suppression of the Hundred Days Reforms in 1898 and the flight of many reformers from the country, merchants in Shanghai, Nanjing, Canton and other areas where the reform groups had been active became sponsors of publications and speakers supporting constitutionalism (in theory, the orthodox position of the Qing court and its supporters). Merchants had the capital to sustain most of the industries, particularly the railways, built and managed by foreigners, but the provisions of the treaties made it impossible for them to dislodge the foreign owners. The treaties became the topic of frequent public denunciation and protest, and merchants as well as intellectuals hoped that a constitution would revive the reputation of the Qing government sufficiently for the foreign powers to negotiate revisions of the treaties. This had been a primary goal of Qing reformers after the Taiping War, and Xiaoqin and other spokesmen for the court frequently suggested that reform of the government would be a step toward achieving it. From the time that Xiaoqin began to make her public statements regarding the creation of a constitution, merchants and local organizers in the provinces started campaigning for acquiring legal ownership, or virtual ownership through management, of foreign-owned railroads in China.

Both Yuan Shikai and Zhang Zhidong were wary of private Chinese ownership of railways and mining, which they thought were of national strategic interest and should be in the control of the state – or, from Yuan's perspective, the Beiyang Intendancy as a proxy for the state. Zhang himself had been keenly interested in the problem, partly because of practical concerns about the development of his iron and steels works near Hankou, and partly because of his understanding of the importance of Chinese ownership of the industrial infrastructure. In 1905 he arranged a deal to purchase the Hankou-Canton line, which had been developed and managed by the American China Development Company since 1902. The financing and the subsequent management scheme bound the provincial government and private shareholders together in a delicate financial partnership. The Qing government was delighted to receive the backing of Chinese merchants in its new industrial enterprises, but Zhang and others worried that crowds agitated by a fervor for Chinese control of industry might become unruly in a way reminiscent of the Boxers. Merchants and political activists in other provinces soon began to attempt their own purchases of existing railroads (or rights to railroads contracted but not built). The necessity to combine government pressure on foreign companies with persuasive investment packages caused some campaigns to falter or fail. In Zhejiang, Jiangsu, Henan and Hubei provinces, landowners and merchants banded together to nurture popular movements for rights recovery. A parallel movement for the recovery of mining and oil drilling rights also arose. New mining companies in Shanxi, Heilongjiang, Hubei and Yunnan competed against British companies to open new sites, and in order to prevent foreign investors buying control they sold shares only to Chinese. The movement became truly popular after 1907, when housewives, students, retired people, farmers and laborers all over China began saving to make their contribution to rights recovery.

The number of heavy industrial enterprises absorbed or generated in the rights recovery movement exceeded the ability of either the merchant investors or the government to provide the money to keep them going at the rate that the public had hoped. Actual completion of the financial arrangements and the industrial building necessary to realize native control was slow. In several instances in Zhejiang and Jiangsu, the British government proved less willing than the American government to give up development rights. In 1908, near the end of Zhang Zhidong's life, the government attempted to move things along by setting up a series of re-grants that would essentially use partial British financing to allow Chinese companies to complete the region's railways. Sheng Xuanhuai, the communications minister who now represented the government in negotiations, was viewed by activists as a traitor for including foreign money in the deal. When resourceful organizers found a way to complete the railway lines without the government loans, a political war developed in which Zhejiang and Jiangsu railway company officers and rights recovery activists attempted to remove Sheng's authority over the projects, and Sheng in turn attempted to have the railway company's officers fired.

In 1910 Sheng succeeded in his goal, which sparked huge public demonstrations and brought the provincial assembly into action. Popular protest over the incidents combined demands for a constitution with demands for private ownership and management of the railroads. In Sichuan province, a similar dispute had arisen over government and private competition for control of the railroads. When a private company attempting to build the railway performed poorly, Qing officials moved to regain control, intending to use foreign loans to revitalize the project. Protests against the loans turned into protests against taxes, for a constitution and against the officials themselves, who in Sichuan were Mongol and Manchu bannermen. The protest turned violent, government soldiers fired on the crowds, and activists fled in all directions. They sought reinforcements, particularly among the militia and the secret societies (most widely represented the Gelao hui, believed to be a descendant of the White Lotus cells), to combat the government forces. Unrest spread through the industrial cities of the Yangtze and south China, and government forces ordered to quell the uprisings were increasingly hampered by desertions among the New Army units, by militia uprisings, and by the intervention of armed, trained secret society members joining the anti-Qing forces. Sun Yatsen's dashing follower Wang Jingwei attempted to assassinate Zaifeng (Prince Chun) in Beijing, but was foiled and jailed. Huang Xing attempted to organize an armed uprising at Canton, but never managed to coordinate among the diverse groups – soldiers, militia, secret societies and students – necessary to bring it off.

Weeks later, in October of 1911, New Army forces rebelled and seized the city of Wuchang, quickly taking Hankou and Yichang as well. They declared a provisional revolutionary nationalist government, with Li Yuanhong (once a protegé of Zhang Zhidong) as president. Word of the uprising spread quickly, and in both urban and rural settings throughout southern China and western China – areas only thinly under the influence of the Beiyang governors – revolts broke out in a chain reaction. Militiamen, officers and recruits of the provincial armies as well as the secret societies primed by years of contact with Sun's League of Alliances seized weapons and ammunition stores and set off in search of government officials. Eight Banner garrison communities were particularly vulnerable, being populated mostly by women, children and the elderly, with active soldiers undertrained and usually unarmed. The search for Manchus in particular began the day of the outbreak at Wuchang, where 800 Manchus of all ages and sexes were quickly killed and the search continued for more. Three weeks later, the largest massacre of Manchus took place at Xi'an, where revolutionary mobs surrounded the garrison for days, starving its inhabitants, then broke into the compound and killed 20,000 people, virtually the entire Manchu population of the city. Documents later collected by the republican government attest a minimum of 50,000 casualties on the revolutionary side, and losses among Manchus and government forces could hardly have been less, suggesting a minimum of 100,000 direct casualties, most of them occurring during October and November of 1911. In December the revolutionaries captured Nanjing and nominated Huang Xing as military dictator. He declined, however, and insisted they send to Sun Yatsen, then on a fund-raising lecture tour in the USA, to accept the post of president of the new republic.

Sun Yatsen's background was something new in Chinese political history. He was not a traditional literatus, like Kang Youwei or Liang Qichao; he was not a militarist like Yuan Shikai; he was not a bandit like the founders of some earlier imperial dynasties. He came from a farming family in Guangdong province. His older brother emigrated to Hawaii as an agricultural laborer, and arranged for Sun to go to Hawaii, while still a boy, to study in the British and American schools there; like Yung Wing, he won an English prize, though when he started school he knew no English at all. Sun converted to Christianity, and in 1883 went to Hongkong and married. He subsequently had two sons and attended medical school. In 1894 he attempted to find a bureaucratic post in the Beiyang Intendancy, by outlining plans for establishing commercial agriculture. He did not receive an appointment, however, and went back to Hawaii, where he and other young Chinese students and professionals formed a political association, the Society for the Revival of China (*Xingzhonghui*). After China's defeat by Japan in 1895, Sun went back to Hongkong with the idea of starting a movement to overthrow the Qing. It was quickly smashed. Sun headed for London, hoping to plead his cause and raise funds among Chinese workers and British sympathizers. Officials in the Qing embassy to London found out he was there and kidnapped him, holding him prisoner in the embassy for almost two weeks while arranging to have him sent to China. But a sympathizer helped him get word to the British authorities, who freed him. The result was an international incident which brought Sun tremendous support, allowing him to stay in Britain for almost a year before he set out for Canada, and later Japan. In Yokohoma and Tokyo, Japanese military agents, who were eager to use movements for nationalism and industrialization in China to promote a dependence upon Japanese advisors and money, greeted Sun warmly, helping him establish a residence and office for himself in Tokyo. From that city, he aided or managed schemes to recruit revolutionaries both within the Beiyang Intendancy and within the secret societies of south China from 1900 to 1905. A few uprisings occurred in the south, but with no result (apart from arrest and execution of leaders when discovered).

In 1905, the anti-American boycott proved to be an international phenomenon, its geographical contours corresponding to the map of Chinese commercial and labor migrations in the late nineteenth century. Kang Youwei was in Los Angeles during the boycott, whence he sent talking points via cable to organizers in Shanghai and Yokohama, where Liang Qichao was leading the organizing. Publicity was an essential element, as the political associations involved initiated their own newspapers, and worked assiduously to convince periodicals in the USA, Europe and the British colonies of India, Burma, Singapore and Hongkong to publish comments or editorials by Kang or Liang. These organizations, born to sustain boycotts, were quickly adapted to become networks for the transmission of information on the employment, treatment and cultural comfort of millions of overseas Chinese. Sun Yatsen was not a leader of this internationally-based Chinese boycott of foreign goods, but he clearly was impressed by the profound possibilities for garnering money, organizational support and potent publicity from the growing web of global Chinese communities. In 1905 he founded, with the financial support of his Japanese sponsors, the League of Alliances) (*Tongmenghui*) in Tokyo and a journal, *People's Gazette* (*Minbao*). From its inception, the League of Alliances provided a unique point of articulation for the diverging and converging movements among journalists, merchants and students. More important, it linked the rising politicization of these worlds to the illegal and sometimes violent societies of south China whom Sun had involved in his attempted uprisings; these included weapons smugglers, whom Sun was able to call upon not only to arm sporadic uprisings in China but also to arm Filipino resistance to American colonialism. In 1907, the Japanese government became uncomfortable with their public association with the rising tide of violence against the Qing government and officials in China, and gave Sun a financial grant to leave Japan and set up operations elsewhere. He first tried to transfer to Hanoi, where the Chinese merchants and their associations were well established, but the French government insisted he move on. Britain would not allow him to make Hongkong his base. He ended up in the USA, on a tourism and lecturing visa, periodically inciting revolts in Guangdong that demonstrated the increasing threat to the Qing but did not succeed in igniting nationwide revolution.

When the large revolutionary outbreak occurred in 1911 and spread to Nanjing, Sun accepted the summons (received by cable in Denver) to become president of the new republic, and arrived in Nanjing within weeks. He and his political advisors realized that their position was untenable. Support from militia and secret societies in south China was very well, but the military governors of the Beiyang Intendancy controlled the north, and nothing much could be done about it. Yuan Shikai personally held the fate of the Qing empire in his hands, and probably that of all China. Yuan would decide whether the Beiyang Intendancy would deal the Qing a death blow. Sun's representatives contacted Yuan, promising him the presidency of a new republic if he would force the abdication of the Qing child emperor. Members of the Qing court, led by Puyi's father Zaifeng, also attempted to enlist Yuan to their side. When they were unsuccessful, they agreed to issue a statement of abdication (largely dictated by Yuan) in which they proclaimed a Chinese republic, with Yuan Shikai as its president, and transferred sovereignty to it. Yuan assumed the presidency, and declared his capital at Beijing. Sun and his supporters acquiesced, on the understanding that a Parliament (*Yuan*) would be established after elections, to be held in early 1913.

When the elections were held, Sun Yatsen's Nationalist Party (*Guomindang*, usually known by the Wade-Giles transliteration acronym KMT) swept the Parliament. They were led by Song Jiaoren, Sun Yatsen's leading political aide at the time. Yuan appears to have been shocked by the outcome of the vote. His agents assassinated Song at a Shanghai train station a month after the elections. Yuan then began to bribe or intimidate other Nationalist Party members, and the Parliament collapsed. Sun Yatsen was packed off to Japan by his supporters to keep Yuan from killing him. Yuan replaced Parliament with a Council of State, led by the commander of the Beiyang Army, Duan Qirui. The new government's plan was to reorganize the provinces. The grip on power by governors or regional military magnates was both the foundation of Yuan's power (in the north) and a threat to his power (in the south); in either case, in the long term Yuan did not plan to survive as a lily pad, like the Qing court, bobbing on a turbulent pond. His plan was to drain the pool, and put his regime on solid ground. Civil governors were displaced by overtly military governors (*dudu*, a title for military governor with a very long history) of Yuan's own selection. But a strong central government could not administer the provinces effectively. Each governor collected his own taxes, administered his own army, industries and schools. Yuan collected a share of each of the governors' proceeds, and expected to handle foreign policy for the entire group. As a substitute for a state, the Intendancy's organization had a fatal flaw: It did not exert sufficient control over the former Qing peripheries to prevent politically disastrous subversion of those territories by foreign powers, a fact that contributed to the downfall of Yuan Shikai in 1916.

Yuan's plans for control through militarized governorships were extensions of the basic structure of the Beiyang Intendancy to the entirety of the country. It left intact the secret societies that had been a source of Nationalist power in the south, as well as the industrial, military and financial patterns that had developed in Shanghai and northern China in the previous four decades. It was sufficient to stop the civil war in 1912, but ineffective for reunifying the country. In the post-imperial period, the outlook of the Beiyang Intendancy remained much the same as it had been in the days of Li Hongzhang: The Northeast was important; Mongolia, Xinjiang and Tibet were not. In the late nineteenth century, the history of Qing administration in Xinjiang was very different from the pattern in other border areas. The persistence of a strong Qing garrison in the province and the defeat of Russian attempts to intrude, as well as creation of a centralized province in 1884, produced a relatively strong Qing presence, compared to the fading authority in Tibet and Mongolia. After the fall of the Qing, Xinjiang continued for some time to evince the same stability that had characterized it in the very late Qing period. In 1912 the Qing governor of Xinjiang, like many other governors, fled his post. His former military commander, Yang Zengxin, assumed control of the province, and quickly stated his solidarity with the Republic of China – meaning the new state regime of Yuan Shikai. He was strong supporter of Yuan's attempt to establish a monarchy in 1916 (see below), and celebrated it by rounding up protestors against Yuan and beheading them. When the Yuan interlude drew to a close, Yang remained in firm control of the province.

The Qing administration in Tibet had always been thin, and during the nineteenth century Tibetans, under the Dalai Lama and the Banchen Lama, had organized the best they could to deal with troubles coming over the border from Burma, Nepal and the Punjab region of India. After the restructuring of British rule in India in 1857, British expeditions had begun mapping Tibet and establishing communications with the religious hierarchy. Both British and Indian merchants and mercenaries worked in Tibet to swing the region to the British side in the competition with Russia to control Central Asia. In 1903 members of a British expedition numbering about 10,000 entered Tibet under the command of Francis Younghusband. The next year they opened fire on Tibetan militiamen with rifles and Maxim guns, killing about a thousand. The Dalai Lama was taken by his guards to Urga, in Mongolia, for safety. The de facto leaders of Tibet signed a treaty with Britain that required an opening of the border with India, free access to Tibetan markets by British and Indian merchants, tariff-free imports of British and Indian goods and an indemnity to be paid to Britain (presumably by the Qing empire) of 2.5 million rupees. In 1906, the Qing signed anagreement with Britain affirming the terms of the 1905 agreement, and requiring that no other nation except Britain could enter into communications or negotiations with Tibetan leaders. The next year Britain and Russia signed a protocol acknowledging Qing rule in Tibet, and promising to go through the Qing government in future communications. The Dalai Lama was brought back to Tibet. Beiyang general Zhao Erfeng, then the military governor of Sichuan province, was assigned by the Qing court (upon instructions of Yuan Shikai) in 1908 to take his forces into Tibet to reassert Qing authority there. Resistance from Tibetans, who had become accustomed to ruling themselves, was strong, and Zhao's occupation was brutal. When the Dalai Lama protested in 1909, Zhao's troops drove him out of the country again; he found refuge in Darjeeling, in India. In 1911, the troubles over the railroad in Sichuan quickly spread to Tibet and combined with other issues to cause widespread uprisings. Zhao was killed after a revolt by his own troops. After the abdication of Puyi, the last Qing officials in Tibet either fled or surrendered to Tibetan leaders. The Yuan government never seriously considered expending its military resources on establishing any authority over Tibet, and in 1914 representatives of Britain, Tibet and the Republic of China met at Simla, in Punjab. In principle they agreed that the Republic of China would govern the northern part of Tibet (most of the Tibetan plateau), and British India would govern southern Tibet (which is called Anuchal Pradesh by Indian historians), including Tawang. Though the talks at Simla seemed to indicate agreement by all sides, when the terms were learned by Yuan's government in Beijing they were rejected. In ensuing decades the unresolved geographical and political status of Tibet's various regions led to an independent government emerging at Lhasa under control of the Dalai Lama, with quasi-autonomous regional control by various generals and tribal leaders.

Mongolia, like Tibet, had showed signs of deep alienation from the Qing in the middle nineteenth century. The Qing policy of permitting Chinese farmers, merchants and financiers to dominate Mongolia's trade centers and land development had left Mongol nomads poor and angry. The living lama, Bogda Gegegen Jebsundamba Khutukhtu, became the lightning rod for Mongol separatists, and in July of 1911 they declared independence from the empire. When the national revolt in China took place in November, four thousand Mongols surrounded the office of the Qing official at the Mongol capital, Urga, nabbed him, and sent him back to China. The Jebsundamba Khutukhtu was declared the temporal as well as spiritual ruler of Mongolia. Mongol militiamen systematically seized the last remaining Qing official offices in Mongolia, sending each official back to Beijing. By the end of 1912, Mongol communities on the Tibetan border, in Qinghai province, had joined the theocratic state of Mongolia. A parliament derived from both the traditional Mongol *khuriltai* and the British parliamentary model was created to meet at Urga in 1914, and a legal code was promulgated soon after. At the same time that the institutions of independence were being completed, the first manifestations of a long period of growing Russian influence occurred. In 1915 Russian soldiers threatened to invade if the Mongol government did not agree to a treaty resembling the British treaty with Tibet in 1905. Mongolia acceded to the demand, and the country began its slide into Russian domination.

The situation in the Northeast was, perhaps, more complex than any other border region. On the ground, Japanese industries, military guards and spies of the Southern Manchuria Railway were thick. The nine provinces of the region were under the direct control of military governors connected to the Beiyang Intendancy, and in 1911 Zhao Erxun was transferred to the province at the instigation of the Beiyang headquarters (with the signature of the Qing court). But all the governors and their armies had to come to terms with the presence and growing influence of Japan. At the time of the revolution an apparent secessionist movement emerged under the leadership of a young bannerman, Zhang Yong, who had come to command his own band of armed men, and who occasionally supplied information both to the Qing governors and to Japanese agents. When the revolution broke out in China, Zhang began to agitate for a separate political entity based in the Northeast. In 1912 Zhang was assassinated at a public event by agents of Zhao Erxun. The collapse of the Yuan regime in 1916 left the Japanese without the formal acknowledgement of their privileges and interests in Manchuria that they had hoped to gain. In Fengtian province (modern Liaoning), the mercenaries and militiamen answered to Zhang Zuolin, a wily native of the province who had worked his way up through the ranks of bandits, revolutionaries and secret societies. He carefully negotiated his way between the Japanese and the Beiyang élites, finally gaining acknowledgement as governor in his own right in 1916. After the fall of Yuan, Zhang even added the small group of intellectuals and old Qing officials gathering around Puyi to his list of possible allies.

Pressures from Japan that had become part of the fabric of political and economic life in the Northeast became urgent for Yuan in early 1915. Japan delivered a written demand to Yuan's government to concede to Japan extraordinary territorial and financial privileges. The outbreak of the First World War in Europe had thrown open to question the European concessions throughout China. Japan had made the war a "world war" by declaring itself on the side of Britain, France and the other Allied powers. The written demands to Yuan in 1915, now referred to as the "Twenty-One Demands," could be grouped into several distinct categories. Because of Japan's declaration of war against Germany, Japan claimed for itself the German colonies and railway lines in Shandong province. Japan's growing industrialization of the Northeast and the scope of the Southern Manchuria Railway were, according to Japan's demands, to constitute the basis for a formal Japanese claim over the Northeast and eastern Mongolia. In addition, Chinese industrial centers that had been funded with Japanese loans, still unpaid, were to be surrendered to Japanese control (including the Han Ye Ping complex created by Zhang Zhidong in Hubei province). China was required to not award any territories to any power except Japan. Japanese advisors were to be assigned to the Yuan government, to major Chinese religious organizations (particularly Buddhist), and to the Chinese police forces. Yuan was astounded at the demands. But he also perceived that Japan's own government was not entirely stable, as the Meiji founders were either dead or elderly, while political leaders and military commanders were in fatal competition for control. Yuan rejected the demands, and the Japanese actually withdrew the stipulations for control over China's government, police and religious organizations. But the remainder of the demands were returned with an ultimatum from Japan that rejection would mean war. Since Yuan was already nearly overwhelmed by his plans to centralize government and assert military authority, he accepted the demands, hoping that they would not become public until he had made more progress with consolidating his regime.

Word of the Yuan's acceptance of the Twenty-One Demands (now Thirteen Demands) roughly coincided with his attempt to reform Chinese government again. Opinion had circulated loosely in China, Japan and the USA that China's political turmoil might be resolved by a new emperorship. Traditional emblems of authority could be used to calm the public, while the instabilities of parliamentary or representative government could be avoided for at least a time. Creation of a new monarchy for Yuan would make formal and public the transformation of the Beiyang Intendancy into a state. In November of 1915 Yuan declared himself the Hongxian emperor of the Chinese Empire. Political and public reaction against both the new emperorship and capitulation to Japan's demands sparked public demonstrations and riots on an unprecedented scale. Sun Yatsen, in Japan, publicly declared that he was leading a new revolution to overthrow the new empire. Yunnan military governor Cai E led a military and political campaign to convince the southern governors, en masse, to declare that they would secede in order to protect the republic. The foreign press denounced Yuan, and several foreign governments – including Japan – announced that they would cease aid to and cooperation with the Yuan government. For good measure, Japan supplied funds to Sun Yatsen to aid in the rebellion. Yuan demurred from a public ceremony of accession, hoping that public outrage would subside. But when he attempted to mobilize his Beiyang military subordinates Duan Qirui and Feng Guozhang to go to war against Cai and the southern governors, they refused. In March of 1916 Yuan not only abandoned his plans for monarchy but resigned as president. Governors continued to declare independence as Yuan completely withdrew from public life. On June 15, he died. Remnants of Beiyang organization would continue to function in north China for some years, but with Yuan's death the true infrastructure of late Qing – or Beiyang Ascendancy – government at last collapsed.

Further reading

On trade and economy in the late Qing, see: Feuerwerker, *The Chinese Economy* (1969); Cochran, *Big Business in China* (1980); Goodman, *Tobacco in History* (1994); Wyman, "Opium and the State in Late-Qing Sichuan" (2000); McMahon, *The Fall of the God of Money* (2002); Ji, *A History of Modern Shanghai Banking* (2003); Zheng, *The Social Life of Opium in China* (2005).

On reform, industrialization, the Beiyang Intendancy and Yuan Shikai, see: Li, *The Political History of China, 1840–1928* (1956); Rawlinson, *China's Struggle for Naval Development, 1839–1895* (1967); Ch'en, *Yuan Shih-k'ai* (1972); Ch'en, *State Economic Policies of the Ch'ing Government* (1980); Kwong, *Mosaic of the Hundred Days* (1984); Reynolds, *State-sponsored Reforms and China's Late-Qing Revolution* (1995); Thompson, *China's Local Councils in the Age of Constitutional Reform, 1898–1911* (1995); Rawski, *The Last Emperors* (1998); Karl and Zarrow, *Rethinking the 1898 Reform Period* (2002).

For print, news media and popular literacy, see: Drege, *La Commercial Press de Shanghai* (1978); Rawski, *Education and Popular Literacy* (1979); Drege and Hua, *La Revolution du Livre dans la Chine Moderne* (1979); Arnove and Graff, *National Literacy Campaigns* (1987); Lee and Nathan, "The Beginnings of Mass Culture" (1987); Bailey, *Reform the People* (1990); Judge, *Print and Politics* (1996); Sinn, "Fugitive in Paradise" (1998); Wagner, "The *Shenbao* in Crisis" (1999); Wagner, "The Early Chinese Newspapers and the Chinese Public Sphere" (2001); Reed, *Gutenberg in Shanghai* (2004); Keulemans, "Printing Storyteller's Performance" (2004).

On popular movements, rebellion and revolution, see: Fang, "Tsou Jung" (1943); Hsüeh, *Huang Hsing and the Chinese Revolution* (1961); Jansen, *The Japanese and Sun Yat-sen* (1970); Chi, "Shanghai-Hangchow-Ningpo Railway Loan" (1973); Li, *China's Quest for Railway Autonomy, 1904–1911* (1977); Schiffrin, *Sun Yat-sen* (1980); Spence, *The Gate of Heavenly Peace* (1981), Crossley, *Orphan Warriors* (1990); Lum and Lum, *Sun Yat-sen in Hawai'i* (1999); Bergère, *Sun Yat-sen* (2000); Rankin, "Nationalistic Contestation and Mobilization Politics" (2002); Li, "Popular Culture in the Making of Anti-Imperialist and Nationalist Sentiments" (2004).

11

Cultural Revolution

Hᴜ sʜɪʜ (Hu Shi) was born to a farming family in Anhui province in 1891. When he was 15, his family arranged for him to be engaged to an illiterate and foot-bound girl from a neighbor family. Hu was very bright, was tutored by an uncle from the age of 4, and received some education in boarding schools, finishing in Shanghai. In 1909 he passed a special examination for a scholarship, funded by indemnities paid to the USA by the Qing empire after the Boxer rebellion. He received the scholarship, and arrived at Cornell University in 1910 to study agronomy. He quickly became attracted to the study of philosophy, however, and in 1914 entered the graduate program at Columbia University, where the pragmatist John Dewey taught. In later years Hu became a leading philosopher, public intellectual, academic administrator and advocate for women's rights in China. He looked back, in 1933, on the power of education to transform a society's outlook:

> The old education was purely classical and literary, and was intended only for those who were to take the literary examinations and to become officials. The sons of the ordinary fanner and artisan, if they went to school at all, wanted to know no more than a few hundred characters; only exceptionally clever boys were encouraged to go beyond that. But the new education, however inadequate and bookish, was meant for everybody who came to take it; it was planned as education for citizenship. The content has become so different that a new world, far more interesting and far more intelligible than the moralizings of the ancient sages, is brought within the comprehension of the average boy and girl. New ideas and ideals are consciously instilled and new ambitions developed in the minds of the school children as well as in their parents. If the education does not give the pupils new capabilities, it has at least taught them to be dissatisfied with their lot and with their old environment. They know enough to see that foot-binding of the girls is bad, that marriage arranged by parents is bad, and that superstitions of all kinds are bad.

In 1917, after returning to China with his Columbia PhD, Hu married his village fiancée. He later wrote, "Ours is an intermediate generation that must be sacrificed both to our parents and to our children."

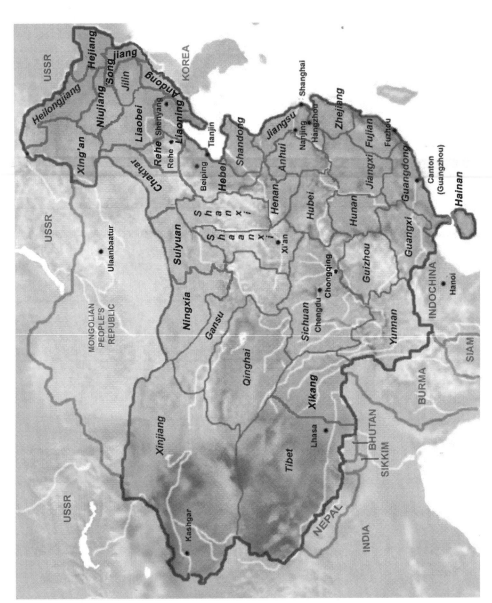

Map 8 Republican China, *c.* 1930

The complexity of the economic, social and political forces converging to strangle the Qing empire and to hobble the republic that attempted to replace it was equaled by the complexity of the ideological sources that informed political change between 1896 and the middle of the twentieth century. Some roots lay in Chinese tradition, some in a variety of foreign influences, others were newly sprouted from a mix. Kang Youwei, the guide for many traditional élite scholars who sought a new path after the Treaty of Shimonoseki, might have sided with the traditionalism of many of his peers. He came from a wealthy family in which the men were educated in classical Chinese language and literature, and Kang successfully passed the traditional examinations in 1895. But Kang's thought was already mutating into something new. Conditions in Kang's home province of Guangdong meant that not even the most traditional home could be impervious to Christianity and other foreign influences. In 1883 Kang began a campaign to persuade the rural population to give up foot-binding, and by 1890 he had begun to see the ancient texts from which Confucius had drawn his teachings as sources of revelation. He interpreted Confucius not as a champion of tradition and of social hierarchy, but as an iconoclast who sought to make his society more humane and more egalitarian. Kang denied the authenticity of certain texts that portrayed Confucius as reflexively conservative, and argued that in the true classics a new world was fore-seen, one in which war and injustice would be banished. The notion was not a new one – Wang Tao had mentioned in a lecture at Oxford in 1856 that Confucius had predicted a social transformation resulting in the Great Harmony (*datong*), the same phrase that Kang cited from the philosophical classics. The idea was widespread among scholars who, like Wang Tao and Kang himself, were grounded in the classics and incidentally influenced by Protestant Christianity. But Kang had worked to systematically document the interpretation. By the time he reached Beijing to sit for the 1895 examinations, Kang was already known for his "new text" philosophical ideas, and for his campaigns for social reform. In aspect Kang appeared to be the traditional élite male in a long robe and the queue prescribed by Qing law. In philosophy, he was a champion of the idea of a new social world (not only for China), foreseen by the classics, but dependent upon the actions of righteous élites to achieve.

Liang Qichao was eighteen years younger than Kang, but born close to Kang's home county in Guangdong province. Despite a brilliant beginning for his academic career, by 1890 Liang was losing enthusiasm for the examination route. He was an acolyte of Kang Youwei's social reform activities, and a proponent of Kang's "new text" approach to traditional philosophy. After failing the national examinations a second time, Liang left for Hunan, where the reformist governor Chen Baozhen was attempting to put many of Kang's ideas into place (see chapters 8 and 10). Liang remained in solidarity with Kang Youwei's idea that a constitutional monarchy, led by the Guangxu emperor and a group of enlightened advisors, could overcome the weight of traditional attitudes and guide China's uneducated, mistrustful, conservative majority to a new society and a new status in international relations. As all educated Chinese were painfully aware after 1895, this model had already permitted Japan to throw off its traditional government and pursue a spectacularly successful program of industrialization, educational reform, cultural receptivity, economic expansion and formidable military advancement.

When Kang received the invitation from the Guangxu emperor (see chapter 10) to become an imperial advisor, Liang came along. When Kang and Liang evaded their death sentences, they escaped into an international network of Chinese communities. All had intense connections to global patterns of Chinese labor migrations and financial transfer, many had radicalizing political organizations, most had several newspapers published by reform associations, and all were closely connected by cable communications – Berlin, Paris, London, New York and San Francisco had been connected since the late nineteenth century; Hongkong, Shanghai, Yokohama and Honolulu were connected as of 1903; and Vancouver and Sydney were added a few years later. Before 1908, their ideas competed in this milieu against the more radical ideas of Sun Yatsen, and against the less well-known but even more radical ideas of Zhang Binglin.

Sun Yatsen had entered this transnational field earlier, when his failure to secure a post with the Beiyang Intendancy caused him to return to Hawaii to become a full-time organizer for overthrow of the Qing. After Shimonoseki, Sun's rhetoric was strongly laced with vicious denunciation of the Manchus and of the Qing court. He recalled and recited the accounts of the massacres in the Yangtze delta during the Qing conquest two and a half centuries before; he held living Manchus responsible for atrocities of the past; and he blamed the current weakness of China on the self-serving, predatory Manchu imperial state. When Liang and Sun met each other for the first time in Vancouver in 1899, Liang – though still an adherent of Kang's constitutional monarchist movement – clearly felt that Sun had hit upon an effective racial rhetoric for uniting the politically indifferent behind a revolutionary movement. He himself played with racist invective for the purpose of gaining attention and exciting his audiences. But the degree of his racism differed from Sun's, whose attitudes would also, over time, grow distant from those of their nationalist competitor, Zhang Binglin.

Zhang Binglin (Zhang Taiyan) was the son of prominent scholarly family in the intensely scholarly city of Hangzhou, in Zhejiang province in the Yangtze delta. At the age of 28 in 1896, Zhang had gone to Shanghai to join the local chapter of Kang Youwei's Self-Strengthening Society. While Kang and Liang were at the Guangxu emperor's side, Zhang continued the work in Shanghai, writing newspaper articles for the society's journals and lecturing. In 1898 Zhang fled to Taiwan (then a new Japanese colony) and became a journalist. In 1901 he returned to China to teach and write under an assumed name. He wrote for the dissident journal *Subao* in Shanghai, until the British government agreed to shut it down in 1903 (see chapter 10). Zhang traveled between Shanghai and Tokyo until he was arrested by British authorities and jailed until 1906. When released he went back to Japan, lecturing Chinese expatriates on Chinese linguistics, archeology, Buddhism and radical nationalism. In 1907, the Japanese government banned radical Chinese nationalist publications and Sun Yatsen's League of Alliances was expelled. Zhang stayed on in Tokyo as a private tutor, developing his own nationalist philosophy.

Racial thinking in China was not a product of European or Japanese influence exclusively. Racism is not a matter of only noting that some groups are different from others, or preferring one's own group. The cosmology of racial thinking proposes that differences in human appearance are connected to essential, categorical differences throughout the natural world. These essential differences defining human groups were considered to be comprehensive, affecting not only appearance but esthetic sensibilities, moral character and temperament. According to this logic, a people may learn the culture of another group, behave like them or even come to look like them, but their essential nature will never be changed through the process of assimilation. These ideas can be attested widely in many parts of the world between 1400 and 1800. Their generation may have been due to a combination of the rising instances of first contacts between widely different cultures and the revival of classical or neoclassical philosophies of the natural world. Whatever the explanation, scholars in seventeenth century China had developed a strong theory of essential racial differences, at the same time that such ideas were being spread throughout Europe and Japan. Scholars of that era who had written treatises on the eternal differences between the Chinese and Mongols, or Chinese and Manchus, were studied by Zhang Binglin, Liang Qichao and their students. Zhang and Liang worked to publish the writings of these early thinkers (including Wang Fuzhi), which had been strenuously banned by the Qing empire.

These ideas, Zhang appreciated, not only proved the injustice of the Qing empire (in which Manchus ruled over and exploited Chinese), but also had fundamental implications for the kind of government that should come after the empire was gone. For Zhang, any state that attempted to govern a society in which Chinese lived together with alien peoples would necessarily be unjust and unsuccessful. People with the same ancestry, in Zhang's view, shared the same understanding of justice, and could agree on a form of government that would serve their interests. Minorities within such a society would either become dissatisfied and unruly or would be forced to live without complaining in a system that was unfair to them. When the Qing empire dissolved, Zhang argued, the best solution would be for "China" to occupy the historical confines of China proper (see chapter 4), while Manchus, Mongols, Muslims and Tibetans left for their homelands, where they could develop governments that were, in their own eyes, just. Zhang was never explicit about how this great transfer – of Chinese to China, of minorities from China to their ostensible "homes" – would be accomplished.

Liang Qichao and Kang Youwei, who supported a constitutional monarchy before the Guangxu emperor's death in 1908, could hardly agree with Zhang's thesis. Their reasons were not only practical, but rooted in traditional philosophy. They argued that Confucius' primary belief was that education, or self-perfection, could completely transform not only individuals but also entire cultures. They found Zhang Binglin's ideas to be irreconcilable with Confucius' teachings, something with which Zhang himself would have agreed (since he considered the ancient classics were mostly of historical interest and did not have the revelatory qualities that Kang and Liang thought they had). Empires, for Kang and Liang, were not necessarily bad. Bringing together peoples of different background through moral education, which they regarded as the essential mission of any empire, could be not only good but necessary. Liang Qichao called this kind of government "national empire," and he could point to two new empires, both operating on this principle, then sweeping the old empires out of the Pacific: Japan and the USA. Japan in Korea and Taiwan considered itself on a civilizing mission, and the USA claimed to be doing the same thing in Hawaii and the Philippines. In Liang's view, China's future would be one of a new civilizing empire, bringing harmony and justice not only to its own lands but to those of neighbors.

The fact that both Zhang Binglin and Liang Qichao, with their radically different philosophies and concepts of what a new Chinese state would look like, are both considered well within the scope of Chinese nationalism is a demonstration of how large and confused the problem of nationalism was, and remains. It is not surprising that the great nationalist movements of the late nineteenth and early twentieth century occurred within the umbrella of the great empires. As the Qing, Russian, Ottoman, French and British empires began to disintegrate, leaders of many regional cultures and linguistic groups sought to create smaller states in which their peoples could develop national forms they regarded as suitable for themselves and strong enough to fight for their interests against other national groups. Historians often think of nationalism as a European phenomenon, drawn from many different veins of eighteenth-century thought – rationalism, romanticism, historical linguistics, early folklore studies – but shaped as a political concept in the aftermath of the invasion and domination of discrete cultural spheres by Napoleonic France. From Europe, nationalism is seen as being transmitted to late imperial regional societies in Asia, the Middle East, Africa and Latin America. This seems, however, to be primarily true with respect to the vocabulary used in nationalist struggles and in new education. In East Asia, for instance, Japanese translations of German political works of the eighteenth and nineteenth centuries produced a vocabulary including *minzoku* (a primary or majority genealogical/cultural group), *kokka* (the state), *kokutai* (the polity). The travel of students and scholars between Japan and China in the late nineteenth-century allowed these terms to quickly enter the vocabulary of scholarly and journalistic writing, producing the modern Chinese terms *minzu* (from *minzoku*), *guojia* (from *kokka*), *guoti* (from *kokutai*), and so on. The appeal of nationalist ideas in late nineteenth-century China was enhanced by the use of this new vocabulary. But elements of the idea were old. Zhang Binglin argued that the knowledge needed to define a Chinese people was present in the classics, in the imperial histories produced during the preceding 2,000 years, in traditional studies of the Chinese language and its writing system, all of which were accessible in their full meaning to an educated modern Chinese. Even for scholars like Liang Qichao who were not essentialists, the key to understanding the experience and the rights of the Chinese people were to be found in the histories – all produced by the empire that the nationalists intended to destroy. Destruction of the empire was all that nationalists agreed upon in late nineteenth- and early twentieth-century China. What form the new state would take – a constitutional monarchy, an authoritarian republic, a representative democracy – and what its geography was to be were open to debate.

Sun Yatsen was not a philosopher. While Liang and Zhang debated the meaning of cultural differences and the correct form for a new state in China, Sun was forging increasingly influential networks for financing, publishing, lecturing and finding political allies to aid in overthrow the Qing empire. His political ideas seem to have been crafted on the basis of practicality and rhetorical appeal. Before 1910 he adhered to simple slogans of racial unity of the Chinese against the Manchus and against imperialism. He compared the imperialist nations of Europe who had established treaty superiority over China, as well as ruling areas of Chinese residence in Hongkong, Singapore, Malaya, Indonesia and elsewhere, to silk farmers who nurtured their silk worms only as long as they produced silk, and fed them to the fish if they stopped. Canceling the privileges of imperialists in China was a popular message among Sun's Chinese audiences, but Japanese agents who were financing much of Sun's work were discomfited enough to distance themselves from him in 1907–08, when his newspaper was shut down and he was expelled from the country. The economic milieu in which Sun was supporting himself caused him to turn his mind to the practical issues of managing the Chinese economy in such a way that the extreme gaps in income and education between the cities and countryside might be lessened, and markets managed to make sure that farmers got a good return for their produce. He had some interest in the ideas of Henry George, which were debated in newspaper editorials and lecture halls all over the world in the early years of the twentieth century. George's "agrarian socialism" proposed that the state protect farmers, using laws against land speculation or other intrusions by urban financiers to keep farmers free of the pressure of rents, high land prices or low wages. The USA had seen many political movements of this type during the nineteenth century. None had succeeded to any significant degree, but Sun followed the general idea that the majority of the population, who in most societies in the first decade of the twentieth century were farmers, should be protected from a predatory minority.

In 1903 Sun's speaking and writing showed his ideas clustering around what he called the "Three People's Principles" (*sanmin zhuyi*). His discussion of them was general. *Minzu zhuyi* (usually translated as "nationalism"), the first principle, basically meant that China should be ruled by the Chinese, and not by foreign governments, industrialists or merchants. *Minquan zhuyi* (usually translated as "people's rights"), meant that the majority of the population should have the right to determine, or at least influence, government policy. *Minsheng zhuyi* (usually translated as "people's livelihood") meant that policy should be designed around providing for the economic health of the majority. Beyond that, his ideas had not developed any specificity, and so they did not alienate any particular part of his following. In 1905, the Three People's Principles were promulgated as the official slogans of the League of Alliances.

The origins of the nationalist movement, and Sun's attempt to distill principles he thought both nationalist and progressive, took place against the background of a competing school of thought and action: anarchism. In casual speech anarchy connotes a state of chaos, but at the turn of the twentieth century it was a complex and influential philosophy that had peculiar resonances with Chinese social patterns and political crises. At root anarchy is the theory that justice is generated from a community outward, and that impositions upon a community from an external force – a national government, a provincial government, a municipal government, social or economic elites with coercive powers, or a rigid and unquestioned tradition – result in injustice, exploitation and war. Late nineteenth-century anarchists in Europe and in Russia, many of whom had some influence in China, were opponents of monarchy, of imperialism, and of kinds of nationalism that envisaged large, centralized states enforcing their authority militarily.

Anarchism as a political theory immediately struck some Chinese scholars as describing perfectly the self-sustaining communities on which the Qing empire had supported itself at its height. They suggested that Confucian and Daoist texts, alike, were rooted in the belief that the community is the source of moral and economic order; outside impositions were, in this interpretation, necessarily despotic, and should be resisted by all necessary means. Nationalists such as Sun Yatsen and Liang Qichao echoed many anarchist themes when they argued against imperialism as an unjust, chaos-making trespass against the community of Chinese. Zhang Binglin's ideas of the innate sympathy of people of one ancestry for another closely paralleled some

4.   A formal portrait of Sun Yatsen, one of many taken for publicity purposes.

anarchist thinking, and he rejected the idea of a large, centralized state forcing peoples
of different cultures to follow identical laws and obligations. Kang Youwei's idea of
the ultimate Great Harmony strongly echoed both agrarian socialism and anarchy, as
it foresaw a world in which communities and individuals would be self-governing.
Although pure anarchism did not go on to become a major political philosophy in
China, an anarchist theme was often grafted by Chinese writers onto socialist, nationalist, and anti-imperialist ideology. Not only the history of local independence, but
the philosophy of local independence, became fundamental to political thought and
action in twentieth-century China.

The ideas of Kang, Liang, Zhang and Sun also showed the imprint of perhaps the
most pressing concept of the era, Herbert Spencer's "survival of the fittest," sometimes popularized as "social Darwinism." In an age of imperialism and resistance to it,
Spencer's idea that the ability to dominate others is a sign of superiority, of nature's
favor, was potent. Yan Fu, a supporter of reform who was banished in 1898 along
with the reformers (see chapter 10), had spent years studying in England and made a
point of translating Spencer, John Stuart Mill and other English philosophers of gradual social change. From Yan and Spencer, reformers and revolutionaries alike had
absorbed the specifics of a life and death struggle between China and the foreign powers. They also, of necessity, joined Spencer's ideas of virtuous dominance to newly
imported discourse of race. In the first decade of the twentieth century, biological – or
"environmental" or "scientific" – racism was a global phenomenon. Academics,

diplomats, journalists and opinion makers almost everywhere insisted that racial characteristics were the result of climate in the remotest early eras when the races were formed. According to Spencer's logic, the races were in a hierarchical relationship to each other, the logical outcome of their essential qualities. "Caucasians" were at the top of the global hierarchy because their superior intelligence and industry had allowed them to colonize most of the world. Asians were next, since they had succeeded in protecting at least a part of their domain (mostly Japan, Thailand and parts of China) from colonization; and Africans were at the bottom, their entire continent (except, by 1900, Ethiopia) devoured by superior forces. These qualities, the environmentalists insisted, could not be changed. All that could be hoped for was a more humane world in which the weaker were not continually exploited by the stronger. Liang Qichao and his contemporaries subscribed to the general outlines of Spencerianism. But a "new text" theme continued in their thought, as they proposed that a cultural and political transformation in China could unleash the strengths of the Chinese that had not been evident in the past hundred years. Japan, they acknowledged, had demonstrated that Asians belonged at the top of the hierarchy along with Caucasians. China would have to undertake the same road to industrial and military strength if it were to prove that Caucasians were not eternally, universally, superior.

Following the death of the Guangxu emperor in 1908, Liang and Kang Youwei were eclipsed as prospective political leaders, since their idea of constitutional monarchy had difficulty gaining traction with the child Puyi as the prospective monarch. Both became supporters of Sun Yatsen and the League of Alliances. Zhang Binglin was officially a supporter, too, though he grew impatient with Sun's political practicalities and lack of a clear philosophy of a Chinese republic. To the world at large, Sun was the face of Chinese nationalism, and a handsome one. In the age of photography, he was an effective icon of the movement, far more appealing than Liang Qichao with his spectacles and slight overbite, or the apparent eccentricity of traditional dress still worn by Kang and Zhang. More important, he had concrete connections not only to newspapers, writers and merchants but also to gun-running gangs and the popular associations of south China that would prove so crucial to the revolution.

The negotiated ending of the revolution in 1912 put Yuan Shikai in both real and, to the extent it could be determined, legal leadership of China (see chapter 10). Sun Yatsen was soon forced to return to his base in Tokyo, where he campaigned for acceptance of the Three People's Principles and resurrection of his presidency. The Nationalist party continued its existence in China, but was profoundly damaged by the assassination of Song Jiaoren and the displacement of Parliament by Yuan's Council of State. Li Yuanhong, who had been the first provisional president of the revolutionary republic, formed a political party that co-opted some of Sun's rhetoric but actually supported Yuan Shikai and his authoritarian approach. Yuan never allowed Li real influence in the new government. After Yuan's aborted emperorship and his death, Duan Qirui and other Beiyang élites who assumed control of the government appointed Li president, assuming that his connections to the revolution in the south would neutralize southern resistance to a resurgence of Beiyang control. Li was able to make gestures toward reviving the republic. Parliament was called back into session in August of 1916, and Li's political comrades proceeded to embarrass Yuan Shikai's successor as the last Beiyang Intendant, Duan Qirui, over the matter of the newly-revealed loans from Japan (see chapter 10).

Even after Yuan's disastrous imperial adventure, ambivalence regarding the idea of a republic was still evident in Beijing and other parts of China. The compromise that ended the revolution left the Qing imperial lineage surviving as a legal entity. Puyi and a small court still resided in the northern part of the Forbidden City with a small contingent of bannermen, and a "treaty of favorable treatment" promulgated in the aftermath of Puyi's abdication specified that the property, persons and livelihoods of Manchus, Mongols, Tibetans and Muslims should be protected. Japanese agents were funding a prospective rebellion by the Mongol prince Babojab to restore Puyi to the throne in 1915, and the Manchu nobleman Shanqi – once an opponent of the Boxers and of Xiaoqin, and the first head of the reformed police force – continued, until his death in 1921, to solicit both Japanese and German funding for a restorationist coup. The only actual restoration happened for about two weeks in 1917, in response to Li Yuanhong's appeal for help in resisting Duan Qirui's army. When Li scored a political point by linking Duan Qirui to the Japanese loans, Duan decided to use force to eject Li from office. For protection Li turned to a former bannerman, Zhang Xun, who had been appointed as Yuan Shikai's military governor of Anhui, and was called by his contemporaries the "pigtailed general" because he continued to wear a queue of the sort the Qing had required. Zhang was willing to bring his army to Beijing to protect Li, but only if Li dissolved Parliament and allowed a restoration of Puyi (then almost 12 years of age) to the throne. Kang Youwei announced his support for the restoration. The troops, the emperor and his supporters were barricaded inside the Forbidden City, but were eventually driven out when Duan's units used biplanes to drop bombs into the imperial compounds. Li, Kang, and Puyi himself were all released by Duan's forces, though Li and Kang were banned from political activities and Puyi was kept under strict observation.

Constitutional monarchy as an ideal did not collapse even after the Zhang Xun farce. Hu Shih, back in China and beginning his appointment at Peking University, applied for permission on several occasions to visit Puyi. In 1919 Reginald Johnston (who had been in China in various colonial offices since 1898), was appointed as a tutor to Puyi, teaching him English language and English literature, history and basic science. Puyi became a favorite subject of foreign photographers, and in the 1924 was visited in the Forbidden City by Rabindranath Tagore, then at the height of his fame as a Nobel Prize winner and anti-imperial activist. The visit was arranged by Liang Qichao, who while no longer wholly dedicated to constitutional monarchy was nevertheless in favor of allowing the emperor a political role if Puyi could evince signs of a progressive consciousness. Some élite who continued to wear traditional robes and maintain traditional families were clearly sympathetic to the idea of restoring the empire and its late institutions, but there is no evidence that on a popular level there was any interest in a restoration, or any response to the emperor as a symbol of authority. The warlord government of Beijing, however, was annoyed by the apparent interference of Puyi, Johnston, Jinliang and others connected with Puyi in politics. They were also alarmed at the idea that Puyi could sell the imperial treasures collected over the centuries – J.P. Morgan's secretary Belle d'Acosta Greene nearly put together a million dollar (USD)offer in 1912 – and turn the proceeds into a political war-chest. In 1923 Parliament passed a law nationalizing the treasures, and in 1924 warlord armies forced Puyi and his party out of the Forbidden City. The Japanese government offered the imperial remnants shelter at its consulate in Tianjin. From 1924, political thinking in China moved irrevocably toward the establishment of a stable, national republican government.

Sun Yatsen returned to China in 1917. Nanjing was now firmly under the control of Beiyang-connected armies, so he set up his capital in Canton, reorganizing the Nationalist party and setting up an alternative to the Duan Qirui government in the north. His primary support came from Chiang Kaishek (Jiang Jieshi), who decades before, as a military cadet, had become enamored of the anti-Qing movement, and had joined the League of Alliances in 1906. In 1917, Chiang was commanding a military force of his own; he took over the protection of Sun Yatsen and the further consolidation of military forces under his command. In 1915, Sun married Soong Ching-ling (Song Qingling), though his first marriage was still legal. Ching-ling was a daughter of Charlie Soong (see chapter 10), who was Sun's major source of money. All the children of Charlie Soong had been educated in the United States. Ching-ling's sister Ai-ling, once a secretary of Sun's in the League of Alliances, married H.H. Kung (Kong Xiangxi), who had taken a master's degree in economics from Yale in 1907 and then returned to China to make a fortune in commercial shipping. Her brothers were all bankers, and the eldest brother T.V. Soong (Song Ziwen) was becoming China's wealthiest financier. Her youngest sister, May-ling (Song Meiling), not yet 20 in 1917, was just graduating from Wellesley College; ten years later she would be the wife of Chiang Kaishek. The Sun, Kong, Soong and Chiang families would remain at the center of a financial and political complex through the entire period of the Nationalist republic in China, and beyond.

Around them swirled diverse ideological and political trends, from capitalist to fascist to socialist and communist. Sun's military and financial resources in 1917, though formidable, were not sufficient to permit the possibility of going against the northern warlords. Japan, once a funder and advisor to Sun's movement, could not be approached for help, since Chinese public anger at Japan would have quickly stained Sun's Nationalist party. But a new resource suggested itself after the events in Russia of 1917–19, resulting not only in the creation of a communist government in Russia, but also in the inauguration of the Third Communist International (Comintern), an organization for advancing communist revolution outside Russia through bourgeois, or nationalist, revolution.

The timing coincided with an outbreak of social turmoil and ideological ferment, usually called in English the May Fourth Movement, but in Chinese, the Cultural Revolution (*wenhua geming*). The background to the event lay in two pieces. One was the insuperable expansion of Japanese industrial and military operations in China since Japan had defeated Russia – and appropriated Russia's industrial facilities in the Northeast – in 1905. Taiwan was in Japanese hands, undergoing modernization of industry, transportation and education. Japanese influence in the Northeast and northern China was growing. Japan's incursions into what were technically Qing territories before 1912 brought it no opprobrium from the foreign powers. In 1911 Japan's only unequal treaty, the Kanagawa Treaty of 1858 with the USA, was renegotiated, ending all special American privileges of trade and residence. But China's unequal treaties all remained in force despite the efforts of statesmen since the days of

Zeng Guofan and Wenxang to ameliorate them. Now, Japanese collaboration with Qing restorationists in Mongolia, Manchuria and Beijing had been exposed. And the story of the Twenty-One/Thirteen Demands (see chapter 10) was being revealed to an outraged public.

The second piece was the independent decisions in China and in Japan to declare war on Germany by joining the Allies in the First World War. In China the decision had been controversial, but had been undertaken with the understanding that German concessions in Shandong province would be surrendered to China if Germany were defeated. As many as 140,000 Chinese laborers entered the war as cooks, housekeepers, medics and factory laborers attached to British forces in France. Chinese representatives went to the Paris Peace Conference in early 1919 in the glow of victory and with the expectation that Woodrow Wilson's globally publicized principle of "self-determination" would mean that German colonies, railroads and industrial facilities in Shandong province would be handed over to China. However, when the document that would become the Treaty of Versailles was concluded, it not only awarded to Japan all German concessions in China, but implied endorsement of Japan's colonization of Korea and its increasing powers in China. The two Chinese representatives to the conference left without signing the document, and in September of 1919 the Duan Qirui government unilaterally ended its war against Germany.

The first massive public reaction to the treaty was in Korea, where Japan had been using harsh police tactics to keep the population restrained while it took mineral resources, grain and labor from the country and built such industrial facilities as were necessary to maximize its extraction. On March 1, 1919, crowds of students, laborers and housewives congregated in downtown Seoul, where organizers read a declaration of independence for Korea, then alerted the local police to their own actions. It is possible that over the year that demonstrations broke out and were suppressed in the country as many as two million people participated; at least 7,500 were killed, 16,000 wounded and nearly 50,000 arrested. On May 4, 1919, demonstrations started at Peking University, whose chancellor Cai Yuanpei had studied in Germany and was now spokesman for anti-imperialism and progressive reform in China. Compared to the Korean movement, the size of Chinese gatherings was modest at first, only a few thousand at a time. The government paid very little attention (a fracture was opening in the Beiyang coalition, see chapter 13), and as the gatherings became more frequent they also became more organized. Street demonstrations including students of all levels and a number of laborers carrying signs in Chinese as well as English (for the benefit of photographers from international news syndicates) were frequent during latter 1919 and the early part of 1920. But as the movement became institutionalized, with series of speakers, informal classes and increasing numbers of publications, it became consciously a "new culture" (*xin wenhua*) movement.

China's universities, in particular, became nodal points in the converging public discussion of culture, history and politics, which continued for years. Hu Shih's notion of a "new culture movement" that would expand literacy, scour ideas of élitism and deference from received tradition and instill in the general population a knowledge of and respect for science, was taken up by a wide range of writers – scholars, poets, and novelists – for decades. An emerging light was Zhou Shuren (Lu Xun), who as a youth had been a student in Japan, and had been galvanized to stop studying and start working for revolution when he saw a photograph of young, strong Chinese men gathering to enjoy the execution of a fellow Chinese who had been caught spying on Japanese installations in the Northeast. Zhou became a disciple of Zhang Binglin for a time, and a scholar of ancient Chinese literature. After the revolution of 1911/12 Zhou was back in China teaching school. In 1918 he published his first work of short fiction, "Diary of a Madman," under the pseudonym Lu Xun. In later works Zhou continued to develop his theme that traditional Chinese culture and Chinese social organization promoted in modern individuals an indifference to – even a predilection to – exploit and annihilate strangers, acquaintances and the society in general. Like many intellectuals of the 1920s, Zhou had a deep hope that communism might bring with it a new culture based upon compassionate regard for all people, particularly the poor and helpless. Jiang Bingzhi (Ding Ling), a young woman writing essays and short stories advocating rejection of traditional women's roles and behavior, joined the communists after her husband was executed by the forces of Chiang Kaishek in 1932. Like many "new culture" activists, she hoped that communism would create a world of equality for women.

The primary advantage of the movement to the Nationalist government of Sun Yatsen was the widening and deepening condemnation of the militarists and the military governments of North China. The failure to create a civil government that could rein in the power of the militarists, or use it to promote the general welfare, produced profound despair in the universities, the newspaper offices, the missionary societies and some small-merchant associations. Hu Shih, in particular, organized gatherings and lectures focused on the problem of creating a sustainable political culture. He was among many younger Chinese academics, often educated in the USA, who were convinced that no great change in governance could be achieved without a revolution in public education. Together with some of his fellow Chinese alumni of Columbia, Hu invited his mentor John Dewey to come to China in 1919 to lecture on his philosophy of pragmatism (in Chinese, experimentalism, *shiyan zhuyi*). Dewey proposed – and Hu continued to argue afterward – that there was no transcendent, universal truth, but only approaches to revealing facts. Constant comparisons of the results of one technique against another would ultimately prove which techniques worked, and were therefore in one sense true. Science, education and politics could, according to Hu, all be reconciled through these principles. But education of the percipient was primary; only informed and critically skilled observers could tell good results from bad.

Hu particularly criticized the elitist educational traditions of China, which had for centuries restricted the ability to read to a tiny portion of the population. He advocated the use in teaching of a limited vocabulary and vernacular grammar, more resembling the writing styles coming from newspapers and popular fiction than from the classical texts. Hu and his colleagues became the fount of a widespread movement of voluntary teaching and school creation across China, including in rural areas; by 1920 over 150,000 new schools for both boys and girls had been created. Missionary traditions, merchant donations and new philosophies joined to form a movement for universal elementary education that continued, with stops and starts, for decades. In the countryside, the reconstruction activist Jimmy Yen (Yan Yangchu) – a 1918 Yale graduate and 1920 Princeton magister, who had been an interpreter and reading tutor for Chinese laborers in France after the World War I – created a rural literacy project, based on the same idea of using only the most common words and vernacular grammar. Yen worked on his Mass Education Movement in the villages steadily, avoiding most of the political turmoil of the cities in the 1920s. Primers developed for his programs inspired publications for popular education that were later reproduced both by the Nationalist government and by the Communist government. His programs attracted international attention and support until he was forced to leave China in 1950. Like Hu Shih, Yen associated the practicality of literacy with the ultimate goal of democracy: He told a gathering in New York City in 1928, "Democracy and illiteracy cannot stand side by side. One of the two must go ... Illiteracy must go and democracy must stand."

Hu Shih's association of scientific training with the ability to conduct a democracy paralleled the May Fourth Movement's slogan (from a 1919 essay by Chen Duxiu), "only [Mr. Science and Mr. Democracy] can save China from the political, moral, academic, and intellectual darkness in which it finds itself." The movement for universal education strongly reinforced ideas, such as Liang Qichao's, that only after a revolution in universal education and the inculcation of liberal values could the public be trusted to support a political system based on voting and representation. Liang's characterization of Sun Yatsen and the Nationalist party as the leading force for anti-imperialism and progressive social transformation in China drew the attention of international literati, including George Bernard Shaw. Liang's own commitment, however, to democracy as it would have been understood by political thinkers in either Britain or the USA was murky. His writings before 1920 show interest in justice, social reform, nationalism and anti-imperialism, but little specific determination to bring a democratic political process to the country (a distinct difference between him and Jimmy Yen). After 1920, when Liang began being more specific about democracy, it appeared to mean primarily rule by the majority. The protection of political minorities that was explicitly at the center of American democratic institutions, and implied in the practice of British democracy, was barely hinted at in Liang's discussions.

For Liang, democracy in China was a distant prospect, far down a road where the first hurdles would be wresting China free from imperial domination, defeat of the continual menace of domestic militarism and establishment of a level of minimal well-being for the increasing number in rural poverty. He saw a period of political authoritarianism as the necessary prelude to any democracy in China. When democracy would arrive, if it only meant shifting the powers of legislation and decision away from a tiny minority to the majority, with or without representative institutions, it would be revolution enough. Before that time, a government with a strong, if civil, mandate to guide education, gradually expand political institutions of representation, and develop media capable of keeping the entire public informed would have to be carefully managed by educated and progressive élites. Liang speculated that the Nationalist party could create such a government, if it were to enjoy the support of foreign governments and be able to command sufficient military and police powers.

Imperialism in China and the collapse of the Yuan Shikai's government, combined with a social conformation that very loosely corresponded to Russia's in 1917, convinced Comintern strategists in Moscow to send Mikhail Borodin to Canton. Borodin's personal history paralleled many of those in the Nationalist party, since in the last days of the Russian empire he had also taken refuge in the United States to continue his studies and organize on behalf of a Russian revolution. To Sun Yatsen,

Borodin represented the likelihood that Russia would become an ally of China against Japan, if necessary, and a source of educational and technical advisors to his government once he unified the country. Borodin's advice to Sun was, first, to think about the Leninist revolutionary principles. Unlike Marx, Lenin had argued – and practiced – that the transition from capitalism to socialism and eventually to communism was not determined solely by the large objective forces of history, but could be accelerated by the dedicated actions of a vanguard. Not unlike Liang Qichao, Borodin argued for not only the importance of a tight, well-trained, dedicated revolutionary team, but also the continuing tutelary role of the state, as it guides the population toward revolutionary consciousness. Second, Borodin advised Sun to strike an alliance with the small but enthusiastic Chinese Communist Party for purposes of opposing the militarists in the north.

The formal creation of a communist party in China was a product of the May Fourth movement. Socialist ideas, of the sort that Sun Yatsen had espoused during his years in Canada and the USA, were not new. The theory that farmers and agriculture should be the first priorities in state economic planning was at least a hundred years old, and its main theoretical tracts had been translated into Chinese in the nineteenth century. Marx's thought, and the theories of Lenin, were less well known before 1918. A major conduit of their influence was Li Dazhao, a professor of economics and head librarian at Peking University who had spent some years studying in Japan, where a socialist movement was gaining strength. Redactions of Marx's writings had been translated into Japanese, and Li was able to retranslate them from Japanese into Chinese. Li's understanding of Marxism, moderated by Li's own teacher Kawakami Hajime, allowed for the incorporation of Leninist ideas of revolutionary action. It also left aside the ideas of both Marx and Lenin that revolution would necessarily spread from industrialized Europe to the less industrialized parts of the world. He did not emphasize Marx's idea that only the proletariat (the urban laboring class) could drive a revolution, but instead thought in terms of the widely oppressed, which would include farmers. In Li's view a socialist revolution focused solely on China was possible, and it could accommodate many features of Chinese culture. In the environment of swirling ideas at Peking University and elsewhere around 1920, many students, philosophers and journalists could see how Kang Youwei's dream of the coming "great harmony" might be the same as Marx or Lenin's theory of universal socialist and communist transformation. In 1920 Li organized a socialist study group, and in July of 1921 they formed the Chinese Communist Party.

The group who composed the original party were men of very diverse backgrounds. Chen Duxiu was the closest to Li Dazhao, and both had been involved in publishing the magazine *New Youth* (*Xin Qingnian*) since 1915. Chen had been a student in Japan for eight years, and a supporter of the League of Alliances. Once he returned to China to start teaching in 1908, he had become a public speaker on behalf of revolution; once the revolution ended he became a public opponent of Yuan Shikai; once Yuan was dead, he became the publisher of a vernacular journal pressing for social and political reform. In 1920 Chen was a professor of literature and dean of the humanities at Peking University. Li Dazhao's Marxist study group appears to have converted him to socialism, and he became the first chairman of the Chinese Communist Party. Chen Gongbo was also in attendance; he was a Cantonese philosophy student who was enthusiastic about communism for about a year, then left for the United States.

5. May Fourth demonstrators with posters and flags crowded the streets of Beijing and congregated in Tiananmen Square.

Zhang Guotao, a young Zhejiang native of 23, had been a student at Peking University since 1916, and had been a prominent organizer in the May Fourth demonstrations of 1919; he was entrusted by the first CCP meeting with overseeing education of the revolutionary élite, starting the organization of labor unions and publishing a new journal, "Red Flag" (*Hongqi*, still the journal of the CCP) to spread the word to urban workers. Liu Shaoqi and Mao Zedong were also present. They were both graduates of the same technical school in their home province of Hunan, both trained as elementary school teachers, and both were in Beijing not as students, but drawn by the excitement of the May Fourth Movement to live and work near the university and audit classes. Before the CCP was created, Liu and Mao had both been active in organizing a socialist movement among students and workers in Beijing. Of the two, Liu was less brilliant but more sociable and accommodating. Mao had already been a soldier, having fought with the Hunan militia during the revolution of 1911/12. He was a tall man with a strangely childish face and a high-pitched voice. He came to the first meeting with very strong opinions. He wanted no part of foreign travel or training, he wanted a national revolution with a communist goal and he wanted, like Li Dazhao, a revolution with the broadest base, which meant one based upon agrarian activism. Liu Shaoqi, not surprisingly, was selected in preference to Mao to spend a short training period at Comintern headquarters in Moscow.

The Comintern had a correspondent, Henk Sneevliet, at the first CCP meeting. He immediately reported to Moscow that the CCP was not ready for serious political work, recommending that the Comintern put its emphasis on the Nationalist party instead. It was with this thought in mind that the Comintern sent Borodin to Canton, intending to promote a policy of permitting CCP members to become members of the Nationalist party. In 1922 the so-called "First United Front" was formed. Chen

Duxiu, Zhang Guotao, Liu Shaoqi, Mao Zedong and others of the CCP became members of the Nationalist party, and attempted to work out a strategy for dislodging the warlords from the north. They were joined by handsome and elegant Zhou Enlai, who had had a singular career to that point. Zhou came from a wealthy Zhejiang family. In the early stages of the May Fourth Movement he had been living in Tianjin (ostensibly as a literature student at Nankai University), but had actually been occupying himself with political organizing and editing a new culture journal. He had been an advocate of women's rights, and was accompanied in his work by his lover Deng Yingzhao, whom he would marry in 1925. In 1920 the Comintern had encouraged Zhou to go to Beijing to join the CCP, but he had resisted, and instead went to France as a labor organizer among the young Chinese who were in the country as contract laborers. It is probable he joined the CCP while in France; he stayed on as a student in France and in Germany for a time. In 1924 he arrived in Canton as both a CCP and Nationalist party member. He went straight to the top of the United Front heirarchy and together with Chiang Kaishek started the Whampoa Military Academy, a wing of Sun's Nationalist government.

Problems immediately became apparent. Chen Duxiu despised the Nationalists for their traditional prejudices, their dependence on the rich financial families of Shanghai and Canton, and their apparent subservience to the Russians. Zhang Guotao had never thought the United Front was a good idea, but was criticized by Chen and others for doing the work well and becoming trusted by the Nationalists. The original CCP members disliked Zhou Enlai and questioned his revolutionary credentials. Mao and Li Dazhao were successful at their Nationalist careers and rose quickly to important committees, but they hated Borodin and thought the ideas, such as they were, of his communist colleagues were pretentious and ahistorical. What the CCP members got most advantageously from the United Front was crisp military education, and an intimate knowledge of the strengths and weaknesses of the Nationalist organization and its personalities. They also had a freedom to study and preach Marxism that they could never have enjoyed under the watchful eye of the warlord governors of Beijing and Nanjing. Sun Yatsen, whose early ideas were partly inspired by agrarian socialism, was sympathetic to the goals of increasing the welfare of the countryside, and was open to Borodin's strategy of the United Front, no matter how much it was opposed by Chiang Kaishek and the young generals he was gathering around him.

Within Sun's inner group, discomfort with the new coalition with the CCP combined with more urgent tensions to make 1923 an uneasy year. The main cause was Chen Jiongming, a trained lawyer who had been a firebrand League of Alliances supporter before and during the revolution of 1911/12. Soon after the compromise with the north that ended the war, Chen had become military governor of Guangdong, in which position he had provided critical protection and support to Sun Yatsen both in 1913 and again after 1917. But after 1920 the two were on a collision course. Sun thought that though the militarists in Beijing were corrupt, exploitative and less than patriotic, they nevertheless had one correct idea: That the complexities and the disparities of China – whether in geographical space, cultural diversity or economic status – required a strong, militarily overwhelming central authority to control. If Sun could succeed in breaking the power of the northern warlords and uniting the country, he intended to rule it thoroughly and for at least a time ruthlessly from the center, with a single party government. Chen objected to this concept. He used the slogan "Canton Province for the Cantonese," by which he meant not an independent state in Guangdong province but a federal system in which the provinces exercised sovereignty while the central government remained relatively weak, and multiple parties competed for influence in the Parliament. Like others before him, Chen saw a dependence upon local coherence as the shortest route to establishing a viable central government.

The disagreement was largely theoretical until 1922, when the Beiyang coalition began to decay. Following the debacles of the public acknowledgement of the Twenty-One/Thirteen Demands and the humiliation in the Treaty of Versailles, Duan Qirui began to lose credibility as head of the Beiyang military forces and of the remaining coalition of Beiyang governors. Commanders inside the coalition began to form themselves into cliques, competing against Duan and against each other for influence. In 1920 a "Zhili clique" based around Beijing, led by Cao Kun and Wu Peifu, defeated Duan and his allies. Duan fled to Japanese protection in Tianjin. Almost immediately, another group of military governors based in Manchuria, the "Fengtian clique" led by Zhang Zuolin, challenged the Zhili group for control, and they went to war – mostly in and around Beijing – in 1922. To the strategists around Sun Yatsen, this was the perfect time to prepare to make a move against the fractured north. Chen Jiongming suggested that war might be avoided if both the nominal president (Xu Shichang) set up by the northern warlords and Sun Yatsen would cede their presidential ambitions to some third party, most likely Li Yuanhong, and gain the acquiescence of the provincial governors by promising each a large degree of local sovereignty. Sun rejected the plan, insisting instead that Chen begin making war on Hunan province, to push the boundaries of Nationalist control further north. Chen then enacted a coup against Sun, driving the Nationalists out of Canton; they temporarily set up another capital at Huizhou, to the east. For almost three years the two camps warred over control of Canton, while Sun and his followers attempted to recentralize themselves and plan a campaign toward the north. In 1925 Chen was defeated; he and those allies of his who could escape made their way to Hongkong.

Sun Yatsen died of cancer in March of 1925. The southern camp was in the process of disintegration. Chiang Kaishek moved quickly to consolidate his role as successor, pushing aside several left-leaning Nationalist acolytes – including Wang Jingwei, who had been released from prison after the revolution of 1911/12 was concluded – whom Sun had seemed, at times, to prefer. Chiang's role as military commander of the Nationalist forces made his leadership essential, since supporters of Chen Jiongming remained in Guangxi and Yunnan, to the west, and moved quickly to challenge Chiang's authority. Once Chiang had repulsed them, he mustered his forces to undertake the Northern Expedition that Sun had dreamed of for so long. His plan was to move through Hunan to the Yangtze, take Nanjing and Shanghai, and move north to Beijing. If Chiang could succeed in accumulating forces, weapons and money as he went, there was a chance that he could unite China under a single government, a genuinely unified government, for the first time since the 1860s.

Chiang hated the instructions of the Comintern, hated Borodin and hated the Communists. He saw the CCP not as the helpful partners that the Comintern had suggested, but as a second front within his own government – traitors and spies who would plot to kill him, as would Wang Jingwei or Chen Jiongming, if he gave them the chance. The hatred was for the most part reciprocated. The CCP members knew of Chiang's intentions for a northward campaign and expected the United Front to fall apart after Sun's death. Some, such as Mao, paid little attention to their assigned duties, and pursued the labor organizing in both the city and countryside that had always been the CCP's fundamental activity. Mao developed a theory he had picked up from Li Dazhao regarding the role of the farmers in the revolution. Marx, Mao was continually reminded, had stated that "peasants" could not be revolutionary. They were tied to the land, they were deferential to landowners, they were unable to escape their perspectives and sacrifice themselves in the interests of social transformation. They were volatile, but only in the interest of righting wrongs or getting relief from immediate pressures. Li Dazhao had been skeptical of the principle, but mostly out of necessity: In all of China there were, perhaps, two million urban physical laborers. If Marx was right, Russia could not have had a revolution and China would not be able to in future. Politicizing farmers was, in the view of Li and Mao, absolutely essential to any hope of a revolution. Mao's history of labor organizing in Beijing and in Changsha piqued his interest in understanding how rural organizing worked. He was able to learn from a fellow CCP-Nationalist party member, Peng Pai, who had been assigned to run the rural support organizations in Guangdong.

Peng Pai, a Hakka, was working to organize farmers in an area of Guangdong close to the old heartland of the Taiping Heavenly Kingdom. He had studied in Japan when younger, and returned to Guangdong in 1920 to teach school. However, his views on social reform and economic justice soon prompted the local landlords to have him dismissed from his teaching job. By 1922 he had organized about 200,000 farmers and farm laborers into associations of mutual aid and protection. In 1924 the Nationalists asked Peng to come to Guangdong to establish a night school for agricultural laborers, and he invited both Mao and Zhou Enlai to lecture. He left Canton in 1925 to go back to his base in the countryside, and Mao took over his work with the farmer's institute. Both the Nationalists and the CCP were impressed with the military potential of Peng's rural organizing, and Chiang counted heavily on coordinating with Peng in planning the Northern Expedition. For Mao, Peng's creation of a sophisticated rural base, interweaving work, study, military drilling and political indoctrination, pointed the way to tapping China's deepest historical resource to effect the broadest transformation. But as Chiang's movement northward in 1925 began, Mao's disagreement with his fellow CCP members was still latent; it was difficult to define or delineate against the glare of the coming conflict between the CCP and the Nationalist party.

The focus of Peng Pai and Mao Zedong on labor organizing was an important facet of the May Fourth Movement. In addition to inspiring widespread experiments and reforms in education and changes in the condition of women, the May Fourth Movement had also fueled a vigorous labor movement. Most of the communists, including Mao, Peng and Liu Shaoqi, had been labor organizers, leading dock workers and farm laborers alike to demand higher wages and better working conditions. Chiang and other enemies of the CCP regarded the labor movement as a pernicious threat to industrial advancement and a constant source of nourishment for the CCP. In mid-May of 1925, labor organizers in Shanghai announced a strike to protest the killing of a Chinese worker by a Japanese factory manager. Crowds of supporters joined the strikers, eventually mounting daily protests against continuing

European and American economic privileges in China, the failure to revise the unequal treaties, and the willingness of KMT financiers and landlords to act as collaborators. Beijing writers, political activists and labor organizers went to Shanghai to aid in the massive demonstrations planned for May 30. The Shanghai Chamber of Commerce printed pamphlets in support of the strikers and paid for publications of the movement. Students in the major eastern cities set up clubs to collect money to fund the rents and food for the strikers. Trade unions in the Soviet Union and some cities of Europe sent funds to sustain the strike. Leaders of the Shanghai protests scheduled May 30 as the culmination of the movement, when they expected strikes to shut down the city.

At the time, the Shanghai police forces were still managed as an independent municipal authority created by the British and other imperial powers, and sometimes staffed by Sikh or British officers. On May 30 the police standing outside their station on Nanjing Road, in Shanghai, fired on the demonstrators. The city erupted in chaos. Railroads, newspapers, markets, docks and schools suspended operation. The British city authorities appeared to be surrounded by the political sea of anti-imperialist anger flowing from merchants, workers and students. Sympathy strikes and demonstrations arose in all China's major cities, including the industrial centers on the Yangtze, the largest cities in the Northeast, Beijing, Tianjin, Qingdao, Taiyuan in Shanxi, Chongqing in Sichuan, Changsha in Hunan and the coastal cities of Canton, Xiamen and Fuzhou. In early June, the city authorities attempted to part the waters by cutting off electricity to Chinese firms in the city until the strikes and demonstrations would end. Merchants did, in fact, largely abandon the movement within a few days, seriously undermining the financial resources available to strike organizers. The Duan Qirui regime in Beijing made a donation to the Shanghai strike organizers, but other attempts by protestors to wrest support from newspapers and small shopkeepers faded quickly.

The Nationalist authorities in Shanghai, whose jurisdiction was very limited, allowed the strikes and demonstrations to proceed without much interference, and the movement lasted through the summer. Li Lisan, a CCP member and a prominent organizer of the movement, eventually undertook negotiations with the Shanghai city authorities to bring the disorders to an end. Japanese representatives agreed to compensate the family of the worker killed at the factory in mid-May, and both Japan and Britain agreed to slightly improve working conditions. But the lightning spread of popular unrest in May, compared to the dissipation of support and organization in the following months, indicated to many that the energies drawn from the May Fourth movement for nationalist organizing and solidarity were being gradually strangled by combined pressures: on the one hand, the struggle between workers, farmers, students and writers on the left and bankers, factory owners and landlords on the right; and on the other hand, the deepening and dangerous tensions with Japan. Many historians take the May Thirtieth Movement as the final phase of the May Fourth Movement.

Within a few years of Sun's death, the varieties of visions for the new Chinese state had been devoured by the exigencies of armed struggle between factions, between parties and ultimately between nations. Li Dazhao would be executed in 1927 by warlords and Peng Pai by the KMT in 1929, Kang Youwei and Liang Qichao would die of natural causes in 1927 and 1929, respectively. Chen Duxiu would be expelled from the CCP for his deepening Trotskyite convictions. Chen Gongbo returned to China in 1925, but decided to join a leftist faction of the Nationalist party rather than return to the CCP. As China entered the 1930s, it would reach another road of bifurcation, not unlike that which followed the suppression of the Boxers in 1900. At the earlier impasse, the road of liberal reform ended. Only conservative loyalism and revolutionary radicalism were left. In the decade after Sun Yatsen's death, political activists, philosophers, essayists, poets and fiction writers who yearned for a path to liberal reform of the republic, a path to strong parliamentary institutions, progressive education, agricultural land reform and a civil society in which the free exchange of ideas was valued, found the path blocked by an irresolvable conflict between entrenched local militarism and a powerless rump government unable to restore a balance. From that point diverged two opposing futures: fascism or communism. Scholars, activists, and writers who attempted to live in the closing space between them found their options gradually eliminated.

Further reading

The Hu Shih quotation is from "The Chinese Renaissance" (1933). The quotation from Jimmy Yen is from Bieler, *Patriots or Traitors?* (2004) and the Chen Duxiu quotation is from Gu, *Who Was Mr Democracy?* (2001).

On liberalism, pragmatism, constitutional monarchism, nationalism, literary trends and the May Fourth movement, see Chow, *The May Fourth Movement* (1960); Gasster, *Chinese Intellectuals and the Revolution of 1911* (1969); Grieder, *Hu Shih and the Chinese Renaissance* (1970); Hsiao, *A Modern China and a New World* (1975); Lin, *The Crisis of Chinese Consciousness* (1979); Spence, *The Gate of Heavenly Peace* (1981); Schwarcz, *The Chinese Enlightenment* (1990); Crossley, *Orphan Warriors* (1990); Liu, *Translingual Practice* (1995); Zeng, "A Chinese View of the Educational Ideas of John Dewey" (1998); Rhoads, *Manchus and Han* (2001); Gu, *Who Was Mr Democracy?* (2001); Xu, *China and the Great War* (2005); Chen, *From the May Fourth Movement to Communist Revolution* (2007); Wang, *John Dewey in China* (2007); Chow *et al.*, eds., *Beyond the May Fourth Paradigm* (2008).

On Liang Qichao and Zhang Binglin specifically, see Levenson, *Liang Ch'i-ch'ao and the Mind of Modern China* (1953); Chang, *Liang Ch'i-ch'ao and Intellectual Transition in China* (1971); Huang, *Liang Ch'i-ch'ao and Modern Chinese Liberalism* (1972); Wong, *Search for Modern Nationalism* (1989); Shimada, *Pioneer of the Chinese Revolution* (1990); Laitinen, *Chinese Nationalism in the Late Qing Dynasty* (1990); Dikötter, *The Discourse of Race in Modern China* (1992); Tang, *Global Space and Nationalist Discourse of Modernity* (1996); Crossley, *A Translucent Mirror* (1999); Fogel, *The Role of Japan in Liang Qichao's Introduction of Modern Western Civilization to China* (2004).

On Lu Xun, Ding Ling and other writers of the New Culture Movement, see Ding, *The Sun Shines over the Sangkan River* (1954); Lu, *Silent China* (1973); Semanov, *Lu Hsün and his Predecessors* (1980); Link, *Mandarin Ducks and Butterflies* (1981); Lu, *The Complete Stories of Lu Xun* (1981); Ding, *Miss Sophie's Diary and Other Stories* (1985); Lee, *Lu Xun and his Legacy* (1985); Lee, *Voices from the Iron House* (1987); Ding, *I Myself Am a Woman* (1990); Lu, *Diary of a Madman and*

Other Stories (1990); Alber, *Embracing the Lie* (2004); Feuerwerker, *Ding Ling's Fiction* (1982); Shi, *The Lure of the Modern* (2001).

On Marxism, socialism and anarchism, see Schwartz, *Chinese Communism and the Rise of Mao* (1958); Meisner, *Li Ta-Chao and the Origins of Chinese Marxism* (1967); Bernal, *Chinese Socialism to 1907* (1976); Nakamura, "The Influence of Kemuyama Sentarō's Modern Anarchism" (1984); Fogel, *Ai Ssu-ch'i's Contribution to the Development of Chinese Marxism* (1987); Godley, "Socialism with Chinese Characteristics" (1987); Min, *National Polity and Local Power* (1990); Zarrow, *Anarchism and Chinese Political Culture* (1990); Chinese Communist Party Central Committee, *History of the Chinese Community Party* (1991); Dirlik, *Anarchism in the Chinese Revolution* (1993); Smith, *Like Cattle and Horses* (2002).

On Chinese expatriates, Chinese-Americans and efforts at reconstruction in China after the Qing, see: Cohen, *The Asian American Century* (2002); Bieler, *Patriots or Traitors?* (2004).

12

Essay
Manchus as Minorities

Although contemporary figures show the portion of the PRC population that identifies itself as "non-Han" is less than 10 percent, through history China has absorbed both immigrant populations and immigrant cultures. In some cases this has resulted in expansive changes in China's popular and élite cultures. Buddhism and Islam, both imports, have changed Chinese cultures and the lives of many millions of Chinese individuals. During the period of Mongol occupation in the twelfth and thirteenth centuries, the language at the capital of Beijing changed, while the arts and entertainments were deeply transformed by the tastes of the Mongol court. And it is not only conquerors who have had an effect. South China's regional cultures and dialects still strongly reflect the influences of the indigenous peoples who once dominated the area, but who were gradually driven into remote pockets or into Southeast Asia by the steady influx of Chinese farmers over the past two thousand years. The Miao, Yao, Naxi, Li, Zhuang, Dai and others who represent south and southwest China's earlier cultures are now recognized as among the 55 officially identified "minority nationalities" of the PRC.

In the earlier twentieth century, historians were fond of pointing to the Manchus – the military caste of the Qing empire – as examples of the axiom that "China conquers its conquerors." At the time of the Qing conquest of north China in 1644–5, Manchus were all enrolled in the Eight Banners, and so were often called "bannermen." Many Mongols were also in the Eight Banners, as were the cultural group known to the Qing as the "Chinese-martial" bannermen (*hanjun baqi*), who had complex genealogies but all spoke Chinese and had ancestors from the Chinese-speaking or Korean-speaking regions of Manchuria. By the nineteenth century, few Chinese-martial had survived the policy changes of the Qing court, and to all appearances the Chinese-martial could not be distinguished from civilian Chinese. Manchus, however, were under strict legal obligations to speak Manchu, study military arts, marry other Manchus and either live in the segregated garrison communities or gain permission to reside just outside them. The evidence is overwhelming that Manchus had a preference for speaking the local Chinese language, working at any trade in which they could support themselves, and marrying whomever they or their families thought best. The condition of Manchus before the middle nineteenth century contrasted strongly to the condition of the Hui Muslims. Manchus were prescribed a language and culture that were prized by the

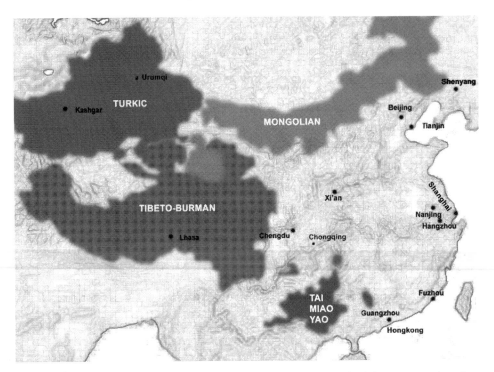

Map 9   Modern cultural variation. Areas of modern China in which languages other than Chinese are prevalent

court; they could be penalized if they did not follow this culture, and indirectly rewarded if they did. The Hui, like other Muslims in China, were objects of Qing government fear and contempt. When they exhibited devotion to their religion, used Arabic for religious purposes, dressed distinctly or gathered as a community to perform religious rituals, they were vulnerable to punishment or being placed at a disadvantage by the government. Nevertheless, a majority of Manchus failed to live up to government expectations that they sustain their difference from the majority, and a majority of Hui sustained their difference in defiance of government strictures.

The situation for many Manchus changed in the nineteenth century. As the government became impoverished, so did the Manchus who were required to live off a government stipend (often unpaid). As the government became weaker and the need to survive economically became stronger, more Manchus ignored legal obligations and left the garrisons to fend for themselves. However, when the Taiping War raged, many Manchu bannermen (as well as Mongol) volunteered to serve, under the Chinese civil governors who formed novel military organizations if necessary, to defend the empire. We can never be sure to what extent Taiping invective against the Manchus (see Chapter 7), and horrific Taiping assaults upon banner communities that required women and elderly men to take up arms to defend their families inspired a new sense of Manchu separateness and pride in some communities, but it must have had a role. After the war, many Manchus moved to the forefront of both the reform and the "self-strengthening" movements (see Chapter 10). Manchu identity in the nineteenth century was clearly what we would now call "layered" or "multi-valent." It did not depend upon the simplistic criteria of language or geographical segregation that the Qing court had once tried to impose (and which the PRC also bases its "minority" identities upon). Speaking Chinese, serving under the new civilian leadership or marrying Chinese did not necessarily contradict a sense of Manchu historical consciousness and obligation.

Despite the past claims of historians that Manchus were all assimilated by the beginning of the twentieth century, Chinese nationalists insisted that racial identities – including Manchu – could not be obliterated by culture. Even Manchus who were allies of the nationalists were often rejected, and when the revolution of 1911/12 broke out, there were repeated instances of mass murder of Manchu families. Some Manchus – like Mongols, Tibetans, and Uighurs – felt that the only option in the world after the empire was to separate themselves from the Chinese and form separate states. Others recognized China as their home and stayed, though usually concealing their Manchu heritage. In Republican China, historians tended to blame all of China's ills upon the Qing empire and the Manchus as a people. Admitting Manchu ancestry could be dangerous, and so when historians and sociologists sought Manchus in the 1930s through the 1970s, few or none could be found. In the later twentieth century, Manchus began to reclaim their historical identities. Many have applied themselves to learning to read Manchu, often to help in the archiving and preservation of a million Qing historical documents in Manchu. Others eagerly visit the few remaining locations in northeastern China where the Manchu language is still spoken, and some Manchu traditions are still observed.

The Manchus are now officially recognized as a minority nationality. Like other minority nationalities, they are – in theory – eligible to have more than one child, and may be eligible for preference in university admissions or employment. In practice, many minorities find that while it may be practical to receive permission to have more than one child, enjoying actual preference in education and employment may be impractical. Nevertheless, PRC citizens who claim minority nationality – which is voluntary, if an individual is eligible by ancestry – risk attracting the anger of Chinese colleagues who are chafing under the one-child policy, or the contempt of colleagues who see no importance in celebrating historical differences. The importance of those differences, however, may be shown in the fact that the proportion of "non-Han" PRC citizens is steadily rising, partly from increasing choice of minority registration and partly from increasing birth rates.

Though experiencing polar opposite pressures to be different or be the same in the eighteenth century, today the Manchus and Hui share an identical distinction, as the two "minority nationalities" that are heavily urban and professional. While many minority nationalities find it comfortable, profitable or politically convenient to continue to inhabit autonomous zones and entertain tourists with traditional dress, Manchus and Hui tend to treat their identities as what in other countries would be called "ethnicity" – a consciousness of difference that does not affect life in the economic and professional mainstream. As the PRC becomes more comfortable with this tone of personal difference, the implications for diversity in many areas of modern Chinese life may be profound.

Further reading

Crossley, *Orphan Warriors* (1990); Crossley, *The Manchus* (1997); Elliott, *The Manchu Way* (2001); Rhoads, *Manchus and Han* (2001); Ying and Conceison, *Voices Carry* (2008).

13
War

Research on World War II causes us to occasionally revise our estimates of the losses. Fifty-five nations now existing were involved in the war either as theaters of combat or as contributors to the deployed forces. Total estimates of about 70,000,000 deaths worldwide are still regarded by some historians as too low. Fatalities for Britain, France and the USA together equal about 1,000,000, and each country lost much less than 1 percent of total population. Historians agree that Russia (then the Soviet Union), with fatalities ranging between 12 and 15 percent of the entire population, suffered the greatest blow of all nations involved in the war. In absolute numbers, China's estimated 20,000,000 deaths rank second after the Soviet Union, but China's population of well over 500,0000,000 going into the war renders a percentage loss for China of about 4 percent, which might sound modest. The statistics for China are normally based upon a chronology from 1937 to 1945, and overwhelmingly relate to fighting between Chinese troops and Japanese, prisoner of war deaths (400,000 Chinese in Japanese custody) and related civilian casualties – the last-named accounting for 80 percent of the total, with three quarters of all civilian deaths attributed to famine. But the war beginning with the Japanese invasion of China in the 1930s was the middle phase of a period of prolonged war in China. Warfare on a significant scale began in China with the Northern Expedition in 1926. It continued after Japan's surrender, in the form of the final civil war between the Chinese communists and the Nationalist party, which officially concluded in 1924. Its final phase was the military consolidation of CCP power, coterminous with the war between China and the USA in Korea. Between 1926 and 1953, some part of China was always afflicted with organized large-scale armed combat. Famine related to failed government maintenance of infrastructure leading to the collapse of transport and the frequency of floods was widespread in the late 1920s and worsened in the 1930s and 1940s. For the two and half decades of conflict, total casualties among Chinese may have been as high as 40,000,000, probably overshadowing the losses in the Taiping War. As devastating as these losses were to individuals, families and communities, the period of continuous war had an equally shattering effect on the ability of the society to regenerate a state, and to construct a vital relationship between that state and the communities. Yet the destruction and disintegration of this period may have been the necessary crucible in which China's reunification was cast.

Following Sun Yatsen's death in 1925, succession was not clearly vested in Chiang Kaishek, but seemed suspended among Liao Zhongkai (American born and educated), Hu Hanmin, Wang Jingwei and Chiang. A few months later Liao was assassinated and Hu Hanmin was suspected as the killer, which reduced the field of active leaders to two. Chiang Kaishek moved quickly to implement the Northern Expedition of which Sun had dreamed, which marginalized Wang. In essence, the Northern Expedition would be both an instrument for securing Chiang's leadership of the Nationalist government and a war against the remnants of the Beiyang warlord network that still dominated north China. In the summer of 1925 Chiang collected his forces as the National Revolutionary Army, lectured them on the grand strategy of establishing a political base on the Yangtze, then consolidated forces for a move north. He broke off the Nationalist relationship with the Comintern in 1926, dispensing with the Russian strategists who had helped draw up the design of the Northern Expedition. The Nationalist government was now a one-party government, and the international press used the term "KMT" (the acronym of the old transliteration of Guomindang, the Nationalist party) variously for the party, Chiang's government and his military forces.

The Chinese Communist Party (CCP) was the next target of Chiang's housecleaning, and in the same month that he broke with the Comintern he banned CCP members from serving on KMT committees. The CCP nevertheless were ordered by the remote Comintern to lend their aid on the battlefield, in espionage and in guerilla organizing to the Northern Expedition. By 1926 Chiang controlled China from the Yangtze south, and east of Tibet. With the occupation of Shanghai, he felt confident in the power of the forces he controlled directly, and decided to purge the party, government and army of communists. Reports of a communist plot to assassinate him in 1926 also may have convinced him that co-existence with the CCP was impossible. The CCP, however, together with sympathizers from the left wing of the KMT under the leadership of a hero of the revolution, Wang Jingwei, still held the industrial center at Wuhan. Between 1926 and 1927 Chiang's new capital, Nanjing, and Wuhan were at war. The leftist KMT at Wuhan expelled the communists, hoping to avert Chiang's wrath, but in 1927 his troops occupied Wuhan and brought unified military governance to the entire Yangtze.

The warlords of the north were well armed and determined to resist Chiang if possible. Throughout China, warlords north and south had been assiduously arming themselves in preparation for the struggle. Rents, tribute from landlords, tribute from criminal gangs and, most important, opium all provided tremendous wealth to militarists for the purchase of weapons. Between the world wars, when there was no central government capable of handling systematic and legal weapons purchases, expenditures on light and heavy weapons from provincial militarists in China may have accounted for as much as 15 percent of global sales. The value of Chinese purchases is believed to have risen from about $300,000 in 1920 to $4,200,000 in 1927. Regional generals were well supplied with cars, trucks, horses, explosives, all manner of firearms and airplanes.

Chiang proceeded to press a ferocious, brutal campaign of extermination against communists and trade unionists. The simultaneous operations, in history called the "White Terror" (white contrasting to red, for communist), were surprise attacks in Shanghai, Canton, Nanjing and other cities, most in the Yangtze basin or on the southeast coast. In Shanghai, the overlord of the crime syndicates (and a member of the Green Gang, which claimed to be a Tiandihui descendant), Du Yuesheng, was enlisted to terrorize the unions while KMT security forces went after the communists; the civil government (once under the domination of Northeastern warlords) was dissolved. A few hundred people were shot in the streets by gangsters before dawn on April 12, while the bodies of thousands of summarily executed communists were left in the courtyards and alleyways. In the aftermath of the White Terror, Shanghai remained under the domination of Du Yuesheng and his gangster colleagues for decades. Similar massacres occurred throughout the cities under Chiang's control, with tremendous violence in Canton. China's enemy warlords in the north feared that communists fleeing the White Terror would infiltrate their territories and work to undermine them. Zhang Zuolin, for instance, who was in control of Beijing, heard that Li Dazhao (see chapter 11) had fled Shanghai for Beijing and taken refuge in the Soviet embassy; Zhang's troops stormed the grounds, assassinating Li and killing nineteen other people. Deaths were in the tens of thousands, and CCP histories would later report that 80 percent of CCP members were killed in the attacks. Surviving communists fled the cities for the relative safety of the countryside. The savagery of the attacks caused problems between Chiang and the Soong family, into which he was hoping to marry. Sun Yatsen's widow Soong Ching-ling (whom Chiang had already tried unsuccessfully to marry) was furious at Chiang and wanted him kicked out of the Nationalist party. Her brother T.V. Soong, the family's star financier, distanced himself publicly from Chiang for a time. Yet within months Chiang had not only convinced the family to accept his political tactics, but had also smoothed over tensions caused by his complicated marital history by sending one of his previous wives to the USA to earn a doctorate. He married Soong May-ling in late 1927.

Following the wars among warlords around Beijing from 1922 to 1924 (see chapter 11), there was no recognizable power center at Beijing. Duan Qirui and his "Anhui clique" lost their domination of the Beijing civil appointments after a military challenge from Zhang Zuolin and Cao Kun. The main combatants in the war, Zhang Zuolin's "Fengtian clique" and Cao Kun's "Zhili clique," decided to recognize each other's territory and political prerogatives, once most of Duan Qirui's old territories had been absorbed by Cao, the nominal victor. They lived in uneasy neutrality with other cliques, including the Shanxi clique of the reform-minded governor Yan Xishan. The destabilizing presence in their ranks was Feng Yuxiang. He had come up through the Beiyang Intendancy armies in the days of Yuan Shikai, and still believed in the old ways – military first, all the new weapons that could be bought, careful discipline of the troops, education and training of each individual, political leadership in Beijing and Tianjin, suspicion of Japan. In 1914 he had been converted to Christianity, and liked to think that his troops were all Christian, too (he baptized them en masse with a fire hose). When the Intendancy disintegrated after Duan Qirui was deposed, Feng threw his loyalty to Cao Kun, whose territories and alliances encompassed the greater part of the old Intendancy. But Feng was open to plenty of influences – including the Comintern, which made contact with him in 1924. At the time Feng was in charge of his own army, the "national people's army" (*Guominjun*). He was persuaded in late 1924, either by the Comintern or by Zhang Zuolin's son Zhang Xueliang – or by both – that leaving the Zhili clique in power in the north was a mistake. He and his army defected from the Zhili to the Fengtian side. In a brief but decisive war, the Fengtian clique reversed the previous result, and assumed command and tribute rights over the former

Zhili territories, including Beijing. The Forbidden City was seized by Feng Yuxiang himself, who made sure Puyi and his court were safely escorted out of Beijing.

Chiang Kaishek, now consolidating his hold over the Yangtze, had previously considered the Zhili clique to have conserved most of the power of the Beiyang Intendancy. He now saw the greatest warlords of the north defeated by their own underlings, and pressed forward with his plans to proceed north. Ironically, to get to Beijing he had to go through the armies of Feng Yuxiang and Yan Xishan. The two considered their positions, then signed on to Chiang's campaign against the Fengtian clique. As Chiang established himself north of the Yangtze and gathered more allies on his way to Beijing, the northern warlords gradually sought a way to accommodate the inevitable. Chiang commanded a force of not less than 2,000,000 men, while even the largest warlords of the north had armies of a hundred thousand. Zhang Zuolin was a holdout. In 1926, as many generals of the north shifted their weight either toward neutrality or toward Chiang Kaishek, Zhang seized control of Beijing and asserted his intention to remain independent in the north. Japanese agents warned him to return to the Northeast, where his cooperation had been essential to previous economic and industrial development. In 1928, as Chiang's forces approached the capital, Zhang attempted to return to Shenyang (which the Japanese called by its Manchu name of Mukden) by train. A bomb, planted by a Japanese army officer, exploded during the train's passage under a bridge. Zhang Zuolin was killed. The Southern Manchuria Railroad company kept the news a secret for almost two weeks while installing Zhang's son, Zhang Xueliang, as the new lord of the Northeast. Part of their haste to murder the elder Zhang was their conviction that the younger would be a pliant puppet in their hands. Young Zhang's first act was to declare allegiance to Chiang Kaishek.

The death of Zhang Zuolin removed the last obstacle to Chiang Kaishek's conquest of Beijing in 1928. For the first time since the middle nineteenth century, real and legal power were predominantly in the hands of one man, and the country was under the apparent political leadership of a single capital. The human cost had been considerable; a two-year struggle through a finite corridor of territory had left at least 300,000 dead in its wake. The achievement was profound, but it depended upon a studiously superficial approach to the regional and provincial powers entrenched in north China. Chiang's military title, "Generalissimo" (*jiangren da yuanshi*), was both in Chinese and in English a term for a supreme campaign commander, a general overseeing and coordinating the activities of other generals. Only provinces ruled by Chiang directly paid taxes to the government; other provinces collected their own taxes and made their own disbursements, an arrangement that did not differ greatly from the days of the Beiyang Intendancy. He did not assume the presidency, but was styled "chairman" of the KMT government as he had been chairman of the party since the death of Sun Yatsen. The Council of State – one of Yuan Shikai's innovations that had lived on after him – and other political institutions in Beijing were of little interest to Chiang. The city of Beijing became, in official KMT terminology, Beiping – "northern pacification," with the "capital" element removed from the name. Chiang intended to seat his government at Nanjing, and to run it as a military dictatorship. In his view, this accorded with the plans of Sun Yatsen, who thought that a nationalist military occupation of the country would be necessary for the government to begin its long work of re-education of the population, which would itself be a necessary prelude to the creation of a civil, and perhaps representative, government.

The nominal presidencies that had fronted for warlord government in Beijing since Yuan Shikai's resignation in 1916 were abolished, as were the premierships of the State Council. Instead, an Executive Cabinet (*xingzheng yuan*) was created at Nanjing, with departments dedicated to defense, finance and communications. From 1928 to 1947 Chiang was briefly president of this cabinet four times; during other periods it was presided over by his brothers-in-law H.H. Kung and T.V. Soong or their political front men. Chiang made the decisions, but was spared the distraction of administrative affairs. He devoted himself to maintaining his military hegemony, and pursuing the support of foreign governments.

During one extraordinary passage from 1932 to 1935, the Executive Cabinet was presided over by the charismatic Wang Jingwei, a decided political enemy of Chiang. Despite his tentative alliance with the CCP against Chiang in 1926, Wang had escaped, physically, from the collapsing Wuhan government and had escaped, politically, from being labeled a communist. In fact, it appears that his politics moved sharply to the right. Wang had been genuinely suspicious of the communists' ties to the Comintern, and after the White Terror seems to have been careful to position himself as remotely as possible from leftists, socialists and labor supporters. Once Wang had been a contender to succeed Sun Yatsen as head of the party, but he had been pushed aside by Chiang. After 1928, Wang seemed to be pushing back. His greatest resources were the mercurial Feng Yuxiang and the progressive Yan Xishan. Both had capitulated to Chiang during the Northern Expedition, but both harbored reservations about Chiang's political program and resentments over their relative loss of power. In 1929 Chiang attempted what the Qing had not attempted in the aftermath of the Taiping War: He promulgated a command that the military governors disband their forces and enroll them in a national army, under Chiang's own command. Feng and Yan decided to attempt a coup against Chiang. Wang joined them as the political frontman and sympathizers were widespread, including the former Guangdong warlord Chen Jiongming, who hated Chiang's one-party system of military dictatorship. Bai Omar Chongxi, the Muslim warlord dominating part of Guangxi, along with two other Guangxi warlords, formally refused Chiang's demands in March of 1929. By May the rebel warlords, led by Feng Yuxiang's "People's Army," were in open combat with Chiang's troops. Other regional governors, and some high-ranking members of Chiang's bureaucracy in Nanjing, defected. In early 1930 Yan Xishan demanded that Chiang Kaishek give up his power as head of government. The Guangxi generals headed for Hubei and seized Wuhan. Yan Xishan directed his forces from his base in Shanxi toward Nanjing.

Much of the country was wracked by famine. Organizers of rural support relief and defense organizations were far more dependent on the local warlords than on Nanjing, and many feared that Chiang's plans would inevitably mean the diversion of local resources from their counties and provinces into the Nationalist coffers. In the early months of fighting, momentum was on the side of the renegades, but within weeks the impossibly distant deployment tactics of their forces opposing Chiang began to take a toll. By June of 1930 Chiang was beginning to reverse the course of the war, and in September he received the decisive advantage of Zhang Xueliang's decision not to join the Wang Jingwei party but to support Chiang Kaishek against them. By the end of the year the war had been negotiated to a close. The significance of the rebellion of 1930 is out of proportion to its length. In a matter of months, a minimum of

300,000 more deaths had been added to the mounting casualties from warfare. The rebellion inspired others, most notably Hu Hanmin's attempt to foment a Guangdong secessionist government in 1931. Chiang arrested Hu, but later released him under pressure from Nationalist generals. Thereafter, Hu's organization in Canton remained a lightning rod for anti-Chiang discontents. The Chiang regime had been shown to be built on an unsteady alliance with heavily armed militarists jealous of their power; government attempts to dismantle that power in order to stabilize the government only threatened the stability of the government more. At the conclusion of the war, the generals all once again swore allegiance to Chiang Kaishek, and in return he made Wang Jingwei president of the Executive Cabinet.

Surrounded by political challenges from within, rebel base areas, secessionism and foreign invasion in the early 1930s, Chiang Kaishek seemed in need of a guiding political idea. A program for resocialization, to pry rural people in particular away from their loyalties to their local governors, would also divert them from the appeal of communism. Beginning in Jiangxi province (where Mao's Soviet base area – see below – was rapidly reorganizing some elements of rural life), word of Chiang's "New Life Movement" was spread via telegram, poster, pamphlet, public lectures and organizing of mass "demonstrations." By 1935 New Life instructional committees were established in more than 1,100 counties, and the message was being spread energetically by Nationalist party agents. According to Soong May-ling, the New Life Movement was "the only path for the salvation of the country."

The central tenet of the movement, apparently inspired by (the American educated) Soong May-ling herself, was personal hygiene. By washing hands, brushing teeth and wearing clean clothes, Chinese would transform themselves and the nation. The program progressed from the simple to the complex and comprehensive. Keeping clean required getting up early in the morning to make the preparations. That demanded a strict organization of one's personal schedule. The necessary self-discipline, once ingrained, would militate against opium addiction, gambling or laziness. The growing dedication to order would extend to public life. In 1936 a KMT official reported that the movement had reached its zenith: "There is no wandering or shuffling about the streets, no stopping in the middle of the road, no gaping about and no blocking the traffic. The people ... always keep to the left when walking about the streets. Smoking in the streets is considered undesirable and slovenly. Spitting in public places calls for a reprimand, not from the police but from followers of the New Life Movement." These New Life members, going about enforcing a distinctly American public space discipline on Chinese, wore crisp blue shirts, traveled in committees and made detailed reports on their achievements in correcting social deviation. Men, women and children had their own organizations. All were encouraged to report on the relative orderliness of their neighbors and alert the authorities to what was regarded as deviant speech or action. In the teaching materials distributed to them (ostensibly authored by Chiang Kaishek), they were advised to see their fellow Chinese as alien creatures who ate like animals and walked like zombies. Wang Jingwei, then well on the way to fascist enthusiasms, denounced the traditional Chinese lack of discipline and ambition.

Ideas of hierarchy and respect for authority, attributed to Confucius, were thrown into the teaching materials. The highest virtue was complete subordination of the individual to the group. Critics such as Hu Shih denounced the movement's trivialization of political culture. New Life politics were strictly those of the regimented, militarized, obedient "new citizen." Particles were lifted from the Beiyang military reforms, the Three People's Principles, rural reconstructive education and Christian missionary schools, all in the service of transforming local autonomy into a national, and industrious, uniformity. But even when Chiang Kaishek, Soong May-ling and their supporters were putting the most energy into the New Life movement between 1934 and 1936, the impact of the program was slight. Local officials were careful to say correct things, but beyond the enclave of Nanjing the challenges of survival and the primacy of local structures muffled any impact that state propaganda could have. Outside the circles of wealth and comfort where the Chiangs nested, it was avoiding drought and famine and earning the next meal while staying on the healthy side of local landlords, criminal syndicates and the provincial armies that were the daily tasks; ironing clothes, walking on the left and informing on seedy neighbors never traveled to the top of most people's priorities.

The urgency with which the Chiangs pushed New Life was clearly related to the scope as well as the nature of the challenge from the CCP. From the middle 1920s, Mao and a minority of the CCP had been fighting a combined ideological and strategic battle against a majority in the party – that majority being largely educated and international, having traveled or studied in Moscow, France, England or Japan. The Comintern tended to play all sides of any internal conflict in China; both Mao and his rivals among the party orthodox received encouraging messages from Moscow, though Mao's rivals received more. Li Lisan, who had a history as a crack labor organizer in the mines of Jiangxi province, was the leader of the party during much of the later 1920s, and sometimes its actual chairman. Zhang Guotao, Zhou Enlai, Liu Shaoqi and other veterans sided with him against the rural anarcho-socialists led by Mao.

In the middle 1920s, when still based in Canton, Mao had found that the rural organizing of Peng Pai was an example of how revolution would be realized. Communist party cells based on historic communities, comprehensively woven into the fabric of work, defense, education and social life, would create a geography of revolution that could be gradually expanded to the entire country. Peng and Mao blended agrarian socialism, anarchism and Marxist-Leninist theory (see chapter 11) into a science of rural transformation. When the White Terror extermination campaign against the communists was unleashed, many CCP members fled the cities for the countryside, becoming more or less willing adherents of Mao's strategy, if not his ideology. Peng joined other CCP members in briefly attempting to hold out in the city of Nanchang, Jiangxi, against Nationalist forces in August of 1927. Zhou Enlai, Zhu De, Ye Jianying and He Long mustered their forces to support him and declared their combined troops as the People's Liberation Army (PLA). KMT forces quickly dispersed the group. Before the end of the year Peng was back in his home county of Haifeng in Guangdong province, and announced the creation of the Guangdong Soviet, with its own governing committees and defense forces. The Nationalists were too engrossed in gaining control of the cities and dealing with the unpredictable giants among the northern warlords to notice. Mao left his wife, Yang Kaihui (who would be captured and tortured to death by the KMT in 1930), and two young sons in Shanghai, and went to the Jinggang mountains in Jiangxi province to set up his own soviet among the friendly villages there. Chen Jiongming, the warlord of Guangdong, set his troops against both of the soviets. Peng's fell within weeks, and he fled Canton where he lived incognito until 1929, when he was executed in Shanghai after trying to lead another uprising against the KMT.

Chen Jiongming did not succeed in dislodging Mao's Jiangxi soviet, nor the smaller soviets which were dotted around southeast China. In the ensuing years Mao expanded his territory and strengthened his military. Deng Xiaoping, a tiny Sichuanese who had joined the CCP while a laborer and student in France after the First World War, attempted to create his own soviet in Guangxi province in 1928; when it collapsed, he and his followers took refuge in Mao's base area. Mao still professed allegiance to the CCP, which was under the leadership of Li Lisan until he was pushed out by a fresh troop of Comintern-minted revolutionaries led by Wang Ming in 1929. The arrival of Wang and his "Twenty-Eight Bolsheviks" plunged the mainstream CCP into years of turmoil. Li Lisan loyalists, veterans who disliked being condescended to, and party members annoyed by Wang's personality and style began to resist his leadership. In 1931, as the party prepared for a national congress, Wang Ming was called back to Moscow, where he stayed until 1937.

In November of 1931 CCP members gathered at Ruijin, Jiangxi for an all-party summit, a "plenum." The local committees and the Comintern had agreed that there was no safe place in China for communists to assemble except in the heart of Mao's Jiangxi soviet. Mao used the event to take the extraordinary step of transforming his guerilla base area into a state, the Chinese Soviet Republic (*Zhonghua sulianyi gong-heguo*). The new country had a population of about 3,000,000 people. Mao was declared head of state, both as "national chairman" (*guojia zhuxi*) and as prime minister. The CCP, which made its permanent home there, remained a separate organization, under General Secretary Bo Gu. Plans were put into place to create a central bank with its own currency; the bank went into business in 1932, with Mao's brother as its director. A land reform program provided that the landless or owners with negligible land received plots sufficient to maintain them, taken from large landholders. Suspicion of the criteria used for classification brought resistance from farmers, however, and Mao resorted to a flat tax on land that was marginally less (at about 38 percent of the realized harvest) than the tax imposed by the Nationalist government. Shopkeepers were also taxed to provide the area with amenities, including repaired roads to take goods safely to market. Economically the majority of residents in the CSR were living at a higher level than those outside their limits. The prosperity of the CSR benefited neighboring regions, in part because its silver coins corresponded in size and valuation to the Mexican dollars that had been used continually throughout China since the middle nineteenth century. Better quality of life, regardless of the form of ideology of political control that accompanied it, made the CSR attractive to surrounding villages in both Jiangxi and interior Fujian, so that the area had the potential of expanding rapidly. The city of Ruijin and a few outlying towns had electricity, cable communications and telephones, amenities little known in China outside the largest cities. The CCP set up a radio broadcast enterprise, in addition to its printing operations. In 1931 a constitution was promulgated. In addition to protecting the property of the residents, it explicitly recognized the property rights, cultural independence and political participation of the Miao, Yi, Li and Zhuang nationalities who lived in the region. The right of cultural minority areas to secede was explicitly guaranteed. An added marriage law forbade arranged marriages, outlawed dowries and made divorce possible at the request of either party.

The People's Liberation Army, which at the time was a standing force of about 140,000 (comparable to the forces of any single northern warlord, though much smaller than Chiang's growing Nationalist army), was put under the command of Zhu De, a Hakka farmer's son from Guangdong who had begun life as an accomplished traditional scholar before switching to a military career as both a member of Sun's League of Alliances and of the Gelaohui secret society in 1912. He had served during the Yuan Shikai period as an enforcer for warlords in lawless Guangxi, been addicted to opium and thrown it off, and finally joined the CCP while a student in Germany. Zhu was one of Mao's first supporters in the Jiangxi base area, credited with not only making the soviet secure, but also developing the Red Army as an unusually advanced fighting force. The CSR had sufficient cash to buy its share of the weapons that circulated everywhere in the country. And though his army lacked some of the heavy artillery that could be commanded by the Nationalists, it ranked with Chiang's best units – and above most of the warlord armies – in its advanced cable and radio communications. To exploit its military advantages for the sake of greater strategic leverage, some CCP military commanders left the CSR to set up base areas of their own, expecting to some day annex the territories to the CSR. Zhang Guotao, for instance, took his forces to Sichuan and set up a base. He Long created a small base in western Hunan and Hubei. In essence, the new bases worked off land and social policies that paralleled those of the CSR.

The emergence of a fully fledged state in the interior of the country alarmed and infuriated Chiang Kaishek. Though he was in the process of dealing with the secession of Feng Yuxiang and Yan Xishan, Chiang attempted to pre-empt the congress and creation of the CSR in the last weeks of 1930 and the early winter of 1931. The base areas held, partly because of the aid of the villagers in sabotaging KMT communications and transport. In subsequent campaigns during the autumn of 1931, KMT forces were more concentrated and made more progress, but sudden Japanese seizure of the Northeast (see below) caused Chiang to break off the attack. Advisors to the Chiangs argued that the Japanese attack had changed the strategic environment, and suggested that Chiang consider a second united front with the CCP for purposes of driving Japan out of the Northeast. As Chiang hesitated, Japan bombarded Nanjing in 1932 and Japanese forces were being landed at Shanghai. To some of Chiang's advisors, including Feng Yuxiang, a rapprochement with the CCP was urgent and imperative. Chiang saw the situation another way: Complete elimination of the communists, first, would permit him to turn his full attention to defending China against Japan afterward. It might also buy time to reinforce China's material defense-works and improve its communications systems.

By 1933 the conflicts with Yan, Feng and Wang Jingwei were resolved, and Chiang collected his forces for a full assault on the CSR in the spring. Zhu De's defending troops allowed the Nationalists to gain ground. The leadership of the CCP, including Zhou Enlai, denounced Mao and Zhu for their strategies, and removed them from command. When the Nationalist troops arrived in September of 1933, Bo Gu, Zhou Enlai, and the Comintern advisor Otto Braun had taken control of military strategy. For months the armies clashed on all fronts of the CSR, with the Nationalists steadily gaining ground. By September of 1934 it was clear to Zhou Enlai (who was also the chief of intelligence for the CSR) that the Nationalist forces were going to overrun the base area, and probably engage in another mass slaughter of the CCP. Eighty-six thousand people – overwhelmingly members of the CCP and of the

People's Liberation Army, among whom were only 35 women – organized for an exodus out of the area before the KMT forces arrived.

The Long March, the trek of CCP members and supporters from Jiangxi to Shaanxi province, took slightly more than a year. In outline the story is fairly simple: Nearly 90,000 people were driven of Jiangxi, a little over 8,000 arrived at the destination after walking about 6,000 miles. Those who participated, such as Mao Zedong, Zhu De, Zhou Enlai and Deng Xiaoping, would go on to enjoy long-lasting power in the state created in 1949. Critical events along the way would consolidate Mao's almost unshakable grip on the party and its ideology. The method of living, fighting and working evolved during the Long March would shape a revolutionary culture that would inform Chinese life in the 1950s and 1960s. Both the heroism and the canniness demonstrated by the Red Army would win the hearts of the Chinese public and provide the unity and determination to first defeat Japan, then the KMT, then to confront the imperial powers. Some of this myth bears up under historical examination, but there is more to the story of the Long March.

One essential theme is the relationship of China to its border areas, and the ongoing attempts to reconstitute the strategic frontiers of the Qing empire. The route of the march does not go from Jiangxi to Shaanxi in a straight line (that would be only

Map 10 Communist spaces, 1928–49. Major CCP base areas, 1933–7, and the Long March to Yan'an

about 2,000 miles). The march to the west, and then to the north, follows a path through which the CCP could draw upon the resources of disaffected border areas. The Zunyi "conference" was really a series of consultations and confrontations at the Guizhou-Sichuan border region, as well as cable communications, between January and September of 1935. Nearly half the Guizhou population was not Han Chinese, but were instead Miao, Yao, Qiang, Zhuang, Tibetan, Muslim (Hor) or a half dozen other groups. He Long, the CCP general whom Mao was expecting to meet at Zunyi, was himself a member of the Tujia group who had inhabited the highlands between Hunan and Guizhou for many centuries. Like Yunnan to the west, the region had been only lightly governed since the late nineteenth century. Traditional village organizations, farming cooperatives and plentiful smuggling operations kept the residents fed and secure, and interference from the Chinese central government, or governments, was not appreciated. Guizhou and Yunnan, together with Guangxi, had been a reservoir of resistance to Chiang personally and to the KMT generally. Its warlords were quick to assert independence, and were slow to support Chiang against his Beiyang challengers. Their territory, or at least the outer perimeters of it, was hospitable ground for the wandering communist rebels.

To the north and west of Zunyi lay Xinjiang province, a prospective path for CCP relocation. From the revolution of 1911/12 to 1928, the province had been under the iron fist of Yang Zengxin. He had come to power by capturing and executing local revolutionaries, which had endeared him to Yuan Shikai. In return, Yuan had permitted Yang to maintain a personal fiefdom in Xinjiang. After Yuan's death the Duan Qirui government had been uneasy about Yang's power, but had generally left him alone. He tolerated no social disorders, harshly excluded any consideration of Muslim dietary, social or economic values from his policy decisions, and welcomed Soviet trade, advisors and weapons. In 1928 Yang had celebrated Chiang Kaishek's triumph in the Northern Expedition, but then had been almost immediately murdered by a local political rival. Yang's lieutenant Jin Shuren seized power and continued Yang's policies, while the Nationalist government seemed unwilling or unable to assert its influence. Jin's selective demand for taxation on Uighurs and appropriation of their land, as well as intrusion into traditional selection of local leaders, sparked an uprising at Kumul (Hami) in 1931. In response, Jin's subordinate Sheng Shicai led both local troops and reinforcements from the Soviet Union against the rebels. The revolt was suppressed, and in the aftermath Sheng decided to use his impressive combined force to establish himself as warlord of Xinjiang. In 1933, a year before the CCP armies began moving toward their Zunyi summit, Jin was driven out of the province, possibly to the Soviet Union, and Sheng assumed control. The cities of Khotan and Kashgar declared an independent state, the Turkish Islamic Republic of Eastern Turkestan. The rebel state was poor and lacking modern communications. The Soviet Union, the KMT government in Nanjing, Sheng Shicai himself and local Muslim warlords who were loyal to Sheng were all determined to stamp it out. By February of 1934 the rebel cities had been retaken by Sheng or his Soviet military allies, and the aspiring nationalists had dispersed to India, Afghanistan and the Yunnan/Guizhou/Guangxi border areas which the Long March was approaching. The fact that Xinjiang was, at the time of the Zunyi conference, all but a client state of the Soviet Union suggested to many CCP strategists that the province could be a good place to escape Chiang's clutches and rebuild the CCP revolution.

The strategic role of Xinjiang could not be considered without the context of Tibet and Mongolia. The Yuan Shikai regime had showed very little interest in Tibetan affairs after the 1914 Simla agreement (see chapter 10). The Canton government of Sun Yatsen made a half-hearted attempt to regain control of the Kham territory of Tibet in 1917, but afterward pursued reconciliation with Tibet by offering the Dalai Lama national honorifics and inviting leading Tibetan militarists to become members of the KMT. The response was negligible, though by the early 1920s the Sun government and the British government had come to a sort of understanding. Britain ceased its attempts to encourage Tibetan independence, and tended to describe Tibet as a distinct entity "under Chinese suzerainty." For his part, Sun spoke near his death of a policy of "self-determination" for the peoples of distinct culture, which was understood to mean Tibet above all. In the meantime, fighting in the Tibetan areas bordering Xinjiang, Gansu, Sichuan and Yunnan was constant. Chinese warlords, Muslim warlords and Tibetan warlords, big and small, competed for the strategic areas of water sources, trade routes, agriculture and, now, railway development. In 1933, the thirteenth Dalai Lama died under unclear circumstances, and the hunt for the fourteenth Dalai Lama would take seven years. It was an opportunity for ambitious warlords to declare independence, and that happened almost immediately in Kham, where a pair of Tibetans attempted to establish a state distinct from both Tibet and China. Western Sichuan warlords immediately invaded the area to put an end to the claims. The CCP group traveling from Jiangxi to Zunyi entered the general zone of the quarrel just as the rebels were being mopped up. CCP strategists must have noted that while Nationalist fragmentation left Tibet open to British influence and permitted individual Tibetan militarists to exert influence over a wide swathe of territories that were ostensibly Chinese, the strategic importance of the Tibetan plateau demanded that any regime hoping to unify China find a way to bind Tibet inalienably to China.

Mongolia, on the northern side of the Gansu corridor, was also an influence on Xinjiang. Many groups of western Mongolia, such as the Kazakh and the Dzunghars, moved frequently between the two regions because of herding or trade; and in times of trouble, either region could be fled to from the other. More pertinent to the prospects for the CCP, the region often called "Outer Mongolia" had been an independent theocracy from 1911 to 1924. For the last three years of that period the theocracy had been fiction, as a result of the fact that Mongolia had become a battle ground in the consolidation of communist control over Russia. After the November Revolution of 1917, "White" Russian holdouts against the Bolsheviks had attempted to take refuge in Mongolia and use it as a staging area for battling the revolutionary troops. The Mongolian religious ruler, the Bogd Khaan, had granted permission, hoping to gain an ally against Chinese warlords who from time to time invaded the country and demanded that the Bogd Khaan capitulate to them. But the White Russians occupied the Mongolian capital at Urga in 1920 and 1921, toppling the government of the Bogd Khaan. Mongol guerillas hoping to drive the Russians from the country appealed for aid to the Bolsheviks, and formed a Mongolian Communist Party to formalize their alliance. In 1921 the Mongols under the command of Sukhbaatar drove the Russians out, and restored the Bogd Khaan to titular power while they formed a new government on the Soviet model. In 1924, the Bogd Khaan abdicated and gave his blessing to the Mongolian People's Republic, the first "people's republic" in history. The country's economic planning came under the influence of the Soviet Union, and in the late 1920s there was unrest throughout the region, as herdsmen resisted collectivization of herds and lands, and destruction of religious centers.

The increasing domination of Mongolia, as well as Xinjiang, by the Soviet Union might have suggested to the CCP that Mongolia would be a good haven, but it was far too remote and underdeveloped in communications to be a good revolutionary base. A more appealing prospect was Inner Mongolia (then called Chakhar after its largest Mongolian dialect group), the long half-moon of traditionally Mongol territory that historically had been an economic province of China. Its main city – Hohhot (Qing period Guihua and Suiyuan) – had had a large population in the sixteenth century, already mostly composed of Chinese merchants. The proximity of Chakhar to the Northeast gave rise to frenzied organizing of patriotic militia guerilla groups to resist further Japanese encroachment. None other than Feng Yuxiang had turned up to lead the effort in 1933. Within months he had assembled a force in excess of a hundred thousand men, stopped the Japanese advance at the Chakhar borders and established a new base for himself at Zhangjiakou, just inside Hebei province. The territories now controlled by Feng were thick with people, weapons and easy communications to the major cities of north China. They were also the corridor to confronting the Japanese in the Northeast. The only drawback of aiming for Chakhar was Feng's inconstant politics. The chances that he would welcome the CCP with open arms one day and turn them out the next were high. Of course, Mao and his colleagues were aware that this was also true for Feng's relationship with the KMT.

When Mao and his followers, now reduced to 15,000, reached the Zunyi area, they intended to join up with the armies of Zhang Guotao and He Long. Within his own group, Mao's supremacy was now unquestioned – previous skeptics, particularly Zhou Enlai, were either vocal supporters of Mao's ideological and strategic views or learned not to voice dissent. The arrival of the Zhang and He armies changed this. He Long's comparatively small force was easily amalgamated with Mao's, and He himself became a staunch follower. But Zhang Guotao was different. He arrived in the area with a complement of soldiers five times the size of Mao's and he seemed intent on seizing control of the migration. The groups fought side by side in a few engagements with local KMT forces, but in the background lay their political rivalry and their strategic disagreements. Zhang challenged Mao's entire concept of the future of the trek, arguing that the way was not north into Shaanxi but south into Sichuan, further into the protection of the hill peoples. Mao pointed out that the troubles in Kham had brought a concentration of troops and conflict into the area; he wanted to go away from it, not toward it. Mao was, moreover, sensitive about wearing out the welcome of the local non-Han peoples. It is possible that when Zhang became convinced that Mao would not defer to him, Zhang decided to have Mao arrested or worse, and that Zhang's lieutenants Ye Jianying and Yang Shangkun saved Mao by giving the plot away. Whatever the details, the upshot was that Mao and his supporters, not greatly increased in number, left the camp in the direction Mao had determined. For good measure, Mao had CCP headquarters circulate resolutions that officially declared Zhang Guotao to be a "splittist," an "opportunist," and probably an aspiring warlord. Contrary to his orders, Zhang took his troops south and east, and in a year of fighting lost almost three quarters of his force. After he finally turned to head north toward the base area Mao had established at Yan'an, he lost most of his remaining force in fighting against warlords who tried to stop him crossing the Yellow River. When Zhang dragged into Yan'an, Mao received him and gave him a bureaucratic title with the local party organization, but made his life miserable. Zhang defected from the communist cause in 1938.

Yan'an, where Mao brought his migration to ground, was a relatively calm area, with a natural isolation from the densely populated Wei River Valley directly to the south. The Wei River valley, and the city of Xi'an, had been the political center of China for the thousand years before the capitals had shifted east to Beijing and Nanjing. Some of the earliest states of China, and all its early empires, had placed themselves somewhere on the Wei River which diverged from a great bend in the Yellow River. Yan'an was outside the belt of prosperity and nestled on the edge of what had been the diverse and under-populated borderlands of the Qing, now loosely controlled or independent regimes.

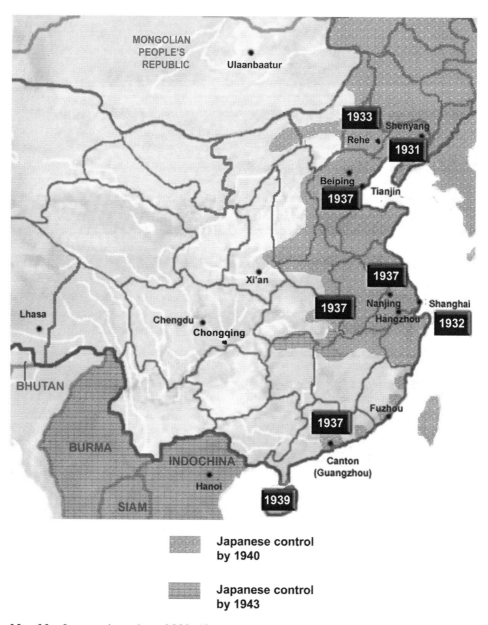

Japanese control by 1940

Japanese control by 1943

Map 11 Japanese incursions, 1932–43

Yan'an was a historic rebel base. It had been used by both Li Zicheng and Zhang Xianzong (see chapter 2) in their massive revolts that ended the Ming dynasty. When Mao and the CCP arrived at the end of 1935, it was controlled, to the extent it was controlled at all, by bandit gangs and Muslim warlords. Mao and his forces were able to assert control quickly. Sichuan warlords, to the south, were still engaged in mopping up Tibetan rebels. The highlands of Qinghai (actually the eastern piedmont of the Tibetan plateau) separated Yan'an from dangerous Sheng Shicai in Xinjiang. To the east and north lay the territory of Yan Xishan, the progressive dictator of Shanxi, and beyond that the Chakhar corridor controlled by Feng Yuxiang. Mao had hopes of cooperating both with Yan and with Feng, and to a degree it worked. In time Yan welcomed communists from the Yan'an base into his province to aid in agricultural development, and both Feng and Yan not only listened to Mao's ideas with some interest, but also permitted a certain amount of lecturing to their farmers and soldiers. In 1933, Chiang Kaishek sent a large force against Feng, whom he feared had either become a communist or was permitting communists to infiltrate the Chakhar armies. In 1934 Feng resigned his command and was sent by Chiang to aid in the training of troops near Beijing.

Historians argue whether Japanese military and economic encroachment on China from the late nineteenth century to the early twentieth century was the cause of Chinese disunity and vulnerability, or the other way around. It might be best to see them as two tires on the same bicycle. The fall of centralized political authority in the late Qing permitted the hypertrophy of local and regional regimes, the two greatest of which were the Beiyang Intendancy and the Japanese military empire growing in the Northeast, northern China, and parts of coastal China. Both wove their commercial, intelligence and military operations into provincial and county life. Both grew stronger as the Qing government grew weaker. Both smothered the development of national civil government after the fall of the empire. Each stimulated the growth of the other while diminishing the resources and the strategic space for any centralized entity in China. Beiyang forces overwhelmed the Qing remnants in 1912, but lost their final battles in 1928, when Japanese agents assassinated Zhang Zuolin, and Chiang Kaishek forced northern militarists to accept his supremacy.

The assassination of Zhang Zuolin in 1928 had clearly marked a determination by Japanese operators to control the Chinese leadership in Manchuria, since their expectation was that Zhang's son, the 27-year-old "young marshal" Zhang Xueliang, would be their puppet governor of the province. Zhang immediately expressed his loyalty to the KMT, but that was only to be expected, and the Japanese were confident he would conform to their military agenda. As a manager and strategist, Zhang proved to be a very practical. Nevertheless, he was caught unprepared by the Japanese assault on Mukden, his provincial capital, in September of 1931. An explosion on a Japanese rail line leading into the city was blamed by the Southern Manchuria Railway Company on Chinese terrorists, and regiments of the Kantôgun – the mercenary army loosely authorized by the Japanese government to safeguard Japanese industrial sites in Manchuria – immediately deployed artillery weapons already secreted inside the city. Zhang Xueliang's airplanes were destroyed on the ground, and his troops fled the city in shock. From Nanjing, Zhang decided to not resist the Japanese coup, but to withdraw with as many men, supplies and weapons as he could move to nearby Chakhar; when Japanese troops made an incursion a few months later into Rehe (Chengde of the Qing period), Zhang Xueliang stood down. But the Northeast and the eastern edge of Mongolia were effectively in Japanese hands.

At that moment Chiang Kaishek was dealing with dissent and secessionism within the KMT, as well as the unsuccessful assault against the Chinese Soviet Republic. He did nothing to resist the Japanese forces as they consolidated their control over the Northeast, integrated it with their colonial industries in Korea and linked it to their facilities in Shandong province. Popular reaction in China was immediate and continued to build for months. Anti-Japanese riots broke out across the country, but most intensely in the eastern coastal cities. Warlords in most areas, and the KMT government in Nanjing and Shanghai, suppressed the disorders, but in January of 1932 five Japanese Buddhist monks were beaten to death by a crowd in Shanghai. Riots spread, as well as calls for a boycott of Japanese goods – especially the new mass-produced Japanese textiles that were for the first time outselling Chinese cotton and silk in the department stores of the world. The Japanese demanded reparations, on top of a cessation to all boycott threats and violence against Japanese nationals.

When the response from Chiang Kaishek was slow, the Japanese response was, again, nearly immediate. A Japanese aircraft carrier – the first ever deployed in East Asia – launched fighter planes which strafed targets in Nanjing and Shanghai. Three thousand Japanese troops were landed in the vicinity of Shanghai, ostensibly to protect the Japanese treaty concession zone in the city. Britain and France, each of which had valuable assets in Shanghai, attempted to negotiate a Japanese withdrawal, but without success. Chiang's Nineteenth Route Army undertook the main task of defending Shanghai, and managed a stalemate until Japan landed another 90,000 troops in the city. Chiang directed his best-trained and best equipped units toward Shanghai, though he would have preferred to keep them harassing the CSR. On the last day of February, the Japanese forces outflanked the KMT armies, and Chiang ordered his commanders to withdraw from Shanghai. Negotiators from the League of Nations designed an agreement that, in effect, gave Japan the right to police Shanghai and forbade the KMT government to keep any troops in the city; both Japan and the Republic of China signed it in May. It is possible that Chiang's Nineteenth Route Army never forgave what they saw as his capitulation to Japan. When he redeployed them to Fujian to fight the CSR, they struck a truce with Mao and attempted to set up their own "people's government" in Fujian. Chiang was tasked to fight them as well as the communists. He defeated the Nineteenth Route rebels in 1934, after which they either escaped to Hongkong or caught up with the Long March.

Puyi, the last Qing emperor and at one time a small hope to the constitutional monarchists, had been living under Japanese protection in Tianjin since he had been expelled from the Forbidden City in 1924. The Japanese government now invited him and his entourage to take up residence in the "New Capital" (Xinjing, modern Changchun in Jilin province), as President Henry Puyi of the state of Manchukou ("Manchu Land"). Puyi accepted, though many of his former attendants stayed behind in China (see chapter 12). The new country had a ready-made industrial base, ample production of wheat and timber, and extraordinary reserves of coal and iron. It was, in addition, instantly supplied with imported Japanese industries for publishing, radio broadcasting and film and newsreel production. Japan immediately announced its recognition of the new state, as did – to the fury of both Chiang and Mao – the Soviet Union, which welcomed a Manchukuo embassy to Moscow (even while it furiously expanded its fortification along the Amur River, and in Vladivostok). But other nations, and the League of Nations, demurred. Victor Bulwer-Lytton, a former governor of Bengal and likely an expert on things colonial, reported to the

League in 1932 that Manchukuo was a puppet state of Japan. When the League of Nations refused to admit Manchukuo to membership, the Japanese delegation left the floor, and Japan withdrew from the League. Under the circumstances, there was nothing to lose in upgrading Manchukuo to an overt empire, so in 1934 Puyi became emperor of the Manchu Empire (though in English it continued to be called Manchukuo). As an empire, Manchukuo became popular. It was recognized by El Salvador and the Vatican before the full-on Japanese invasion of China in 1937, then by all the Axis powers of Europe and the nations under their occupation, then by more Japanese puppet states in China (see below) and the Philippines, and finally by Thailand after the latter was forced to sign a mutual recognition treaty with Japan in 1943. And though no government (not managed by Japan) or warlord in China recognized the state, trade between China and Manchukuo was voluminous from the start. Manchukuo was a large, industrialized, modern country, with rich resources, a vibrant market and a smashing public relations operation.

In 1933 Nationalist representatives signed the Tanggu Truce, which established a demilitarized zone between Manchukuo and north China. The zone included the Great Wall and extended almost to the suburbs of Beijing. Wang Jingwei and others in the Nationalist government bemoaned that they were "forced to be Li Hongzhang," helplessly formalizing Japanese seizures of what was regarded as Chinese territory, while searching for ways to slow or halt the seemingly inexorable Japanese advance. Chiang Kaishek was hoping to eradicate the communists quickly enough to turn his guns toward Japan before a full invasion could begin, but the events in Shanghai of 1932 indicated to others in his government that time was running out very quickly. In 1933 T.V. Soong was in the USA seeking support for the Chiang regime. At the time the American government was restricted by its own Neutrality Act from becoming involved in foreign wars, but Soong thought it possible the USA would apply indirect economic pressure on Japan to stop it seizing Chinese territory; he advised that the KMT government be less accommodating to Japanese demands. Chiang, however, was beginning to make progress against the CSR by late 1933, and did not heed recommendations to make opposing Japan his first priority.

The breakdown of CSR defenses and initiation of the Long March only deepened the skepticism in Chiang's government and in his armies. The uprooting of Mao, Zhang Guotao and He Long caused many Nationalist commanders, with Chiang's blessing, to send their troops to the west in pursuit. As a result, Nationalist forces in the east, where the Japanese forces were gathering, were thinned. By the time Mao reached Yan'an in late 1935, Zhang Xueliang had lost confidence in Chiang's strategies. That year the Nationalist government, under Chiang's order to resist battling the Japanese forces, signed an agreement recognizing the former "demilitarized zone" as, in fact, territory under Japan's control. Barely a year later, the Japanese began to set up a series of puppet states in Chakhar. Wang Jingwei and others in the Executive Council were aware that the National government's apparent capitulations to Japan were driving a deep wedge between the government and the public, which was daily becoming more nationalistic, more frenzied in its hatred of all things Japanese and more impatient with the KMT.

Zhang Xueliang established secret communications with Zhou Enlai at Yan'an, and it is possible, but unconfirmed, that Zhang professed to be a supporter of communism. In December of 1936, his forces were fighting the Red Army in Shaanxi province, in the general vicinity of Yan'an. Chiang Kaishek had started the practice, during the Japanese attack on Shanghai in 1932, of using the Wei River Valley as a retreat. In December, Chiang, his military advisors and his civil officials were all at the Huaqingchi resort, a natural hot spring which had been a favorite spa of the Tang emperors. With Mao, Zhou, Chiang and himself all within close proximity, Zhang executed a bizarre plan. He and a few other KMT generals, including Yan Xishan, arrested Chiang and his entire staff in the middle of the night. Chiang awakened in only his pajama bottoms, with his teeth in a glass by his bedside and his glasses in a drawer. He sprinted up the side of Lishan, the rocky, partially wooded mountain standing behind the springs, and Zhang's soldiers found him wedged between two boulders. The Chiang party were whisked away to Yan'an, where the CCP leader and the KMT leader confronted each other.

Chiang's entourage was held two weeks in Yan'an. Soong May-ling harangued Zhang Xueliang by telephone and by cablegram, insisting that her husband be freed. Chiang's Blue Shirt élite guards were preparing to storm Yan'an. International dailies carried reports that the Generalissimo was dead, was alive, was in communication, was incommunicado. It is possible that Mao considered trying and executing Chiang, but was persuaded by cables from Moscow to keep Chiang alive and pursue a new united front. Zhou Enlai worked daily to persuade Chiang that the CCP and KMT should lay aside their differences until the war against Japan had succeeded. At length Chiang agreed, and his party was released to fly back to Nanjing. Zhang Xueliang surrendered himself to Chiang, who declined to condemn him for treason, but kept him in custody permanently. Chiang came under pressure from his generals to abide by the Yan'an agreements, and there is no credible evidence that he considered not keeping his

6. Zhang Xueliang, Soong May-ling, Chiang Kaishek, Yan Xishan. The four posed for a photo with troops in 1935, a year before Zhang kidnapped Chiang to force negotiations at Yan'an.

word. The world was informed that the Generalissimo had now assumed command of a united campaign to save China from Japanese invasion and domination.

In a matter of months, the full-scale Japanese assault on China began. The Japanese-controlled territories now pressed against the Beijing city limits. Japanese rail lines into and out of Beijing were guarded by Japanese marines. South of Beijing, at the town of Wanping, the "Marco Polo Bridge" (*Lugouqiao*) remained the only means of rail access to the capital by Chinese forces. At the beginning of July, 1937, Chinese and Japanese forces were amassed on both sides of the bridge, the Japanese ostensibly to conduct military training maneuvers and the Chinese for vigilance. Shots were fired and a Japanese soldier was declared dead. The Japanese demanded clearance to search Wanping; the Chinese refused. After a show of force by the Japanese commander, both sides called for a truce. Japanese forces were augmented, and the next day a battle broke out. The Japanese quickly seized the bridge, cutting off rail communications to Beijing. They swept through the city, and seemed for the time content to add it to the western perimeter of their growing zone of control inside the Great Wall.

Chiang Kaishek, however, with the enthusiastic support of his generals and of the CCP, declared war on Japan. He chose Shanghai as the first theater of engagement. Seizing control of the Yangtze River and paralyzing transport had been a favored tactic of the treaty powers, and Chiang expected that Japan would follow the same logic. He began amassing his forces outside Shanghai, and the Japanese – who still controlled a great deal of the city and had full access to its ports – did the same. In August the shooting began. Troops from both sides swarmed through Shanghai, and planes (which Japan had in abundance) dropped bombs on soldiers and civilians alike. For nearly four months Chiang attempted doggedly to drive the Japanese out of Shanghai, but the invaders kept increasing their troop strength and firepower. Chiang's commanders feared that the Japanese forces would outflank them and attack the capital, Nanjing, but Chiang was determined to remain focused on Shanghai. At the end of November the Chinese lines collapsed, and the worst happened: Japanese forces set upon Nanjing, with few Chinese military units in place for defense.

Chinese officers in Nanjing hurried to organize a militia defense. Chiang, his family and his officials were escorted by troops westward; they eventually established a wartime capital at Chongqing, far up the Yangtze River. The Japanese dropped leaflets into Nanjing from the air, stating that their forces were insuperable and demanding that the city of Nanjing be surrendered. The KMT forces in the area surrounded Nanjing to make sure that the citizens could not leave. The next day, Japanese commanders began the siege. Realizing the hopelessness of the situation, Chinese forces destroyed everything in the city that could be of use to the Japanese – buildings, grain stores, pack animals, hospitals – and withdrew. For six weeks, Japanese troops roamed almost unopposed through the city. They rounded up isolated Chinese soldiers and militia men and machine-gunned them to death. Other groups of Chinese were buried alive. Civilians, including women and children, were shot, stabbed, hacked or burned to death, many before or after being raped. Atrocities of every sort, imaginable and unimaginable were reported as being suffered by the civilians. Survivors were forced to dispose of the bodies. Historians now estimate a total of a million casualties in the Nanjing region for the period from late November of 1937 to March of 1938, with a likely total between 200,000 and 300,000 killed in Nanjing during the weeks of the Japanese rampage (see under "Further Reading" below).

The KMT forces moved west along the Yangtze, hoping to regroup. Invading forces also made more gains in northern China, absorbing part of Shanxi province. From Chongqing, Chiang sought a way to repel the Japanese both in northern China and in the Yangtze delta. He anticipated that the Japanese would use the Yellow River to transport troops and materiel deeper into China and ordered that in June of 1938 the dams controlling the levels of the river be bombed by his own forces. The Yellow River was diverted from its path, and was useless to Japan. It may or may not also have been part of the plan to devastate the region's agriculture and population, depriving the Japanese occupiers of even more resources (a strategy that resembled the use of fire in Nanjing). About 1,200 square miles of active farmland in three provinces was ruined, tens of thousands of people were drowned outright and hundreds of thousands were made homeless. The effect was only for Japanese forces to concentrate more intensely on exploitation of the Yangtze during the invasion. The eastern Yangtze, from Shanghai to Wuhan, quickly fell into Japanese hands. While consolidating on the ground, the Japanese launched an air campaign that inflicted instant, grievous damage on cities as widely dispersed as Changsha, Xi'an, Canton and Chiang's new capital at Chongqing. The Japanese commanders now found, as earlier invaders of China had found, that actually controlling the populations, communication systems, economies and criminal associations of the territories under their domination was nearly impossible. The ground forces were overextended and encountering their first defeats, as of 1940, in Hunan.

The reasonable solution was to set up an occupation authority under native leadership. Wang Jingwei came forward. He had followed Chiang Kaishek to Chongqing, intending to continue his rivalry for leadership of the KMT, but fled to the French colony of Indochina after nearly being assassinated. When France fell to Germany in 1940, the Vichy collaborationist government granted Japanese militarists and industrialists free access to what had been French Indochina, and Wang came into communication with Japanese war planners. Despite his earlier, strident calls for Chiang Kaishek to resist encroachments by Japan, Wang now felt that the Chiang regime offered no hope for either defeating Japan or reviving Chinese unity. He had a long-term fascination with fascism, finding it both a practical means to improve the nation's material life and also psychologically appealing. In 1940 Wang accepted the Japanese invitation to head his own government in Nanjing. It assumed the same name as the Republic of China (*Zhonghua minguo*), occupied the same capital and had many of the same officials – members of the left wing of the KMT who felt themselves at risk in Chiang's domain, centrists and rightists who thought Wang's regime offered more opportunities than Chiang's, military officers who had become disgusted by Chiang's tactics or demoralized by defeat, New Life Movement educators and propagandists who were looking forward to continuing their work.

The population of Wang's provinces – most of Jiangsu, Anhui and Zhejiang – was vastly diminished as a result of the number of people dying or fleeing, and probably totaled just over 60,000,000. Under Wang's occupation state, the locals policed themselves and enjoyed the benefits of a temporary relief from the immediate horrors of war. The economy of the Nanjing Nationalist government was controlled by the objectives of the Greater East Asian Co-Prosperity Sphere – the Japanese program for coordinating the import and export roles of the economies of Korea, Manchukuo, the Mongol Military Government. Taiwan and the occupation states of China and Southeast Asia for the greater industrialization of Japan and the specialized supply of resources or labor by the subordinated economies. Later, the Provisional Government of Free India, the Empire of Vietnam, the nationalist regime in Thailand under Plaek Pibulsonggram and the kingdoms of Laos and Cambodia would be added. The ideology of the occupation was simple, corresponding more or less the personal philosophy of Wang Jingwei: opposition to communism and opposition to Chiang Kaishek.

By the end of 1940 the Japanese incursion into China stalled. The existence of multiple occupation states within the borders of the former Qing empire provided only marginal aid to the Japanese efforts to protect their resources. Chinese guerillas, some associated with the CCP, some with the KMT, and some independent, were persisting in sabotaging or blowing up Japanese railroads, warehouses, and cable communications. Japanese occupiers responded with a scorched earth practice that superficially resembled the tactics used by the KMT when leaving Nanjing or flooding the Yellow River – the systematic destruction of all material resources that could aid the enemy. But in the Japanese practice, later known as the "three alls" – kill all, burn all, loot all – the wholesale destruction was followed by forcing local residents to construct what were essentially internment camps for themselves, complete with moats and barbed wire. Men between the ages of 15 and 60 were all suspected guerillas, and if not killed were imprisoned, starved, and in some cases used for research into new weapons of mass destruction. The center for such research was the so-called "Unit 731" at Harbin in Manchukuo. It received prisoners – overwhelmingly Chinese and Korean, but occasionally Mongolian, Russian or American – for experiments involving vivisection, amputation, burning by flame or by chemical, freezing, infectious disease, lethal gas, shooting and explosion.

Chiang Kaishek and his generals were still holding interior Fujian, Jiangxi, Guangdong and the entire center and west of the country. Supplies were thin, partly because access to not only the coasts but also the major railways had been lost. Chiang's generals extracted what they needed in the way of grain, cash and uncompensated labor from their own troops and from the cities and villages under their dominance. Self-enrichment by the generals was rampant, and as the war persisted many of them began to feel independent. Some simply ignored Chiang's commands, others engaged in their own small wars against the CCP, and still others actually joined the CCP forces in resisting the Japanese. The principles upon which the Nationalist war effort were based were not greatly different from the principles that provided coherence to the Nationalist military center after the Northern Expedition: Chiang needed to convince his generals that he could either defeat them or enrich them, and this remained true as Japan occupied and brutalized the entire eastern perimeter of the country. Even in areas that Japan had not conquered, the Chinese population generally was in extreme distress. North China had been struck repeatedly by famine during the 1920s and 1930s. Many young Chinese men joined the Nationalist forces thinking that, as in recent decades, the militarists would provide grain, shelter and perhaps even a salary. When recruits discovered that in fact they were being starved and robbed to enrich their commanders, many melted away from the war effort. A majority of Nationalist recruits did not stay more than a few weeks; of those who remained to become regular troops, nearly half eventually deserted, and 20 percent starved to death at some time during the war.

Chiang's ability to provide his generals supplies that they needed – weapons, grain, intelligence, personal security – was partly dependent upon what he could be supplied from abroad. The KMT, like the CCP, had during their history received state aid only from the Soviet Union, though help from churches and other private groups in Britain and the United States had also been influential. In 1941 the Soviet Union signed a non-aggression pact with Japan. Beginning in the late 1930s, a group forming in the USA attempted to persuade the American Congress to come early to the support of China against Japan. Hu Shih, then the Chinese ambassador to the USA, wrote and gave lectures constantly on the intensifying Japanese occupation. Both T.V. Soong and his sister Soong May-ling were frequently in the USA, attempting to use newspapers, radio and the lecture circuit to gain aid. Henry Luce, the publisher of *Time Magazine*, had been born in China and was a vigorous supporter of the Chiang Kaishek government; in 1937, the Chiangs were the magazine's "people of the year," and Chiang Kaishek, with or without Soong May-ling, was featured on at least nine other covers of the magazine during his lifetime. Frank and Harry Price, sons of a missionary to China, formed a committee to pressure Congress to lift the strictures of the Neutrality act with regard to China. It is possible that these efforts were partly financed by T.V Soong and H.H. Kung. The United States attempted in 1939 to restrain Japan's aggression by refusing to supply Japan with oil or scrap metal, but the Neutrality Act forbade the USA from participating in the war directly.

In 1940 a cooperative effort by the Chiang government (mostly T.V. Soong) and the American government provided training and aircraft to the volunteer group, the Flying Tigers. Though the Flying Tigers, based in Burma (which was being gradually conquered by Japan), were active in flying and escorting supply missions to Chongqing, they were also trained from the beginning as fighter pilots. They were ready for combat before the USA was attacked by Japan at Pearl Harbor on December 7, 1941, and a little more than a week after the attack they were engaging Japanese pilots over China. Also ready for combat was Joseph Stillwell, who had been the military attaché at the American embassy in Beijing from 1935 to 1939; afterward he returned to the USA to train troops for eventual participation in the war in Europe. Within weeks after the USA declared war on Japan, the Nationalist forces with American air support were able to clear Hunan province of Japanese troops, and Stillwell was preparing to return to China as an advisor to Chiang. In his public pronouncements in the weeks after the USA entered the war, Franklin Roosevelt constantly invoked China and the Chiang government as essential partners in the struggle to defeat the Axis Powers (Germany, Italy and Japan). Because of the Japanese conquest of Burma in 1942, supplies to China had to be flown from India, which was primarily undertaken by the USA, still financed by T.V. Soong. In 1943 Chiang attended conferences with Roosevelt, Churchill and Stalin at Cairo and Tehran, and signed the Potsdam Accord, at every step hailed by Roosevelt as an equal partner in the war effort. In acknowledgment, Britain and the USA signed new treaties with China abrogating all extraterritorial rights.

It was an essential element of the American war strategy that the China front not collapse and allow Japan to concentrate its forces against the USA in the Pacific. Stillwell began by training Chinese refugee forces in India, and later coordinated their airlift back to southwest China. When Stillwell himself arrived in China, he began to criticize Chiang – both to his face and in his reports back to Washington – for delaying combat against Japan, for being unable to discipline his commanders and his troops, and for absorbing huge amounts of American cash ($1.6 billion) and weapons without showing progress. Stillwell was unimpressed by Chiang's argument that expending his troops in fighting the Japanese would leave him open to an assault by the armies of

Mao Zedong; on the contrary, Stillwell continually advised Chiang to live up to the united front and share his supplies with the communists. A great deal of Stillwell's attention was focused on attempting to retake Burma and re-open ground supply lines to China from Southeast Asia and India – an objective that British allies and other American commanders did not agree with, and which Chiang resisted. Not until 1945, when the Japanese war effort was all but exhausted (and Stillwell had been reassigned out of China), did a combined Chinese and British force manage to re-open Burma to supply traffic between India and Chongqing. Between 1942 and 1945, the failure of Japan to make more progress in China was primarily due to the strains of conducting the war in the Pacific and Southeast Asia, of failing to exert control over areas of China already conquered and of flagging material support from industries in Japan and Korea. In August of 1945 the Soviet Union finally agreed to enter the Pacific war and invaded Manchukuo. The USA dropped atomic bombs on the Japanese cities of Hiroshima and Nagasaki on August 6 and 9, and Japanese militarists began to turn against their own government. Japan surrendered on August 15, and both the KMT and the Red Army began to take Japanese prisoners in China.

For the CCP, Yan'an had functioned as a wartime capital, in the style of – and not greatly distant from – Chiang Kaishek's capital at Chongqing. Despite the rigors of the Long March, Mao and his followers had set to work with urgency in 1936 to complete their control over the party and over the Yan'an region. The battles, both military and political, of the Long March had winnowed the party leadership to those who, like Zhu De and Lin Biao, were enthusiastic Mao supporters, and those like Zhou Enlai who had reconciled themselves. At Yan'an, the forced implementation of land reform had won the CCP the loyalty of the poor majority, but tens of thousands of landowners may have been killed in the process. Zhou had been entrusted by Mao with not only the primary propaganda and negotiating efforts (whether with warlords, criminal gangs or foreign governments) but also with intelligence gathering. Mao was keen to know who might be plotting against him, and Zhou was to watch the study groups organized at Yan'an, as well as to listen to conversations, to pick up any troubling dissension. Liu Shaoqi, once Mao's friend in adolescence but now a rival for power within the CCP, had a subversive operation of his own in the Beijing-Tianjin area. He visited Yan'an from time to time; Mao received him cordially but offered him no status at the base. In 1938 Wang Ming arrived in Yan'an, after living in Moscow and working for the Comintern for almost seven years. Some of his "Twenty-Eight Bolsheviks" had been soldiers on the Long March; Yang Shangkun, for example, and others had turned against Zhang Guotao and joined Mao's clique. This time Wang brought a fresh face, Kang Sheng. In the ensuing years, Kang's ingratiation of himself with Mao, and his successful effort to replace Zhou Enlai as Mao's security chief, made him a hated and feared figure in the party.

After the creation of the second united front with Chiang in 1936, communist guerilla organizers and the Red Army concentrated on engaging the Japanese forces in north China, from which Chiang Kaishek had largely withdrawn. Mao was aware of the disgust with which Chinese farmers and city dwellers regarded the predatory practices of the KMT troops. He strictly instructed his troops never to take the property of civilians, and to provide a helping hand whenever possible. The communist forces, whether regular Red Army or guerilla forces, were effective at sabotaging Japanese installations and harassing Japanese troops. Chakhar Inner Mongolia west of Rehe was still successfully resisting the Japanese, partly thanks to the base created by

Feng Yuxiang. Though Feng himself had been reassigned to other parts of the war theater by Chiang Kaishek, many of his remaining officers and soldiers cooperated with the communists in defending Chakhar and northern Zhili provinces. Shanxi province, under the rule of Yan Xishan, was almost entirely lost to Japanese forces by 1940, but Yan withdrew to the extreme northwest corner of his province and held the line, thanks in part to aid from communist forces. Altogether the communist troops were never as numerous as the Nationalist forces during the war, and they did not have direct foreign aid from the USA, but they were effective at their smaller operations and, equally important, were masters of image.

Yan'an could be reached by air, and during the war years it was frequently visited by international journalists, activists – including Japanese and Russian communists, the American doctor George Hatem and the Canadian doctor Norman Bethune who died in 1939 while attending to Red Army soldiers – and photographers. The highlands of Shanxi are marked by bare sandstone and loess-covered highlands. The winds have carved hollows and caves out of the hillsides, and the CCP took up their residence in these caves. Following local tradition, they built attractive half-timber and heavily papered fronts, with carved wooden doors and glass windows. The insides were clean, and warm when heated by coal stoves. Farmland had been redistributed, and labor collectives formed for farming, evening study (of Marxism, of Mao's essays on class conflict and revolution, of basic medicine and engineering, and adult literacy), and military training. The work week was punctuated, especially when journalists were visiting, with dances and folk music. Mao, Zhou, and other leaders of the party would join the local farmers in doing the *yangge*, a traditional fertility dance, accompanied by suggestive movements that most Americans would not see in public until the 1960s. Ample photographs and memoirs attest to the unusual sense of camaraderie perceived by foreign visitors in wartime Yan'an. In 1944, the American government decided to make a comprehensive assessment of the communist war effort. A team of military analysts, soldiers, political analysts and technicians (including Japanese-American George Nakamura), took up residence in Yan'an. From there, they supplied the American government with constant reports (many of them read by Chiang Kaishek and T.V. Soong) regarding the military readiness of the Red Army. Overall the American advisors thought that the best troops of Chiang Kaishek were much better than the best troops of the Red Army. But they recognized that guerilla tactics and political acumen had given the communists an influence that outweighed their numbers. They also felt that American training and American weapons could raise the value of the communists as fighters against the Japanese. Patrick Hurley, the new ambassador to China, visited Yan'an as an exploratory measure to begin a program to assure cooperation between the CCP and the KMT. By the time the Japanese surrendered, however, the differences between the CCP and the KMT were not diminishing, they were growing.

At the conclusion of the war against Japan, China, its people and its environment had been ravaged in a way that could be compared only to the Taiping War of a century before. Of the minimum 20,000,000 deaths, only a little over 3,000,000 occurred as a result of military conflict. The remainder resulted from the sickness as a result of debilitation, and from starvation. Persisting drought and flood were worsening in their own vicious cycle even before the Japanese invasion. But the war had cut off supply and market roads, destroyed dams, irrigation systems and farmland. The fertile, delicately terraced hillsides of Sichuan were nearly all destroyed in the struggles of 1942–3. There were virtually no medicines for use by the civilian population anywhere.

The economy had been ravaged by hyperinflation, reducing most families to barter, many to begging. Cities such as Beijing and Nanjing which had enjoyed a brief respite from war while under Japanese occupation were assaulted again in 1945, as advance forces of the KMT and the CCP competed to gain control and seize Japanese weapons and supplies. The exhausted population had little to celebrate, even as the war ended. Internationally, Chiang Kaishek's reputation was high, as he was hailed as one of the heroes of the war. Among his military staff, his authority rested on his ability to continue to bring in American aid and arms and to grant the Americans lucrative new privileges in the country. But Chiang could never be sure of their loyalty. Only the outbreak of open war between the CCP and the KMT would clarify the issue.

There had been occasional skirmishes between the Red Army and the Nationalist forces during the war, particularly when Chiang Kaishek insisted (usually successfully) that the Red Army avoid holding Chinese areas that had once been independent communist base areas in Jiangxi. But generally Chiang and Mao had both preferred to refrain from expending resources fighting each other, hoarding the supplies and waiting for the Japanese war machine to die. When Japan surrendered, the scramble was on by both sides to take and hold territories. The terms of the Japanese surrender to the USA required that Japanese soldiers in China and Manchuria surrender to the KMT only, since was the legal government of China. But the Soviet Union was on the ground in the Northeast, and rounded up nearly a million Japanese soldiers, industrial managers, spies and suspected Chinese collaborators, as well as Puyi himself; these individuals remained in Soviet custody, and were not transferred to the KMT. Moreover, there were tens of thousands of Koreans in the Northeast, most of them former Japanese mining and agricultural slaves, now freed and allied with the communist anti-Japanese guerillas of Korea, who were ready to lend their support to the Chinese communists in seizure of the Northeast. It was apparent to the USA that the danger existed that the Northeast, as virtually an entire industrial, economic and national unit, could became an instant CCP state. While Patrick Hurley organized summit talks between Mao and Chiang, American forces transported KMT troops by air and sea to Beijing, Tianjin, Shenyang (Mukden), Dairen (Port Arthur) and other northern cities. For good measure almost 50,000 American marines were sent along to the Northeast to prevent a communist assault. The Soviet Union was entreated to not make a gift of the Northeast to the CCP.

Fighting between the CCP and KMT troops broke out in many locations in China, but perhaps most revealing was the conflict in Shanxi. Yan Xishan had regained his province after the collapse of the Japanese occupation, and he looked forward to a return to the pre-war circumstances in which he was the sole authority in his domain. Cooperation with the communists before and during the war seems to have weighed heavily with Yan. He was a reformer in his own right, but had felt threatened by the social and economic reforms the communists had carried out in his province. With the Japanese threat gone, Yan took it upon himself to rid Shanxi of the communists by force, but the Red Army units – one of them led by Deng Xiaoping – were more than his match: Yan lost nearly 40,000 men in three weeks of fighting. The events alarmed Hurley and Chiang, but made Mao confident enough to refuse most of the compromises Hurley suggested. Yan Xishan, in the meantime, refused to concede, and for over a year battled the Red Army and communist guerillas at virtually every site in his province. By late 1947, Yan had lost 300,000 men, all his weapons and Shanxi to the CCP. He fled south toward Nanjing, and eventually to Guangdong.

In broad outline, Yan's route described the progress of the civil war. The more advanced weapons supplied to the KMT were quickly captured by the CCP, yet their value may have been negligible since neither side had the ability to train soldiers in use of the weapons, nor the means to maintain them and continue to manufacture ammunition. The CCP tactics of guerilla warfare better suited the material conditions of a ruined and starving countryside and chaotic cities, though their technological level rose quickly as KMT officers defected to them, along with tanks, trucks and artillery. Perhaps more important, the CCP political appeal was overwhelming. The KMT had led China for years while caught in the vice of being unable to materially resist Japanese encroachment on the one hand, and being unable to quell popular outrage at the economic and military depredations of Japan on the other. Any government attempting to protect China from Japanese predation between 1915 and 1935 could only have been discredited and alienated from the angry and terrified public.

KMT political and military leaders had only compounded their woes by demonstrating very little compassion toward rising public misery. They unapologetically lived in enclaves of luxury – well fed, well groomed, well clothed, and well armed, flaunting their comforts in front of hungry, sick, frightened citizens. It is estimated today that food production declined about 30 percent during the 1940s, and a ruined infrastructure prevented distribution of what was produced. As KMT government in China dissolved in 1949, the average life expectancy in the country was 32 years. Where the CCP armies arrived, there also arrived food (even if forcefully taken from wealthier hoarders), and basic medical care. The Red Army built shelters for the homeless. While KMT élites became more invested in the system of endless compromise with Japan on the one hand and endless aid from overseas Chinese, the American public and ultimately the American government on the other, the overwhelming majority of Chinese lost all investment in the system, enduring privation and death in China surpassed only by Russia during the war. Though Chiang Kaishek started the war against the CCP in 1946 with a much larger army, better communications and a promise of fresh weapons, cash and advisors from the USA, the CCP gained ground in the cities and in the countryside almost inexorably during 1947 and 1948. The early communist hold over north China was firm. As the CCP expanded its domain, the KMT were forced further south – ironically, back to the region where Sun Yatsen had once been contained. By 1947 they were abandoning Beijing, taking as many valuables and treasures as possible from the Forbidden City, from the banks, from the libraries, to carry along with them to their temporary headquarters in Canton. Their advance forces started to transfer to Taiwan, now liberated from Japanese colonial domination. By late spring of 1949 the CCP had taken Nanjing, and were moving toward the last KMT holdouts in Canton. Accompanied by a total population – military and civilian – of 2,000,000, the Nationalists completed their transfer to Taiwan in late 1949. In October, Mao stood atop the Forbidden City's Qianmen Gate, overlooking Tiananmen Square – heavily lighted for the cameras, heavily miked for radio and resplendent in a new tailored blue suit – to announce that the People's Republic of China was born.

Further reading

Soong May-ling's New Life quotation and the excerpt from the field report on the New Life Movement are from Dirlik, "The Ideological Foundations of the New Life

Movement" (1975). The reference by Chinese politicians to themselves as "Li Hongzhang" is from Barrett and Shyu, *Chinese Collaboration with Japan* (2001). The discussion of opium revenue and arms purchases is largely from Van de Ven, *War and Nationalism in China* (pp. 73–4).

On the Nationalists, Nationalist politics, Chiang Kai-shek, Soong May-Ling and foreign supporters of the Chiangs, see Tang, *America's Failure in China* (1963); Tuchman, *Stillwell and the American Experience in China, 1911–45* (1971); Lary, *Region and Nation* (1974); Dirlik, "The Ideological Foundations of the New Life Movement" (1975); Sheridan, *China in Disintegration* (1977); Garver, *Chinese-Soviet Relations, 1937–1945* (1988); Schoppa, *Blood Road* (1998); Fenby, *Generalissimo* (2003); Waldron, *From War to Nationalism* (2003); Chu and Kennedy, *Madame Chiang Kaishek and Her China* (2005); Herzstein, *Henry R. Luce, Time, and the American Crusade in Asia* (2005); Zarrow, *China in War and Revolution* (2005); Lary, *China's Republic* (2007); Dikötter, *The Age of Openness* (2008); Taylor, *The Generalissimo* (2009).

For accounts of war, discussions of technology and strategy, atrocities and memoirs from the field see Tuchman, above; Schaller, *The U.S. Crusade in China* (1979); Chan, *Arming the Chinese* (1982); Myers and Peattie, *The Japanese Colonial Empire* (1987); Williams, *Unit 731* (1989); Hsiung and Levine, *China's Bitter Victory* (1992); Harris, *Factories of Death* (1994); Gold, *Unit 731* (1996); Schoppa, *Blood Road* (1998); Van de Ven, above; Latimer, *Burma: The Forgotten War* (2004); *A Plague Upon Humanity* (2004); Rummel, *China's Bloody Century* (2007); Shiu, "Modern War on an Ancient Battlefield" (2009). On the Nanjing massacre, see Chang, *The Rape of Nanking* (1998); Brook, *Documents on the Rape of Nanjing* (1999); Yang, "Convergence or Divergence?" (1999); Fogel, *The Nanjing Massacre in History and Historiography* (2000); Zhang, *Eyewitnesses to Massacre* (2001); Askew, "New Research on the Nanjing Incident" (2003); Latimer, *Burma: The Forgotten War* (2004); Wakabayashi, *The Nanking Atrocity* (2007); MacKinnon, Lary and Vogel, eds., *China at War* (2007).

On the warlords, see Sheridan, *Chinese Warlord*, 1966; Gillin, *Warlord* (1967); Pye, *Warlord Politics* (1971); Lary, 1974, above; Chi, *Warlord Politics in China* (1976); Nathan, *Peking Politics* (1976); Sheridan, *China in Disintegration* (1977); Chan, above; Lipman, "Ethnicity and Politics in Republican China" (1984); Lary, *Warlord Soldiers* (1985); Waldron, above; MacKinnon, Lary and Vogel, above. On places during the Republican period see, as examples, Gamble, *Peking: A Social Survey* (1921); Strand, *Rickshaw Beijing* (1989); Wakeman, *Policing Shanghai* (1995); Li, Dray-Novey and Kong, *Beijing* (2008).

On the communists and other opposition forces during the war years, see North, *Moscow and Chinese Communists* (1963); Schram, *Mao Tse-Tung* (1967); Chang, *The Rise of the Chinese Communist Party* (1971); Chesneaux, *The Chinese Labor Movement* (1980); Braun, *A Comintern Agent in China* (1982); Shum, *Zhu De (Chu Teh)* (1982); Galbiati, *P'eng P'ai and the Hai-Lu-Feng Soviet* (1985); Salisbury, *The Long March* (1987); Chinese Communist Party Central Committee, *History of the Chinese Community Party* (1991); Dirlik, *Anarchism in the Chinese Revolution* (1993); Han, *Eldest Son* (1994); Goodman, *Deng Xiaoping and the Chinese Revolution* (1995); Deng, *Deng Xiaoping* (1996); Saich and Yang, *The Rise to Power of the Chinese Communist Party* (1996); Short, *Mao: A Life* (1999); Spence, *Mao* (1999); Smith, *A Road is Made* (2000); Chang and Halliday, *Mao* (2005).

14

The Ubiquitous Center

Iɴ 1959 ᴛʜᴇ leading members of the government of the PRC decided to hold their conference in Lushan, Jiangxi. The town had been created as a summer retreat for foreigners in southern China in the middle nineteenth century. Between 1928 and 1934 it had been within the boundaries of the Chinese Soviet Republic, but after the CSR had collapsed, Chiang Kaishek and Soong May-ling used it as a retreat from the summer heat and political discord in Nanjing. Mao returned to it after 1949. For the July meeting planned for 1959, Lushan was the perfect scene – high and cool, but well fitted with gracious and comfortable housing. The setting, however, contrasted profoundly with the worry, almost panic, of the party, and the heated debates that would ensue. On July 2 the meetings of the Central Committee Political Bureau – the Politburo – began. Famine and economic breakdown on a scale unprecedented in peacetime had gripped the country. At almost the same time, a political hunt for "rightists" had swept the party, the universities and publishing houses. Factions had sharpened their differences, and as they assembled in Lushan they may also have been sharpening their knives. Mao saw that a historic campaign to rebuild China from the ground up as an extension of the central state was approaching a precipice, and could be lost without a ruthless assertion of control. His enemies saw a society in near-total ruin and for the first time believed that Mao was sufficiently weak in credibility and political support to be vulnerable to removal as head of government. The showdown prolonged the plenum well into August, and for most of the period the advantage see-sawed from one side to the other. But when the meeting was dissolved on August 16, Mao, incredibly, had driven his enemies to the wall, and was free to push his extraordinary vision to its ultimate conclusion.

Between 1947 and 1949, the Nationalist forces streaming toward Taiwan included not only Chiang Kaishek and Soong May-ling, but also a fragment of the former KMT military backers – former Shanxi warlord Yan Xishan, for instance, was the last premier of the Republic of China in China, and then the first in Taiwan, and Xinjiang warlord Sheng Shicai retreated to the island as a private citizen. Others had not come along. Feng Yuxiang denounced Chiang and attempted to emigrate to the Soviet

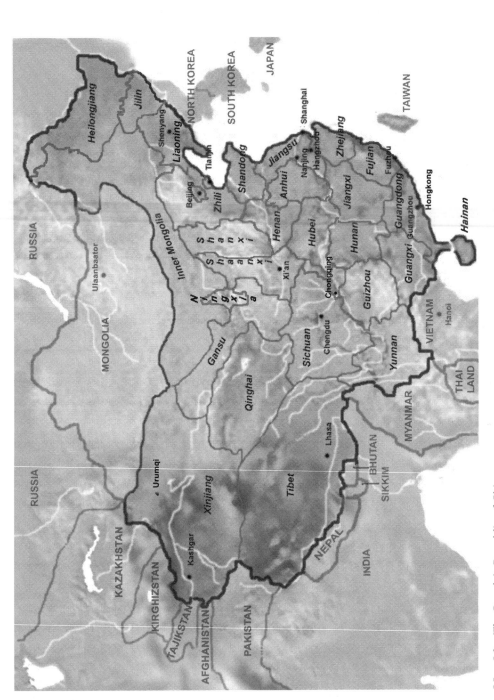

Map 12 The People's Republic of China

Union, but died in a ship fire en route. Zhang Guotao, Mao's hated rival from the Long March who had defected to the KMT from Yan'an, went to Hongkong in 1949 and later moved to Canada.

Those who arrived with the Chiangs found the ground well prepared. Nationalist soldiers had been in Taiwan since the surrender of Japan and its military forces, installing a provincial government. The Cairo pact of 1943 had stated the intention of the Allied powers that Taiwan would be returned to China after the defeat of Japan, but in fact Japan had surrendered its possessions to the USA (the formalities of Japanese renunciation of sovereignty over all the islands around Taiwan was protracted, concluding only in the 1950s). The clear expectation of the USA was to transfer Taiwan to Chinese control, but in the years following the war what and where legal China was appeared to the USA and some other nations to be unclear. When Mao declared the People's Republic of China (PRC) founded in October of 1949, Chiang Kaishek declared the Republic of China (ROC) still in existence, and temporarily transferred the capital from Nanjing to Taipei, which had been the capital of the Japanese colony in Taiwan. When PRC forces did not immediately seize Taiwan, the USA considered its previous alliance with the ROC to be transferrable to the government in Taipei, and so Taiwan became the object of post-war reconstruction aid to "China" from the USA (about US $4 billion in economic and military subsidies between 1950 and 1965). When the United Nations was founded in 1945, the ROC government was not only recognized as the government of China, but it was placed permanently on the security council, being the fifth member along with France, the Soviet Union, Britain and the USA; the Soviet Union strongly protested the seating of the ROC, and boycotted UN meetings for years. The size of Taiwan and its economy made it possible for the KMT economic planners to solve problems that in China were too pervasive and too profound to be ameliorated through government intervention. The gold reserves from Nanjing, entirely transported to Taiwan, allowed the KMT to float its own currency (still in *yuan* units), protecting the Taiwan economy from the hyperinflation that had poisoned the Chinese economy before and during the war. Low agricultural taxes and compensated land distribution allowed poorer settlers from "the mainland" to set up as farmers, and softened the blow for local farmers who were encroached upon. Nevertheless, the effects of the disorganization and corruption of the KMT managers created a crisis of high rice prices and reinforced the influence of the black market even before the Nationalist immigration was complete in 1949.

Vigorous opposition to the KMT in Taiwan was widespread. Japan had found it hard to establish its control over Taiwan after gaining title to it in the Treaty of Shimonoseki. The majority population were descendants of settlers, primarily from Fujian province across the Straits of Taiwan, who had flaunted Ming and Qing law, braved the sea and its pirates, and then fought with the aboriginal population (descendants of the ancestors of all the peoples of the Pacific islands) to settle the rich farmlands of Taiwan's piedmonts. When Japanese colonial forces landed on the island in 1896, they confronted not only these farmers and merchants, but also the aboriginal remnants (now pushed toward the mountains in the island's center and the east coast) and the complex networks of pirates and smugglers active from the Philippines to Okinawa. In time the Japanese not only established their colonial regime but brought to Taiwan modern education, railroads, cable networks, telephone, radio, trolleys and medicine. By 1945 a large proportion of the male population of Taiwan was bilingual in their own Fukienese dialect and in Japanese.

Making way for a new population of 2,000,000 people who spoke standard northern Chinese, evinced contempt for the locals and were backed by a military force that assured their access to land and housing was difficult. The KMT forces seized Japanese property, including factories, farms and mansions, and sold them to the incoming "mainlanders" at bargain prices. Disappearance of the Japanese regime meant disappearance of its bonds and its currency, leaving many formerly prosperous locals with nothing. In 1947 an altercation between a local woman cigarette peddler and a KMT military officer who claimed to be seizing contraband ended with the woman having her skull fractured and the Nationalist officer leaving with her life savings. A crowd attempted to stop the soldier from leaving; he pulled his pistol and killed a bystander. Overnight a larger crowd surrounded the governor's office, and the next morning troops turned machine guns on the gathering. The governor declared a curfew, and his soldiers set about finding curfew violators, saboteurs of government installations or property of Nationalist immigrants, or those ideologically opposed to the KMT government. Nevertheless, the locals far outnumbered the mainlanders, and within weeks they had gained control of radio stations and government buildings, and were prepared to cut off supplies to KMT garrisons. Leaders of the local opposition appealed for international support and negotiation, some suggesting that a plebiscite should decide Taiwan's future. As the locals crowds quieted and hoped for international political pressure to undo the KMT appropriation of the island, Chiang's military forces regrouped, and struck the local organizers in a pattern reminiscent of the "White Terror" of 1927. Nationalist troops ran rampant through the cities and countryside; foreign witnesses described behavior resembling (or mimicking) the behavior of Japanese troops in at Nanjing in 1937. Historians generally agree on a death toll of between 3,000 and 4,000. At the end of the purge, the KMT was firmly in control of government installations, and the whole country was put under indefinite martial law.

With the arrival of the Chiangs in 1949, a formal government apparatus was completed. Chiang was president, a national assembly validated his authority, a legislative parliament validated his edicts and an Executive Cabinet (dating back to the days following the success of the Northern Expedition) aided him in formation of policy. Overall those policies were fairly simple. The ROC was now a police state, designed around the suppression of two great conspiracies – communism and Taiwan independence. Police were empowered to use virtually any means to eradicate these enemies and to protect the property and persons of Nationalist immigrants. In 1949 as in 1939, the ROC was a one-party state. The school system was centralized for the pursuit of its main goals of indoctrinating students with a Nationalist passion for reconquering the mainland. Speakers of Fukienese dialect were to learn northern standard Chinese and to use it. Aboriginal peoples were to be forced to learn standard Chinese, adopt Chinese dress and family structure and abide by KMT land laws.

As violent and protracted as KMT consolidation of control over Taiwan was, it was dwarfed by the complexity and the scale of the PRC programs to gain control over China and its border territories. Driving the Nationalist government out of the country had not made China communist. There remained an estimated 2,000,000 armed men (and possibly women) not connected to the CCP or the Red Army in the country;

about 600,000 were KMT fighting a rearguard action, and an equal number were simply armed criminals. These forces needed to be quelled. The ruined countryside had to be put back into production. The urban economy had to be provided both a currency that was not hollowed out by inflation and a means of being supplied with food and building materials. A government had to be created.

Management of all these problems was aided by the almost immediate outbreak of war with the USA, in Korea. Before the Japanese surrender in 1945, the allies had decided to divide Korea north and south (at the famous Thirty-Eighth Parallel). The north became the Democratic People's Republic of Korea, under the presidency of Kim Il-sung and the protection of the Soviet Union. The south became the Republic of Korea under the presidency of Syngman Rhee and the protection of the USA. The plan was that in five years Korea would be governed by a state whose form would be determined by popular choice. Korean reception of the agreement was uneasy, with repeated protests against continued foreign domination of the country and the imposition of an artificial dividing line. Border clashes were frequent, as each government jockeyed to gain more territory and more credibility before the scheduled end of the occupations. In June of 1950, armies of North Korea crossed the Thirty-Eighth Parallel, claiming it was retaliating against an incursion by the South. The United States immediately declared its support for the South and mobilized its Pacific forces. With representatives of the ROC attending and the Soviet Union absent (due to its boycott in protest of the seating of the ROC as "China"), the common membership of the UN passed a resolution blaming the North and demanding an end to hostilities. Instead, the North launched a full attack on the South, whose forces rapidly retreated until nearly the whole peninsula was under Northern control. A month later, American forces arrived in Korea to defend the South. They were supplied from the American occupation bases and supply depots in Japan. Reinforcements from Britain, Turkey, Australia, Canada, France, Thailand, Greece, the Netherlands, Colombia, Ethiopia, the Philippines, the Benelux countries, New Zealand and Japan (defense forces) came to ostensibly enforce the UN resolution to end hostilities by containing or punishing North Korea. Within a short time, the North was once again contained above the boundary, but in October the allied forces pushed into North Korea. The People's Republic of China decided to join the war on the side of North Korea.

Both the ROC and the PRC recognized the potential of the war in Korea to aid in their efforts to consolidate their new governments. The ROC had asked to join the UN forces in Korea when the North first crossed into the South, but American diplomats had ruled against it, fearing it might provoke the PRC to enter the war. In the PRC, a portion of the CCP leadership were very reluctant to confront the USA in Korea, with so many issues of consolidation and development pending at home. But Mao and his closest military advisor, Peng Dehuai, were quick to define Korea as part of China's strategic perimeter and to mobilize forces. The Red Army had been renamed as the People's Liberation Army (in honor of the first use of the name at Hunan in 1927); its reorganization and professionalization was a major goal of Peng, and the Korea engagement was a chance to keep the troops organized and employed. In the event, the PRC enjoyed the ironic benefits of a foreign war – stimulating the economy through industrial production, concentrating the public's nationalist support on the war effort, and keeping millions of potentially demobilized young men from crowding the ranks of the unemployed or the criminally employed, all while ripping up somebody else's terrain instead of their own.

The logic of PRC deployment in the war – rather than simply supplying the North with food and weapons, which they were doing from the summer of 1950 – also depended upon the previous placement in the Northeast of a large standing Chinese force of about 300,000 men. The same advantage of placement that had allowed the Qing to repeatedly defeat Russia in Turkestan allowed the PRC to intervene in Korea. The Soviet Union was not regarded in 1950 as a strategic threat, taking Chinese attention off its enormous internal border for the first time in centuries. The previous strategic frontier of Manchuria, which the Qing had had to defend against both Russia and Japan, had now shifted to the Yalu River and its southern littoral. PRC strategic interests in Korea all but dictated that it would enter the Korean conflict once the allied forces had crossed into North Korea. Yet, the PRC – like all other parties in the Korean conflict – carefully observed the fiction that no international war was occurring. The armies of the USA and its allies were performing a "UN peacekeeping mission," China was mobilizing not the PLA but the People's Volunteer Army (all seconded from the PLA, of course). Their nominal commander in Korea was Zhu De (now 65 years old), but operations were actually under the command of Peng Dehuai.

The first battle between Chinese and American forces occurred in November. The PRC had a tiny air force, all flying Soviet-built planes. But the Soviet air support the PRC was depending on came rather little and rather late. By 1951 total PRC soldiers in Korea were well over a million. Their only real advantage over the better-equipped UN forces was numbers, the use of night attacks and experience in guerilla tactics. The Chinese marched fast and attacked unrelentingly, despite taking huge casualties as a result of the "human wave" assaults that shocked and terrified the UN allies. The methods were effective. One entire American army was almost destroyed; others narrowly escaped by evacuation to sea. Even after American forces and particularly weapons were heavily augmented in mid-1951, the UN forces could do little more than advance just north of the Thirty-Eighth Parallel. Peace negotiations began, but continued for two years before a ceasefire was announced in July of 1953. It has largely held to the present day, though no formal agreement among all the combatants has ended the conflict.

The costs to the PRC would have crippled the development of many countries. Official figures given by the PRC government cited about 150,000 deaths, though historians estimate that the true figure was between about 400,000 and 900,000 (including one of Mao's estranged sons, Mao Anying). The cost of mobilization for the PRC totaled US $2.5 billion (compared to about $20 billion for the USA). But the advantages to the state were considerable. In American eyes, the PRC had lost the war. The Korean peninsula was still divided, South Korea still existed, PRC losses had been the largest compared to any group of participants except the people of South Korea, and the American Seventh Fleet had been brought to East Asia, where it would indefinitely protect Taiwan. But in the eyes of Mao and his fellow PRC strategists, the losses were small when compared to the devastation of the past two decades, and all the material damage had been done outside China. The world watched the PRC fight to a standstill a country that had just waged atomic war against another Asian country, and had threatened the PRC itself with nuclear weapons tested in the Pacific during the war. Mao was known in China to have sacrificed his own (perhaps unwilling) son in the patriotic struggle against the USA. The new state in the PRC had a mesmerizing nationalist theme around which to organize its economic campaigns, its media and entertainments, and its educational programs. China was sentimentally unified in a way that transcended the complications and ideological splits of the previous 30 years.

This theme of a country at war against an imperialist aggressor was useful at a time when consolidation of the CCP control over the countryside was still developing. Like Taiwan, the mainland was effectively under martial law as of 1950. Military officers, and military political commissars, were in charge of pacification in most provinces (an exception were the three heavily-garrisoned provinces of the Northeast, which were governed directly from Beijing). An initial wave of land reform, modeled on earlier practices at Jiangxi and Yan'an, was pushed in most provinces to expose opponents of the regime and improve productivity. Party cadres went deep into the countryside, rousing villagers to identify prostitutes, landlords, and opium growers, smugglers or users. Class backgrounds were recorded – poor peasant, middle peasant, rich peasant, landlord, bourgeois, capitalist. Land was taken from the land-rich and given to the landless. Bourgeois and capitalist could admit their crimes and ask forgiveness; the recalcitrant were imprisoned or executed, depending on the verdict of the party cadres and the villagers. PRC law as of 1950 called for the "elimination" of the landlords as a class, though commentary indicated this to mean that landlords would be redeemed and take up life as farmers, or perhaps even as party cadres, should their inner transformation be thorough enough. In fact, many landlords appear to have been eliminated in a more literal way. Estimates of the number of people killed in these campaigns range from many hundreds of thousands to a few million. The point was made: Members of the CCP increased from about 3,000,000 in 1947 to about 6,000,000 in 1953. Enemies of the party became very few, and very silent. Farmers reclaimed and reopened abandoned or ruined land, workers became busy in the state factories churning out weapons and vehicles for use in Korea. A unified currency, backed by a state bank, was in place by 1951. By 1952, the society was functioning (if at a low level in some areas), Chinese were enjoying the novelty of life without domestic warfare for the first time in more than three decades, and the country was making its mark on international affairs.

The demands of rural remodeling, industrial revitalization and international competition were lessened by the simplifications of military government, but Mao's announced plan was to move as soon as possible toward constitutional, civilian rule, and toward a heavy emphasis on programs that would materially improve the conditions of the majority of the population. Mao was emphatic that unless the state reassured the public, all would be lost: "If we know nothing about production and do not master it quickly, if we cannot restore and develop production as speedily as possible and achieve solid successes so that the livelihood of the workers, first of all, and that of the people in general is improved, we shall be unable to maintain our political power, and we shall be unable to stand on our feet; we shall fail."

The guiding civil principles were the "organic law" that made the CCP the government and the "common program" that allowed practice to be affirmed as regulation. Under the Common Program, the party announced its intention to proceed gradually with the transition from capitalism to socialism. Though the CCP was the state, it permitted non-party members to have high rank. Sun Yatsen's widow Soong Chingling had not accompanied her family to Taiwan, but had stayed in Shanghai. She was not a member of the CCP (though she joined just before her death in 1981), but she became vice-president of the PRC and headed the All China Women's Federation, which advocated for women's employment and equality. The China Democratic League, an umbrella organization that had been formed in 1939 to create a political platform for the smaller political parties advocating rural education and land reform, as well as socialism outside the Marxist-Leninist model, was made legal, and proved useful in organizing many of the programs for rural advancement. CDL member Shen Junru was appointed first president of the Supreme People's Court (though the body had little to do at the time), and many others affiliated with the CDL were appointed to head ministries of education, industry, trade and agriculture. Industrialists who decided to stay in China (and there were many in Zhejiang and Jiangsu provinces particularly) were invited by the CCP to sell to the state an annually increasing percentage of their industries, and to stay on as managers and trainers. City landlords with large apartment buildings were also invited to share in their properties to the state on an increasing schedule, and to remain in their own apartments within their former buildings. In domestic and international trade and manufacturing, pre-1949 corporations still existed, but the state created its own firms to compete with them for an increasing share of the market. In transportation and mining, the PRC simply assigned the old KMT monopolies to itself. The moderation of the Common Program was no doubt responsible, in combination with the Korean War, for allowing the PRC to reach a surprisingly high degree of stability within a short time.

In 1954, the Common Program was ended with the promulgation of a constitution, which most historians feel was a conscious emulation of the USSR constitution of 1936 – with the major exception that the Soviet constitution had implied sovereignty (or at least a right to secede) for distinct societies and cultural minorities, and the PRC constitution (in contrast to the constitution of the CSR in 1931) insisted upon a centralized, unified state that monopolized sovereignty. Strikingly, the constitution formalized a transition from military to civilian rule. The new state structure put military officials under party committees and reporting to party liaisons, while military officers were given only a modest number of appointments in the highest party committees. The constitution declared that all individuals had rights of free speech, correspondence, public demonstration and religious belief. Complaints of abuse by private individuals or by state officials could be lodged with the appropriate agencies. Women were guaranteed legal equality. The constitution ratified the National People's Congress (which had already been meeting since 1953) and established the methods for citizens to be elected. The structure of the state was formalized, with the CCP, its Secretariat and the Politburo technically distinct from the National People's Congress and the State Council. Mao Zedong was "elected" Chairman of the CCP and President of the PRC; Liu Shaoqi was chairman of the Standing Committee of the National People's Congress; and Zhou Enlai was premier of the State Council. In practice, the distinction between state and party was obscured by the practice of giving government leaders appointments in both the party and the state. Liu Shaoqi, for instance, was both vice-chairman of the CCP and vice-chairman of the National People's Congress. Additionally, the power of the top three individuals – Mao, Liu and Zhou Enlai – was amplified by the fact that each had multiple appointments. Zhou, for instance, had important powers over domestic policy, but was also the official primarily responsible for foreign relations. The legal system was left obscure, but committees were created to further the work of establishing a system of courts, judges and lawyers.

Prior to 1952, the CCP had drawn much of its life and effectiveness from its ability to graft itself onto the structures of traditional social and economic organization, and to transmute those structures only at opportune moments, for specific reasons. Rural communist cells were based on villages, their work and debt cooperatives, and even the cults attached to religious shrines. Peng Pai had used such as approach when organizing farmers against landlords and rents in Guangdong, and Mao had studied such techniques both in Guangdong and in his native Hunan. In intensely commercialized environments, communist organizers worked with market and transport organizations, first promoting the profitability of products, then attempting to shift the attention of merchants and peddlers toward restructuring relations between producers and consumers. Even the land reform programs in Jiangxi and Yan'an had evinced this basic chameleon property, since they were designed to identify and act out the agenda of the majority of distressed farmers. The Common Program was in some ways the climax of this style of CCP traveling on the crest of long-standing rural and market-village organizations. In the immediate post-World War II period, it simplified and speeded the efforts of the CCP to establish itself in every town and village as a credible force for the majority – a truly revolutionary call, of the sort that had not been heard since the days of Mao's Yan'an predecessors, Li Zicheng and Zhang Xianzhong. The cohesion of the villages was combined with the energy of unleashed social rage to create a crucible for the political reorientation of the countryside; land reform and the "suppression of counter-revolutionaries" became one process, generated from the surviving social order. Land redistribution was modest, and private property remained the abiding value in the villages.

In 1952 the CCP began very deliberately to apply some of its own pressure to the reshaping of rural organization, with the introduction of "mutual aid teams" (MATs). Mutual aid, in many forms, had been familiar for centuries in rural China (see chapter 2), as among farmers everywhere. Banding together to harvest each other's crops in series, or lending each other handtools, plows or an ox, was traditional. The state's intrusion was to register the teams, influence the size and membership, and ultimately to encourage areas without organized teams to create them. It was not until the promulgation of the "First Five Year Plan," to begin in 1953 and continue to 1957, that the hand of the state began to lie more heavily on the countryside. First, mutual aid teams were superseded by "agricultural producer's cooperatives" (APCs) in which the pooled items used on a loan basis by the mutual aid teams became the permanent property of the APC itself. By 1956 all MATs had been transformed into APCs. Apace with this development, early APCs became "advanced producers' cooperatives." Members no longer took proceeds directly from their own land, but instead pooled their produce and distributed it on a work-unit basis to all who had participated in planting, weeding and harvesting. The size of the cooperatives still corresponded more or less to the size of a traditional village. But many cooperatives saw land on all sides of them being bought by the state and reorganized into "state farms." Farmers residing on such land worked the land without owning it, and received disbursements of grain or cash on the basis of a cadre's calculations. The policies allowed the state to invest a tiny proportion – on the order of 2 percent – of its total budget in the countryside, while putting most of its resources into the Korean War and into development of the industrial sector. Historians now estimate that agricultural productivity rose in this period, with crop cultivation increasing 25 percent from 1952 to 1957, forestry increasing almost 300 percent, animal husbandry increasing about 35 percent, and fish farming rising by more than 100 percent. Diversification of secondary products was also marked. Cotton, chicken and pork, fish, and sugar all increased; only oilseed output declined slightly.

The foundation of industry in the early PRC was built upon the earlier enterprises of the KMT and of the Japanese in the Northeast, Shandong and Shanghai, as well as the late nineteenth-century governors' industries at Wuhan. Railroads, telephone communications and radio broadcasting systems had mostly been either in Japanese hands before being seized by the KMT in 1945, or had been monopolized by the KMT from the early 1930s. Machine tool installations were critical. They were concentrated in the Northeast, where Russians and Japanese had been developing them for half a century. Industrial mining was well developed in the Northeast, in contrast to the traditional handtool mining done in other parts of China (see chapter 15). The strategy of the early PRC planners was to open as many new mines as possible, providing fresh supplies of coal not only for industrial purposes but also to provide heat, for part of the year, to households in north China. Iron, steel and concrete were essential to reconstruction, and facilities to produce them were soon widely distributed across the country. Under the Common Program, industrialists in China could use their remaining capital to start up new enterprises. Some industrialists who did not have enough of their own capital entered into partnership with the state. Despite the fact that the law permitted private corporations to compete with the state-owned or partly state-owned enterprises, in practice the competition was hopeless. Any remaining personal capital was declining during the early years of the 1950s, and officials had numerous tactics for obstructing the progress of private enterprises. By 1956 there were no private enterprises at all. Fully state-owned enterprises accounted for about 70 percent of all industry, and state-private partnerships accounted for 30 percent, with the trend in the direction of the former. Overall industrial production rose almost 20 percent each year during the First Five Year Plan, vastly outrunning the increases in agricultural production percentages, even though agriculture remained the country's primary industry for the remainder of the twentieth century.

Military policy in the era of the Common Program was focused on domestic pacification but also on learning to become formidable enough that the United States would never consider invading China. For the first purpose, China was divided into thirteen military regions, where soldiers could be centrally located for purposes of quelling internal disorder or defending against external attack. For the second purpose, a heavy reliance upon Soviet training and supplies introduced a modest degree of modern weaponry. The use of military airplanes in China dated back to the days of Duan Qirui, at the latest, and many CCP officers had long histories with the warlord forces, the KMT armies and the war against Japan that acquainted them with the use of airplanes for bombing and, in the 1930s, for strafing. Fighter planes acquired from the Soviets immediately after the creation of the PRC required intense training of pilots, which the Soviet Union also supplied. The few Chinese pilots who got into the air in the Korean war acquitted themselves very well. Yet at the end of the war they were still a tiny part of the overall military force, being perhaps 10,000 personnel together (including maintenance and support) among a total military force of over 4,000,000.

PRC military planners carefully linked military industrial production to general industrial planning in the First Five Year Plan. During the earliest years of the PRC, and particularly during the Korean War, Peng Dehuai as supreme military commander and effectively minister for defense was able to keep military prestige high and military priorities funded, and by 1956 the PRC was manufacturing its own fighter planes (on Soviet designs). The army was, during 1950 and 1951, pruned to eliminate the many militiamen and volunteers who had fought the Japanese or the KMT without benefit of training or regular attachment to an established force. The standing army was reduced by almost a third, to a little over 4,000,000, and military academies were established to train officers and infantry, with instructors returned from the Korean War. A naval branch of the army was founded in 1950, 60,000 soldiers were enrolled to be retrained as sailors, and a naval academy was founded at Dalian (once Dairen, Port Arthur, in the Lushun peninsula). Universal male conscription was enacted in 1954, requiring each recruit to serve a minimum of three years, but allowing soldiers with aptitude to apply for longer enlistments or lifetime careers.

Though the military planners were given generous portions of the state budget to undertake these programs, their political influence was each year diminished in the highest planning councils. When the Korean War ended a political rivalry started between Peng Dehuai and Lin Biao, with Lin insisting that Peng's tactics had increased Chinese casualties in the war. By the middle 1950s Mao was also becoming wary of Peng's insistence that military officers should be given advanced training specific to their branch of service, and promoted on the basis of performance regardless of their class background or level of ideological edification. Lin Biao's criticisms, many of which were strident and bordering on irrational, were not a real problem for Peng. But Mao's suspicions of a highly specialized military, insulated from civilian control or ideological conditioning, were to prove dangerous to Peng in the coming years.

In this same period, before 1957, the PRC worked energetically to increase its influence abroad. The ROC's role at the UN and the Olympics gave it a distinct public relations advantage. In the USA, the Luce publications and the lobbying activities of T.V. Soong (who had moved to New York City), together with the practical strictures on public speech during the McCarthy anti-communist campaigns of 1950 to 1954, left no window for changes in American opinion regarding China. In fact, American communists or development activists were in China with many other foreign residents, mostly working in publishing or teaching. By 1950 Song Ching-ling was supervising foreigners at the Foreign Languages Press in Shanghai. Among their publications was *China Reconstructs*, a spectacularly-illustrated magazine published in English, French, Spanish, Arabic and German in addition to Chinese, each month reporting, sometimes with significant exaggeration, on the latest Chinese advances in agriculture and industry. Other foreigners were active in promoting agriculture or developing medical services. American Joan Hinton and Polish-born Israel Epstein were writers and editors in Shanghai; American George Hatem was a high-ranking health official who over the years made great progress in containing leprosy, schistosomiasis and venereal disease. Other foreign residents were children or grandchildren of missionaries, who had been raised in China and stayed after 1949 primarily because it was their home. Mao was proud of the image of the revolution as being an international achievement. His moving essay on the death of Norman Bethune was known to all high school students, and he was frequently photographed with foreign residents.

Mao was particularly delighted when foreign intolerance, such as the McCarthy fanaticism in the USA, drove foreign "experts" into the arms of the CCP. Joan

Hinton's brother William had lived in China since the 1930s and served with the American government's information service in China during World War II. He stayed to observe the early stages of land reform and assertion of communist control over the rural sector, but wished to return to the United States after the Korean War to write a memoir. Political persecution made it impossible for him to make a living in the USA and the American government forced him to surrender his research notes, but he managed to write *Fanshen*, his classic celebration of rural transformation, which became an international bestseller in 1966 and brought the CCP enormous prestige and credibility. But it was not only foreign talent that was cemented to the CCP during the years of radical anti-communism in the USA. Qian Xuesen (Tsien Hsue-shen) had gone to the USA in the 1920s to do graduate work in physics and engineering, and finished a Ph.D. at California Institute of Technology in 1939. He was an outstanding researcher in rocketry, and helped the American army develop techniques for assisting the take-off of very heavy aircraft (such as the B-29 "flying fortresses" used to drop atom bombs on Japan). By the end of World War II, Qian was at the Pentagon, and within a few years worked out the concept that would one day make the space shuttle possible. But in the early 1950s anti-communist investigators in the USA targeted Qian because of his Chinese ancestry. He was forbidden to work, and waited years for a verdict on his status before he was deported in 1955. He had nowhere to go but to the PRC, where he was instantly recognized as a national treasure. American Undersecretary of the Navy Dan Kimball famously remarked afterward, "It was the stupidest thing this country ever did. He was no more a Communist than I was, and we forced him to go." The effects of Qian's contributions began to be evident in China immediately, and continue to be reflected in the Chinese space program at the beginning of the twenty-first century.

In Asia, the PRC moved quickly to position itself as a leader of the developing nations of Asia and Africa. Due in part to the decolonization trend after World War II, new nations were emerging that wished to avoid being client states of either the USA or the Soviet Union. Particularly after the death of Stalin in 1953, Mao showed an increasing willingness to criticize the Soviet Union, and in his policies emphasized making China completely independent of Soviet technological tutelage as soon as possible. Mao was one of a generation of Asian leaders – including Ho Chi Minh in Vietnam, Kim Il-Sung in Korea, Sukarno in Indonesia – who had led guerilla movements in the countries against Japanese occupation, and in the post-war era were advocates for "self-reliance" in their developing countries. Indonesia had taken the lead in defining the "non-aligned" movement. In 1955 Sukarno invited representatives of 29 countries to come to Bandung to write and sign a declaration condemning colonialism and discussing strategies for independent development. Though Sukarno had expected to establish himself as the leader of the movement, he was quickly overshadowed by Jawaharlal Nehru, the prime minister of India, and Zhou Enlai, who attended in his role as premier of the PRC. Zhou's ability to charm and persuade was well known in China and to American diplomats by the end of World War II, but his appearance at Bandung made a spectacular impression, challenging the equally charismatic Nehru. Zhou proposed that, having made its point in Korea, the PRC would now be content with "peaceful co-existence" with the dominant powers, the USA and the USSR. He suggested that China would be generous with its knowledge and its foreign aid. And for good measure, he announced in Indonesia – a country with a huge minority of Chinese origin – that the government of the PRC considered all Chinese descendants living in other countries to be, fully and completely, citizens of those countries. Zhou's debut as an international leader – backed by the material achievements of the PRC since 1949 and the stunning public images from *China Reconstructs* and other products of the vigorous publishing and film industries – marked China's emergence as a global presence.

The steady development of the PRC during the early 1950s was, for Mao, a problematic achievement. He was convinced that without meeting the expectations of the public for material improvement, consolidation of CCP power could not be accomplished. On the other hand, he disliked the relationship between improving education and incomes on the one hand and the emergence of new élites on the other. The potential for such élites and interest groups to gain the upper hand in policy and to determine the fates of apparently supreme leaders was manifest in Chinese history. The state could never free itself of dependency on local communities and interest groups until those basic granular patterns on which Chinese society rested could be controlled from the center. The reunification of China, which Chiang Kaishek had attempted but fallen far short of in 1928, could never be realized until the state became the matrix in which every individual, family and community was recast. The process by which this was to be achieved was indistinguishable from the path which Mao described as the path to communism. It led through collectivization of all historic associations of economic, social and cultural activity in China to some other sort of total transformation that, as of 1955, Mao probably did not see with clarity. But he did know, as all the state planning councils knew in 1955, that the First Five Year Plan was only the prelude to the serious business of transformation. As the First Five Year Plan drew to a close, Mao looked to the two quarters where he was likely to experience resistance: the military and the "intellectuals."

The military had not been idle since the Korean War. In 1954 the ROC had attempted to place large numbers of troops, and build fortifications, on the islands of Jinmen (Quemoy) and Mazu (Matsu) in the straits between the mainland and Taiwan. PRC forces immediately moved to dislodge the KMT troops by shelling the islands from its ships and planes. The USA warned the PRC to desist, but got no response. In January of 1955, Congress passed the Formosa Resolution, requiring the USA to defend the ROC against any attack. Allen Dulles, then American Secretary of State, let it be known that the use of atomic weapons was being considered. In 1955 the PRC ceased shelling Jinmen and Mazu, but occupied other islands in the Straits of Taiwan not covered by the Formosa Resolution. In 1956 Mao began to modify his earlier advice to the military to catch up with international military standards by following the standards and practices of the Soviet Union. He began to suggest that, in fact, the PLA should revive its revolutionary guerilla culture, emphasize its social role of spreading literacy by increasing recruitment, and concentrate less on rewarding the technocrats and specialists in the ranks. He elevated critics of Peng Dehuai, such as Liu Bocheng and Lin Biao, to positions high enough to challenge Peng's policies, and watched the two sides set upon each other. Peng won the early rounds, and continued with plans that saw the first launch of a Chinese-manufactured submarine in 1956 and further reduction in the size of the standing force, to about 2,500,000. But the faction opposing Peng, led by Lin Biao, solidified, awaiting a chance to politicize the military and cripple Peng's political influence.

The fate of the military was strongly tied to the development of relations with the Soviet Union. Mao realized that accelerated collectivization in China would inevitably attract criticism of the Soviet Union. Mao noted that in the Taiwan Straits crisis, support from the Soviet Union for the PRC position had been tepid. This combined with frustration with the fact that the Soviet Union refused to share its atomic and nuclear secrets with China to convince Mao that since the death of Stalin the Soviet Union had been following a revisionist, counter-revolutionary, rightist road. The Soviet system was to establish new educational and professional élites, to concentrate material and cultural resources in the great cities, and to compete with the United States for technological domination of other societies; this was now derided by Mao as "Khrushchevism." In 1956 Mao prominently sided with Eastern European protestors against Soviet domination of their societies. He was prepared to pursue global leadership of the non-aligned movement, particularly if it led to weakening of the dominance of both the USA and the USSR.

Like the military, "intellectuals" were a difficult problem, and also not divorced from Mao's growing disenchantment with the Soviet Union. Few of the great writers or philosophers of the 1920s and 1930s had survived KMT purges or the rigors of the long wars. The generation of the previous revolution had passed away: Kang Youwei had died in 1927, Liang Qichao in 1929, and Zhang Binglin in 1936. Lu Xun (see chapter 11), whom the CCP falsely claimed as a convinced communist (though they might truthfully have considered him a humanist who for a time put his hopes on communism), had also died in 1936, of tuberculosis; the CCP was free to institutionalize him as a cultural icon, a repudiation of the liberal, bourgeois thinking that had been represented by Kang and Liang, or by Hu Shih (who had gone to Taiwan and become a leading educator). The living were a more complicated matter. Ding Ling (see chapter 11) had found her way to Yan'an in the late 1930s; though she had wandered to the wrong side of a cultural debate with Mao in 1942, she had avoided more serious trouble by denouncing herself. She stayed on in the PRC after 1949 as a publicly committed communist, though her frequent allusions to sexism among party leaders made some uneasy. Qian Zhongshu, the globally acclaimed novelist educated in France, returned to China in 1938 and spent the early part of the decade translating Mao's works into French and English (the apparent obsequiousness of the gesture made Mao suspicious). Another survivor was Guo Moruo, an archeologist and iconoclastic poet who had fled to Japan during the KMT purge of communists in 1927, but returned after the Japanese invasion to join the fight on the side of the CCP. In the early 1950s Mao had assigned him to head various ministries and committees of culture and education, but thought him unpredictable and abstruse. There was also Fei Xiaotong, the fearless social researcher who had been working rural China since the 1930s, chronicling the worlds of the poor and the culturally disparate. Fei, unlike Guo, was not a professed communist, and was in many ways a product of the Common Program, which had permitted the politically neutral to survive in, and Mao feared, dominate, the small and poor universities of China.

In the early years of consolidating CCP power, campaigns in the countryside had rooted out not only landlords but the politically uncommitted. In the middle 1950s the cities, and particularly the schools, had not yet been thoroughly cleansed. It was true that individuals who did not do manual labor – teachers, accountants, engineers, printers – had been put on notice that their contributions were negligible and merited only negligible rations of pork, rice and cotton. But Mao felt as he approached a steeper rate of collectivization that these thinkers would be likely to carp against the program, to spread news of any temporary setbacks, and become a source of political friction. In 1955 intellectuals were terrorized by a sudden party campaign against Hu Feng (Zhang Mingzhen), who had suggested that literature could have uses not limited to socialist transformation; public criticism of Hu was intense, he lost his university position, and party spokesmen declared their intention of finding his sympathizers in the academy.

Mao was concerned that academics, or intellectuals as a community, would identify with Hu, and seek safety in withdrawal. He intended to isolate Hu by enticing the rest of the academics and professionals to lower their defenses. Zhou Enlai opened the campaign to discipline the intellectuals with a speech in January 1956, in which he appeared to extol the contributions of the intellectuals and advocate their greater participation in the work of socialist transformation. In effect, the speech served to identify intellectuals as an object of politicization. In Zhou's view, intellectuals were high school teachers and technicians in addition to college professors and writers. He estimated that there were about 150,000 of them in the country. In May of that year Mao gave a speech in which he underscored Zhou's points and added that the intellectuals should feel free, very free, to criticize the government and officials. Mao may, like the Qing emperors, have felt that open criticism was a good way of enhancing the ability of the center to root out corruption and inefficiency. But he was clearly also curious what the cryptic and self-censoring intellectuals would come out with if unmuzzled. He invoked the days of philosophical competition in ancient China, quoting, "Let the hundred flowers bloom, let the hundred schools of thought contend." Still the audiences held back, evidently suspicious of the party's motives; writers and academics in particular remembered the vicious ideological struggles during Mao's cultural sessions at Yan'an, which had occasionally resulted in humiliation or, in a few cases, death. Mao renewed the call to criticism in early 1957, saying criticism was better than mindless obedience. Criticism, he implied, would be rewarded, and praise would not.

The CCP succeeded in opening the floodgates of public opinion, and the Hundred Flowers Movement gathered steam. Students and teachers, writers, and workers with opinions now participated with enthusiasm via letter, poster and street declamations. Party cadres were criticized for their sense of superiority and abuse of privileges, the Soviet Union was criticized as a hypocritical and ungenerous partner and the USA was denounced for its protection of the KMT in Taiwan. Perhaps Mao did not really expect the accompanying complaints: Teachers and writers felt bullied by the party; Marxist theory predicted that the state should wither away, but it seemed to be thickening up instead; long-term officials and leaders should abdicate; or, Marxism was simply the wrong path, and better methods could be found in pragmatism or in models from Chinese history. Mao, signaling that his patience with the experiment was at an end, revised and republished his Yan'an period essay "On Correct Handling of Contradictions among the People." In July, he declared that, in essence, the Hundred Flowers had all bloomed; the record would be reviewed, exposed contradictions would be adjusted, and those who had deviated would be rectified. Hu Feng was sentenced to prison indefinitely. Ding Ling was accused of never having had much devotion to communism, being more focused on petty criticisms and promoting herself as a cultural authority; she was expelled from the party and denied all party privileges. Many other authors of her generation, some veterans of the Long March or of the Yan'an community, were criticized as being a drag on the public mood, just when optimism and good humor were needed for continued collectivization. Fei Xiaotong was forced to denounce himself for questioning communism and pursuing researches of a bourgeois and selfish nature. Many of the accused turned to lawyers to protect them; the civil legal system was suspended and lawyers were given other work. Six months after Mao declared the Hundred Flowers Movement concluded, 300,000 people had been condemned as rightists, losing party membership, employment, housing, and educational opportunities for their children. The search for rightists continued, since the main work of establishing total control over the localities – not only spatial, but educational, professional, and political – had really only begun. For good measure, the party completed construction on Qincheng prison, near the Ming tombs, where in coming decades PRC citizens protesting centralization and curbs on freedom would be incarcerated.

In January of 1958, Mao Zedong announced the initiation of the Great Leap Forward (GLF). The Soviet model of five year plans for graduated industrialization was regarded by Mao as narrow-minded and dogmatic. What was needed in China was a bold advance to complete the socialist transformation. Collectivization in the countryside would be completed with creation of communes and the abolition of private property. The principles of rural collectivization would be applied to industrial advancement. The party would unite around the demands of the moment, as the risks of interference from the Soviet Union or the United States would be high. The cautious types in the party, Mao fulminated – naming Zhou Enlai and many others – would just have to renew their revolutionary fervor and get on board. There would be no guiding authority except the "dictatorship of the people." The survival of the people was at stake, and resistance would be treason. The motives behind Mao's great plan have been an object of speculation among historians. Productivity on virtually all fronts had been high during the First Five Year Plan, and no looming economic crisis demanded the action. Strategically the GLF seemed to have little effect except to invite criticism from Khrushchev and possibly convince him that the Soviet Union was wasting its aid on the PRC. Many historians point to the GLF as primarily designed to tighten Mao's grip on power, since initiation of a grand but perilous development gamble meant that there was no margin for dissent or even uncertainty.

More practical considerations may also have been relevant. For instance, greater collectivization would demand a reshaping of the infrastructure; dams and irrigation systems would be repaired and extended, roads would be redrawn, bridges built. The labor demands would anchor the rural population and minimize illegal migration to the cities by the underemployed. Additionally, the degree of collectivization introduced during the First Five Year Plan had raised agricultural productivity markedly while depending on very little state investment. Mao may have been supposing that collectivization of industry would in like manner produce continued gains in productivity but with even lower state investment. But more likely Mao was attracted to the idea of simply reducing state investment in local industries altogether.

Mao often depicted the GLF as a form of radical decentralization, so complete that even the CCP would be reduced to a set of independent commune-level units, united mainly by their revolutionary determination. In fact, the logic of the GLF was to obliterate the difference between the center and the locality, submerging the center in all the localities, transforming all the localities through their immersion in the center. Mao's writings make it clear that the state-local dichotomy was a problem for him. In the style of an old fashioned agrarian socialist, or an anarchist (see chapter 11), Mao thought that farmers were complete political individuals – self reliant, naturally orderly, but full of revolutionary energy. They were to him the antithesis of the predatory elites he feared would emerge from the army, the party, and professions if they were permitted to concentrate themselves in certain cities or regions. He was more ambivalent about the farmer's tendency to form communities that resisted broader influences for change, destruction and creativity. Such traditional granular resistance he regarded as "counter-revolutionary."

The persisting shapes – both administrative and political – of provinces and counties annoyed Mao. The First Five Year Plan had vested decision-making in provincial committees and provincial governors, a practice Mao planned to end. The Northeast, whose three provinces were supposed to be under direct control from the capital, was a particular target of his charges of "mountain top-ism," or the pursuit of local interests in neglect of the party or national agenda. Mao had suspected that the commissioner for the Northeast, who died in 1954, had explored the possibility of making the Northeast into a Soviet satellite state, like the Mongolian People's Republic. The Northeast was the seat of China's industrialization and much of the mining industries. So long as those industries remained concentrated in the Northeast the rest of the country was vulnerable. But take those industries, smash them, and redistribute the pieces all over the country, and there would be no grounds for any locality to indulge in the creation of its own interest groups, or identities. The society could be remade from the ground up, and the PRC could be unified in the only meaningful way that could occur in modern history. It would not be a matter of the state rearranging the localities; it would be obliteration of the distinction between state and locality that historically had been the source of China's political coherence and incoherence. The state would be the locality, and the locality the state. For Mao and others of his generation who suffered the worst effects of China's period of profoundest fragmentation, the vision of a society in which imperialism and warlords were impossible, in which parasitic élites could not gain leverage over the majority, may have been compelling in its own right.

Attributing the GLF to Mao himself cannot explain the rapidity and thoroughness with which collectivization was achieved, or the extremes to which the process was ultimately pushed. Mao predicted spectacular achievements – famously, iron production surpassing Britain's in fifteen years – but his plan for the GLF was notably absent specific methods by which this would be achieved. The country should "walk on two legs" (agriculture and industry) and find its resources internally, freeing itself of dependence on outside help. He invited officials and cadres to find ways of implementing his ideas. In the spring, he visited Henan province to see the first accomplished commune. As with those to come, it was organized in levels for decision making. At the bottom was the team, about 30 families. Teams reported to the brigade, and the brigades reported to the commune, which could be the size of several traditional counties. In the fall, Mao was shown how an enterprising team had started to smelt iron themselves. They found scrap metal, heated it in a large cauldron over a fire of wood taken from window frames, gates, bridges (later some smelters would use coffins), charcoal and dung, and then ladled it into molds they had stamped in the sand. Mao considered the idea inspired. He declared that this practice should be emulated by all the communes, once they were formed. He described the process of innovation and emulation as the "communist wind" that would blow down the ruins of "feudalism." Within three months, about 700,000,000 of the country's roughly 800,000,000 people had been organized into 27,000 communes. In each of them, private property was abolished and residents ate in communal dining halls instead of in their homes. The communes ran their own schools and hospitals, their own weaving and clothes manufacture and, of course, did their own iron smelting. They all had plans to build their own factories for the production of bicycles, motorcycles, trucks, tractors and electrical appliances. When the communes were freshly established in 1958, they maintained about 600,000 smelting furnaces and nearly 3,000,000 factories for the production of textiles or machines. Mao kept touring the communes, and talking with the amateur enthusiasts of industry. He also became an amateur agronomist, passing wisdom he had been given by farmers at one commune on to those at another: planting more closely was more efficient, plowing more deeply encouraged root growth, killing sparrows would improve the rate of sprouting (in fact, killing sparrows caused infestations by the insects they normally ate).

Problems were encountered in some localities immediately, and in others it took some time. In many communes it was discovered that referring decisions on production to the commune level was cumbersome. Brigades and teams began to make their own decisions, threatening a return to the political economy of the traditional village. The steel and iron produced in the micro-smelting operations was almost unusable, and most heavy construction still required that the iron and steel components be made in the large iron works of the Northeast. Nevertheless, good weather and considerable reserves from the previous year allowed the communes to report to the party at the end of the year that 1958 had been successful despite the disruption of radical political and social reorganization; indeed, the official figures claimed a spectacular 55 percent jump in agricultural productivity. The same was not true of 1959. Weather across most parts of northern China, Inner Mongolia and Xinjiang was cold and rainfall was below average. Nothing much had been done to repair the Yellow River, and it flooded, causing drought in neighboring areas. The state had no effective central way of managing reserves, and residents of the affected areas began to starve. In Tibet, the forced reorganization of villages to make way for the communes had disrupted production in more fertile areas, leaving the drier areas cut off and without grain. Lhasa residents gathered to protest their conditions, and in some areas Tibetans resorted to the guerilla tactics that had kept the region effectively independent for 40 years before 1950. The PLA was dispatched to Tibet, and a series of skirmishes killed about 80,000 protesters and guerillas. The autonomous government that had been set up in Tibet in 1950 was rescinded. The Fourteenth Dalai Lama and his government went over the mountains to India, and the CCP set up the Banchen Lama as the region's governor. Xinjiang and parts of Inner Mongolia were also trouble spots. Nomads resisted the confiscation of their lands for incorporation into the communes. The harsh weather and diminished food distribution quickly brought intense distress to Xinjiang in particular. Protests and riots ensued, as tens of thousands petitioned to emigrate to the republics of Soviet Central Asia. Troops fired into crowds, crowds fought back.

As the news of riots, starvation, floods, famines and overwhelmed army units came to the party leaders, they gathered for their Eighth party plenum in the artificial calm of Lushan. The magnitude of what was happening was hard for everyone to grasp, including Mao. Agricultural output had fallen by 14 percent, nearly 10,000,000 people had died of starvation. The cities were desperate and some areas were becoming ungovernable. Peng Dehuai saw another sinister development, which he thought should alarm Mao: Most communes had begun to form and train their own militia, who were prepared to fight with the PLA and with each other, over water and food. In a written plea, Peng asked Mao to step down as head of government, and to end or significantly amend the GLF program.

In conference, Mao referred to Peng's letter, using it as a launching pad for an aggressive speech, the essence of which he would elaborate in the series of meetings ahead. The GLF had made missteps, Mao conceded, and the micro-smelting schemes had been among them. But the concept of the GLF was correct, and would bring glorious results if pursued. Peng's criticism of Mao's excesses, Mao claimed, was actually evidence of Peng's own "rightist tendencies," not so very different from the rightest tendencies in all sectors that Mao had been combating since 1957. Peng had been a long-time critic of any policy that diverted resources from the army, or undermined a Soviet-style élitism and specialization within the military. For all he knew, Mao intoned, Peng was an active agent of the Soviet Union, undermining the GLF in order to discredit Mao and take advantage of the leadership crisis to launch an attack. Mao reminded his listeners that he was the leader who had led them out of the clutches of the KMT when Zhang Guotao had failed. He had led the party and the army to victory against the Japanese. He had foreseen that opposing the USA in Korea was possible. He was the genius of the revolution, and if the party did not support him now, he would go back to his own revolutionary base, form his own revolutionary army, and start the Chinese revolution over again. It took weeks of debate for the plenum to come to its conclusion: Peng Dehuai was dismissed as minister of defense and all his committee appointments, and he was to be placed under house arrest (he was eventually taken to Chengdu); Lin Biao was his successor. Sympathizers of Peng Dehuai, including Zhang Wentian, were to be sought out and punished; most lost their positions, and some – such as Mao's personal secretary Li Rui, who had added his voice to the critics – received long prison sentences. Qincheng prison, which was already full of Tibetan and Uighur protesters and Chinese farmers who resisted the confiscation of their grain, began to make room for the CCP élite.

Mao saved his position in 1959, but nothing could halt the cascade of bad news about the effects of the GLF. In 1960 weather conditions worsened further, and the cities began to suffer because food was not being transported from the countryside. In some cases, the failure of food deliveries was due to neglected roads and bridges, as well as defective vehicles. But increasingly through 1960 the communes, brigades and teams were fighting to keep their food to themselves, to preserve their own lives. The commune structure prevented the rural population from shifting in response to local conditions, meaning that those with inadequate production needed food transported to them; the absence of market mechanisms for distributing food in the traditional way led to attested waste of food in the communes in 1958 and early 1959, reducing emergency stores. Henan province, which had led the way in total collectivization, was among the regions suffering most intensely, as were the normally poor provinces of Anhui and Gansu. Sichuan, once among the most productive provinces, had become a model of GLF collectivization of industry in 1958, and may have suffered the greatest provincial losses. Party élites and local committees hoarded food. Riots in the cities as well as the countryside became endemic, and the army itself could not be fed. Anecdotal reports depicted the population eating bark, leather and the flesh of other people. Between 1959 and 1960, grain production fell 30 percent, and food consumption in the countryside may have declined nearly 25 percent. A healthy individual needs about 2,100 calories daily, but research now indicates that the average consumption in China from 1959 to 1961 was about 1,500 calories per day. The number of deaths that occurred by 1961 is still debated. A government census of 1964, which was not available to scholars until the 1980s, implied a near doubling of the normal death rate, and about 15,000,000 deaths for the GLF period. Demographers calculating the number of missing births put the mortality figures at 25,000,000 to 30,000,000. A recent study done from original documents, interviews, and a review of media reports suggests a total of 36,000,000. In absolute numbers the death totals rivaled that of the Taiping War (which lasted fourteen years), though the rise in population from about 400,000,000 in the nineteenth century to about 650,000,000 left the Taiping War, proportionally, as the most fatal single episode in Chinese history. Nevertheless, the loss of something on the order of 36,000,000 people without a war, merely as a result of ideological misguidance and economic mismanagement, in less than three years, is a unique atrocity in human history.

The GLF was not Mao's only setback in 1960. In the heady days of GLF success in 1958, Mao had ordered the PLA to resume aerial bombardment of the Jinmen and Mazu islands, while whipping up a new anti-American propaganda campaign and resuming threats to invade Taiwan. The USSR sent Andrei Gromyko to meet with Mao and caution moderation, which Mao rejected. The bombardments ceased only after improved missiles, supplied by the USA, were put into service by the ROC air force. Mao privately denounced the Soviet Union for appearing to prefer the new "peaceful co-existence" policy over supporting the PRC. Khrushchev met with American president Eisenhower in Paris that year, despite the fact that the USA had admitted violating Soviet airspace with its U-2 high altitude surveillance planes. Mao sniped at Khrushchev's willingness to meet with the USA, and Khrushchev sniped back that the GLF was an inane departure from proven communist development strategies. The discord continued for months, and Khrushchev finally announced that PRC leaders were so confused about the basics of industrial management that the USSR was wasting its aid resources. The 1,400 Soviet industrial and scientific advisors were ordered withdrawn. They took their designs and manuals with them, and even tore out the machine tools they had installed in major factories in the Northeast and trucked them back to the Soviet Union. Mao, determined to demonstrate that the split was good riddance, decided to fully repay the outstanding PRC debt to the USSR, a sum in cash and grain that was equal to 12 percent of the military budget.

The PRC military was stunned, and Mao's opponents in the CCP added this to the devastation of the GLF in their case against Mao. In late 1960 Mao indicated that he would be willing to relinquish his planning role in the GLF and allow Liu Shaoqi (who assumed the state presidency) and Deng Xiaoping to take the lead. During 1960 and 1961 the economic planners took emergency measures to improve food production and access. Collective eating in the communes had already been abandoned, now a degree of private land income was introduced in order to create incentives for farming to resume. About 25,000,000 city dwellers were sent into the countryside to allow them to aid in production and have direct access to food. Industrial activities for the most part returned to the industrial centers. Liu and Deng ordered a review of local-level party operatives, dismissing the radically collectivist and replacing them with developmentalists of their own type. These cadres allowed both consumption and production to revert more to villages, lineages and households. Communes were no longer required to maintain high stores of grain, permitting it to be bought in local markets.

At the commune level, industrial enterprises that were unproductive or produced below quality were sold, and the workers were sent back into agriculture. A priority was placed on restoring transportation and policing, so that food and textiles could be safely delivered to distribution points. With these policies and some good luck with the weather, China's economic recovery was remarkable. Industry had not experienced the collapse that agriculture had between 1959 and 1961. By 1965 total industrial production was double what it had been in 1957, and agricultural production was back to what it had been in 1957. Liu and Deng placed economic planning for the communes under control of the CCP central planning committee. They moved management of grain and textile distribution from the commune level to the level of the team, the lowest local unit. The more successful rural industrial enterprises – mostly in concrete and fertilizer production, not in iron or steel – were allowed to continue, and were given state aid if needed. Military research, which may have been protected from the ravages of the GLF by the relative isolation of the research facilities in Qinghai province and by the military's independent sources of supply, continued.

In 1962 it seemed clear that the unmitigated disaster of the GLF and the visible success of the recovery efforts under Liu and Deng had shifted the direction of the party away from radical collectivization and decentralization and toward centralized planning, distribution via market mechanisms, professionalization of the military – and probably toward a rapprochement with the Soviet Union. Mao remained chairman of the party, and public announcements by Liu and Deng usually began with obsequious references to the brilliance of Mao's revolutionary leadership. Mao knew that he was being turned into a figurehead, to legitimate policies he despised. Still residing at the chairman's residence in Zhongnanhai inside the Forbidden City, he had few companions to commiserate with. One was Jiang Qing (Li Shumeng), a Shanghai film actress in the 1930s, then a communist supporter, and in 1938 Mao's fourth wife and mother of his daughter Li Na. Another was Kang Sheng, who had been Mao's ideological enforcer at Yan'an. In the 1950s Jiang Qing had been put to work at the Ministry of Culture. As at Yan'an, Kang had been Mao's main source of intelligence during the 1950s, though he did not take a public role until Peng Dehuai's dismissal in 1959, which Kang had helped to manage. Mao, Jiang and Kang knew that though the successful recovery efforts under Liu Shaoqi (whose portrait was now seen publicly everywhere that Mao's had been displayed) had shifted them off the pinnacle of power, they were not without resources. Liu and Deng Xaioping were both ruthless political operators who had generated their share of resentment over the decades. The party was still replete with undimmed disciples of Mao and his ideas. The post-GLF policies had allowed inequalities of privileges to emerge in the countryside, creating new tensions between collectivists and developmentalists. Lin Biao, a champion public booster of Mao, was still minister of defense. Deng had appointed both Jiang and Kang to the party secretariat, probably as a way of mollifying Mao. There was fuel to start another fire, regain the political center and punish Liu and Deng.

Mao attended the Tenth Plenum of the Chinese Communist Party Central Committee in September of 1962, and amid all the optimist assessments of the recovery under Liu he reminded the party "never forget class struggle!" Mao demanded that the party authorize a new campaign, the "four cleansings" (*si qing*). The relaxation of collectivization and group decision making had, in Mao's view, created a new class of empowered cadres in the countryside (most placed by and beholden to Liu and Deng) who were not only engaging in corrupt practices of their own (mostly running black markets in grain) but were corrupting the revolutionary dedication of the farmers. The campaign, usually called the "Socialist Education Campaign" (SEC) in English, was authorized, and during 1962 and 1963 inspectors and instructors (many vetted by Mao and associates) canvassed the countryside looking for corrupt, inept and ideologically casual cadres, who were given bad reports and subjected to seminars. En masse, farmers were gathered and lectured on their own newly-noticed failings. Only in 1964 did the SEC become a program for dismissal and punishment of miscreants. Many offenders were "struggled," a practice that went back at least to Yan'an. In personal interrogations or in public denunciation, targets were subjected to intense psychological abuse, and sometimes to physical harassment. Upon review, the CCP found that the effects of the campaign were overall deleterious; cadres had become paralyzed by fears of being targeted, while the necessity to form factions for mutual protection had riven the ranks of both the cadres and the SEC investigators. With Mao's grudging agreement, the party instructed SEC operatives to return to the instruction and hortatory of the earlier period. In 1965 and 1966, the SEC had become a shadow of Mao's hopes to re-establish class struggle and revolutionary purity as the central goals of all policy.

But Mao and his associates were working on other fronts to encircle his enemies in the party. Probably due to the influence of Jiang Qing, Mao decided to steer his approach through culture. He had engaged in intense debates with writers, poets and painters at Yan'an, primarily over the issue of whether the purpose of art was to advance revolution and improve the material well-being of the people, or whether it was to satisfy the subjective urges of the artist. Ding Ling had been demoted for her views but later professed to agree with Mao; other writers had been exiled, and at least one had been executed at the rebel base. Mao's awareness of and interest in the arts had never been dampened, nor had his conviction been blunted that art is a critical battlefield of the revolution.

Jiang Qing was originally from Shanghai, and still maintained connections with writers and playwrights there. In 1961 Mao was chafing under the success in Beijing of the play "Hai Rui Dismissed from Office" (*Hai Rui Ba Guan*). The author, Wu Han, was a major historian of the Ming period, who had helped in the heroic removal of the students and facilities of Peking University, Tsinghua University and Nankai University to safer locations in Guizhou province after the Japanese occupation of Beijing (see chapter 13). He had stayed on in China after 1949 as a member of the China Democratic League and, like several CDL members, received a high political post – in his case, vice-mayor of Beijing. Probably in 1951 Wu first composed a play based on the story of Hai Rui, a Ming official who was punished and forced into retirement after criticizing the emperor. In 1960 the play was produced in Beijing as an opera, and was a popular success. Public consensus as of 1961 was that the play was a veiled reference to the dismissal and arrest of Peng Dehuai in 1959. During the traumas of 1960 and earlier 1961 Mao had been little affected by the idea that Beijingers were nightly reveling in a play that indirectly glorified Peng and ridiculed Mao. But in 1962 Jiang Qing complained that Wu Han had written the play as a subversive attack on the party chairman – an accusation that was clearly wrong with respect to Wu Han, but may have been true of the producers of the opera derived from Wu Han's original play.

In 1965, Jiang Qing persuaded the Shanghai literary critic Yao Wenyuan to write a denunciation of the Hai Rui play in the Shanghai newspaper *Wenhuibao*. Yao's Shanghai colleague, Zhang Chunqiao, was a former editor of the CCP theoretical journal *Jiefang*, who had vociferously called for the abolition of private property in 1958, and repeatedly criticized the reintroduction of modified private property rights under Liu Shaoqi. Zhang now connected the dots between Wu Han and Liu Shaoqi – Wu Han's administrative superior Peng Zhen, the mayor Beijing, was a long-time associate of Liu and an outspoken developmentalist, also connected to Deng Xiaoping – and demanded that the Beijing bureaucracy isolate and punish Wu Han. Peng Zhen ignored the demands, which in the view of Zhang Qunqiao confirmed his claim that the Beijing bureaucracy was engaged in a surreptitious campaign to discredit Mao and glorify Liu Shaoqi. Zhang began to echo Mao's complaints, first aired in 1962, that the Liu clique was abandoning class struggle and allowing new comfortable elites to control state policy. By 1965 Jiang and Zhang had linked Wu Han together with the editor Deng Tuo and novelist Liao Mosha as a cabal they called the "Three Family Village." It was telling that Mao's propagandists chose the image of the traditional village – in their view in-bred, insular, self-sufficient and defiant of outside control – as their metaphor for counter-revolutionary subversion. Activists in the SEC were able, in early 1966, to use gatherings for discussion of anti-corruption and anti-élitist temptations to introduce a rhetoric calling for a "Great Proletarian Cultural Revolution" (in contrast to the original "cultural revolution," the May Fourth Movement) to specifically combat political parochialism: "We must unmask all anti-party, anti-socialist 'Three Family Village' freaks and monsters in the whole country, the whole province and in our own localities and home units. Whether they are in the towns or the villages, below us or above, we must strike them all down and uproot them...." By the summer of 1966, Mao had publicly called for the production of posters and "big character" placards acclaiming the Great Proletarian Cultural Revolution, and repeating the need to find bourgeois, counter-revolutionary, "Three Family Village freaks and monsters" everywhere.

Jiang Qing proclaimed an ideological struggle had emerged between the Liu establishment and the champions of class struggle. She formed the "cultural revolution small group." At a series of meetings in 1966, Mao, Kang Sheng, Zhang Qunqiao and a few sympathizers began to demand a reorganization of the Beijing government. Practitioners of "bourgeois" (sentimental, subjective, romantic, classless) literature and theater should be identified, denounced and given a chance to redeem themselves. Zhang and Yao set up a "Shanghai commune" that was intended to reproduce revolutionary culture of the Yan'an style, complete with class struggle, in the city. A security guard in a Shanghai factory, Wang Hongwen, became a fanatical supporter of the commune and the new Cultural Revolution. Young and relatively good look- ing, with a pleasant voice, Wang provided to the movement a great deal that was missing. In May of 1966, the mood changed when Lin Biao declared at a high level meeting of the CCP that Peng Zhen and three associates were actually plotting a coup. There was no evidence for the charges, but Zhou Enlai stated in a speech a few weeks later that even if Peng and his friends were not planning a coup, they were certainly working for counter-revolutionary ends, and they were the kind of people who needed to be exposed. The Beijing officials were all dismissed, replaced either by clients of Mao or of Zhou Enlai.

With concrete results, the campaign to find freaks and monsters was on. The universities were quickly hit after Mao replied to a letter from a Peking University lecturer with the phrase, "To rebel is justified." Big-character placards reproducing the phrase were soon all over the campus, and students began denouncing their pro- fessors and their fellow students for counter-revolutionary sentiments. The movement spread to other campuses. Within a short time the confrontations became physical, as targets of the campaigns began to be "struggled." Faculty accused as counter- revolutionaries were surrounded by hostile crowds of angry students, then forced to wear signs announcing their freakiness and monsterhood, then wear dunce caps and be paraded across the campus, then forced to clean the latrines, then beaten, and in some instances finally killed. The movement spread to other campuses, and eventually to high schools. Faculty fearful of being denounced rushed to become the denouncers of others. Traces of counter-revolutionary identity were professed to be found in indi- viduals' household objects – books, paintings, grand pianos, correspondence with foreign friends and family. Houses became the new centers of investigation and judg- ment. Pets – evidence of bourgeois indulgence – were killed, books and art burned, musical instruments destroyed. After private homes had been gutted, activists moved on to museums and historical buildings (in some cases, temples or ruins of very ancient buildings), all remnants of the feudal China that Mao and his new revolutionaries intended to eradicate.

The shock troops of the new revolution were the Red Guards. The first units appear to have been organized at a high school in Beijing in 1966, among students who were mildly punished for writing acid criticisms of "Hai Rui Dismissed from Office," but were energized when Mao publicly took their side. Liu Shaoqi was disturbed by the spreading disorders associated with proliferating Red Guard organizations, and sent CCP counselors into the city to try to calm the teenagers. Mao, Jiang and Kang all denounced Liu for having terrorized the righteous Red Guards, and demanded that they be permitted to organize themselves and pursue their revolutionary actions without interference. University students and factory workers organized their own Red Guard units, seeking counter-revolutionary ene- mies in their university administrations and in the city government. In the factories, swarms of Red Guards were sometimes met with organized resistance from the workers, with violent scenes. Mao ordered the PLA to escort the Red Guards on their outings, and to provide them transportation if necessary. In the months of the Red Guard rampages in Beijing, historians now estimate that about 1,700 people died. Shanghai and Beijing Red Guard units were quickly integrated, and between them organized rural Red Guard units to seek out the developmentalist cadres put in place by Liu and Deng.

Mao enjoyed the adulation of the crowds of hundreds of thousands of Red Guards who gathered to hear his speeches in Beijing; but he was already planning on having the Red Guards suppressed, since their growing violence threatened to discredit him in the party and give ammunition to his enemies. In early 1967 the PLA was turned against the Red Guards in the major cities. Young guards were accused by Maoist party leaders as "left-deviationists," or worse – closet counter-revolutionaries and rightists who had exploited the revolution for their own personal satisfaction. Hard cases – murder or manslaughter convictions – were imprisoned, hundreds of thousands of others were sent to the countryside for reform through labor.

Accusations and purges spread through the party and the cities, then through the countryside. In retrospect, historians see that violence and casualties of 1966–76 were not even distributed throughout the country. Provinces such Guangdong, whose provincial leadership attempted to keep self-proclaimed "revolutionaries" off of important provincial committees (see chapter 17), had a much higher degree of radical activity and disorder. More pragmatic provinces, which compromised with Mao's faction, experienced less disruption and bloodshed. In many localities, Red Guards on the run from the PLA acquired weapons and organization enough to engage in low-grade warfare before being taken into custody. There were a few instances (in Guangdong and Guangxi, famously) of Red Guards becoming involved in armed gang fights with each other. Some commandeered jeeps or trucks and roamed the countryside, "making revolution" – abusing farmers, peddlers, prostitutes and anybody else who caught their eye. As the crackdown on the Red Guards spread outward from Beijing, Red Guards moved southward toward Canton, or westward into Gansu, Qinghai and Xinjiang. The regional cultures of the borderlands were hit hard by the rampages of Red Guards and party operatives associated with the Mao and Jiang. The ideology of the Cultural Revolution condemned regional cultures as "bourgeois" and in some cases – for instance, Tibet – as "feudal." Red Guards flew themselves into Lhasa in 1967, intending to destroy temples and monasteries (which happened), and immediately catalyzed furious fighting between groups in Tibet separated by complex social tensions. Cultural revolution fervor mixed, in some cases, with Tibetan secular passions, producing the Nyemo revolt of 1969 in which Tibetan "Red Guards" – actually millenarian radicals – slaughtered traditional Tibetans and set off a chain of uprisings that brought battalions of the PLA into Tibet to attempt to restore order.

In Xinjiang, where many of the local party functionaries had personal histories going back to the days of the warlord Sheng Shicai and where Muslims excited the Cultural Revolution contempt for cultural diversity, Red Guards from Shanghai arrived to begin to expose the counter-revolutionary essence of the province's officials. The Red Guards infiltrated the provincial militia and instigated widespread revolt. Through 1967 and 1968 a provincial civil war raged in the province. PLA units dispatched to quell the rebels joined them instead, and more units were sent to replace them. The complexly derived militia/Red Guard/PLA rebels included a large number of Uighurs, and before long the rebels were denouncing "great Han chauvinism" (a catchphrase of the party) and proclaiming an East Turkistan People's Revolutionary Party, hoping to revive the Islamic Republic of Eastern Turkestan (see chapter 13). Violence in Xinjiang was not quelled until the end of 1969, significantly later than in other regions. In Inner

Mongolia, the Red Guards arrived in 1967, and the fighting there was particularly vicious. Young Chinese revolutionaries regarded all Mongols as feudal and secessionist by nature. The party deposed the provincial governor, Ulanfu, who had an almost perfect revolutionary history going back to Yan'an. Monuments relating to Buddhism or to Mongol history were demolished, and a significant portion of the total casualties of the Cultural Revolution – perhaps as much as 10 percent – occurred in Inner Mongolia.

In the nation-wide conflagration of the Cultural Revolution, the famous and powerful had no protection if they fell afoul of Mao, his colleagues, their subordinates or the gangs of roving revolution-makers they unleashed. The displacement of the Beijing bureaucrats in 1966 inspired Mao and his group – with the acquiescence of Zhou Enlai – to fling charges at Liu Shaoqi, Peng Dehuai, Deng Xiaoping and thousands of their associates. Liu, Peng and Deng were all removed from their posts. Liu and Peng were imprisoned, and both died of the effects of imprisonment and lack of medical care (Liu in 1969, Peng in 1974). Deng was physically abused and humiliated, then sent to work in a tractor factory in Jiangxi; his son Deng Pufang was "struggled" out of a second-story window on the campus of Peking University and disabled for life. Many other party members died in obscure or ambiguous circumstances, and all that can be said for certain is that when the Cultural Revolution ended they were indeed dead. He Long died, perhaps of untreated diabetes, in prison in 1969. Wu Han died in jail shortly after Liu Shaoqi, though whether from disease or abuse is unclear. So-called "minority nationalities" very rapidly attracted the suspicion and punishment of the activists. Puyi, the last emperor of the Qing, former president and emperor of Manchukuo, had been turned over the PRC by the Soviet Union after World War II, subjected to years of interrogation and re-education, then released to live in Beijing as a gardener; he died in 1967, evidently as a result of a violent assault by Red Guards or ruffians posing as Red Guards. The Uighur historian Jian Bozan – criticized by name by Mao for his attempts to inject questions of cultural difference into historical study – and his wife committed suicide in 1968 rather than submit to the humiliations of the Red Guards. Artists and scholars who survived nevertheless experienced life-threatening abuse, sometimes mixed with public humiliation and the privations of imprisonment. Both Fei Xiaotong and Qian Zhongshu were physically abused, had all their books destroyed, and were forced to work as janitors. The actor Ying Ruocheng – whose family was both Manchu and Roman Catholic – was jailed for three years on suspicion of his loyalties. Few could avoid the expanding perimeter of accusation, very few could muster any defense against the vague and contradictory charges once they were leveled, none could escape the arbitrary, endless punishments visited on them if convicted.

By 1969 the PLA had restored order in most regions (except Xinjiang), and the Cultural Revolution took a different turn. With the public conditioned by the terrors of the previous three years, the Cultural Revolution was rapidly institutionalized. Despite the partial dismantling of communes in the early 1960s, from 1967 many were revived, and urban communes were formed. Reformed Red Guards as well as young people truly convinced of the righteousness of Mao's new revolution were sent to the countryside as laborers, and many continued their political activism. Each commune had committees, working with party cadres, for the systematic investigation, public trial, and conviction (the three being inevitably in chain) in every locality.

Nearly 300,000 additional counter-revolutionaries were unmasked in 1970 alone, and those who were convicted of denouncing Mao or the party were executed. A period of profound and pervasive institutionalized paranoia took hold in all communities and in many families. The best way to avoid suspicion was to accuse others. Neighbors recommended that neighbors be investigated, and particularly revolutionary children informed on their parents. Academics, farmers, soldiers and party members themselves found that the safest course was the one of hollow speech, crisp obedience to the cadres and committees, passivity in all other things. Popular culture at the end of the century would take a long look back on this as a period of alienation, loneliness, emotional sterility, wasted time and corrosive boredom.

From the time they entered school, students were taught to literally sing the praises of Mao and the Party. Their lessons consisted of learning tales of the Long March, of Yan'an, of the war against Japan and of the war in Korea against the USA. High school education was based on reading and memorizing the aphorisms and abridged essays of Mao Zedong, now conveniently published in the "little red book," a plastic-covered volume exactly the dimensions of (and with the bookmark tassel and the same feel to the pages) of the new testaments distributed worldwide by Gideons International since the beginning of the century, and very familiar to Mao from his youth in Changsha. University courses were dedicated to the study of revolutionary history, China's "feudal" history (before 1949), imperialism, Mao Zedong thought, and redacted Marxism/Leninism. Medical practice was focused on "barefoot doctors," medical technicians able to give inoculations, set broken bones and advise peasants on sanitation and hygiene. Advanced medical care was not a priority. Many people, of all political convictions and all ranks, who died of what might be regarded as treatable diseases elsewhere (diabetes, tuberculosis, cancer, hypertension) were afflicted with diseases which, from the perspective of the Cultural Revolution, were not actually treatable, since they were diagnosed in a small minority of the population and demanded expensive and sometimes exotic protocols. In the world of the Cultural Revolution, diseases to treat were malaria, schistosomiasis, malnutrition including rickets and anything else that could be ameliorated through the use of cheap and available folk remedies. Engineering was largely a matter of consultation between those with some knowledge and those with no knowledge. Trial and error – even with the advantage to error – was encouraged by Mao, who cheerfully opined that "truth comes from facts;" dams broke, irrigation systems leaked or flooded the wrong areas, bridges collapsed and steel works sank into swampy ground as work teams attempted to transform the aphorism into practice.

Despite Mao's unprecedented supremacy within the party, political contests continued to disturb the inner sanctums. Not many details are known. Zhou Enlai, never a supporter of Mao's radical policies for collectivization or for thought control, was clearly vulnerable to accusation as an enemy of the revolution. His historical pattern was to shift quickly to Mao's side when his diffidence threatened his influence, or the well-being of his wife, Deng Yingzhao. It had been his way before Mao's ascendance, when he confessed "weakness and error" in support of Li Lisan sincerely enough to Comintern representatives that he was retained on the politburo while Qu Qiubo was dropped in 1931. It had been his way in 1935 when Mao blamed him for strategic mistakes that had led to the collapse of the CSR, and Zhou was contrite enough to be appointed Mao's colleague in the creation of a new strategy that would take them to

Yan'an. It was his way after Mao threatened him in 1958 if he should try to obstruct the GLF, it was his way in 1966 when he endorsed the persecution of the Beijing government. Though Zhou was once hailed by historians as a nearly unstained hero of humanity and humanism in Mao's regime, biographers now find evidence of the same profoundly ruthless instincts for personal preservation that were evident in Mao. Zhou signed a warrant for his own brother's prosecution, and may have sent many other friends and family into the meat-grinder of the hunt for counter-revolutionaries. He used the feared Kang Sheng as an informant and as a surveillance agent, perhaps even running his own operation to identify victims of the next round of purges.

Mao immediately apprehended Zhou's weaknesses – as he apprehended the weaknesses of most people he met – and appears to have enjoyed watching Zhou humbling himself. With the arrest of Liu Shaoqi in 1966 Zhou was perceived as the unchallenged premier and second man in the party, but Lin Biao was clearly eager to usurp Zhou's place. At Lushan in 1959, when Zhou Enlai was working to avoid Mao's wrath without having to whole-heartedly endorse the coming failure of the GLF, Lin had passionately thrown himself into the campaign against Peng Dehuai. When Peng was dismissed, Lin assumed his former position. A constitutional conference of 1969 officially identified Lin as Mao's successor as party chairman. Zhou could not have been alone in realizing the disaster likely to befall the whole country (now a fully-fledged nuclear power) and perhaps a large part of Asia if Lin should in fact succeed Mao. Lin was a life-long neurotic, probably wending toward full-blown madness. In September of 1971, the party made a public announcement that Lin Biao had died in a plane crash. Subsequent reports indicated that the plane had crashed in the Mongolian People's Republic, suggesting that it had been flying toward the Soviet Union. In 1972, news surfaced in a roundabout way that Lin Biao had in fact attempted a military coup against Mao, and when the coup failed fled to the Soviet Union in a plane with an inadequate fuel supply.

The news was a shock to the public; evidently it had originally been a shock to Mao too, who took to his bed, depressed, for days. The idea that even an ambitious and perhaps mad general would attempt a coup against an elderly leader whom he was already assured to succeed appeared bizarre. But recent research suggests that Zhou was not slow in attempting to even the ground between him and Lin after 1969. Lin may have overplayed his hand by attempting to increase the political influence of the army, something that would have alienated Mao and played into Zhou's hands. Lin's apparent attempt to flee to the Soviet Union suggested that he may have been an agent of the hated enemy, with whom the PRC had had border skirmishes in 1968 and 1969, and whom Mao frequently claimed was planning a nuclear annihilation of China. More certain, Lin fiercely opposed the willingness of both Mao and Zhou as of 1970 to open communications to the USA (see chapter 17). Debate over the policy clearly damaged Lin's standing with Mao in the months leading to the crash. Whether the demonstrably unstable Lin could have attempted a coup when he realized his status as successor was not in fact secure, or whether Lin fled for another reason and the coup was a fable generated to explain his death, is unknown. Evidence of a coup attempt involving anybody other than Lin's son Lin Liguo (who may have been the actual instigator) is very hard to find. Either way, with Lin dead and discredited, Zhou Enlai assumed again the role of facilitator and filter to Mao. His ascendency lasted only about two years, however, as bladder cancer caused his health to deteriorate.

When the severity of his illness was clear, Zhou arranged (apparently with the consent of Mao) for Deng Xiaoping to be released from his tractor factory and reassigned as Zhou's personal assistant. From 1974, the push to succeed Mao, extend the Cultural Revolution and send Deng Xiaoping back to the countryside was on, led by Jiang Qing, publisher Zhang Chunqiao, literary critic Yao Wenyuan and public agitator Wang Hongwen.

As in all other periods of twentieth century Chinese history, policy initiatives were accompanied by massive publishing and distribution, backed by continued attempts to raise the literacy rate which in the 1960s was about 80 percent. Major cities all had newspapers with large circulation, the party ran its own newspaper (*People's Daily*), policy journal (*Red Flag*), and theoretical journal (*Liberation*). Academics were not forbidden to publish, on the contrary they were forced to publish. Often written by committee and under a collective pseudonym, journals of economics, sociology, literary theory, and history were published in huge numbers, in the "simplified" characters and with the limited vocabulary that the PRC had adopted to make reading easier. Essays were formulaic, always opening with a quote from Marx, Lenin or Mao or with didactic set pieces on the contradictions among feudalism, capitalism and socialism, and always underlining the Cultural Revolution theme of class struggle. Topics were chosen to illustrate these problems, and essays concluded with an affirmation of the ultimate triumph of communism over imperialism or feudalism. Editors vetted their colleagues thoroughly, hoping to avoid unwelcome attentions from the state censorship bureaus. Beginning in 1969, and accelerating after 1971, history became an obsession. In 1973 the journals, across the horizon, took up the theme of Lin Biao (and his vague "clique") as contemporary avatars of feudalism, and of the pernicious influence of Confucius, a strange connection that during 1974 took on even stranger permutations.

The theme, as developed in all state journals of 1974 to 1976, was that Confucius lived on in the plots of current CCP operatives to bring back "feudalism." Mao himself was depicted as the living heir of the First Emperor, Qin Shihuang, who in 221 BCE succeeded in destroying China's ancient social hierarchy and created the first unified – and, to the extent he could manage it, uniform – empire. At the time outsiders and probably many insiders read the tropes as shallow mottos, justifying the persecution of one faction by another. Yet, they were chosen for a reason, and for educated Chinese of the age of Mao and Zhou they may have had actual content. In the rhetorical scheme established in these years, the entire period of Chinese history before 1949 was "feudal," and feudal elements were still present in Chinese society, even in the party. Feudalism meant many things in this discourse, but it primarily indicated decentralization, class stratification, deference, power exercised by élites over the common people, and protection of exploitative social systems. In the strictest historical sense there was nothing feudal about China in, say, 1936, but in the Cultural Revolution rhetoric, feudalism encompassed all the elements that had prevented central government from evolving during the first half of the twentieth century. Warlords were feudal, they protected their own domains from intrusion by national or revolutionary forces, they used armies to keep their élites in power, they exploited the majority as soldiers and serfs. They had this power because the "feudal" Qing had not prevented itself deteriorating into a decentralized set of fiefdoms, some ruled by Li Hongzhang and his subordinates, some by Zhang Zhidong and his. The Japanese were feudal because they functioned in China as foreign warlords. Lin Biao – the "Lin Biao" constructed in Cultural Revolution image play – was feudal because he was willing to smash the state and the party in order to gain more power for his own fiefdom, the army. Liu Shaoqi was feudal because he wished to protect his favored sectors – research, military development, economic planning – from being intruded upon by the egalitarianism of the party and of Mao.

The only antidote to Confucius and feudalism, in Cultural Revolution rhetoric, was the ruthless, total centralization attempted by the First Emperor. He destroyed the aristocracy, divided the country into new administrative units, and set his own officials, bound by his law, in the stead of the former feudal barons and landowners. When the Confucians complained, he burnt their books and buried them alive. He destroyed feudalism and united the country, and if his successors had stuck to the path instead of compromising with the feudal remnants, China would have been strong and united. Foreign invaders – the Mongols, the Manchus, the Japanese, the treaty powers – would never have been able to invade if China had not been perpetually weak, divided by region and by class, according to the prescription of the feudalists. In the search to root out "feudalism," Cultural Revolution activists, in practice, targeted everything that appeared divisive, reserved, regionalist, or exclusive: elitist tastes, large vocabularies, historical monuments, Islam, Buddhism, Christianity, foreign cultures or foreign travel, hobbies and shyness (both of which drew people away from the group and toward themselves), arts such as musical performance that required long periods of relative seclusion.

Historians have speculated for decades on the motivations of Mao in catalyzing the Cultural Revolution. Among the earliest theories, Robert J. Lifton proposed that Mao was unnerved by the realization that death was approaching, and chose to live vicariously through the juvenile Red Guards, smashing the static system that seemed to be imprisoning him and his meaning in Chinese society, setting in play a new revolution that would be as a new life to him. Others have seen Mao as vengeful, a narcissist, a sadist. For many authors, while Mao remains the indispensable element in the Cultural Revolution, the real answer lies is some defect in Chinese culture, producing a mass "authoritarian personality," easily led into mob murder and frenzied devotion to a heroic, fatherly leader. It is possible, however, that as obvious as it may seem, recent history leading up to the Cultural Revolution may provide part of the explanation. As much as many authors would like to describe the Cultural Revolution as a unique production of Mao himself – with regard to whom the worst personal assessments can be amply supported by evidence – that does not bear much consideration. The Cultural Revolution required the willing, indeed the enthusiastic, participation of many millions of people. Mao struck the right note and provided many of the catchphrases, but the idea that without Mao there would have been no Cultural Revolution is as historically weak as supposing that without Hitler there would have been no Holocaust or World War II. The process by which the CCP triumphed in China was one by which it worked as thoroughly as possible to transform the local societies it encountered from the ground up – using land reform to create a completely new object of loyalty among the poor farmers, killing landlords who would not cease playing the role of local magnates. The Great Leap Forward was Mao's attempt to implement a similar plan on a national scale, obliterating old lines of local affiliation and replacing them with larger structures, all articulated at the level of the party-state. So widespread was the enthusiasm for this, so resonant was this goal with adults across the country, that collectivization was actually achieved more quickly than Mao had expected – perhaps too quickly to permit new management skills and administrative structures to appear before disaster struck. The failure of the plan was, to Mao, an abortion of the imperative to recentralize China and permanently prevent a reversion to the narrow loyalties of place and region that had poisoned the country for so long – and which the developmentalists would have perpetuated with their centers of resource concentration, their enclaves of specialists and professionals.

When Mao was able to resume his programs, he aimed deeper than he had in the GLF – this time transforming not the structures of the localities, but the psychological and cultural structures that he thought had made militarized regionalism ("feudalism") possible in the first place. His personal targets were instructive, since they included many valiant fighters in the cause of communism whom Mao thought had, since the establishment of the state, been too ready to create enclaves of their own within it. Ulanfu was accused of defining the interests of Inner Mongolia distinctly from the rest of the country; He Long was accused of being a "warlord" for his supposed encouragement of a faction to resist Cultural Revolution encroachment upon the ministry of foreign affairs. Their crimes resembled the supposed crimes of Liu Shaoqi, Peng Zhen and Deng Xiaoping, each of whom would have protected an evolving interest group from Mao's demands for total centralization. As in the case of the GLF, Mao's rhetoric was instantly accepted by interested groups. The Red Guards have received most of the attention, and their activities were the most dramatic, but in fact a large portion of the party and the society responded. This is not to suggest that everybody endorsing Mao's programs either in the 1950s or the 1960s were all responding to the same element of appeal. And it is not meant to ignore that Mao was a master manipulator, quickly sensing the insecurities and ambitions in others that made them easy to exploit. It is only to suggest that along with Mao's narcissism and psychopathy came a keen sense of history. It strongly affected those who experienced the two decades leading up to 1949, and it was rather precisely encoded in the otherwise bizarre rhetoric of the Cultural Revolution. Mao's obsession with history and his mania for monism both had the same root: The century in which China had been subjected to increasingly malign, predatory local militarism.

It will be many years before the exact scope and major elements of the Cultural Revolution can be described with confidence. Our histories of the period sometimes do not make clear that people were doing other things besides terrorizing and abusing each other for the decade of the Cultural Revolution. In 1966 and 1967, city industries were widely disrupted, as were mines. Red Guards pre-empted transportation needed for food transport in order to travel to their next site of political agitation. Outside committees assumed control of key points of manufacture and distribution. As a result 1966 was a disastrous year across all sectors, except agriculture where production was merely poor. After violence had been quelled, many of the most disruptive political appointees were replaced by "rehabilitated" professionals, and key industries such as fertilizer were opened to foreign investment and to foreign advisors. The industrial sector recovered significantly. From 1970 on, it showed roughly 8 percent growth for the remainder of the Cultural Revolution, and agriculture about 4 percent. Estimates of the death toll range from 500,000 to 7,000,000. In a decade, the physical toll of the Cultural Revolution was clearly less than for the Great Leap Forward in three years. But the cultural, social and political toll for the PRC was enormous, and the personal cost for many tens of millions of people was all but unbearable. It was the cost, of attempting – and only attempting – to purge local self-sufficiency, and parochial priorities, and negotiated disunity that Mao and many of contemporaries considered the source of all Chinese suffering.

Further reading

Mao's quotation regarding early PRC economic development is from his Report to the Second Plenum of the Seventh Central Committee of the Chinese Communist Party, March 1949. It is quoted here from the *Joint Publication Research Service-CRF-86-021* (October 29 1986), "China Report," p. 6. The quotation from Dan Kimball is from Iris Chang, *Thread of the Silkworm*, p. 200.

For general histories of the 1950s and 1960s, see MacFarquhar, *The Politics of China* (1997); Zheng, *Party vs. State in Post 1949 China* (1997); Lawrance, *China since 1919* (2004); Brown and Pickowicz, *Dilemmas of Victory* (2007); Lee and Yang, *Re-envisioning the Chinese Revolution* (2007); Strauss, *The History of the PRC* (2007) .

On the Korean War and development of the PLA, see Whiting, *China Crosses the Yalu* (1960); Cumings, *The Origins of the Korean War* (1981); Hastings, *The Korean War* (1987); Chen, *China's Road to the Korean War* (1994); Zhang, *Mao's Military Romanticism* (1995); Kaufman, *The Korean Conflict* (1999); Li, Millett and Yu, *Mao's Generals Remember Korea* (2001); Stueck, *The Korean War* (2001); Zhang, *Red Wings over the Yalu* (2002); Stueck, *The Korean War in World History* (2004); Li, *A History of the Modern Chinese Army* (2007); Worthing, *A Military History of Modern China* (2007).

On the Great Leap Forward and rural development, see Kane, *Famine in China, 1959–61* (1988); Bachman, *Bureaucracy, Economy, and Leadership in China* (1991); Yang, *Calamity and Reform in China* (1996); Becker, *Hungry Ghosts* (1997); Teiwes, *China's Road to Disaster* (1999); Chan, *Mao's Crusade* (2001); Shapiro, *Mao's War against Nature* (2001); Li, *Village China under Socialism and Reform* (2009).

On the Socialist Education Campaigns and the Cultural Revolution, see Baum, "Revolution and Reaction in the Chinese Countryside" (1969); Baum, *China in Ferment: Perspectives on the Cultural Revolution* (1971); Hinton, *Turning Point in China* (1972); Dittmer, *Liu Shao-ch'i and the Chinese Cultural Revolution* (1974); Domes, Myers and von Groeling, *Cultural Revolution in China* (1974); Ahn, *Chinese Politics and the Cultural Revolution* (1976); Maitan, *Party, Army and Masses in China* (1976); Lee, *The Politics of the Chinese Cultural Revolution* (1978); MacFarquhar, *The Origins of the Cultural Revolution* (1983–99); Hemmel and Sindbjerg, *Women in Rural China* (1984); Schram, *The Thought of Mao Tse-tung* (1989); Schoenhals, *China's Cultural Revolution, 1966-1969* (1996); Perry and Xun, *Proletarian Power* (1997); Chong, *China's Great Proletarian Cultural Revolution* (2002); Chang, *Wild Swans* (2003); Ma, *The Cultural Revolution in the Foreign Ministry of China* (2004); Starr, *Xinjiang* (2004); Brown, *The Purge of the Inner Mongolian People's Party in the Chinese Cultural Revolution* (2006); Esherick, Pickowicz and Walder, *The Chinese*

Cultural Revolution as History (2006); MacFarquhar and Schoenhals, *Mao's Last Revolution* (2006); Berry, *A History of Pain* (2008); Clark, *The Chinese Cultural Revolution* (2008); Ying and Conceison, *Voices Carry* (2008); Andreas, *Rise of the Red Engineers* (2009); Goldstein, Jiao and Lhundrup, *On the Cultural Revolution in Tibet* (2009). On CCP leaders and their relationships before and during the Cultural Revolution, see MacFarquhar, *China under Mao* (1966); Mao, *The Secret Speeches of Chairman Mao* (1989); Deng, *Deng Xiaoping* (1996); Tiewes and Sun, *The Tragedy of Lin Biao* (1996); Jin, *The Culture of Power* (1999); Barnouin and Yu, *Zhou Enlai* (2006); Tiewes and Sun, *The End of the Maoist Era* (2007); Ji, *The Man on Mao's Right* (2008).

On PRC foreign relations before 1971, see Van Ness, *Revolution and Chinese Foreign Policy* (1970); MacFarquhar, *Sino-American Relations, 1949–1971* (1972); Hsüeh, *China's Foreign Relations* (1982); Snow, *The Star Raft* (1988); Xia, *Negotiating with the Enemy* (2006); Ampiah and Sanusha, *Crouching Tiger, Hidden Dragon?* (2008); Ji, above; Large, "Beyond 'Dragon in the Bush'" (2008); Luthi, *The Sino-Soviet Split* (2008); Szonyi, *Cold War Island* (2008); Radchenko, *Two Suns in the Heavens* (2009); Snyder, *China's Rise and the Two Koreas* (2009).

15

Essay
Minerals

CHINA IS RICH in coal and iron deposits, but poor in copper. Some of the earliest archeological evidence for the use of coal as a heat source comes from China, perhaps 6,000 years ago. Through China's early history, coal was by far China's most important mining product. Deposits are widely distributed throughout the country, but concentrated in the north, particularly in Shanxi province, and in the southwest, stretching from Sichuan through Yunnan. The greatest challenge, both historically and in the present, has been the fact that geological processes have made a majority of China's coal deposits discontinuous, often interrupted by faults and vulnerable to flooding by groundwater. This has caused many coal seams to be on or near the surface, but they are quickly exhausted and deeper pits had to be dug to follow the seam. A thousand years ago China was already a world leader in coal production, which is essential to the creation of iron and steel, both of which China was then producing at a rate that may rival nineteenth-century Britain. Today, China remains the world's largest producer of coal, accounting for about 35 percent of the total.

Historically, transportation of coal has been very expensive. Buying coal in areas where it is not mined, or where a major waterway does allow it to be moved cheaply, was been beyond the reach of most common people before 1949. Mixing coal dust with any binding agent – clay, mud, or animal dung – created cakes that workers and farmers might be able to afford; such cakes, now mixed with clay, are still a major source of heat in north China during the winter. Since the nineteenth century, the Yangtze has been a critical conduit of coal from the southwest, one of the reasons that cities facing onto the river have been central points of industrialization. At present, the PRC also uses coal for power generation, though efficiency in burning is still low enough that PRC coal-powered electric stations produce 20 percent more carbon dioxide than producing the same energy would produce in the USA (and 80 percent more than in Japan). However, in recent years the PRC government has concentrated on improving the efficiency and lessening the greenhouse gas emissions from new facilities.

Mining is dangerous everywhere, but in China it appears to kill more miners than anywhere else, accounting for about 80 percent of the global total during the first decade of the twenty-first century. Mine owners often bribe local officials to not

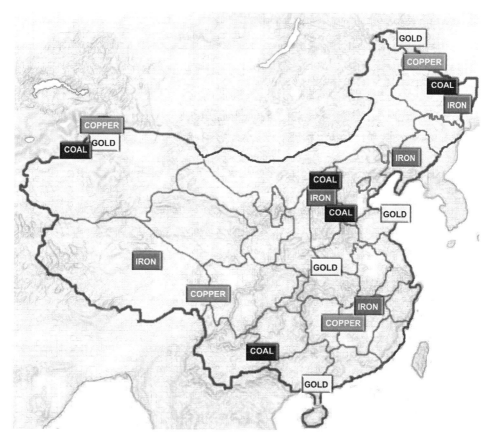

Map 13 Known mineral deposits. Distribution of major deposits of common minerals

report or to minimize reports of fatalities. Miners are paid very little and compensation for deaths is negligible. The push by mine owners for profits is, moreover, increased by the PRC determination to compete globally as an exporter of coal, despite the fact that production barely meets domestic demand. As a result, production is so intense a priority that safety and environmental protection do not figure greatly in mine planning and operation. In 2008, government statistics acknowledged nine deaths a day from coal mining accidents; industry observers consider that the real total is twice that, at a minimum.

Moreover, the ferocious push by the PRC to maximize coal production has ravaged much of the countryside. Beginning in 1980, TVEs (see chapter 17) were permitted to buy into government mines and to open their own mines; by the end of the century 75% of mines were run by TVEs. Safety regulations are lax, and practices much more lax. Open pits have pushed aside farmland and polluted rivers with their run-off. Because of the geological qualities of China's deposits, mining with modern machines creates seismic disturbances and threatens the architectural stability of thousands of towns and villages; natural earthquakes and mud-slides take a much higher toll in such areas. Because of the exhaustion of surface deposits, mines are dug deeper and deeper. Perpetual underground fires affect many of China's mines, injecting methane or carbon dioxide into the atmosphere. Coal processing plants acidify ground and water with their wastes and release oxides into the air, creating acid rain not only across China but also across the Pacific and parts of North America. The multitude of direct damages to the environment by mines has produced constant popular pressure for change – demonstrations, riots, sabotage and sometimes direct attacks upon mine officials. The government is demanding improved safety practices and more environmentally sound methods of coal processing, though whether these demands will have a significant effect is not yet clear.

In addition to its lead in coal production, China is now also the leading producer of gold. In 2006 China surpassed South Africa, where wage negotiations and improved safety measures have decreased production. But when it comes to the minerals now critical to modern technologies, the PRC has attempted to withdraw from the export market, because its reserves now do not meet its own demands. The PRC has claimed that export restrictions have targeted the minerals whose processing is most damaging to the environment – bauxite, coke, molybdenum, magnesium, rare earth, zinc, indium, and wolfram, among them – but foreign governments have claimed that the precious minerals being restricted are in fact the ones most in demand in the industrialized world. They accuse the PRC of driving up world prices by restricting exports, thus enjoying cheap access to the materials themselves (and enhancing their advantages through agreements with African nations also rich in precious minerals). Since this is a violation of the principles of the World Trade Organization (which the PRC joined in 2001), the USA and the European Union are suing China in the WTO court to have the restrictions lifted.

Further reading

Needham and Golas, *Science and Civilization in China, Volume 13* (1991); Freese, *Coal* (2003).

16

Essay
Health Risks

CHINA HAS A distinguished place in medical history, primarily for pharmacological discoveries, some dating back 2,000 years. Chinese students led the world fifteen hundred years ago, and Chinese invention of variolation – a means of stimulating an immune reaction – inspired European experiments with immunization in the late eighteenth century. But in the twentieth century, the confluence of foreign invasions, environmental disaster and civil wars produced almost unprecedented rural poverty and disruption of normal government services. The early PRC put its public health policy emphasis upon curing opium addiction (PRC law very severely forbade selling or using the drug); instructing the public in basic hygiene; preventing the spread of malaria, smallpox and schistosomiasis; limited immunization; basic obstetrics; and emergency care of wounds. Children and adults alike were instructed in eye exercises and discouraged from wearing glasses. Tuberculosis sufferers, who have been very numerous in twentieth-century China, were quarantined but not otherwise treated. Advanced medicine such as sophisticated antibiotics, radiology and chemotherapy were reserved for a small segment of the party and military élite. The popular measures were successful in dramatically limiting the scope and severity of infectious and contagious diseases in the 1950s, but uninformed medical practice occasionally spread disease rather than limiting it.

Since the 1980s, as the government began to withdraw from health care administration, infectious diseases such as schistosomiasis, all strains of hepatitis and tuberculosis have rebounded. At present, China's tuberculosis rate is second only to India's. Preventive action is also largely absent. Smoking is extremely widespread among Chinese men, with the estimated consumption in the early 1990s being ten times, per individual, what it was in the 1950s. Its effects are estimated to kill about a million people a year, from cancer, emphysema and COPD combined, and the costs – lost productivity, out-patient and in-patient care – are estimated to be more than US$7 billion per year. Yet the government does little by way of education or health monitoring to decrease smoking. At present, less than 10 percent of Chinese have private health insurance; the rest are required to pay at the door for medical care.

In the later twentieth century, China like the rest of the world was confronted with new health challenges – avian flu, SARS and HIV/AIDS. Popular indifference to preventive care and government avoidance of responsibility for public health combined to allow all of them to spread with little interference. Only at the point of public panic did the government take measures, sometimes illogical ones such as the culling of huge numbers of healthy animals or quarantining of huge numbers of individual suspected of being infected. It appears to have been particularly difficult for the government to admit that it shared, with the rest of the world, an epidemic of HIV/AIDS.

The venues of HIV/AIDS transmission were assumed to be congruent with corners of public life that were not only illegal, but which the government of the PRC insisted did not exist – homosexuality, drug use and prostitution. As a consequence, the government delayed in admitting a problem and addressing it in strategic ways. The first recorded symptoms and deaths in China of AIDS patients occurred in the early 1980s, contemporary with the discovery of the disease in other countries. Chinese officials insisted that AIDS was a disease of homosexuals, and that China had no AIDS because it had no homosexuals. The government was being advised by doctors that AIDS was being transmitted in China by the blood supply, and in 1985 the PRC banned the importation of foreign blood products, suggesting that foreign homosexuals were the source of the infection. In fact, doctors were reporting to the state that contamination of the blood supply originated with Chinese intravenous drug users, and was being amplified by poor practices among China's blood banks. In the 1990s, the PRC changed its public position, acknowledging a danger from AIDS and beginning public education campaigns against drug use and dangerous sexual practices. But it was not until the end of the decade that the government banned commercial solicitation of blood and systematically reformed the practices of blood donation, preservation and distribution, instituting needle exchange programs and free condom distribution. By then, HIV had been widely distributed through blood products. At end of the century, it is probable that over a million people in China were HIV positive, and that half of them had been infected since 1997. The government now reports that HIV/AIDS claims about 8,000 lives a year.

The symbol of the stand of China's health professionals against the history of government bungling of the HIV/AID issue is Gao Yaojie, who was born in Henan province in 1927. She was trained as a gynecologist and has worked her whole life in her native province. In the early 1990s she and other doctors became alarmed at the growing business of collecting blood at street kiosks and small clinics, for sale to hospitals in China and other parts of Asia. As she and her colleagues predicted, the practice resulted in an explosion of local HIV/AIDS cases, and by 1995 they had convinced the provincial government to shut down the operations. Gao discovered, however, that the increased number of AIDS patients had no medical care, since they were shunned by hospitals and medical professionals. She set up her circuit practice to care for HIV/AIDS patients in the surrounding towns and villages, and wrote and paid to distribute pamphlets educating the local population on prevention of HIV infection and care for AIDS patients. With grants from foreign charitable foundations and the work of local volunteers, she was able to set up homes for children whose parents had died of AIDS.

Gao's treatment by her own government was a warning of the risks to health professionals of contradicting government pronouncements and shaming the government with virtuous private actions. Fear of people who are HIV/AIDS positive in China is deep, and superstitions relating to blood reinforce the rejection and exclusion of gays and lesbians that the government prefers. Colleagues of Dr. Gao's who attempted to hold public information conferences on AIDS were put under house arrest, and Gao herself was briefly under house arrest in 2007 after she was invited to Washington, DC, to accept a public service award. She maintains a web site and weblog, which have been disrupted many times by hackers who appear to have government or commercial connections. She wrote, "I was lucky with my difficulties in working in the villages. When I was in trouble, journalists, both local and international, helped me. With their help, the Henan AIDS crisis was revealed to the public ... I would like to say that what I did is what I should do as a citizen."

Further reading

Quotation from 2003 response to the Ramon Magsaysay Award for Public Service, www.rmaf.org.ph/Awardees/Response/ResponseGaoYao.htm. See also Guo, *China in Search of a Harmonious Society* (2008).

17

Gravity

A POORLY SUBSTANTIATED STORY claims that Mao ordered a fireworks display to celebrate the death of Zhou Enlai in April of 1976. The evidence that Mao and Zhou were not friends is inexhaustible. Mao considered Zhou comprehensively effete. The man who became premier of the People's Republic of China (PRC) had carefully cultivated a striking physical appearance his whole life. He was almost invariably well-coifed, well-barbered and well-dressed from youth to old age. He was the kind of man who did not shrink from posing in a coyly traditional-chic studio portrait with his wife in the colonial city of Shantou, Guangdong province, in 1926. His full beard produced striking photos of him in military garb, looking the dashing freedom fighter; Mao could have passed for anybody's eccentric aunt in military drag. Foreigners took Zhou seriously, regarding him as a paragon of what they admired (personal dignity, education and polish, international experience) and a past master of what they would like to practice (diplomacy, realism, humanity, courtesy); they regarded Mao as bizarre and inexplicable, a precocious but unsettling child who must be humored. Zhou was the kind of public figure about whom people accepted with no corroboration a story that his opinion on the French Revolution was that "it's too early to tell"; if Mao had said it, scholars would be pounding the memoirs trying to confirm that he knew what the French Revolution was. Zhou came from the cities, from a certain amount of wealth (though his childhood circumstances had been hard), he had studied in Europe. Mao came from the unappealing (especially to him) class of comfortable rustics, disliked by their poorer neighbors and despised by city-dwellers.

Zhou was fundamentally in agreement with the developmental ideas of the USSR, echoed later in the policy initiatives of Liu Shaoqi, calling for centralized management of industry and the military, toleration of a new élite of technocrats and professionals, and reliance on local initiatives for distribution of goods and services; Mao had been battling that crew since he first joined the party in 1921. Zhou's embodiment of the urban, privileged, cosmopolitan, élitist, collaborationist China that Mao wanted to kill probably distorted the relationship between the two men as much as any issues of policy or power. Many, many times in their decades of collaboration Mao delivered to Zhou an ultimatum to betray his policy views, his colleagues and even his family or face destruction, and Mao seemed to take a sadistic satisfaction in watching Zhou obey in each instance.

Mao may have been responding to more than a simple dislike of Zhou's personality. Zhou's political approach and his facade of enlightened evolution were literally anathema to Mao's incarnation of the earthy, radical, eternally unfolding, leveling, recentralizing, unsentimental absolute of revolution. Mao may have felt that keeping Zhou in his power was keeping the revolution protected from the seeds of Chinese society and economy that threatened to reset their roots and regrow the foliage of local interests, local power and local identities that had obscured the ambitions of so many aspiring despots, whether malevolent or benevolent. It was a historical reality, epitomized in Zhou, that Mao could neither tolerate nor dispense with. Seeing Zhou die before him (which Mao probably ensured by denying Zhou care for his cancer) may, for Mao, have meant that the transforming center had ensured its future. But, in fact, it was Zhou who was the link to modern Chinese leadership. It was Zhou who continued to work for reconciliation with Taiwan, secretly maintaining intermittent communications with Chiang Kaishek between 1949 and Chiang's death in 1975. It was Zhou who looked the way that men of China's future would aspire to look. It was Zhou who had the capacity to be convincingly sympathetic with the public. It was Zhou who, if necessary, could have been elected to office. And it was Zhou who provided a successor, when Mao did not; Zhou opened the channels through which Deng Xiaoping (Mao's revolution on the outside, Zhou's government on the inside) navigated his way to captaincy of China, the China that is now a global power on the level of the greatest empires of China's past.

Relations between the USA and the PRC had followed an uneven path since 1969. In that year, American president Richard Nixon and his security advisor Henry Kissinger conceived the notion that the PRC might be helpful in extricating the USA from the war in Vietnam. In addition, the break between the USSR and the PRC in 1960 left the PRC as an unattached and therefore – in Kissinger's view – unexploited resource in the ongoing strategic competition between the USA and the USSR. Nixon encouraged the Congress to pass laws modifying the previous restrictions on trade with and travel to the PRC, and in 1971 supported a United Nations resolution giving the PRC the seat on the Security Council that had previously been occupied by the ROC on Taiwan. The fact that the USA did not recognize the PRC, and had no means of communicating with its government directly, was regarded as a minor problem. Pakistan president Muhammad Yahya Khan was the most important intermediary in conveying the message to Zhou Enlai that the USA would like to conduct talks with the PRC. With Mao's consent, Zhou quickly replied that the PRC would be pleased to discuss with the USA the withdrawal of American military defense forces in and around Taiwan. In 1971 Kissinger made a diplomatic trip to Pakistan, and took a secret side trip to Beijing. He returned to the USA with an invitation for Nixon to visit China. The public reaction in the USA was extremely positive. American governments had given up hyperbolic propaganda against communism in the late 1960s. PRC publicization of the Cultural Revolution had a left a vivid impression in many foreign countries, and in the USA, where sentiment against the Vietnam War was strong, the PRC seemed a fresh new partner. Nixon enjoyed a sharp rise in popularity as planning for his trip to China began. Internationally the reaction was positive, except for the USSR, Japan and South Korea. In early 1972 Nixon and Kissinger arrived in China to meet with Mao and Zhou. Photographs of China's magnificent scenery and architecture, its charming children, catchy music, fine food, the endearing duo of the eccentric Mao and the suave Zhou, all combined to give Americans a new view of the PRC. It was now a friendly power. The good feelings were further developed shortly afterward with exchanges of ping-pong players and the arrival in the USA of a juvenile panda pair, both of whom lived all their lives at the Washington Zoo.

The result was a public relations windfall for both sides. Zhou Enlai was able to follow up his coup of the UN seat in 1971 with the potential to reel in the USA as a strategic and economic partner, perhaps a connection that would bring protection against the USSR; Nixon's visit confirmed in the eyes of the Chinese public that China was now a recognized center of international power politics. For Nixon, the opening to China was an iconoclastic release from the strictures of the Cold War, and the key to a possible solution in Vietnam. But substantial advances were not part of the agenda. Nixon signed onto the "Shanghai Communiqué," affirming that there is "one China." Zhou regarded it as an important concession because within American strategic circles the possibility that Taiwan could become an independent state had been regarded as a desirable solution to the conundrum of an unrecognized PRC and the fading fantasy that the ROC government on Taiwan was actually "China." To Kissinger and Nixon, the Shanghai Communiqué seemed negligible, since it did not specify where or what the one China was. Liaison offices were established between the two countries, and the normalization process was supposed to begin.

When the excitement over the opening to China died down, the relationship between the USA and the PRC seemed suddenly complicated. The PRC continued to support North Vietnam, but was not actually in a position to bring them to negotiations with the USA. For that, the USSR would have been more important. The PRC continued to support the Khmer Rouge in Cambodia and the Pathet Lao in Laos, and in its press acidly criticized the USA for extending the Vietnam War to those countries with its bombing campaigns of 1970. Most problematically, Nixon was crippled as a political actor by the Watergate investigations of 1973 and forced from office in 1974, frustrating any immediate follow-up in the development of relations with China. His successor, Gerald Ford, visited the PRC in 1975 to confirm that the USA intended to proceed with normalization of relations, but it did not happen during his term, which meant it did not happen in the lifetime of either Mao or Zhou. In 1976 James Earl Carter was elected president of the USA, and after he took power in 1977 he began in earnest to seek realization of the plan to normalize relations. The details were agreed in 1978, and in 1979 Deng Xiaoping travelled to the USA to sign the accord. In 1981, the two countries became allies in backing Afghan resistance fighters against the USSR.

A major factor in the delay in concluding the normalization was Taiwan. Perhaps most trivial, there was a lingering question of which country would go to the Olympics. In the 1950s, the PRC had been invited to the Olympics along with the ROC, but had refused to participate if athletes from Taiwan were present and claiming to represent "China." In 1958, Mao broke off relations with the Olympics, and never considered sending another delegation. The question came up again in the 1970s, as the ROC teams continued to attend the Olympics. The PRC demanded that the ROC teams be disqualified, but the USA hesitated, and for the 1970s neither the PRC nor the ROC participated. In 1980, the PRC returned to the Olympics (Taiwan athletes today compete as well, but with a team called "Chinese-Taipei").

More serious, the ROC had been one of the founders of the United Nations, and remained a permanent member of the Security Council. Loss of the seat in 1971 had angered a remaining base of support for Chiang Kaishek in the USA, a base that was primarily Republican. Nixon had to mollify this constituency. American lawyers, diplomats and politicians were also concerned about the implications of the 1955 mutual security pact signed by the USA and the ROC. Since the ROC was still in existence, many argued that the treaty was still valid, and that its unilateral termination by the USA would be dishonorable or perhaps illegal. Soon after signing the pact normalizing relations with the PRC in 1979, Carter also signed the Taiwan Relations Act, which carried over the essential features of the 1955 treaty. The PRC was more concerned about American arms sales to Taiwan, which actually increased after the normalization of relations with the PRC. In 1982 the USA agreed to gradually reduce its arms sales to Taiwan. In practice, the USA linked its arms sales to Taiwan to PRC behavior toward the Straits of Taiwan and to PRC arms purchases. Neither was much of an issue through the 1980s, but after the resumption of PRC and USSR relations in 1989, the PRC began to purchase advanced fighter planes. This stimulated new sales of American weapons to Taiwan, which raised more tensions in the American relations with the PRC. These issues remain unresolved today, and frequently surface when American diplomats broach the subject of PRC cooperation in limiting arms sales to the Middle East and to Africa. They also surfaced in 2001, when an American surveillance plane was accused by the PRC of violating its airspace, forced to land, and the crew detained while Chinese experts inspected the plane's technology. American president George W. Bush retaliated by sale to Taiwan of missiles, defense systems, artillery, helicopters and submarine designs.

At the end of the first decade of the twenty-first century, American policies on Taiwan, sales of military arms, environmental regulation and international trade tend to shift with the degree of PRC involvement in the American economy. At the time of normalization in 1979, this was an unimagined and unimaginable issue. Emphasis at the time was put upon the prospects for sales of American manufactured goods in China, and exploitation of Chinese labor to lower the manufacturing cost of goods to be sold in the USA. At the time of normalization, Chinese exports to the USA were about a third the value of Chinese imports from the USA, in line with the expectations of the American government. But by 1983 the direction of trade had reversed, with China exporting more to the USA than it was importing. Since then, the magnitude of the American trade deficit with China has grown from US$71 million in 1983 to $22.8 billion in 1993, to $266 billion in 2008. There has also been a qualitative change in the goods involved in trade. During the 1980s and 1990s, the USA and other developed nations attempted to avert the effects of lowered trade barriers by virtually monopolizing highly profitable technologies such as military weapons, computers, automobiles and aircraft, while allowing developing nations to provide most of their textiles, manufactured furniture, inanimate toys and other products with low profit margins. The PRC was one of many developing nations that gradually moved out of the low-margin box. Japan, once itself assigned to the low-margin economic role, moved into electronics, and as the wages of Japanese workers rose too high to maintain desired profit margins, component manufacture was contracted out to China, Taiwan, the Philippines and Vietnam. Automobile companies in both Japan and the USA followed a similar strategy, building numerous factories in China, transferring technology and expertise. In addition, China began manufacturing its own weapons early, partly as a result of the split with the Soviet Union, and then as a result of uneven relations with the USA over the questions of arms sales. Through technology transfers, both legal and illegal, China had become a major arms manufacturer by the end of the twentieth century. It has also moved into computers, advanced electronics and automobiles, which it will imminently begin to export to the USA. At the same time, China continues to enjoy its advantage in the manufacture of inexpensive clothing, shoes, furniture and toys, since many developed nations virtually ceased to manufacture such items by the end of the twentieth century. In 2005, imports from China to the USA were led by electrical machinery, with clothing and shoes second. Among all imports into the USA, those from the PRC accounted for about 3 percent in 1990, and over 15 percent in the first decade of the twentieth-first century. All of China's trade partners have experienced a similar pattern in their deficits. Since 1987, the world's trade imbalance with China has risen from about US $7.5 billion to about $120 billion in 1997, to over $400 billion in 2007.

The rapid growth of the PRC's income since the 1990s is also reflected in the volume of its investment in the debt of Europe and the USA. Public debt in the USA has been growing at a modest rate since the 1990s and very rapidly since 2001. Historically the greatest foreign holder of American public debt was Britain, but in the late twentieth century Britain was surpassed by Japan. The PRC is now the major foreign creditor of the USA, holding a percentage that is normally well above 20 percent of all American government securities purchased by foreign governments, with Japan a distinct second and Britain a rather distant third. The holdings are significant enough that by 2008 the administration of George W. Bush reversed its arms policy of 2001, and the American government became a supporter (in spite of American public opinion) of PRC entry into the World Trade Organization (WTO), as well as modifying international standards of environmental protection in China's favor. A similar pattern can be observed with respect to Britain. In the 1980s, when Britain agreed to return Hongkong to China, the hope was that this would open opportunities for British firms to invest in China. Britain indeed became a participant in the joint-venture enterprises, though a little after Japan, West Germany (as it was then) and the USA. British trade deficits with China followed the general pattern of the European Union as a whole, with modest rises in the late 1980s and early 1990s, and extremely rapid acceleration at the transition from the twentieth to the twenty-first century. The two countries had tense relations in the early 1990s, as the PRC accused Britain of sabotaging the planned return of Hongkong by first instituting full democracy in the colony. Hongkong's Legislative Council was enlarged, and Britain negotiated a Basic Law for Hongkong in 1990 that appeared to guarantee that its democratic institutions would continue after 1997, when Hongkong became a "special autonomous region" (SAR) of the PRC.

The normalization of relations with the USA which precipitated the transformation of economic relations between the PRC and the world was an important milestone in the development of the PRC's foreign relations, but it was only a fragment of the story. The PRC's diplomatic trajectory after the Bandung conference in 1955 was not completely derailed by the country's concentration on domestic issues in the Great Leap Forward. Zhou Enlai and a small entourage traveled through South and Southeast Asia immediately after Bandung to consolidate relations, at roughly the same time as the Soviet Union's suppression of dissent in Eastern Europe, and the attempts of Britain and France to undermine the government of Abdul Gamel Nasser in Egypt. In 1960 Zhou added Mongolia and the Himalayan nations to his diplomatic destinations, shoring up support in the region for the PRC's border disputes with India, which flared into a brief conflict in 1962. During that war, the Soviet Union and the USA appeared to favor India, and Pakistan was predictably vocal in support of the PRC. These alignments – India, the USA and the USSR on one side and China and Pakistan on the other – have endured into the twenty-first century, though sometimes taking subtle forms. The PRC has repeatedly accused India of aiding Tibetan independence activists, and in the 1950s cut off trade routes between Tibet and northern India. The two countries fought again in 1967 when rebels in Sikkim attempted unsuccessfully to establish a communist government. Chinese leaders and Indian leaders exchanged visits during the 1980s, though sporadic outbreaks of fighting at the border sometimes ruptured relations. Serious attempts to solve the border issue were undertaken in the early 1990s, and relations were good until India tested a nuclear device in 1998, explicitly identifying the PRC as its primary threat. Relations between India and the PRC at the end of the century were calm, though underlying tensions involve still unresolved border disputes, and China's plans to dam the Brahmaputra (Yarlung Zangpo) River, which originates on the Tibetan plateau but flows through India and Bangladesh to the sea. Indian authorities estimate that the dam would divert 60 percent of the water volume now depended upon by countries south of Tibet (see chapter 9).

In the early 1960s Zhou sought to consolidate relationships with key North African nations in addition to Egypt. Zhou's theme was anti-colonialism, as most of the nations of the region were recently independent. But he also hoped that their ties to France remained strong enough that they would do as France had done and recognize the PRC. Through the 1960s and 1970s, the PRC imported African ivory to the point that the UN banned the sales because they endangered the survival of the African elephant; this ban was recently lifted, with the approval of the USA. Soon, China added timber to its African imports; by the end of the century, 70 percent of all timber imported into China came from Africa. In the 1980s China began to send advisors, and often investment, to aid in the development of railroads. Many of the railroads were mapped to mines from which China bought diamonds, gold, coltan, molybdenum and many other precious industrial minerals. As China's industrialization and commercialization took off at the end of the twentieth century, its need for oil increased very dramatically; demand in 2008 was 35 times higher than in 1998. In the early twenty-first century, a third of China's imported oil comes from Africa, and a third from the Middle East. Most of the African oil supplied to the PRC comes from Angola, Equatorial Guinea, Nigeria, Republic of Congo and Sudan, with Sudan having direct relations with the PRC going back to the early 1960s. Zambia, Nigeria, Mali and Egypt are the largest recipients of direct foreign investment from the PRC.

Southeast Asia has also been an important focus of PRC diplomacy, strategic planning and economic relations. To consolidate its border claims against India, the PRC began in the very early 1960s to pursue close diplomatic and trade ties with Nepal, Cambodia and Laos; Burma remained hostile to the PRC in this period, since it was struggling to suppress a communist insurgency. North Vietnam was formally an ally, but because of North Vietnam's close relationship to the USSR, connections to the

PRC were stiff after 1960. At the conclusion of the Vietnam War in 1975, the PRC remained allies with Cambodia and Laos, and in 1979 went to war against Vietnam to attempt to force Vietnamese troops out of these two countries. Vietnam prevailed, however, ending the regimes of the Khmer Rouge and the Pathet Lao. In the ensuing decades, China has maintained strong economic relations with Cambodia and Laos, to the extent that Laos is now virtually an extension of the economy of southwestern China. A coup in Burma in 1988 installed a military dictatorship that sought, and received, substantial arms sales from the PRC. To the present, the PRC remains a supporter of the Burmese government, which is believed to have allowed the PRC to establish intelligence outposts within its possessions.

The means by which this wide influence has been achieved by a country that was, per capita, one of the poorest in the world in the early 1970s, and which during the later twentieth century suffered spectacular natural disasters and political crises, are complex. Once Deng was back in government, Jiang Qing and her colleagues were anxious to discredit both Zhou and Deng. Their fury was piqued by the Tenth Party Congress in 1973, at which Mao (visibly weakened by Parkinson's disease and possibly mild dementia) was treated like an immortal figurehead, while developmentalist policies favored by Zhou and Deng were affirmed with Deng's restoration to the Central Committee of the CCP. For a time in 1973 and 1974 the "criticize Confucius" campaign began to harp on Confucius' occasional remarks to the effect that the lineages as well as the practices of the early Zhou dynasty (*c.* 1050 to 771 BCE) should be revived. In 1973 one PRC official above all others was known for having recalled and rehabilitated discredited party members (and, by implication, their children); his name happened to be the same as Confucius' favorite dynasty, Zhou. Jiang Qing, with the assistance of Kang Sheng, created a task force of more than 30 scholars from Peking University and Tsinghua University who were assigned to comb the classics, hunting up good metaphors and analogies with which to pummel Zhou. By 1974 the campaign was filling up the pages of state journals, and Jiang Qing was leading a lecture campaign to spread the word to the army. It is possible that the screeching fanaticism of Jiang Qing and her friends annoyed Mao, who was reported to have told them not to become a "gang of four" (*siren bang*) alienating important party members with their sanctimony and obsessive personal attacks. Certainly, Mao never acceded to their demands that Zhou be driven out of government. Good managers were hard to find after 1966, and Zhou happened to be one. When Zhou was so debilitated that he could no longer do his jobs more than a fraction of each day, he shifted his responsibilities to Deng Xiaoping, and Mao did nothing to prevent it. By 1975 Deng was a member of the Politburo again and, effectively, the state executive of the PRC. Zhou virtually announced that policy had been reoriented when he lectured to the National People's Congress on "the four modernizations" – agriculture, industry, military, and science and technology.

In January of 1976, Zhou Enlai died. As his replacement Mao named Hua Guofeng (Su Zhu), probably on the suggestion of Deng Xiaoping. Hua had a long history as a revolutionary fighter and provincial party functionary. In the late 1950s he appeared to eagerly side with Mao against the developmentalists. During the Cultural Revolution Hua had appeared radical enough to avoid trouble and, in fact, rise higher in the bureaucracy. But since 1970 he had defined himself as an opponent of Lin Biao and a protégé of Zhou Enlai. Jiang and her colleagues had a political center at

Shanghai – specifically the Shanghai Commune that Zhang Chunqiao had had a hand in founding, and in the publishing houses. They tried to organize a revolutionary militia in other cities and provinces, but could not inspire sufficient interest. When Deng quietly succeeded to Zhou's powers while Hua succeeded to his rank, Jiang Qing could do little more than raise the volume of anti-Confucius rhetoric. Mao had tacitly assented to Deng's return; senior members of the party either welcomed Deng or did not wish to act in opposition to Mao's authority.

Deng had long-standing ties to the PLA, which he had refreshed since his return to government. Mao, in his weakened state, was the major weapon that Jiang Qing could use. Until April of 1976 Mao had been an obstruction to their plans to discredit and if possible purge Deng. But in April things changed. A gathering in Tiananmen Square combined the traditional festival in memory of the dead with impromptu memorials to Zhou Enlai. Protest messages directed at Jiang and her fellow radicals appeared, some couched in obscure historical references (but some more obviously ridiculing the "woman emperor," Wu Zetian, of the Tang empire); one such message painted on a T-shirt irked the authorities, who tried to clear the square. Protesters and onlookers were enraged, and filled the square again. Jiang Qing and others beseeched Mao, insisting that Deng Xiaoping was behind the disorders, and that he was attempting a coup. Mao gave assent for Deng to be deprived of his offices and powers. In July, the military hero Zhu De died. Weeks later a magnitude 7.8 earthquake struck the industrial city of Tangshan, not far from Beijing; an aftershock of similar magnitude made it the single most deadly earthquake of the twentieth century. The immediate death toll was well over half a million, with hundreds of thousands of injuries. The PRC's refusal (probably at the insistence of Jiang Qing) to accept international aid is believed to have aggravated the level of death and injury.

In September, Mao himself succumbed to a heart attack, and the party leadership passed the chairmanship to Hua Guofeng. Since Zhou's death, Hua had hardly established a reputation for standing up to Jiang Qing and the radicals, but with Mao dead he realized that he was vulnerable to a coup from them, and called upon the army to take control of the situation. Jiang Qing was arrested at home and her colleagues were summoned to a supposed emergency session of the Politburo and arrested there. Soldiers and police went through Peking University and Tsinghua University to take the radical propagandists into custody. Leading supporters of Jiang in the provinces were also arrested. Within weeks, government publications were denouncing the "Gang of Four" for a variety of crimes, including a plot to seize the government after Mao's death. Deng Xiaoping reappeared in the capital. He may not have been surprised that Hua did not offer to relinquish either the party chairmanship or the premiership, but he may been less prepared for Hua's determination to gain and hold real power. Hua had minimal interest in Zhou's "four modernizations," and seemed more engaged in not only looking like Mao (Hua had a round, childish face and a high, scratchy voice reminiscent of the late chairman) but in replicating Mao's rhetoric on the glories of collectivization and the sacred duty to protect the revolution.

In 1977 Deng ascended to the vice-chairmanship of the party, giving him an active public speaking schedule. He used it to openly encourage students and workers – the people who had created the Tiananmen movement of April 1976 and got him bounced out of government – to speak openly about their dissatisfactions with the party and the state. Mao had invoked earlier philosopher's maxim of "seeking truth from fact," and now Deng suggested that the first fact was popular opinion. When it emerged that a major frustration for the public was the class identity system – which barred descendants of Republican-era landlords or KMT officers from high office and often from university admission – Deng ordered the system dismantled. He quickly discovered that with the shrilling of the Gang of Four muzzled, overt cancellation of policies central to the ideology of the Cultural Revolution not only did not arouse the indignation of the public, it drew support which constituted a potentially useful political tool. Deng used it to extend his influence in the party. In 1978, as he claimed more and more public support for his policies as contrasted to Hua's, reform activists supporting Deng started using the brick wall along Xidan Street, a major thoroughfare to the west of the Forbidden City in Beijing. By the middle of the year, Deng had regained power over the Central Committee, with approval of the army and of vociferous public opinion calling for economic development, depoliticization of work and study and repayment for the abuses of the Cultural Revolution. In 1978 Deng was able to get the Four Modernizations affirmed again as state policy, and by the end of the year Hua appeared content to be a figurehead, even being sent on a world diplomatic tour in 1979 while Deng Xiaoping began to reform the PRC government in earnest.

Deng's intended reforms were interlocking. Using incentives to accelerate agricultural expansion would generate disposable income, which would stimulate a consumption dynamic in the PRC for the first time in almost twenty years. Markets would facilitate the distribution of goods and, eventually, services. The relationship with the USA, which Deng would complete, would provide capital for further development and markets for manufactured goods. The universities would open new programs in science and technology, from which professionals would emerge to lead the economy and the army to new sophistication. Population restriction through a one-child policy (promulgated in 1979) would rebalance the current imbalances in labor, compensation, housing costs, and educational opportunities. Given the PRC's depressed levels of agricultural and industrial growth between 1966 and 1977, Deng guessed correctly that a return to management and incentive programs that resembled those before the GLF would allow a steep improvement in production, consumption, and military security. The challenge would be to keep the public tolerant of the program. Expectations had to be managed to keep people satisfied with the rate of improvement, but optimistic enough to continue to work and to purchase. Deng had grasped that extreme public dissatisfaction had been a force for ending governments and transferring leadership; for those who wished to remain secure, curtailing public frustration by keeping public demands modest and isolating those likely to express discontent was essential. Deng's first action in the management of expectations was to shut down "Democracy Wall" in Xidan in 1979. The postings were removed. Wei Jingsheng, whose essay claiming that democracy was the fifth modernization, first posted in Xidan Street, had made him a national celebrity, was sentenced to fifteen years in jail. Other authors went underground, or found ways to continue publishing criticisms in less prominent settings; the government pursuit of them did not cease, and arrests of dissidents continued into the early 1980s.

It appears that Deng was surprised at the speed with which the countryside began to reorganize itself once the strictures of collectivization were relaxed. Anhui province was experiencing an extreme drought in 1978, and in an attempt to keep incentives high, retain produce in the village and keep the farmers on the land, a village leader convinced his neighbors to sign an agreement to divide up the former production team lands (which were the property of the state), and in return fulfill the divided grain tax quota individually. If they should fail to make the quota, the statement continued, they were "willing to be decapitated" (perhaps intended to be read as an allusion to the deep traditional roots of village initiatives). The notion of substituting individual contracts for collective grain production obligations and allowing farming households to keep any surplus above the tax obligation spread very quickly. State bureaucrats were at first unwilling to allow the structures of the communes and production teams to evaporate in the heat of popular enthusiasm for seizing management of state lands. Critics claimed the system was capitalist in nature and would corrupt the ethics of farmers while possibly endangering grain supplies to the cities. In essence, the agreement turned the farmers into tenants, since they did not own the land but were in practice leasing it through the grain tax obligation. Only in 1980 did Deng publicly and unequivocally endorse this "household contract responsibility system" (HCRS), calling it compatible with his "socialism with Chinese characteristics" formulation. Agricultural production and distribution increased steadily for nearly a decade. A new constitution promulgated in 1982 stated: "Working people who are members of rural economic collectives have the right, within the limits prescribed by law, to farm private plots of cropland and hilly land, engage in household sideline production and raise privately owned livestock." After 1982, farmers began to build new houses for themselves at their own expense, even though the policy of the PRC was to guarantee housing to everyone. In fact expenditures on rural housing could be diminished somewhat as farmers decided to spend their own funds rather than live in dilapidated state housing.

HCRS reforms created village market distribution systems, as farmers sold their grain to those supplying it to town and city markets (a new business enterprise). With cash becoming available in the villages, farmers began to explore other ways of pursuing the light industries that had been previously been under commune and brigade management. Farmers pooled money to buy tools or start up small companies. They bypassed state investment agencies, and occasionally went to local banks if they needed a loan. Textiles in particular were suitable for village production, as they had been in Qing and Republican times. In 1978 and 1979, these "town and village enterprises" (TVEs) came to the attention of national authorities, especially since they had begun to compete with the "state-owned enterprises" (SOEs) – industrial facilities either newly created through state investment or inherited from the communes and now run from a central planning and finance authority. Some of the SOEs were in the heavier industries – machine tools, tractors, military hardware – but others were in light industries where they were meeting unexpected competition from the TVEs. The value of TVE production, nation-wide, rose from about 50 million *yuan* in 1978 to 170 million in 1984, and 1.2 billion in 1991. The number of TVEs, however, peaked in 1984, and fell significantly during the ensuing decade. The competition with state-owned enterprises was not appreciated by the CCP, and many applications to create new TVEs were rejected after the middle 1980s. More important, some TVEs were increasing in efficiency, in the process eliminating more inefficient TVEs that were too large or too small.

After his retirement in 1992, Deng commented, "In the rural reform the most rewarding gain entirely out of our expectation is the development of TVEs, which have suddenly emerged engaging themselves in commodity economy and in running small enterprises of various trades. It is really a new force suddenly coming to the fore. It is not the merit of our central authorities." One of the reasons Deng was so delighted with the function of the TVEs was that they had provided a solution for rural underemployment. During the years when the economy had been managed on Mao's guidelines, salaries were equalized and all adults received them, even when there was not enough work for all who received salaries. The result was a rural economy in which a large portion of the population was reporting to work and being paid, but not actually producing. During a transition to compensation based on productivity, some significant portion of the population would necessarily be underemployed or unemployed. Even if the state were to pay support to adults without employment, the level of compensation would quickly fall below what neighbors and relatives who were working productive land or successful industries were being paid. The danger of massive migration to the cities in search of more remunerative work, or social disorder as a result of disappointed expectations, was unsettling to Deng and the party. His leading economic advisors, Zhao Ziyang and Hu Yaobang, knew that to best match expectations and rewards, decollectivization would have to be managed carefully, something that made them resistant to the phenomenon of spontaneous, informal innovation from the countryside up. But in fact, during the 1980s, TVEs had absorbed much of the surplus labor that agriculture alone could not use. By the end of the 1980s half of the rural population were employed in TVEs, in addition to the increasingly productive agricultural sector. As Deng later commented, "Myself and many other comrades have never predicted the outcome. It suddenly brought about such a striking effect … Many good things in the rural reform have all been created from the grassroots, we just take them and then refine them to be the guidelines for the whole country."

Transferring the lessons to the cities was not easy. Major industries remained under the management and long-term planning of the state. Differential compensation was introduced, slowly, to raise production and create incentives for training and education. Virtually all employment in the cities in the early 1980s was in the "state-owned enterprises" (SOEs). The transition to partial privatization began with a book-keeping technique, by which continued state investment in the SOEs became ostensible loans (which in practice were never paid back). The state thus began to accumulate assets in the form of loans to the SOEs that were sometimes worthless. Deng and his planners were unsure how long the state could continue to support a workforce that was not being compensated, reorganized or redistributed to meet criteria for efficiency. Farmers could feed themselves and manage their businesses at the household level if necessary. Urban workers labored, mainly, in large factories or offices, and were dependent upon state-owned apartments for housing. That housing was also a virtually insoluble dilemma. Urban workers paid virtually nothing for housing – normally much less than a dollar a month for an apartment. The government of the PRC, still with virtually no cash reserves and no significant income in the early 1980s, was undertaking to house the world's largest population at its own expense.

In 1980 Deng arranged for Zhao Ziyang to become premier, and the next year Hu Yaobang became chairman of the CCP. Zhao's father had been a communist in the

1940s, but was executed by CCP officials before 1949. Zhao himself had been a communist from a young age, and after the creation of the PRC he had become a provincial official in Guangdong, at the age of 30. Through the 1950s his sympathies were with the developmentalists, and in 1962 he had been among the more thorough decollectivizers in hopes of softening the effects of the famine in his province. Until 1966 he rose quickly in the Liu Shaoqi regime. During the Cultural Revolution, however, Zhao was quickly targeted as a capitalist-roader, publicly humiliated and sentenced to forced labor. After 1970 he was among the officials Zhou Enlai rehabilitated and brought back into government. He joined Deng Xiaoping on the Central Committee in 1973. After the fall of the Gang of Four, Zhao was one of the most energetic provincial reformists, welcoming local innovation and amplifying it with his own restructuring of industry and administration. Hu Yaobang had been with Mao in the Chinese Soviet Republic, but for various reasons had never been trusted by Mao and his supporters. He went on the Long March, but joined Zhang Guotao's disastrous alternate route, barely surviving battle with and imprisonment by Muslim warlord forces. Like Deng, Hu's primary functions were as a political attaché to the army. Though Hu was not as prominent as Zhao in supporting the developmentalists during the 1950s, his views were known, and in the Cultural Revolution he was quickly purged. Zhou's rehabilitations of the early 1970s included Hu, and when Deng was looking for supporters to staff his government Hu came quickly to mind. Zhao and Hu became the administrators of two new strategies for getting cash into the cities, both ratified in a new economic law of 1979. One was a program of partnerships between the CCP and foreign investors, to underwrite the development of heavy industry. The other was the creation of special economic zones, to facilitate commercial development and exports in ways that normal PRC economic law would not tolerate.

During Deng's visit to the USA in January of 1979, the primary theme had been opportunities for American investment in China. Later in the year, American companies began to enter into join-venture contracts with the CCP. Japanese and West German firms were already preparing to enter into open manufacturing plants. The basic scheme seemed mutually beneficial. Foreign companies would rely upon CCP managers to open factories in China, and benefit from the cheap labor. China would receive the benefits of foreign investment, a certain amount of technology transfer, and the training of its managers and some workers in the modern industrial techniques. In reality, problems with joint-venture enterprises emerged over the years. Chinese workers, while available for very low wages, were unaccustomed to the expectations of foreign managers for promptness and quality control, and often needed to undergo prolonged training in basic technology and safety practices before they could begin work. Dissatisfaction among the workers sometimes led to work actions, with the cooperation of CCP officials. Delays in production drove up the storage costs of foreign manufacturers, and sometimes led to invalidation of contracts. Perhaps most troubling, CCP partners of the foreign investors continually demanded high informal, or customary, payments – bribes. Frequent payments for cooperation in managing the workforce, for the supply of electricity and water to the factories, and access to higher CCP officials able to negotiate new contracts also drove up the costs of foreign partners, often to a level that eradicated all profits. In 1987 the PRC government admitted publicly that only a third of all joint-ventures were profitable, probably an inflated assessment. Japan was the first of the joint-venture companies to publicly announce that the business climate in China was "not advantageous." In that instance, the PRC foreign ministry issued a blistering denunciation, reminding Japanese of their war crimes in China in World War II and implying that Japan had an obligation to invest in China, regardless of profitability. But West Germany, Britain, France and eventually the USA all lessened involvement with joint ventures during the 1990s.

The special economic zones (SEZ) were a distinct, but related, approach. They were originally designated as areas where the normal tax policies, residence requirements, and joint-venture partnership laws were suspended or modified for purposes of stimulating development. The original SEZ was Shenzhen, once a sleepy customs outpost for travelers passing between Hongkong and Canton. In 1980 Shenzhen was opened to direct foreign investment. Hongkong entrepreneurs swept into the city, and within a short time Shenzhen was a hub for small electronics manufacture, textiles and shoes specially produced for the foreign market, and plastic toys. Shortly after, two more Hongkong-oriented SEZs were opened at Shantou and Zhuhai; a Taiwan-oriented SEZ was created at Xiamen (Amoy), in Fujian province. The success of the SEZs in attracting foreign capital and producing profitably for the foreign market was almost immediate. By the end of the 1980s, over two dozen SEZs had been created at various points of coastal China, the state had opened its own special economic zones in the interior where special laws for encouragement of entrepreneurs were in force, and over 50 concentrated areas for industrial and scientific enterprises had been established. The Pudong district of Shanghai, a sort of super-SEZ, has become one of the most concentrated zones of capital investment in the world.

The SEZs and similar enclaves created in the 1980s and 1990s have grown in number and in wealth in direct proportion to the PRC's emergence as an export economy. On the surface, the SEZs resemble the treaty ports of the Qing period. Some of the SEZs were even described by the PRC government at the time of their creation as intended to connect to a specific nation of investment origin – Shenzhen linked to Hongkong, Xiamen to Taiwan, SEZs of Shandong province and the Northeast to South Korea or Japan. Foreign residents have tax advantages they would not have elsewhere in China, and they can run their own banks and legal firms. But unlike the treaty ports, low tariffs and reduced taxes on foreign enterprises do not in fact siphon money away from the government. Chinese living in the SEZs are among the wealthiest in China, and all pay income taxes. Firms profiting from the international trade are also taxed. The opening of the Beijing stock market in 1985 and a planned Shanghai stock market create opportunities for foreign investment firms to thrive in the SEZs, and widen the scope for foreign capital to enter China.

By the middle 1980s, the rapid economic changes had begun to stir discontent, in just the way that Deng Xiaoping had feared. Decollectivization had left health care and its financing adrift. In some areas the rural poor could have only the treatment they could find and afford on their own, while the wealthy and well-connected had the advantage of increasingly sophisticated care in the cities. It is believed that by the middle 1980s life expectancy in the countryside was around 64 years, four years shorter than in the cities. The rapid influx of investment and income from exports caused significant inflation, which only got worse in the later decade. In the countryside, inequalities of income and wealth that had not been seen in PRC history had become widespread. Many government officials put themselves into positions as managers or virtual owners of the TVEs, creating a new predatory élite not unlike the landlords and officials of a century before. Disorder broke out occasionally, as farmers protested their lands being appropriated for industry, or their investments in TVEs being fraudulently converted. In the cities, the problems were more widespread. Employees working for the state-owned enterprises were paid much less and lived in much worse housing than the residents of the SEZs. But more damaging was the fact that many members of the CCP had monopolized investment and partnership opportunities with the new industries for themselves. Some were assumed to have used unsecured "loans" from the government, in the style of the state-owned enterprises, to set themselves up in lucrative positions. Many enriched themselves by accepting large bribes from foreign firms. The CCP members, their children, and their grandchildren now constituted a new class. The usual privileges of preferred housing, tailored clothing, modern healthcare and university admissions for children were now augmented by wealth hugely out of proportion to the general population. These "princes" and "princesses" began, in the 1980s, to extend their enclave, reserving shops, restaurants and hotels exclusively for themselves. Popular indignation over the increasingly visible effects of "corruption" was sharp. Deng responded in the middle 1980s with a campaign against "spiritual corruption," meant to assure both Maoist senior members of the CCP and the public that the aping of foreign attitudes and pastimes, as well as conspicuous consumption of luxury goods, were to be criticized.

Hu Yaobang thought that pressure could be relieved by the government creating new avenues for the reception of public opinion, and by officials showing sympathy for popular complaints. He had pushed hard in the early 1980s against the remnants of Maoist philosophy in the party, and he did not appear to share Deng's sensitive ear on discontentment from the conservative ranks. In 1986, students in Beijing cited Hu's expressed openness to their views in a series of demonstrations demanding better food, better dormitories, fairer admissions policies, rights of free speech and "democracy" in China. When the demonstrations persisted for weeks, Deng dismissed Hu from his post as head of the CCP. Zhao Ziyang took his place, and Li Peng was appointed to Zhao's former position as premier. Li was a decade younger than both Zhao and Hu, and was an adopted son of Zhou Enlai. He had been a teenaged communist, and had studied in Moscow. Li had a great interest in development, and no interest in public opinion.

By the end of 1987, many men (for such they were) at the top of Chinese government realized that something serious was going on. Dissatisfaction and anxiety were simmering virtually everywhere in China. Wages had doubled since 1977, while the government subsidized products such as grain and pork to keep prices low. But for those purchasing any but staples, inflation was still eating away at purchasing power. Zhao Ziyang, finally approaching the impossible problem of housing the whole nation, had introduced modest rent charges (equivalent to 3 or 4 US dollars per month) for tenants of large apartments in the center of some major cities. The streets were almost instantly flooded with protesters, waving signs proclaiming "Socialist Wages, Capitalist Rents." Zhao backed down on the experiments of 1987, but rent rises were still on the agenda for the government, and news of it (or fears of it) spread widely. Approaching the problem of subsidies from another angle, the government attempted to lessen its support for pork producers; the result was refusal of the suppliers to deliver pork to markets in the major cities. Anger over the corruption and arrogance of officials and their families continued to build. Because of the large network of families involved, almost no official was above suspicion, including Deng Xiaoping. As 1988 opened, the economic and the political situations grew worse. The well-heeled – executives in the travel industry, managers in foreign firms, CCP-connected investors – were buying luxury apartments in the SEZs and in the major cities, poor people were paying 50 percent more for food. Students, many of them in the provinces, blamed the problem on CCP complacency and corruption. The advice of Zhao Ziyang was to placate public opinion and go slow on further reforms, delaying lifting price controls on groceries, cigarettes and alcohol. Li Peng's was to forge ahead, regardless of opposition. Deng tended in the direction of Zhao, but watched anxiously for any signs of organized opposition or incipient social disorder.

In 1988 a confluence of international trends resonated with problems in China and its borderlands to bring the PRC as a whole to a high rate of tension. Student protests late in 1988 at Peking University over bad food and shabby dorms developed into a series of teach-ins, or "salons." Fang Lizhi, an astrophysicist, and Ren Wanding, who had been an activist in the days of the "democracy wall" in 1978, drew the attention of the students to larger issues of reform and democracy. The students and the intellectuals inspiring them were all riveted by events in Eastern Europe and the Soviet Union. Mikhail Gorbachev announced in 1985 that the basic economic plan in the USSR would be supplemented by political reforms and "openness" (*glasnost*). By 1988 effective freedom of speech had become a theme and, to a certain degree, a practice of Gorbachev's government. In Poland and Hungary, authoritarian reformers were being challenged by popular organizations (in Poland, the fabled Solidarity) who were inspired by economic liberalization but angered by a lack of political liberalization. Street demonstrations, enthusiastic international press, and Gorbachev's own tolerance for public dissent put the Polish and Hungarian governments in a precarious situation, and most observers speculated that they had only months to survive. The reach of Gorbachev's influence was not limited to far-away Europe. The USSR had withdrawn its armed forces from the Mongolian People's Republic in 1986, and in 1987 the PRM had opened relations with the USA as well as American oil companies and banks; already in the PRM there was a small but loud reform movement demanding "openness." More ominous in some ways for Deng's government, the USSR had withdrawn from Afghanistan, and militant Muslims had seized the government; the dangers that such a government would inspire or perhaps aid Muslims of Xinjiang and other western perimeter provinces to revolt was increasing. In Hongkong, Deng's victory in gaining a promise from Britain to return the colony was being eroded by British reforms intended to make Hongkong democratic before it would revert 1997. Hongkongers who had never before shown an interest in politics were debating issues and preparing elections in the planned Legislative Council. In Taiwan Chiang Kaishek's son Chiang Ching-kuo, who had inherited the leadership of the KMT after his father's death in 1975, lifted martial law in 1987 and made the opposition Democratic Progressive Party legal. Chiang also made himself popular by choosing a local native, Lee Teng-hui, as president. In 1988 Chiang died, and Lee engaged in a thorough-going reform of the government, making it more local and less like the "mainlander" regime Chiang Kaishek had established in 1949. Elections for the presidency were promised for 1996.

As 1989 opened, Deng and his government were surrounded at home and abroad by public opinion casting them as totalitarian hold-outs in a world moving toward democracy. The "salon" movement in Beijing was generating specific activist points, moving out of the haze of aimless verbosity that Deng probably wished it would remain in. The most persistent and concrete call was for the release of Wei Jingsheng. Through the spring, and when events in the center of Beijing began to get complicated and distracting, leading activists – including Fang Lizhi and the poet Bei Dao – and then student leaders continued to petition for Wei's release, and eventually for the release of all political prisoners. Equally concrete was the direction of their petitions – to the National People's Congress. Suggesting that the NPC could release political prisoners was tantamount to demanding that the NPC should have the power to release political prisoners. The prospect of the NPC as an executive body, and perhaps even a legislative body, was very far outside the imagination of Deng or his colleagues.

It seemed that Deng was being slowly squeezed by pressures emanating from the USSR and the USA. Gorbachev's policies had brought him celebrity status in the USA, and his plan to bring American investment to the USSR's limping economy was paying immediate dividends. The PRC, on the other hand, was becoming an object of criticism and ridicule because of the obstruction to foreign investment and profit caused by the corruption of CCP members. In February George H.W. Bush visited Beijing, mostly a personal victory tour in which the newly-elected president revisited the scene where he had once been an ambassador and where his family and friends were pursuing huge investments. It should have been a low-pressure event for Deng, but Bush invited Fang Lizhi to the American embassy for a talk, and the PRC authorities prevented Fang from going. The result was another black eye delivered to Deng's government by world opinion. Earlier the same month Deng welcomed a Soviet representative to China for the first time since 1959, when Eduard Shevardnadze visited; the meeting was cordial, but it was clear that the USSR, in the glow of Mikhail Gorbachev's reforms, was keen to push a fraternal line with the PRC on the value of openness and reform. Deng was uncomfortable with the prospect of the statically-charged Gorbachev in China, but he was resolved to heal the rift with the USSR despite high risk, and agreed that Gorbachev would come to China in May.

In March, Muslim students at the National Minorities University (*Minzu xueyuan*) in Beijing peacefully demonstrated in the streets against a new book purporting to expose the secrets of Muslim sexual behavior. Slogans of the brief movement demanded dignity and equality for Muslims in China. Officials in Beijing tensely watched for a spread of the protests to other cities, and particularly to Xinjiang, but it seemed that the excitement was brief. Nevertheless, the combination of the falling threshold for popular expression of discontent and the rising official anxiety about disorder prompted many discussions in the Politburo regarding the appropriate response to public calls for government reform. Zhao Ziyang, Hu Yaobang and Zhao's associate Bao Tong all suggested, at various times, that the government express its interest in public opinion, and consider some concrete responses, even including release of a political prisoner or two. Li Peng and others insisted that rewarding demonstrations and petitions would only encourage more. The disagreements sharpened in early April when Wang Dan, a history student at Peking University, wrote a widely-distributed editorial calling for a political movement, in the spirit of Poland's Solidarity, in China.

Placards, t-shirts and headwraps with mottoes echoing Wang's theme appeared immediately in the streets. At a heated Politburo meeting Hu Yaobang had a heart attack.
On April 15 Hu died, and while the government issued a respectful commemorative
statement, they made no mention of a state funeral.

Within days, students had begun camping out in Tiananmen Square, displaying
memorial photos of Hu and placards describing him as a hero of democracy. On April
18 tens of thousands of students gathered outside CCP headquarters in Tiananmen
Square, demanding an end to corruption and an end to Deng's campaign against
"spiritual pollution." The government announced that a state funeral for Hu would,
after all, be held, but that Tiananmen Square would have to be vacated on April 21 to
allow the ceremonies to take place at the Great Hall of the People. The funeral was
held, but the students refused to vacate. Their leaders celebrated a victory against the
government. The same week, the Politburo received reports of sympathy demonstrations in the city of Xi'an, in Shaanxi province. The students in Tiananmen Square
announced that they would not be returning to class, but would stay in the square
until they got a government response they regarded as satisfactory. By the end of the
month, it was clear that Deng's hope that the protests would burn themselves out, or
evaporate after Hu's funeral, were empty.

Foreign journalists, and many foreign observers, were puzzled that the government seemed to be neither suppressing the movement nor responding to its demands.
The idea of a government simply spectating while the public spaces of its capital were
occupied by rapidly growing numbers of angry, confident and increasingly organized
citizens seemed to suggest that the government was giving up, and was only dither-
ing over the details of its demise. No Chinese official of the generation of Deng, or
even the generation of Zhao Ziyang and Li Peng, could be in any doubt that a movement which successfully integrated the interests and the aspirations of a the majority
would be a force that few governments could survive. But they also had behind them
the peculiar period of Mao, which over two decades attacked and may have profoundly eroded the social practices that permitted local organizations the vitality and
the complexity to both sustain public order and resist government excess. Deng had
been surprised that his decollectivization directives had actually been anticipated by,
and so speedily transformed by, local initiatives that could only have been generated
by intact (or restored) village and lineage organizations. The instant success of the
rural reforms suggested that resilient localities were once again a part of China's
economic constitution. It may have been unclear whether they had also become a
part of China's political fabric, and it was even more unclear whether Tiananmen
Square, with its large but homogeneous population of rootless students, was a locality at all. Deng remained equivocal, while Li Peng and Zhao Ziyang staked out positions on opposite sides of the issue of a government response. Li argued that the
government had attempted to bargain with the students by granting Hu a state funeral,
and the students had shown no willingness to reciprocate by leaving the square. Zhao
thought that a state funeral for Hu was only fair, and that a true response to the students would address the issues of corruption and release of Wei Jingsheng at a minimum. Li denied that the demonstrations in Tiananmen Square were a true popular
uprising. He claimed that a small group of conspirators was shrewdly manipulating
the crowd, for purposes of its own. The accusation may have struck home. Deng
knew that, however a public movement starts, it eventually becomes good for those

who want power, and bad for those who wish to retain power. He had given it a spin himself, one way in 1978, and the other way in 1979.

It is not difficult to understand why the CCP had doubts whether the movement in Tiananmen had yet taken on the attributes of a true opposition organization. The group had leaders. Wuerkaixi (Urkesh Dawlat), a Uighur student who was the son of CCP members and Xinjiang provincial officials, was prominent, as were Wang Dan, and Chai Ling who had recently graduated from Peking University with a degree in psychology. They were the spokesmen for the students in the square and held a strong sense of symbolism and theater. They knelt at the Great Hall of the People to present their petition for reform, in the same posture as scholars petitioning the Qing emperor to reform the country 92 years before. When they were summoned to meet with Li Peng in the Great Hall of the People in May, they bowed elaborately, again imitating scholars of old, and presented their petition with bowed heads (Wuerkaixi still in hospital togs). They were careful at all times to explicitly reject calls for violence, and to prevent or quickly punish the desecration of venerated objects in the square, particularly Mao's portrait hanging on Qianmen. The students' grasp of imagery and publicity seemed far better than that of the leaders of the CCP; the protesters organized a press bureau to keep a steady stream of interviews and photographs emanating from their headquarters in the square. But their political sense may have seemed to Deng to be inadequate. They had resolutely prevented workers from joining the movement, physically pushing them out of the square in April. And they were known to have disagreements among themselves. Some, including at various points Wang Dan and Wuerkaixi, were willing to return to the university to take their examinations, or otherwise abandon the square before the point of no return was reached. Chai Ling, on the other hand, remained a firebrand for standing their ground, and repeatedly hectored the crowd into staying in Tiananmen even after it had become almost uninhabitable because of hygiene problems, and after the government had announced that an attack was imminent. In an interview in late May she declared that her strategy was to push to the point of bloodshed – of the creation of martyrs – in order to foment an even larger uprising.

In the larger picture, the power of Tiananmen and its magnitude as a historical event were rooted in its support by the existing and evolving communities on the perimeter of the square. It is not an accident that the most indelible image from the events of June, 1989 is a normal Chinese worker walking home with his groceries, who stopped a line of four tanks for almost half an hour by simply standing in front of them. The belief on the part of the population that the PLA would not have the nerve to kill them without provocation was very strong, and in the days before the military attack on the square brought hundreds of thousands of confident supporters into the movement. The workers rejected by the students in April formed their own protest organization just outside the square. They echoed the demands for an end to corruption, but added more demands that meant something to the people passing them on the street. They called for an end to inflation and restoration of food subsidization. They formed a union – illegal, since in the workers' dictatorship that was the PRC no unions were necessary. When they finally joined the students in Tiananmen Square in May, they magnified the number of protesters hugely, driving the number toward a million by the end of the month. Deng may have hoped that the public nuisance would wear out the public welcome. Instead, residents of Beijing began to visit the

7. Deng welcomes Michail and Raisa Gorbachev, whose visit he dreaded, on May 15, 1989.

square, bringing food, clothing and medicine to the protesters, and spread the spirit of the demonstration to their own neighborhoods. By mid-May it was not the students in Tiananmen Square who were staging a protest. The city of Beijing was engaging in a peaceful protest that was weakening the work force, emptying the schools, and far exceeding the ability of the police to control. And it was not only Beijing. Protests, strikes or clashes with police were being reported from perhaps as many as 400 cities. Shanghai was extensively affected, as was Canton, and Chengdu in Sichuan province. Inner Mongolia, Xinjiang and Tibet were all reporting dangerous new protest movements. Demonstrations in Hongkong expressed sympathy with the Beijing protesters and demanded that democracy in Hongkong be preserved in the future.

Gorbachev arrived for his short visit on May 15. The student protesters in the square announced a hunger strike, specifically demanding that Li Peng withdraw his accusation that they were subversives attempting a coup d'état. During the Gorbachev visit the media presence in Beijing, and in Tiananmen, was enormous, and the government was on its best behavior. But its course had already been decided. When Gorbachev left the capital, martial law would be declared. Zhao Ziyang would resign as premier and be succeeded by Jiang Zemin. Li Peng would lead the government in its suppression of the protests. Zhao Ziyang visited Tiananmen on May 19 with Li Peng and Wen Jiabao, who had been brought into the Central Committee by Hu Yaobang. Zhao pleaded with the students to see his visit as a gesture of compassion and goodwill by the state. He argued that their point had been made, and they should now go home and get on with their lives. The students were respectful, and very many were inclined to comply. But Chai Ling gave a rousing speech that resolved a great part of the crowd – perhaps 300,000 people – to remain in the square. The next day, Li Peng made a public speech saying that the time was drawing near when the government would resolve the Tiananmen impasse by force. Zhao Ziyang was purged from the party and put under house arrest, where he remained until his death in 2005. Bei Dao, Fang Lizhi, and other writers who the year before had been heroes to the students also visited the square to advise that the protests end, but left without effect.

Officials calculated that army units from Beijing or its environs might be reluctant to shoot into the crowd. Time would be needed to transfer infantry from outlying regions. The community in Tiananmen Square decided to form a defense force, with Chai Ling as commander. Residents of neighborhoods on all sides of the square began to barricade the streets and make provisions for feeding themselves and the protesters if the city should be attacked. On May 21 truckloads of soldiers entered the city and tried to move toward the square, but were stopped by the debris piles that residents had deposited. In famous television scenes, elderly residents scolded the army drivers through their truck windows, demanding that they turn around and leave the city in peace. After the interval purchased by Beijing defenders, protesters again appeared ready to leave the square, but Chai Ling convinced a majority that to leave would be to admit defeat. The protesters were joined by a small number of party officials, such as Zhao Ziyang's associate Bao Tong (who had just resigned as General Secretary of the CCP, in protest against martial law), who hoped their presence might prevent an attack against the students by the military until a withdrawal could be organized. But during the night of May 29, a huge plaster and styrofoam statue of a "Goddess of Democracy," was moved to the square by students from a Beijing arts school. Academic and cultural celebrities, including the rock star Hou Dejian, come to the square to join in the hunger strike and protest martial law. On June 3, army infantry platoons entered the square, as other units attempted to clear the citizen barricades to make way for trucks and tanks to follow. Open battle broke out between citizens outside the square and the soldiers. Rocks were thrown, and at least one vehicle was burned with the soldiers still inside. Soldiers fired upon civilians. In the middle of the night, the troops cut off escape routes from Tiananmen Square. Again, the protesters inside the square debated whether to withdraw and Chai Ling convinced them to stay. Hou Dejian and others negotiated with the military commanders, arriving at an agreement that if the students left before dawn the army would allow them to withdraw. Just before dawn, the protesters were apparently leaving the square when, for unknown reasons, the troops began to fire.

During the days of June 4–6, the PLA systematically occupied the city of Beijing and the CCP began busily releasing its own reports on casualties and the progress of the restoration of order. Most sources agree that several dozen soldiers died, clearly as a result of resistance from the Beijing population, though the government claimed that armed criminals had infiltrated the protesters and were responsible for most of the army deaths. The number of civilian deaths and where they occurred is a continuing matter of dispute. Government statistics issued in July stated that nobody had been killed inside Tiananmen Square, and that a few hundred deaths and many more casualties had occurred in the side streets and in a few other neighborhoods of Beijing. Eyewitness accounts described deaths from gunshot inside the square, and incidents of people being crushed by tanks in Chang'an Street. Long after the event, testimony even from CCP members would acknowledge hundreds of deaths in the square and many more outside. The Red Cross attempted a canvass of hospital emergency rooms,

8.   Tiananmen Square on the first day of June, 1989.

and estimated a minimum 1,500 deaths in the city; witnesses claimed to see stacks of corpses in hospital courtyards and at some intersections. Estimates by journalists in Beijing at the time of the suppression have ranged from 1,500 to 5,000 deaths. The city was effectively cut off from international communications and travel out of Beijing by any means, including air, was suspended. Deng declared the PRC under martial law indefinitely. When news began to filter out after a passage of days, it was clear that Bao Tong was under arrest, and likely to be charged with revealing state secrets for having told the students that an armed attack was coming. Wuerkaixi had escaped Beijing and surfaced in Paris. Chai Ling and Wang Dan were missing, but were believed to be fugitives in China. The PRC government spokesmen avidly recounted the absconding of the leaders to safety while their followers were left to face the army. Within a year it would emerge that Wang Dan had been arrested by the Chinese authorities and was being held for trial. Chai Ling had been smuggled to Hongkong, had plastic surgery, then showed up in Paris, then went to Princeton, then joined an American consulting firm that eventually made her wealthy.

Deng and Li were clearly willing to bear the public excoriation of world governments. If their assumption was that the public reactions would have much less substance that the economic reactions, they were confirmed. In the USA, the Congress was aflame with indignation, reporting overwhelming, impassioned support of their constituents for the Beijing protesters. President George H.W. Bush publicly denounced the Deng government as despots, and declared suspension of all "government-to-government" weapons sales, as well as a ban on commercial weapons sales to the PRC. The Deng government protested to the American embassy and cancelled expected visits from American military officials. At the end of June the American government sent two very senior diplomats, secretly, to Beijing to compliment the Deng government on its mild response to the new sanctions, and to look past the complications of the present to the long-term benefits of mutual cooperation. When the American Congress passed a bill that would have permitted Chinese students in the USA to remain there until martial law was lifted in the PRC and there was no threat that they would be arrested or persecuted, Bush vetoed it. Similar reactions came forth from Britain, France, Australia, West Germany and the Soviet Union. Leaders described their reactions as shock and disgust; within weeks or months, normal economic and diplomatic relations were resumed. A possible exception was arms sales embargoes by the USA and by the European Union. In both cases the embargoes were qualified, always able to be overridden by executive decision. The volume of arms sales from the USA and the European Union to China did in fact decrease after 1989, but this may have been a function of China's own development as an arms manufacturer in the 1990s.

The outcome of the so-called "pro-democracy" movements in the PRC in 1989 can be seen in retrospect as a significant contrast to developments elsewhere, many of which seem to have had an influence on the speed and direction of the Tiananmen protests. The fate of the Ceaucescu regime in Romania must have confirmed the worst fears and any doubts among CCP conservatives about the handling of Tiananmen. The regime fell violently in December when the army turned against the president, who was executed together with his wife. But in other cases, peaceful transitions put previously communist countries on a path to development from which the PRC markedly diverged. A pro-democracy movement in Mongolia, evincing public protests and hunger strikes that resembled Tiananmen, led to resignation of the government and the end of the Mongolian People's Republic; in March of 1990 the Republic of Mongolia was founded. In Poland, Solidarity became a legal party and replaced the former communist government after national elections. In Hungary, the communist party dissolved itself, and began to compete in elections against a variety of other parties. East Germany was urged by the Soviet Union to adopt political reforms that would halt the exodus of its population and make it a suitable trade partner with its reforming neighbors; the result was virtual evaporation of the East German state, which was unified with West Germany in 1990. In the Soviet Union, party conservatives failed to prevent by force the election of and assumption of office by Boris Yeltsin. In the aftermath, the constituent republics declared independence, and the Soviet Union ended, becoming the Commonwealth of Independent States (with gigantic Russia wielding the most economic and political influence).

The PRC remained the only major communist state in the aftermath of 1989–91. Party leaders declared themselves still dedicated to reform, but with market controls and single-party government. Deng had resigned the last of his official ranks in 1989, and in 1992, at the age of 88, he announced that he would no longer control policy. His final doubts on the dedication of Jiang Zemin to market liberalization were satisfied by then, and in 1993 Jiang became president. The policies and practices of the early 1980s, however, were no longer adequate to assure continued growth. Agricultural productivity under the HCRS leveled off in the late 1980s, and in 1993 began to contract in real terms. In the cities the state-owned enterprises had nearly disappeared, between competition from the "TVEs" on the one hand

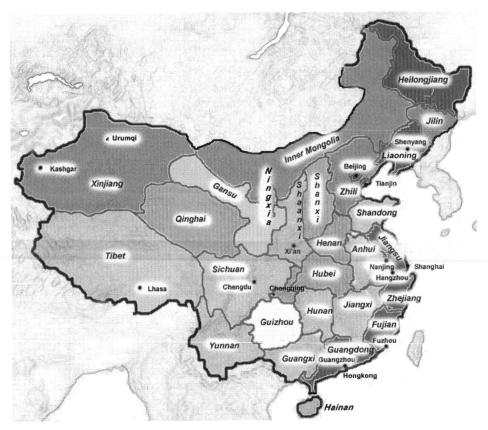

Map 14 Income disparities by province. Relative income of contemporary PRC provinces. (High to low represented by dark to light.)

and foreign-owned firms on the other. In 1997, the year that Deng Xiaoping died, rural employment – which was primarily in TVEs, and not in agriculture exclusively – began to contract for the first time, and in 1998 it plunged 20 percent. Urban unemployment in 1997 was 40 percent. Much of it was due to the demise of the SOEs; much more was caused by uncontrollable migration from the countryside to the cities. The unemployed and the homeless were a rich resource for criminal organizations, which were growing unchecked in both the cities and the country-side. The bond and stock markets that Deng had authorized never gained credibility; stock prices were manipulated by party officials for their own gain and fraud against investors was rampant. Both the government and the public agreed that corruption was out of control, and in terms of volume was clearly the greatest of any time in Chinese history.

And there was a new challenge, a peculiar religious sect, Falungong – whose practices resemble a strange amalgam of traditional Chinese therapeutic exercise, American-style pyramid sales schemes for religious paraphernalia, and personal moral perfection – was becoming widespread in China after 1992. The tight organization of the believers and their sophisticated use of the Internet were disturbing to the CCP. So was their emphasis on *qigong*. Qing period rebellions, from White Lotus to the

Boxers, had all incorporated some belief in practices related to *qigong*; the belief that rebel leaders could fly or make themselves impervious to bullets had contributed significantly to the cohesion and confidence of the movements. There is some evidence that the PRC government did not consider *qigong* powers to be merely superstition, and that it has spent some money researching whether mental and physical advantages might be gained through its use. But religious conversion in the PRC, by any group, was illegal, and in the late 1990s the PRC security forces began breaking up Falun gong worship and study meetings. The Jiang government passed a new law in 1999 affirming that "heterodox religions" (a peculiar phrase once used in the Qing period, implying that there are "orthodox" religions) were illegal. In 1999 Falungong believers began public protests against the persecution, most of which were met by the state with arrests, sometimes with beatings or worse. Falungong campaigns for religious freedom in the PRC, and the PRC campaign to eradicate what it considers subversive organizing by the Falungong, continue today.

Under Jiang, the primary government response to the faltering economy and new challenges to PRC restrictions on freedom were publicity campaigns designed to calm and cheer the public. State involvement in the economy was gradually diminished. Safety regulation in most industries was rescinded or neglected. Real estate practices in the SEZs, and ultimately in the cities near to them such as Canton, Shanghai and Tianjin, created completely new opportunities for property sales, building contracts, bonds for the financing of new development and leases. Members of the CCP, their relatives and friends were generally at the center of the lucrative exchanges, and by the late 1990s a hugely speculative interface of real estate and banking had created many millionaires in the coastal cities. Further impositions on the credit system came from financing of the extension and repair of railways that had drifted into the private ownership of the crony class. Combined with the residual "assets" that banks held from empty or defunct SOEs, analysts estimated that by the middle 1990s the concatenation of bad loans and fraudulent real estate estimates in China constituted an authentic bubble that would ultimately burst. But on paper, China's economy seemed to enjoy double-digit annual growth rates.

Only when Zhu Rongji became premier in 1997 did the government begin to fight the high-level instability of the economy with regulation. By keeping interest rates high and raising standards for credit, he attempted to restore the health of banks. When other Asian economies were struggling with a currency crisis in the late 1990s, Zhu focused on domestic consumption. He worked out a social security system to keep the unemployed able to purchase, dissolved TVEs that were inefficient and lowered taxes on farmers (the taxes were later eliminated by the government of Hu Juntao and Wen Jiabao). Foreign investment, and industrial presence – already a major part of the state's plans for economic stability – were further encouraged by favorable tax policies. Zhu's associate Wen Jiabao was assigned to survey the banking system, exposing empty loans and establishing new credit regulations. Perhaps most important, Zhu aimed to expand both the volume and the scope of Chinese exports by joining the WTO. Admission would, in theory, mitigate foreign claims that China's own market was not open to imports, and result in lower tariffs on Chinese goods abroad. Continued investment in China, and a continuing expansion of China's exports, could buy time to stabilize the most fragile elements of the Chinese economy before disaster could strike. But to join the WTO, the PRC would need the backing of the USA.

In 1999, American public opinion hugely opposed the admission of the PRC to the WTO, on economic, moral and political grounds. As part of its application to the WTO, the PRC substantially lowered its import tariffs in the 1990s, took some steps toward modifying laws for foreign direct investment outside the SEZs, and expanded its purchases of American public debt. In 2002 the PRC became a fully-fledged member of the WTO, obliged to permit imports to be sold on substantially the same basis as domestic products.

Though foreign trade has been a profoundly important element in the amazing wealth accumulation in China in the past twenty years, government strategies for lowering public expenses while lowering taxes somewhat, have also been important. Through the 1980s and early 1990s, government expenditures on education, health care and retirement pensions had remained high. Under Premier Zhu Rongji, the approach was to shift as many costs as possible to local governments and to private organizations. Laws were altered to allow approved local organizations to raise their own funds to finance building, educational programs and pension schemes. Local governments were forbidden to borrow development funds from the central government, but could borrow from local banks or private investment firms. The result was that about 70 percent of government functions (and about the same percentage of all government appointments) were apportioned to the local governments. The central government's responsibility for supporting housing, education, health care and retirement was gradually withdrawn, so that at present these matters are overwhelmingly in the hands of private individuals, their families, the firms for which they work and local savings societies to which they might belong. The central government now maintains a workforce of just over 10 million officials, while the totality of government-like work done in the country seems to rest with a minimum of about 40 million people, meaning that about three-quarters of government and administrative work is privatized and localized. Communities, many of which do not date much earlier than the period of decollectivization in the 1980s, are once again the foundation of economic, social and political organization. In addition to portending a changing relationship between the state and the localities, the policies may shape and be shaped by the contours of income distribution. Though the PRC is the world's second largest economy, its per capita purchasing power ranks 163rd in the world, below Uganda and above Mali (Taiwan ranks 25th, and Hongkong is virtually even with the USA at 6th). If the poor populations of the localities are required in future to carry the burdens of government, either they will demand their cut of the wealth concentrated in the small elite, or government will fail.

China's new-found wealth and power, combined with its firm domination of borderlands in Tibet, Xinjiang and Inner Mongolia, sometimes tempt foreign writers to describe it as an "empire." They are referring to its lack of democracy and its harshness toward the distinct societies that lay within its boundaries, particularly the military occupation of Tibet. They are referring to the destruction of communities in the Mao period, and to the brutal suppression against the population of Beijing in 1989. They are referring to the unbridled self-indulgence of its predatory élites. But being large, diverse, undemocratic and on occasion harsh does not make a polity an empire. The differences between the Qing empire and the PRC are profound enough that they should discourage even frivolous equation. Under an empire like the Qing, the emperorship was the point of integration, transcending the diversities of language, culture and religion of which the empire was composed. In such an empire, loyalty and status are not absolutely determined by a relationship to culture or history, but by one's relationship to the emperor.

When the empire was gone, the criteria for inclusion and enfranchisement shifted, so that the necessity to define oneself in relation to "Chinese" – in or out – became critical. Because the PRC is not an empire, and because it frequently resorts to nationalist cheerleading when tensions arise, it can never dispense with a basic construction of Chinese identity as its threshold of inclusion. The huge areas under the domination of the PRC – that is, under domination of Chinese via the mechanism of the PRC – must continue to be construed as culturally and historically convincing only in the context of their cultural and historical relationship to China. There are alternatives, in theory. In the USA, affiliation and enfranchisement are based less on cultural identity than on fidelity to values such as the Constitution, liberty, capitalism and democracy. Communism might function the same way, as some believe it to have done in the Soviet Union. But Maoism was not communism, it was a communistically-inspired anarcho-socialism strongly laced with old-fashioned nationalism. It could never be universally applicable to all the peoples who lived under the PRC, even if there were early periods in his career when Mao might have thought it would be. Its ideological cognate in the post-Mao era has been an even less nuanced nationalism, combined with the demonstrated power to dominate and exploit its strategically-critical borderlands. Deng Xiaoping and his successors have added little if any unifying ideology apart from an enthusiastic validation of comfort and wealth as an end in themselves. Should the PRC in future become frankly dedicated to the pursuit of wealth to the exclusion of any other moral values, then everybody wishing to enrich themselves as their first and only goal in life will become candidates for equality in the PRC. Until then, the best it can offer its citizens in terms of inclusion and enfranchisement is assimilation. Those who resist and remain cultural minorities will live as minorities. For generations some of the districts of the PRC have known no other kind of political life and may have no other expectations. This is emphatically not comparable to cultural life under the Qing empire. Political inclusion defined around a designated cultural majority necessarily and irremediably marginalizes minorities.

More important, the PRC and the Qing empire bear no resemblance as administrative presences. The PRC sits on roughly the same expanse of terrain and cultural complexity as the Qing empire, and its administrative work is facilitated by modern telecommunications and weaponry. Yet it is roughly 435 times the size of the Qing government in terms of personnel and budget. When we remember that the current population of China is three times greater than the Qing, that very crudely translates to more than 150 times less space between the state and the individual, with more than 150 times less space for the community to mediate. This is most meaningful as an index of the profound dependency of the Qing empire, and the Ming before, on local coherence in the maintenance of public order and well-being. Modern government operatives have new functions, particularly relating to direct surveillance of persons and of communications, that would have been impossible for the Qing empire to attempt. Nevertheless there is a curve to government presence and intrusiveness in the modern PRC. Mao's attempt to substitute the party and the state for the local community was a deviation from the historical pattern, and since the death of Mao the state has moved gradually, but steadily, back toward dependence on the local communities for management of local welfare and local order. In a very interesting development, the government of Wen Jiabao has even begun to use the old Qing tactic of unfunded mandates – laws requiring local communities and agencies to provide social support, without receiving grants from the central government. The "new" policy is a reminder of the continuities in the geo-spatial dynamics of governing the former Qing territories, and the way, over time, they produce similar behaviors in governments which are fundamentally different. The expanse of the country, the tremendous disparities in regional resources and regional wealth and the deep divide between the cultures of the cities and of the countryside virtually require that every government allow its decision-making to devolve to the locality. When that is combined with a degree of financial independence at the local level – perhaps forced upon it by a bankrupt or overly-thrifty state – the pendulum that swings between state dependence on the locality and state fear of the locality is set in motion.

Most observers of China have abandoned the iron equation of increasing wealth and increasing political liberalization when it comes to predicting the political future of the PRC. The rule comports with much of the history of Europe, but is not uniformly applicable elsewhere. The quote that opened this book invokes a historical fact, that in the USA no government has allowed the central spaces of its capital to be occupied by dissidents. In the USA, long-standing institutions of liberal representation, combined with a profound political culture defining the rights and obligations of the enfranchised, allows every individual to mediate his or her interests through such institutions; each individual may address the state directly, through the ballot box, through the courts, or through elected representatives. Mass movements, though implied to be protected under the Constitution, are not historically regarded as part of the compact between the state and the society. In China it is different. It has historically been impossible, and is impossible now, for a state based in China to rule with consent of the governed, since there are no institutions through which individuals or the public en masse can grant consent. But ruling with the toleration of the governed was manifestly the practice of the Qing. Attempts to radically alter that compact through force of arms, as in the days of Yuan Shikai and his successors, or by a universalization of the party-state, as under Mao, have all been defeated by the centrifugal forces that have allowed the intolerance of the public to be mediated through mass movements, mass protests (from Democracy Wall to the modern Internet), and the cultural institutionalization of dissent. It is not democracy, it cannot emulate democracy, and it seems unclear whether it can lead to democracy. Neither is it despotism, except in those periods of central hypertrophy in which the state makes a direct assault upon the coherence of local organization. It is a field of political negotiation that, in comparison to the political environs of some other countries, looks uncommonly hazardous for individuals, strenuous for local associations of all kinds and perilous for the head of state who loses a challenge with the rest of the country. But it is a pattern that contemporary China is demonstrating is difficult or impossible to eradicate, and may be a mode of state survival in the present as it was in the past.

Further reading

The reference to Mao considering fireworks to celebrate the death of Zhou is from Gao, *Zhou Enlai*, p. 308. Deng's quotation on the origin of the TVEs is from Qi, "Deng Xiaoping's Ideas on Chinese Township and Village Enterprises," p. 86.

On political development since 1976, see Domes, *China after the Cultural Revolution* (1977); Blecher, *Micropolitics in Contemporary China* (1979); Nathan, *Chinese Democracy* (1986); Goodman and Segal, *China Deconstructs* (1994); Lieberthal, *Governing China* (1995); MacFarquhar, *The Politics of China* (1997); Tien and Zhu, *China under Jiang Zemin* (2000); Hughes and Wacker, *China and the Internet* (2003); Kuhn, *The Man Who Changed China* (2004); Lam, *Chinese Politics in the Hu Jintao Era* (2006); Shirk, *China* (2007); Ji, *The Man on Mao's Right* (2008); Pan, *Out of Mao's Shadow* (2008). On the Tiananmen Incident of 1989 and related issues, see Davis and Vogel, *Chinese Society on the Eve of Tiananmen* (1990); Oksenberg, Sullivan, Lambert and Li, *Beijing Spring, 1989* (1990); Barmé and Jaivin, *New Ghosts, Old Dreams* (1992); Schell, *Mandate of Heaven* (1995); Zhang, Nathan, Link and Schell, *The Tiananmen Papers* (2002); Zhao, *The Power of Tiananmen* (2004); Wu, *Remaking Beijing* (2005); Marchetti, *From Tian'anmen to Times Square* (2006).

On normalization and subsequent growth of the US-China relationship, including trade, see Nathan and Ross, *The Great Wall and the Empty Fortress* (1998); Tyler, *A Great Wall* (2000); Suettinger, *Beyond Tiananmen* (2003); MacMillan, *Nixon and Mao* (2007); Shirk, above; Tucker, *Strait Talk* (2009).

On domestic, social and economic issues since 1976, see Naughton, *Growing Out of the Plan* (1996); Yeung and Sung, *Shanghai* (1996); Vermeer, Pieke and Chong, *Cooperative and Collective in China's Rural Development* (1997); Zweig, *Freeing China's Farmers* (1997); Lardy, *China's Unfinished Economic Revolution* (1998); Oi and Walder, *Property Rights and Economic Reform in China* (1999); Barmé, *In the Red* (2000); Lubman, *Bird in a Cage* (2002); Peerenboom, *China's Long March toward Rule of Law* (2002); Brettell, *The Politics of Public Participation* (2003); Naughton and Yang, *Holding China Together* (2004); Weller, *Discovering Nature* (2006); Pei, *China's Trapped Transition* (2008); Zhang, *Chinese Human Smuggling Operations* (2008).

For other foreign relations since 1971, see Shirk, above; Ji, above; Johnston, *Social States* (2008); Horner, *Rising China and Its Postmodern Fate* (2009); Michel and Beuret, *China Safari* (2009); Raine, *China's African Challenges* (2009); Wishnick, *Russia, China, and the United States in Central Asia* (2009).

Bibliography

Adler, Joseph A. (2004) "The Qianlong Emperor and the Confucian 'Temple of Culture' (*Wen miao*) at Chengde," in Millward et al., eds., *New Qing Imperial History*, pp. 109–22.

Ahn, Byung-joon (1976) *Chinese Politics and the Cultural Revolution: Dynamics of Policy Processes*. Seattle: University of Washington Press.

Alber, Charles J. (2004) *Embracing the Lie: Ding Ling and the Politics of Literature in the People's Republic of China*. Westport: Praeger.

Allen, Robert C. (2005) "Real Wages in Europe and Asia: A First Look at the Long-Term Patterns," in Allen et al., eds., *Living Standards in the Past*, pp. 111–30.

Allen, Robert C. (2005) Jean-Pascal Bassino, Debin Ma, Christine Moll-Murata and Jan Luiten van Zanden, "Wages, Prices, and Living Standards in China, Japan and Europe, 1738–1925," GPIH Working Paper No. 1, Version: October.

Allen, Robert C., Tommy Bengtsson and Martin Dribe, eds. (2005) *Living Standards in the Past: New Perspectives on Well-being in Asia and Europe*. Oxford: Oxford University Press.

Alvin, Austin (2007) *China's Millions: The China Inland Mission and Late Qing Society*. Grand Rapids: Eerdmans.

Ampiah, Kweku and Sanusha Naidu, eds. (2008) *Crouching Tiger, Hidden Dragon? Africa and China*. Scottsville: University of KwaZulu-Natal Press.

Andrade, Tonio (2007) *How Taiwan Became Chinese*. New York: Columbia University Press.

Andreas, Joel (2009) *Rise of the Red Engineers: The Cultural Revolution and the Origins of China's New Class*. Stanford: Stanford University Press.

Antony, Robert J. (1993) "Brotherhoods, Secret Societies and the Law in Qing-Dynasty China," in Ownby and Heidhues, eds., *'Secret Societies' Reconsidered: Perspectives on the Social History of Modern South China and Southeast Asia*, pp. 190–211.

Antony, Robert J. (2003) *Like Froth Floating on the Sea: The World of Pirates and Seafarers in Late Imperial South China*. Berkeley: Institute for East Asian Studies, China Research Monographs, No. 36.

Antony, Robert J. and Jane Kate Leonard, eds. (2002) *Dragons, Tigers and Dogs: Qing Crisis Management and the Boundaries of State Power in Late Imperial China*. Ithaca: Cornell University Press.

Arnove, Robert F. and Harvey J. Graff (1987) *National Literacy Campaigns: Historical and Comparative Perspectives Edition*. New York: Springer.

Askew, David (2003) "New Research on the Nanjing Incident," *The Asia-Pacific Journal: Japan Focus*. Online: www.japanfocus.org/-David-Askew/1729.

Auslin, Michael R. (2006) *Negotiating with Imperialism: The Unequal Treaties and the Culture of Japanese Diplomacy*. Cambridge, MA: Harvard University Press.

Austin, Alvyn (2007) *China's Millions: The China Inland Mission and Late Qing Society*. Grand Rapids: Eerdmans.

Baark, Eric (1997) *Lightning Wires: The Telegraph and China's Technological Modernization, 1860–1890*. Westport: Greenwood Publishing Group.

Bachman, David M. (1991) *Bureaucracy, Economy, and Leadership in China: The Institutional Origins of the Great Leap Forward*. Cambridge: Cambridge University Press.

Bailey, Paul J. (1990) *Reform the People: Changing Attitudes towards Popular Education in Early Twentieth-Century China*. Edinburgh: Edinburgh University Press.

Barenblatt, Daniel (2004) *A Plague Upon Humanity: The Secret Genocide of Axis Japan's Germ Warfare Operation*. New York: HarperCollins.

Barmé, Geremie (2000) *In the Red: On Contemporary Chinese Culture*. New York: Columbia University Press.

Barmé, Geremie and Linda Jaivin (1992) *New Ghosts, Old Dreams: Chinese Rebel Voices*. New York: Times Books.

Barnouin, Barbara and Changgen Yu (2006) *Zhou Enlai: A Political Life*. Hongkong: Chinese University Press.

Bartlett, Beatrice S. (1991) *Monarchs and Ministers: The Grand Council in Mid-Ch'ing China, 1723–1820*. Berkeley: University of California Press.

Barrett, David P. and Lawrence N. Shyu (2001) *Chinese Collaboration with Japan, 1932–1945: The Limits of Accommodation*. Stanford: Stanford University Press.

Bastid, Marianne (1988) "Qingyi (Disinterested Counsel) and the Self-strengthening Movement," in *Proceedings of the Conference on the Self-strengthening Movement in Late Ch'ing China, 1860–1894*. Taipei: Academia Sinica, Institute of Modern History, pp. 873–93.

Baum, Richard (1969) "Revolution and Reaction in the Chinese Countryside: The Socialist Education Movement in Cultural Revolutionary Perspective," *The China Quarterly*, No. 38 (Apr.–Jun.): 92–119.

Baum, Richard, ed. (1971) *China in Ferment: Perspectives on the Cultural Revolution*. Englewood Cliffs: Prentice-Hall.

Becker, Jasper (1997) *Hungry Ghosts: Mao's Secret Famine*. New York: Free Press.

Beeching, Jack (1975) *The Chinese Opium Wars*. London: Hutchinson.

Bello, David A. (2005) *Opium and the Limits of Empire: Drug Prohibition in the Chinese Empire, 1729–1850*, Cambridge, MA: Harvard University Asia Center.

Belsky, Richard (2005) *Localities at the Center: Native Place, Space, and Power in Late Imperial Beijing*. Cambridge, MA: Harvard East Asian Monographs.

Beng, Tan Chee, Colin Storey and Julia Zimmerman, eds. (2007) *Chinese Overseas: Migration, Research and Documentation*. Hong Kong: University of Hong Kong Press.

Benson, Linda (1990) *The Ili Rebellion: The Moslem Challenge to Chinese Authority in Xinjiang, 1944–1949*. Armonk: M.E. Sharpe.

Bergère, Marie-Claire (2000) (J. Lloyd, trans.) *Sun Yat-sen*. Stanford: Stanford University Press.

Bergholz, Fred W. (1993) *The Partition of the Steppe: The Struggle of the Russians, Manchus, and the Zunghar Mongols for Empire in Central Asia, 1619–1758: A Study in Power Politics*. Grand Rapids: Peter Lang.

Bernal, Martin (1976) *Chinese Socialism to 1907*. Ithaca: Cornell University Press.

Bernhardt, Kathryn (1987) "Elite and Peasant During the Taiping Occupation of the Jiangnan, 1860–1864," *Modern China* 13: 379–410.

Bernhardt, Kathryn and Philip C.C. Huang (M. Zelin and M.A. Allee, contributors) (1994) *Civil Law in Qing and Republican China*. Stanford: Stanford University Press.

Berry, Michael (2008) *A History of Pain: Trauma in Modern Chinese Literature and Film*. New York: Columbia University Press.

Bianco, Lucien (2005) *Jacqueries et révolution dans la Chine du XXe siècle*. Paris, Editions de La Martinière.

Bianco, Lucien (2004) *Peasant Without the Party: Grass-Roots Movements in Twentieth-Century China*. Armonk: M.E. Sharpe.

Bieler, Stacy (2004) *"Patriots or Traitors?": A History of American-Educated Chinese Students*. Armonk: M.E. Sharpe.

Blecher, Marc J. (1979) *Micropolitics in Contemporary China: a Technical Unit during and after the Cultural Revolution*. Armonk: M.E. Sharpe.

Braun, Otto (1982) *A Comintern Agent in China, 1932–1939*. Stanford: Stanford University Press.

Brettell, Anna M. (2003) *The Politics of Public Participation and the Emergence of Environmental Proto-Movement in China*. College Park: University of Maryland Press.

Brokaw, Cynthia J. and Kai-wing Chow (2005) *Printing and Book Culture in Late Imperial China*. Berkeley: University of California Press.

Brook, Timothy, ed. (1999) *Documents on the Rape of Nanjing*. Ann Arbor: University of Michigan Press.

Brook, Timothy and Bob Tadashi Wakabayashi, eds. (2000) *Opium Regimes: China, Britain and Japan, 1839–1952*, Berkeley: University of California Press.

Brown, Jeremy and Paul G. Pickowicz, eds. (2007) *Dilemmas of Victory: The Early Years of the People's Republic of China*. Cambridge, MA: Harvard University Press.

Brown, Kerry (2006) *The Purge of the Inner Mongolian People's Party in the Chinese Cultural Revolution, 1967–69: A Function of Language, Power and Violence*. Folkstone: Global Oriental.

Carr, Caleb (1995) *The Devil Soldier: The American Soldier of Fortune Who Became a God in China*. New York: Random House.

Ch'en, Jerome (1972) *Yuan Shih-k'ai* (2nd edn.). Stanford: Stanford University Press.

Ch'en, Jerome (1980) *State Economic Policies of the Ch'ing Government, 1840–1895*. New York: Garland Publishing.

Chan, Alfred L. (2001) *Mao's Crusade: Politics and Policy Implementation in China's Great Leap Forward*. Oxford & New York: Oxford University Press.

Chan, Anthony B. (1982) *Arming the Chinese: The Western Armaments Trade in Warlord China, 1920–1928*. Vancouver: University of British Columbia Press.

Chang, Chung-li (1962) *The Income of the Chinese Gentry*. Seattle: University of Washington Press.

Chang, Hao (1971) *Liang Ch'i-ch'ao and Intellectual Transition in China, 1890–1907*. Cambridge, MA: Harvard University Press.

Chang Hsin-pao (1964) *Commissioner Lin and the Opium War*. Cambridge, MA: Harvard University Press.

Chang, Iris (1996) *Thread of the Silkworm*. New York: Basic Books.

Chang, Iris (1998) *The Rape of Nanking: The Forgotten Holocaust of World War II*. New York: Penguin.

Chang, Jung (2003) *Wild Swans: Three Daughters of China*. New York: Simon & Schuster.

Chang, Jung and Jon Halliday (2005) *Mao: The Unknown Story*. London: Random House/ Jonathan Cape.

Chang, Kuo-t'ao (Zhang Guotao) (1971) *The Rise of the Chinese Communist Party: 1928–1938*. Lawrence: University of Kansas Press.

Chao, K'ang (1986) *Man and Land in Chinese History*. Stanford: Stanford University Press.

Chen, Jian (1994) *China's Road to the Korean War: The Making of the Sino-American Confrontation*. New York: Columbia University Press.

Chen, Xiaoming (2007) *From the May Fourth Movement to Communist Revolution: Guo Moruo and the Chinese Path to Communism.* Albany: SUNY University Press.

Chen, Yung-fa (1986) *Making Revolution: The Communist Movement in Eastern and Central China, 1937–1945.* Berkeley: University of California Press.

Chen, Yung-fa and Gregor Benton (1986) *Moral Economy and the Chinese Revolution: A Critique. Publikatieserie Zuid-ed Zuidoost-Azie, No. 32.* Amsterdam: Anthropological-Sociological Centre, University of Amsterdam.

Cheng, Pei-kai and Michael Lestz (1999) *The Search for Modern China: Documentary Collection.* New York: W.W. Norton.

Chesneaux, Jean (1970) (C.A. Curwen, trans.), *Peasant Revolt in China 1840–1949.* London: Thames and Hudson Ltd., 1973. (Cf Jean Chesneaux (dir.), *Mouvements populaires et sociétés secrètes en Chine aux XIXe et XXe siècles,* Paris, Maspéro).

Chesneaux, Jean (1980) (H.M. Wright, trans.), *The Chinese Labor Movement, 1919–1927.* Stanford: Stanford University Press.

Chesneaux, Jean, Marianne Bastid and Marie Claire Bergere (1976) *China: From the Opium Wars to the 1911 Revolution.* New York: Pantheon Books.

Chetham, Deirdre (2002) *Before the Deluge: The Vanishing World of the Yangtze's Three Gorges.* New York: Palgrave Macmillan.

Cheung, Gordon C. K. (2004) "Chinese Diaspora as a Virtual Nation: Interactive Roles between Economic and Social Capital," *Political Studies* 52 (4): 664–84.

Chi, Hsi-sheng (1976) *Warlord Politics in China, 1916–1928.* Stanford: Stanford University Press.

Chi, Madeleine (1973) "Shanghai-Hangchow-Ningpo Railway Loan: A Case Study of the Rights Recovery Movement," *Modern Asian Studies* 7: 85–106.

Chinese Communist Party Central Committee (CCPCC) (1991) *History of the Chinese Community Party: A Chronology of Events (1919–1990).* Beijing: Foreign Languages Press.

Chong, Woei Lien, ed. (2002) *China's Great Proletarian Cultural Revolution: Master Narratives and Post-Mao Counternarratives.* Lanham, MD: Rowman & Littlefield.

Chow, Kai-Wing, Tze-ki Hon, Hung-yok Ip and Don C. Price, eds. (2008) *Beyond the May Fourth Paradigm: In Search of Chinese Modernity.* Lanham: Rowman & Littlefield.

Chow, Tse-tsung (1960) *The May Fourth Movement: Intellectual Revolution in Modern China.* Cambridge, MA: Harvard University Press.

Chu, Samuel C. and Kwang-ching Liu, eds. (1994) *Li Hung-chang and China's Early Modernization.* Armonk: M.E. Sharpe.

Chu, Samuel C. and Thomas L. Kennedy (2005) *Madame Chiang Kaishek and Her China.* Norwalk: Eastbridge.

Clark, Paul (2008) *The Chinese Cultural Revolution: A History.* Cambridge: Cambridge University Press.

Coble, Parks M. (2005) "Rethinking Modern Chinese History: War and History," paper prepared for the International Conference on Rethinking Modern Chinese History, Institute of Modern History, Academia Sinica, June 29–July 1.

Cochran, Sherman (1980) *Big Business in China: Sino-Foreign Rivalry in the Cigarette Industry.* Cambridge, MA: Harvard University Press.

Cohen, Paul A. (1963) *China and Christianity: The Missionary Movement and the Growth of Chinese Anti-Foreignism, 1860–1870.* Cambridge, MA: Harvard University Press.

Cohen, Paul A (1988) *Between Tradition and Modernity: Wang T'ao and Reform in Late Ch'ing China,* Cambridge, MA: Harvard University Press.

Cohen, Warren I. (2002) *The Asian American Century.* Cambridge, MA: Harvard University Press.

Conroy, Hilary (1960) *The Japanese seizure of Korea, 1868–1910: A Study of Realism and Idealism in International Relations.* Philadelphia: University of Pennsylvania Press.

Croll, Elisabeth J. (1978) *Feminism and Socialism in China.* London: Routledge.

Crossley, Pamela Kyle (1990) *Orphan Warriors: Three Manchu Generations and the End of the Qing World.* Princeton: Princeton University Press.

Crossley, Pamela Kyle (1997) *The Manchus.* Oxford: Blackwell Publishers.

Crossley, Pamela Kyle (1999) *A Translucent Mirror: History and Identity in Qing Imperial China Ideology.* Berkeley: University of California Press.

Crossley, Pamela Kyle, Helen F. Siu and Donald S. Sutton, eds. (2006) *Empire at the Margins: Culture, Ethnicity, and Frontier in Early Modern China.* Berkeley: University of California Press.

Cumings, Bruce (1981) *The Origins of the Korean War: Liberation and the Emergence of Separate Regimes, 1945–1947.* Princeton: Princeton University Press.

Curthoys, Ann and Marilyn Lake, eds. (2005) *Connected Worlds: History in Transnational Perspective.* Canberra: Australian National University.

Curwen, Charles A. (1977) *The Deposition of Li Hsiu-ch'eng.* Cambridge: Cambridge University Press.

Dai, Yingcong (2001) "The Qing State, Merchants, and the Military Labor Force in the Jinchuan Campaigns," *Late Imperial China* 22: 2 (December): 35–90.

Dai, Yingcong (2005) "Yingyong Shengxi: Military Entrepreneurship in the High Qing Period, 1700–1800," *Late Imperial China* 26: 2 (December): 1–67.

Davis, Deborah and Ezra F. Vogel (1990) *Chinese Society on the Eve of Tiananmen: The Impact of Reform.* Cambridge, MA: Harvard University Council on East Asian Studies.

de Crespigny, Rafe (1975) "Political Protest in Imperial China: The Great Proscription of Later Han, 167–184," originally published in *Papers on Far Eastern History,* 11 (March): 1–36, later revised and posted at www.anu.edu.au/asianstudies/decrespigny/Proscription_1975.doc.

Deng, Maomao (1996) *Deng Xiaoping: My Father.* New York: BasicBooks.

Dikötter, Frank (1992) *The Discourse of Race in Modern China.* Stanford: Stanford University Press.

Dikötter, Frank, ed. (1997) *The Construction of Racial Identities in China and Japan: Historical and Contemporary Perspectives.* Honolulu: University of Hawai'i Press.

Dikötter, Frank (2002) *Crime and Punishment in Modern China, 1895–1949.* New York: Columbia University Press.

Dikötter, Frank (2008) *The Age of Openness: China before Mao.* Berkeley: University of California Press.

Dikötter, Frank, Lars Peter Laamann and Zhou Xun (2004) *Narcotic Culture: A History of Drugs in China.* London: C. Hurst & Co.

Ding, Ling (1954) *The Sun Shines over the Sangkan River.* Peking: Foreign Languages Press.

Ding, Ling (1985) (W.J.F. Jenner, trans.) *Miss Sophie's Diary and Other Stories.* Beijing: China International Book Trading Corp.

Ding, Ling (1990) *I Myself Am a Woman: Selected Writings of Ding Ling,* trans. and ed. Tani E. Barlow and Gary J. Bjorge. Boston: Beacon Press.

Dirlik, Arif (1975) "The Ideological Foundations of the New Life Movement: A Study in Counterrevolution," *The Journal of Asian Studies* 34 (4) (August): 945–80.

Dirlik, Arif (1993) *Anarchism in the Chinese Revolution.* Berkeley: University of California Press.

Dittmer, Lowell (1974) *Liu Shao-ch'i and the Chinese Cultural Revolution: The Politics of Mass Criticism.* Berkeley: University of California Press.

Domes, Jürgen (1977) *China after the Cultural Revolution: Politics between Two Party Congresses,* trans. A. Berg and D. Goodman. Berkeley: University of California Press.

Domes, Jürgen, James T. Myers and Erik von Groeling (1974) *Cultural Revolution in China: Documents and Analysis.* Brussels: Centre d'étude du sud-est asiatique et de l'extrême-orient.

Drege, Jean-Pierre (1978) *La Commercial Press de Shanghai, 1897–1949*. Paris: Memoire de l'Institut des Hautes Études Chinoises.

Drege, Jean-Pierre and Hua Chang-Ming (1979) *La Revolution du livre dans la Chine moderne*. Paris: Publications Orientalistes de France.

Dreyer, June Teufel (1976) *China's Forty Millions: Minority Nationalities and National Integration in the People's Republic of China*. Cambridge, MA: Harvard University Press.

Economy, Elisabeth (2005) *The River Runs Black: The Environmental Challenge to China's Future*. Ithaca: Cornell University Press.

Edgerton-Tarpley, Kathryn (2008) *Tears from Iron: Cultural Responses to Famine in Nineteenth-Century China*. Berkeley: University of California Press.

Eastman, Lloyd (1967) *Thrones and Mandarins: China's Search for a Policy during the Sino-French Controversy, 1880–1885*. Cambridge, MA: Harvard University Press.

Elleman, Bruce (2001) *Modern Chinese Warfare, 1795–1898*. London: Routledge.

Elliott, Mark C. (2001) *The Manchu Way: The Eight Banners and Ethnic Identity in Late Imperial China*. Stanford: Stanford University Press.

Elman, Benjamin A. (1990) *Classicism, Politics, and Kinship: The Ch'ang-chou School of New Text Confucianism in Late Imperial China*. Berkeley: University of California Press.

Elvin, Mark (1973) *The Pattern of the Chinese Past*. Stanford: Stanford University Press.

Elvin, Mark (2006) *The Retreat of the Elephants, An Environmental History of China*. New Haven: Yale University Press.

Elvin, Mark and Liu Ts'ui-jung (1998) *Sediments of Time: Environment and Society in Chinese History*. Cambridge: Cambridge University Press.

Epstein, Israel (1956) *From Opium War to Liberation*. Beijing: New World Press.

Esherick, Joseph W. (1987) *The Origins of the Boxer Uprising*. Berkeley: University of California Press.

Esherick, Joseph W. and Mary Backus Rankin, eds. (1990) *Chinese Local Elites and Patterns of Dominance*. Berkeley: University of California Press.

Esherick, Joseph, Paul Pickowicz and Andrew George Walder, eds. (2006) *The Chinese Cultural Revolution as History*. Stanford: Stanford University Press.

Fairbank, John K. (1973) *The Chinese World Order: Traditional China's Foreign Relations*. Cambridge, MA: Harvard East Asian Series.

Fairbank, John K. (1953) *Trade and Diplomacy on the China Coast: The Opening of the Treaty Ports, 1842–1854*. Stanford: Stanford University Press.

Fang Chao-ying (1943–44), "Tsou Jung," in Hummel, ed., *Eminent Chinese of the Ch'ing Period*, p. 769.

Fay, Peter Ward (1975)*The Opium War, 1840–1842: Barbarians in the Celestial Empire in the Early Part of the Nineteenth Century and the War by which They Forced Her Gates Ajar*. Chapel Hill: University of North Carolina Press.

Fenby, Jonathan (2003) *Generalissimo Chiang Kai-Shek and the China He lost*. New York: The Free Press.

Ferguson, Niall (1999) *The House of Rothschild: Money's Prophets, 1798–1848*. New York: Viking.

Feuerwerker, Albert (1958) *China's Early Industrialization: Sheng Hsuan-huai (1844–1916) and Mandarin Enterprise*. Cambridge, MA: Harvard University Press.

Feuerwerker, Albert (1969) *The Chinese Economy ca. 1870–1911*. Ann Arbor: Center for Chinese Studies, University of Michigan.

Feuerwerker, Albert (1996) *Studies in the Economic History of Late Imperial China: Handicraft, Modern Industry, and the State*. Ann Arbor: University of Michigan Press.

Feuerwerker, Yi-tsi Mei (1982) *Ding Ling's Fiction: Ideology and Narrative in Modern Chinese Literature*. Cambridge, MA: Harvard University Press.

Fletcher, Joseph (1978) "The Heyday of the Ch'ing Order in Mongolia, Sinkiang and Tibet," in John K. Fairbank, ed., *The Cambridge History of China: Late Ch'ing 1800–1911, Part I.* Cambridge: Cambridge University Press.

Flory, Wendy Stollard (2003) "Confucius against Confusion: Ezra Pound and the Catholic Chaplain at Pisa," in Qian, Zhaoming, ed., *Ezra Pound and China.* Ann Arbor: University of Michigan Press.

Fogel, Joshua A. (1987) *Ai Ssu-ch'i Contribution to the Development of Chinese Marxism.* Cambridge, MA: Harvard University Asia Center.

Fogel, Joshua A., ed. (2004) *The Role of Japan in Liang Qichao's Introduction of Modern Western Civilization to China.* Berkeley: Institute of East Asian Studies, University of California Berkeley, Center for Chinese Studies.

Fogel, Joshua, ed. (2000) *The Nanjing Massacre in History and Historiography*, Berkeley: University of California Press.

Folsom, Kenneth E. (1968) *Friends, Guests and Colleagues: The Mu-fu System in the Late Ch'ing Period.* Berkeley: University of California Press.

Forbes, Robert Bennet (1878) *Personal Reminiscences.* Boston: Little, Brown & Company.

Frank, Andre Gunder (1998) *Reorient: Global Economy in the Asian Age.* Berkeley: University of California Press.

Freese, Barbara (2003) *Coal: A Human History.* Cambridge, MA: Da Capo Press.

Friedman, Edward (1974) *Backward Toward Revolution: The Chinese Revolutionary Party.* Berkeley: University of California Press.

Friedman, Edward, Paul G. Picowicz and Mark Selden, with Kay Ann Johnson (1991) *Chinese Village, Socialist State.* New Haven: Yale University Press.

Galbiati, Fernando (1985) *P'eng P'ai and the Hai-Lu-Feng Soviet.* Stanford: Stanford University Press.

Gamble, Sidney D. (1921) *Peking: A Social Survey.* New York: George H. Doran Company.

Gao, Wenqian (2007) *Zhou Enlai: The Last Perfect Revolutionary*, trans. P. Rand and L.R. Sullivan. New York: PublicAffairs.

Garrett, Valery M. (2002) *Heaven is High and the Emperor Far Away: Merchants and Mandarins in Old Canton.* New York: Oxford University Press.

Garver, John W. (1988) *Chinese-Soviet Relations, 1937–1945: The Diplomacy of Chinese Nationalism.* Oxford: Oxford University Press.

Gasster, Michael (1969) *Chinese Intellectuals and the Revolution of 1911: The Birth of Modern Chinese Radicalism.* Seattle: University of Washington Press.

Giersch, C. Pat (2006) *Asian Borderlands: The Transformation of Qing China's Yunnan Frontier.* Cambridge, MA: Harvard University Press.

Gillin, Donald G. (1964) "'Peasant Nationalism' in the History of Chinese Communism," *Journal of Asian Studies* 23 (2): 269–89.

Gillin, Donald G. (1967) *Warlord: Yen Hsi-shan in Shansi Province, 1911–1949.* Princeton: Princeton University Press.

Godley, Michael R. (1987) "Socialism with Chinese Characteristics: Sun Yatsen and the International Development of China," in *The Australian Journal of Chinese Affairs* 18 (July): 109–25.

Gold, Hal (1996) *Unit 731: Testimony.* North Clarendon: Tuttle Publishing.

Goldman, Merle, ed. (1977) *Modern Chinese Literature in the May Fourth Era.* Cambridge, MA: Harvard University Press.

Goldstein, Melvyn C., Ben Jiao, and Tanzen Lhundrup (2009) *On the Cultural Revolution in Tibet: The Nyemo Incident of 1969.* Berkeley: University California Press.

Goodman, David (1995) *Deng Xiaoping and the Chinese Revolution: A Political Biography.* London: Routledge.

Goodman, David and Gerald Segal (1994) *China Deconstructs: Politics, Trade and Regionalism.* London: Routledge.

Goodman, Jordan (1994) *Tobacco in History: The Cultures of Dependence*. London: Routledge.

Graham, S. Gerald (1978) *The China Station: War and Diplomacy, 1830–1860*. Oxford: Oxford University Press.

Grieder, Jerome B. (1970) *Hu Shih and the Chinese Renaissance: Liberalism in the Chinese Revolution, 1917–1937*. Cambridge, MA: Harvard University Press.

Gu, Edward X. (2001) *Who Was Mr Democracy? The May Fourth Discourse of Populist Democracy and the Radicalization of Chinese Intellectuals (1915–1922)*. Cambridge: Cambridge University Press.

Guo, Sujian and Baogang Guo, eds. (2008) *China in Search of a Harmonious Society*. Lanham: Rowman & Littlefield.

Guo, Yingjie and Baogang He (1999) "Reimagining the Chinese Nation: The "Zeng Guofan Phenomenon," *Modern China* 25: 142–70.

Guy, R. Kent (1987) *The Emperor's Four Treasuries: Scholars and the State in the Late Ch'ien-lung Era*. Cambridge, MA: Harvard East Asian Monographs.

Hail, William James (1927) *Tseng Kuo-fan and the Taiping Rebellion*. New Haven: Yale University Press.

Han, Suyin (1994) *Eldest Son: Zhou Enlai and the Making of Modern China, 1898–1976*. New York: Hill & Wang.

Hanes, Travis III, and Frank Sanello (2004) *The Opium Wars: The Addiction of One Empire and the Corruption of Another*. Napierville: Sourcebooks.

Harris, Sheldon H. (1994) *Factories of Death: Japanese Biological Warfare 1932–45 and the American Cover-Up*. London: Routledge.

Harrison, James P. (1972) *The Long March to Power: A History of the Chinese Communist Party, 1921–72*. New York: Praeger.

Hastings, Max (1987) *The Korean War*. New York: Simon & Schuster.

Hemmel, Vibeke and Pia Sindbjerg (1984) *Women in Rural China: Policy towards Women before and after the Cultural Revolution*. London: Curzon Press.

Herman, John R. (2007) *Amid the Clouds and Mist: China's Colonization of Guizhou, 1200–1700*. Cambridge, MA: Harvard University Press.

Herzstein, Robert Edwin (2005) *Henry R. Luce, Time, and the American Crusade in Asia*. New York: Cambridge University Press.

Hevia, James Louis (1995) *Cherishing Men from Afar: Qing Guest Ritual and the Macartney Embassy of 1793*. Durham: Duke University Press.

Hevia, James Louis (2003) *English Lessons: The Pedogogy of Imperialism in Nineteenth-Century China*. Durham: Duke University Press.

Hinton, William (1972) *Turning Point in China: An Essay on the Cultural Revolution*. New York: Monthly Review Press.

Ho, Ping-ti (1959) *Studies on the Population of China, 1368–1953*. Cambridge, MA: Harvard University Press.

Hoe, Susanna and Derek Roebuck (1999) *The Taking of Hong Kong: Charles and Clara Elliot in China Waters*. London: Routledge.

Horner, Charles (2009) *Rising China & Its Postmodern Fate: Memories of Empire in a New Global Context*. Atlanta: University of Georgia Press.

Hsiao, Kung-chuan (1975) *A Modern China and a New World: K'ang Yu-wei, Reformer and Utopian*, 1858–1927. Seattle: University of Washington Press.

Hsiung, James Chieh and Steven I. Levine (1992) *China's Bitter Victory: The War with Japan, 1937–1945*. Armonk: M.E. Sharpe.

Hsü, Immanuel Chung-yüeh (1965) *The Ili Crisis: A Study of Sino-Russian Diplomacy, 1871–1881*. Oxford: Clarendon Press.

Hsüeh, Chün-tu (1961) *Huang Hsing and the Chinese Revolution*. Stanford: Stanford University Press.

Hsüeh, Chün-tu (1982) *China's Foreign Relations: New Perspectives*. New York: Praeger.

Hu, Shih (1933) "The Chinese Renaissance: Social Disintegration and Readjustment" from the Haskell Lectures (University of Chicago).

Huang, Pei (1974)*Autocracy at Work: A Study of the Yung-cheng Period, 1723–1735*. Bloomington: Indiana University Press.

Huang, Philip C. (1972) *Liang Ch'i-ch'ao and Modern Chinese Liberalism*. Seattle, University of Washington Press.

Hughes, Christopher R. and Gudrun Wacker (2003) *China and the Internet: Politics of the Digital Leap Forward*. London: Routledge.

Hummel, Arthur, ed. (1943–44) *Eminent Chinese of the Ch'ing Period*. Washington, DC: USGPO.

Hunter, W.C. (1965) (original publication 1882) *The Fan Kwae at Canton Before Treaty Days*. Taipei: Chengwen Publishing Co.

Inglis, Brian (1976) *The Opium War*. London: Hodder & Stoughton.

Iriye, Akira (1967) *Across the Pacific: An Inner History of American-East Asian Relations*. Chicago: Harcourt, Brace.

Iriye, Akira (1967) "Public Opinion and Foreign Policy," in A. Feuerwerker et al. (eds.), *Approaches to Modern Chinese History*. Berkeley: University of California Press, pp. 216–38.

Jansen, Marius B. (1970) *The Japanese and Sun Yat-sen*. Stanford: Stanford University Press.

Jen, Yu-wen (assistance of Adrienne Suddard) (1973) *The Taiping Revolution Movement*. New Haven: Yale University Press.

Ji, Chaozhu (2008) *The Man on Mao's Right: From Harvard Yard to Tiananmen Square, My Life Inside China's Foreign Ministry*. New York: Random House.

Ji, Zhaojin (2003) *A History of Modern Shanghai Banking: The Rise and Decline of China's Finance Capitalism*. Armonk: M.E. Sharpe.

Jin, Qiu (1999) *The Culture of Power: The Lin Biao Incident in the Cultural Revolution*. Stanford: Stanford University Press.

Johnson, Chalmers A. (1962) *Peasant Nationalism and Communist Power: The Emergence of Revolutionary China 1937–1945*. Stanford: Stanford University Press.

Johnston, Alastair I. (2008) *Social States: China in International Institutions, 1980–2000*. Princeton: Princeton University Press.

Judge, Joan (1996) *Print and Politics: 'Shibao' and the Culture of Reform in Late Qing China*. Stanford: Stanford University Press.

Kahn, Harold L. (1971) *Monarchy in the Emperor's Eyes: Image and Reality in the Ch'ien-lung Reign*. Cambridge, MA: Harvard University Press.

Kane, Penny (1988) *Famine in China, 1959–61: Demographic and Social Implications*. London: Macmillan.

Karl, Rebecca and Peter Zarrow, eds. (2002) *Rethinking the 1898 Reform Period : Political and Cultural Change in Late Qing China*. Cambridge, MA: Harvard University Asia Center.

Kaufman, Burton Ira (1999) *The Korean Conflict*. Westport: Greenwood Publishing Group.

Keulemans, Paize (2004) "Printing Storyteller's Performance: Publishing Martial-Arts Fiction for an Expanding Middlebrow Audience in the Late Nineteenth Century," *Twentieth-Century China* 29 (2) (April): 7–37.

Kuhn, Philip A. (1970) *Rebellion and Its Enemies in Late Imperial China: Militarization and Social Structure, 1796–1864*. Cambridge, MA: Harvard University Press.

Kuhn, Philip A. (1977) "Origins of the Taiping Vision: Cross-Cultural Dimensions of a Chinese Rebellion," *Comparative Studies in Society and History* 19 (3) (July 1977): 350–66.

Kuhn, Philip A. (1990) *Soulstealers: The Chinese Sorcery Scare of 1768*. Cambridge, MA: Harvard University Press.

Kuhn, Philip A. (2002) *Origins of the Modern Chinese State.* Stanford: Stanford University Press.

Kuhn, Philip A. (2006) "Why China Historians Should Study the Chinese Diaspora, and Vice-Versa," *Journal of Chinese Overseas* 2 (2): 163–72.

Kuhn, Philip A. (2008) *Chinese Among Others: Emigration in Modern Times.* Lanham: Rowman & Littlefield.

Kuhn, Robert Lawrence (2004) *The Man Who Changed China: The Life and Legacy of Jiang Zemin.* New York: Crown Publishers.

Kuo, P.C. (1935) *A Critical Study of the First Anglo-Chinese War with Documents.* Westport: Hyperion.

Kwong, Luke K.S. (1983) "Imperial Authority in Crisis: An Interpretation of the Coup d'État of 1861," *Modern Asian Studies* 17 (2): 221–38.

Kwong, Luke K.S. (1984) *Mosaic of the Hundred Days: Personalities, Politics, and Ideas of 1898.* Cambridge, MA: Harvard East Asian Monographs.

Laitinen, Kauko (1990) *Chinese Nationalism in the Late Qing Dynasty: Zhang Binglin as an Anti-Manchu Propagandist.* London: Curzon Press.

Lam, Willy Wo-Lap (2006) *Chinese Politics in the Hu Jintao Era: New Leaders, New Challenges.* Armonk: M.E. Sharpe.

Lan, Feng (2005) *Ezra Pound and Confucianism: Remaking Humanism in the Face of Modernity.* Toronto: University of Toronto Press.

Lardy, Nicholas R. (1998) *China's Unfinished Economic Revolution.* Washington, DC: Brookings Institution Press.

Large, Daniel (2008) "Beyond 'Dragon in the Bush': The Study of China–Africa Relations," *African Affairs* 107: 45–61.

Larsen, Kirk W (2008) *Tradition, Treaties, and Trade: Qing Imperialism and Chos&ocaron;n Korea, 1850–1910.* Cambridge, MA: Harvard University Asia Center.

Lary, Diana (1974) *Region and Nation: The Kwangxi Clique in Chinese Politics, 1925–1937.* Cambridge: Cambridge University Press.

Lary, Diana (1985) *Warlord Soldiers: Chinese Common Soldiers, 1911–1937.* Cambridge: Cambridge University Press.

Lary, Diana (2007) *China's Republic.* Cambridge: Cambridge University Press.

Latimer, Jon (2004) *Burma: The Forgotten War.* London: John Murray.

Lawrance, Alan (2004) *China since 1919: Revolution and Reform: A Sourcebook.* London: Routledge.

Lee, Ching Kwan and Guobin Yang (2007) *Re-envisioning the Chinese Revolution: The Politics and Poetics of Collective Memories in Reform China.* Stanford: Stanford University Press.

Lee, Hong Yung (1978) *The Politics of the Chinese Cultural Revolution: A Case Study.* Berkeley: University of California Press.

Lee, James and Wang Feng (1999) *One Quarter of Humanity: Malthusian Mythology and Chinese Realities, 1700– 2000.* Cambridge, MA: Harvard University Press.

Lee, James (2004) *The Political Economy of a Frontier: Southwest China, 1250–1850.* Cambridge, MA: Harvard East Asian Monographs.

Lee, Leo Ou-Fan, and Andrew J. Nathan (1987) "The Beginnings of Mass Culture: Journalism and Fiction in the Late Ch'ing and Beyond," in David G. Johnson, Andrew J. Nathan and Evelyn S. Rawski, eds., *Popular Culture in Late Imperial China.* Berkeley: University of California Press.

Lee, Leo Ou-fan, ed. (1985) *Lu Xun and his Legacy.* Berkeley: University of California Press.

Lee, Leo Ou-fan (1987) *Voices from the Iron House: A Study of Lu Xun.* Bloomington: Indiana University Press.

Leonard, Jane Kate (1996) *Controlling from Afar: The Daoguang Emperor's Management of the Grand Canal Crisis, 1824–1826*. Ann Arbor: Center for Chinese Studies, University of Michigan.

Leong, Sow-Theng (Tim Wright, ed.) (1997) *Migration and Ethnicity in Chinese History: Hakkas, Pengmin, and Their Neighbors*. Stanford: Stanford University Press.

Levenson, Joseph Richmond (1953) *Liang Ch'i-ch'ao and the Mind of Modern China*. Cambridge, MA: Harvard University Press.

Lewis, John W. (1969) "A Review of John K. Fairbank, ed., The Chinese World-Order," *American Political Science Review* 63: 549–51.

Li, Chien-nung (1956) (S.Y. Teng and Jeremy Ingalls, trans.), *The Political History of China, 1840–1928*. Stanford: Stanford University Press.

Li, Danke (2004) "Popular Culture in the Making of Anti-Imperialist and Nationalist Sentiments in Sichuan," *Modern China* 30 (4): 470–505.

Li, Xiaobing (2007) *A History of the Modern Chinese Army*. Lexington: University Press of Kentucky.

Li, En-han (1977) *China's Quest for Railway Autonomy, 1904–1911: A Study of the Chinese Railway-Rights Recovery Movement*. Singapore: Singapore University Press.

Li, Huaiyin (2009) *Village China under Socialism and Reform: A Micro History, 1948–2008*. Stanford: Stanford University Press.

Li, Lillian M. (1981) *China's Silk Trade: Traditional Industry in the Modern World, 1842–1937*. Cambridge, MA: Harvard East Asian Monographs.

Li, Lillian M. (2007) *Fighting Famine in North China: State, Market and Environmental Decline, 1690s–1990s*. Stanford: Stanford University Press.

Li, Lillian M., Alison Dray-Novey and Haili Kong (2008) *Beijing: From Imperial Capital to Olympic City*. New York: Palgrave Macmillan.

Li, Xiaobing, Allan R. Millett and Bin Yu, trans. and eds. (2001) *Mao's Generals Remember Korea*. Lawrence: University Press of Kansas.

Liao, Yiwu (2008) *The Corpse Walker: Real Life Stories: China from the Bottom*. New York: Pantheon Books.

Lieberthal, Kenneth (1995) *Governing China: From Revolution to Reform*. New York: W.W. Norton,

Lin, Man-houng (2006) *China Upside Down: Currency, Society, and Ideologies, 1808–1856*. Cambridge, MA: Harvard University Asia Center.

Lin, Yu-sheng (1979) *The Crisis of Chinese Consciousness: Radical Antitraditionalism in the May Fourth Era*. Madison: University of Wisconsin Press, 1979.

Lindley, August F. (1866) *Ti-ping Tien-kwo: The History of the Ti-ping Revolution, A Narrative of the Author's Personal Adventures*. London: Day & Son (Ltd), Lithographers & Publishers.

Link, Perry (1981) *Mandarin Ducks and Butterflies: Popular Fiction in Early Twentieth-Century Chinese Cities*. Berkeley: University of California Press.

Lipman, Jonathan N. and Stevan Harrell (1990) *Violence in China: Essays in Culture and Counterculture*. Albany: SUNY University Press.

Lipman, Jonathan N. (1984) "Ethnicity and Politics in Republican China: The Ma Family Warlords of Gansu," *Modern China* 10: 285–316.

Lipman, Jonathan N. (1997) *Familiar Strangers: A History of Muslims in Northwest China*. Seattle: University of Washington Press.

Little, Daniel (1992) *Understanding Peasant China Case Studies in the Philosophy of Social Science*. New Haven: Yale University Press.

Liu, Kwang-ching (1970), "The Confucian as Patriot and as Pragmatist: Li Hung-chang's Formative Years, 1823–1866," *Harvard Journal of Asiatic Studies* 30: 5–45.

Liu, Lydia He (2004) *The Clash of Empires: The Invention of China in Modern World Making*. Cambridge, MA: Harvard University Press.

Liu, Lydia He (1995) *Translingual Practice: Literature, National Culture, and Translated Modernity–China, 1900–1937.* Stanford: Stanford University Press.

Low, C. P. (1905) (2nd edition 1906) *Some Recollections of Captain Charles P. Low, commanding the Clipper Ships "Houqua," "Jacob Bell," "Samuel Russell" and "N. B. Palmer," in the China Trade, 1847–1873.* Boston: Geo. H. Ellis Co. (entire text available via Internet).

Lu, Xun (Gladys Yang, ed.) (1981) *The Complete Stories of Lu Xun.* Bloomington: Indiana University Press; Beijing: Foreign Languages Press.

Lu, Xun (1973) *Silent China: Selected Writings of Lu Xun,* trans. and ed. Gladys Yang. London & New York: Oxford University Press.

Lu, Xun (1990) *Diary of a Madman and Other Stories,* trans. and ed. William A. Lyell Honolulu: University of Hawaii Press.

Lubman, Stanley B. (2002) *Bird in a Cage: Legal Reform in China after Mao.* Stanford: Stanford University Press.

Lum, Yansheng Ma and Raymond Mun Kong Lum (1999) *Sun Yat-sen in Hawai'i: Activities and Supporters.* Honolulu: University of Hawaii Press.

Luthi, Lorenz M. (2008) *The Sino-Soviet Split: Cold War in the Communist World.* Princeton : Princeton University Press.

Ma, Jisen (2004) *The Cultural Revolution in the Foreign Ministry of China.* Hong Kong: Chinese University Press.

McKeown, Adam M. (2008) *Melancholy Order: Asian Migration and the Globalization of Borders.* New York: Columbia University Press.

MacFarquhar, Roderick (1966) *China under Mao: Politics Takes Command.* Cambridge: Massachusetts Institute of Technology Press.

MacFarquhar, Roderick (1972) *Sino-American Relations, 1949–1971.* New York: Praeger.

MacFarquhar, Roderick (1997) *The Politics of China: The Eras of Mao and Deng.* Cambridge: Cambridge University Press.

MacFarquhar, Roderick (1983–99) *The Origins of the Cultural Revolution,* 3 vols. New York: Columbia University Press.

MacFarquhar, Roderick and Michael Schoenhals (2006) *Mao's Last Revolution.* Cambridge, MA: Harvard University Press.

MacKinnon, Stephen R., Diana Lary and Ezra F. Vogel, eds. (2007) *China at War: Regions of China, 1937–1945.* Stanford: Stanford University Press.

McMahon, Daniel (2005) "The Yuelu Academy and Hunan's Nineteenth-Century Turn Toward Statecraft," *Late Imperial China* 26 (1): 72–109.

McMahon, Keith (2002) *The Fall of the God of Money: Opium Smoking in Nineteenth-Century China.* Lanham: Rowman & Littlefield.

MacMillan, Margaret (2007) *Nixon and Mao: The Week that Changed the World.* New York: Random House.

Maitan, Livio (1976) *Party, Army and Masses in China: A Marxist Interpretation of the Cultural Revolution and its Aftermath,* trans. G. Benton and M. Collitti. London: Verso/NLB.

Mancall, Mark (1971) *Russia and China: Their Diplomatic Relations to 1728.* Cambridge, MA: Harvard University Press.

Mao, Zedong (1989) *The Secret Speeches of Chairman Mao: From the Hundred Flowers to the Great Leap Forward,* ed. Roderick MacFarquhar, Timothy Cheek, Eugene Wu, Merle Goldman, Benjamin I. Schwartz R. Macfarquhar, T. Cheek and E. Wu. Cambridge, MA: Harvard University Council on East Asian Studies.

Mao, Zedong (1989) *The Secret Speeches of Chairman Mao: From the Hundred Flowers to the Great Leap Forward.* Cambridge, MA: Harvard University Council on East Asian Studies.

Marchetti, Gina (2006) *From Tian'anmen to Times Square: Transnational China and the Chinese Diaspora on Global Screens, 1989–1997.* Philadelphia: Temple University Press.

Marks, Robert (1984) *Rural Revolution in South China: Peasants and the Making of History in Haifeng County, 1570–1930*. Madison: University of Wisconsin Press.

Marks, Robert (1998) *Tigers, Rice, Silk, and Silt: Environment and Economy in Late Imperial South China*. Cambridge: Cambridge University Press.

Mayhew, Nicholas (1999) *Sterling: The Rise and Fall of a Currency*. London: Penguin Press.

Meagher, Arnold (2008) *The Coolie Trade: The Traffic in Chinese Laborers to Latin America, 1847–1874*. Bloomington: Xlibris.

Meisner, Maurice (1967) *Li Ta-Chao and the Origins of Chinese Marxism*. Cambridge, MA: Harvard University Press.

Michael, Franz (1971) *The Taiping Rebellion: History and Documents*, 3 vols. Seattle: University of Washington Press.

Michel, Serge and Michel Beuret (2009) *China Safari: On the Trail of Beijing's Expansion in Africa*. New York: Nation Books.

Miles, Steven B. (2004) "Celebrating the Yu Fan Shrine: Literati Networks and Local Identity in Early Nineteenth-Century Guangzhou," *Late Imperial China* 25 (2) (December): 33–73.

Millward, James A. (1998) *Beyond the Pass: Economy, Ethnicity, and Empire in Qing Central Asia, 1759–1864*. Stanford: Stanford University Press.

Millward, James A., Ruth W. Dunnell, Mark C. Elliott and Philippe Forêt, eds. (2004) *New Qing Imperial History: The Making of Inner Asian Empire at Qing Chengde*. London: RoutledgeCurzon.

Min, Tuki (1990) *National Polity and Local Power*. Cambridge, MA: Harvard University Press.

Morse, Hosea Ballou (1926) *Chronicles of the East India Company Trading to China*, 4 vols. Oxford: Clarendon Press.

Munn, Christopher (2000) "Hong Kong Opium Revenue," in Brook and Wakabayashi, eds., *Opium Regimes*, pp. 105–26.

Murray, Dian (1987) *Pirates of the South China Coast, 1790–1810*. Stanford: Stanford University Press.

Murray, Dian (1994) *The Origins of the Tiandihui: The Chinese Triads in Legend and History*. Stanford: Stanford University Press.

Myers, Ramon and Peattie, Mark, eds. (1987) *The Japanese Colonial Empire, 1895–1945*. Princeton: Princeton University Press.

Nakamura Tetsuo (1984) "The Influence of Kemuyama Sentarō's Modern Anarchism on the Chinese Revolutionary Movement," in: Etō, Shinkichi and Harold Z. Schiffrin, eds., *The 1911 Revolution in China – Interpretive Essays*. Tokyo: University of Tokyo Press, 1984: pp. 95–105.

Naquin, Susan (1976) *Millenarian Rebellion in China: The Eight Trigrams Uprising of 1813*. New Haven: Yale University Press.

Naquin, Susan (1981) *Shantung Rebellion: The Wang Lun Rebellon of 1774*. New Haven: Yale University Press.

Naquin, Susan (2000) *Peking: Temples and City Life, 1400–1900*. Berkeley: University of California Press.

Naquin, Susan and Evelyn S. Rawski (1989) *Chinese Society in the Eighteenth Century*. New Haven: Yale University Press.

Nathan, Andrew J. and Robert S. Ross (1998) *The Great Wall and the Empty Fortress: China's Search for Security*. New York: W.W. Norton.

Nathan, Andrew J. (1986) *Chinese Democracy*. Berkeley: University of California Press.

Nathan, Andrew J. (1976) *Peking Politics, 1918–1923: Factionalism and the Failure of Constitutionalism*. Berkeley: University of California Press.

Naughton, Barry, (1996) *Growing Out of the Plan: Chinese Economic Reform, 1978–1993*. New York and Cambridge: Cambridge University Press.

Naughton, Barry and Dali L. Yang, eds. (2004) *Holding China Together: Diversity and National Integration in the Post-Deng Era*. New York: Cambridge University Press.

Needham, Joseph and Peter J. Golas (1999) *Science and Civilization in China*, vol. 13. Cambridge: Cambridge University Press.

Ni, Shawn and Pham Hoang Van (2006) "High Corruption Income in Ming and Qing China," *Journal of Development Economics* 81: 316–36.

North, Robert Carver (1963) *Moscow and Chinese Communists*. Stanford: Stanford University Press.

Oi, Jean C. and Andrew George Walder (1999) *Property Rights and Economic Reform in China*. Stanford: Stanford University Press.

Oksenberg, Michel, Lawrence R. Sullivan, Marc Lambert and Qiao Li (1990) *Beijing Spring, 1989: Confrontation and Conflict: The Basic Documents*. Armonk: M.E. Sharpe.

Ownby, David, and Mary Somers Heidhues (1993) *"Secret Societies" Reconsidered: Perspectives on the Social History of Modern South China and Southeast Asia*. Armonk: M.E. Sharpe.

Paine, S.C.M (2003) *The Sino-Japanese War of 1894–1895: Perception, Power, and Primacy*. Cambridge: Cambridge University Press.

Pan, Philip P. (2008) *Out of Mao's Shadow: The Struggle for the Soul of a New China*. New York: Simon & Schuster.

Parreñas, Rachel Salazar, and Lok C. D. Siu (2007) *Asian Diasporas: New Formations, New Conceptions*. Stanford: Stanford University Press.

Peerenboom, Randall P. (2002) *China's Long March toward Rule of Law*. Cambridge: Cambridge University Press.

Pei, Minxin (2008) *China's Trapped Transition: The Limits of Development Autocracy*. Cambridge, MA: Harvard University Press.

Pepper, Suzanne (2004) "The Political Odyssey of an Intellectual Construct: Peasant Nationalism and the Study of China's Revolutionary History – A Review Essay," *The Journal of Asian Studies* 63 (1) (February): 105–25.

Perdue, Peter C. (1987) *Exhausting the Earth: State and Peasant in Hunan*. Cambridge, MA: Harvard University Press.

Perdue, Peter C. (1996) "Military Mobilization in Seventeenth and Eighteenth-Century China, Russia, and Mongolia," *Modern Asian Studies* 30: 757–93.

Perdue, Peter C. (2005) *China Marches West: The Qing Conquest of Central Eurasia*. New York: Belknap Press of Harvard University Press.

Perry, Elizabeth (1976) "Worshipers and Warriors: White Lotus Influence on the Nian Rebellion," *Modern China* 2 (1) (January): 4–22.

Perry, Elizabeth J. (1980) *Rebels and Revolutionaries in North China 1845–1945*. Stanford: Stanford University Press.

Perry, Elizabeth J. and Li Xun (1997) *Proletarian Power: Shanghai in the Cultural Revolution*. Boulder: Westview Press.

Peyrefitte, Alain (1992) (Jon Rothschild, trans.) *The Immobile Empire: The Great Collision of East and West and the Astonishing History of Britain's Grand, Ill-fated Expedition to open China to Western Trade*. New York: Alfred Knopf.

Platt, Steven R. (2007) *Provincial Patriots: The Hunanese and Modern China*. Cambridge, MA: Harvard University Press.

Polachek, James M. (1992) *The Inner Opium War*. Cambridge, MA: Council on East Asian Studies, Harvard University.

Pomeranz, Kenneth (2000) *The Great Divergence: China, Europe, and the Making of the Modern World Economy*. Princeton: Princeton University Press.

Pomeranz, Kenneth (2005) "Standards of Living in Eighteenth Century China: Regional Differences, Temporal Trends, and Incomplete Evidence," in Allen et al., eds., *Living Standards in the Past*, pp. 23–54.

Pomeranz, Kenneth (2009) "The Great Himalayan Watershed: Agrarian Crisis, Mega-Dams and the Environment," in *New Left Review* 58 (July–August). Online at www.newleftreview.org/?page=article&view=2788.

Pound, Ezra (1969) *Confucius*. New York: New Directions Publishing.

Pye, Lucian W. (1971) *Warlord Politics: Conflict and Coalition in the Modernization of Republican China*. New York: Praeger.

Qi, Hantang (2004) "Deng Xiaoping's Ideas on Chinese Township and Village Enterprises," *China Report* 40: 77–90.

Qian, Zhaoming, ed. (2003) *Ezra Pound and China*. Ann Arbor: University of Michigan Press.

Radchenko, Sergey (2009) *Two Suns in the Heavens: The Sino-Soviet Struggle for Supremacy, 1962–1967*. Washington, DC: Woodrow Wilson Center.

Raine, Sarah (2009) *China's African Challenges*. Abingdon: Routledge for the International Institute for Strategic Studies.

Rankin, Mary Backus (1982) " 'Public Opinion' and Political Power: Qingyi in Late Nineteenth Century China," *Journal of Asian Studies* 41 (3): 453–84.

Rankin, Mary Backus (2002) "Nationalistic Contestation and Mobilization Politics: Practice and Rhetoric of Railway-Rights Recovery at the End of the Qing," *Modern China* 28 (3) (July): 315–61.

Rawlinson, John L. (1967) *China's Struggle for Naval Development, 1839–1895*. Cambridge, MA: Harvard University Press.

Rawski, Evelyn S. (1979) *Education and Popular Literacy in Ch'ing China*. Ann Arbor: University of Michigan Press.

Rawski, Evelyn S. (1998) *The Last Emperors; A Social History of Qing Imperial Institutions*. Berkeley: University of California Press.

Reed, Christopher A. (2004) *Gutenberg in Shanghai: Chinese Print Capitalism, 1876–1937*. Vancouver: University of British Columbia Press; Honolulu: University of Hawaii Press.

Reilly, Thomas H. (2004) *The Taiping Heavenly Kingdom: Rebellion and the Blasphemy of Empire*. Seattle: University of Washington Press.

Reynolds, Douglas R. ed. and trans. (1995) *China, 1895–1912: State-sponsored Reforms and China's Late-Qing Revolution: Selected Essays from Zhongguo Jindai Shi (Modern Chinese History, 1840–1919)*. Armonk: M.E. Sharpe.

Rhoads, Edward J.M. (2001) *Manchus and Han: Ethnic Relations and Political Power in Late Qing and Early Republican China, 1861–1928*. Seattle: University of Washington Press.

Rhoads, Edward J.M. (2005) "In the Shadow of Yung Wing," *Pacific Historical Review* 74 (1): 19–58.

Roux, Alain (2006) "Lucien Bianco, Jacqueries et révolution dans la Chine du XXe siècle," *China Perspectives*: 64; online at www.chinaperspectives.revues.org/document612.html (December 21, 2008).

Rowe, William T. (2001) *Saving the World: Chen Hongmou and Elite Consciousness in Eighteenth-Century China*. Stanford: Stanford University Press.

Rowe, William T. (2007) *Crimson Rain: Seven Centuries of Violence in a Chinese County*. Stanford: Stanford University Press.

Rowe, William T. (1989) *Hankow: Conflict and Community in a Chinese City, 1796–1895*. Stanford: Stanford University Press.

Rummel, R.J. (2007) *China's Bloody Century: Genocide and Mass Murder Since 1900*. New Brunswick: Transaction Publishers.

Saich, Tony and Bingzhang Yang (1996) *The Rise to Power of the Chinese Communist Party: Documents and Analysis.* Armonk: M.E. Sharpe.

Salisbury, Harrison (1987) *The Long March: The Untold Story.* New York: McGraw-Hill.

Schaller, Michael (1979) *The US Crusade in China, 1938–1945.* New York: Columbia University Press.

Schell, Orville (1995) *Mandate of Heaven: The Legacy of Tiananmen Square and the Next Generaton of China's Leaders.* New York: Simon & Schuster.

Schiffrin, Howard Z. (1980) *Sun Yat-sen, Reluctant Revolutionary.* New York: Little, Brown & Company,

Schoenhals, Michael, ed. (1996) *China's Cultural Revolution, 1966–1969: Not a Dinner Party.* Armonk: M.E. Sharpe.

Schram, Stuart R. (1967) *Mao Tse-tung.* New York: Penguin.

Schram, Stuart R. (1989) *The Thought of Mao Tse-tung.* Cambridge: Cambridge University Press.

Schrecker, John E. (2004) *The Chinese Revolution in Historical Perspective* (2nd edn.). Westport: Greenwood Publishing Group.

Schwarcz, Vera (1990) *The Chinese Enlightenment: Intellectuals and the Legacy of the May Fourth Movement.* Berkeley: University of California Press.

Schwartz, Benjamin I. (1958) *Chinese Communism and the Rise of Mao.* Cambridge, MA: Harvard University Press.

Schoppa, R. Keith (1998) *Blood Road: The Mystery of Shen Dingyi in Revolutionary China.* Berkeley: University of California Press.

Schoppa, R. Keith (2002) *Song Full of Tears: Nine Centuries of Chinese Life at Xiang Lake* (revised edition). Boulder: Westview Press.

Scott, James C. (1976) *The Moral Economy of the Peasant: Rebellion and Subsistence in Southeast Asia.* New Haven.: Yale University Press.

Selden, Mark (1971) *The Yenan Way in Revolutionary China.* Cambridge, MA: Harvard University Press.

Semanov, V.I. (1980) *Lu Hsün and his Predecessors*, trans. and ed. Charles J. Alber. White Plains: M.E. Sharpe.

Seymour, James D. and Richard Anderson (1999) *New Ghosts, Old Ghosts: Prisons and Labor Reform Camps in China.* Armonk: M.E. Sharpe.

Shapiro, Judith (2001) *Mao's War against Nature: Politics and the Environment in Revolutionary China.* Cambridge: Cambridge University Press.

Sheridan, James (1977) *China in Disintegration: The Republican Era in Chinese History, 1912–1949.* New York: Simon & Schuster.

Sheridan, James (1966) *Chinese Warlord: The Career of Feng Yu-hsiang.* Stanford: Stanford University Press.

Shi, Shumei (2001) *The Lure of the Modern: Writing Modernism in Semicolonial China, 1917–1937.* Berkeley: University of California Press.

Shimada, Kenji (1990) *Pioneer of the Chinese Revolution: Zhang Binglin and Confucianism*, ed. J. Fogel. Stanford: Stanford University Press.

Shirk, Susan L. (2007) *China: Fragile Superpower.* Oxford: Oxford University Press.

Shiu, Victor Chiang Cheng (2009) "Modern War on an Ancient Battlefield: The Diffusion of American Military Technology and Ideas in the Chinese Civil War, 1946–1949," *Modern China* 35 (1): 38–64.

Short, Philip (1999) *Mao: A Life.* New York: Henry Holt.

Shue, Vivienne (1980) *Peasant China in Transition: The Dynamics of Development toward Socialism, 1949–1956.* Berkeley: University of California Press.

Shue, Vivienne (1988) *The Reach of the State: Sketches of the Chinese Body Politic.* Stanford: Stanford University Press.

Shum, Kui-Kwong (1982) *Zhu De (Chu Teh)*. Queensland: University of Queensland Press.

Sinn, Elizabeth (1998) "Fugitive in Paradise: Wang Tao and Cultural Transformation in Late Nineteenth-Century Hong Kong," *Late Imperial China* 19 (1) (June): 56–81.

Skinner, G. William, ed. (1977) *The City in Late Imperial China*. Stanford, CA: Stanford University Press.

Skinner, G. William (1987) "Sichuan's Population in the Nineteenth Century: Lessons from Disaggregated Data," *Late Imperial China* 8 (1) (June): 1–79.

Smith, Jonathan Z. (1972) "The Wobbling Pivot," *The Journal of Religion* 52 (2) (April): 134–49.

Smith, Stephen Anthony (2000) *A Road is Made: Communism in Shanghai, 1920–1927*. Honolulu: University of Hawaii Press.

Smith, Stephen Anthony (2002) *Like Cattle and Horses: Labor and Nationalism in Shanghai, 1895–1927*. Raleigh: Duke University Press.

Snow, Philip (1988) *The Star Raft: China's Encounter with Africa*. London: Weidenfeld & Nicolson.

Snyder, Scott (2009) *China's Rise and the Two Koreas: Politics, Economics, Security*. Boulder: Lynne Rienner Publishers.

Spector, Stanley (1964) *Li Hung-chang and the Huai Army: A Study in Nineteenth-Century Chinese Regionalism*. Seattle: University of Washington Press.

Spence, Jonathan D. (1966) *Ts'ao Yin and the K'ang-hsi Emperor: Bondservant and Master*. New Haven: Yale University Press.

Spence, Jonathan D. (1975) "Opium Smoking in Ch'ing China," in Frederic Wakeman and Carolyn Grant, eds., *Conflict and Control in Late Imperial China*, Berkeley: University of California Press.

Spence, Jonathan D. (1981) *The Gate of Heavenly Peace: The Chinese and their Revolution, 1895–1980*. New York: Viking Press.

Spence, Jonathan D. (1996). *God's Chinese Son: The Taiping Heavenly Kingdom of Hong Xiuquan*. New York: W.W. Norton.

Spence, Jonathan D. (1999) *Mao Zedong*. New York: Viking.

Spence, Jonathan D. (2001) *Treason by the Book*. New York: Viking.

Starr, Frederick, ed. (2004) *Xinjiang: China's Muslim Borderland*. Armonk: M.E. Sharpe.

Strand, David (1989). *Rickshaw Beijing: City People and Politics in the 1920s*. Berkeley: University of California Press.

Strauss, Julia C. (2007) *The History of the PRC (1949–1976)*. Cambridge: Cambridge University Press.

Stueck, William Whitney (2001) *The Korean War: An International History*. Princeton: Princeton University Press.

Stueck, William Whitney (2004) *The Korean War in World History*. Lexington: University Press of Kentucky.

Suettinger, Robert (2003) *Beyond Tiananmen: The Politics of U.S.-China Relations, 1989–2000*. Washington, DC: Brookings Institution Press.

Szonyi, Michael (1997) "The Illusion of Standardizing the Gods: The Cult of the Five Emperors in Late Imperial China," *Journal of Asian Studies* 56 (1) (February): 113–35.

Szonyi, Michael (2002) *Practicing Kinship: Lineage and Descent in Late Imperial China*. Stanford: Stanford University Press.

Szonyi, Michael (2008) *Cold War Island: Quemoy on the Front Line*. Cambridge: Cambridge University Press.

Tang, Tsou (1963) *America's Failure in China, 1941–50*. Chicago: University of Chicago Press.

Tang, Xiaobing (1996) *Global Space and Nationalist Discourse of Modernity: The Historical Thinking of Liang Qichao*. Stanford: Stanford University Press.

Taylor, Jay (2009) *The Generalissimo: Chiang Kai-shek and the Struggle for Modern China*. Cambridge, MA: Harvard University Press/Belknap Press.

Teng, Ssu-yü (1970–71) "Hung Jen-kan, Prime Minister of the Taiping Kingdom and His Modernization Plans," *United College Journal* 8: 87–96.

Teng, Ssu-yü (1971) *The Taiping Rebellion and the Western Powers: A Comprehensive Survey*. Oxford: Clarendon Press.

Teng, Yuan Chung (1963) "Reverend Issachar Jacox Roberts and the Taiping Rebellion," *The Journal of Asian Studies* 23 (1) (November): 55–67.

Thaxton, Ralph (1983) *China Turned Rightside Up: Revolutionary Legitimacy in the Peasant World*. New Haven: Yale University Press.

Thaxton, Ralph (1997) *Salt of the Earth: The Political Origins of Peasant Protest and Communist Revolution in China*. Berkeley: University of California Press.

Thaxton, Ralph A. Jr. (2008) *Catastrophe and Contention in Rural China: Mao's Great Leap Forward Famine and the Origins of Righteous Resistance in Da Fo Village*. Boston: Cambridge Studies in Contentious Politics.

Thompson, Roger R. (1995) *China's Local Councils in the Age of Constitutional Reform, 1898–1911*. Cambridge, MA: Harvard University Asia Center.

Thornton, Patricia M. (2007) *Disciplining the State: Virtue, Violence, and State-Making in Modern China*. Cambridge, MA: Harvard University Asia Center.

Tien, Hung-mao and Yunhan Zhu (2000) *China under Jiang Zemin*. Boulder: Lynne Rienner Publishers.

Teiwes, Frederick C. (1999) *China's Road to Disaster: Mao, Central Politicians, and Provincial Leaders in the Unfolding of the Great Leap Forward, 1955–1959*. Armonk: M.E. Sharpe.

Tiewes, Frederick C. and Warren Sun (2007) *The End of the Maoist Era: Chinese Politics during the Twilight of the Cultural Revolution, 1972–1976*. Armonk: M.E. Sharpe.

Tiewes, Frederick C. and Warren Sun (1996) *The Tragedy of Lin Biao: Riding the Tiger During the Cultural Revolution, 1966–1971*. Honolulu: University of Hawaii Press.

Trocki, Carl A. (1999) *Opium, Empire and the Global Political Economy: A Study of the Asian Opium Trade, 1750–1950*. London: Routledge.

Tsai, Lily L. (2007) *Accountability Without Democracy: Solidarity Groups and Public Goods Provision in Rural China*. Cambridge: Cambridge University Press.

Tsang, Steve Yui-Sang (2004) *A Modern History of Hong Kong*. London: I.B. Tauris.

Tuchman, Barbara W. (1971) *Stillwell and the American Experience in China, 1911–45*. New York: The MacMillan Company.

Tuck, Patrick J.N., Earl Hampton Pritchard and Hosea Ballou Morse (1926) *Britain and the China Trade*. Oxford: Clarendon Press.

Tucker, Nancy Bernkopf (2009) *Strait Talk: United States-Taiwan Relations and the Crisis with China*. Cambridge, MA: Harvard University Press.

Tyler, Patrick (2000) *A Great Wall: Six Presidents and China: An Investigative History*. New York: Public Affairs.

Van de Ven, Hans J. (2003) *War and Nationalism in China, 1925–1945*. London: Routledge.

Van Ness, Peter (1970) *Revolution and Chinese Foreign Policy; Peking's Support for Wars of National Liberation*. Berkeley, University of California Press.

Vermeer, Eduard B., Frank N. Pieke and Woei Lien Chong (1997) *Cooperative and Collective in China's Rural Development: Between State and Private Interests*. Armonk: M.E. Sharpe.

von Glahn, Richard (2007) "Foreign Silver Coins in the Market Culture of Nineteenth Century China," *International Journal of Asian Studies* 4 (1): 51–78.

von Glahn, Richard (1996) *Fountain of Fortune: Money and Monetary Policy in China, 1000–1700*. Berkeley: University of California Press.

Wagner, Rudolf G. (1999) "The Shenbao in Crisis: The International Environment and the Conflict Between Guo Songtao and the Shenbao," *Late Imperial China* 20 (1) (June): 107–43.

Wagner, Rudolf G. (2001) "The Early Chinese Newspapers and the Chinese Public Sphere," *European Journal of East Asian Studies* 1: 1–34.

Wakabayashi, Bob Tadashi (2007) *The Nanking Atrocity, 1937–1938: Complicating the Picture.* Oxford: Berghahn Books.

Wakeman, Frederick E. Jr. (1985) *The Great Enterprise: The Manchu Reconstruction of Imperial Order in Seventeenth-Century China*, 2 vols. Berkeley: University of California Press.

Wakeman, Frederic E. Jr. (1993) "The Civil Society and Public Sphere Debate: Western Reflections on Chinese Political Culture," *Modern China* 19 (2) (April): 108–38.

Wakeman, Frederic E. Jr. (1995) *Policing Shanghai, 1927–1937.* Berkeley: University of California Press.

Wakeman, Frederic E. Jr. (2001) "Boundaries of the Public Sphere in Ming and Qing China," in *Daedalus* 127 (1998); revised as "Boundaries of the Public Sphere in Ming and Qing China," in Eisenstadt, Shmuel Noah et al., eds., *Public Spheres & Collective Identities.* New Brunswick: Transaction Publishers.

Waldron, Arthur (2003) *From War to Nationalism: China's Turning Point, 1924–1925.* New York: Cambridge University Press.

Waley, Arthur, (1959) *The Opium War through Chinese Eyes.* London: George Allen & Unwin and Macmillan.

Wang, Dong (2002) *China's Unequal Treaties: Narrating National History.* Lanham: Lexington Books.

Wang, Gungwu (2002) *The Chinese Overseas: From Earthbound China to the Quest for Autonomy.* Cambridge, MA: Harvard University Press.

Wang, Jessica Ching-Sze (2007) *John Dewey in China: To Teach and to Learn.* Albany: State University of New York Press.

Wang, Yeh-Chien (1973) *Land Taxation in Imperial China, 1750–1911.* Cambridge, MA: Harvard University Press.

Wasserstrom, Jeffrey N. and Elizabeth J. Perry, eds. (1994) *Popular Protest and Political Culture in Modern China: Learning from 1989.* Boulder: Westview Press.

Weller, Robert Paul (2006) *Discovering Nature: Globalization and Environmental Culture in China and Taiwan.* New York: Cambridge University Press.

Whitbeck, Judith (1983) "Kung Tzu-chen and the Redirection of Literati Commitment in Early Nineteenth-Century China," *Ch'ing-shi wen-t'i* 4 (10) (December): 1–32.

Whiting, Allen S. (1960) *China Crosses the Yalu: The Decision to Enter the Korean War.* New York, Macmillan.

Wiemer, Calla (2004) "The Economy of Xinjiang," in S. Frederick Starr, ed., *Xinjiang: China's Muslim Borderland*, pp. 163–89.

Will, Pierre-Étienne and R. Bin Wong with James Lee, Jean Oi and Peter Perdue (1991) *Nourish the People: The State Civilian Granary System in China, 1650–1850.* Ann Arbor: Center for Chinese Studies.

Williams, Peter (1989) *Unit 731: Japan's Secret Biological Warfare in World War II.* New York: Free Press.

Williams, S. Wells (1856) *A Chinese Commercial Guide, Consisting of a Collection of Details and Regulations Respecting Foreign Trade with China, Sailing Directions, Tables, &c.* Canton: Printed at the Office of the Chinese Repository.

Wills, John E. Jr. (1974) *Pepper, Guns, and Parleys: The Dutch East India Company and China, 1662–1681.* Cambridge, MA: Harvard East Asian Series.

Wishnick, Elizabeth (2009) *Russia, China, and the United States in Central Asia: Prospects for Great Power Competition and Cooperation in the Shadow of the Georgian Crisis.* Carlisle Barracks: Strategic Studies Institute, U.S. Army War College.

Withers, John Lovelle II (1983) "The Heavenly Capital: Nanjing Under the Taiping, 1853–1864," Yale University PhD dissertation.

Wong, John W. (1998) *Deadly Dreams: Opium, Imperialism, and the Arrow War (1856–1860) in China*. Cambridge: Cambridge University Press.

Wong, R. Bin (1982) "Food Riots in the Qing Dynasty," *The Journal of Asian Studies* 41 (4) (August): 767–88.

Wong, R. Bin (1998) *China Transformed: Historical Change and the Limits of European Experience*. Ithaca: Cornell University Press.

Wong, Young-tsu (1989) *Search for Modern Nationalism: Zhang Binglin and Revolutionary China, 1869–1936*. Hongkong: Oxford University Press.

Worthing, Peter M. (2007) *A Military History of Modern China: From the Manchu Conquest to Tian'anmen Square*. Westport: Praeger Security International.

Wu, Hung (2005) *Remaking Beijing: Tiananmen Square and the Creation of a Political Space*. London: Reaktion Books.

Wyman, Judith (2000) "Opium and the State in Late-Qing Sichuan," in Brook and Wakabayashi, eds., *Opium Regimes*, pp. 212–27.

Xia, Yafeng (2006) *Negotiating with the Enemy: US–China Talks during the Cold War, 1949–1972*. Bloomington: Indiana University Press.

Xu, Hongxin (2003) "Growth of the Yellow River Delta over the Past 800 Years, as Influenced by Human Activities," in *Geografiska Annaler* 85A (1): 21–30.

Xu, Yamin (2008) "Urban Communities, State, Spatial Order, and Modernity: Studies of Imperial and Republican Beijing in Perspective," *China Review International* 15 (1) (November): 1–38.

Xu, Guoqi (2005) *China and the Great War: China's Pursuit of a New National Identity and Internationalization*. Cambridge and New York: Cambridge University Press.

Yang, Dali L. (1996) *Calamity and Reform in China: State, Rural Society, and Institutional Change since the Great Leap Famine*. Stanford: Stanford University Press.

Yang, Daqing (1999) "Convergence or Divergence? Recent Historical Writings on the Rape of Nanjing," *American Historical Review* 104 (3) (June): 842–65.

Yeung, Yue-man and Yun-wing Sung, eds. (1996) *Shanghai: Transformation and Modernization under China's Open Policy*. Hong Kong: Chinese University Press.

Ying Ruocheng and Claire Conceison (2008) *Voices Carry: Behind Bars and Backstage during China's Revolution and Reform*. Lanham: Rowman & Littlefield.

Yung, Wing (1909) *My Life in China and America*. New York: Henry Holt.

Zarrow, Peter (1990) *Anarchism and Chinese Political Culture*. New York: Columbia University Press.

Zarrow, Peter (2005) *China in War and Revolution, 1895–1949*. London: Routledge.

Zelin, Madeleine (1984) *The Magistrate's Tael: Rationalizing Fiscal Reform in Eighteenth Century China*. Berkeley: University of California Press.

Zeng, Baosun (2002) *Confucian Feminist: Memoirs of Zeng Baosun (1893–1978)*, trans. and ed. Thomas L. Kennedy. Darby PA: DIANE Publishing.

Zeng, Zida (1998) "A Chinese View of the Educational Ideas of John Dewey," *Interchange* 19 (3–4) (September): 85–91.

Zhang, Liang, Andrew J. Nathan, Perry Link and Orville Schell (2002) *The Tiananmen Papers: The Chinese Leadership's Decision to Use Force Against Their Own People In Their Own Words*. New York: PublicAffairs.

Zhang, Kaiyuan, ed. (2001) *Eyewitnesses to Massacre*. Armonk: M.E. Sharpe/East Gate Books.

Zhang, Sheldon (2008) *Chinese Human Smuggling Operations: Families, Social Networks, and Cultural Imperatives*. Stanford: Stanford University Press.

Zhang, Shuguang (1995) *Mao's Military Romanticism: China and the Korean War, 1950–1953*. Lawrence: University Press of Kansas.

Zhang, Xiaoming (2002) *Red Wings over the Yalu: China, the Soviet Union, and the Air War in Korea*. College Station: Texas A&M University Press.

Zhao, Dingxin (2004) *The Power of Tiananmen: State–Society Relations and the 1989 Beijing Student Movement*. Chicago: University of Chicago Press.

Zheng, Shiping (1997) *Party vs. State in post-1949 China: The Institutional Dilemma*. New York: Cambridge University Press.

Zheng, Yangwen (2005) *The Social Life of Opium in China*. Cambridge: Cambridge University Press.

Zweig, David (1997) *Freeing China's Farmers: Rural Restructuring in the Reform Era*. Armonk: M.E. Sharpe.

Index

Adams, Jonathan 9
Afghanistan 67, 190, 248, 260
Africa 160, 218, 242; PRC trade and
   investment 251
agriculture 27, 28, 30, 31, 35, 45–6, 49,
   55–6, 59, 63, 66, 100, 110, 116, 117,
   118, 121, 123, 126, 138, 149, 161, 173,
   175, 210, 214–16, 223, 225, 227, 237,
   252, 268–9; corn and new crops 49, 50
Ai Weiwei 12
Alcock, Rutherford 83, 89
Amherst, William Pitt 70–1, 78
anarchism 161–2, 186, 223
Anhui province 50, 100, 105, 112, 116,
   117, 121, 122, 164, 199, 225–226; Anhui
   clique 182; Anqing 100, 122; Anhui
   army (Huaijun) 112, 122
Arrow War (Second Opium War) xv,
   83, 113
Australia 80, 102, 211, 267; Sydney 158
Austro-Hungary 86, 139

Babojab 164
Bai Omar Chongxi 184
Banchen Lama 35, 38, 48, 151, 224
Bangladesh 45, 251
Bao Tong 261, 265–266
Baoyun 89
Bei Dao 261, 265
Beijing xii, xv, xvi, xvii, 7, 9–10, 11, 24, 36,
   41, 50, 54, 56, 60, 61–2, 63, 71, 83, 84,
   85, 86, 91, 95, 101, 109, 134, 135,
139–41, 148, 164, 166, 170, 172, 174,
   177, 182–3, 193, 196, 201, 202, 204,
   228–9, 234, 260–267; Beiping 183–4;
   Forbidden City xii, 87, 136, 139, 141,
   164–5, 183, 195, 205, 227; Great Hall of
   the People 262, 263; Imperial City 59;
   Legation Quarter 87; Lugouqiao/Marco
   Polo Bridge 198; Olympics at, 7, 11, 15;
   Qianmen 205; stock market 258; Temple
   of Heaven 139; Tiananmen 87; *Yihe dian*
   (Haidian) Summer Palace 123, 138;
   Zhongnanhai 227
Beiyang Intendancy 118, 122–4, 133–54,
   158, 163–5, 166, 172, 181–3, 186,
   190, 194
Belgium 86, 211; legation in Beijing 87
Bethune, Norman 203, 217
Bianco, Lucien 15, 17
*Biographies from Our Nation's Female
   World* 99
Bo Gu 187, 188
Borodin, Mikhail 168, 170, 171, 172
Boxers or Boxer Rebellion xv, 10, 138–40,
   147, 164
Braun, Otto 188
Britain xiii, xv, xvii, 39–40, 59, 61, 62,
   71–2, 73–82, 83, 84, 85–6, 89, 91, 92,
   99, 101, 102, 107, 109, 113, 115, 117,
   120, 121, 137, 147, 152, 153, 162,
   174, 186, 191, 195, 201, 209, 211, 223,
   258, 260, 267; British empire 68, 77,
   79, 141, 150, 151–2, 158, 160, 174;

Britain (*Cont'd*)
  George III 41; legation in Beijing 87,
    139; London 75, 120, 140, 149, 158;
    Parliament 70–1, 72, 75, 77, 81, 89;
    Royal Asiatic Society 70; Queen
    Victoria 76, 77, 80
Bruce, James (Lord Elgin) 83
Brunei 38
Bulwer-Lytton, Victor 195–6
Burgevine, Henry 115
Burlingame, Anson 88, 89
Burma (Myanmar) 21, 25, 34, 38, 68, 91,
  102, 120–1, 143, 149, 151, 201–2, 251–2
Bush, George H. W. 261, 266
Bush, George W., 249

Cai E 127, 153–4
Cai Yuanpei 166
California Institute of Technology 218
Cambodia 38, 45, 200, 248, 251–2; Khmer
  Rouge 248
Canada 149, 169, 203, 209, 211;
  Vancouver 144, 158
Canton (Guangzhou) xiii, 39, 40, 41, 59,
  64, 70, 72, 73–8, 79, 80, 82, 86, 89, 93,
  102–3, 113–14, 121, 123, 134, 135, 142,
  144, 146, 148, 165, 168, 171, 172, 174,
  181, 185, 186, 187, 191, 199, 231, 264
Cao Kun 172, 182
Carter, James Earl, Jr., 248
Cen Yuying 120–1
Central Asia 38, 39, 51, 54, 67, 68, 85, 151
Chai Ling 263, 264–6
Chen Baozhen 127, 136, 138, 157
Chen Duxiu 168, 169, 170–1, 174–5
Chen Jiongming 171–2, 184, 186–7
Chen Shui–bien 9
Chen Tianhua 141
Chen Xiwen 10
Chen Yucheng 112
Chen Yunlin 9
Cheng Gongbo 169, 175
Chengde (Jehol, Rehe) 35, 36, 60, 83, 86,
  109, 194, 202
Chesneaux, Jean 17
Chiang Ching-kuo 260
Chiang Kaishek (Jiang Jieshi) xvi, 165, 171,
  172, 173, 180, 181–6, 188, 190,
  194–205, 207, 209–11, 219, 249, 260

China Democratic League 214, 228–9
Chinese Communist Party (CCP) xvi, 7, 12,
  18, 127, 169–71, 172, 174, 175, 181,
  184, 186–8, 190, 191–2, 200, 210, 213,
  220, 222, 230, 236–7, 257, 259, 262–3,
  265; 10th Party Congress, xvi; Central
  Committee 257; Politburo 1, 15, 207,
  214, 253, 261–2; Secretariat 214; White
  Terror xvi, 181–2, 184, 186, 210; *see also*
  Lushan Plenum
Chinese Soviet Republic xvi, 185, 186–8,
  195, 196, 207, 214, 233, 257
Chonghou 90–2, 118
Churchill, Winston 201
Colebrooke, Henry Thomas 70
Columbia University 155
Comintern (Communist International) 127,
  165, 168, 170–1, 172, 181, 182, 184,
  186, 187, 188, 233
Communist revolution 68, 101, 190
compradors 72–3; hong 73, 80, 96
Confucianism xiii, 16–17, 32, 35, 119, 126,
  127, 136, 157, 159, 161; Confucius 110,
  185, 252; New Text 157; anti-
  Confucius 252
constitutions and constitutionalism,
  including constitutional monarchy 140,
  145, 146–8, 157–9, 160, 163, 164,
  187, 214
contract labor 121–2, 146, 149, 171
Cornell University 155
crime, organized 51, 63, 73, 75, 102–3,
  107, 143–4, 163, 181–2, 186, 268; *see
  also* secret societies; smuggling
Cultural Revolution (GPCR) xvi, 68,
  229–38, 252, 254, 257; Red
  Guards 230–2

Dai 53, 69
Dalai Lama 38, 68–69, 151;
  Fourteenth 191, 224
Daoguang emperor (Minning) 59, 60–1,
  75, 78, 82, 93, 105
Daoguang reign period xv, 61–3, 107, 137
Davis, John Francis 74
demonstrations 5, 10–11, 13, 14, 17, 55,
  136, 153, 166, 173–4, 185, 211, 224,
  242, 259, 263; Charter 08 xvii;
  Democracy Wall (Xidan Street) xvi, 254

Deng Pufang 232
Deng Tuo 229
Deng Xiaoping xvi, xvii, 15, 128, 187, 189,
    226–9, 231, 232, 235, 237, 247, 252–62,
    266–8, 271
Deng Yingzhao 171, 233
Deng Yujiao 12–13
Dent, Lancelot 76
Dewey, John 155, 167
Ding Ling (Jiang Bingzhi) 167, 220,
    221–2, 228
disease and medical care 4, 217, 220,
    232–3; HIV/AIDS 69, 243–5
Dong Fuxiang 139, 140
Du Wenxiu 120, 124
Du Yuesheng 182
Duan Qirui 150, 154, 163–4, 165,
    166, 172, 174, 182, 190, 216
Duke University 143
Dulles, Allen 219
Dzungars, Dzungaria 34, 36, 191

East India Company 39–40, 42, 63, 70–2,
    73–6, 78, 79, 80, 102
education and schools 16, 26–7, 142, 155,
    166–8, 173, 175, 182, 183, 186, 209,
    210, 214, 219, 220–2, 224, 268; *see also*
    examinations
Eight Banners 10, 21, 24, 25, 26, 27, 30,
    33, 49, 53–4, 55, 57, 58, 59, 63, 77, 80,
    83, 85, 86, 104, 107, 112, 118, 137, 139,
    148, 149, 152, 164, 177–8; banner
    livelihood 54; Chinese-martial 53, 177;
    niru 22; *see also* Manchus
Eisenhower, Dwight David 226
Eldemboo (Eledengbao) 21–2, 35, 36, 37,
    38, 54, 58
Elliot, Charles 75–9
embassy system, "tribute system"
    (*zhigong*) 37–9, 41, 55; kowtow 39, 41
Empress Dowager Cixi: *see* Xiaoqin
environmental deterioration 4, 5, 10, 29,
    32, 49–50, 131, 224, 241–2, 243;
    deforestation 50, 56, 223–4; endangering
    of African elephant 251
Epstein, Israel 217
Esherick, Joseph 17
Eulenberg, Friedrich Albrecht zu, 86
eunuchs 24, 59, 64, 124

Europe, including European Union 15, 37,
    39, 41, 51, 54, 56, 60, 62, 82, 94, 96,
    101, 104, 119, 135, 140, 143, 158–9,
    161, 174, 246, 267, 272; Franco-Prussian
    War 135; medieval xiii, 81; Rothschild
    family 73; weapons 92, 126
Ever Victorious Army 115–16, 119
examinations 16, 26, 29, 30, 103, 136, 142,
    155; Taiping 110; *see also* education

famine 35, 56, 58, 63, 104, 109, 143, 180,
    184, 186, 200, 207, 223–6, 257
Fang Lizhi 260, 261, 265
Fei Xiaotong 220, 222, 232
Feng Guifen 118
Feng Guozhang 154
Feng Yunshan 103, 105
Feng Yuxiang 182–3, 184, 188, 192, 194,
    202–3, 207–8
Fontanier, M.-H. V. 90
Ford, Gerald 248
Four Treasuries (*siku chuanshu*) 36
France xiii, 72, 75, 78, 79, 82, 84, 85, 86,
    88, 90, 91, 92–3, 95, 101, 102, 107, 109,
    115, 117, 120, 121, 123, 139, 140, 153,
    160, 186, 195, 199, 209, 211, 246, 251,
    258; Chinese laborers in 166, 167, 171,
    187, 267; Paris 93, 158, 226, 266
Freeman, Charles W., Jr. 1
Fujian province 49, 50, 51, 52, 64, 73, 87,
    113, 117, 137, 195, 200, 209; Fuzhou,
    80, 93, 118, 123, 134, 174, 187;
    Xiamen 80, 174, 258

Galdan 34
Gansu province 21, 34, 49, 68, 101,
    119–20, 121, 191, 225–6, 231;
    Jinjibao 119; Lanzhou 119
Gao Yaojie 244–5
Genghis Khan 23, 34
George, Henry 161
Germany 92, 95, 137, 138, 140, 153, 160,
    164, 166, 171, 187, 199, 201, 257–8,
    267; Berlin 158; *see also* Prussia
Gladstone, William 77
Gorbachev, Mikhail 260, 261, 264
Gordon, Charles 115
governors, imperial 30, 57, 64, 88,
    107, 118, 123, 127, 133, 139, 142;

governors, imperial (*Cont'd*)
  military 150–1, 153–4, 164,
  165, 167, 171, 181–5, 190, 191,
  192, 235
Grand Canal xv, 61–2, 78, 81, 82,
  107, 109, 130
Great Leap Forward xvi, 222–6, 227, 234,
  237, 238, 250
Great Wall 23, 68, 196, 198
Greene, Bell d'Acosta 164
Gromyko, Andrei 226
Guangdong province 4, 5, 9, 10, 49,
  50, 53, 64, 82, 87, 98, 99, 102–3,
  117, 136, 144, 148, 157, 171–2,
  173, 184, 185, 186, 188, 200, 204,
  215, 231, 246, 257; *bendi* 102;
  Dongzhou 5–6; Guangdong
  Soviet 186–7; Haifeng 186;
  Huizhou 172; Humen 79; Jiaying 116;
  Niubailing 98; Pearl River or delta 49,
  102; Quanbi 78, 79; Sanyuanli 79;
  Shantou 246, 258; Shenzhen 258;
  Taishan 4, 14; Zhuhai 258; *see also*
  Canton
Guangxi province 53, 82, 99, 102–5,
  107, 114, 116, 126, 172, 184,
  188, 190, 231; Guangxi Soviet 187
Guangxu emperor (Zaitian) xv, 91, 95,
  119, 123, 124, 136–8, 140, 141, 158,
  159, 163
Guangxu reign period xv, 91
Guangzhou: *see* Canton
Guizhou province 5, 21, 36, 49, 53,
  58, 64, 120, 190, 228;
  Zunyi 190–2; Weng'an 5
Guo Moruo 220
Guo Songtao 127
Gurkhas 77

Hainan 144; Hainan Incident xvii
Hakka 53, 102–4, 173, 187
Hamberg, Theodore 114
Han empire xiii, 14, 45, 51
Hart, Robert 87, 88
Hatem, George 203, 217
Hawaii 80, 102, 149, 158, 159;
  Honolulu 144, 158
He Long 186, 188, 190, 192, 196,
  232, 237

Hebei province 13, 192; Dingzhou 13;
  Shanhai Pass 24, 66; Tangshan 253;
  Zhangjiakou 192
Heilongjiang province 85, 147; *see also*
  Northeast, the
Henan province 147, 223, 225–6, 244–5;
  Luoyang 1–2, 3; Zhengzhou 109
Heshen 36, 42, 57, 58
Himalayan Mountains 34, 68, 251
Hinton, Joan 217
Hinton, William 218
Ho Chi Minh 218
Hong Renda 113
Hong Renfa 113
Hong Ren'gan 100, 101, 103–4, 112,
  113–16, 137
Hong Xiuquan 98, 103–5, 108, 110,
  112–16, 124
Hong Xuanjiao 98–9, 110
Hongkong xv, xvii, 71, 77, 78, 80, 84, 94,
  100, 104, 114, 135, 138, 149, 150, 158,
  160, 172, 195, 209, 260, 264, 266;
  Legislative Council 250, 260
Hou Dejian 265
household contract responsibility system
  (HCRS) 255, 267
Hsü, Immanuel 101
Hu Feng (Zhang Mingzhen) 221
Hu Hanmin 181, 185
Hu Linyi 109, 127
Hu Shih 155, 164, 166, 167, 168, 185,
  201, 220
Hu Yaobang 255, 257, 259, 261–2
Hua Guofeng (Su Zhu) 252–3, 259
Hualianbu 118
Huang Xing 141, 148, 149
Hubei province 3, 10, 58, 64, 107, 147,
  153, 184, 188; Daye 10; Hankou 123,
  134, 142, 147, 148; Hanyang (Han Ye
  Ping Ironworks) 142, 147, 153;
  Wuchang 105, 108, 123; Wuhan xv, 181,
  184, 199, 216; Yichang 130, 148;
  Xiangyang 58
Hui (Chinese Muslims) 54, 106, 119,
  177–8; *see also* Muslims
Hunan province 6, 10, 21, 57, 58, 64, 105,
  107, 121, 122, 126–8, 140, 157, 170,
  172, 190, 199, 211, 215; Changsha 105,
  107, 116, 126, 127, 134, 136, 141, 173,

174, 188, 199, 201, 233; Hunan Army
  (Xiangjun) 107, 112, 127; Hunan
  University 126; *Shiwu xuetang* 136–7;
  Xiang River 126; *see also* Yuelu Academy
Hundred Days Reforms xv, 127, 137–8,
  140, 141, 146, 158
Hundred Flowers Campaign xvi, 221–2
Hung Taiji 23, 24, 30, 34, 38
Hurley, Patrick 203–4

Ignatiev, Nicholai Pavlovich 85
Ilham Tohti 11
imperialism and anti-imperialism 71, 81,
  96, 159, 160, 161, 162, 164, 166,
  168, 195, 196
indemnities and reparations 80, 84, 90, 91,
  92, 94, 95–6, 107, 121, 139–40, 151
India xvi, 45, 62, 68, 69, 70, 73, 75, 78,
  149, 151, 190, 202, 224, 251;
  Bengal 195; border conflicts with
  China 251; Calcutta 73, 83;
  Darjeeling 151; Bombay (Mumbai) 39;
  Provisional Government of Free 200;
  Punjab 151
Indian Ocean 49
Indonesia 38, 70, 102, 160, 218;
  Bandung 218–19, 250
Inner Mongolia province 67, 68, 192, 224,
  264, 270; Chakhar 192, 194, 196,
  202–3, 231–2; Hohhot 68; *see also*
  Chengde, Mongolia
Internet 5, 7, 11, 12, 13, 272
Italy 86, 139, 140, 201; Rome 41

Japan xiii, xvi, 9, 24, 37, 39, 51, 69,
  79, 89, 94, 117, 121, 135–7, 139,
  140, 141, 142, 144–5, 149, 150,
  158–60, 163, 165–6, 169, 173,
  186, 209, 212, 220, 247, 257–8;
  boycott 146, 195, 211, 216;
  Greater East Asia Co-Prosperity
  Sphere 199–200; Hiroshima and
  Nagasaki 202; Meiji emperor 94, 136;
  military aggression toward or conflict with
  China 68, 94, 95, 123, 145, 152–4,
  164–6, 169, 172, 173, 174, 180, 188,
  192–205, 209, 213, 215, 217,
  225; Tokyo 137, 140, 141, 144, 149,
  158, 163, 220, 235, 258; Unit 731

200; and World War I 153, 166;
  Yokohama 149, 158; *see also*
  Nanjing Massacre; Okinawa;
  Russo-Japanese War; Sino-Japanese
  War; Southern Manchuria Railway
  Company; Twenty-One Demands
Jehangir 61, 82
Jen Yu-wen (Jian Youwen) 101
Jian Bozan 232
Jiang Qing (Li Shumeng) xvi, 227–9,
  230–1, 235, 252–3; gang of four 252–3;
  Wu Zetian 253
Jiang Zemin 10, 267
Jiangnan Arsenal 101, 122
Jiangsu province 110, 117, 121, 147, 199,
  214; Suzhou 11; Yangzhou 89;
  Zhenjiang 79
Jiangxi province 50, 113, 121, 185, 186,
  189, 191, 200, 215, 232; Jinggang
  Mountains 186; Jiujiang 108;
  Nanchang 186; Ruijin 187; *see also*
  Chinese Soviet Republic; Lushan Plenum
Jiaqing emperor (Yongyan) 21, 36,
  58–60, 72
Jiaqing reign period xv, 21, 60
Jilin province 57; *see also* Northeast, the
Jin Shuren 190
Jingdezhen 55
Jinliang 164
Johnson, Tim 2–3
Johnston, Reginald 164

Kang Guangren 137, 138
Kang Sheng 227–8, 229, 230, 234
Kang Tongbi 145
Kang Youwei 136, 137, 138, 146, 148, 149,
  157–9, 162, 163, 164, 169, 174, 220
Kangxi emperor (Xuanye) 25, 26, 30, 34,
  35, 36, 39, 57, 60
Kawakami Hajime 169
Kazakh 54, 191; Kazakhstan 68, 85
Ketteler, Clemens von 139
Khan, Muhammad Yahya 247
Khrushchev, Nikita 220, 222, 226
Kim Il-sung 211, 218
Kim Ok-kyun 95
Kimball, Dan 218
Kirghiz 54, 61
Kissinger, Henry xvi, 247

KMT (Nationalist Party) xvi, 18, 98, 150, 163, 168, 170–1, 173, 174, 175, 181–92, 194–200, 207, 209–11, 214, 216, 217, 220, 221, 225, 254; Blue shirts 197; *see also* New Life Movement, Republic of China

Korea 37, 38, 71, 80, 81, 89, 90, 94–6, 122, 124, 159, 166, 195, 199–200, 202, 211–13, 218; Democratic People's Republic of Korea 211; Koreans 22, 37, 200, 204; Donghak movement 95; King Gojong 95; March First Movement 166; Myeongseong 95–6; Republic of 211, 247, 258; Seoul 95

Korean War xvi, 211–13, 217, 218, 219, 225, 232

Kung, H. H. (Kong Xiangxi) 165, 184, 201

Kunlun Mountains 34

Laos 38, 45, 200, 251–2; Pathet Lao 248

law and lawyers 11, 12, 33, 35, 39, 51, 64, 71, 72, 75, 76, 77, 81, 82, 84, 101, 143, 222; extraterritoriality 80–1, 91; international 41, 75, 76, 84; Qing legal code 70

League of Alliances (*Tongmeng hui*) 144, 149–50, 158, 161, 163, 165, 169, 171, 187

League of Nations 195–6

Lee Teng-hui 260

Lenin, V. I, 169, 186

Li Dazhao 169, 171, 173, 174, 182

Li Hengsong 115

Li Hongzhang 90, 93, 94, 95, 96, 112, 115, 116, 118, 119, 120, 122–5, 133, 135–7, 138, 139, 141, 142, 151, 196, 235

Li Lisan 174, 186, 187, 233

Li Na 227

Li Peng 259–60, 261, 262, 264, 266

Li Rui 225

Li Xiucheng 112, 113, 114, 115–16

Li Xubin 127

Li Yuanhong 148, 163–4, 172

Li Zicheng 14, 24, 25, 56, 58, 194, 215

Liang Afa 103

Liang Qichao 127, 136, 137, 138, 148, 149, 157–64, 168, 169, 174, 220

Liao empire 36

Liao Mosha 229

Liao Zhongkai 181

Liaoning province 22; *see also* Northeast, the

Lifton, Robert J. 236

Lighdan Khan 23, 34, 38

Lin Biao 202, 217, 219, 225, 228, 230, 234, 235, 236, 252–3

Lin Liguo 234

Lin Miaoke 14

Lin Zexu 64, 75–8, 80, 107, 126, 137

Lincoln, Abraham 88

Lindley, August and Mary 112

Liu Bocheng 219

Liu Changyou 127

Liu Kunyi 127, 140

Liu Rong 127

Liu Shaoqi xvi, 127, 170, 171, 173, 186, 202, 214, 226–9, 230, 231, 232, 236, 237, 246, 257

Lolo 53

Long March xvi, 189–92, 195, 196, 202, 209, 222, 232, 257; Zunyi conferences 190

Lu Xun (Zhou Shuren) 166–7, 220

Luce, Henry 201, 217

Luo Zenan 127

Lushan Plenum xvi, 207, 225–6

Ma Hualong 119

Ma Ying-jeou 9

Macao 39, 70, 72, 76, 78, 144

Macartney, George 40, 70, 71, 78

magistrates (imperial government) 27–31, 39, 46–7, 51, 56, 57–8, 59, 64, 89–90, 104

Major, Ernest 134

Malaysia 49, 70, 160; Penang 144

Malthus, Thomas 46

Manchukuo xvi, 195–6, 199, 200, 202

Manchuria: *see* Northeast, the

Manchus 21–2, 24, 25, 30, 32, 35, 36, 51, 58, 61, 82, 83, 85, 86, 87, 104, 107, 112, 117, 126, 137, 140, 141, 148, 149, 158–60, 164, 177–9, 232, 235; *see also* Eight Banners, Jurchens

Mao Anying 212

Mao Zedong 127, 170, 171, 173, 185–92, 195, 196, 197, 202, 203, 204–5, 207, 209, 212–15, 217–27, 246–8, 252–4, 271, 272; and First Emperor (Qin shihuang) 235–6

Martin, W. A. P. 86, 88

Marx, Karl or Marxism 15, 71, 169, 173, 186, 203, 214, 221, 233, 235

May Fourth Movement xvi, 165–75, 229

May Thirtieth Incident xvi, 173–4

Meadows, Thomas Taylor 112

Mekong River 34

Miao (Hmong) 21, 38, 53, 58, 69, 87, 102, 104–5, 120, 126, 177, 187, 190

migration 48–50, 52, 53, 55, 63, 68, 117, 131, 143, 222, 256; *huiguan* (provincial associations) 49; *see also* population

Mill, John Stuart 162

Ming empire xii, 16, 22–5, 26, 27, 31, 33, 36–8, 39, 45, 48, 49, 51, 52, 54, 55–6, 58, 60, 62, 63, 66, 68–9, 86, 102, 110, 194, 209, 228, 270

mining and miners 4, 6, 14, 15, 25, 32, 55, 60, 62, 120, 147, 186, 216, 223, 237, 240–2

Mongolia xii, 23, 34, 37, 38, 49, 51, 53, 54, 55, 57, 67, 81, 85, 133, 151, 152, 154, 166, 191–2, 194, 267; Jebsumdamba Khutukhtu 152; Mongol Military Government 199; People's Republic 191, 223, 234, 251, 260; Republic of 68, 267; theocratic state, Bogd Khaan 152, 191; Urga 151, 152; *see also* Inner Mongolia

Mongols xii, 32, 35, 38, 55, 58, 61, 68, 69, 80, 85, 87, 107, 148, 159, 164, 178, 200, 235; Khalka 85

Morgan, J. P. 164

Morrison, Robert 103

Mujangga 78, 107

Mukden: *see* Shenyang

Muslims and Islam 8, 21, 34, 54–5, 68, 69, 87, 90, 91, 101, 119–21, 139, 159, 164, 177, 184, 190, 191, 231, 236, 260, 261; Hor 190; Sufis 34, 119; *see also* Hui; Uighurs

Nakamura, George 203

Nanjing Massacre 198–9, 204

Nanjing xv, xvi, 82, 84, 86, 89, 92, 99, 100, 108, 110, 113, 114, 116, 136, 146, 149, 150, 165, 172, 181–4, 186, 188, 190, 193, 195, 198–200, 204, 207, 209; wartime regime 199–200

Nankai University 171, 228

Nanyang Intendancy 118

Napier, William 72–3, 74, 76, 78

Naquin, Susan 17

Nasser, Abdel Gamal 251

National Minorities University (*Minzu xueyuan*) 261

nationalism 127, 140, 158–63, 174, 270–2

Nationalist Party: *see* KMT

Nationalist revolution (1911–12) xv, 18, 127, 148–9, 179

Naxi (Nakhi) 177

Nehru, Jawaharlal 218

Nepal 79, 151, 251

Netherlands 37, 39, 40, 49, 72, 86, 211

New Life Movement 185, 199

New Zealand 211

newspapers or publishing 133–5, 136, 144, 146, 149, 154, 160–1, 163, 166, 167, 171, 174, 195; *Beijing News* 12, 13–14, 24; China General Publishing Company (*Zhonghua yinwu zongju*) 135; *China Mail* 134; *China Reconstructs* 217, 219; Commercial Press (*Shangwu*) 135; Foreign Languages Press, 217; *Guangming Daily* 13; *Liberation* (*Jiefang*) 229, 235; *Jingbao* 134; *New York Times* 10; *New Youth* (*Xin Qingnian*) 169; *Newsweek* 9; *North China Herald* 134; *Pearl River Evening News* 12; *People's Daily* (*Renmin ribao*) 13, 235; *Red Flag* (*Hongqi*) 170, 235; *Shenbao* 134; *South China Morning Post* 10; *Southern Daily* 13; *Southern Weekly* and *Southern Weekend* 12; *Subao* 141, 158; *Time Magazine* 201; *Wenhuibao* 229

Nian rebels 99, 106, 108, 109, 117, 119

Nineteenth Route Army 195

Nixon, Richard xvi, 247

Northeast, the (Manchuria) 22, 25, 30, 36, 37, 53, 54, 55, 57, 63, 67, 96, 108, 137, 140, 145, 151, 152–3, 165, 166–7, 174, 177, 179, 183, 188, 192, 194, 204, 212,

Northeast, the (Manchuria) (*Cont'd*)
    213, 215–16, 223, 226, 258; Amur
    River 34, 67, 85, 195; Fort Kumarsky 85;
    Changbaishan 85; Changchun 2, 3, 195;
    Evenks, Nanai, Orochens 85;
    Fengtian 153; Fengtian clique 172, 182;
    Harbin 200; Lüshun (Dairen, Port
    Arthur) 95, 137, 204, 217; Shenyang
    (Mukden) 23, 183, 194, 204; *see also*
    Heilongjiang province; Jilin province;
    Liaoning province; Southern Manchuria
    Railway Company
Northern Expedition xvi, 175, 180–1, 184,
    190, 210, 219
Northern Grand Battalion 108, 112
Nurgaci 22–3, 30

oil 68, 147, 251
Okinawa 38, 94, 209; Liuqiu (Ryûkyû)
    38, 94
Olympics xvii, 7, 15, 217, 248
opium 42, 62–4, 70, 71, 73–8, 80, 84, 92,
    101, 102, 113, 120, 142, 143–4, 181,
    185, 187, 243
Opium War xv, 61, 69, 71, 77–80, 107,
    124, 126; *see also* Arrow War
Ottoman empire 61, 79, 81, 90, 160
Oxford University 157

Pakistan 45, 247, 251
Palmerston, Viscount (Henry John
    Temple) 72, 75–7
Panthay sultanate xv, 90, 92, 102, 106,
    120–1
Parker, Peter 72, 89
Peel, Robert 77, 80
Peking University 137, 164, 166, 169–70,
    228, 230, 232, 252, 260, 261
Peng Dehuai 211–12, 217, 219, 225, 219,
    225, 229
Peng Pai xvi, 173, 174, 186–7, 215
Peng Zhen 229, 230, 237
People's Liberation Army 6, 186, 188,
    211–12, 216; air corps 212, 216, 219,
    253; navy 217, 219; People's Volunteer
    Army 212; Red Army 188–9, 196, 202,
    204–5, 210
People's Republic of China xvi, 1–12, 67,
    69, 177, 205, 207–48, 265; budget 215,
226; agricultural producer's
    cooperatives 215; Common Program xvi,
    213–16; exports 249–50, 254; First Five
    Year Plan 215, 219, 223; investments in
    foreign countries 250; joint venture
    companies 257; mutual aid teams 215;
    one-child policy 254, 178–9; Public
    Security Bureau (*Gong'an ju*) 2;
    purchasing power 270; Socialist
    Education Campaign xvi, 228, 229;
    special economic zones (SEZs) 257–60,
    268–9; State Council 68, 214; state-
    owned enterprises (SOEs) 255–6, 268
Perry, Elizabeth 17
Philippines 24, 39, 49, 51, 149, 159, 196,
    209, 211; Manilla 144
piracy 39, 42, 73, 77, 78, 80, 209; *see also*
    crime, organized; smuggling; secret
    societies
population 44–8, 50, 55; "floating
    population" 49, 63; *see also* migration
porcelain 37, 39, 55, 73, 121
Portugal 37, 39, 86
Pottinger, Henry 79
Pound, Ezra xi, xiv
Price, Frank and Harry 201
Princeton University 167, 266
Prussia 86; German Customs Union
    (Zollverein) 86; *see also* Germany
Puyi xv, 141, 150, 152, 153, 163, 164–5,
    183, 195–6, 204, 232

Qian Xuesen (Tsien Hsueh-shen) 217–18
Qian Zhongshu 220, 232
Qianlong emperor (Hongli) 34, 35–6, 41,
    49, 54, 57, 58
Qianlong period 37, 57, 60
Qincheng prison 222, 225
Qing empire xiii, 10, 16–42, 44–63,
    68–150, 155, 159, 160, 161, 165, 177,
    179, 189, 192, 193, 194, 195, 200, 209,
    212, 267–8, 270; *baojia* 31, 33, 110;
    Board of Punishments (*xingbu*) 28;
    budget or treasury 29, 36, 55, 57, 58,
    101; court xiii, 50, 105, 118, 123, 135,
    151, 152, 158, 164; Foreign
    Ministry 142; Frontier Administration,
    Department of (*lifan yuan*) 38, 81;
    granaries 27, 63, 110; Grand

Council 137; Green Standard Armies 26, 27, 33, 112; Hanlin Academy 87; Imperial Maritime Customs Service 87, 102; *lijia* 31; officials 26, 27, 41, 42, 52, 55, 63–4, 72, 73, 118, 138–40, 152; political reforms 141–3; *Tongwen guan* 86, 117
Qinghai province 10, 34, 194, 227, 231
qingyi 14, 61, 136
Qishan 78, 79
Qiying 78, 79, 82

railroads 133, 134, 136, 137, 138, 140, 142, 146–8, 151–152, 153, 166, 174, 198, 200, 209, 214, 251, 268; rights recovery 147
rebellion (imperial era) 14, 17, 21, 24, 25, 33, 35, 47, 52, 57–9, 60–1, 82, 90, 91, 98–9, 100–19, 191, 194; Autumn Harvest Uprising 127; Eight Trigrams 59, 60, 80; Jinchuan 35, 36, 57, 58; military 141, 148, 149; Small Sword Society 99, 108, 112, 114; Three Feudatories 24–5; *see also* Boxer; Nian; Taiping; White Lotus
religion 268–9; Baptists 103; Buddhism 34, 51, 127, 136, 153, 158, 177, 195, 231, 232, 236; Catholicism 60, 232; China Mission Society 103; Christianity 54, 60, 72, 82, 89, 100, 103–5, 110, 112, 114, 139, 149, 182, 186, 236; Daoism 51, 161; Falungong 17, 268; heterodox in the PRC 268; Jesuits 39, 41, 54, 60, 87; missionaries 72, 89–90, 100, 103, 113, 114, 115, 134, 138–9, 144, 167, 186; Taiping 82, 103
Ren Wanding 260
Republic of China (ROC) xvi, xvii, 9, 11, 67, 68, 69, 98, 151, 152, 174, 179, 187, 189–205, 209–11, 217, 219, 226, 248–9, 254, 260; Council of State 150, 163, 183; Democratic Progressive Party 260; Executive Cabinet 184, 196, 210; National People's Congress 214, 252, 261; Parliament 150, 163, 164, 165, 172; *see also* KMT
Rhee, Syngman 211
Richard, Timothy 136
riots 4–10, 11, 13, 14, 17, 33, 55, 63, 89–90, 95, 153, 210, 224, 226, 242;

antiforeign 93–4, 195; *see also* demonstrations
Roberts, Issachar Jacox 103–4, 110, 114–15
Rong Hong: *see* Yung Wing
Ronglu 137–8, 139, 140
Roosevelt, Franklin 201
Roosevelt, Theodore 88
Russia 67, 79, 81, 152, 161, 169, 191, 200, 216; Commonwealth of Independent States 267; Maritime Province, Vladivostok, Ussuriysk 85, 195; Moscow 96, 186, 187, 195; St Petersburg 91, 92; revolution 165; Russian empire xiii, 26, 34, 38, 39, 61, 68, 83, 84, 85, 86, 90–1, 92, 95–6, 101, 117, 120, 122, 137, 139, 140, 144–5, 151, 160, 212; *see also* USSR
Russo-Japanese War 144–5

Sasser, James 10
secret societies 21, 51–3, 57, 58, 104, 105, 138, 139, 144, 148, 149, 150, 151; Gelaohui 148, 188; *see also* crime, organized; Tiandihui
Selden, Mark 17
self-strengthening movement 92, 123, 127, 136, 158
Sengge Renchin 83, 118, 119
Shaanxi province 14, 49, 50, 58, 119–20, 121, 189, 192, 196, 262; Huaqingchi 197; Wei River Valley 197; Xi'an xvi, 14, 139, 149, 193, 199, 262; *see also* Yan'an base area
Shandong province 50, 57, 59, 109, 121, 129, 138–9, 153, 166, 195, 258; Ji river 109; Qingdao 137, 174, 216; Weihai 137
Shanghai Communiqué 248
Shanghai xiii, xvi, 11, 12, 80, 83, 86, 92, 93, 95, 100, 101, 102, 108, 112–15, 117, 121, 123, 134–6, 138, 140, 143, 144, 146, 149, 150, 151, 155, 158, 171–4, 181–2, 184, 187, 188, 195, 196, 197, 198, 213, 216–17, 228, 230, 253, 264; Nanjing Road 174; Pudong 258; Shanghai Commune 229–30, 253; stock market 258; *see also* Yangtze delta
Shanqi 164

Shanxi province 11, 123, 139, 147, 184, 194, 203, 204, 207; Shanxi clique 182; Taiyuan 174

Shen Jin 140, 141

Shen Junru 214

Sheng Shicai 190, 194, 207, 231

Sheng Xuanhuai 142, 147

Shevardnadze, Eduard 261

Shi Dakai 105, 108, 112, 113, 115

Shunzhi emperor 24

Siberia 35, 67, 68, 85

Sichuan province xvii, 4, 6, 21, 24, 34, 49, 53, 57, 59, 64, 115, 137, 144, 148, 151–2, 187, 188, 190, 191, 192, 203, 226; Chengdu 56, 134, 225, 264; Chongqing 130–1, 174, 198–9, 201; Dazhou 4; Gaodong 6

Sikkim 251

Simla agreement 152, 191

Singapore 39, 78, 80, 144, 149, 160

Sino-Japanese War (1894) 95

slavery 30, 51, 55, 60, 102, 144

smuggling 39, 40, 42, 51, 52, 53, 62, 63, 69, 70, 73–4, 76, 87, 92, 102, 113, 122, 143, 146, 209; *see also* crime, organized

Sneevliet, Henk, 170

socialism 161, 169, 186, 223

Song empire xii, 27, 67, 126

Song Jiaoren xv, 150, 163

Soong Ai-ling (Song Ailing) 165

Soong Ching-ling (Song Qingling) 165, 182, 213, 217

Soong May-ling (Song Meiling) 165, 182, 184, 186, 196, 197, 201, 207

Soong, Charlie (Han Jiaozhun) 144, 165

Soong, T. V. (Song Ziwen) 165, 182, 184, 196, 201, 203, 217

South China Sea 39, 69

Southeast Asia 38, 45, 49, 50, 51, 81, 93, 144, 202; PRC trade and investment 251

Southern Grand Batallion 108, 112

Southern Manchuria Railway Company 145, 152, 153, 183, 194

southwest China 33, 35, 54, 68, 143; *see also* Yunnan, Guizhou, Guangxi

Spain 37, 86, 87

Spencer, Herbert 162–3

Stalin, Joseph 201, 218, 220

Staunton, George (Thomas) 41, 70–1, 77

Staunton, George 41

Stillwell, Joseph 201–2

Sukarno 218

Sun Yatsen xv, xvi, 130, 144, 148–59, 153–4, 158, 160–3, 165, 168–9, 171–3, 174, 183, 184, 187, 191, 205, 213; Three People's Principles 161, 162, 186; *see also* League of Alliances

Supreme Court (*zuigao renmin fayuan*) 11–12, 14, 214

Sushun 117

Swedish-Norwegian Union 82

Tacibu 118

Tagore, Rabindranath 164

Taiping rebel kingdom and war xv, 82–3, 86, 87, 88, 98–9, 100–19, 120, 121, 122, 124, 127, 134, 137, 143, 146, 173, 178, 184, 203; Bible 110; religion compared to Mormonism 110; Society of God-Worshippers 104–5, 107; symbols to nationalists and revolutionaries 98, 141

Taiwan xvi, xvii, 9, 21, 24, 25, 34, 36, 37, 39, 49, 50, 51, 52, 53, 57, 69, 81, 87, 93–4, 159, 165, 199, 209–11, 213, 226, 247, 248–9, 260; 2–28 incident 210; Danshui/Tamshui 84; Jinmen and Mazu 219, 226; Straits of 209, 219, 220, 249; Tainan 39; Taipei 209; *see also* Republic of China

Tajiks 54

Tan Sitong 127, 136, 137

Tang Caichang 127, 140

Tang empire xiii, 36, 67, 68

taxation 10, 14, 26, 28, 31, 42, 44, 45, 47, 48, 59, 62–4, 68, 73, 80, 112, 117, 143, 148, 150, 182, 187, 268–9; amnesties 63; *lijin* 107, 121, 143

tea 39, 40, 62, 71, 100, 121

textiles 55, 121, 195, 255; silk 37, 73, 121, 195; silkworm metaphor 160

Thailand (Siam) 38, 45, 93, 196, 200, 211; Plaek Pibulsonggram 200

Thaxton, Ralph 17

Three Gorges Dam xvii, 130–1

Tiananmen Incident of 1976 15, 253; of 1989 xvii, 1, 14, 262–7

Tiandihui 52–3, 57, 58, 63, 72, 102, 104, 109, 144, 182; *see also* secret societies

Tianjin 62, 71, 83, 87, 89–90, 92, 93, 118, 121, 123, 127, 134, 144, 165, 171, 172, 174, 182, 195, 202, 204

Tibet and Tibetans xii, xvi, xvii, 7–8, 9, 11, 25, 34, 35, 36, 56, 68–9, 129, 133, 151–2, 181, 190, 191, 224, 225, 231, 251, 264, 270; Anuchal Pradesh/ Tawang 152; cultural communities 35–6, 54, 55, 57, 120, 159, 164; Kham 191, 192; Lhasa 7, 68, 225, 231; Nyemo revolt 231; *see also* Banchen Lama; Dalai Lama; Simla agreement

Tientsin Massacre xv, 89–91

tobacco, snuff and cigarettes 143, 144, 210, 243, 260

Tocqueville, Alexis de 71

Tongzhi emperor (Zaichun) 88, 117, 119

Tongzhi reign period xv, 118; restoration 89

town and village enterprises (TVEs) 241, 255–6, 259, 267–8

treaties and conventions: Chefoo Convention 121; Convention of Peking 84–6, 87; Convention of Tientsin 94, 95; Tanggu Truce 196; Treaties of Tientsin 83, 84–6, 113; Treaty of Aigun 85; Burlingame Treaty xv, 88, 92, 145; Treaty of Canton 82; Treaty of Favorable Treatment 164; Treaty of Kanagawa 165; Treaty of Kanghwa 94; Treaty of Khiakta 38, 85; Treaty of Kokand 61, 85; Treaty of Kuldja 85; Treaty of Livadia 91; Treaty of Nanking xv, 71, 79, 81, 82, 85, 102; Treaty of Nerchinsk 34, 85; Treaty of Paris xvi; Treaty of Peking 115; Treaty of Shimonoseki xv, 95–6, 133, 135–6, 137, 158, 209; Treaty of St Petersburg 92; Treaty of The Bogue 71, 79, 80, 81, 82; Treaty of Versailles xvi, 166, 172; Treaty of Wanghia 82; Treaty of Whampoa 82

Tripartite Intervention 95–6, 135

Tsinghua University 228, 252, 253

tuanlian 33, 58, 80, 107, 110, 115

Tujia 126, 190

Turkestan (Eastern) xii, 34, 54, 67, 68, 80, 81, 85, 91, 92, 120, 212;

Turkish Islamic Republic of, 190, 231; *see also* Xinjiang; Kashgar

Turkey 73, 211

Twenty-One Demands xvi, 153, 166, 172

Uighurs 8–9, 11, 32, 34, 55, 68, 190, 225, 231, 263; Turkestani Muslims 54–5, 61

Ulanfu 232, 237

United Nations xvi, 209, 211–12, 217, 247, 248–9

USA xvii, 1, 9–10, 69, 72, 73–5, 82, 83, 84, 85, 88, 91, 92, 94, 96, 99, 100, 101, 102, 104, 107, 113, 114, 117, 119, 121, 135, 139, 143, 144, 146, 149, 159, 161, 168, 169, 174, 182, 185, 200, 201–2, 203, 204, 205, 209, 211–12, 216, 217, 218, 220, 226, 249, 251, 258, 260, 261, 266, 272; A. A. Low Brothers firm 73; American China Development Company 146, 147; Belgrade embassy bombing xvii, 9–10; Boston 73; boycott 145–6, 149; California 80, 102; Central Intelligence Agency 69; Chinese Exclusion Act xv, 92, 138, 145–6; copyrights 140; Denver 150; Formosa Resolution 219; Flying Tigers 201; Illinois 103; imports from China 249–50; Los Angeles 149; McCarthy period 217, 218; Neutrality Act 196, 201; New York City 88, 158, 168, 217; normalization of relations 234, 247–50; Open Door Notes 140; Pearl Harbor 201; Pentagon 218; Republican party 249; Russell & Company 73; San Francisco 144, 158; Seventh Fleet 212; Taiwan Relations Act 249; Tennessee 103; weapons 92; Wilsonianism 166

USSR xvi, 165, 168, 174, 180, 182, 190–2, 195, 201, 202, 203, 207, 209, 211, 216, 220, 221, 222, 223, 224, 226, 227–8, 246, 247–8, 251, 260, 261, 267; *see also* Comintern; Russia

Uzbek 54; Uzbekistan 68; Kokand 61, 90

Vietnam xvii, 38, 49, 53, 92, 218, 248, 252; Annam 38, 81, 92–3, 102, 116, 120, 123; Cochinchina 92–3; Empire of 200;

Indochina xv, 93, 199; Hanoi 92, 150; Tonkin 92–3
Vietnam War 247–8

Wade, Thomas 83, 91
Wang Dan 261–1, 263, 266
Wang Fuzhi 126, 159
Wang Hongwen 230, 235
Wang Jingwei 148, 172, 181, 184, 185, 188, 196, 199–200
Wang Lixiong 11
Wang Ming 187, 202
Wang Tao 113, 134–5, 137, 145, 157
Wang Xiuying 7
Ward, Frederick Townsend 86, 88, 115
warlords: *see* governors, military
Wasserstrom, Jeffrey 17
water 5, 129–32; floods 14, 47, 50, 59, 69, 101, 107, 109, 129, 131, 192, 203; management 16, 25, 29, 30, 50, 56, 61–2, 70, 142, 224; pollution 5, 6, 10, 13, 131, 241; *see also* environmental deterioration
Wei Jingsheng 254, 261, 262
Wei Yuan 126
Wellesley College 165
Wen Jiabao 10, 14, 264, 268, 272
Weng Tonghe 117, 123
Wenxiang 83–4, 86, 87, 89, 91, 118, 119, 165
Whampoa Military Academy 171
White Lotus sect or rebellion xv, 21–2, 33, 51–2, 57–8, 72, 80, 101, 108, 268–9
witchcraft 35, 52, 57
women 32, 102, 105, 108, 110, 111, 127, 134, 140, 173, 189; All China Women's Federation 213–14; education 127, 142, 167; foot-binding 32, 55, 102, 155, 157; marriage 48, 54, 155, 187; matrilineality 35; rebel leaders 51, 98–9, 108, 110, 112; rights 167, 171
World Trade Organization (WTO) xvii, 250, 269–70
World War II 180–204, 218; Cairo pact 201, 209; Potsdam 201
Wu Bingjian 73–4, 80, 134
Wu Chongyue 73, 76
Wu Dianying 7

Wu Han and/or *Hai Rui Dismissed from Office* 228–9, 230, 232
Wu Peifu 172
Wu Sangui 24–5
Wu Yue 141
Wuerkaixi (Urkesh Dawlat) 263

Xianfeng emperor (Yizhu) 82, 83, 85, 86, 88, 107, 108–9, 117
Xianfeng reign period xv
Xiao Chaogui 99
Xiaoqin (Empress Dowager Cixi) xv, 88, 109, 117, 118, 123–4, 135, 137–40, 141, 146–7, 164
Xiaozhen 117
Xinhua news agency 5, 13
Xinjiang xvii, 8–9, 11, 34, 36, 38, 54–5, 57, 59–63, 68, 69, 78, 81, 82, 85, 90–1, 92, 101, 117, 119–22, 133, 151, 190–1, 224, 231–2, 260, 261, 263, 264, 270; *bingtuan* 68; Ili 34, 85; Kashgar xv, 8, 9, 39, 61, 82, 90–1, 107, 120, 190; Khotan 190; Kumul (Hami) 190; Ürümqi 8; *see also* Turkestan (Eastern)
Xu Shichang 172
Xuantong reign period xv

Yakub Beg xv, 90–1, 92, 106, 120, 122, 124
Yale University 73, 89, 165, 167
Yalu River 95, 212
Yan Fu 145, 162
Yan Xishan 182, 183, 184, 188, 194, 197, 203–5, 207
Yan'an base area xvi, 192–4, 196–7, 202–203, 209, 215, 220, 221, 222, 228, 230, 232, 234
Yang Jia 11–12
Yang Kaihui 186
Yang Peiyi 14
Yang Shangkun 192, 202
Yang Xiuqing 99, 113
Yang Zengxin 151, 190
Yangtze River and/or Delta 21, 24, 25, 28, 29, 30, 33, 36, 39, 49, 50–1, 58, 61–2, 77, 78, 81, 82, 84, 86, 87, 93, 95, 100, 101, 105, 107–9, 112, 113, 114, 115, 116, 126, 129, 130–1, 143, 148, 158, 172, 174, 181, 198–9, 240; *see also* Shanghai
Yao 38, 53, 87, 120, 126, 177, 190

Yao Wenyuan 229, 235
Yarlung Zangbo (Brahmaputra) 129, 251
Ye Jianying 186, 192
Ye Mingchen 82, 83
Yellow River 28–9, 34, 45, 50, 61,
    101, 105, 109, 123, 129, 131, 192, 193,
    199–200, 224
Yen, Jimmy (Yan Yangchu) 167–8
Yi 69, 187
Yihuan (Prince Chun) 92, 109, 117, 123–4
Ying Ruocheng 232
Yixin (Prince Gong) 84, 86, 87, 89, 90, 92,
    109, 117, 124
Yongluo emperor xii
Yongzheng emperor 28, 30
Younghusband, Francis 151
Yuan empire xii, 36, 45, 58, 67, 68, 69, 177
Yuan Shikai xv, 94–5, 127, 137, 139, 141,
    147, 148, 150–4, 163, 164, 168, 169,
    182, 188, 190, 191, 272
Yuanming yuan (Summer Palace) 83
Yuelu Academy 126–7, 137
Yung Wing 89, 100–1, 114, 121, 125, 137,
    138, 149
Yunnan province xii, 21, 25, 36, 37, 38,
    49, 53, 56, 59, 62, 64, 67, 68, 69, 90,
    91, 92, 101, 102, 120–1, 144, 153–4,
    172, 190, 191; Dali 120–1

Zaifeng (Prince Chun) 141, 148, 150
Zeng Guofan 89–90, 91, 92, 100–1,
    107–8, 112, 113, 115–19, 121, 122,
    125, 127, 136, 141, 165
Zeng Guoquan 127
Zeng Jing 36
Zeng Jize 91, 93
Zhang Binglin 158–60, 161, 162,
    163, 166, 220
Zhang Chunqiao 229, 235, 253

Zhang Guotao 170, 171, 186, 188, 192,
    196, 202, 209, 225, 257
Zhang Longping, 3, 6
Zhang Luoxing 108
Zhang Wentian 225
Zhang Xianzhong 24, 25, 56, 194, 215
Zhang Xueliang 182, 183, 184,
    194, 196–7
Zhang Xun 164
Zhang Yong 152
Zhang Zhidong 90, 91, 92, 93, 122–3,
    140, 142, 147, 148, 153, 235
Zhang Zuolin 153, 172, 182, 183, 194
Zhao Erfeng 151–2
Zhao Erxun 142, 152
Zhao Ziyang 255, 256–7, 259–62, 264–5
Zhejiang province 50, 64, 110, 113, 115,
    117, 121, 146, 158, 170, 171, 199, 214;
    Hangzhou 116, 117, 134, 135, 146, 158;
    Ningbo 80; Zhapu 39, 79
Zheng Chenggong 24
Zhili province 59, 123, 203; Dagu 83;
    Wanping 198; Zhili clique 172, 182–3
Zhongyong xi
Zhou Enlai xvi, 15, 128, 171, 186, 188–9,
    192, 196–7, 202, 203, 214, 218–19, 221,
    222, 230, 233–5, 246–8, 250–3, 257;
    Four Modernizations 253–4
Zhou Xiuying 99
Zhoushan Islands 77, 81
Zhu De xvi, 186, 188–9, 202, 212, 253
Zhu Rongji 128, 268–70
Zhuang 69, 177, 187, 190
Zongli Yamen 86, 87, 90, 91, 117, 118,
    137, 142
Zou Rong 140–1
Zunyi conferences xvi
Zuo Zongtang 91, 92, 118, 119–20, 122,
    127, 139

89562279R00183

Made in the USA
Middletown, DE
17 September 2018